Fourteenth Century

Fourteenth Century

Fifteenth Century

Fifteenth Century

Early Sixteenth Century
(1500–1550)

Early Sixteenth Century
(1500–1550)

Late Sixteenth Century
(1550–1600)

Louis XIII Period
1610–1643

Louis XIII Period
1610–1643

Louis XIV Period
1643–1715

Louis XIV Period
1643–1715

Fairchild's Dictionary
of FASHION

Fairchild's Dictionary
of FASHION

by
Dr. Charlotte Calasibetta, Ph.D.

former Professor of Fashion Merchandising,
Bernard M. Baruch School
City University of New York

Edited by
Ermina Stimson Goble

former art director and fashion editor,
Women's Wear Daily

Lorraine Davis

feature associate,
Vogue Magazine

Fairchild Publications, Inc.
New York, New York

Cover Design: Beverly Gerstl

Standard Book Number: 87005-133-4
Library of Congress
Catalog Card Number: 74-84805

Printed in the United States of America

About the Illustrations

Except in the cases she has mentioned in her preface, the drawings in this book are by Charlotte M. Calasibetta; many of those depicting the 19th and early 20th centuries were adapted from her own collection of old prints and periodicals, including *Godey's Lady's Book, Peterson's Magazine,* and *Demorest's Magazine.* Fashions from earlier periods were drawn, whenever possible, from the art of the time. The Greek figures and Roman man in the fashion-history section and the himation, chiton, and chlamys were redrawn from *Costumes of the Greeks and Romans* by Thomas Hope, published by William Miller in 1812 and by Dover Publications, Inc., New York, in 1962.

The color illustrations, unless otherwise noted on the page, came from these sources (number refers to the number of the illustration): 1. Shawabty Figure of Yuya: The Metropolitan Museum of Art, New York; The Theodore M. Davis Collection, Bequest of Theodore M. Davis, 1915. 2. Offering Bearers: The Metropolitan Museum of Art, New York; Rogers Fund, 1920. 4. Carolingian costume, *The History of Fashion in France,* C. Hoey, J. Lillie; New York: Scribner and Welford, 1882. 7. "Paradise," by Giovanni de Paolo: The Metropolitan Museum of Art, New York; Rogers Fund. 8. Detail of the princess from "Saint Georges Terrassant le Dragon:" Musee Unterlinden, Comar. 10. "Wife of Tommaso Portinari," by Hans Memling: The Metropolitan Museum of Art, New York. 11. English costume of the Middle Ages, *English Costume of the Later Middle Ages,* I. Brooke; London: A & C Black Ltd., 1935. 13. "Adoration of the Magi," from the *Belles Heures of Jean de France, Duke of Berry:* The Metropolitan Museum of Art, New York; The Cloisters Collection. 14. "Queen Elizabeth I:" The Metropolitan Museum of Art, New York; gift of J. Pierpoint Morgan, 1911. 15. "Louis XIV," by Hyacinthe Rigaud: Louvre, Paris. 16. "The Fortune Teller," Caravaggio: Louvre, Paris. 17. English costume of the Elizabethan Age, *English Costume in the Age of Elizabeth,* I. Brooke, London: A & C Black Ltd., 1933. 18. "The Three Magi," German, 16th century: The Metropolitan Museum of Art, New York; Joseph Pulitzer Bequest. 20. English dress of the 1690's: The Metropolitan Museum of Art, New York. 22. Japanese teahouse maid by Kitagawa Utamaro: The Metropolitan Museum of Art, New York. 25. "George Washington," Charles Willson Peale: The Metropolitan Museum of Art, New York. 28. Sea-side dress, 1826; *La Belle Assemblée.* 29. Hairstyle of 1872: *La Mode Illustrée.* 30. Promenade dresses, 1872: *Revue de la Mode.* 31. Clothes for afternoon wear, 1899: *The Delineator.* 32. Men's attire, 1854, *Le Progrés.* 34. Dressing Gown, 1922; *Journal des Dames:* The Metropolitan Museum of Art, New York; Costume Institute. 35. Dresses by Marie Marielle, 1928: *Trés Parisien.* 36. The St. Moritz look, 1925: *Trés Parisien.* 39. Felt hat by Rose Descat, 1932; *Femina:* The Metropolitan Museum of Art, New York;

v

Costume Institute. 40. Afternoon and evening dresses, Mutine, 1927: *Trés Parisien*. Dress by Beer; The Metropolitan Museum of Art, New York; Costume Institute.

In the photo sections in the Appendix, the following have provided very useful material, for which we are most grateful:

Eleanor Lambert Inc. for most of the style pictures on designers from the United States; Barbara Trister Public Relations for the style pictures on Rudi Gernreich.

Women's Wear Daily and Fairchild's Photo Department for photos of the designers and for most of the photos on styles by designers from England, France and Italy.

Joe Lieberman of Vera Maxwell Inc. for the Vera Maxwell style photos; Helen O'Hagan of Saks Fifth Avenue for photos of Emilio Pucci styles.

Author's Preface

Fairchild's Dictionary of Fashion presents clothing terminology from both historical and contemporary viewpoints. The book is intended to be used along with *Fairchild's Dictionary of Textiles,* edited by Dr. Isabel B. Wingate; fabrics are included in this volume but are not discussed in depth. It is hoped that this book will be useful to students of fashion, design, and retailing; to people involved in productions for theater, movies, opera, or television; to newspaper, magazine, and advertising writers and editors; to retailers, buyers, and sales people—all of them should find it a useful reference. The book should prove interesting, too, to the person who cares about fashion for fashion's sake.

Fairchild's Dictionary of Fashion evolved from a college course in fashion. In an attempt to teach students a vocabulary of fashion terms that would not become outdated, lists were assembled of collars, necklines, sleeves, skirts, and so on, and each considered in the light of the existing fashion trends: Which were "in;" and which, "out?" The basic categories for this book grew from those lists; the addition of historical terms and some of the vocabulary of clothing manufacture rounded out the entries.

Fashion is thought by some people to be a superficial kind of knowledge; but, when investigated thoroughly, it can be found to intersect many different fields of learning. Understanding man-made textiles requires a knowledge of chemistry; the various aspects of color take one into the realm of physics; information on gems involves the field of mineralogy; to understand mink mutations, it is necessary to grasp something about genetics. The history of fashion involves the whole sweep of world history and the people who made it; fashion is part of the sociology, culture, and art of every era. How people have lived and what they have thought has been reflected in what they wore. Where people have lived, what their occupations and avocations were, these have affected their clothes. So strong is fashion's influence that even the powers of religion and the law have been overruled by the dictates of fashion. People have worn whatever was in style, even when they were faced by state fines or chastisement by the Church.

It would be impossible to thank everyone who offered suggestions or gave help during the compilation of the *Dictionary of Fashion,* but special thanks are due to the following: To Dr. John W. Wingate and Dr. Isabel B. Wingate for their inspiration and encouragement. To Charlotte Fisher, who, with her knowledge of Greek and Latin and her large collection of dictionaries, helped to verify terminology and to check historical references. To Irene Wiener, Janis Best, and Arnold Waldman, who read some of the manuscript in preliminary stages and offered suggestions. To Emily Mankey Williamsen, for drawings of Chinese pajamas and swimsuits and for many preliminary drawings leading to the illustrations. To Betty Garrabrant, for filing the thousands of reference illustrations and data gathered from an estimated fifteen thousand publications. To Veronica Di Chiara and Dale Pleckaitis Corsello, for typing the thousands of reference cards. To Rose Ulrich and Rose Natale, for patient typing and retyping of the manuscript. To Sarah Brady for tabulation of the illustrations and help in proofreading.

Much appreciation and thanks go to the staff of Fairchild Publications, beginning with Edward Gold, Manager of Fairchild Books and Visuals, for his unfailing enthusiasm and his ardent belief that the *Dictionary of Fashion* would make a definite contribution to the fashion field as a reference source and for his untiring efforts to make the book a reality. To editors Donna B. Sessa, Marjorie Lewis, and Shelly Ruchlin, for their interest and diligence during the production of the book. To Merle Joy Thomason, head of the Fairchild costume library, for her conscientious help in selecting references for checking research material. To editors Cynthia Benjamin and Kenneth Rothstein who showed outstanding ability in coordination of the printing.

More thanks to Beverly Gerstl, for her ingenuity and originality in the design of the cover and the pages of color photographs. And particular thanks to Ermina Stimson Goble, who is the author of the appendix of fashion designers, and to Lorraine Davis, for her enthusiasm, keen fashion insight, and considerable literary ability in editing the last revision of the manuscript.

Gratitude is owed to my family, for their sympathetic understanding and many suggestions: To my mother, Katharine Laux Mankey, who used her keen memory to help in checking many of the terms from the early 1900's. To the memory of my father, Fred W. Mankey, who always encouraged me to further my education. And particular thanks to my husband, Dr. Charles J. Calasibetta, for his patience, understanding, and constant encouragement during the more than six years the book has been in progress . . . it is due to him that it was finally finished.

C.M.C.

Williamsport, Pennsylvania
February, 1975

Publisher's Notes

Consider these notes supplementary to Dr. Calasibetta's *Author's Preface*. Hopefully, they will be brief and to the point.

First, our reason for publishing this ambitious work despite extraordinary problems over a production period of six years: on the basis of talks with fashion professionals, educators and librarians, the evidence was that a tome of this scope was sorely needed and sadly missing from fashion literature. Also, our involvement with the fashion world, through our association with *Women's Wear Daily* in particular, made such a project a "natural" for us.

Secondly, a word about our good fortune with the author and senior editors. Dr. Calasibetta was unrelenting in her search, facing every setback, ambiguity, or difficult decision with good grace. She also contributed the mammoth collection of black and white sketches which covers about 15 per cent of the work. Senior editors Lorraine Davis and Ermina Stimson Goble, in terms of professional and emotional involvement, treated the book as if it were their own. Their combined efforts represented the very best fashion talent any publisher could hope for.

Finally, thanks to some people not yet mentioned, who helped with advice, research and typing to complete the project: June Weir, Fashion Editor of *Women's Wear Daily,* for judgments on designers; Stanley E. Gellers, fashion specialist on *Men's Wear Magazine;* Prof. Rosalie Kolodny of Fashion Institute of Technology, for help in relating art to definitions; Al Samuels, Editor, and Vivian Infantino, Fashion Director, of *Footwear News;* Phyllis Posnick, Beauty Editor, *Glamour Magazine;* Annalee Gold, fashion author and consultant, for ideas on the scope of the work; editorial staffers Majorie Lewis during the early days of the project and Cynthia Benjamin and Ken Rothstein during the later days of production; and Frances Stahl, my secretary, who helped with the never-ending typing job.

We put the *Fairchild* name on the title of this book purposely; we did it to compliment the book. And we are confident the book will compliment the Fairchild name and the organization behind that name.

E. B. Gold, Mgr.
Fairchild Books

New York City
February, 1975

ix

How to Use This Book

Alphabetical listings:

Fairchild's Dictionary of Fashion is organized in conventional dictionary form, with definitions listed alphabetically. The entry word is printed in **bold type;** the definition is indented. *Key words* in the definitions are printed in *italics,* and the abbreviation *q.v.* (Latin, *quode vide,* which see) refers the reader to related definitions.

Alternate spellings are provided—along with the entry word if they are in comparable usage; otherwise, at the end of the entry. *Plurals* are not shown, unless they differ from the standard English forms. *Pronunciations* are not included, unless they differ radically from a phonetic reading of the English word; *derivations* appear only when needed for full understanding.

Capitalization has been indicated, when possible, for trademarks and proper names. Whether a word that is derived from a proper name—*e.g., chesterfield* coat, *Bedford* cord—shall be capitalized or not remains to some extent a matter of taste. Some of these words seem to have been absorbed totally into the language as common nouns or adjectives; others seem to look better with their proper capitals. Writers and editors will have to consider the context in deciding whether or not to capitalize such words.

Foreign words and phrases have been printed in the same types as English words. Much of the language of fashion is international, and such words are regarded as having been adopted into the English of fashion. It is left to the individual judgments of writers and editors as to whether or not such words as *coiffure en cadenettes* or *cheongsam* should be printed in italics, depending on the context and on who their readers will be.

Categorical listings:

When there are a number of entries in the same basic category, the words have been grouped together and alphabetized within the group. For instance, the alphabetical listing **dress** is followed by a category headed **DRESSES,** with one hundred and ten types of dresses—from **A-line d.** (dress) to **wrap d.**—listed alphabetically. The entry words in the categories are indented along with the definitions—in contrast to the main entries, which extend into the margin. An **INDEX TO CATEGORIES** follows this how-to section, on pages xiii, xiv. Cross references to the categories will be found, as well, in the main alphabetical listings.

Designers appendix:

Biographical sketches of important *fashion designers* around the world, both living and dead, are brought together in an appendix, alphabetized under the names of the countries where they work or worked. Thus, Cristobal Balenciaga is found under FRANCE; since, although a Spaniard, he was a Paris couturier. This section forms a kind of brief history of fashion design. Designers' names are also in the main alphabetical listings, cross-referenced to the appendix with their national groupings. A reader who is not sure of the designer's "nationality" can learn this from the alphabetical listing.

The scope of this book:

Fairchild's Dictionary of Fashion looks at finished clothes from the wearer's point of view. No attempt has been made to include all of the vast technical vocabularies of the clothing trades involved. Clothes as they are worn and have been worn are the subject— a wide and exciting one, quite enough for one book. *L.J.D.*

Index to Categories

Fairchild's Dictionary
of FASHION

A

A 1. Shoe size: Letter indicating a narrow width with AA, AAA, AAAA, AAAAA being successively narrower. 2. Pajama size: Men's size corresponding to 32–36 chest size, 110–135 pounds weight, or shirt sizes 13½–14½. Also called "S" for *small*. 3. Brassiere cup size: Letter A used to indicate small cup size; AA is the smallest size, DD is the largest.

aba 1. Coarse fabric of natural fibers, wool, goat hair, or camel hair—or a blend of these; used by peasants of southern Europe, Asia and northern Africa. 2. Rectangular striped or plain tunic or robe of this fabric, worn by Arabian and North African men; also made of silk for upper classes, sometimes with embroidery at shoulder seams, armholes, edges of neck and the front; fastened at neck with tasseled cords. Also spelled *abba, abayeh, haba.*

abacá (ah-bak-*kah*) Natural durable fiber from a banana-like plant, native to Philippines and Central America, used for "Manila" hats. Also called *Manila hemp* (though unlike true hemp), *Cebu hemp, Davao hemp,* and *Tagel hat braid.* Also spelled *abaka.*

abalone See *mother-of-pearl.*

abilements, abillements See *billiments.*

abito Italian word for *clothes, suit, dress.*

abraded yarn Continuous-filament rayon yarn with fuzzy projections to increase bulk.

abstract cut See *hairstyles.*

abstract design See *prints.*

academic costume Caps, gowns, and hoods, usually black with color trim on hood, worn at commencement exercises; designed by Gardner Cotrell Leonard of Albany, N.Y., in 1887 and adopted in the American Intercollegiate Code of 1894, revised in 1932. Code states style of cap, gown, and hood to be worn by persons with Bachelor's, Master's, and Doctor's degrees along with the colors to be used on the hood. Also called *academic regalia.* See also *Bachelor's, Doctor's,* and *Master's gowns* and *hoods, academic hood,* and *mortarboard.*

academic hood Decorative drape which comes close to neck in front and hangs down the back of academic gowns in various lengths and shapes according to degree held,

1

usually in black with colored facing indicating degree granted. Inside colors represent school colors of institution conferring degree, the outer band of velvet shows field of study, e.g.; Agriculture, maize; Arts and Letters, white; Fine Arts, brown; Law, purple; etc. *Der.* From the *cowl, q.v.,* cape attached to gowns of undergraduates since end of 15th century. See *Bachelor's, Master's,* and *Doctor's hoods.*

accordion pleats See *pleats, handbags. Der.* Named for similarity to pleated bellows of the musical instrument *accordion.*

acetate 1. Generic term for fiber manmade from cellulose acetate. 2. Yarn or thread made from this fiber. 3. Knitted or woven fabrics made from this yarn. Acetates drape well, have a silk-like appearance, resist wrinkles and fading; cost is low. Used for dress and coat linings, blouses, lingerie. See also *triacetate.*

achkan (atch-kan) Full-skirted white cotton coat reaching to knee, buttoned down front; worn by men in India.

Acrilan Trademark of Chemstrand for

wide variety of acrylic fibers manufactured for different end use, each designated by number; type 16 is basic fiber for apparel.

acrobatic slipper See *slippers.*

acrylic 1. Generic name for fibers and yarns man-made from acrylic resins. 2. Knit or woven goods made from acrylic yarns. Acrylics are easy to wash and quick-drying; they have wrinkle resistance, pleat retention, resistance to moths and mildew. Used for sweaters and hosiery and in bonded fabrics for dresses.

action back Term used to describe the extra fullness worked into back of a jacket or coat from shoulder blades to waist permitting freedom of movement.

action gloves See *gloves.*

acton (ak-tun) 1. Padded jacket worn under armor in 13th and 14th centuries. 2. Later, steel-plated jacket worn as armor. Also spelled *aketon, auqueton, hacketon* and *haqueton.*

adaptation Clothing-industry term for copy of an expensive dress, usually from Paris couture, reproduced in less expensive materials with modifications to lower the cost of production.

Adelaide boot Woman's ankle-high side-laced boot with patent-leather, *q.v.,* toe and heel, sometimes with fur or fringed trimming at top. Worn in U.S. from about 1830–65.

Adelaide wool High quality merino wool from southern Australia, used for worsted fabrics; named after Adelaide, the port from which it is shipped.

admiral coat See *coats.*

admiralty cloth See *fabrics.*

Adrian, Gilbert See *designers appendix, United States.*

aegis 1. Shield carried by Zeus, king of the gods in Greek mythology. 2. Later, a type of breastplate made of metal scales with head of Gorgon Medusa and fringe of serpents, worn as a part of armor by Zeus's daughter, Athena, goddess of wisdom.

Aeolian mink See *mink* under *furs.*

aesthetic dress Style of dress advocated by small group of cultured class in England, end of 19th century, who adopted a modified form of 14th-century costume called a *smock, q.v.,* in a protest against tightly corseted contemporary fashion. Called *"greener-yallery, Grosvenor gallery"* costume.

Afghan lamb See *furs.*

Afghanistan jacket See *sport jackets* under *jackets.*

Afghanistan vest See *vests.*

Afghanistan wedding tunic See *shirts.*

Afro Term adopted by Afro-Americans in 1960's to characterize hairdos and fashions with African influence. See *prints, hairstyles, necklaces.*

Afrylic Trademark for specially processed Kanekalon fiber used to make Afro wigs.

after-ski boot See *boots.*

after-ski slipper See *slippers.*

agal (ah-gaul) Thick cord of wool used by Arabians, Bedouins, and desert dwellers to secure the *kaffiyeh,* or head-scarf. See also *kaffiyeh.*

agate See *gems.*

aggravators Term used for semi-curls

AGAL AND KAFFIYEH

near the eye or temple, worn by men from 1830–50.

Agilon Trademark of Deering Milliken Research Corp. for licensed textured processed monofilament yarn, usually nylon, used because of great elasticity for women's hosiery and pantyhose, also for woven goods, sweaters, tricot knits, and men's hose.

aglet Ornamental metal tag, frequently of gold or silver, similar to modern shoelace tip, at end of lacing called a *point,* used in the 15th century for joining men's *doublet* and *hose, q.q.v.;* later used in bunches for a decorative effect. See *aiguillette.*

Agnès See *designers appendix, France.*

Agnès Sorel See *Sorel, Agnès.*

Agnès Sorel coiffure Woman's hairstyle with ribbon bands in front, a knot in back; worn 1830–50.

Agnès Sorel corsage or **bodice** Woman's dress bodice with square neckline front and back, full *bishop sleeves,* or woman's loose-fitting bodice of a *pelisse robe, q.q.v.,* similar to a jacket, fastened high to neck or worn open revealing *waistcoat bosom, q.v.* Worn in 1860's and named after Agnès Sorel, *q.v.*

Agnès Sorel dress Variant of *princess* dress, *q.v.*, worn in 1860's.

agraffe 1. Circular, square, or diamond-shaped clasp, used in pairs to fasten the mantle at neck in Middle Ages; made of bronze, gold, or silver embossed in elaborate patterns, set with jewels. 2. Pin used to fasten slashes in garments in 16th century. Also spelled *agraf* or *agrafe*. Also called *fermails, fermayle,* or *fers, q.q.v. Der.* Norman *aggrape,* clasp on medieval armor.

aigrette (ai-gret) See *feathers.*

aiguillette (ah-gwel-yet) Shoulder decoration made of loops of gilt cord, frequently braided, worn on military dress uniform. *Der.* From square

of leather covered with embroidered coat-of-arms on shoulder of medieval armor, similar to *epaulet q.v.* Also called *ailette* and *aglet.*

aile de pigeon Man's wig styled with smooth top hair pulled to back, with one or two stiff horizontal curls above the ears. Worn in 1750's and 1760's, seen in portraits of George Washington *Der.* French, pigeon wing *q.v.*

Ainu kimono (i-new) Short *kimono* with narrow *obi* sash, *q.q.v.,* wide sleeves tapered to wrist, made of elmbark fabric decorated with bold embroidered appliqué designs and

worn by the Ainu on island of Yezo, north of Japan.

airplane fabrics See *fabrics.*

ajiji Cotton fabric from India similar to muslin, usually containing silk or rayon stripes.

ajour French term for openwork making the design in lace or hemstitching.

aketon See *acton.*

Alaska 1. English yarn made of mixture of cotton and carded wool or other combinations, used for hand-knitting and weaving. 2. British fabric woven of these yarns in twill or plain weave, finished by napping. 3. In early 20th century, an overshoe or storm rubber with a high tongue over the instep.

Alaskan fur seal See *furs.*

alb Full-length liturgical robe worn by

priests at Mass; originally of white linen, now often of blended cotton and man-made fibers; long sleeves, may have a *drawstring* neckline, *q.v.,* or *cowl* hood, *q.v. Der.* Latin, white.

albatross Lightweight wool. See *fabrics.*

albernous Variant of *burnoose, q.v.*

Albert See *fabrics.*

Albert boots Man's side-laced boot with fabric top and *patent-leather, q.v.,* toe, frequently decorated down front with *mother-of-pearl* buttons, *q.v.;* worn 1840–70. *Der.* From fashion popularized by *Prince Albert,* the consort of England's Queen Victoria.

Albert cloth See *fabrics.*

Albert jacket Man's single-breasted jacket with or without waistline seam and side pleats, no breast pocket; worn in mid-19th century.

Albert overcoat Man's loose-fitting mid-calf overcoat with fly front, small shoulder cape, flapped skirt pockets, long back vent, and vertical slit breast pockets; worn in 1840's. Also called *Albert driving sac, cape.*

Albert riding coat High-buttoned single-breasted man's coat with front cut away in slanted style similar to *Newmarket, q.v.,* with broad collar, narrow lapels, and pockets; worn in mid-19th century.

Albert top frock Man's heavy overcoat styled like a *frock coat, q.v.,* made with wide velvet collar and flapped pockets, wide cuffs, and lapels; worn 1860–1900.

Albouy See *designers appendix, France.*

Alençon lace See *laces.*

Alice blue Medium light blue, slight grey-green cast; said to be the favorite color of Alice Roosevelt Longworth, daughter of President Theodore Roosevelt; color was popularized by the song "Alice Blue Gown," introduced by Edith Day in musical *Irene* in 1919.

A-line Term introduced in 1955 by Paris couturier Christian Dior to describe apparel which was narrow through shoulders and stood away from the body, flaring gently to hem like the letter A—popular for *coats, dresses, jumpers, q.q.v.* Also see *silhouettes.*

alligator See *leathers.*

alligator-grained Descriptive of alligator-skin pattern embossed or printed on cowhide or calfskin leather, plastic, or Corfam, *q.v.*

alligator lizard Tanned skins from types of lizards with both rice-like lizard markings and box-like markings similar to alligator. Also see *Lizigator, q.v.,* under *leathers.*

all-in-one See *foundation garment.*

all-over lace See *laces.*

all-over print See *prints.*

all-weather coat See *coats and raincoats.*

alma Silk twill. See *fabrics.*

almain coat or **jacket** Jacket worn by men over doublet in latter 15th and early 16th centuries, close fitting with short, flared skirt and long *hanging sleeves, q.v.,* open at the front seams.

almain hose Full, slashed *trunk hose, q.v.,* with undergarment pulled

5

through the slashes, worn by men in late 16th century. Also called *German hose*. See also *Pluderhose*.

almandine See *gems*.

almoner See *aulmonière*.

almuce 1. A headdress resembling a *cowl, q.v.* 2. A medieval garment with a hood and a fur lining.

aloe See *laces* and *embroideries*.

aloha shirt See *shirts*.

alpaca Yarn made from the fleece of the alpaca, a sheep-like animal of the camel family, related to the llama, native to the Andes in South America (also used for fur).

alpaca fabric See *fabrics*.

alpargata (ahl-pa-gah-ta) See *shoes*.

Alphonsine, Marie See *designers appendix, France*.

Alpine hat See *hats*.

Alpine jacket 1. Waist-length jacket worn with suspender shorts as part of a Tyrolean mountain climber's costume. 2. Late 19th-century Englishman's jacket similar to a Norfolk jacket, made double-breasted with vertical flapped pockets and pleat down center back; worn buttoned to neck, often without a vest.

Alsatian bow Women's native headdress of Alsace-Lorraine: enormous bow of taffeta ribbon placed with knot on top of head, the loops rising like two wings and falling almost to shoulders with longer ends falling down back.

amadis sleeve Sleeve with tight cuff, buttoned at the wrist, worn in 1830's, revived in 1850's, when sleeve was buttoned to elbow, upper sleeve full and pleated into armhole.

Amazon collar Standing collar, similar to a *Chinese collar, q.v.*, with gap in

center front; used on women's blouses in early 1860's and worn with a black ribbon necktie.

Amazon corsage Plain bodice buttoned up front to high neckline; trimmed with small white cambric collar and cuffs; informal style for women in 1840's.

Amazon corset English corset worn for riding in mid-19th century, made with elastic lacings that shortened the garment by three inches when hidden cord was pulled.

Amazone Woman's scarlet riding habit with short waist, full-length skirt; worn in French Empire period. *Der.* From legendary Greek women warriors called Amazons.

Amazon plume See *feathers*.

amber See *gems*.

American buskins Shoes with stout leather soles and knee-high cloth uppers, or leggings, fastened with lacings; worn by American Colonists. Similar to *startups, q.v.*

American coat British term for man's single-breasted full-length coat, usually black, with narrow lapels, wide collar, and full skirt; worn in late 1820's.

American Fashion Critics' Award Original name for the *Coty Award, q.v.*

6

American Indian print See *prints.*

American neckcloth English term for a stock, *q.v.,* plain in center front with vertical pleating on each side, narrow ends brought around to front and tied at base of neck in a *Gordian knot, q.v.;* worn by men in 1820's.

American shoulders English term for padded shoulders popular in U.S. at end of 19th century.

American trousers English term for men's trousers worn without suspenders, pants gathered or pleated into waistband with adjustable strap and buckle in back. Worn from late 1850's on.

American vest British term for man's single-breasted vest, usually with V-neck and no collar, buttoned up center front; worn with a suit from 1860's on.

Amery, Ronald See *designers appendix, United States.*

amethyst See *gems.*

Amies, Hardy See *designers appendix, England.*

amout Sealskin tunic, with hood attached at back to carry an infant; worn by Greenland Eskimo women.

amulet Small object believed to possess magical powers, a good-luck charm as protection against evil, worn by primitive people and surviving to present time in various forms of jewelry.

anadem Wreath or garland of leaves or flowers, worn on hair by women in late 16th and early 17th centuries.

ancient madder See *fabrics.*

Andalouse cape (an-da-looz) Cape, worn outdoors by women in the 1840's, made of silk and trimmed with fringe.

Andalusian 1. Fine worsted dress fabric made in England from Spanish merino wool. 2. English washable silk fabric with *broché* pattern, *q.v.,* popular in early 19th century.

Andalusian casque (an-da-loozian cask) Woman's evening tunic fastened down center with series of ribbons, front of skirt cut away, sloping to knee length in the back; worn over a skirt, in early 1800's.

Andean shift See *dresses.*

androgynous (an-drodg-e-nus) Possessing both male and female characteristics, hermaphroditic. James Laver, fashion historian, says ideal fashion figure of 1920's and late 1960's and 1970's is the androgynous female who resembles a boy. The boy of the 1970's is also androgynous. See *unisex.*

anelace See *anlace.*

anga Man's coat native to India—longer form of the *angharka, q.v.*

angel overskirt Short upper skirt with two long points on either side; worn as part of a woman's daytime dress in 1890's.

Angel Skin Trademark for a smooth waxy finish with dull reflection given some acetate fabrics; term also applied to other dull-appearing acetate fabrics. Also given trademark *Peau d'Ange, q.v.*

angel sleeves Long square panels from shoulders reaching nearly to floor, worn by women in 1889.

angharka (an-gar-ka) Man's semi-fitted jacket with side seams slit up from hem; neckline low, horseshoe-shaped, and bound with braid, exposing high-necked cambric shirt; worn in India at court and by maharajahs for festive occasions.

angiya (an-gee-a) Short-sleeved bodice just covering the breasts, worn by Moslem women in southern India.

angled pocket See *hacking* under *pockets.*

angled shawl collar See *collars.*

angle-fronted coat Variation of man's *morning coat, q.v.,* which was cut away diagonally on each side to reveal triangles of waistcoat; worn 1870–90. Also called *university coat.*

anglesea hat (angle-see) Man's hat with flat brim and high cylindrical crown, worn in mid 19th century.

Angleterre point lace See *point d'Angleterre* under *laces.*

Anglo-Greek bodice Woman's bodice with wide lapels edged with lace and placed far apart, worn in 1820's with *fichu-robings, q.v.*

Anglo-Saxon embroidery See *embroideries.*

angola Corruption of word *augara,* used in England for wool and cotton mixture for shirtings and overcoats and embroidery cloth.

Angora Soft fuzzy yarn made from underhair of Angora rabbit; popular for sweaters in late 1930's and for sweaters and knit dresses in 1970's.

Angoulême bonnet (ahn-goo-lem) Straw bonnet with high pleated crown, broad front brim narrowed at sides, tied down with bow at side; worn by women in French Empire period, and named for Duchesse d'Angoulême, daughter of Marie Antoinette.

Anguilla cotton (ang-gwilla-a) Cotton first produced in West Indies on island of Anguilla; may have been the source of *Sea Island cotton, q.v.*

animal print See *prints.*

ankh Egyptian symbol for eternal life: a *cross, q.v.,* with top bar form-

ing a loop; popular as jewelry motif, especially on necklaces and rings, in late 1960's, 1970's.

ankle boots See *boots.*

ankle bracelet See *bracelets* and *khalkhal.*

ankle jacks Man's low boot, ankle-high and laced up front with five pairs of eyelets; popular in East End of London in early 19th century.

ankle length See *lengths,*

ankle sock See *socks.*

anklet 1. See *bracelets.* 2. See *socks.* 3. See *khalkhal.*

anlace Man's long two-edged dagger, worn hanging from the belt in 14th and 15th centuries.

Annamese band turban Open-crowned wrapped cotton turban with folds sewn into place, wide at sides; native headdress of North Vietnamese women, who originally believed good spirits entered body through open crown.

annular brooch Metal ring with long pin attached, used to fasten clothing in Anglo-Saxon times.

anorak (ah-no-rack) Warm hooded waist-length jacket of sealskin or printed cotton, worn by Greenland Eskimos. Also spelled *anora*.

antelope-finished suede Soft, sueded finish applied to lambskin, calfskin, or goatskin in imitation of antelope skin. See *leathers*.

antelope fur See *furs*.

antelope leather See *leathers*.

antery (an-tery) Waist-length or below-the-knee vest worn by Egyptian and Turkish men over linen shirts.

Anthony, John See *designers appendix, United States*.

antigropolis (an-te-grah-po-lis) Man's long *gaiter, q.v.,* usually leather: over thigh in front, cut away to knee in back; worn in mid 19th century for walking or riding.

antique bodice Long-waisted tight bodice with low décolletage and deep point at front waistline; worn for evening by women in 1830's and 1840's.

antique finish Finish applied to leather giving a shaded effect by dyeing, buffing, wrinkling, waxing, and oiling the surface to resemble old leather.

antique lace See *laces*.

antique satin See *fabrics*.

antique taffeta See *fabrics*.

Antoinette fichu Woman's long shaped scarf which went around the neck, crossed in front, went around the waist, and tied in the back with a bow and long ends; worn in the 1850's. Also called *Marie Antoinette fichu*.

Antonelli, Maria See *designers appendix*, Italy.

Antron Trademark of E. I. du Pont de Nemours & Company for nylon of several types of 66 continuous-filament yarn and staples; used for silky-looking sweaters and lingerie.

Antwerp lace See *laces*.

ao dai Pants suit with long-sleeved mid-calf tunic, slashed on side seams, and full-length pants; worn by women in Vietnam.

Apache (a-patch-e) 1. Styles similar to clothes worn by Indian tribe of American Southwest, mainly Arizona and New Mexico. 2. In France, *apache* (a-pash) means clothes in the style of a gangster or bandit. See also *scarfs, handbags.*

ape drape See *hairstyles.*

apex Originally, the spike of olive wood on the peak of cap worn by Roman flamen (priest of some particular deity); later, the cap was known by this name.

Apollo corset Waist cincher stiffened with whalebone worn by both men and women in early 19th century, similar to *Brummell bodice* and the *Cumberland corset, q.q.v.*

Apollo knot Woman's elaborate evening hairstyle, 1824–1832, made with wired loops of false hair, projecting up from crown of head, finished with decorative comb or flowers or feathers.

apparel industry The manufacturers, jobbers, and contractors engaged in the manufacture of ready-to-wear clothing for men, women, and children. Also called: *garment trade, needle trades, the cutting-up trades,* and *the rag business.*

Appenzell See *embroideries.*

appliqué (ap-plee-kay) Surface pattern made by cutting out fabric or lace designs and attaching them to another fabric or lace by means of embroidery or stitching; also, applied leather designs on shoes and handbags. See *laces.*

après-ski French name for after-ski wear; see *boots, slippers,* etc.

apron Garment worn over all or part of front of body to protect one's clothes or as a decorative accessory, tied around waist or with bib attached to cover bodice. Originated from an extra piece of cloth tied over skirt in Middle Ages, which evolved in 16th century into colored aprons for men to denote specific trades. See *checked-apron men, green-apron men, blue-apron men.* From 17th through 19th centuries became lace embroidered for women. *Der.* From Old French *naperon* or *nappi,* meaning *cloth.* Also see *pinafore.*

APRONS:

barber's a. Long circular cape, fastening at the neckline in back, originally of cotton fabric and now sometimes of plastic, worn to protect clothes while hair is being cut.

bib a. Apron which extends above the bust, held by straps over the shoulders crossing in center back and attached at waistline; first worn in the 17th century.

carpenter's a. Two or more leather or fabric pockets mounted on a belt; worn by workmen to carry nails, small tools, etc.

cobbler's a. Hip-length, large-pocketed apron of stout cloth or leather, originally worn by shoemakers, carpenters, and other workmen to hold nails; worn as woman's fashion in late 1960's, made of leather, suede, or fabrics.

cocktail a. Decorative tiny half-apron made in net, lace, or decorated fabric.

half a. Bibless apron coming only to waist.

Hoover a. Utility wrap-around dress

COBBLER'S APRON

HALF APRON

WORK APRONS, 1892

with two half-fronts and attached strip of material at waist level that goes through slot at each side seam to tie in back; originated during World War I, when Herbert Hoover was food administrator in U.S.A.

work a. Any apron designed to cover the clothes amply while the wearer is working at a job that might soil or harm garments.

apron checks Gingham fabric, *q.v.*, used for aprons made with even *checks*, *q.v.*, of white and a color.

apron dress See *dresses*.

apron swimsuit See *swimsuits*.

apron tongue Extra long leather tongue on shoe that fits behind lacing, then flops over, covering laces completely; often fringed at the end.

aquamarine See *gems*.

araneum lace See *laces*.

Aran Isle sweater See *sweaters*.

arasaid Long gown of *tartan*, *q.v.*, worn, belted at waist, by Scotswoman of early 17th century, with a *tonnag* over the shoulder and a linen *curraichd* on head.

arba kanfoth, kamphoth Undergarment worn by Orthodox Jewish men, a rectangle of cloth about three feet by three feet; slit for the neckline, tassels at the corners.

Arctics See *boots*.

Arcturus mink See *mink* under *furs*.

Argenta mink See *mink* under *furs*.

argentan lace See *laces*.

Argentina borregos lamb See *lamb* under *furs*.

Argentine cloth See *fabrics*.

Argyll, argyl, argyle See *plaids, knits, socks, sweaters*.

Arlesienne coif Headdress native to Arles, France, consisting of white cap worn on crown of head, almost covered by black velvet cap with long broad ribbon extending down back; headdress can be seen in French Post-Impressionist Vincent Van Gogh's painting "L'Arlesienne."

arm bands See *bracelets*.

Armenian lace See *laces*.

Armenian mantle Woman's loose *pelisse*, *q.v.*, without a cape, trimmed

11

with braid *passementerie, q.v.,* in front; worn in mid-19th century.

armhole Section of garment through which arm passes or into which sleeve is fitted. Originally called *armscye* and *armseye.*

armlet See *bracelets.*

armor Protective garments worn by soldiers and knights from early times, especially those made of chain mail and cast metal from Middle Ages through 17th century. For individual items see: *acton, camail, cannon, coif de mailles, cointise, coutes, demi brassard, épauliers, gauntlet, hauberk, jack, jamb, mail, morion, pauldrons, solleret, tabard,* and *vambraces.*

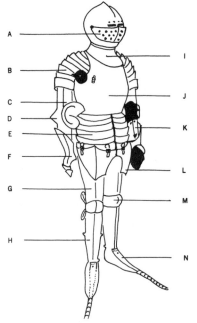

ARMOR c. 1450
A. VISOR; B. PAULDRON; C. REREBRACE; D. COUTES (OR ELBOW COP); E. SKIRT; F. GAUNTLET; G. CUISSE; H. GREAVE; I. GORGET; J. BREASTPLATE; K. VAMBRACE; L. TASSET; M. POLEYN (OR KNEE COP); N. SOLLERET À LA POULAINE.

armozine Heavy corded silk. See *fabrics.*

armscye Older spelling for *armseye.*

armseye Early term for *armhole, q.v.*

armure See *fabrics* and *weaves.*

army blouse See *blouse.*

army cloth See *fabrics.*

Arrasene See *embroideries.*

arrowhead See *embroideries* and *stitches.*

Art Déco Geometric non-representational style of jewelry and fabric design popular in late 1920's and inspired by *Exposition international des arts décoratifs et industriels modernes* in Paris, 1925. Revived in late 1968–69 and used as inspiration for fabric and jewelry design. See also *Art Moderne. Der.* French, *art décoratif,* decorative art.

artichoke See *hairstyles.*

artificial crinoline See *cage petticoat.*

artificial silk Term used before 1925 to describe rayon and acetate. Also called *art silk.*

artillery twill Variant of *whipcord, q.v.*

art linen Linen or linen-and-cotton fabric to be handblocked, screen printed, or embroidered. Also called *embroidery crash* or *linen.*

Art Moderne (ar mod-airn) French design style for jewelry and fabrics that followed the *Arts décoratifs* shown at the 1925 Paris exposition, featuring straight lines and angles.

Art Nouveau (ar noo-vo) Decorative style popular for jewelry and fashions from 1890 to 1900 characterized by use of natural forms in curving designs of climbing vines, leaves, flowers, and women's long hair; revived in 1960's and 1970's. *Der.* French, new art. See also *prints.*

Artois (ahr-twah) Long cloak with lapels and several capes, the longest ending near the waistline; worn by men and women in late 18th century.

Artois buckle Very large ornamental shoe buckle curved over foot, fashionable in late 18th century.

art silk See *artificial silk.*

Ascot Fashionable horse-racing spot, Ascot Heath, in England, for which a number of fashions have been named. See *collars, necklines, scarves, ties.*

Ascot jacket Loose-fitting man's jacket with matching fabric belt pulling in full waistline; worn in late 19th century.

ashes-of-roses Grayed pink color. Also called *bois de rose.*

A-shirt Short for *athletic shirt:* man's undershirt with narrow shoulder straps, worn for gym or sports. See *knit shirts* under *shirts.*

asoosh 17th century term meaning sash-wise or scarf-wise: draped diagonally from shoulder to hip. Also spelled *aswash.*

asterism Ability of a gemstone to project a star-shaped pattern as in rubies, sapphires; produced synthetically in trademarked Linde star and Hope sapphires. See *gems.*

astrakhan (as-tra-kan) 1. Term used for type of lambskin from southern Russia, named for city of Astrakhan. See *furs.* 2. Woven fabric in pile weave imitating curly lamb, used for collars, cuffs, hats, and jackets. 3. Knitted fabric made from curly yarns. 4. Wool fibers from *carakul lambs, q.v.* Also spelled *astrachan.*

aswash See *asoosh.*

asymmetric styles See *dresses* and *silhouettes.*

atef Headdress consisting of tall white cap with two plumes, or feathers, arranged at the sides; symbolic headdress of certain Egyptian gods, particularly Osiris, also depicted as worn by Egyptian kings.

athletic shirt See *knit shirts* under *shirts.*

athletic shorts See *shorts.*

athletic socks See *socks.*

at-home wear See *robes* and *pajamas.*

atours (a-toor) Padded horned headdress worn by women in 14th and 15th centuries.

attifet Woman's headdress arched on either side of forehead to form a "widow's peak" and draped completely with a veil; worn in 16th century and seen in paintings of Mary Queen of Scots.

attire 1. Synonym for *apparel.* 2. Term used since the 15th century for woman's headdress of gold and gems worn on state occasions, later shortened to *tire.*

aubergine (o-ber-jheen) Dark purple color. *Der.* French, eggplant.

Aubusson stitch See *stitches.*

Audubon law Law passed early in 20th century prohibiting use and importation of feathers from rare birds, such as the egret, which were fashionable trim on women's hats from late 19th century to World War I; named for John James Audubon, American ornithologist who died in 1851.

Augustabernard See *designers appendix, France.*

Aujard, Christian See *designers appendix, France.*

aulmoniere (all-mon-y-air) Medieval pouch of silk or leather suspended from girdle, worn by men from the 13th century until the Reformation, to carry alms; women in 14th century also used it to carry mirrors and tweezers for their back hair. Also spelled *aumoniere, aulmonier, almoner.* Similar to *gipser, q.v.*

auqueton (aw-ke-tawn) See *acton.*

aureole (or-e-ole) A white cap tied under chin, with a starched, pleated lace frill framing the face; headdress of women of Boulogne, France.

aurora borealis beads See *beads.*

Australian opossum See *furs.*

Austrian cloth Fine wool. See *fabrics.*

Austrian seal See *furs.*

automobile coat and **cap** Protective wraps worn when motoring in early 20th century, when all cars were open. See *duster.*

automobile veil Wide, sheer, long veil placed over wide-brimmed hat and tied under chin with ends flowing over front of *duster, q.v.;* worn for motoring in early 1900's. Also called *motoring veil.*

Autumn Haze See *mink* under *furs.*

avant-garde (a-vahnt guard) Forward thinking or advanced; when referring to art or costume, sometimes implies erotic or startling. *Der.* French, advance guard.

aviator's jumpsuit See *jumpsuits.*

Avignon French silk. See *fabrics.*

AUTOMOBILE COAT, 1904

AUTOMOBILE CAP, 1907

Avisco Trademark of American Viscose Co. for acetate filament yarn; for rayon filament yarn staple and tow used for woven fabrics, knits, and non-woven disposable fabrics; and for Vinyon H H, which is used as a bonding agent.

award sweater See *sweaters.*

awning stripe 1. Heavy durable cotton canvas with woven stripes used for awnings. 2. Fabric similar to awning canvas, printed or woven in stripes, for sport clothes, handbags. Also see *stripes*.

Ayrshire embroidery See *embroideries*.

azlon Generic term for man-made fibers of regenerated protein from substances such as peanuts, corn, and milk; now made only in Europe.

azoic dyes Group of colors which form directly in the fiber by a chemical reaction. Used on cotton and viscose rayon, low in cost and produce vibrant colors. Also called *naphthol dyes* and *ice dyes*.

Aztec print See *prints*.

Azurene mink See *mink* under *furs*.

B

B 1. Shoe size: letter indicating a width; widths run from AAAAA to EEEEE with A's being the narrowest. 2. Pajama size: men's size corresponding to 36-40 chest size, 135–165 pounds weight, or shirt sizes 14½–15½; also called "M" or *medium*. 3. Brassiere cup size: Sizes run AA, A, B, C, D, DD, with AA being smallest.

babet bonnet Small tulle evening bonnet worn on back of head and covering ears; worn by women in 1830's. Also called *bonnet babet*.

babet cap Woman's morning cap of muslin with ribbon trimming, covering ears and part of cheeks; worn in 1840's.

babouche, baboosh (bah-*boosh*) Heelless slipper of Moroccan leather with pointed toe; worn by peoples of Northern Africa, Turkey, and Armenia. Also spelled *babooch, baboosh, babouch, babush,* etc. Also see *paboudj.*

babushka (bah-boosh-ka) Triangular headscarf, or square folded into triangle, with ends tied under chin. *Der.* Russian word for grandmother —worn by older generation. Also see *scarfs.*

baby blue Delicate pale-blue color, traditionally worn by boy babies, since 1920; earlier, by girls.

baby bodice Daytime bodice introduced in late 1870's with lingerie features similar to baby's dress such

as vertical pleats down front and a wide sash, originally having a square neck, later a high drawstring neckline fastened with ribbon.

baby bonnet See *bonnets.*

baby boot Term used for an infant's *bootee, q.v.,* in second half of 19th century; usually made of fabric and elaborately trimmed with embroidery.

baby bunting Infants outdoor combination blanket-sack with zipper up front and separate or attached hood, frequently made of blanket cloth and bound with satin.

baby cap Woman's *coif, q.v.,* of lawn or lace styled like a baby's bonnet; worn in late 16th and early 17th centuries.

baby combing wool Wool fiber from 2″ to 2½″ that is fine and choice.

baby doll Term used for clothing and accessories similar to clothes worn by childrens' dolls in early 20th century. Also see *nightgowns, shoes, silhouettes.*

baby dress 1. Dresses popular until mid 20th century for infants, regardless of sex, usually made of fine white cotton in shift style and trimmed with tucks, embroidery, and lace. Also see *christening dress.* 2. See *dresses.*

baby Irish See *laces.*

baby lace See *laces.*

baby Louis heel See *heels.*

baby pink Pale tint of pink, traditionally worn by girl babies after 1920; earlier by boys.

baby ribbon Narrow ribbon one-eighth to one-quarter inch in width, sometimes reversible satin; originally used for baby clothes and also to thread through *insertions, q.v.,* of lace and beading in late 19th and early 20th centuries.

baby sash Woman's sash of ribbon tied in bow at back; popular at end of 19th century.

baby skirt Short flared or pleated skirt worn over bathing suit or playsuit during 1930's and '40's.

Baby Stuart cap Classic type of infant's close-fitting cap with narrow chin band, illustrated in portrait of Charles II painted by Van Dyck in 1634.

Bachelor's gown Black *academic gown, q.v.,* of worsted or similar fabric, opening in front, two wide box pleats extending to the hem; large flowing sleeves end in a point;

back and sleeves set into square yoke with *cartridge pleats, q.v.,* worn with the *Bachelor's hood* and *mortarboard q.q.v.,* at graduation by candidates for Bachelor's degrees and former recipients of degree.

Bachelor's hood Black decorative drape, or cape, three feet long in back with a two-inch colored velveteen band around the neck in

front and a pendant tail in the back, turned over to reveal colors of institution granting the degree, worn with the *Bachelor's gown* and *mortarboard, q.q.v.,* by candidates, or former recipients, of Bachelor's degree. Also see *academic hood colors.*

bachlick Woman's fichu of cashmere edged with swansdown, having a hood-like point finished with tassel in back; worn over daytime dresses in late 1860's.

back-combing Hair-dressing technique of lifting each strand of hair and combing or brushing lightly *toward* the scalp to increase bulk; used widely in 1950's and '60's for *bouffant* and *beehive* hairdos. See *hairstyles.*

backed cloth See *fabrics.*

backed weave See *weaves.*

backing Shoe term for extra piece of fabric laminated to flesh side of leather or shoe fabric to give added strength, make it appear plumper.

back pack See *knapsack* under *handbags*.

back stitch See *stitches* and *embroideries.*

back strings Term used in the 18th century for ribbons attached to the shoulders of children's dresses. See *leading strings.*

backtrack Sewing term for reversing stitch on sewing machine and stitching backwards over previous stitching instead of tying threads at end.

back-wrap dress See *dresses.*

badger See *furs.*

bäffchen, beffchen German clerical collar of two white linen tabs hanging over minister's robe at front of neck and tied in back with strings; same as English *short bands, q.v.*

bag 1. Variant of *handbag, q.v.:* an accessory used to carry small possessions. 2. An 18th century wig. See *bagwig.* 3. (plural) Slang term for men's trousers in 19th and 20th centuries. Also see *Oxford bags.*

bag bodice Woman's bodice cut to blouse over belt or waistband; worn in daytime in early 1880's.

bag bonnet Woman's bonnet with soft crown which fitted loosely over back of head; worn in early 19th century.

bag cap Man's cloth or velvet cap, shaped like a turban, trimmed with fur or ornamental band; worn in 14th and 15th centuries.

bagheera Uncut velvet. See *fabrics.*

bag irons Iron, bronze, or silver frames with suspension units made of a crossbar and swivel and lower section of concentric semi-circular rings to act as stiffeners for opening and closing a pouch; used for medieval pouches worn hanging from belt. Also called *bag rings.*

bagnolette (ban-yo-let) 1. Woman's wired hood standing away from face, covering shoulders; worn in 18th century. 2. A woman's hooded, gathered cape; worn in early part of 18th century.

bagpipe sleeve Full sleeve gathered like a pouch on outer side of arm ending in wide band at wrist; worn in 15th century by men and women in the *houppelande, q.v. Der.* From shape of Scottish bagpipe.

bag plastron Woman's bodice with a bloused front panel; worn in mid 1880's instead of *waistcoat bosom, q.v.*

bag rings See *bag irons.*

baguette See *gem cuts.*

bag waistcoat Man's vest, full in front and bloused to form a pouch; worn in 1880's.

bagwig Man's wig style, with hair pulled back, stuffed into a square

black silk bag tied with bow at nape of neck; worn in 18th century. Also called *coiffure en bourse, q.v., crapaud,* or *bag.*

baju Short-sleeved loose Malaysian jacket cut short and open in front; usually made with simple collar and patch pockets on chest.

Bakst, Léon (Lev Nikolayevich) Russian artist who won international fame designing sets and costumes for Ballets Russes produced by *Diaghilev, q.v.,* after leaving Russia for Paris in 1909, and helped to start a wave of Orientalism in women's dresses.

baku, bakou straw (bah-coo) See *straws.*

balayeuse (bah-lah-yuz) Same as *dust ruffle, q.v.*

Balbriggan See *fabrics.*

Balbriggan pajamas Type of winter pajamas popular in 1930's made of knitted *Balbriggan fabric, q.v.,* with wide arms and legs gathered into rib-knit bands at wrists and ankles.

baldachin (bal-da-kin) Medieval fabric of silk interwoven with gold, like modern brocade. Also spelled *baudekin, baudekyn, baldaquin,* etc.

baldric, baldrick 1. Wide decorative metal linked belt to hold dagger, worn at hip level by noblemen and soldiers from 1350 to 1400. 2. From 1400 on, belt worn diagonally from right shoulder to left hip, where sword was placed. See *belts.*

Balenciaga, Cristobal See *designers appendix, France.*

Bali dancer's costume Woman's costume consisting of *sarong q.v.,* skirt, and long strip of elaborate fabric wrapped tightly around the bust, worn with *galungan, q.v.,* and with-

out shoes, by temple dancers on the island of Bali, a part of Indonesia.

ballantine Same as *reticule, q.v.*

ball earring See *earrings.*

ballerina length See *lengths.*

ballerina shoe See *shoes.*

ballerina skirt Full calf-length skirt in gored, gathered, or flared style, adapted from the long-length skirts worn by ballet dancers (see *tutu*) and worn mainly for evening in the 1940's and 50's.

ballet laces Wide satin ribbons used as lacings for ballet slippers, criss-crossed at intervals around ankle and calf and tied in bow; worn in 1870's on bathing slippers and during World War I with high-heeled pumps. See *ballet* under *slippers.*

ballet skirt Tiered skirt of evening dress worn in 1880's, made with three or four layers of tulle of various lengths attached to a silk foundation, sprinkled on top layer with stars, pearls, or beetle wings.

ball fringe Type of braid with little fuzzy balls suspended at regular intervals; used today on beach ponchos and robes, and fashionable in late 1870's and 1880's for dress trimming.

ball gown See *dresses.*

ball heel See *heels.*

ballibuntl straw See *straws.*

balloon cloth Fine cotton. See *fabrics.*

balloon hat Woman's hat with wide brim and large puffed-out crown, of gauze over a wire or straw foundation, fashionable in late 18th century; inspired by balloon flight of

Lunardi. Also called *Lunardi hat* and *parachute hat.*

balloon skirt Full puffed skirt, narrower at hem than at hips, similar to *bubble skirt* and *tulip skirt, q.q.v.* under *skirts.*

balloon sleeve See *sleeves.*

ballroom neckcloth Man's pleated, starched evening neckcloth crossed over in front with ends secured to suspenders on either side and an elaborate brooch in center front to hold it; worn in 1830's.

balmacaan coat See *coats.*

Balmain, Pierre See *designers appendix, France.*

Balmoral or **bal oxford** See *oxfords* under *shoes.*

Balmoral bodice Woman's dress bodice with pleated back peplum; worn in the 1860's. Also called *postillion corsage. Der.* Named for Balmoral Castle, Scotland.

Balmoral boot Woman's short black boot fastened up front with laces, frequently colored; worn from 1850's to 1870's, usually with walking dress.

Balmoral cap or **bonnet** Flat Scottish beret, similar to a *tam-o'-shanter, q.v.,* usually dark blue with a red pompon on top, with crest and badge of the clan on one side; part of traditional Highland dress.

Balmoral jacket 1. Woman's jacket, semi-fitted, belted, double-breasted, with lapels, small-gauntlet cuffed sleeves, similar to a riding-habit coat; worn in late 19th century. 2. Man's jacket, buttoned to neck, front and back shaped to points below waist; worn in late 19th century.

Balmoral mantle Man's cloak of velvet, cashmere, or wool styled like an *Inverness cape, q.v.;* popular for outdoor wear in the 1860's.

Balmoral petticoat Colored petticoat, originally red with black bands,

projecting below a looped-up outer skirt.

Balmoral tartan See *tartans.*

Baltic seal Term used in early 20th century for rabbit fur; considered incorrect terminology since Fur Labeling Act of 1938.

Baltic tiger Term used in early 20th century for rabbit fur; considered incorrect terminology since Fur Labeling Act of 1938.

balzarine French term for light calicoes and muslins printed in ultramarine blue. Also spelled *balzorine.*

balzo Italian woman's headdress composed of a high stuffed turban-shaped roll of gilded leather or copper foil; worn in 16th century, painted in "Isabella d'Este" by Titian.

bamberges Shin guards worn during Carolingian Period, mid 8th to 10th centuries.

bambin or **bambino hat** (bam-been) Woman's halo hat with brim rolling away from the face; worn in the 1930's. *Der.* Italian *bambino*, baby.

band, bands 1. Wide, flat collar, usually linen, lace, or cambric; worn by men and women in 17th century. 2. Clerical collar consisting of two short white tabs fastened by string ties around the neck and hanging down over the front of the black robe worn by ministers. Also called *bäff-chen*, *Geneva bands*, *short bands*, *q.q.v.* 3. See *collars*, *necklines*.

bandanna, bandana 1. Large square handkerchief, usually cotton, traditionally printed in white stylized designs on red or dark blue ground with border pattern; used by cowboys, workmen, and for sportswear, knotted around neck, head, or waist. 2. Silk printed square from India used as neckcloth or snuff handkerchief in 18th century. *Der.* Hindu, *bandhnu,* a method of tie-dying.

bandanna print See *prints*.

band-box 16th and 17th century term for box in which collars, called *bands*, *q.v.*, were kept. 2. Hat box, usually round, of cardboard or thin wood.

band brief See *panties*.

bandeau 1. Narrow piece of ribbon or fabric, sometimes decorated, worn around head, substitute for a hat. 2. See *brassiere*.

bandeau d'amour Woman's hairstyle or wig with high slanting and hanging curls; worn in 1770's and 80's.

bandeau slip Slip with top cut like a *brassiere*, similar to *bra-slip*, *q.v.*

banded agate See *agate* under *gems*.

bandelet 1. Glove term for wide hem at wrist, also called *bord*. 2. 16th

century term for any type of *scarf*, *q.v.* Also spelled *bandelette*.

bandle linen Coarse plain-weave linen about two feet wide, woven in homes in southern Ireland since 1790. *Der.* Irish *bandle*, a two-foot measure.

bandoleer Wide belt having loops to hold cartridges and one or two straps extending over shoulders. Also spelled *bandolier*.

bandore and peak Widow's black bonnet with heart-shaped brim and black veil, draped in back; worn in early 18th century.

banging chignon (sheen-yon) Women's hairstyle of 1770's with wide flat loop of hair hanging from crown of head to nape of neck, often ribbon tied.

Bangkok straw See *straws*.

bangle bracelet See *bracelets*.

bangs See *hairstyles*.

banian Variant of *banyan*, *q.v.*

bani cotton Formerly one of the better varieties of cotton from India; also spelled *banni*.

banjan Variant of *banyan*, *q.v.*

Banlon Trademark of Joseph Bancroft & Sons Inc. for fabrics and apparel made from a crimped, man-made yarn, quality controlled; used for socks, sweaters, knit shirts, and dresses.

bannockburn Wool twill. See *fabrics*.

banyan 1. Man's loose, knee-length coat, sometimes in costly fabrics, worn for informal occasions indoors and out in 17th-century England. 2. Ankle-length dressing gown with center back pleat; worn by men

and women in 18th and 19th centuries. Also spelled *banian* and *banjan*. *Der*. Garment worn by caste of Hindu merchants.

Bara, Theda American silent-film star of 1915 to 1920's, known for exotic harem costumes and jeweled headdresses; her 1915 film *The Vampire* was inspiration for vampire look and slang term "vamp" for a seductive woman.

baracan 1. Heavy warp-ribbed silk or wool fabric with a moiré appearance. 2. Coat or mantle of heavy coarse fabric worn in Russia, Asia, and the Balkans. Also spelled *barracan, berkan, bouracan,* and *perkan*.

barathea See *fabrics*.

barbe (barb) Long piece of linen fabric pleated vertically, worn encircling the chin, with a black hood and long black veil, by widows and mourners from 14th to 16th centuries.

barber's apron See *aprons*.

barbette Term used in the 13th and early 14th centuries for the linen chin band worn pinned on top, or sides, of the head and worn with a small white fillet or *coverchief*. *Der*. Mohammedan veil brought back from Crusades and worn from 12th to 14th centuries.

barbula See *piqué devant* beard.

Barcelona handkerchief Colored or black silk handkerchief made in checks or fancy designs in twill weave; worn around neck or head or carried in hand in 18th and 19th centuries.

Bardot, Brigitte French movie actress who became the sex symbol of the 1950–1960's after the movie *And God Created Woman* (1956), responsible for a wave of interest in tousled hairstyles, tight jeans, body sweaters, and blue and pink checked gingham little-girl dresses.

Bardot hairstyle See *hairstyles*.

bar drop pin See *pins*.

barefoot sandals See *sandals*.

barège Silk-worsted gauze. See *fabrics*.

barège shawl (ba-rezh) Shawls made in France in late 19th century from fabric of silk and imported cashmere in imitation of *cashmere shawls, q.v.* See also *barège* under *fabrics.*

bare-midriff Exposing of the body from under the bust to the waist or hips; style introduced in 1920's, popular through '30's and '40's, revived in mid-1960's. See *dresses, tops.*

bare top See *tops;* also see *topless* under *swimsuits.*

bargello stitch See *stitches.*

bark cloth See *fabrics.*

bark crepe Rough-textured silk-wool. See *fabrics.*

bark tanning Vegetable tannage.

barley corn Geometric basket-weave fabric. See *fabrics.*

barme-cloth Early medieval term for an apron. Gradually replaced by word *apron* after the end of the 14th century. Also called a *barmhatre.*

barmfell 14th to 17th century term for a leather apron. Also called a *barmskin.*

Baronette satin Trademark for lustrous fabric made in satin weave, popular before 1930, made with rayon warp and cotton filling, used for blouses and sportswear. Imitators also spelled *Baronet.*

barong Fiber obtained from the plant, *eugenia apiculata,* in the Philippines; used locally for twine and cordage.

barong tagalog Man's *overblouse* shirt for formal occasions, with no buttons and a vent at the neckline, made from fine sheer fabric and frequently trimmed with embroidery; worn in the Philippines.

baroque (bah-roak) Art style in the 17th century characterized by heavy ornate curves and excessive ornamentation; term is applied to certain jewelry and embroidery designs.

baroque pearl See *beads.*

barouche coat (ba-roosh) Woman's tight-fitting three-quarter-length outdoor coat with full sleeves, fastened in front with gold barrel-shaped snaps and an elastic-type belt with buckle; worn in early 1800's.

bar pin See *pins.*

barracan 1. Fabric of wool, silk, and goat's hair made in a coarse strong weave, used in Eastern countries for mantles; also called *barragon* and *barrong.* 2. Length of striped cloth wrapped around body to form a dress, held by a long woolen sash; worn by Bedouin women.

barre Defect in woven fabric consisting of differences in warps or fillings as to color or texture. Also spelled *barry.*

barré (ba-ray) French adjective for fabrics or knits with horizontal stripes in two or more colors, used for neckwear.

barred buttonholes See *buttonholes.*

barrel Tapered oval shape. See *cuffs, curls, handbags.*

barrel hose *Bombasted trunk hose, q.q.v.,* cut very full and stuffed with horsehair; worn from late 16th to mid 17th centuries. Also called *galligaskins, q.v.*

barrel-knot tie See *Osbaldiston tie.*

barrel-shaped muff Large muff, made of or trimmed in fur, sometimes concealing arms to elbows; illustrated in paintings: "Madame Mole Raymond," by Lebrun and "Mrs. Siddons" by Gainsborough.

barrel sleeve See *sleeves.*

barrel snaps Tubular gilded metal fasteners used for cloaks and pelisses from 1800 to 1830. See *barouche.*

barrette, barret, barette 1. Bar-shaped clasp for hair. 2. Small flat cap similar to *biretta* worn by soldiers and Roman Catholic priests during Middle Ages. 3. Flat Spanish cap of elaborate fabric, slashed, puffed and embroidered. See also *biretta. Der.* French *barrette,* small bar or a biretta. See also *beret.*

barrister's wig White wig with smooth top and sausage curls over ears, tied with ribbon in back; worn by British judges and lawyers.

barrow 1. 19th-century baby's flannel blanket, wrapped around the body and turned up over the feet. 2. Layette item of early 1900's shaped like long wrap-around petticoat with wide band under infant's arms, hem pinned up with big safety pins. Also called *pinning blanket.*

Barrymore collar See *collars.*

Barthet, Jean See *designers appendix, France.*

base Lower portion of a *brilliant-cut stone, q.v.* See also *pavilion* and *girdle.*

baseball cap See *caps.*

base coat Man's jacket or jerkin with skirts, or bases, hanging in unpressed pleats just above the knees; worn in 15th and 16th centuries.

bases 1. Man's separate skirt which hung in unpressed pleats, worn with the padded doublet or armor; worn from late 15th century to mid 16th

century. 2. Skirt of a jacket, or jerkin, hanging in unpressed pleats. See *base coat.*

base socks 16th century term for men's *under-socks.*

basic dress See *dresses.*

basinet Pointed steel helmet worn as armor from 1350 to 1450. Also spelled *bascinet, bacinet, basnet.*

basket Woman's hat resembling a wicker basket, one and one-half feet high; worn in late 16th century.

basket bag See *handbags.*

basketball shoe See *shoes.*

basket button Fashionable button for man's coat in 18th and 19th centuries, either covered with metal in a basket pattern or an interlaced front.

basket stitch See *stitches.*

basket weave See *weaves, stitches.*

baslard, baselard Small, ornamental dagger worn on left side as an accessory by men in 14th and 15th centuries. Also worn by women in smaller size, hanging from jeweled belt along with a mirror, *aulmoniere q.v.,* and pincers.

basque (bask) 1. Originally the part of a man's doublet which extended below the waist; in the 17th century made with a series of vertical slashes forming tabs. The term was extended to mean part of women's bodice that came below waist. 2. By mid 19th century term was extended to mean any woman's bodice that extended below the waistline. 3. In early 20th century a woman's waist-length jacket or dress that fits tightly through waist and rib cage.

25

Basque beret (bask be-ray) See *beret* under *caps.*

basque-habit Bodice with square-cut tabs below the waistline; worn in 1860's.

basque waistband Belt or waistband decorated with five pointed tabs; worn on afternoon dresses by women in latter half of 19th century.

basquina (bas-keen-a) See *basquine.*

basquin body Woman's daytime bodice extended below the waistline with no waistline seam; worn in 1860's.

basquine (bas-keen) 1. Woman's coat with *pagoda sleeves,* fringed trimming and long *basque, q.q.v.;* worn in late 1850's. 2. 1860's outdoor jacket. Also spelled *basquin.* 3. Wide underskirt of rich fabric, held out by hoops; worn in 16th century. Also called *basquina* in Spain.

bast Woody vegetable fibers including flax, ramie, hemp, and jute.

baste To stitch fabrics together, either by hand or with large machine stitches, to hold in place, prior to sewing final seams. After stitching, bastings are removed.

bast hat Straw hat of 17th century made of plaited *bast, q.v.,* or *bass,* the inner bark of the linden tree.

basting stitch See *stitches.*

bateau neckline (ba-toe) See *necklines.*

Bates, John See *designers appendix, England.*

bathing cap See *caps.*

bathing slipper Woman's flat fabric shoe, sometimes laced up leg like ballet slipper, worn in swimming; popular in late 19th century. After 1920, similar shoes, without lacings, have been made of rubber.

bathing suit (or **dress**) or **swimsuit** For women: 1. Originally a costume for outdoor bathing, like a knee-length dress with underpants or bloomers attached, worn with stockings and slippers. 2. Now, a close-fitting garment worn in water for swimming or for sun-bathing, usually of stretchable jersey or lastex and in printed cotton. See *Zouave Marine swimming costume;* contemporary styles are listed under *swimsuits.* For men: 1. One-piece striped jersey suit with knee-length legs, sometimes short sleeves, worn for swimming at turn of century. 2. Cotton boxer trunks or brief jersey pants with no top. See styles under *swimsuits.*

bathrobe See *robes.*

bathrobe cloth Heavy napped fabric. See *fabrics.*

bathrobe dress See *dresses.*

batik (bah-teek) 1. Method of dyeing fabric by drawing the design on silk or cotton, then covering with hot wax all areas which are to remain white, dyeing, and removing wax—resulting in a pattern with a crackled effect; process originated in Indonesia. 2. Fabric dyed in above manner. Also see *batik prints* under *prints.*

bating Tannery term for processing of skins and hides to reveal grain of leather after hair has been removed.

batiste Thin cotton. See *fabrics.*

bat's-wing tie Man's bow tie cut with wide flaring ends; worn in late 1890's.

batt Heavy laced low shoe used for country wear in England in 17th century, sent to New England Colonists in 1630's.

battant l'oeil (bah-tan loy) Woman's cap, worn in 1770's, with sides projecting forward over temples, eyes, and cheeks in exaggerated fashion.

Battenberg jacket Woman's loose-fitting outdoor jacket with large buttons and a turned-down collar; worn in 1880's.

Battenberg lace See *laces.*

battening Weaving term for the pushing of each filling yarn, shot through by the shuttle, tight against the finished cloth on the loom.

batter's cap See *caps.*

batting Matted sheets of fibers used in quilting or stuffing; may be cotton, wool, kapok, spun rayon, spun glass, or *fiberfill, q.v.*

battle jacket See *sport jackets* under *jackets.*

battlements Trimming consisting of square-cut tabs used in same manner as scallops on dresses, skirts, jackets, and basques in the 19th century.

bat-wing sleeve See *sleeves.*

baudekin See *baldachin.*

baum marten See *furs.*

bautte, bautta (bah-oot) Black cloak with hood that could be drawn down over face to form a half mask; worn in 18th century.

Bavarian dress Woman's carriage dress trimmed with bands of fabric down the front; worn in 1820's.

Bavarian lace See *laces.*

bavolet (ba-vo-lay) 1. A veil or curtain at back of woman's bonnet to shade the neck; worn from 1830. 2. Plain cap worn by French peasant women.

bayadere (by-yah-deer) Long narrow scarf of silk or lace worn in early 19th century. *Der.* Costume of East Indian *bayadere* or dancing girl.

bayadere stripe 1. Term used in 1850's for flat velvet trimming used on dresses. 2. See *stripes.*

bayeta Scarlet American Indian blanket, made of Spanish baize fabric, in which Acoma Indians (New Mexico) buried their dead.

beach cloth See *fabrics.*

beach coat See *robes.*

beach pajamas Full-length *culottes, q.v.,* often made of printed fabric, worn sometimes with matching *bolero, q.v.,* for sportswear in 1920's and 1930's; revived in 1970's.

beachwear Items of apparel or accessories specifically for use at the beach. See under *dresses, hats, robes, swimsuits,* etc.

bead (pl.) 1. Pieces of gold, glass, wood, crystal, precious and semiprecious stones, plastic, and other materials, usually round but may be cylindrical, square, disk-shaped, pendant-shaped, etc., and bored through the centers; strung on thread or chain to wear around neck or used for embroidery. See types below. 2. A string of beads, synonym for *necklace,* made and worn since earliest recorded history.

BEADS:

aurora borealis b. (aw-ror-a bore-e-

27

al-is) Glass beads coated with solution causing them to reflect rainbow colors; usually made in Czechoslovakia.

baroque pearls (ba-rok) Pearls of an irregular shape, as opposed to round smooth pearls—may be *simulated, cultured,* or natural *Oriental* (see below), which are prized for shape, color, and luster. Color often blue-gray or off-white.

bubble b. Oversized spherical beads, often hollow, popular for *choker, q.v.,* necklaces in 1950's.

bugle b. Long tubular-shaped glass beads, often black; popular for trimming dresses from last half of 19th century to early 20th century.

cultured pearls Pearls produced by oysters artificially implanted with tiny pieces of mother-of-pearl; first sold in 1921.

cut-steel b. Tiny faceted steel or other metal beads, similar in appearance to *marquisite, q.v.,* stones; popular in last half of the 19th and early 20th centuries.

fresh-water pearls Natural pearls from mussels whose habitat is in rivers of the United States, chalk white in color, not as lustrous as *Oriental pearls, q.v.*

Indian b. 1. Tiny opaque glass beads of various colors used to make necklaces and belts, and for embroidery on moccasins, headbands, belts, and other American Indian clothes. 2. Shell beads used by North American Indians in 16th century as money and called wampum, the amount of trimming on garments indicated wealth. See also *Indian necklace.*

lampshade b. Short strings of tiny beads hung in a fringe from a ribbon tied close to neck, worn by young people in 1970–71. *Der.* Beaded fringe on lampshades popular in late Victorian era.

love b. Tiny multi-color glass beads, a single strand, usually choker length, worn by young girls and men as part of ritual *hippie, q.v.,* costume in late 1960's and early 1970's.

Oriental pearls Highly prized natural pearls from Japan, the Pacific Islands, the Persian Gulf, Australia, Venezuela, and Panama. The most beautiful and expensive of all pearls.

pearl b. See *cultured pearls, fresh-water pearls, seed pearls, Oriental pearls,* and *simulated pearls.*

pop b. or **Poppits** Plastic beads, medium size, each with knob on one side, hole on opposite side, fitting one into another for any length necklace; a fad in 1950's.

rosary b. String of beads arranged on a chain with a pendant cross, used by Roman Catholics for counting the prayers of the Rosary.

rose b. Beads carved out of coral or other soft material in shape of open flower.

seed-pearl b. Tiny genuine or simulated pearls of irregular shapes formerly used in necklaces, now used primarily for embroidery on sweaters or wedding dresses.

simulated-pearl b. Bead made with plastic or glass base and coated with solution called *pearl essence* made from an adhesive combined with fish scales, giving an iridescent luster similar to a natural pearl's.

worry b. Short string of beads, often semi-precious stones, carried in hand to fidget with or worn as necklace. Used by modern Greeks and popular in America in late 1960's. *Der.* From string of thirty-three beads used to count the ninety-nine names of Allah in prayer in Moslem countries.

beaded bag See *handbags.*

beaded sweater See *sweaters.*

beaded velvet See *cut velvet* under *fabrics.*

beading 1. Term used for embroidery in which beads of various kinds are sewn onto blouses, dresses, handbags, or wedding dresses, etc. 2. Term used in late 19th and early 20th centuries for narrow slotted lace or embroidered bands through which ribbon was run.

beanie See *caps.*

beard Hair on man's face permitted to grow, sometimes trimmed and shaped around the jaw and chin, fashionable throughout 19th century and again in the 1960's and 1970's. See *bodkin beard, vandyke, piqué devant,* and *goatee.*

beard box Early American device made of pasteboard, worn at night over beard to keep its shape.

beard brush Term used for small brush used in public to comb the beard; popular during the first half of 17th century.

bearer A padded roll, similar to a *bustle, q.v,* worn under back of skirt by women from late 17th to early 19th centuries.

bearskin 1. See *caps.* 2. Pelt of the bear.

Beatles Avant-garde British rock-music group that became very popular in early 1960's: John Lennon, Paul McCartney, George Harrison, and Ringo Starr; they appeared in *Mod* clothing, *q.v.,* and with long hairstyles that started a trend for young people in England and the U.S. Also see *hairstyles.*

beau (pl. **beaux**) Term used from late 17th to mid 19th centuries for a gentleman who was fastidious about his clothes and accessories, similar to but not as effeminate as a *fop, q.v.*

Beau Brummell See *Brummell, Beau.*

Beaufort coat Man's suit jacket with single-breasted, four-button closing, narrow straight sleeves, seams often double-stitched; worn in 1880's. Also called *jumper coat.*

beau monde (bow mond) French term meaning the world of fashion; literally, the beautiful world.

Beautiful People Term coined by writer Rebecca Warfield in *Vogue* magazine in 1962 for the rich and fashionable. See *couture society.*

beauty spot Mark on the face drawing attention to a good feature, such as a small mole, either natural or artificial. See *mouche, court plaster, patch.*

Beauvais embroidery See *embroideries.*

beaver 1. See *furs.* 2. Hat worn from 14th century by men and women, originally made of beaver skins, later of beaver-hair nap felted over wool-and-rabbit's-hair base. 3. Man's tall hat made of silk in imitation of beaver fur; fashionable in 17th century. Same as *top hat, q.v.*

beaver cloth Napped wool. See *fabrics.*

beaverette Term used in the early 20th century for rabbit fur; considered incorrect since Fur Labeling Act, 1938.

bebe bonnet Tiny outdoor bonnet trimmed with ribbons, flowers, and tulle, with brim turned up showing a cap underneath; worn in late 1870's.

becca Long strip of fabric hanging forward from the *berretino, q.v.,* worn slung over the shoulders; very popular in the reign of Henry VI.

Bedford cord See *fabrics.*

bedgown Dressing gown with loose sleeves worn only in bedrooms, by men and women, in 18th century.

bediya North African vest worn over the shirt, and under the *ghlila, q.v.*

bed jacket See *robes.*

bed socks See *socks.*

beefeater's uniform Tudor-period uniform consisting of red doublet, with ruff at neck, elaborately trimmed with gold and black; red trunk hose, red stockings with garters below knees; black hat with small brim and flat-topped, medium-sized crown; and black shoes trimmed with rosettes. Worn since 1485 by Yeoman of the Guard of the royal household in England, appointed by Henry VII. Same costume worn today by Yeoman Extraordinary of the Guard, appointed Wardens of the Tower of London by Edward VI. *Der.* Name derives from about the middle of the 17th cen-

tury, alluding to English fondness for roast beef. Also see *hats.*

beehive hairstyle See *hairstyles.*

beehive hat 1. Woman's hat with large bubble-shaped crown and narrow brim trimmed with ribbon and tied under chin; worn in 1770's and 1780's. Also called *hive bonnet.* 2. Same style decorated to look like a beehive and fashionable about 1910.

Beene, Geoffrey See *designers appendix, United States.*

Beer See *designers appendix, France.*

beer jacket Short, boxy cotton jacket with patch pockets and brass buttons; originally worn by upper classmen at Princeton University in 1930's, copied by other students.

beetling Pounding or hammering of fabrics made of round linen or cotton yarns to make them flatter and to increase luster.

beige (behzh) 1. Tan or natural color. 2. Term for cloth as it comes from loom in undyed, or greige, state. 3. Serge fabric of natural, black, brown, or grey wool made in Poitou, France. 4. Wool vicuña cloth used in England in the late 19th century. 5. Twill or plain weave worsted or cotton dress goods with mottled grey appearance produced by black-and-white ply yarns.

Belcher handkerchief Blue neckerchief with large white polka dots, each centered with a dark blue eye; worn by men in first half of 19th century. Named after Jim Belcher, a pugilist.

belette Term used from 14th century to mid 16th century for jewel or ornament. Also spelled *bilett*.

Belgian lace See *laces*.

Belgrave shoe Woman's evening shoe cut like a *pump, q.v.,* but coming up

high in the back, fastened in front with gillie lacings; worn in 1870's.

bell Circular cape used as traveling cloak, sometimes hooded, sometimes side and back vents; worn by men and women from late 13th century to early 15th century.

bell-bottom heel See *heels*.

bell-bottoms See *pants*.

bellboy cap See *caps*.

bellboy or **bellhop jacket** See *jackets*.

Belle Époque, La (bell ep-ock) 1. In France period between 1890–1910, corresponding to Edwardian period in England, when social life was especially carefree and clothes were elegant. 2. See *hairstyles*.

bell hoop Dome-shaped hoop-skirt petticoat popular in England in 18th century. Also called *cupola coat*.

Bellmanized Trademark formerly used for starchless finish that gave permanent stiffness to fabrics such as organdy, lawn, and muslin.

bellows pocket See *pockets*.

bellows sleeve Full sleeve, gathered into cuff at wrist, with vertical slit from upper arm to below elbow; could be worn as short hanging sleeve; worn in 14th and 15th centuries.

bellows tongue Shoe tongue stitched to sides of vamp of shoe and pleated so it expands across instep.

bell skirt 1. Woman's full skirt, front fitted by darts rather than gores, sometimes with two buttoned front openings rather than back placket, the hem stiffened with muslin. Popular in late 1800's. 2. See *skirts*.

bell sleeve See *sleeves*.

bell umbrella Dome-shaped umbrella of transparent plastic or of fabric with a plastic window, deeper than most umbrellas, protecting the face. Also called a *bell-shaped umbrella* or a *dome umbrella*.

Bellville, Belinda See *designers appendix, England*.

belly-chete 16th century slang term for apron.

belly piece Stiffened ridge down front of man's doublet lined with buckram, pasteboard, or whalebone; worn from 1620 to 1660.

belt Flexible band, e.g. fabric, leather or chain, usually worn around the waist, below or above it, or over the shoulder in military fashion; worn since the Bronze Age for ornamentation or to hold up clothing. Also called *girdle* or *cincture*.

BELTS:

baldrick (bawl-drick) 1. Belt worn diagonally from one shoulder to opposite hip. 2. 13th century to early 18th century, belt diagonally crossing the chest, sometimes with extension around waist to hold dagger, sword, horn, bugle, or pouch.

black b. See *judo belt*.

body-chain b. Long piece of chain worn around the neck, crossed in front and wrapped around waistline; introduced in late 1960's.

brown b. See *judo belt*.

cartridge b. Low-slung belt holding a row of bullet cartridges, a fad of the early 1970's begun by Ethel Scull, a New York art collector, and others who wore actual military cartridge belts.

chain b. Belt made of chain, usually metal; may be a single strand, of varying widths, or a group of narrow strands joined at intervals.

cinch b. Wide belt worn pulled tight, usually made of elastic or fabric, either laced or clasped in front; popular in 1940's.

CARTRIDGE BELT KIDNEY BELT

CINCH BELT

OBI BELT

SAM BROWNE BELT

PELT BELT

contour b. Curving belt shaped to the body, wider in front or back, first popularized in 1890's.

corselet b. Wide belt sometimes enclosing the rib cage, frequently laced up front in manner similar to peasant's bodice. See also *Swiss belt.*

cowboy b. Wide leather belt, sometimes with tooled designs, worn at top of hip-bone by frontier cowboy to hold gun holster. Adapted in 1960's for men's sportswear.

cummerbund Wide fabric belt, sometimes pleated lengthwise, fastened in back; worn with man's semi-formal dinner suit, and by women. Copied from wrapped cloth belts worn in Eastern countries. *Der.* Hindustani *kamar-band,* loin band.

garrison b. Wide leather belt with metal buckle originally worn by military men, now often worn with *dungarees, q.v.*

gaucho b. Belt made of medallions of leather and metal joined with chain; fashionable in late 1960's. *Der.* From South American cowboys' or *gauchos'* belts.

Greek b. Long narrow belt that winds around waist, crosses over chest and extends over shoulders, worn in ancient Greece and also a fashion in late 1960's. Also called *cross-girdled belt.*

high-rise b. Belt worn above natural waistline.

hip-hugger b. Belt worn below natural waistline, resting on top of hip-bones.

Indian b. 1. Leather belt decorated with woven *Indian beadwork* in bright colors and American Indian motifs. 2. Belt worn by American Indians, composed entirely of woven beadwork, sometimes fringed on the ends.

judo b. Belt worn with *judo clothes, q.v.: black* denoting highest achievement in the sport, *brown* indicating intermediary, and *white* worn by novices.

kidney b. Extremely wide belt similar to a *polo belt,* worn when motorcycling to prevent injury.

macramé b. (ṃak-rah-may) Handmade coarse woven and knotted cord belt.

martingale b. Half-belt worn on back of garment above or below normal waistline. *Der.* Part of horse's harness designed to hold head down.

mesh b. Belt made of extremely small metal links fastened together to form a flexible fabric-like band.

money b. Belt with hidden zippered compartment for money, worn under or over clothes when traveling.

monk's b. Belt of rope, twisted rayon or nylon, with tassels on ends, sometimes wrapped several times around waist; derived from those worn with monks' habits.

obi b. Wide sash worn high under bosom and tied in back in a flat bow, adapted from *obi, q.v.,* worn by Japanese women with kimono.

Pelt-belt Featherweight jacket introduced in 1968, which folds to three-inch-wide belt and can be fastened around waist as emergency protection against weather.

polo b. Wide leather belt covering rib cage, fastened in front with three small buckles on narrow leather straps. Originally worn by polo players for protection.

safari b. Wide belt with attached flapped pockets in front.

Sam Browne b. Sword belt worn around waist with extension strap over right shoulder; worn by U.S. army officers, guards, and some policemen. *Der.* Named for British general, Sir Samuel Browne, who lost his left arm, couldn't support his sword without the special belt.

sash 1. Any belt of soft material that loops over, knots, or ties in a bow rather than buckling.

shoulder b. See *baldrick* and *Sam Browne belt.*

thong b. 1. Wide leather belt with eyelets at each end through which a piece of rawhide is laced. 2. Belt made of braided rawhide.

wampum b. Same as *Indian belt,* def. 2.

webbed b. Belt of heavy canvas webbing, usually wide and fastened with a clip buckle, worn by military men and a women's fashion on bathing suits in 1920's and in late 1960's.

white b. See *judo belt.*

belt bag See *handbags.*

belt buckle Any ornamental or functional device, usually metal, used to fasten a belt. See *buckle.*

beluque Woman's cape or mantle of the 15th century.

Bemberg Trademark owned by Bemberg Industries used for cuprammonium rayon fiber characterized by extreme fineness; used for sheer fabrics.

Ben Casey shirt See *shirts.*

benchwarmer See *sport jackets* under *jackets.*

bend 1. Leather term for the best central section cut from a whole hide.

2. 11th to 15th centuries term for band of fabric on a dress, or fillet for hair or hat band, also synonym for *stripe.*

Ben Franklin glasses See *glasses.*

bengaline Ribbed fabric. See *fabrics.*

Benjamin Overcoat worn by working men in the 19th century. Also called *Benny.* See also *lily Benjamin.*

benjy 1. British slang term used in the 19th century for a man's waistcoat or vest. 2. Straw hat.

Benny See *Benjamin.*

Benoiton coiffure Women's elaborate coiffure with hair parted in center, smooth on top, and chignon and

curls in back; three gold chains were worn over the top of the head and hung in dangling loops under the chin; sometimes garlands of flowers were used instead of chains. *Der.* Named after *La Famille Benoiton,* a play by Victorien Sardou, 1866.

berdash Variant of *burdash, q.v.*

beret (beh-ray) See *caps.* Also see *biretta.*

Berge, Pierre See *designers appendix, France.*

bergère hat Straw hat with wide floppy brim and low crown; worn by women from 1730 to 1800 and again in 1860's. Also called a *milkmaid hat*. *Der.* French, shepherdess.

Berhanyer, Elio See *designers appendix, Spain*.

Berlin gloves Sturdy cotton glove worn by English middle-class men from 1830 on.

Berlin wool Worsted knitting or embroidery yarn from Germany, also called Berlin yarn or German wool.

Berlin work See *embroideries*.

Bermuda collar See *collars*.

Bermuda shorts See *shorts*.

Bernhardt, Sarah (burn-hart) Famous French actress (1845–1923) known as "Divine Sarah," whose elaborate costumes, hairstyle, and jewels influenced fashion in Europe and America in late 19th century, credited with *mousquetaire glove, Bernhardt sleeve* and *mantle, q.q.v.*

Bernhardt mantle Woman's short outdoor cape with loose front and *dolman* or *sling sleeves, q.v.;* worn in the mid 1880's. Named after *Sarah Bernhardt, q.v.*

Bernhardt sleeve Long, fitted sleeve made with a point extending over the hand; worn in the latter part of 19th century and named for *Sarah Bernhardt, q.v.*

bernos, bernose Variants of *burnoose, q.v.*

berretino Square scarlet skull cap with corners pinched in, worn by cardinals of Catholic Church since 15th century. See *biretta*.

berretta Variant of *biretta, q.v.*

bertha Large cape-like collar falling over shoulders and bodice of dress, introduced in mid 19th century as lace ruffle encircling the decolleté neckline of evening dress and fashionable in 1930's as a large cape collar. Usually spelled *berthe*, when first introduced.

bertha pelerine Lace ruffle or *bertha* worn on low-necked dress with ends carried down center front to waist; worn in 1840's. *Der.* French, pilgrim collar.

Berthelot, Gaston See *designers appendix, France*.

Bertin, Rose See *designers appendix, France*.

beryl See *gems*.

Bessarabian lamb See *lamb* under *furs*.

Bethlehem headdress Truncated-cone hat covered with a veil, decorated with rows of dangling coins or jewels across forehead; worn by women in ancient times, copied in 1930's.

betrothal ring 16th century ring, broken in half after wedding ceremony and halves given to bride and groom.

Betsie ruff Lace ruff worn by women in late 19th and early 20th centuries; named after Elizabeth I of England.

beutanol Vinyl-coated lawn. See *fabrics*.

bevel Slanted cut on gemstone, to give light reflection, especially on square-cut gemstones.

bezel (*behz*-el) Upper faceted portion of a brilliant-cut gem such as diamond. Same as *crown*.

bias (by-as) A line diagonally across grain of fabric. See *pleats*, and *bias cut*.

bias binding Narrow strips of fabric cut on the *bias*, *q.v.*, thus pliable for use in covering raw edges of curved

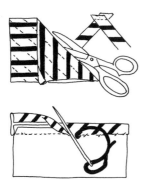

necklines, armholes, etc. or as trimming; hand-cut or sold in packages.

bias cut Way of cutting fabric diagonally across grain of fabric, resulting in a garment that clings and follows body curves closely; •e.g., French couturiere *Vionnet*, *q.v.*, was famous for the bias cut in 1920's.

biaz Glossy, starched, plain-weave white cotton, coarse to fine, in narrow widths, made in Russia and Central Asia.

bib 1. Piece of fabric, square or oval, worn under chin and tied around neck; used to protect clothing while eating, first worn in 16th century. 2. Panel of cloth attached to waist of apron, pants, or skirt, extending upward over chest. See *blouses*, *tops*, and *aprons*. 3. See *necklaces*. 4. See *collars*.

bib cravat Man's wide neckpiece, usually lace-edged, in shape of a bib, usually held by colored string; worn at end of 17th century.

bibi bonnet (bee-bee bun-neh) 1. Small woman's bonnet with sides flaring upward and forward around the face, tied with lace-trimmed ribbons; worn in early 1830's. 2. Name for any tiny, elegant bonnet in late 19th century. See *bebe bonnet*.

bicorn hat Man's hat of the Napoleonic era in shape of a crescent, with front and back brims pressed against each other making points on either side, frequently trimmed with a *cockade*, *q.v. Der.* Latin, *bicornis*, two-horned. Also spelled *bicorne*.

bicycle bal Shoe with protective toe cap and circle stitched over ankle joint, closed with laces extending toward the toes; designed for bicycling in latter part of 19th century and later adopted for other sports. See *basketball shoe* under *shoes*.

bicycle-clip hat See *hats*.

bifocals See *glasses*.

biggin (big-in), **biggonet** (big-on-net) 1. 16th and 17th century term for woman's or child's cap similar to *coif*, *q.v.* 2. Man's nightcap, worn in second half of 16th century through 17th century. 3. Large *mob cap*, *q.v.*, without chin ties, worn in early 19th century. Also spelled *biggon. Der.* French *beguine*, cap worn by religious sect.

BIGS See *space clothes*.

bikini (bee-kee-nee) See *tops*, *swimsuits*, *panties*, and *pantyhose*.

bilett See *belette*.

billfold *Wallet*, *q.v.*, designed to hold paper money, sometimes also credit cards and photos; usually folding in center.

billicock See *billycock*.

billiment 1. 16th century term for the decorative jeweled border of French hood, sometimes made by goldsmiths. 2. Head ornament worn by brides in 16th century. Also spelled *billment* and *bilment*. Also called *habillement* or *abillements* or *borders*.

billycock 19th century colloquial term for man's soft, wide, curved-brimmed hat with low crown. Also spelled *billicock*. Der. 1. From *bullycocked* hat, *q.v.,* of 18th century. 2. From hat worn by Mr. William (Billy) Coke for shooting parties at Holkham, England.

binche (bansh) See *laces*.

binding 1. Sewing term for narrow fabric strips used to cover seams or raw edges of clothing: *e.g., bias binding* and *seam binding, q.q.v.* 2. Glove term for reinforcement or piping of leather or fabric around wrist and placket.

binette See *full-bottomed wig.*

bingle See *hairstyles.*

biological isolation garments See *space clothes.*

bird cage See *veils.*

bird-of-paradise feathers See *feathers.*

birdseye See *fabrics.*

biretta (bi-ret-ah) Stiff square cap with three or four upright projections on top radiating from center, sometimes finished with a pompon; worn by ecclesiastics. Also spelled *birretta, baretta, barrette, beretta, beret,* and *berrette.*

birlet Variant of *burlet.* See *bourrelet.*

birrus 1. Hooded cape of rough cloth, worn in bad weather by Romans of all classes in late Empire period.

2. Coarse brown woolen cloth used for outer garments by lower classes in Middle Ages. Also spelled *byrrus* or *buros.*

birthday suit 1. Man's court suit worn during 18th century on a royal birthday. 2. (slang) Naked, as when born.

birthstone Precious or semi-precious stone assigned to the month of birth, often worn in a ring. January, garnet; February, amethyst; March, bloodstone; April, diamond; May, emerald; June, pearl; July, ruby; August, sardonyx; September, sapphire; October, opal; November, topaz; December, turquoise.

bisette (bee-set) 1. French term for embroidered braid. 2. See *laces.*

bishop collar See *collars.*

bishop sleeve See *sleeves.*

bister, bistre Dark yellowish-brown color.

bi-swing Suit or sports jacket with set-in belt in back and deep pleats extending upward to each shoulder giving freedom of movement, single-breasted closing, and conventional notched collar and lapels; popular in the 1930's for men and women.

BIRETTA

bivouac mantle (biv-wak) Full-length loose cape of scarlet cloth, styled with high collar, padded and lined with ermine; worn in 19th century.

black belt See *judo* under *belts.*

black fox See *fox* under *furs.*

black opal See *gems.*

black tie Brief designation of men's semi-formal evening dress; compare *white tie.* See *ties.*

Black Watch tartan See *tartans.*

black work See *embroideries.*

blade jacket Man's business jacket made with extra fullness at upper arm and back, or shoulder blades, giving broad-shouldered look and freedom of movement; worn in 1930's.

Blake Term used for a shoe utilizing a sole-stitching method invented by Lyman Blake in 1861; same as *McKay method.*

blanchet 1. Originally, long white cotton camisole with sleeves, collar, and fur lining; worn over the shirt in 15th century. 2. Term used from 12th to 14th century for white paint or powder used as a cosmetic.

Blanchot, Jane See *designers appendix, France.*

blanket 1. Fur-industry term for small pieces of fur sewn in a herringbone pattern, in a piece large enough to make a fur coat; generally imported from Greece. 2. Fur-industry term for large beaver skins.

blanket checks See *checks.*

blanket cloth See *bathrobe cloth* under *fabrics.*

blanket plaid See *plaids.*

blanket sleepers See *pajamas.*

blanket stitch See *stitches.*

Blass, Bill See *designers appendix, United States.*

blazer See *sport jackets* under *jackets.*

blazer cloth See *fabrics.*

blazer stripe See *stripes.*

blazer sweater See *sweaters.*

blé d'or (blay-dor) Golden-grain color. *Der.* French, golden corn or wheat.

bleed Tendency of dyed fabric to lose color or run when wet.

bleeding madras Plain weave, yarn-dyed fabric with grey filling and colored warp that bleeds during finishing process. See *madras* under *fabrics.*

blehand, blehant Variants of *bliaut, q.v.*

blend Yarn composed of two or more fibers mixed together, then spun into one yarn. Blend fabrics possess qualities of both yarns, e.g., blended cotton and Dacron polyester produces fabric that is absorbent like cotton but crease-resistant and fast drying like polyester.

blending Fur term for lightly applying dye to long guard hairs of furs, such as mink and sable, to improve the coloring.

bleu drapeau (blur dra-po) French term for flag-blue color.

bliaut (blee-o), **bliaud, bliaunt** Long overgown worn by men and women, from 12th to early 14th centuries. 1. First fitted garment for women made with tight-fitting bodice fastened up sides or back; full skirt attached at low waistline; long wide, sometimes double embroidered sleeves, laced into armholes; embroidered neckline; belt of twisted metal. 2. Narrow-sleeved garment for men, slit from hem to knee, worn under coat of chain mail; loose-fitting version worn by workmen and soldiers was ancestor of farmers' work smock. 3. Costly fabric of middle ages. Also spelled *blehant* and *blehand.*

blind eyelet Shoe-industry term for metal eyelet concealed in the inner surface of leather; outside layer has punched hole through which shoe-string is pulled.

blind stitch See *slip* under *stitches.*

blistered Late 16th and 17th century term for fashion of cutting or slashing sleeves or breeches so that under fabric appeared through holes. looking blistered. Also called *slashed.*

block heel See *heels.*

blocking 1. Process of shaping knitted clothing after completion or after washing, in which garment outline is drawn beforehand on paper and article shaped to conform. 2. Millinery term for molding unformed felt or straw *hood, q.v.,* over a block of wood to get desired shape.

block printing Method of hand-printing fabric by cutting separate wood or linoleum blocks in relief and inking with separate colors. See *hand-blocked* under *prints.*

blonde See *laces.*

blonde de fil See *Mignonette* under *laces.*

bloodstone See *gems.*

bloom Leather-industry term for color of best quality sole leather.

Bloomer, Amelia (1818–1894) Advocate of dress reform for women who lectured on temperance and woman's suffrage in America and abroad in 1851 wearing a Turkish costume, consisting of a knee-length dress

AMELIA BLOOMER, 1850

over full pants gathered at the ankle (originally designed for outdoor work by women). Horace Greeley, editor of the New York *Tribune,* publicized the costume; trousers came to be called *bloomers.*

bloomer dress See *pants-dress* under *dresses.*

bloomer girl Slang term in U.S. and England in late 19th and early 20th century for daring girl who wore *bloomers, q.v.*

bloomers Women's and girls' underpants or gymsuit pants, loose, with legs gathered on elastic, length varying from knee to hip. Last popular in 1920's. *Der.* See *Bloomer, Amelia.* See *panties.*

blouse 1. Loose fitting, lightweight garment covering body from neck to below waist, with or without sleeves, tucked in or over waistband of skirts or pants, usually worn by women and children. Also called *waist.* 2. Man's single-breasted, semi-fitted

39

jacket, part of army or navy uniform. 3. Loose outer garment to waist, hips, or knees worn by peasants in Europe and Russia. See *smock*.

BLOUSES:

JABOT BLOUSE

BOW BLOUSE

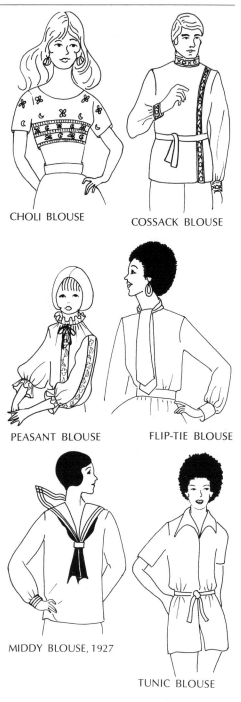

CHOLI BLOUSE

COSSACK BLOUSE

PEASANT BLOUSE

FLIP-TIE BLOUSE

MIDDY BLOUSE, 1927

TUNIC BLOUSE

DRAWSTRING BLOUSE

bib b. Back-buttoned blouse with high band collar and hanging *plastron, q.v.,* in front.

body shirt See *shirts.*

bow b. Blouse with band around neck having two long ends in front that tie in a bow.

choli Blouse worn with Indian sari, reaching just to the ribs, with short

40

sleeves and low neckline; worn by Hindu women and popular in this country in 1968, when bare-midriff styles became popular. Also spelled *cholee* and *coli*. See *sari*.

Cossack b. Overblouse originally worn by Russian Cossacks (horsemen adventurers) having high standing collar, side fastening, often embroidered or braid-trimmed, and secured with belt or sash; sleeves full at wrist and gathered into braided or embroidered band. Worn by men and women. Same as *Zhivago blouse* and *Russian blouse, q.q.v.*

dandy b. Ruffle-trimmed blouse reminiscent of *dandy styles, q.v.,* of early 19th century.

dashiki b. Short version of the African *dashiki,* a long, loose tunic with full, straight-hanging sleeves, usually made in bright printed cotton; worn as a blouse, most frequently over pants, by men and women in U.S. in late 1960's and 1970's as part of *ethnic look, q.v.*

drawstring b. Blouse that fastens at neckline with drawstring, *e.g., gypsy blouse, peasant blouse, q.q.v.*

dueling or **fencing b.** Shirt borrowed from European men's shirts of the 17th century, worn by men and women, generally in white cotton, crepe or jersey, tailored with notched collar, dropped shoulder, long full sleeves gathered into tight cuffs.

flip-tie b. Plain blouse with *scarf collar,* the ends looped over once like a man's *ascot tie, q.v.* Same as *stock-tie blouse.*

gypsy b. Full blouse with drawstring neckline and often short puffed sleeves, originally worn by gypsies; popular in 1960's.. Similar to *peasant blouse. q.v.*

jabot b. (zha-bo) Back-closed blouse having standing band collar with attached ruffle or *jabot, q.v.,* down center front; or a front-buttoned blouse with jabot-like ruffles on either side of opening.

lingerie b. Blouse of thin, often transparent material such as batiste, imitating lingerie's fine tucking, shirring, narrow lace inserts, ruffles and fagoting.

maternity b. Overblouse introduced in 1940's and worn by expectant mothers with maternity skirt or pants, frequently has yoke and hangs straight without belt.

middy b. Slip-on blouse of blue serge or white duck, usually with sailor collar that hangs square in back, tapers to V in front, often has insignia on left sleeve and loop at V of collar through which sailor tie is slipped; worn by men in U S. Navy and by children since 1860, adopted by women from 1910–1940 for wear with bloomers or shorts as a gym suit. (Also called *sailor blouse.*)

overblouse Blouse not tucked inside skirt or pants at the waist but worn outside; may be belted or not.

peasant b. Folkloric woman's blouse, called by national names, such as Rumanian, Polish, Swedish, etc., freely adapted for mass production, usually of white cotton with puffed or long full sleeves and embroidered borders, neckline square and embroidered or round with elastic or drawstring. Also see *gypsy blouse.*

Russian b. See *Cossack blouse.*

sailor b. See *middy blouse.*

shell Women's plain sleeveless blouse, buttoned in back or slip-on, made of knitted or woven fabric and frequently worn with matching skirt and jacket; popular in 1950's and early 1960's.

sissy shirt Woman's frilly shirt with rows of tucks and lace inserts, a ruffled neckline; popular as a reaction against tailored boy-style shirts in 1950's.

slip b. A blouse or shirt attached at the waist to a *half-slip, q.v.,* to eliminate the problem of shirttail's pulling out.

slip-on b. Any blouse, having no full front or back opening, that pulls on over the head.

squaw b. Heavily embroidered blouse resembling *peasant blouse, q.v.* inspired by American Indian styles.

stock-tie b. See *flip-tie blouse.* Also called *stock blouse.*

sweater b. Sweater made of fine yarn and worn as blouse, sometimes having ruffled details or dressmaker styling, may be tucked inside skirt.

tailored b. Woman's blouse in shirting fabric styled like a man's shirt, having front buttoning, long cuffed sleeves, convertible tailored collar; usually worn tucked into pants or skirt, but popular hanging out over *dungarees, q.v.* See *shirts.*

torso b. Overblouse that fits snugly and extends to hips.

tunic b. Wrist-length to mid-thigh length overblouse of woven or knitted fabric, usually long-sleeved,

high necked, and held in by tie-belt; worn by men and women over pants or skirt, e.g., *Cossack blouse.*

wrap b. Blouse made with two bias-cut front sections extended into long sash ends, crossed and wrap-tied around waist.

Zhivago b. See *Cossack blouse.*

blouse coat Coat with V-shaped neckline, *dolman* or *kimono sleeves,* and single-button closing, at waistline; frequently made with slightly flounced skirt and lavish, high fur collar; popular in mid 1920's.

blouse-dress Boys' and girls' dress of 1880's, made with *blouson* top and low waistline; usually short skirt

BLOUSE-DRESS, 1884–87

was pleated. Also called a *blouse costume.* For later versions see *French dress.*

blouse slip See *slips.*

blousette Sleeveless blouse for wear under cardigans or suits; popular in

1930's–40's. Also called *dickey, q.v.*

blouson (blue-sawn) French word for *blouse.* See *dresses, silhouettes, jackets,* etc.

blouson-noir (blue-sawn nwar) French, black shirt, name for a young delinquent.

blucher 1. See *oxfords* under *shoes.* 2. Man's ankle-length riding boot that laces up center front through six pairs of eyelets; worn from 1820 to 1850. *Der.* Named after Field-Marshal von Blücher, Prussian commander at battle of Waterloo, 1815.

blucher bal See *oxfords* under *shoes.*

blue-aproned men English tradesmen of 16th to 18th centuries, who were recognized by their aprons of blue fabric—a color not worn by the upper classes.

blue billy Neckcloth made of blue fabric with white polka dots; introduced by the fighter William Mace and worn from 1800 to 1820.

bluebonnet Small-sized Scotch *tam, q.v.,* of blue wool with narrow *tartan, q.v.,* band fitting around head, long black streamers in back,

colored pompon on top; originally made in leather for protection when fighting. Also called *bonaid,* Scottish word for *bonnet.*

blue coat 1. Coat worn by apprentices and servants from end of 16th to end of 17th centuries, a color avoided by gentlemen as an indication of lower class. Also see *blue-aproned men.* 2. Bluecoat: a policeman.

blue flax Dark linen fiber from Flemish part of Belgium, named for blue color of the plant.

blue fox See *fox* under *furs.*

blue jeans See *pants.*

blue pelt Fur pelt taken in early fall, too soon to be *prime pelt, q.v.*

boa See *scarfs.*

boarded finish Leather finish that makes grain more pronounced, hand-processed by folding the leather with grain sides together and rolling it back and forth while pressing it from top with cork board.

boater British term for man's flat-topped, flat-brimmed straw hat worn from 1880's to 1930's, introduced about 1865 for children, then adopted by women; e.g., the *Henley boater,* popular in 1890's, was blue or grey felt hat of similar shape, named for Henley-on-Thames, England, site of boat races. See *hats.*

boater tie See *ties.*

boating shoe See *shoes.*

boat neckline See *bateau* under *necklines.*

bob See *hairstyles.*

bobbin 1. Small spool such as the one on which lower thread in sewing machine is wound. 2. In textile production, the spool or core on which yarn is wound, with a hole to fit on spindle. 3. Small spindle on which thread is wound when making lace, tatting, or knitting.

bobbinet Hexagonal net. See *fabrics.*

bobbin lace See *laces.*

bobby pin Small flexible piece of metal bent in half with prongs held together by the spring of the metal, worn to keep hair in place or to set hair in *pin curls, q.v.,* under *curls.*

bobby's hat See *hats.*

bobby socks See *socks.*

bobby soxer Slang for teen-ager of the 1940's who followed current fashion fads such as *bobby socks, Sloppy Joe sweaters, saddle shoes, q.q.v.*

bobtailed coat Short-tailed man's coat with narrow revers; worn at end of 18th century and early part of 19th century.

bob-wig 18th century man's wig without queue; long bob covered back of neck, short bob ended at nape of neck.

bodice (bod-iss) 1. 19th century term for close-fitting upper part of woman's dress, cross-laced in peasant dresses. 2. Part of woman's garment above the waist.

bodies, pair of *Stays,* or *coreset,* worn in the 17th century, stiffened with *whalebone, q.q.v.,* steel, or wood and frequently padded.

bodkin 1. Long flat needle with blunt end used to string elastic and ribbon through eyelet insertion, beading, or headings. 2. 16th to 19th century term for long hairpin used by women. 3. Instrument for punching holes in leather or fabric.

bodkin beard Beard with long point in center of chin; worn by men from early 16th century to early 17th century.

body 1. Quality in a fabric that drapes well, hangs well, and stands up under use. 2. Term used from 15th to

17th century to denote woman's *bodice, q.v.*

body boot See *boots.*

body briefer See *body stocking.*

body chain See *belts.*

body coat 19th century men's tailoring term distinguishing a suit coat from an outdoor or overcoat.

body hose See *body stocking.*

body jewelry Highly decorative accessories designed to be worn on all parts of the body, face, and head, over body stockings or clothing, including items which may be pasted on as well as elaborate pieces of metal jewelry and decorative chains, or a cape, dress, cap, pants, coat, or scarf made of loose strands of pearls. Also called *body wrap.* Designed by Bill Smith, Kenneth J. Lane, and Quasar Khanh; also by *Paco Rabanne,* see *designers appendix, France.*

body painting Fad of late 1960's and early 1970's for painting face and body with fantasy flower and geometric designs to show when wearing *bikinis, q.v.,* or semi-nude fashions. See *tattoo* and *caste mark.*

body shirt See *shirts.*

body stocking One-piece knitted body garment, with or without sleeves or legs, having a snap or split crotch; introduced in 1964 as a nude-colored stretch garment without legs, by Warner Foundation Co. In 1967, legs were added and body hose be-

came popular in 1968, particularly for wear under *see-through* dresses, *q.v.* Legless variety also known as *body suit, body shirt, body sweater* or when designed as a control undergarment called *body briefer.*

body suit One-piece fitted garment without legs having a snap crotch;

made in a wide variety of plain, patterned or ribbed knits, sleeveless or with long or short sleeves; substitutes as a blouse or sweater. Also called a *body shirt* or *body sweater.*

Bohan, Marc See *designers appendix, France.*

Bohemian lace See *laces.*

boiled shirt Slang term for man's formal white shirt with stiffly starched front, formerly worn with *tuxedo* or *tails, q.q.v.*

bois de rose (bwa-de-roz) Soft rosy-brown color. Also called *ashes of roses* and *dusty pink;* fashionable in 1920's and 1930's. *Der.* French, rosewood.

Bokhara shawl (bo-kar-a) Shawls made in Bokhara, Turkestan, of camel hair spun into yarn, dyed with vegetable dyes, and woven into 8″ strips of patterned fabric joined invisibly into shawls.

Boldini hairstyle See *hairstyles.*

bolero (bo-lehr-o) 1. Woman's waist-length or rib-length jacket, open in front, with or without sleeves, often embroidered; popular at end of 19th century and again in 1950's and '60's. See *jackets.* 2. Matador's jacket, elaborately embroidered in gold braid and beads, with large epaulets on shoulders; worn by bullfighters in Spain and Mexico. See *suit of lights.* 3. Classic garment in variety of colors and embroideries worn as part of peasant costume in many European and Eastern countries, e.g., Albania and Czechoslovakia.

bolero blouse Long-waisted blouse with attached pieces of fabric forming a false bolero, popular for women during First World War.

bolero cape Elbow-length cape worn by women at end of 19th century, cut like a bolero in front and tapered to waistline in back. Also called *bolero mantle.*

bolero costume Dress with matching *bolero, q.v.,* reaching nearly to the waist or separate jacket and skirt with a shirtwaist; worn from early 1900's to 1920. Some boleros were fitted, some had elaborate full cape sleeves.

bolero toque Woman's small draped hat of fabric or fur, with back trimming extending up over the crown; worn in late 1880's.

Bolivia Velvety coating. See *fabrics.*

bollinger Man's hat of 1860's, having bowl-shaped crown with knob in center and narrow circular brim; first worn by cab drivers, later adopted by gentlemen for country wear. Also called *hemispherical hat.*

bolo tie See *ties.*

bolster collar See *collars.*

Bolton thumb Thumb of glove with

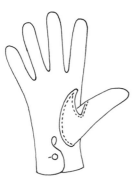

extra point protruding from base of thumb, making more flexibility.

bombanas Fibers obtained from leaves of bombanassa palm; used for straw hats.

bombast Term used in 16th and 17th centuries for garments, especially trunk hose and sleeves, stuffed or padded with horsehair, wool, rags, flax, or cotton. Also called *bombasted.*

bombazine See *fabrics.*

bonaid See *bluebonnet.*

Bonaparte, Napoleon (1769–1821) Emperor of France, 1804–15; encouraged use of French textiles, influenced *Empire styles, q.v.,* as depicted by court painter, J. L. David; cashmere shawls; and military fashions for men and women, e.g., tight cream-colored breeches, *bicorn* hat, high-rolled-collar jackets. See *collars.*

bonbon pink Pastel pink color. *Der.,* French, candy. Also called *candy pink.*

bonding Textile process involving joining of two fabrics into one by means of adhesive or foam; often the backing is acetate tricot. See *backed cloth* and *non-woven fabrics.*

bone lace See *laces.*

bones Stays, q.v., used lightly in a corset, bra, swimsuit bodice, or strapless dress for shaping and stiffening; made of *whalebone, q.v.,* plastic, or steel. Also see *feather boning* and *foundation garments.*

bongrace 1. Separate, stiffened, oblong woman's head covering with drapery in back; worn in 16th and early 17th century, above or over a *coif, q.v.* 2. Pendant flap in back of French hood, which was brought up over crown and fastened so as to project forward over forehead.

bonnaz embroidery See *embroideries.*

bonnet 1. Headcovering for women, children, and infants, usually fitting over back and top of head and tied with strings under chin. 2. Scotchman's cap, e.g., a *bluebonnet, q.v.*

BONNETS:

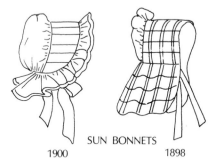

SUN BONNETS
1900   1898

baby b. Infant's cap, sometimes lace-trimmed, fitting to shape of head and tied under chin.

rain b. Accordion-pleated plastic covering for head that ties under chin; folds up to fit in purse when not in use.

sleep b. Any net, snood, or cap worn to bed to protect hairstyle.

sun b. Wide-brimmed bonnet tied under chin, especially worn by infants and children, for protection against the sun.

wind b. Lightweight, fold-up covering, made of *net, point d'esprit,* or *chiffon, q.q.v.,* worn to protect hair.

bonnet à bec Woman's bonnet covering top of head with peak over forehead, lower edge touching the hair; called the *papillon;* worn in early 18th century. Also called *bonnet en papillon.*

bonnet babet See *babet bonnet.*

bonnet en papillon (pah-pe-yon) See *bonnet à bec.*

bonnet rouge (bon-neh rooje) Red wool peak-top cap, symbol of liberty, worn by patriots in French Revolution, late 18th century. *Der.* French, red bonnet. Also called *liberty cap.*

book bag See *handbags.*

bookbinder prints See *prints.*

boots Type of footwear that extends to ankle or above, sometimes as high as the waist; worn, sometimes over shoe, for protection against weather or against hazards of a particular occupation or sport, e.g., *rain boot, stadium boot, wading boot, polo boot, engineer's boot;* or worn in place of shoe, made in a wide variety of leathers, fabrics, or vinyl—styled as stretch pull-ons or laced, zipped or buckled; with various heel heights and shapes of toes. Some 20th-century boots follow.

BOOTS:

ARCTIC BOOT

COWBOY BOOT

ankle b. See *demi-boot, George,* and *pants boot.*

après-ski b. (app-preh skee) Bulky, insulated boot often calf-length and made of long-haired, shaggy furs; worn for warmth after skiing. *Der.*

47

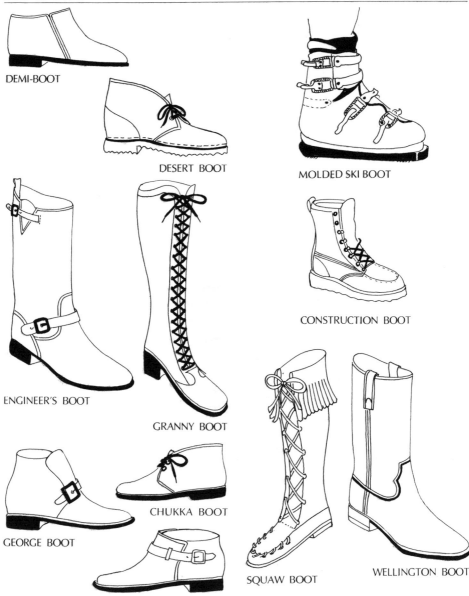

DEMI-BOOT

DESERT BOOT

MOLDED SKI BOOT

ENGINEER'S BOOT

GRANNY BOOT

CONSTRUCTION BOOT

GEORGE BOOT

CHUKKA BOOT

JODHPUR BOOT

SQUAW BOOT

WELLINGTON BOOT

French, after ski. Also called *after-ski boots*. Also see *slippers*.

Arctics 1. Waterproof rubber boots worn over regular shoes, usually with zipper closing; popular in 1940's, revived in 1970's. 2. Over-the-shoe boots introduced in late 19th century made of fabric lined with rubber and with molded rubber soles, fastened in front with series of metal hooks and slotted fasteners; still worn by children and sportsmen. Also called *galoshes*.

body b. Women's long, tight-fitting shoe-boots, reaching to the thigh; introduced in late 1960's.

carriage b. Woman's fur-trimmed winter boots, usually of fabric, sometimes of leather, worn over other shoes to keep feet warm in unheated carriages or automobiles in early 20th century; also used for street wear.

chukka b. Man's and boy's ankle-high boot laced through two sets of eyelets, made of splits of unlined sueded cowhide, with thick crepe-rubber sole; originally worn by polo players and adopted for general wear in 1950's. *Der.* From playing periods of polo game called *chukkers*.

combat b. Ankle-high laced boots worn by U.S. armed forces, made of special retanned leather designed to be waterproof.

construction b. Laced boot of heavy yellow-tan leather, reaching to ankle or a few inches higher, with a heavy rubber sole and wedge-style heel; originally worn by construction workers on the job, a fad for casual wear among young people in early 1970's.

Courrèges b. White mid-calf-length shoe-boot introduced by French designer André Courrèges in fall of 1963, designed to be worn with *mini-skirts, q.v.*

cowboy b. High-heeled, mid-calf-high boot, usually for men, of highly ornate tooled or appliquéd leather, often in two tones; first worn by cowboys of Western United States; now adapted for women and children. Also called *dip-top boots, q.v.*

demi-b. Shoe-boot reaching just to the ankle. Also called *half-boot.*

desert b. Type of *chukka boot, q.v.,* introduced in 1960's, made primarily of sueded cowhide or calfskin, usually lined; laced with two sets of eyelets; rubber sole and heel. Similar to *floats, q.v.*

dip-top b. Man's or boy's 11- or 12-inch boot with high heel, top section cut lower in center front and back, decorated with overlays and stitching in elaborate two-tone leather patterns, often with boot-loops of leather to assist in dressing. Also called *cowboy boot, q.v.*

engineer's b. Man's 12-inch straight-sided boot with low heel, strap across instep; may have leather or elastic gusset at top on outer side.

fishing b. See *waders.*

floats Similar to *chukka boots* and *desert boots, q.q.v.* but with thick crepe soles and a thick pile lining; worn mainly by men and boys, introduced in early 1960's.

galoshes See *Arctics,* above.

George b. Ankle-high boot with one-buckle fastening, similar to *jodhpur boots, q.v.,* and widely accepted for general wear by men in 1969.

granny b. Women's boots laced up the front in imitation of high-topped shoes of 19th century; a 1960's fad.

hip b. See *waders.*

insulated b. Any boot with a lining for protection against cold; may be fur lined, acrylic pile, wool, or foam-bonded fabric.

jockey b. High leather riding boots, worn by jockeys in horse races.

49

jodhpur b. Ankle-high boot fastened with one buckle on the side, worn for horseback riding. Similar to *George boot, q.v. Der.* Named for *Jodhpur,* city in India.

jungle b. *Combat boot, q.v.,* used by U.S. Army in Vietnam; made with heavy steel shank and tiny drainage holes in sides and heel.

kamik ·Calf-length, handmade boot, made of fine leather trimmed with embroidery, worn by Greenland Eskimos.

lumbermen's over Man's heavy laced 10-inch boot with oiled-leather top and rubber vamp and sole; worn over felt liner.

majorette b. Woman's calf-length boots, usually white, with tassels hanging from top centers; worn by drum majorettes, cheer leaders, etc. at athletic events.

mousers Woman's leather stocking-pants reaching to waist with attached chunky-type shoes made of shiny wet-look leather; introduced by Mary Quant, English designer, in 1969.

mukluks (muk-lek) Calf-high boots worn by Alaskan Eskimos, made with moccasin construction of walrus hide or sealskin tanned with hair left on; copied with knitted tops for after-ski and winter at-home wear.

pants b. Ankle-high shoe-boot designed to wear with pants.

rain b. Lightweight plastic or rubber stretch *galoshes* that may be folded and carried in the purse. Same as *Totes, q.v.*

riding b. Boots reaching up to the knee, made of high-quality leather, usually custom-ordered to fit leg; worn with breeches for horseback riding. May have boot hooks for ease in dressing.

rubber b. Moulded rubber waterproof boot, with or without insulated lining but usually fabric-lined, worn over the shoe (especially by children) or in place of the shoe as protection against rain or snow.

ski b. Waterproof thick-soled ankle-high boot of leather or molded plastic, closed with laces or buckles, sometimes with an inner boot, or foam lined, attached to ski by clamp that grips the sole.

squaw b. Below-the-knee boot made of buckskin with fringed turned down cuff at top, soft sole, no heel, worn by American Indian women and popular with young people in 1960's.

squaw bootie Ankle-high American Indian boot, made of buckskin, styled like a moccasin, and trimmed with beads on front and long fringe around top.

stadium b. Calf-high fur- or pile-lined boot worn over shoe, popular for football games in the 1950's.

stocking b. Woman's boot made of stretch vinyl, leather, or fabric with no zipper, and fitting leg closely like a stocking, sometimes reaching to thigh with attached panties; popular in late 1960's.

storm b. Another name for *Artics* or any type of boot worn in snow or rain storms.

Totes Trademark name for lightweight, fold-up unlined rubber boots, worn over shoes. Also called *stretch boots.*

waders Rubber boots for fishing in three heights: *fishing boots,* mid calf; *hip boots,* to hips; *chest-high,* waterproof pants reaching to chest with suspenders over shoulders, made of rubber or lightweight flexible vinyl pressed to cotton jersey and welded to seamless boots.

Wellington b. Man's 14-inch boot usually made of water-repellent leather with oak-tanned soles and rubber heels; may have *boot straps, q.v.* Named for Duke of Wellington, who defeated Napoleon at Waterloo, 1815.

Western b. See *cowboy boots* and *dip-top boots.*

boot blow-up Inflatable plastic or rubber boot form inserted when boots are not being worn to retain shape.

boot cuff Large turned back cuff, reaching nearly to elbow, popular for men's coats in the 1730's used on a *boot sleeve, q.v.*

bootee, bootie 1. Infants' soft knitted, fabric, or leather shoe worn until replaced by walking shoe. 2. See *space clothes.* 3. See *slippers.*

boot garters 18th century term for straps attached to back of boot, which wound around the leg above knee over top of the breeches.

boot hook 1. 19th century term for leather loop attached to back or side of boot at top, which aids in pulling them on. Also called *boot strap.* 2. Long L-shaped piece of metal with a handle used to pull boots on.

boot hose Long stockings of coarse linen with flared tops of lace called *French falls;* worn by men in 15th to 18th centuries to protect silk stockings under heavy boots.

boot-hose tops Decorated borders at tops of boot hose, gold or silver lace, ruffled linen, or fringed silk. Also called *tops* or *French falls.*

boot jack A device of wood and iron to hold boot while wearer withdraws his foot, used extensively in 18th and 19th centuries and still employed by horseback riders.

boot length See *lengths.*

boot pants See *pants.*

boot sleeve Man's coat sleeve with *boot cuff, q.v.;* popular in the 1730's.

boot stocking See *boot hose.*

boot strap See *boot hook.*

border 1. Trimming at edge, or just above edge, on an item of apparel or an accessory. 2. Decorative woven cords or stripes in handkerchiefs. 3. Decorative edge on fabric or one used for identification purposes. 4. (plural) See *billiment.*

border prints See *prints.*

borel 14th-century term for clothing.

bosom flowers Artificial flowers worn by men and women in the 18th century, usually with full evening dress. Also worn by the *Macaroni* or *dandies, q.q.v.,* in daytime.

bosom friends Wool, flannel, or fur chest protectors, which were also bust improvers; worn by fashionable ladies in late 18th century and early 19th century.

bosom knot Same as *breast knot, q.v.*

bosom shirt 1. Man's formal white shirt with starched bib front. 2. Shirt worn in late 19th and early 20th cen-

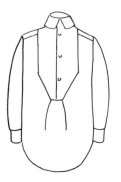

turies, made with collar and bib front of shirt fabric and rest of shirt of inferior fabric, sometimes knitted.

bosses Decorative snoods of gold or linen covering thick coils of braided hair, arranged at each side of face, with a *coverchief, q.v.,* or veil over entire headdress; worn in 13th and 14th centuries. Also called *templers.*

Botany yarn 1. Fine, high-quality worsted yarn. 2. English knitting yarn of coarse quality used in making stockings. *Der.* From Botany Bay, New South Wales, famous for fine quality merino wools. 3. Trademark of knitting yarns.

botews (bot-toos) 15th century term for *buskin, q.v.*

bottine Woman's knee-high riding boot of 16th century.

bouchette (boo-shet) Large buckle used in medieval times to fasten breast plate of armor.

bouclé See *fabrics.*

bouclé yarn See *yarns.*

boudoir cap (boo-dwar) Soft lace-trimmed cap with gathered crown

and ruffled edge; worn over woman's hair in bedroom in 19th and early 20th centuries.

boudoir slipper See *slippers.*

bouffant (boo-fawn) French word meaning full or puffed. See *dresses, hairstyles, skirts, silhouettes,* etc.

bouffant mecanique (mek-can-eek) Sleeve made with hidden spring attached to corset neckline and projected into sleeve to extend it; worn in late 1820's.

bouffant neckwear Lace, linen, or gauze worn around woman's neck and shoulders, and over chest in a puffed *fichu, q.v.;* worn in late 18th and early 19th centuries.

bouillonné (bwee-yon-nay) Crinkled or blistered texture; *Der.* French, bubbled, puffed.

boulevard heel See *heels.*

Boulogne hose English term for round or oval *trunk hose,* frequently *paned* and worn with *canions, q.q.v.,* after 1570. Also called *bullion hose* or *French hose.*

bound With edges covered by narrow strips of fabric. See *buttonholes, hems, pockets.*

Bourbon hat (boor-bon) Blue satin hat decorated with pearls in a fleur-de-lis pattern; popular in 1815 to celebrate Napoleon's defeat, return of Bourbon Louis XVIII to the throne.

Bourbon lock See *love lock.*

bourdon lace See *laces.*

bourette silk See *fabrics.*

bourette yarn See *yarns.*

bourka Man's winter overcoat of thick black cloth woven from goat hair or horsehair: worn in Georgia in the

Russian Caucasus. See also *tcher-keska*.

bournouse See *burnoose.*

bourrelet (boor-lay) 1. 15th century term for padded sausage-shaped roll worn by men and women for head-dresses, or as base of headdress. Also spelled *birlet* or *burlet.* 2. Another name for bustle called *bum roll, q.v.,* worn by women in 16th and 17th centuries. 3. Term used for stuffed, rolled trimming.

bourse 1. Large purse or bag worn in mid 15th until mid 18th centuries, later called a *burse.* 2. 18th century rarely used French term for the black silk bag of a *bagwig, q.v.*

Boussac, Marcel See *designers appendix, France.*

boutique Small shop selling variety of merchandise, including dresses, jewelry, accessories, antique bibelots, or *objets d'art,* etc. *Boutique de la maison couture* originated in Paris in 1929 by *Lucien Lelong, q.v.,* in his *Edition* department, followed by *Elsa Schiaparelli, q.v.,* first couturiere to open a separate boutique, on Place Vendome. Term applied to small shops everywhere since 1950; now such shops often contained within large department stores.

boutonniere (boo-ton-yair) 1. Flower worn in lapel buttonhole, initiated by wealthy boulevardiers and popular for formal functions since the 19th century. 2. Small bouquet, or flower, worn by women on left shoulder or lapel. See *bosom flowers.* Der. French, *buttonhole.*

bow 1. Knot usually having two loops and two ends—often a narrow fabric, ribbon, or string; used for sashes, neckties, or decorative trim. Variant of *bowknot.* 2. See *necklines* and *blouses.*

Bow, Clara American movie star of 1920's, called the "It Girl" in 1926, a round-eyed beauty with small cupid's-bow lips who typified sex appeal and inspired several hats of the late 1920's.

bow dye 17th century term for a scarlet dye. Also called *bowdy.*

bow headdress See *Alsatian bow.*

bowl crop Men's hairstyle of 15th century with hair shaved at back and sides, with longer hair hanging from crown of head in round basin-shaped fashion; a fashion revived in 1970 for young men. See also *pudding-basin cut.*

bowler See *hats.*

bowling shoe See *shoes.*

bow neckline See *necklines.*

bow tie See *ties.*

box bag See *handbags.*

box bottoms Men's close-fitting below-the-knee breeches made with stiffened lining; worn in 19th century.

box calf See *leathers.*

box cape Straight cut elbow- or hip-length cape, with broad padded shoulders and square silhouette, in fur or wool; fashionable in 1930's.

box coat 1. Woman's straight coat with wide shoulders, popular in 1930's and 40's. 2. Heavy, warm overcoat with single or multiple shoulder capes, worn throughout 19th century particularly by coachmen and travelers riding outside coach on the "box." 3. Hip-length woman's double-breasted jacket styled like a *reefer, q.v.,* worn in early 1890's. 4. Unfitted jacket coming to below waistline, styled with *Medici collar, q.v.,* and side closing; worn in mid 1890's. 5. See *Empire jacket.* 6. Three-quarter-length unfitted coat, with shawl collar, not fastened in front, sometimes trimmed lavishly with braid; worn in early 1900's. 7. Double-breasted girl's coat sometimes made with shawl collar, or an extra cape; worn in early 19th century.

boxer panties See *panties.*

boxer shorts See *shorts* and *swimsuits.*

boxes 17th-century term for *galoshes, q.v.*

box jacket See *jackets.*

box loom Loom that has two or more shuttles, used to weave structural designs in various colors, e.g., checked gingham, or for weaving fabrics that have alternating yarns of different types.

box pleat See *pleats.*

boyish bob See *hairstyles.*

boy shorts See *swimsuits.*

boys sizes Run from size 8 to 20, each size coming in slim, regular, and husky. Sizes are determined by height, weight, chest, and waist.

braccae Loose-fitting pants or hose worn by the Romans after the Gallic conquest. Also called *broc, braies, q.v., bracco.*

bracelet Decorative band or circlet worn on the arm, wrist, or ankle, used as ornaments since Biblical times. Also called *armlet, anklet,*

wrist band, wrist belt, wrist cuff. Der. Latin *bracum,* arm.

BRACELETS:

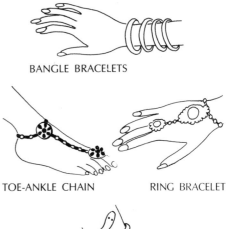

BANGLE BRACELETS

TOE-ANKLE CHAIN   RING BRACELET

SNAKE BRACELET

ankle b. Ornament worn around the ankle; may be *chain, I.D. bracelet,* etc.

bangle b. 1. Narrow, round, rigid bracelet of metal, plastic, wood, or other material, worn singly or several at a time; popular since 1900's, originally worn in sets that jingled when the arm moved. 2. Anklet worn in India and Africa. *Der.* from Hindu *bangri,* a glass ring or bracelet.

chain b. One or more chains of precious metal, in varying widths, worn on the wrist.

charm b. A metal (often gold or silver) chain bracelet on which one or more objects, of matching metal

—"charms," such as disks, zodiac signs, hearts, etc.—are hung, often to commemorate personal events; popular in 1940's.

clip b. Bracelet made of solid metal having one spring hinge allowing it to open wide for removal.

elastic b. Beads or sectional motifs of various types strung on elastic to slip over hand.

expandable b. Spring-link metal bracelet that stretches and needs no clasp; since 1940's frequently used as watch bracelet.

flexible b. A bracelet that is not a rigid circle, such as *chain, elastic, expandable,* etc.

go-go watchband Wide buckled watchstrap of bright-colored leather or plastic, with watch attached by snapped tabs at either side so that band can be changed easily; introduced in 1969. Also called *Mod.*

hoop b. See *bangle bracelet.*

I.D. b. See *identification bracelet.*

identification b. Bracelet of large links attached to oblong metal plaque engraved with name or initials; first used by soldiers in wartime, later adopted by women and children. Also called *I.D. bracelet.*

ring b. Ornate finger ring connected by chain to bracelet worn around wrist, copied from bracelets worn in Eastern countries for centuries and popular in 1880's. Also called a *bracelet ring.* Also see *toe-ankle chain.*

scarab b. Bracelet made of several oval semi-precious stones—such as lapis lazuli or chalcedony—engraved

to look like beetles and connected by gold links. *Der.* Ancient Egyptian sacred beetle. See *scarab.*

slave b. Chain bracelet worn on the ankle.

sleeve b. Ornate bracelet worn around upper arm over full sleeve to make a *double puffed sleeve;* fashionable in England in 1960's.

slide b. Claspless bracelet with small bar of pierced metal through which fine, flat chains are threaded, popular in late 19th century and again in 1960's.

snake b. Metal bracelet in form of a serpent worn coiled around the arm; worn by ancient Greeks and fashionable in 1880's and in 1969.

spring b. Beads strung on flexible wire in a spiral that expands to permit entry of hand.

toe-ankle chain Unusual ankle bracelet with chain attached to toe ring, worn in 1970. Also called *slave bracelet, q.v.*

watch b. Band or strap attached to wrist watch in all types of metals, leather, plastic, fabric, etc., and styles, e.g., bangle, flexible, chain, link.

bracelet sleeve See *sleeves.*

bracelet-tie shoe Woman's ankle-strap shoe with extended loop in center back to hold the strap; worn in 1930's and '40's and again in early 1970's.

braces British term for *suspenders, q.v.,* first worn about 1787. Also called *galluses.*

bracket seaming Type of decorative seam for pockets or yoke, shaped like a double curved bracket, }.

bractiates Type of pin used to fasten garments from 6th to mid 8th centuries.

Bradford system Special process for spinning worsted yarns that results in more sleek, compact yarns than those made on the French system.

bragon braz Full breeches, sometimes accordion pleated, which reflect 16th-century influence, worn as native dress by men in Brittany, France.

braguette Variant of *brayette, q.v.*

braid 1. Narrow woven band for use as trimming, binding, or for outlining lace and embroidery; types described below. 2. (verb) To form a plait of hair, fabric, straw, etc. 3. (Plural) See *hair pieces* and *hairstyles*.

BRAIDS:

coronation braid Firmly woven mercerized cord braid, alternately wide and narrow, used to outline a pattern in embroidery or lace, also for *couching, q.v.*

crocheted b. Lightweight braid of bright colored wool or acrylic yarn worked in continuous links and used for decoration on dresses, blouses, and sweaters.

diamanté b. Bands of fake jewels, such as rhinestones, used as trimming on dresses, blouses, and pajamas.

galloon (gal-*loon*) 1. Narrow tape or braid made of cotton, silk, rayon, wool, or man-made fibers, used for trimming. 2. Double-edged lace made in various widths. *Der.* French *galonner,* to trim with braid or lace. 3. Highly decorative double-edged braid, frequently made of gold thread, sometimes with jewels spaced at regular intervals; used extensively in 1969.

gimp Braid made from heavy *core yarn, q.v.,* arranged in a pattern and stitched to create a raised effect.

Hercules b. Worsted braid, heavily corded, from 1/2" to 4" in width; several widths often used together.

horsehair b. Permanently stiff coarse braid, made originally from horsehair, now of nylon; used for stiffening *bouffant, q.v.,* skirts at the hemline and in millinery.

ladder b. Braid with open stitches crossed by bars creating ladder-like effect, made on a bobbin.

middy b. Narrow, flat glossy braid used to trim collars and cuffs of naval *middy blouses, q.v.,* in white on navy blue or navy blue on white; other colors used for trimming and piping on dresses or coats.

military b. Flat ribbed worsted braid, sometimes a diagonal weave, made in various widths and chiefly gold; used to designate ranks on military uniforms.

rat-tail b. Silk braid of tubular shape used for trimming. See *soutache.*

rice b. Firmly woven, highly mercerized braid with thick parts alternating with narrow to give the appearance of grains of rice. Used for trimming and crochet laces.

rickrack Cotton braid in several widths in zigzag form.

Russian b. Same as *soutache braid, q.v.*

soutache b. (soo-tash) Narrow rounded decorative braid of mohair, silk, or rayon; used for borders and also used in all-over ornamental patterns. *Der.* Hungarian, *sujtas.*

braider Machine that makes braid, consisting of several *bobbins, q.v.,* intertwining yarns to form pattern.

braie girdle (bray) See *breech girdle.*

braies (brays) Loose-fitting trousers, frequently *cross-gartered, q.v.,* worn under the tunic as an undergarment by Romans after the Gallic conquest and in France during the Middle Ages. See also *braccae.*

bra-kini See *foundation garments.*

Brandenburg 1. Man's long, loose winter coat in military style with *frog closings, q.v.;* worn in last quarter of 17th century. 2. (pl.) Term used after 1812 for military trimming consisting of transverse crocheted cording and tassels similar to *frog closing,* worn by women. Also spelled *Brandenbourg* or *Brandenburgh. Der.* Named for braid-trimmed uniforms worn by Brandenburg troops of Prussia.

bra-shift See *dresses.*

bra-slip See *slips.*

brassard 1. 19th century term for mourning band of black cloth worn on upper left arm or for ribbon bow on elbow of evening dress. 2. Wide white silk ribbon bow with streamers worn by first communicants. 3. Furlined half sleeve. 4. 15th century French term for part of sleeve extending from wrist to elbow, attached by ribbons to upper sleeve, called *macheron.* 5. Piece of armor from elbow to shoulder, worn on upper arm for protection, from mid 14th to 15th centuries. Also spelled *brassart.*

brassiere or **bra** Shaped undergarment popularized in 1920's, worn by women to mold and support the breasts, consisting of two cups usually held in place by straps over shoulders and across back; may be padded, wired, or boned; usually has sections of elasticized fabric. Less rigid, less constructed brassieres of soft fabrics with less emphasis on uplifted, pointed lines appeared in the 1960's. *Der.* From French *brassière,* a child's bodice; in French, a brassiere is *soutien-gorge.*

BRASSIERES OR BRAS:

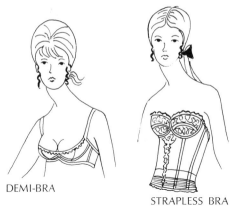

DEMI-BRA

STRAPLESS BRA

bandeau (ban-doe) Synonym for *brassiere. Der.* French, bandage.

Cadoro b. Trademark for decorative metal bra worn with scarf or bikini underneath, consisting of metal cups, frequently filigreed, held on with chains; introduced in 1966. See *body jewelry.*

contour b. Rounded brassiere padded with *fiberfill, q.v.,* or foam.

LEISURE BRA

STRETCH BRA

PLUNGE BRA

décolleté b. (day-kol-eh-tay) Low cut brassiere, for wear with low neck-lines.

demi-b. Half brassiere that exposes upper part of breasts, for wear with low necklines.

French b. Brassiere that fits under bust as an uplift but has no cups, worn with low-necked dresses for natural look.

half b. See *demi-bra,* above.

leisure b. Lightweight unconstructed brassiere, often of stretch lace, de-signed to be worn at home or when sleeping.

long-line b. Brassiere that fits the bust and rib cage, extends to waist: worn with girdle to eliminate waist-line bulges; sometimes strapless.

minimal b. Very brief unconstructed brassiere made of stretch jersey fab-ric with few seams, *e.g.* the top of a bikini swimsuit.

natural b. Popular 1960–70's style made of stretch jersey fabric, some-times in "nude" color, with no stif-fening, boning, or wires, and a mini-mum of seams; often has built-up tank-top, *q.v.,* straps for comfort.

nude b. Brassiere made in light-weight nude-colored fabric with no bones; also called *natural bra* or *minimal bra.*

one-size b. See *stretch brassiere.*

pasties 1. Individual cups that ad-here to breasts; same as *posts, q.v.* 2. Small decorative coverings that adhere over nipples, worn by danc-ers.

plunge b. Brassiere with V-shaped open section in front, separated cups attached to a band, to be worn with a dress with plunging neckline.

posts Cups for the breasts that have no straps or back, fastened in place with adhesive.

push-up b. Brassiere with low-cut front and removable foam bust pads to raise the breasts.

sleep b. Same as *leisure* brassiere.

strapless b. Brassiere constructed so that it stays in place without straps over the shoulders; popular 1940's styles used *boning* or *wired* (see below) cups; 1970's styles made of stretch knit fabrics without added construction.

stretch b. Brassiere of fabric knitted with spandex, elastic straps; permits great freedom of movement; often made in only one size, sometimes in pullover style with no back fastening. Also called *one-size*.

swimbra Molded cups, attached or separate, used inside a bathing suit to shape the bosom.

teardrop b. Minimal brassiere with triangular cups, often the upper part of a bikini swimsuit.

teen b. Brassiere with shallow cups designed for the young girl whose breasts are not fully developed.

wired b. Brassiere with fabric-covered wire under or over the breasts to give added support; often strapless.

bratt 1. Mantle or cape made of coarse material; worn by peasants in Ireland in 9th and 10th centuries. 2. Term used in latter part of 14th century for wrap, or blanket, for an infant. Also called *Irish mantle*. Also spelled *brat*.

brayette Metal *cod-piece, q.v.* worn as armor in 16th century.

braygirdle, braie girdle See *breech girdle*.

breakfast cap See *morning cap*.

breakfast coat See *brunch coat* under *robes*.

breakfast wrapper See *robe de chambre*.

breast kerchief Kerchief worn under doublet or gown, wrapped around neck and shoulders for warmth; late 15th to mid 16th centuries.

breast knot Bunch of ribbons or ribbon bow worn at bosom of woman's dress in 18th and 19th centuries.

Also called *bosom knot*.

breastplates 1. Solid metal brassiere or metal breast ornaments worn by women. See *body jewelry. Der.* From cast metal armor shaped to fit over entire front of chest and reaching from shoulders to waist, worn by soldiers and Spanish conquistadors in 16th century. 2. Ornament made of two sets of long bone beads worn on chest by plains Indians of U.S.

breasts 18th century men's tailoring term for waistcoat buttons.

breech Term used, from late 14th century to early 16th century, to indicate upper part of hose, fitting trunk of body; in 16th century, of contrasting color or fabric. See *breech belt*.

breech belt Waistband of the *breech, q.v.;* see *breech girdle*.

breechcloth *Loincloth, q.v.* worn by American Indians, of cloth or leather about six feet long, decorated with beads and fringe, worn hanging front and back.

breeches 1. Contemporary term for knee-length trousers similar to *knickers, q.v.,* worn by teenage boys in early 20th century and by men for golfing, hunting, etc. 2. Early medieval term for trousers; same as French *braies* and Latin *braccae;* from end of 16th century on, called *breeches* or *hose.* See *cloak bag breeches, knee breeches, slops, galligaskins, petticoat breeches, Spanish hose,* and *Venetians*.

breech girdle Belt, pulled through wide hem of top of *breech. q.v.,* in drawstring fashion, at waist or a little below; worn in 13th to 15th centuries by men.

bregirdle Variant of *bray-girdle, q.v.*

bretelles (breh-tell) 1. Band trimming for blouse or dress bodice, extending from shoulder and narrowing to waist, on front and back of garment; used particularly from 1885–1910, e.g., the *Gibson Girl, q.v.,* shirtwaist. Also called *suspender trimming. Der.* French, suspenders. 2. Revers reaching to waistline front and back, extended over shoulders to resemble capelets; worn in first half of 19th century.

Breton See *hats.*

Breton jacket Fitted hip-length woman's jacket that does not meet in

front but is buttoned on either side to a front panel, with tailored collar and lavishly trimmed with wide braid, frequently shorter in center back; in the late 1870's, when worn with matching skirt, was called a *Breton costume.*

bretonne lace See *laces.*

Breton work See *embroideries.*

Brewster green Dark blue-green color, used for coachman's livery in Victorian era.

brick stitch See *stitches.*

bridal dress See *dresses.*

bridal veil See *veils.*

bride lace 1. 16th and 17th centuries term for blue ribbon used to tie sprigs of rosemary given as wedding favors; originally worn on arm, later on hat. 2. See *bridal* under *laces.*

brides 1. Term used in 1830's and '40's for ribbons attached to inside brim of bonnet or broad-brimmed hat, which were loosely tied or hung free. 2. Connecting threads joining lace designs where there is no net ground; also called *tie bars.*

bride's garter See *wedding garter.*

bridesmaid's dress See *dresses.*

bridles 18th century term for strings attached to *mobcap, q.v.,* tied under chin. See also *kissing strings.*

briefcase See *handbags.*

briefs See *panties.*

brilliant cut See *gem cuts* under *gems.*

brim Rim of hat attached to crown and shading the face; narrow to wide, worn level or turned down or up at a variety of angles.

brin See *bave.*

Brioni See *designers appendix, Italy.*

Bristol blue Intense blue color of Bristol glass, similar to peacock blue.

britches See *breeches.*

British warm British army or navy officers' heavy double-breasted overcoat, knee-length or shorter; copied for civilian wear in 1950's and '60's.

broadbrim Wide-brimmed, low-crowned hat worn by members of the Society of Friends, called Quakers; term *broadbrim* is a soubriquet for one of these members.

broadcloth See *fabrics.*

broadtail lamb See *furs.*

broc (plural *brec*) Anglo-Saxon term for trousers similar to Roman *braccae, q.v.;* plural developed into *breech,* then *breeches.*

brocade See *fabrics.*

brocade embroidery See *embroideries.*

brocatelle See *fabrics.*

broché (bro-shay) 1. Paisley type shawl made in Scotland, woven in alternating stripes of pattern and plain color. 2. A French term for pattern produced by swivel and lappet weaving. 3. A fabric decorated with special threads introduced into the warp or weft but not really part of the structure.

brodekin 1. Lightweight shoe worn in Middle Ages inside of boots. 2. Scottish term for man's calf-length boots of 15th to 17th centuries, called *buskin* in England. Also spelled *brodkind* or *brotiken.*

broderie anglaise See *embroideries.*

brogan See *shoes.*

brogue See *shoes.*

bronzed leather Copper-colored kid or calfskin.

brooch See *pins.*

Brooks, Donald See *designers appendix, United States.*

broomstick skirt See *skirts.*

brown belt See *judo* under *belts.*

brown George Late 18th-century colloquial term for man's brown wig said to look like coarse brown bread.

Bruce tartan See *tartans.*

Bruges lace See *laces.*

Brummell, Beau English dandy, George Bryan Brummell (1778–1840), arbiter of men's fashions during the Regency; leader of the *beaux,* who advocated unobstrusive dark-blue

fitted coats, cream trousers, elaborately tied cravats, absence of showy fabrics or excessive decoration, impeccable grooming.

Brummell bodice Whalebone *waist cincher,* or *corset,* worn by English *dandies, q.q.v.,* of Regency period, 1810–20.

brunch coat See *robes.*

Brunswick Close-fitting riding coatdress with mannish collar; worn by women in 18th century, said to have originated in Brunswick, Germany.

Brunswick gown *Sack*-backed, *q.v.,* gown with front-buttoned bodice, long sleeves; worn by women from 1760–80. Also called *German gown.*

brush Bushy tail of an animal, usually a fox, used as trimming.

brush cut See *crew cut* under *hairstyles.*

brush-dyeing Coloring of fur or leather by placing skins flesh side down on metal table and applying dye to fur or to grain side with brush; desirable for black kid used for gloves, as inside remains white.

brushed fabric Knitted or woven fabric brushed to form nap on face.

Brussels lace See *laces.*

Brussels net See *laces.*

brusttuch Elaborately embroidered oblong plastron, fastened around neck; worn by Jewish women in Poland in 19th century.

Brutus head or **wig** Man's own hair worn closely cropped or brown unpowdered wig, both worn disheveled; popular from 1790–1820 and inspired by the French Revolution.

bruyère (bru-yer) Pinkish-purple, color of heather. *Der.* French, heather.

Bruyère See *designers appendix, France.*

bubble Popular term to describe many fashions in 1950's. See *beads, caps, hairstyles, curls, silhouettes, skirts.*

Buchanan tartan See *tartans.*

buck clothes 16th- and 17th-century term for clothes placed in buck baskets to be laundered.

bucket-top boot Man's boot with very wide, exaggerated cuff top; worn in early 17th century.

Buckinghamshire lace See *laces.*

buckle A clasp, usually of metal, wood, or plastic, consisting of rectangular or curved rim, often with one or more movable tongues or a clip device, fixed to end of a strap, used to fasten to other end or to another strap; used since earliest times for belts, shoes, knee breeches, etc.

buckled wig 18th-century man's wig with tightly rolled *sausage curls, q.v.,* arranged horizontally near ears. *Der.* French *boucle,* curl.

buckles d'Artois Knee buckles of enormous size worn during early 18th century, named after the Comte d'Artois, later Charles X of France.

Bucko calf See *leathers.*

buckram See *fabrics.*

bucksain Man's padded overcoat, with wide sleeves; worn in 1850's.

buckskin 1. Deerskin tanned by *buckskin* method, *q.v.,* then buffed. See *leathers.* 2. Sheepskin treated to resemble above. 3. (plural) From 15th to 19th centuries, term for buckskin gloves, breeches, or riding gaiters. 4. See *fabrics.* 5. See *jackets.*

buckskin tannage Type of primitive tannage of animal skins used by American Indians; hair and skin side were scraped, skins immersed in solution of lye made from wood ashes, lubricated with brains and liver of animals, and hung in smoke-filled tepee.

bucky pelts Fur peltry taken in spring months when skins are not fully furred and tend to be tough and unyielding. Also called *springy pelts.*

budget Wallet or extra pocket hanging from belt; used in 17th century.

buff coat Man's leather jacket, made of ox or buffalo hides, sometimes with shoulder wings or sleeves of fabric; worn in 16th and 17th centuries, originally a military garment worn during civil wars in England, later adopted by civilians and American Colonists. Also called *buff jerkin* or *leather jerkin.*

buffed finish Finish produced on leather by abrading with emery wheel.

buffins, pair of English term for men's *trunk hose* similar to *slops,* or *round hose, q.q.v;* worn in 16th century.

buffon Woman's large scarf or neckerchief of gauze or fine linen draped around neck and shoulders and puffed out over the chest, sometimes supported by wire framework; worn in 1780's. Also spelled *buffont.* See *bouffant neckwear.*

bug-eyed glasses See *sunglasses* under *glasses.*

bugle beads See *beads.*

built-up heel See *stacked heel* under *heels.*

built-up slip See *slips.*

built-up straps Shoulder straps constructed in continuous curve as part of garment, usually a *slip* or *bathing suit, q.q.v.* Also called *tank top.*

bulgare pleat Term used in mid 1870's for double *box pleats* kept in place with elastic on inside of skirt.

bulking Several procedures used for crimping, curling, or looping yarn to make it bulkier.

bull-dog toe See *toes of shoes.*

bull head Woman's hairstyle with fringe of thick curls across forehead; worn late 17th century. Also called *taure. Der.* French *taureau,* bull.

bullion embroidery See *embroideries.*

bullion hose See *Boulogne hose.*

bullion lace See *laces.*

bullion stitch See *French knot* under *stitches.*

bully-cocked 18th century term for man's cocked hat, usually broad brimmed and three-cornered; worn by gentlemanly blackguards known as Bloods or Mohocks. Also called *kevenhuller hat, q.v.*

bum See *bum roll*

bumper Cap worn in the Netherlands by children, fitted at back of head, with wide, thick roll of yarn around the face for protection. Also see *child's pudding* and *bumper brim.*

bumper brim 1. Term for hat brim that rolls back from the face, used in various widths on different styles of hats. 2. Hat with this brim. See *hats.*

bumper collar See *collars.*

bum roll Padded roll worn around hips to hold out skirt in the tub-shaped French *farthingale, q.v.;* worn in England during 16th and 17th centuries. Also called *hausse-cul* in Netherlands, about 1600.

bun See *hairstyles.*

bundle Garment-trade production term for cut-out pieces of dresses, shirts, etc., tied together with cord or elastic.

bundle stitch See *stitches.*

bundle system Garment-trade term for method of production using an unorganized flow of sectionalized work, each employee bundling his finished work. See also *development bundle system.*

bunny suit See *pajamas.*

bun snood or **bun-warmer** See *chignon cap.*

buntal Fiber from Philippines used for *ballibuntl straw, q.v.*

bunting 1. Same as *baby bunting, q.v.*
2. Name of loosely woven lightweight cotton fabric in red, white,
and blue flag colors; used for patriotic decorations and costumes. 3.
18th century English worsted fabric.

Burberry 1. Trademark for a heavy or
lightweight British fabric treated to
resist the congealing of snow and
penetration of wind. 2. By extension, a term used for a raincoat in
Great Britain. 3. Clothing worn by
Arctic explorers, c. 1914, consisting
of boots made with tops of this fabric, Burberry outer helmets, Burberry overalls, and Burberry jackets.
4. Clothing made of this fabric worn
in 1920's for skiing.

burdash Fringed sash worn by *beaux,
q.v.,* over the coat, in late 17th and
early 18th centuries. Also spelled
berdash.

burka Voluminous ankle-length garment completely covering the head
and figure, the top fitting close to
head with veiled opening for the
eyes; worn in India by Muslim wom-
en. Also spelled *bourkha, burga* and
burkha.

burlap Jute sacking. See *fabrics.*

burlet See *bourrelet.*

burnet 1. 17th-century term for *hood* or
headdress, q.q.v. 2. 13th-century
term for fine black or brown woolen
fabric. Also spelled *burnette.*

burn grace See *bongrace.*

burnoose 1. Traveling cape of plain or
striped camel's-hair fabric, circular,
with a square hood tasseled at the
corners; worn by Moors and Arabs in
northern Africa. Also called a *selham.* 2. A cloak or wrap, sometimes

without front opening; worn in Palestine, Turkey, and Arabia. 3. Woman's sleeveless evening wrap like
shawl with a small hood; worn from
1830's to 1870. Also spelled *bernos,
burnouse, burnose, bournouse,* etc.

Burnsides Side whiskers and full moustache with clean-shaven chin; worn
from 1860's to end of 19th century.
Der. Named for Major General Am-
brose Everett Burnside, commander
of Army of the Potomac in 1862.

burnt-out fabric See *fabrics.*

burnt-out lace See *laces.*

burnt-out print See *prints.*

burnt sienna (see-en-a) Dark, rust-
brown color.

burnt umber Dark, yellowish color approaching mustard.

burse Same as *bourse, q.v.*

burunduki See *furs.*

busby See *hats.*

bush coat or **jacket** See *safari jacket* in
sport jackets under *jackets.*

busheling Retail-store term formerly
used for the alteration or repair of
men's clothing.

bush hat See *hats.*

bush shirt See *safari shirt* under *shirts.*

business suit See *suits.*

busk 1. Term used from second half of
16th through 19th century to indicate pieces of cane, wood, whalebone, steel, and sometimes horn
used as stiffeners for woman's *bodice* or *stay, q.q.v.* 2. Men's clothing
thus stiffened. Also called *buske.*

buskin 1. Calf-length thick-soled laced
boot worn by men in ancient Greece
and Rome; same as *cothurnus.*

2. High boots, sometimes to knees, often made of patterned silk, worn in Middle Ages by men and women; copied in 1960's and 1970's for women. Same as *brodekin, brodkin,* or *brotiken, q.q.v.* 3. Leather riding boots; worn in 17th century for traveling. 4. Women's low-cut shoe with elasticized gores at sides of instep; worn in early 20th century.

busk point Metal tip or tag of a lacing that secures ends of the *busk, q.v.*

bust bodice *Boned, q.v.,* garment, laced up front and back, worn over *corset* to support breasts; introduced in late 19th century and forerunner of the *brassiere, q.q.v.*

Buster Brown Comic-strip character of early 20th century whose haircut, collars, shoes, etc. were widely copied for children's wear; now a trademark for children's shoes. See *collars.*

Buster Brown haircut See *hairstyles.*

bust extenders Ruffles used by women to pad bosom in early 20th century.

bust form Padding or wire covered with muslin used by women to emphasize the bust in 1890's

bust improvers Pads of wool and cotton used by women to fill out bosom; introduced in mid 1800's.

bustle Pad, cushion, or arrangement of steel springs creating a bulbous projection below the waist in back of woman's dress; so named in mid 19th century and popular in various

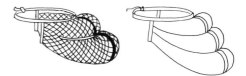

forms to end of century. See *bearer, cushionet, cushion pad, dress improver, figure improver, frisk, Nelson* and *quizzonet.* Also see *silhouettes.*

bustle back Puffs of ribbon, or bows at back of hat, popular in 1930's. Also see *skirts.*

bustle curls See *curls.*

bust pads Foam-rubber or stuffed fabric pads used inside the brassiere to make the breasts appear larger.

butcher-boy Woman's blouse, hip-length or longer, shaped like a smock, usually yoked and buttoned either front or back; popular in 1940's and used later for *maternity blouses, q.v. Der.* garment worn by French butchers' delivery boys.

butcher linen See *fabrics.*

Butch haircut See *hairstyles.*

butterfly bow Length of stiffly starched lace, resembling outstretched butterfly wings, fastened to front of shoe at end of 17th century. Any similar bow.

butterfly cap Woman's small lace cap wired in shape of a butterfly worn perched above forehead with lappets, jewels, and flower trimmings frequently added for court wear; worn in 1750's and '60's. Also called *fly cap*.

butterfly glasses See *sunglasses* under *glasses*.

butterfly headdress 16th-century term for a 15th-century towering head-dress made of sheer gauze and wired to stand out like wings and supported by a fez-shaped cap; worn today by an order of nuns in Normandy, France.

butterfly sleeve See *sleeves*.

button 1. Disk, knob, ball, etc., used as fastening or ornament on garments, bags, etc., attached by sewing through *holes* punched in center or through *shank* on back, inserted through buttonhole or loop to close; may be made in many sizes, shapes and materials, e.g., brass, gold, wood, leather, shell, plastic, jewels, crochet or fabric covered. *Der.* French *bouton*, bud or knob. 2. Glove term indicating length of glove, e.g. one-button is one centimeter measured from base of thumb, two-button is wrist-length, six-button is halfway to elbow, 14-button is almost to shoulder.

button boots Short boots buttoned up outer side with black japanned or mother-of-pearl buttons; worn in 19th century by men and women.

button-down See *collars* and *shirts*.

button earrings See *earrings*.

buttonhole Opening through which *button, q.v.,* is inserted to secure the garment; originated in 15th century. Generally a *bound* or *worked buttonhole, q.q.v.* below.

BUTTONHOLES:

barred b. *Worked buttonhole, q.v.,* with straight bar embroidered across ends.

bound b. Buttonhole with edges fin-

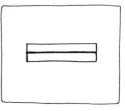

ished with stitched-on fabric or leather binding.

eyelet Round opening *worked* with *buttonhole stitch, q.q.v.* or *overcast,* used for laced closings.

piped b. *Bound buttonhole, q.v.,* with contrasting binding, sometimes with corded edge.

tailored b. *Worked buttonhole* with

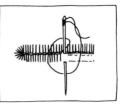

rounded end toward edge of garment, a *bar* at other end.

worked b. Buttonhole finished by hand by embroidering with *buttonhole stitch, q.v.,* or with similar stitching done by a sewing machine.

buttonhole stitch See *stitches*.

button hook 1. Small metal hook attached to long handle formerly used to pull buttons through buttonholes of shoes or gloves. 2. (pl.) Small metal hooks first used in 1860's instead of eyelets on shoes, the laces winding around hooks, criss-crossing to fasten shoes; used now on skating and other types of boots and called *speed lacers*.

button shoe See *high button shoe*.

B.V.D.'s 1. Trade name for man's *union suit* popular from early 19th century up to World War II, consisting of one-piece, wide-legged, knee-length

garment with U neck, buttons down front and an adjustable back flap, usually made of checked cotton dimity. 2. Trademark for underwear and other men's clothes made by B.V.D. Company.

bycocket High-crowned hat with a wide brim peaked well forward in front, and turned up in back; worn by men in last half of 15th century. 2. Similar hat called a *student bycocket*; worn by Italian students in mid 20th century. Also spelled *bycoket*.

Byrd cloth See *fabrics*.

Byrne, Kiki See *designers appendix, England*.

Byron collar See *collars*.

Byron, Lord *George Gordon Byron, 6th Baron (1788–1814)*, English poet who became a fashion influence by 1812, especially copied were the open-necked shirt with long pointed collar, the freehanging hair; his travels to Turkey and Greece inspired him to wear Turkish caftans, slippers, Ottoman dressing gowns, Indian jewelry, and Oriental perfume. See *Byron collar* under *collars, Byron tie*.

Byron tie Short, narrow string necktie made of silk; worn in 1840's and 1850's. Named for *Lord Byron, q.v.*

byrrus Same as *birrus, q.v.*

byzance See *necklaces*.

Byzantine embroidery See *embroideries*.

Byzantine stitch See *stitches*.

C

C 1. Shoe size: Letter indicating a width; widths run from *AAAAA* to *EEEEE* with *A*'s being the narrowest. 2. Pajama size: Men's size corresponding to 40–44 chest size, 165–185 pounds weight, or shirt sizes 15½–16½. Also called "L" for Large. 3. Brassiere cup size: Letter used to indicate medium size cup, with sizes running *AA, A, B, C, D, DD; AA* being the smallest.

caban (ka-ban) Believed to have been the first fitted European coat with sleeves, having a closed front, sleeves wide at the armhole, and sometimes a belt. See *gaberdine.* Also see *templar cloak.*

cabaña set (cah-ban-ya) See *swimsuits.*

cabas (kah-bas) Version of *Phrygian cap, q.v.,* made of beaver or velours, draped across forehead to conceal hair and ornamented in back; created by Sally Victor, New York milliner, in 1956.

cabbage ruff Large ruff falling in irregular folds, like leaves of a cabbage; worn by men in early 17th century.

cabbage-tree hat Broad brimmed hat made of plaited or woven leaf fibers from the cabbage tree or palm; worn in Australia.

cabin-boy breeches Tight-fitting pants laced below the knees; worn for sportswear by women in 1940's; named after an employee on ocean vessel who waits on officers and passengers.

cable hatband Band of gold yarn twisted to resemble a rope or cable; worn in the late 16th century.

cable net See *fabrics.*

cable stitch See *stitches.*

cabochon (kab-a-shon) See *gem cuts.*

cabretta (ka-bret-ah) See *leathers.*

cabriole headdress Rare fashion *c.* 1755, lasting only a few years, consisting of a miniature coach-and-six or post chaise worn by women on head instead of a cap; coach was made of gold thread and six dappled gray horses were made of blown glass. Also spelled *caprioll.*

cabriolet bonnet (kab-ree-o-leh) Large bonnet with brim extended forward framing the face like a carriage top, but cut away in back to show hair; popular from about 1820 to 1850. *Der.* Named for two-wheeled carriage.

cache-chignon (cash sheen-yon) A velvet bow attached to jeweled pin, used to hold loose ends of back hair in place; worn in 1840's and 1850's.

cache-folies (cash fo-lee) Short-haired wig worn by women in Paris to cover the cropped *Titus coiffure, q.v.,* after the French Revolution in the early 19th century.

cache-laid (cash lade) Term used for mask worn in Paris to conceal a plain or unattractive face; fashionable about 1650, during reign of Louis XIV. *Der.* French, hide-ugly.

cache-peigne (cash pain) Snood of net and ribbon worn by women to hold hair back, in the 1850's and '60's. *Der.* French, hide-comb. See drawing, next page.

CACHE-PEIGNE

CADOGAN NET

Cacherel, Jean See *designers appendix, France.*

cack Heelless shoe with soft leather sole, made for infants in sizes one to five.

caddie See *bush hat* under *hats.* Also spelled *caddy.*

cadenette (cad-net) French term for a lock of hair. See *coiffure en cadenettes.*

cadet blue Light bluish-gray color, similar to uniforms worn by cadets at U.S. Military Academy at West Point, N.Y., and other academies.

cadet cloth See *fabrics.*

cadmium yellow Brilliant yellow artist's pigment or dye resembling this color. Other cadmium colors include a strong green, brilliant orange, and bright red.

Cadogan See *catogan hairstyle* and *catogan wig.*

cadogan net Snood, *q.v.,* sometimes made of knotted silk yarn, worn over crown of head and enclosing the hair hanging down the back in *catogan* style, *q.v.;* popular in late 1870's and early 1880's, particularly for young women and girls.

Cadoro bra See *brassieres.*

café (ka-fay) Dark-brown coffee color. *Der.* French, coffee.

café au lait (ka-fay o leh) Brownish beige, like coffee with milk—the exact French meaning.

caftan 1. North African or Mid-Eastern garment (sometimes called *farasia* in Morocco), a long, full robe with slit neckline, decorated with embroidery, and long, full, bell-shaped sleeves; worn in U.S. since 1960's as at-home and evening dress by women and sometimes by men. See *dresses* and *robes.* 2. Egyptian and Near Eastern striped coat-like garment with long sleeves; worn by men with sash around waist. 3. Russia: Long overcoat, formerly worn by men. Also spelled *kaftan, kuftan, gaftan,* or *cafetan.*

cage 1. Overblouse or dress made out of lattice-like or transparent fabric. See *dresses.* 2. Shortened name for the *cage petticoat, q.v.,* below.

cage-americaine Hoop-skirt petticoat, the upper part made of hoops connected with vertical tapes and lower part covered with fabric; worn in 1860's. See *cage petticoat.*

cage empire Cage petticoat made

with graduated hoops of steel, shaped into a slight train in back, for wear under a ball gown; worn in the 1860's.

cage petticoat Hoop-skirt petticoat made of a series of whalebone or wire hoops graduated in size from waist down and fastened together vertically with tapes, making it flexible, lighter in weight than layers of petticoats; worn by women in 1850's and 1860's. Also called *cage* or *artificial crinoline, q.q.v.* Variant of *cage-americaine, q.v.*

caging Fur-cleaning process, in which furs are revolved in cage-like wire drums that permit the sawdust used for cleaning to fall out through the wire mesh.

cagoule (ka-gool) Cloth or fur semicircular cape with attached hood; worn by peasants in 11th to 13th centuries in France.

cai-ao Long chemise-type garment worn in Vietnam, by both men and women, which closes on one side and is slashed to hips revealing trousers or skirts. Worn with *caiquan* as part of *ao dai, q.q.v.*

cainsil (kane-sil) See *chainse.*

caiquan (kay-kan) Long black trousers worn in North Vietnam by men and women under the *cai-ao,* to form *ao dai, q.q.v.*

cairngorm See *gems.*

cake hat Man's soft felt hat with a low oval crown; worn in late 1800's. Similar to *Alpine hat, q.v.,* under *hats.*

calash Large hood made with hinged arches of *whalebone, q.v.,* or cane

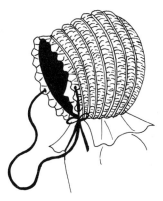

covered with fabric in manner similar to folding top of convertible car, stood away from head and protected bouffant hair styles; worn in 18th and 19th centuries. *Der.* Named after hood of French carriage called *calèche.* Also spelled *calèche.*

calasiris See *kalasiris.*

calcarapedes Self-adjusting rubber galoshes, worn by men in the 1860's.

calceus patricius (cal-se-us pa-trish-e-us) Calf-high Roman boot, essentially a low shoe with straps wrapping high on leg; worn by Emperor Nero and Roman senators.

calèche See *calash.*

calendering Running a finished fabric between hot metal rollers under pressure to make it shiny or give embossed effect.

calf-length See *lengths.*

calfskin Hide from young cows or bulls, tanned for use either as leather or fur. See *leathers* and *furs.*

calico See *fabrics* and *prints.*

calico button Metal ring covered with calico, sometimes with metal eyelets in center; used mainly for underclothes in 1840's.

California embroidery See *embroideries.*

calimanco shoes Heavy twilled-cotton shoes worn by American women in Colonial days. Also spelled *calamanco, callamancoe, calliman, callimancoe,* and *calmanco.*

calisthenic costume Knee-length dress worn with Turkish trousers similar to *bloomer costume, q.v.,* worn in late 1850's by women and girls for such sports as archery, ice skating, and exercising with dumbbells. Later version

of this dress was called *gymnasium costume.*

calk 1. Device on heel or sole of shoe or boot to prevent slipping or give longer wear; may be a metal plate with sharp points. 2. In Colonial America, *clog, q.v.,* with spiked sole.

Callot Soeurs See *designers appendix, France.*

calotte (ca-lot) 1. Woman's small skull cap; worn in 1940's and '50's, sometimes with large pinned jewel badge. 2. A cap worn by school-boys, called *beanie, q.v.* under *caps,* or *dink.* 3. Tiny, close-fitting skullcap cut in shaped gores, often with a tab at center of top; worn by Roman clergy and by priests and monks in early Christian orders. Also called *zucchetto, q.v.* 4. Black silk skullcap, worn by Chinamen; red cord knot on top indicating a married man, a white knot worn for mourning. Also spelled *calot* and *callot.* 5. See *yarmulka.*

calpac Large black sheepskin or felt cap; worn by men in Near East, Turkey, and Armenia. Similar to *Cossack hat, q.v.*

calypso chemise (ca-lip-so) Woman's dress of 1790's, made of colored muslin, worn under a loose robe.

calypso shirt See *shirts.*

camail (ka-mail) 1. Shoulder cape of chain mail laced to helmet, worn as part of armor during first half of 14th century. 2. Woman's waist-length or three-quarter-length cape-like cloak with small turned-down collar, arm slits, and fringe trimming, made of padded satin or velvet in winter and lined silk in summer; worn in 1840's.

Camargo (ka-mar-go) A woman's jacket with draped fullness around hips, worn over waistcoat or vest in late 1870's. *Der.* Named after Marie Ann de Camargo, *q.v.*

Camargo hat Small woman's evening hat with brim raised in front; worn in mid 1830's. *Der.* Named for Marie Ann de Camargo, see below.

Camargo, Marie Ann de Cupis de (1710–1770) Celebrated dancer, born in Brussels of Spanish descent; she shortened the ballet skirt and removed the heels from her dancing shoes, was a fashion influence in shoes, coiffures, hats, etc.

camauro (ka-mor-o) Red velvet, ermine-trimmed cap slightly larger than a skullcap; formerly worn by Pope of Roman Catholic church.

cambric Fine cotton. See *fabrics.*

Cambridge coat Three-button, single- or double-breasted man's suitcoat, made with three seams in back and a vent; worn from 1870.

Cambridge paletot (pal-e-toe) Man's knee-length overcoat, cut with wide cape collar, large turned-back cuffs, and wide lapels extending almost to hem; worn in 1850's. *Der.* Old English *pattok,* peasant's coat.

camelaurion (kamel-lo-ree-on) Coronet with closed crown, worn in Byzantium in 12th century.

camel hair 1. Fibers from the Arabian-Asian camel, producing soft luxurious yarn that is resistant to heat and cold. 2. Cloth made of these fibers.

camel suede See *fabrics.*

cameo Raised design carved on a stone that has more than one layer, such as onyx; used in jewelry. See *gems* and *pins.*

cameo necklace A *cameo,* see above, mounted in gold and suspended from velvet ribbon tied around the neck; worn by women in the 1850's and popular again in late 1960's and 1970's.

Cameron tartan See *tartans.*

cames See *chemise.*

camis Blouse worn by Mohammedan women of India with the baggy *chudidar paejamas, q.v.*

camisa (kah-mee-sah) 1. Blouse worn by women in the Philippines, made of sheer fine *rengue* cloth woven from pineapple fibers, with gathered set-in sleeves hanging wide and free to the elbow or below and elaborately embroidered at the lower edge. See *butterfly* under *sleeves.* 2. Chemise, shirt, or blouse, worn in Southwestern U.S. by women. 3. See *chemise. Der.* Spanish *camis,* blouse.

camise See *chemise.*

camisia Synonym for *chemise, q.v.,* in England in the Middle Ages.

camisole (kam-ih-sole) 1. Lingerie: waist-length gathered top with straps, trimmed with lace or embroidery; worn with a petticoat under a sheer blouse in late 19th and early 20th centuries. 2. Short bodice or vest with built-up straps, worn over corset or stays; introduced in early 1800's. Also called *chemise, corset cover,* or *petticoat bodice.* 3. Woman's dressing *sacque, q.v.* 4. Sleeved jacket or jersey formerly worn by men. 5. See *slips.*

camisole top Blouse of a dress, styled like a *camisole, q.v.,* usually cut straight across, gathered with drawstring, and held up with wide straps. See *necklines.*

camlet Fine fabric of mixed materials such as silk, wool, linen, goats' and camel hair, usually costly and used continuously for clothing from 12th century through 19th century. Also spelled *camelot, chamblette. Der.* Place of manufacture on banks of River Camlet in England or possibly from its camelhair content.

camouflage Fabric colored to resemble hues seen in surrounding terrain so that person wearing fabric becomes invisible; used by soldiers in World War I and II, surplus fabrics used for men's sport jackets, pants, and hats.

campagus (kam-pa-gus) 1. Shoe worn by bishops in Western Church, particularly Roman Catholic, sometimes Episcopal. 2. Shoe worn during Byzantine period and the Middle Ages, high in back to the ankle and fastened with ribbon or strap around ankle; revived in 1960's and 1970's as part of *hippie* dress, *q.v.*

campaign coat Originally a long military overcoat worn by the rank and file from about 1667, and later adopted by men for civilian wear in late 17th century.

campaign hat Broad-brimmed field hat worn first by Union soldiers in Civil War and later issued to entire American Army; worn by soldiers in World War II with four dents in top of crown.

campaign wig Periwig with full curls above forehead, one long curl on either side of face, one in back with the ends turned up and tied; worn by European soldiers from late 17th through 18th centuries. Also spelled *campaigne*. Also called *traveling wig.*

canadienne (ka-nah-dee-en) Woman's hip-length, double-breasted, belted coat; designed in Paris during the 1940's, copied from coats worn by Canadian soldiers.

canary breeches See *hunt breeches* under *pants.*

candlewick Cotton fabric of loose weave through which loops of soft cotton yarn are pulled from the back in rows and then clipped to form tufts; originally used for bedspreads, now used for women's and children's robes. See also *embroideries.*

candys See *kandys.*

candy stripes See *stripes.*

cane Staff or stick to assist walking or to carry as a fashionable accessory, varying from rough rustic wood for country use, e.g., *shillelagh,* to polished woods with elaborately decorated heads, for gentlemen, e.g., *Malacca cane* and *rattan cane, q.q.v.,* carried from 16th to 20th century by men and occasionally women. See also *constable.* Also called *walking stick.* See *swagger stick.*

canezou (can-zoo) 1. Woman's waist-length jacket, usually sleeveless and made of lace or richly embroidered; worn in early 19th century. Also called *canegous.* 2. In 1830's, a cape cut short and pointed, covering front and back but not the arms. Also called *Canezou pelerine.* 3. By mid 19th century, an elaborate *fichu, q.v.,* of muslin, lace, and ribbons covering bodice of dress.

caniche See *fabrics.*

canions Tight-fitting cuffed tubular garments worn on the thighs as extensions of men's *trunk hose, q.v.,* frequently of different fabric or color; worn about 1570 to 1620.

canned dress Trade name for simple printed nylon-knit shift dress packaged in a tin can for sale; brief popularity in 1967.

cannele *Warp-wise, q.v.,* cord effect in fabric with woven-in ribs, e.g., *piqué, q.v.* under *fabrics.* Also spelled *canale, canelle, canele, canile,* and *canellee.*

cannetille (can-tee) 1. Military braid, of gold or silver thread, that looks like lace. Also spelled *cantile.* 2. Fine spiral-twisted gold or silver thread, used for embroidery. 3. French warp-ribbed dress fabric.

cannon 1. See *canons.* 2. Piece of protective plate armor for the upper arm or forearm, cylindrical or semi-cylindrical.

cannon sleeve Woman's padded and boned sleeve, swelled at shoulder and tapered to wrist, giving appearance of a cannon; used in women's gowns from about 1575 to 1620. Also called *trunk sleeve.*

canons Frills of lace or bunches of ribbons (also called *fancies*) that fell down over tops of wide boots; worn by men during most of the 17th century. Also worn with low shoes and *petticoat breeches, q.v.* Also spelled *cannons* or called *port canons.*

canotier (kan-o-tee-ay) 1. Man's stiff flat oval-crown straw hat with straight brim, fashion of early 20th century and identified with actors Maurice Chevalier, Buster Keaton, and Harold Lloyd. Same as *boater, q.v.* 2. French term for fabric made in a twill weave and used for sportswear and yachting clothes. *Der.* French, boatman.

Canton crepe Silk or rayon crepe. See *fabrics.*

Canton flannel Napped cotton. See *fabrics.*

Canton silk Silk yarn from southern China from small domesticated silk worms, weaker than Japanese silk but lustrous and of even diameter. *Der.* Canton, China.

cantouche See *kontush.*

Cantrece (can-treess) Trademark for a resilient self-crimping nylon yarn, used for hosiery and pantyhose.

canvas See *fabrics.*

canvas, embroidery See *embroidery.*

cap Head covering, often fits snugly, brimless but may have front visor, usually of fabric but may be of vinyl plastic, leather, or fur; often worn by men for *sports* such as baseball, hunting, etc. and by jockeys, policemen, engineers, army, navy, air-force personnel. Caps for children and women are often knitted or crocheted. See various historical caps under alphabetical listing; contemporary caps listed below. See also *hats.*

CAPS:

army c. Variety of caps, usually in khaki or olive-drab fabrics, cotton twill or wool: 1. *Baseball, q.v.,* type with visor, called *fatigue* or *forage cap.* 2. Flat-folded cloth cap with lengthwise pleat in center of crown, called *overseas cap* or *garrison cap.* 3. Dress cap with stiff round flat top and visor, called *service cap.*

baseball c. Close-fitting cap with visor to shade the eyes, crown frequently cut in gores and with button on top; worn by baseball players. See also *batter's cap.*

BASEBALL CAP

GLENGARRY CAP

TAM-O'-SHANTER

TROOPER CAP

BEARSKIN CAP

NEWSBOY CAP

MORTARBOARD

KEPI

NURSES CAP

OVERSEAS CAP

YACHTING CAP

bathing c. Tight-fitting cap made of rubber, with or without strap under chin, often elaborately decorated with rubber flowers, fringe, or other trimmings; worn to protect hair while swimming.

batter's c. Duck-bill visored cap with hard crown for protection, worn by baseball players when taking turn at bat.

beanie Skullcap cut in gores to fit the head; worn by children and by freshmen students as a part of hazing by upperclassmen. Also called *dink* or *dinky*.

76

bearskin c. Tall cylindrical cap of black bear hide with a chain or strap under lower lip or the chin, worn by some personnel of the British army and by military guards of Buckingham Palace in London and Parliament buildings in Ottawa. See *shako* under *hats.*

bellboy c. Small fabric *pillbox, q.v.,* often trimmed with gold braid, sometimes with chin strap; worn by hotel or restaurant bellboys. Also called *bellhop cap.*

beret Round wool cap, woven in one piece, that lies flat, stretches to cover the head closely; traditional man's black or navy headgear in the Basque country of southern France, adapted for sportswear by men, women, children. See *pancake beret.* See also *tam* and *tam-o'-shanter.*

chapel c. Small circle or triangle of lace, often with ruffled trim, carried folded in the handbag by Roman Catholic women to wear when entering a church when head is not otherwise covered.

Davy Crockett c. Coonskin (raccoon fur) hat with tail of animal hanging down back; worn in Colonial America by woodsmen and pioneers and named after David Crockett, frontiersman and politician, who fought and died at the Alamo in Texas in 1836; popular for young boys in 1950's and '60's after wide exposure on television programs.

deerstalker Checked or tweed cap, similar to *jockey's cap, q.v.,* with visor both front and back and ear laps that can be buttoned or tied to top of crown. Associated with pictures of Sherlock Holmes, the fictional detective created by Sir Arthur Conan Doyle. Also called *fore-and-aft.*

dink or **dinky** See *beanie,* above.

Dutch-boy c. Cap with visor and soft wide crown, usually made of navy-blue wool. Also called *schoolboy cap* and made popular for young men and women by Russian dancer Rudolf Nureyev in 1960's.

engineer's c. Round cap with visor worn by railroad workers, usually of blue-and-white striped cotton, the crown box-pleated onto the band; worn in 1960's by young people as sportswear.

Eton c. Close-fitting cap with a short visor, modeled after those worn at Eton College in England, popular in fabrics to match coats for young boys in the U.S. in 1920's, '30's.

fatigue c. See *army cap,* above.

forage c. See *army cap,* above.

French beret Same as *pancake beret, q.v.,* below.

French sailor c. See *hats.*

garrison c. See *army caps,* above.

Glengarry c. Military cloth cap, creased to fold flat like an *overseas cap, q.v.,* usually with tartan band at edge, regimental badge at side front, and two black ribbon streamers in back; part of the uniform of Scottish Highland regiments and adapted for sportswear by women and small boys in late 19th century. Also see *casquette.*

hunting c. Bright-red, sometimes fluorescent, visored cap, enabling hunter to be clearly seen by other hunters.

jockey c. Visored cap with crown usually of bi-colored sateen cut in gores, similar to baseball cap but with deeper crown, worn by race-track jockeys. Similar caps worn by women in mid 1960's.

Juliet c. *Skullcap, q.v.,* of rich fabric, worn for evening or with wedding veils. May also be made entirely of pearls, jewels, or chain. *Der.* Medieval costume of Juliet in Shakespeare's play *Romeo and Juliet.*

kepi High-crowned, flat-topped, visored cap, sometimes decorated with a feather cockade in center front, worn by French military and by American marching bands as part of uniform.

Legionnaire's c. Cap with visor and stiff flat crown, sometimes with a cloth curtain or *havelock, q.v.,* attached in back; worn by French Foreign Legion. See *kepi,* above.

military c. Caps similar to the styles described under *army caps,* above; also worn by the U.S. Navy, Marines, other military groups.

miner's c. Stiff cap with short duck-bill visor and battery-powered light attached to front of crown.

mortarboard Large, square, flat, cloth-covered board attached to a skullcap that comes down to a point in front and back, with tassel hanging from top center over side; worn with *academic costume, q.v.,* at colleges, universities. See drawing, page 76.

newsboy c. Soft fabric cap with flat bloused crown and visor that some-times snaps to the crown; formerly worn by newsboys and made famous by child actor Jackie Coogan in films between 1916 and 1919, revived in exaggerated form in 1960's–'70's, called various names, e.g., *Carnaby, bebop, soul,* or *applejack.*

nurses c. White fabric cap, often stiffly starched, awarded to Registered Nurses at graduation and worn with uniform, pinned on the crown of the head, while nurse is on duty; each teaching hospital has its distinctive style of cap.

overseas c. See *army caps* above.

pancake beret Flat wool *tam, q.v.,* often in navy blue, wider than original Basque beret, to be worn tilted and shading the eyes.

sailor c. See *hats.*

scarf c. 1. Scarf attached to visor and tied around head; worn in late 1960's. Also see *scarf hat,* under *hats.* 2. Long tubular knitted or crocheted scarf with opening for head in one end, similar to *stocking cap, q.v.*

Scout c. 1. Boy Scout—green fabric cap shaped like *overseas cap, q.v.* 2. Cub Scout—blue fabric visored cap. 3. Girl Scout—green wool beret with insignia. 4. Brownie Scout—brown wool beanie.

skullcap Gored cap, usually made in eight sections, which fits tightly to crown of the head; often part of ecclesiastical garb or national costume. See *yarmulka.*

stocking c. A knitted or crocheted cap coming to a long pendant point, often with a tassel on the end; originally made by folding back the cuff of a stocking and pulling it over the head as a cap.

tam-o'-shanter 1. Traditional Scotsman's headgear, a flat cap made of two circles of wool fabric sewed together, opening for head in one circle; frequently made of shaggy striped wool fabric cut in gores so stripes form a mitred pattern and with a pompon at center of crown. 2. Similar cap for women or children, often knitted or crocheted. Also called *tam*. See *beret* and *blue-bonnet*. *Der.* Named for character in Robert Burns poem.

tea-cozy c. Cap introduced in late 1960's that fits head like a bell or *cloche* hat, covering hair completely. *Der.* Named for quilted padded cover for teapots.

trooper c. Man's or boy's cap of leather or leather-like plastic with fur or pile lining and a flap around sides and back that can be folded down to keep ears warm or up to reveal lining; originally worn by state policemen or "troopers," now used by mailmen, policemen, etc.

yachting c. Cap, usually white cotton, with flat crown and black or navy-blue visor, decorated with yacht-club emblem; similar to a naval officer's cap; worn by yacht-club members on boats.

watch c. Knitted cap, fitting closely over head, with turned-up cuff, made of navy-blue wool yarn; worn by sailors on watch or for other work duty or as a replacement for white duck hat. Adapted in other colors for sportswear by men, women, and children.

capa 1. Wide, circular, full-length hooded cape worn by Spanish men from Middle Ages to early 17th century; in the Romantic Era (1820–1840) in France it was called *cape à l'espagnole* and worn in evening by women. 2. Full cape worn by bullfighters in Spain, used to secure bull's attention. *Der.* Latin *capa,* hooded cloak.

cape Sleeveless outer garment of various lengths, usually opening in center front; cut in a full circle, in a segment of a circle, or on the straight; may have slits for arms. Classic type of cloak worn in one form or another from Roman times to the present by both men and women. For other cape items, see under categories, e.g., *coats, collars.*

CAPES:

capelet Any small cape, e.g., a cape collar, attached or detachable, on a coat, dress, or suit. See *tippet.*

capote Full, circular cape with wide *cape collar, q.v.,* and red lining, used as a working cape by matadors at Spanish and Mexican bullfights. Also spelled *capot.*

clerical c. Three-quarter-length cape, of wool melton with satin lining, small velvet collar, and braided frog closing, worn today by clergy of Catholic and Episcopal churches and other denominations.

cope 1. Originally a hooded cloak designed as a rain cape, sometimes with sleeves and fastened in center front. 2. Semi-circular mantle, without sleeves or armholes, fastened at the neckline; worn by ecclesiastics

COPE

OPERA CAPE

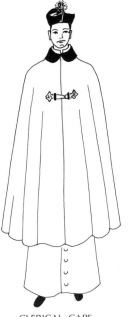

CLERICAL CAPE

French policeman's c. Circular-cut knee-length cape worn by French policemen, made of heavy black wool and rubber and heavy enough sometimes to be swung like a billy club. Authentic cape was sold as sportswear in boutiques and Army surplus stores in U.S. in late 1960's. Also called *gendarme* cape.

mozetta (mot-ze-tah) Shoulder-length cape with ornamental hood hanging in back, worn by cardinals and church dignitaries. *Der.* From Italian *mozzare,* to cut short.

nurse's c. Three-quarter-length cape of navy-blue wool, brass buttoned and lined in red; worn by nurses with their uniforms.

and by British monarchs as one of the *coronation robes, q.v.*

officer's c. Three-quarter-length cape in navy-blue worsted with

• **1** Shawabty Figure of Yuya, Egyptian, XVIII Dynasty, about 1400 B.C. See *wig, kohl.*

2 Offering Bearers, Funerary Model from Tomb of Meket-Re, Egyptian, XI Dynasty, about 2000 B.C. See *shendyt, history of fashion.*

3 Egyptian kings and priests and images of gods 1600–1100 B.C. See *history of fashion.*

4 (right) Carolingian costume of the 9th and 10th century. See *mantle, crakows, headband, braid.*

5

6

• **5** Gallo-Roman, 1400.
See *stola, sudarium, pearls.*

6 (below) English costume
of the Middle Ages, 1250.
See *crown, mantle, tunic, surcoat.*

7

7 (left) "Paradise," by Giovanni
di Paolo, Sienese, about 1445.
See *tights, fur, monk's robe,
nun's habit, wimple.*

small standing collar; part of dress uniform of officers in U.S. Navy.

opera c. Man's full, circular knee-length black worsted cape, sometimes lined in red satin; worn for formal occasions with *tail coat* and *top hat, q.q.v.,* and also favored by magicians and circus ringmasters.

cape à l'espagnole (les-pan-yol) See *capa.*

cape coat See *coats.*

cape collar See *collars.*

cape hat See *hats.*

capelet See *capes,* above.

capeline (cap-eh-leen) 1. Wide wavy-brimmed hat popular in 1930's and again in 1970, either in straw or felt. 2. Late 19th century hood with attached cape, worn by women in country. 3. Late 18th century woman's feather-trimmed wide-brimmed hat. 4. Iron or steel skull-cap worn by foot soldiers in Middle Ages. See *hats.*

capeskin See *leathers.*

capless wig See *wig.*

cap of dignity Same as *cap of maintenance, q.v.* below.

cap of maintenance Cap carried on a cushion before British sovereigns in coronation processions, sometimes used for mayors: usually made of scarlet velvet with ermine trim and symbolizing high rank. Also called *cap of dignity* or *cap of estate.*

capot (ka-pot) Man's loose coat with turned-down collar and cuffs; worn at end of 18th century. Also spelled *capote.*

capote (kah-poat) 1. See *capes.* 2. Hooded coat or cloak worn from Middle Ages on. 3. Popular bonnet of 19th century, with stiff brim, framing the face, soft gathered crown, and ribbon bows tied at side or under chin; by 1890, worn mostly by older women. 4. French term for fabric with napped surface used for sailor's clothes and waterproof coats.

capot-ribot Black velvet hat with long "curtain" or veil hanging below shoulders at sides and back; popular in France after Napoleonic campaign in 1798 and worn by ladies of high rank; still worn in Brittany.

cappa floccata (kap-pa flo-kah-ta) Round cap of hairy fabric, worn by Greek shepherds.

caprice (ka-preece) Loose, sleeveless short woman's evening jacket, tapered to rounded point below the waist in back; worn in mid 19th century.

Capri-length panty girdle (ka-pree) See *girdles.*

Capri pants (ka-pree) See *pants.*

Caprolan Trademark for Allied Chemical Company's nylon 6, used for apparel and hosiery as well as for draperies, rugs, etc.

cap sleeve See *sleeves.*

Capucci, Roberto See *designers appendix, Italy.*

capuche (cap-poosh) 1. Cowl worn by Capuchin monks. 2. Woman's hood attached to cloak; worn in 17th century. 3. Woman's silk-lined sunbonnet of mid-19th century. Also spelled *capouche.*

Capuchin (kap-yoo-chin) 1. Hood worn outdoors from the 13th to 17th centuries. 2. Hood and shoulder

cape or long cloak, sometimes lined in colored or striped silk, worn by women in 18th and 19th centuries for traveling. *Der.* From *capuche,* cowl worn by Capuchin monks of Franciscan order. Also spelled *capuchon, capucine,* and *capuche.*

Capuchin cowl Continuous roll collar on a wrap-over front bodice with a V-neckline, worn by women in the late 18th and early 19th centuries. Also called a *Capuchin collar.*

capuchon (ka-poo-shon) 1. See *Capuchin.* 2. Woman's waist-length outdoor evening mantle with wired hood and long tight sleeves; worn 1830's–'40's. Also called *carmellette.* 3. Tiny bonnet made of flowers.

capucine (*kap*-u-seen) Yellow-orange color. *Der.* French, nasturtium.

Capulet (cap-yew-let) Small hat conforming to shape of head and placed back from brow, sometimes with cuffed brim in front: named for Juliet Capulet, heroine of Shakespeare's play *Romeo and Juliet.*

caraco (kar-a-ko) 1. Fitted hip-length suit jacket with peplum, made by French designer Yves Saint Laurent in 1969, said to derive from jackets in Toulouse-Lautrec paintings. 2. Thigh-length jacket or bodice, fitted to body with no waist seam, flaring below, popular for women from mid 18th century on, called *caraco corsage.* See *casaquin.* 3. Hip-length bodice, tight fitting and often sleeveless, worn in French provinces as part of regional costume.

caracul See *furs.*

caravan Small type of collapsible bonnet similar to the *calash, q.v.,* made of semi-circular hoops that, when opened, drop a veil of white gauze called *sarcenet* over the face; worn in 1875.

caravan bag See *safari bag* under *handbags.*

carbatina Ancient Roman sandal made of single piece of untanned hide as sole, overlapping sides of foot and held on by leather thongs; worn by majority of citizens in first two centuries *A.D.,* but forbidden to slaves. Copied in 1950's to 1970 as barefoot summer sandal worn everywhere by young people. Similar to *calceus patricius, q.v.*

carbuncle See *garnet* under *gems.*

carcaille (kar-kiyuh) 15th century standing collar, which flared upward to the ears, used on *houppelande* and *pourpoint, q.q.v.*

car coat See *coats.*

Cardigan, 7th Earl of James Thomas Brudenal (1797–1868), Lieutenant General in English army who led the "charge of the light brigade" in battle of Balaklava in Crimean War in 1854 and needed an extra layer of warmth over his uniform. *Cardigan jacket* and related garments were named after him. See *coats, dresses, jackets, necklines, sweaters.*

Cardin, Pierre See *designers appendix, France.*

cardinal 1. In 18th and 19th centuries, three-quarter-length scarlet cloak with hood, which resembled the *mozetta, q.v.* worn by cardinals in Roman Catholic church. 2. Woman's waist-length red cloak with hood or collar, worn from 17th through first quarter of 19th century; gave name to tale of Little Red Riding Hood.

cardinal pelerine Large lace *bertha, q.v.,* with collar, open in center front; worn on evening dresses in 1840's.

carding Textile term for first process used on cotton, wool, and spun synthetic fibers when making yarn in which extraneous matter and short fibers are removed, leaving a filmy weblike mass.

careless Loose-fitting, caped man's overcoat with spreading collar and no seams at waistline; worn in 1830's.

carma Tall conical hat made of silver, gold, or brass—similar to the *henin, q.v.,* worn by Algerian women in Tunisia in 18th and 19th centuries. Also see *tantoor.*

carmagnole (car-man-yole) 1. Provincial ceremonial jacket worn by Italian workmen in southern France in late 18th century. *Der.* Named for Carmagnola, Italy. 2. Jacket or short-skirted coat with wide collar, lapels, and rows of metal buttons; worn with black pantaloons and red *liberty cap, q.v.,* by French Revolutionists in 1792–93.

Carmelite cloth See *fabrics.*

carmine Rich red color, purple cast.

Carnaby look Synonym for *Mod* look, name derived from Carnaby Street in London, where this look first appeared in many small boutiques catering to *avant-garde* young customers. The first *mini-skirts, granny* dresses, wide use of *leather fashions* and *boots q.q.v.,* started here in early 1960's.

Carnaby shift See *dresses.*

Carnegie, Hattie See *designers appendix, United States.*

carnelian See *gems.*

carnival collar Collar made of wide loops of bright printed fabric arranged in an unstarched *ruff, q.v.,* as on a clown's costume.

carnival lace See *bridal lace* under *laces.*

Caroline corsage Woman's evening bodice with lace ruffles forming a V in front, extended around shoulders into small cape; worn in 1830's.

Caroline hat Man's hat of Caroline beaver, imported from Carolinas in the Colonies; worn in England from late 17th to 18th centuries.

Caroline sleeve Daytime dress sleeve full from shoulder to elbow and fitted to wrist; worn in 1830's.

carpenter's apron See *aprons.*

carpet bag See *handbags.*

carpet slippers See *slippers.*

carpincho See *leathers.*

carriage boot See *boots.*

carriage parasol Small umbrella, sometimes fringed, popular accessory for ladies when driving in open carriages in late 19th and early 20th centuries.

carriage suit Three-piece set for infant, consisting of jacket, pants, and hat; worn outdoors in baby carriage.

carriage trade Term coined by merchants during the horse-and-buggy era, 1890–1910, for customers wealthy enough to come to stores in their own carriages.

carrick Man's or woman's full-length duster, styled like a coachman's coat with three capes, similar to an *Ulster, q.v.;* worn from 1810 to 1870's. Also called *box coat.*

Carrickmacross lace See *laces.*

carryall Open-top bag similar to a *tote, q.v.* under *handbags,* carried by women to hold small purchases when shopping.

carryall clutch Woman's wallet designed to hold coins, bills, photographs and credit cards, usually the size of U.S. paper money, with snap closing on long edge and purse-like section for coins.

cartoon fashions Fad of the late 1960's and early '70's of imprinting comic-strip and cartoon characters on clothing and accessories, e.g. Mickey Mouse shirt or wrist watch — a 1930's children's watch revived for adults.

cartridge belt See *belts.*

cartridge pleats See *pleats.*

cartwheel See *hats.*

cartwheel ruff Extremely large, starched *ruff, q.v.,* set in regular convolutions; worn from 1580 to 1610. A wire frame called *supportasse, q.v.* was used for support.

Carven, Mme Carmen Mallet See *designers appendix, France.*

casaque (ka-sack) 1. Fitted jacket usually buttoned down the front, worn by women from mid 1850's to mid 1870's; early types had *basque, q.v.,* effect to hips sometimes longer; later types had skirts draped in *polonaise* style, *q.v.* 2. French term for jacket worn by jockeys, usually made in bright colors of their stables. 3. Girl's coat cut on princess lines; worn in 1860's. 4. See *cassock, #3.*

casaquin (kas-a-kan) One of the earliest jackets (late 18th century) worn as top part of a dress; fitted, long-sleeved and waist-length in front, longer in back, similar to *caraco, q.v.*

casaquin bodice Tight-fitting bodice for daytime dress similar in cut to man's *tail coat, q.v.,* closing with buttons down front; worn in late 1870's.

casaweck (kasa-wek) Woman's short, quilted outdoor mantle made with close-fitting velvet or silk collar and sleeves and frequently trimmed with fur, velvet, or lace; worn from mid 1830's to mid 1850's.

cascade 1. Trimming used in 19th and early 20th centuries, made by

84

cutting a narrow piece of fabric on *bias, q.v.,* pleating it to form repeated shell designs. 2. Ruffles bias-cut from fabric in circular manner, falling in graceful folds. 3. Jet pendants or beads in a zigzag edge used at waistline of dress or bodice in 1860's. 4. See *collars.*

cased body 1. Man's sleeveless *jerkin* worn over *doublet, q.q.v.,* in latter part of 16th century. 2. Woman's *bodice* with series of horizontal pleats or shirrings across the front, called *casings;* worn in early 19th century.

cased sleeve Woman's long sleeve made of sections of fabric alternating with bands of *insertion, q.v.;* worn about 1810–1820.

cashambles See *chaussembles.*

Cashin, Bonnie See *designers appendix, United States.*

cashmere An extremely soft, luxurious yarn made from hair of the cashmere goat, native to Kashmir in northern India, and to Tibet, Turkestan, Iran, Iraq, and China; obtained from combing rather than clipping the animal; knit for sweaters and dresses and woven for suits and coats for men and women. Also spelled *Kashmir* and *cachemire.* See *sweaters* and *fabrics.*

Cashmere shawl Large square or oblong wrap made in the Kashmir valley in northwest India from hair of a Tibetan goat that produces fine yellow, white, or black hair called *pashm;* woven under direction of the maharajah and confined to India from late 16th to late 18th centuries, popular in Western world during late 18th and early 19th century. Characteristic pattern was the cypress, a cone-like design often done in red, green, gold, and silver. Shawls again popular in 1969–70 for day and evening. Also see *shawls.*

cashmere work See *embroideries.*

casings See *cased body* and *cased sleeve.*

casque (cask) A hat shaped like a helmet. *Der.* French, helmet.

casquette (kass-ket) 1. Cap with visor, similar to military officers' caps, adapted for women's headwear. 2. Woman's straw cap of mid 1860's, similar to a *Glengarry, q.v.,* with additional short brim front and back, trimmed with black velvet ribbon and ostrich feathers.

cassimere See *fabrics.*

Cassini, Oleg See *designers appendix, United States.*

cassock 1. Full-length liturgical robe, like coat with standing collar, worn by clergy, altar boys, and choirs, sometimes under white *surplice* or *cotta.* Also called *soutane.* See illustration, page 86. 2. Short jacket, buttoned front; worn by clerics. 3. Long loose overcoat with a cape collar; worn from late 16th through 17th century by men and women for hunting and riding and by foot soldiers. Also called a *casaque, q.v.*

cassock mantle Knee-length short-sleeved cloak with shirring at shoulders and down the center back; worn by women in 1880's.

castellated Describing a garment with squared "scallops" at edges,

CASSOCK

particularly the sleeves or hem; used in 14th and 15th centuries. Same as *dagged*.

caste mark 1. Red mark worn in center of forehead by women of India, originally to symbolize and identify caste membership, now serving a decorative function. 2. Paste-on "caste marks" were introduced in United States as body jewelry for women in 1968. Also called *tika*, *tikka*.

Castillo, Antonio See *designers appendix, France*.

Castle, Irene American ballroom dancer, married to her dancing partner, Vernon Castle; together they made tea-dancing the rage pre-World War I, and by 1914 she had started many fashion fads — among them, bobbed hair, Dutch-lace caps, slashed hobble skirts, and laced-up dancing shoes. See *Irene Castle bob* under *hairstyles*.

castor 1. Man's beaver hat. 2. Perfume ingredient obtained from the castor beaver used as a fixative for spicy odors. *Der.* Latin, beaver.

casula Latin name of *chasuble, q.v.*

catch stitch See *stitches*.

cater cap (kay-ter) In 16th and 17th centuries term for square cap worn at universities, now called *mortarboard, q.v.*

Catherine II Wife of Peter III of Russia, married in 1745; Peter III ascended throne in 1762, was deposed, and his crown usurped by Catherine. She influenced fashion: One of her dresses, worn to receive the Turkish ambassador in 1775, was trimmed with many diamonds and 4,200 magnificent pearls; during her reign, coiffures were limited in height to one arm's length.

Catherine-wheel farthingale See *wheel farthingale*.

catiole Shoulder-length French marriage coif made of elaborate bands of lace sewed together and hanging in long *lappets, q.v.,* pinned up half their length.

Catlin, George American artist, traveler, and author (1796–1872), whose portraits and sketches of American Indians of over forty different tribes are a good source of their distinctive details; collection of his works is in the National Museum in Washington, D.C., and in the American Museum of Natural History in New York.

catogan (ka-to-gan) Woman's hairstyle with cluster of ringlets or braids of hair hanging at back of head, tied at nape of neck with wide ribbon; worn in 1870's and resembling male *catogan wig, q.v.* of 18th century. Bow at nape revived by French coutouriere Gabrielle Chanel in 1960's. Also called *Cadogan* and also spelled *catagan. Der.* Misspelling of name of Earl of Cadogan.

catogan wig (ka-toé-gan) Man's wig with broad, flat, club-shaped *queue, q.v.,* turned under and tied with black ribbon that sometimes came around to front and tied in bow under chin; worn from 1760 to

1790's much favored by the *Macaroni, q.v.,* in 1770's *Der.* Name a misspelling for British General, 1st Earl of Cadogan, 1675–1726. Also called *club wig.* Also spelled *cadogan* or *catagan.*

cat's eye See *gems.*

cat stitch See *stitches.*

cattlehide See *leathers.*

caubeen (caw-been) Irish slang term for any hat, particularly when shabby and old.

caul (kol) 1. Mesh cap similar to a *snood, q.v.,* frequently the work of a goldsmith, or made of silk, and held to sides of head by a *crespine,*

q.v.; worn usually by unmarried girls from late 14th to 17th century. 2. Late 17th and 18th centuries, foundation on which wig was made. 3. 18th and 19th centuries, soft crown of bonnet or cap.

cauliflower wig Short-bobbed wig, all-over tightly curled; worn by coachmen in latter half of 18th century.

caution fee Fee paid by American designer or manufacturer to attend showing of a Paris couturier, which may be equal to cost of one or two items, to be applied to purchases.

Cavalier 1. A partisan of Charles I of England (1625–1649), who wore exaggerated plumed hat, wide flared cuffs, wide-cuffed boots, and swinging cloak, making these styles popular. 2. A wide-brimmed velvet hat trimmed with ostrich plumes. 3. Brimmed hat with one side turned up, worn by Theodore Roosevelt and his Rough Riders in Spanish American War. 4. See *collars.*

Cavalier sleeve Sleeve slashed and fastened along outer edge by ribbon bows, full at shoulder and close-fitting on forearm; used on women's daytime dresses in 1830's.

cavalry twill See *fabrics.*

Cavanagh, John See *designers appendix, England.*

cavu shirt See *shirts.*

cawdebink See *caudebec.*

caxon Man's wig, always white or pale yellow, hair drawn back and curls tied in back by black ribbon; worn as undress or informal wig by professional men in 18th century.

ceint (sant) Man's or woman's belt or girdle; worn in the 14th and 15th centuries. Also spelled *seint*.

Celanese (sel-ah-neeze) Trademark of the Celanese Fibers Co., applied to acetate and nylon yarns used in apparel and industrial fabrics.

cellophane Generic name, once a trademark, for thin transparent film made of acetate; used in ribbon-sized strips to cover paper fibers imitating straw or used alone as synthetic straw for hats and hand-bags, etc.

Celluloid collar Detachable shirt collar made of Celluloid (trademark for a

highly flammable plastic made of nitrocellulose and camphor); popular for men in the early 20th century.

cellulose Basic ingredient in all vegetable fibers and certain man-made fibers including *acetate* fibers, e.g., rayon is classified as *regenerated cellulose*.

cendal Silk fabric similar to *taffeta* or *sarcinet, q.v.,* widely used during Middle Ages; by 17th century used only for linings.

cendré (sahn-dray) Pale-gray color. *Der.* French, ashen.

cerise (se-reese) Intense pink-red color. *Der.* French, cherry.

cerulean (seh-roo-le-an) Sky blue, pale and slightly greenish.

Cerulean mink See *mink* under *furs*.

ceruse Term used from 16th to 19th centuries for cosmetic used by men and women to whiten the face, originally made of white lead and poisonous.

cervelliere (ser-ve-li-air) Close-fitting steel cap, usually worn under helmet during Middle Ages. *Der.* French *cervelle,* brains.

ceryphalos (ser-rif-a-los) Wide head band, or fillet, worn by women in ancient Greece.

cevennes silk (seh-ven) Top-grade French raw silk used to make laces.

chabaori Japanese jacket similar to the *haori, q.v.,* but shorter; made popular after World War II by Osuka Sueko, Japanese designer.

chaconne (shak-kon) 1. Ribbon cravat tied with ends dangling over chest, named for dancer Pecourt, who in 1692 danced a *chaconne* with his cravat tied in this manner. *Der.* From name of 17th century dance.

chadar, chaddar, chadder, chaddah, or **chudder** 1. Long, narrow scarf worn by Hindu men around shoulders or waist. 2. Indo-Iranian shawl or mantle about three yards long, somber-colored or flowered, worn like a veil by Mohammedan women. Also called *uttariya.* 3. Shapeless black outdoor wrap worn by Iranian women, enveloping wearer from head to toe with only a slit for the eyes. 4. British fabric, half-bleached cotton with colored borders, exported to India and Africa. Also called *chadder ulaya.*

chaffers (chaf-ers) 16th-century term for embroidered hanging side flaps, called *lappets,* of *English hood, q.q.v.*

chaharbagh See *kasabeh* under *fabrics*.

chaharkhana 1. Handwoven 54-inch-wide *cashmere, q.v.,* dress fabric in *leno weave, q.v.* made in Kashmir and worn by the wealthy. 2. Handmade 18-inch-wide checked fabric; half gray cotton, half dyed tussah silk; made in Bengal, India.

chain Series of connected loops or links made of gold, silver, brass, aluminum, tortoise shell, etc., used for *closings* and worn as ornamental accessory in form of *necklace, braclet,* or *belt,* by men and women. Chain links can be shaped round, called *balloon* links, elongated, called *bugle,* simulated *rope* or *flat* or *double.* See *closings.*

chain loafers See *shoes.*

chain mail See *mail.*

chainse Full-length, fine white linen woman's under-tunic, sometimes pleated, with long tight-fitting sleeves showing beneath full *hanging sleeves* of the dress or *bliaut, q.q.v.,* worn during Middle Ages.

chain stitch See *stitches.*

chalcedony See *gems.*

chalk stripes See *stripes.*

challis See *fabrics.*

chamarre (shah-mar) In the 14th and 15th centuries, an academic robe; a long, full coat made with sleeves full at the shoulders, usually fur-lined and decorated with braid and *passementerie, q.v.,* introduced about 1490 in England; later, a judge's gown. Also spelled *chammer;* see also *simar.*

chambord See *fabrics.*

chambord mantle Three-quarter-length hooded woman's cloak, resembling a shawl, with fullness in back, made of satin or velvet; worn in 1850's. Also called *chambard mantle.*

chambray Yarn-dyed cotton. See *fabrics.*

Chambre Syndicale de la Couture Parisienne An association of Parisian couturiers founded in 1868, outgrowth of old medieval guilds, that regulates its members in regard to dates of openings for collections, number of models presented, relations with press, questions of law and taxes. May comprise approximately 30 or more couture houses and is the most renowned of the several groups into which the syndicate is divided; educational program, started in 1929, teaches the needle-trade skills in a three-year course.

Chambre Syndicale de la Mode French official organization of milliners operating like the *Chambre Syndicale de la Couture Parisienne, q.v.*

Chambre Syndicale des Paruriers An association which comprises approximately 20 or more accessory houses in Paris, producing bags, belts, feathers, flowers, gloves, and umbrellas.

chameleons (ka-me-le-on) Ladies shoes and boots with cutouts to show colored stockings underneath, worn in late 1850's.

chamois (sha-mee, or French, shah-mawh) 1. Sueded sheepskin tanned by the chamois method. See *leathers* and *chamois tanning.* 2. Yellow color of chamois skin.

chamois cloth See *fabrics.*

chamois tanning Type of primitive tannage, used by American Indians, called *buckskin tanning, q.v.*

chanchanko Sleeveless, padded short coat worn by Japanese country children in winter.

chandelier earrings See *earrings.*

Chanel bag See *handbags.*

Chanel bow Black velvet ribbon about one-and-one-half inches wide tied in large bow and worn at the nape of neck; fashion reintroduced by French couturière Gabrielle Chanel in 1960's. See *catogan.*

Chanel, Gabrielle See *designers appendix, France.*

Chanel jacket See *jackets, necklines,* and *suits.*

Chanel shoe See *shoes.*

changeable earrings See *earrings.*

change purse See *handbags.*

ch'ang-fu Informal Chinese robe worn by all classes, from Emperor down, in Manchu dynasty, 1644–1912. Men: followed style of *chi-fu robe, q.v.,* usually made of monochrome patterned damask. Women: gown had wide loose sleeves finished with sleeve bands and made of fabric with woven or embroidered patterns. Contemporary Chinese dress for men and women derives from these robes.

channel setting See *gem settings* under *gems.*

chantahi See *kasabeh.*

chantilly lace See *laces.*

ch'ao-fu Long Chinese robe worn during Manchu dynasty, 1644–1912, by Emperor and Mandarins and their wives for formal state occasions.

Man's robe had kimono sleeves which flared into "horse's hoof cuffs," close-fitting neckband and second attached collar with wing points extending to shoulders, full pleated or gathered skirt attached to a set-in waistband. Prescribed colors and motifs that indicated rank included dragons, clouds, mountains and waves. The Emperor's robe was bright yellow with 12 imperial signs embroidered on it, while other officials wore a stone-blue color. Woman's robe was made in long straight lines with no waist-line; over the main robe, a jumper-like knee-length garment with wide epaulets over the shoulders.

chaparajos See *chaps.*

chap-de-sol Bright-colored parasol carried by the Portuguese woman as protection from the sun.

chapeau bras (sha-po bra) 1. Man's flat three-cornered hat, evenly *cocked, q.v.,* or crescent shape, made expressly to be carried under arm; worn from 1770's on in France, England, and America. Also called *broken hat* and *opera hat.* 2. Woman's crush bonnet or *calash, q.v.,* which folded to be carried under arm; worn to concerts and opera in early 19th-century England and America. *Der.* French, arm-hat.

chapeau claque (sha-po klack) See *Gibus hat.* Also called *crush hat* or *opera hat* or *claque. Der.* French *claque,* slap.

chapeau cloche Small crowned hat with wide drooping brim worn by women in 1860's to protect face from the sun.

CHAPEAU CLOCHE

chapel cap See *caps.*

chapel de fer (sha-pel de fehr) Armor for head, a skullcap of iron or steel, sometimes with brim; worn by medieval knights. *Der.* French, cap of iron.

chapel-length train See *lengths.*

chapel veil See *veils.*

CHAPERON AND LIRIPIPE

chaperon 1. Anglo-French term for a fitted hood cut in one with a shoulder cape; worn from Crusades to end of the 15th century. 2. Draped version of the chaperon achieved by rolling the cape and tying it with the extended tail of the hood, called the *liripipe, q.v.;* popular in the 14th and 15th centuries. 3. Woman's soft hood in the 17th century. Also spelled *chaperone* and *chaperonne.* Also called *cappuccio.*

chapiney See *chopine.*

chapkan A type of *angharka, q.v.,* worn by servants and palace guards in India; called by this name when made of heavy, colored material and belted with *cummerbund, q.v.*

chaplet 1. Originally a garland of flowers for the head worn by men and women on festive occasions by Anglo-Saxons. 2. In 15th century, such a garland, worn only by a bride. 3. Circlet or metal band set with gems, worn by women in 14th and 15th centuries; also called a *coronal of goldsmithry.* 4. Late 14th and 15th centuries, a headband of twisted silk or satin wound around a padded roll. 5. 17th century term used for a short rosary or set of beads worn on the neck.

chaps Cowboys' leather leggings, worn over ordinary trousers to protect legs when riding. See *pants. Der.* Spanish *chaparejos,* undressed sheepskin.

chaqueta (cha-kee-ta) Spanish word for jacket, often of leather, worn by cowboys in the southwestern U.S.

chargat (shar-gaht) Triangular indoor kerchief of sheer muslin, worn fastened with pin under chin by Persian women.

Charlotte Woman's hat with full, gathered crown attached to brim covered with wide ruffle, named for Princess Charlotte, daughter of England's George IV and Caroline, his queen, in early 19th century; popular until early 20th century.

Charlotte Corday bonnet or **cap** Woman's headdress consisting of high, puffed muslin crown gathered to a ribbon band above a frilled narrow lace ruffle framing the face, with ribbons hanging in back; worn as an indoor cap in 1870's and 1880's. *Der.* Named after Charlotte Corday, who stabbed Jean Paul Marat, French Revolutionist, in his bath and was guillotined.

Charlotte Corday fichu Long woman's scarf of *grenadine, q.v.,* trimmed with a ribbon threaded through a wide hem; placed around the neck, crossed in front, and tied in the back; worn in mid 1850's. See above.

charm bracelet See *bracelets.*

Charmeen See *fabrics.*

charmeuse See *fabrics.*

charro costume See *traje charro.*

charro pants See *pants.*

chartreuse (char-troez) Tint of yellow-green or greenish-yellow similar to the liqueur of same name made by Carthusian monks.

Charvet See *fabrics.*

Chase, Edna Woolman Editor of *Vogue* magazine from 1914 to 1952; considered one of the most able and competent fashion authorities. One of her outstanding achievements was the introduction in 1914 of a society-sponsored fashion show with live models called Fashion Fete, beginning of her long promotion of American designers. In February, 1938, *Vogue's* first Americana issue was published and was repeated for a number of years.

chasembles Variant of *chaussembles, q.v.*

chasing Jewelry term for fine lines engraved on metals.

chasseur jacket Fitted, hip-length, military-inspired women's jacket, made with standing military collar,

slashings at hem, and elaborately trimmed with braid and *Brandenburgs, q.v.;* worn in early 1880's.

chastity belt Belt-like device worn by women in the Middle Ages to insure marital fidelity.

chasuble (chaz-u-behl) Sleeveless clerical garment with round neckline, open sides, sometimes with Y-shaped band from neck to hem called the *orphrey, q.v.;* worn as part of vestments at the celebration of Mass in the early Christian church, now worn by priests over the cassock. *Der.* Latin *casula,* cloak.

chatelaine (shat-eh-len) Ornamental chain of oxidized silver, silver-plated metal, or cut steel, suspended at woman's waistline or hooked to belt, holding small items such as scissors, thimble case, tape measure, penknife, or button hook; worn in last half of 19th century. *Der.* French, lady of the castle.

chatelaine bag Small handbag trimmed with lace or beads, hung from waist

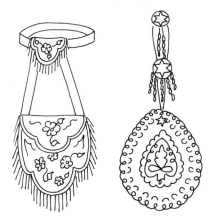

by ornamental chain and hook; popular in 19th century.

chatelaine pin See *pins.*

chatoyancy (sheh-toy-ent-see) Jewel quality in certain gems that causes a single streak of light to move as the stone is turned, e.g. tiger's-eye and cat's-eye gems. *Der.* French verb *chatoyer,* to change luster, as a cat's eye.

chausons (show-son) French equivalent of English *braies, q.v.,* or breeches; worn from the 5th century through the 13th century.

chausse Synonym for *epitoga, q.v.* Also called *chausse hood.*

chaussembles (show-som-bl) Man's hose with attached soles of leather or whalebone; worn by nobility in Middle Ages. Also spelled *chausembles, cashambles.*

chausses (shos) 1. Stockings of *mail, q.v.,* worn by knights and soldiers in last quarter of 13th century. 2. Stockings and trunks cut in one piece, similar to contemporary tights; first worn in Norman period 1066–1154; later in Middle Ages, fastened to *doublet* by means of *points, q.q.v.*

chausses en bourses (shos awn boorce) Breeches boned and padded so they were fuller at bottom—making a flattened balloon shape; worn in 17th century. *Der.* French, bag breeches.

chausses en tonnelets (shosawn ton-leh) See *Venetians.*

chaussures à crics (shaw-sir ah kree) Shoes with high heels worn in the 17th century. *Der.* French, shoes on lifts. Also called *chaussures à Pont-Levis.*

Chavacete (shah-va-set) Trademark for French silk-like solution-dyed filament yarn made of textured acetate.

cheat 1. Men's waistcoat or vest, of 17th century, with expensive fabric on front and poorer quality in back. 2. 19th century term for shirt front with collar attached, worn as a *dickey, q.v.*

check Fabric design of colored squares alternating with white, similar to a checkerboard; or a plaid design produced by stripes of color crossing at right angles, printed or yarn-dyed. *Check* often applies to a plaid of one color with white.

CHECKS:

blanket c. Very large squares of color used originally in blankets, sometimes made with an *overcheck*.

checkerboard Even squares of two colors, alternating in rows.

district c. Yarn-dyed checks of Scottish origin, used to distinguish the various counties and districts of origin. See *tartans*.

gingham c. Yarn-dyed checks of one inch, one-half inch, one-eighth inch, or one-sixteenth inch, made in a color alternating with white. Also called *apron check*.

glen, Glen Urquhart c. See *plaids*.

gun club c. A three color, double check design consisting of a large check over a smaller one; used in wool and worsted fabrics.

harlequin c. Medium sized diamond-shaped colored motifs alternating with white.

hound's-tooth c. Irregular colored one-half-inch to two-inch check like a square with points at the corners, alternating with white, produced by a yarn-dyed twill weave. In France, called *coq;* because it looks like a chicken foot. *Der.* From resemblance to pointed dog's tooth.

overcheck See *overplaid*.

pincheck Very tiny squares, also called *micro checks.*

shepherd's c. Uniform checks about ¼ inch wide of white and one color, usually black, in twill- or basket-weave wool, worsted, cotton, etc. *Der.* From four-yard lengths of plaid worn by Scottish shepherds. Also called *shepherd's plaid.*

tablecloth c. Large plain-weave check, usually in stripes of red or blue alternating with white, crossing at right angles, producing a third shade where color crosses white; color-white square may have woven design—fleur-de-lis, etc.

tattersall c. Colored lines (sometimes one color in each direction or alternating colors) on light background. See *tattersall plaid.*

windowpane c. Dark horizontal and vertical bars crossing over light background, giving effect of a window divided into small panes. Also called *windowpane plaid.*

checked-apron men English barbers of 16th century distinguished by the checked pattern of their aprons.

checkerboard See *checks.*

cheeks-and-ears See *coif.*

cheek wrappers Side flaps of woman's *dormeuse, q.v.,* or *French night cap;* worn in second half of 18th century.

cheesecloth See *fabrics.*

cheetah Spotted cat. See *furs.*

Chelsea collar See *collars.*

chemise (sheh-meez) Linen garment worn by men and women in Middle Ages, next to the skin, with long sleeves, straight hanging, and as long as garment worn over it. By 14th century man's chemise called *shirt* or *sherte, q.q.v.:* woman's chemise called *smock, q.v.,* later called *shift* in the 17th century and *chemise combinations q.v.,* in late 18th century. Also called *camise, camisia, cames, kemse, robe linge.* See *camisole* and *dresses.*

chemise gown See *perdita chemise.*

chemisette (shem-ee-zet) 1. *Scarf* or *fichu q.q.v.,* of cambric, tulle, or muslin fabric worn as fill-in for low-necked gown in 18-19th century. Also called a *chemise tucker.* 2. Sleeveless blouse worn under a suit, in early 20th century. Also see *partlet* and *tucker.*

chemisette à jabot (ah zha-bo) Embroidered or pleated ruffle worn as a fill-in at front opening of the *redingote, q.v.,* showing from neck to waist; worn in 1850's and 1860's.

chemisette garter Vertical supporter for hose attached to the corset in 1830's and '40's.

chenille See *yarns.*

chenille embroidery See *embroideries.*

chenille lace See *lace.*

cheongsam (chong-sam) Traditional everyday dress worn by Chinese, Korean, and Hong Kong women, consisting of straight *chemise, q.v.,* side slit, with standing band collar and front closing slanted to side with buttons or *frogs, q.v.* Adapted by Westerners for *housecoats* and summer dresses. See *dresses.*

Cheruit, Madame See *designers appendix, France.*

cherusse or **cherusque** (sher-oose, sher-oosk) Starched lace *collarette* forming a standing border for low-cut necklines on women's gowns; worn during the Revolutionary period in France and later at Napoleon's court in Empire period. Also called *collarette à la lyonnaise.*

Chesterfield, 4th Earl of Philip Dormer Stanhope, (1694–1773), British author and statesman after whom the chesterfield overcoat and other garments were named.

chesterfield coat See *coats.*

chest measurement 1. Men: distance around body at fullest part of upper torso, one of the measurements by which suits are sold. 2. Women: measurement across front of body from armhole seam to armhole seam at point above bust; differs from the *bust measurement* taken at fullest part of bosom.

Cheviot See *fabrics.*

Cheviot shirtings See *fabrics.*

chevron 1. Motif consisting of two straight lines meeting to form an inverted V. 2. Badge of these V stripes worn on sleeve by policemen, firemen, the military to indicate rank. 3. (pl.) Trimming for women's clothes introduced in 1820's, usually a zig-zag band near bottom of skirt.

chic (sheek) Almost indefinable noun meaning *style* or adjective meaning *smart* or sophisticated: a flair for assembling a costume with the proper accessories. *Der.* French, stylish; or German, *Geschick,* skill.

chicken-skin gloves Thin, strong leather gloves treated with almonds and spermaceti; worn at night as cosmetic aid to keep hands soft and white, by women from the end of 17th century to early 19th century.

chiffon See *fabrics.*

chiffon taffeta See *fabrics.*

chiffon velvet See *fabrics.*

chi-fu Ankle-length robe worn by chinese Mandarin men and women for regular court wear; made with loose sleeves, high collar, and diagonal closing extending under right arm and elaborately embroidered with motifs of dragons, clouds, mountains, and waves to symbolize rank. Man's robe was slit up front and back for walking. Emperor's robe was bright yellow; nobles wore blue. Also called *dragon robes. Der.* From Chi Fu, seaport of North China.

chignon (shee-n yon) Heavy coil or knot of hair, natural or false, worn at nape of neck or high on head; a contemporary style also popular in 16th century and 1850's and 1860's, often revived. See *hairpieces* and *hairstyles.*

chignon cap Small cap made in a variety of colors and fabrics for wear over the chignon, *q.v.*, in 1930's and '40's and popular again in 1960's and '70's—then called a *bun-warmer* or *bun snood, q.v.*, usually of crocheted wool.

chignon strap Band of ribbon fastened to woman's hat that passes around back of head and under the chignon to hold hat firmly; worn in the 1860's and '70's and again in 1940's and '50's.

child's pudding Small, round padded cap worn by infants and small children to serve as shock absorber in a fall. Also see *bumper.*

chima Pleated skirt, worn by Korean women, with waistline just under bust and moderately full; worn over petticoat and trousers, with a full-sleeved brief jacket, *chogorit, q.v.*

chimere (cheh-mir) Full-length sleeveless robe, similar to an *academic robe, q.v.*, worn by Anglican bishops, with full lawn sleeves attached to armholes. Also spelled *chimer.*

chimney-pot hat 1. Man's high-crowned hat with extremely narrow brim worn from 1830's on, replacing *beaver hat, q.v.*, made by felting rabbit hair on top of silk and applying steam and pressure until it was smooth and shiny. 2. Sarcastic name for a conservative citizen as opposed to revolutionaries who wore round *liberty cap, q.v.* in late 18th century.

China blue Lavender-blue similar to that in Chelsea dinnerware.

China grass Bast fiber consisting of stiff ribbons of ramie from three to six feet in length, very strong and durable but difficult to extract; used in Asian countries for *grass cloth, q.v.* under *fabrics.*

China ribbon Narrow ribbon, about ⅛-inch wide, woven with a plain edge; popular in mid 19th century for *China ribbon embroidery*

China silk See *fabrics.*

chinchilla See *furs.*

chinchilla cloth See *fabrics.*

chin cloak Term used from about 1535 to 1660's as synonym for *muffler*, or *scarf, q.q.v.* Also called *chin clout, chin cloth,* and *chinner.*

chiné Textile term for warp-printed fabrics. *Der.* French, mottled.

Chinese styles Characterized by bound feet, *calotte, ch'ao fu* ch'ang-fu, chi-fu, coolie hat, finger-nail shields, ma-coual, Mandarin headdress or Mandarin hat, Mandarin court robe, p'u-fang, and p'u-fu, q.q.v. Also see modern adaptations under collars, dresses, necklines, pajamas.

Chinese design Design composed of motifs such as dragons, lanterns, clouds, mountains etc., in the style typical of Chinese paintings and embroideries.

Chinese dog See furs.

Chinese dress Simple, straight-lined dress with standing-band collar and closed diagonally to side, slashes up side seams from the hem. See dresses and cheongsam.

Chinese embroidery See embroideries.

Chinese jacket See jackets.

Chinese knot Ornamental knot of covered cord used as trimming on apparel, copied from traditional ornaments on Chinese robes.

Chinese lamb See caracul under furs.

Chinese Mandarin court robes See ch'ang-fu, ch'ao-fu, and chi-fu.

Chinese slippers See kampskatcha slipper.

Chinese stockings Short stocking of heavy woven cotton with a separate compartment for big toe; worn in China with sandals. See tabi.

Chinese trousers Trousers of blue cotton fabric cut rather full at bottom, sometimes quilted for warmth, worn by men, women, and children in China.

chino See fabrics.

chinos See pants.

chin stays Term used in 1830's for ruffles of tulle or lace added to bonnet strings forming a frill when tied under chin. Also see mentonnieres..

chintz Printed cotton. See fabrics.

chip straw See straw.

chique-tades Same as slashings, q.v.

chirinka Highly prized square of silk or muslin with metallic embroidery, sometimes edged with gold fringe or tassels; an accessory formerly carried by women in Russia.

chiripa South American garment, made by wrapping a blanket around legs and loins; worn by the Araucanian Indians of central Chile and formerly worn by Argentine gauchos, or cowboys.

chiton (kee-tehn) Linen, cotton, or woolen open-sided tunic worn by ancient Greeks; made of a large rectangle hung in folds from the shoulders; where back and front were pinned by fibulae, q.v. The Doric chiton was folded and belted

in a variety of ways, sometimes with two belts in a double *blouson* effect; the *Ionic* chiton was made of sheerer fabric and sewn at the sides, sleeves were formed by pinning with *fibulae.*

chitterlings (chit-er-lings) Popular term used in the 18th and 19th centuries for frills or ruffles on front of man's shirt.

chlaine (klain) Woolen cape worn in Greece during Homeric period by shepherds and warriors.

chlamys (klay-mis or klahm-is) Oblong mantle approximately five or six feet by three feet, fastened in front or on one shoulder with a pin; worn in ancient Greece by travelers, youths, soldiers, and hunters and in Greek mythology by the god Hermes.

choga Knee-length overcoat fastened with a few loops above the waist, made of cotton, brocade, or cashmere; worn by Moslem men of India.

chogori Rib-length jacket worn by Korean women.

choir-boy collar See *collars.*

choir robe Ankle-length closed robes, similar to *bachelors' academic gown, q.v.,* originally black or red; worn by singers in church choirs. Copied for women's tops and children's pajamas.

choker See *necklaces.*

choker collar See *collars.*

choker neckline See *necklines.*

Chola hat Hat similar to man's *derby, q.v.,* but with larger, higher crown and wider brim, faced with band of another color and with ribbon trim and tailored bow on

CHOIR ROBES

side; worn by Chola Indian women of Peru with long braids hanging beneath it. Also called *Chola derby.*

choli Short, midriff-baring blouse with short tight sleeves, frequently made of fine silk and sometimes trimmed with gold braid or embroidery; worn by women in India under the *sari, q.v.* See *blouses.*

choori-dars See *pants.*

chop Mark used in China and Japan to identify maker of an item; similar to a trademark in this country. Also called *chop mark.*

chopine (cho-pin or chop-in) Wooden or cork *clog, q.v.,* covered with leather, sometimes 18″ high, fitted with toe cap and used as a *patten, q.v.,* or *overshoe;* worn in 16th and 17th centuries. Also spelled *chopin* and *chopiney.*

chou or (pl.) **choux** (shoo) 1. Frilly

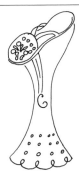

CHOPINE

pouf of fabric used at neckline. 2. Soft, crushed-crown hat similar to *mobcap, q.v.* 3. Large rosette used to trim gowns in late 19th and early 20th century. 4. Late 17th-century term for *chignon, q.v. Der.* French, cabbage.

chou rouge (shoo rooz) Deep reddish-purple color. *Der.* French, red cabbage.

christening dress Extremely long dress elaborately trimmed with tucks,

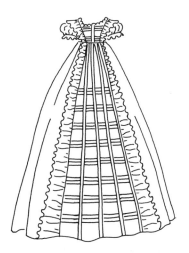

lace, beading, or hand embroidery, worn by infants for baptism. Also called a *christening robe.*

Chromspun Trademark owned by Eastman Chemical Products, Inc.

for solution-dyed acetate continuous filament yarn and staple fiber; also fabric made of this yarn.

chrysolite See *peridot* under *gems.*

chubby See *jackets.*

chudder See *chadar.*

chudidar paejamas Pants, full at top, similar to *jodhpurs, q.v.,* but tightly fitted at lower leg, worn by Mohammedan women in India with *camis* and *chadar, q.q.v.*

chukka boot See *boots.*

chukka hat See *hats.*

chukka shirt Same as *polo shirt.* See *knit shirts* under *shirts.*

chullo (chew-yo) A cap worn by Peruvian Inca Indians; the *chullo* is a helmet-shaped stocking cap with high peak and large rounded ear flaps and is worn under a black hat with wide upward flaring brim lined with color, having attached ribbons knotted under the chin.

chunky heels See *heels.*

chunky shoes See *shoes.*

ciclaton See *cyclas.*

cidaris Assyrian headdress shaped like a truncated cone, trimmed with a band or fold of fabric at the base.

ciel (see-el) Pale-blue color. *Der.* French, sky.

cinch belt See *belts.*

cinch closing See *closings.*

cinched waistline See *waistlines.*

cincture (sink-cher) A belt or girdle. See *belts.*

cinglation See *cyclas.*

cingulum (sin-gyeh-lehm) 1. Belt, or girdle, worn under the breasts, by women in ancient Rome. 2. Belt worn by men in Rome on tunic to adjust the length of garment. 3. Roman sword belt. 4. Belt worn with liturgical garments.

cinnamon stone See *garnet* under *gems.*

Circassian See *fabrics.*

Circassian round robe Evening dress of gossamer gauze, neckline low and square cut with fabric decoration of Indian lotus at center front; sleeves short, waistline high, skirt elaborately decorated down the front and above the hem with festoons of knotted ribbon; worn in early 1820s. *Der.* Caucasian tribe of Circassia.

Circassian wrapper Loose wrap cut somewhat like a *chemise, q.v.,* worn by women for daytime in Empire Period, 1813.

circassienne Late 18th-century version of the *polonaise, q.v.,* worn by women just before French Revolution.

circular Long cape or mantle of silk, satin, or other fine fabric in extra wide widths, frequently lined with rabbit or gray squirrel combined with bright fabric; fashionable in late 19th century.

circular-knit hose Stockings without seams; knitted in tube form, then shaped. See *hose.*

circular knitting See *knits.*

circular ruffle Ruffle cut from circle of fabric rather than straight across the grain, which makes graceful folds, less bulky than gathered ruffle; similar to *cascade ruffle, q.v.*

circular skirt See *skirts.*

circumfolding hat Man's dress hat

with low crown, made to fold flat to be carried under arm; worn in the 1830's. See *chapeau bras.*

Ciré (cee-ray) Trademark for a very shiny fabric in several weights or for its patented finish; popularized in 1969 as the *wet look, q.v. Der.* French, waxed. See *fabrics.*

ciselé velvet See *fabrics.*

CityPants Term coined by the garment-trade newspaper *Women's Wear Daily* in 1968 for women's pants suitable for town wear. See *pants* and *shorts.*

civet Perfume ingredient with a strong, musk-like odor consisting of waxy substance secreted by the civet cat, known and used since Middle Ages.

civet cat See *furs.*

claft Head scarf of heavy fabric, frequently striped, fastened around head and allowed to fall in a single formal, outward flaring fold at either side of face; worn in ancient Egypt and seen on Egyptian sphinxes and statues of pharaohs. Sometimes spelled *klaft.*

clam diggers See *pants.*

claque (clack) Man's *opera hat, q.v.,* with crown that folds flat. Same as *Gibus* and *chapeau claque q.q.v.*

Clarence Man's laced ankle-high boot of 19th century made of soft leather with triangular gusset at the side, forerunner of *elastic-sided boot, q.v.*

Clarissa Harlowe bonnet Large leghorn-straw woman's bonnet lined with velvet, trimmed with a large ostrich feather; worn with brim forward shading the brow, in late 1890's. *Der.* From popular novel

Clarissa, or the History of a Young Lady, by Samuel Richardson, published in 1747–8.

Clarissa Harlowe corsage Evening-dress bodice with off-the-shoulder neckline with folds caught at the waist by band of ribbon, short sleeves trimmed with two or three lace ruffles; worn in late 1840's. *Der.* See above.

Clark, Ossie See *designers appendix, England.*

classic Any style that remains in fashion for a considerable length of time, serving as a standard or guide for its category, e.g., a *cardigan sweater, polo coat,* a *shirtwaist dress.*

claw-hammer coat Colloquial name for the swallow-tailed coat, named for shape of coattails, which are cut straight across resembling claws of a hammer.

clays Worsted serge. See *fabrics.*

clear-finishing Finishing process, including fulling and shearing, applied to worsteds to remove all fuzzy fibers, thus revealing and emphasizing weave and color.

cleats Projections attached to soles of sport shoes of plastic, wood, rubber, or metal; used particularly on football, golf, and baseball shoes to prevent slipping.

cleavage 1. Ability of gemstone to break along the crystalline structure lines; especially important in cutting valuable diamonds. 2. Separation between a woman's breasts seen when a low neckline is worn.

Cleopatra (klee-o-pa-tra) Queen of Egypt 51–49 and 48–30, B.C., mis-

tress of Julius Caesar and Mark Antony, and one of the notorious beauties in history whose jewelry, hairstyles, facial makeup, and clothes sum up the exotic Egyptian style of dress. Depictions of Cleopatra on stage and screen by Vivien Leigh, 1951, and Elizabeth Taylor, 1968, influenced fashion fads in 1950's and 1960's.

Cleopatra blue Brilliant Oriental blue color with a greenish cast.

clerical cape See *capes.*

clerical clothes See above, plus *alb, cassock, cotta, Geneva robe, soutane, surplice,* etc.

clerical collar See *collars.*

clip 1. One season's growth of wool taken from a sheep. 2. Jewelry with a spring-held fastening; often an ornament similar to a *brooch.* See *bracelets, earrings.*

clip closings See *closings.*

clip hat See *hats.*

clip-on tie See *ties.*

cloak Loose outer garment used from Anglo-Saxon times; name used for any type of outer garment that might also be classed as *cape, mantle,* or *coat, q.q.v.,* particularly during last half of 19th century.

Cloak and Suit Industry Name given manufacturers of coats and suits when first census of the clothing industry in the U.S. was made in 1860, a category making up half the total of manufacturing establishments. Originally called *Cloak and Mantilla Manufacturers,* later called *coat and suit industry.*

cloak bag breeches Full oval-shaped men's breeches, fastened above or below the knee with decorative *points, q.v.,* or bows; worn in early 17th century.

cloche (kloshe) See *hats.*

clock 1. Ornamental design, frequently embroidered, running vertically up a sock or stocking on inside or outside of ankle. *Der.* From a triangular

gore inserted into a stocking, cape, or collar to make it wider and embroidered over the joined seams, worn in 16th and 17th centuries.

Clodagh See *designers appendix, Ireland.*

clog See *shoes, sandals.*

cloisonné (kloi-zeh-nay) Jewelry term for small areas of colored enamel separated by thin metal bands and forming a pattern. *Der.* French, partitioned.

cloqué (klo-kay) French word meaning blistered, applied to a fabric such as *matelassé, q.v.,* under *fabrics.* Also called *cloky.*

close coat Term used in 18th and 19th centuries for a buttoned coat.

closed seam Shoe seam, similar to a simple fabric seam, stitched on the inside, edges pressed back, usually used for joining the shoe at center back.

close-plate buckles Shoe buckles made of an alloy—part tin, part copper—known as *tutania;* cast by street peddlers in molds in about fifteen minutes, in late 1660's to '80's.

close stitch See *stitches.*

closing 1. The fastening together of two parts of a garment. 2. The devices used to close a garment.

CLOSINGS:

buckled c. See *buckles.*

buttoned c. See *button.*

chain c. Laced closing using a metal chain instead of a lacer, used on vests and blouses; novelty of the late 1960's.

cinch c. Double-ring closing; strap pulls through both rings, then back through second ring to fasten; borrowed from fastenings on horse bridles and saddle straps, used mainly on belts and cuffs of sleeves.

clip c. Metal fastener with a spring-backed device on one side of garment and a ring, eyelet, or slotted

DOUBLE-BREASTED CLOSING

FLY-FRONT CLOSING

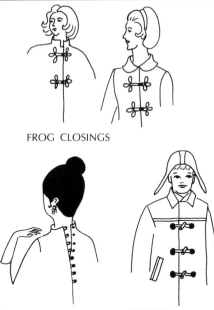

FROG CLOSINGS

LOOP-AND-
BUTTON CLOSING

TOGGLE
CLOSING

fastener on other side; used mainly on raincoats, jackets, car coats.

double-breasted c. Closing lapped deeply across front of garment, fastened with parallel rows of buttons on either side of center front; men's garments lap from left to right, women's from right to left.

fly-front c. Buttonholes, or zipper, inserted unseen under a placket; developed in latter half of the 19th century and used for overcoats, particularly the chesterfield, and on men's or women's trousers.

frog c. An ornamental coat fastening consisting of intricately knotted cord forming a loop through which a button passes. Typical Chinese closure on *Mandarin robes, q.v.;* popular in the West since last quarter of 18th century. Also called *Brandenburgs, q.v.*

galosh clip Hinged metal hook on one side clipped through a slotted metal fastener with graduated slots to adjust the degree of fit. Used for *galoshes, q.v.,* beginning in early 20th century and for raincoats, coats, and jackets from 1950's on.

grippers Heavy metal snaps attached to garment by pressure, without sewing; used primarily on children's and infants' clothes, *e.g.,* crotch of infants' pajamas, panties, and pants, for easier dressing, undressing; also used on adults' jackets and raincoats.

hook-and-eye c. Small metal hooks sewn onto garment and fastened through corresponding sewn-on metal bars or loops or through embroidered thread bars or loops; almost entirely replaced in contemporary clothing by the *zipper, q.v.,* except where great flexibility is desired or on adjustable closings, such as those on brassieres.

laced c. Leather thong or cord laced through small metal or embroidered *eyelets, q.v.,* popular method of fastening garments in Middle Ages and in late 1960's. See also *points.*

loop-and-button c. Closing with series of corded loops fastened over covered or rounded buttons, used for decorative effect.

single-breasted c. Conventional closing with single row of buttons on suits, jackets, skirts, blouses and coats.

snap Round metal fastener in which a sphere-topped post of one half snaps into a hole in a corresponding half, sewn only through facing on top side of garment opening, making neat invisible closing and used where there is little strain.

tabbed c. Added pieces of fabric that lap across opening and button; popular closing for *car coats* in middle 1960's.

tied c. A sash at waist or paired strips of fabric that can be tied together, used on bathrobes, wrap dresses, and skirts to hold the garment closed.

toggle c. Rod-shaped button, usually of wood, attached by rope loop on one side of garment, pulled through similar loop or *frog* on opposite side.

Velcro Trademark for closing consisting of a tape woven with minute nylon hooks that mesh with loops on opposite tape; used on children's clothing and adult sportswear. Used inside space capsules to help astronauts remain upright when there is no gravity; part of capsule is lined with one type of Velcro and opposite tape is on soles of men's bootees.

wrap c. Closing by wrapping one side of garment over the other and holding with a belt, sash, button, or snap.

clot Heavy shoe with thin iron plates on the sole; worn by workmen in the 15th century. Also called *clout-shoen.*

cloth Synonym for fabric, *q.v.*

cloth beam Cylinder at front of the loom on which finished cloth is wound. Also called *cloth roll.*

clothe 1. To put on garments. 2. To provide with clothing.

cloth embroidery See *embroidery.*

clothing industry Same as *garment industry* or *apparel industry.*

clothing wool Term used in grading wool for fineness and length of fiber, applied to wool fibers which may be made into woolen fabrics.

clout-shoen See *clot.*

club 1. Heavy stick carried by men since earliest times, fashionable in 1730's instead of a cane and also in the early 19th century. See *canes.* 2. Name for a *catogan wig, q.v.*

Cluny lace See *laces.*

cluster curls See *hairpieces.*

cluster pleats See *pleats.*

cluster ring See *ring.*

clutch coat Woman's coat with no fasteners in front, worn open or held clutched together; popular in 1950's and early 1960's.

clutch purse or **bag** See *handbags.*

coachman green See *Brewster green.*

coachman's coat See *coats.*

coal-scuttle bonnet Large, stiff scoop-brim bonnet with flat-topped crown, resembling a coal bucket; worn in mid 19th century.

coal-tar colors Dyes produced chemically from the thick black liquid distillate of bituminous coal, including analine, naphthalene, phenol, and other distillates. Term applied broadly to any synthetic organic dye.

coat Outdoor garment for both sexes designed to be worn over other clothing, made with sleeves and at least hip length, usually longer; the fitted coat was introduced at end of 18th century and called a *redingote* or a *pelisse, q.q.v.,* called *cloak* until late 19th century.

COATS AND RAINCOATS:

admiral c. Double-breasted *reefer, q.v.,* style coat, frequently with gold buttons, adapted from naval coats.

A-line c. Coat close and narrow at the shoulders, flaring gently from under arms to hem like letter A, made in single or double-breasted styles with or without a collar; introduced in 1955 by Paris designer Christian Dior.

all-weather c. Waterproofed or water-repellent coat, sometimes with zip-in lining to adapt to various temperatures.

balmacaan (bal-ma-kan) *Raglan-sleeved, q.v.,* loose-fitting style with small collar and buttoned up front to neck, frequently of tweed and

MAXI-COAT

INVERNESS COAT

BALMACAAN

CHESTERFIELD COAT, 1927

PEASANT COAT

CUTAWAY

REGENCY
COAT

PANTS
COAT

WRAP-AROUND
COAT

CHILD'S
TOGGLE COAT

CHILD'S
PRINCESS COAT

TENT COAT

water-repellent. Names for an estate near Inverness, Scotland.

beach c. See *beach robe,* under
robes.

bench c. See *bench-warmer jacket* in *sport jackets* under *jackets*.

bush c. Same as *bush jacket* or *safari jacket, q.q.v.*, in *sport jackets* under *jackets*.

cape c. 1. Coat with sleeves and an attached or separate cape. 2. Combination of cape and coat, the back falling like a cape, the front with sleeves and looking like a coat. See also *dolman*.

car c. Sport or utility coat, cut shorter than the average from hip- to three-quarter length; comfortable for driving a car and popular with the station-wagon set in suburbia in late 1950's and 1960's. See *bench-warmer* in *sport jackets* under *jackets* and *duffel coat* below.

cardigan c. Coat with no collar, fastened down center front. See *cardigan*.

chesterfield c. Semi-fitted, straight-cut classic man's or woman's coat in single or double-breasted style, with black velvet collar, sometimes a fly-front closing; introduced in 1840's as a man's coat by the 4th Earl of Chesterfield.

classic A coat style that has been popular for a long period of time with little change, e.g., a *chesterfield* coat, a *polo* coat, a *balmacaan, q.q.v.*

coachman's c. Double-breasted coat with large, wide lapels, fitted waistline, and flared skirt, frequently having a cape collar and brass buttons; copied from English coachmen's coats of mid 19th century.

convoy c. See *duffel coat*, below.

coolie c. Short, boxy coat reaching slightly below waist, with standing band collar and sleeves cut in one with front and back in *kimono, q.v.*, style, fastened with frogs; worn by Chinese workmen and frequently copied as beach or lingerie coat. *Der.* Chinese *kuli,* unskilled workman.

cutaway Man's formal black one-button jacket with peaked lapels, skirt cut away from waist in front to knees in back in slanting line, back vent topped by two buttons; worn with waistcoat and striped trousers in daytime. Called *morning coat. Der.* From 19th century riding coats made by cutting away fronts of frock coats instead of folding the skirts back for horseback riding. Called *Newmarket coat, q.v.*

dirndl c. Woman's coat cut with fitted torso, the skirt gathered at a low waistline; popular in the mid 1960's. *Der.* From gathered skirt and fitted bodice of the Tyrolean peasant called a *dirndl.*

dress c. See *swallow-tailed coat.*

dressmaker c. A woman's coat that is not sharply tailored, with soft lines and intricate details more like those of a dress; may have a set in belt and such details as tucks, pleats.

duffel c. Short woolen coat with a hood and fastened with *toggles, q.v.*, rather than buttons; worn by men in British navy during World War II, adapted as a sport coat for men and women in 1950's. See *car coat. Der.* Named for the fabric, a heavy napped woolen originally made in Duffel, Belgium. Also called *convoy coat.*

duo-length c. Full-length or midi-length coat with a strip at the hem that zips off to make a shorter length; often of fur.

duster Woman's loose, lightweight, dress-length coat, frequently of faille or bengaline; popular in 1940's. See *robes*.

Edwardian c. Man's top coat or overcoat, knee-length and double-breasted, with large deep-notched collar with a high roll, raised nipped-in waistline, deep vent in back; inspired by coats of *Edwardian* era in England, *q.v.*, popular in 1960's.

fold-up rain c. Lightweight coat for men or women, of thin plastic or water-repellent fabric, that can be folded into a small envelope when not in use; sometimes has a matching head scarf or hat; used for travel.

greatcoat Heavy voluminous overcoat worn by men and women, originally with fur lining, similar to *ulster, q.v.*

guardsman c. Double-breasted, half-belted coat with inverted box pleat in back, slashed pockets, and wide collar; adapted from coats of British guardsmen. Also called *officer's coat.*

happi c. See *robes*.

hunt c. See *pink coat.*

Inverness c. Knee-length coat with long removable cape or half-capes over the shoulders, like those worn by men in late 19th century. *Der.* From Scots county Inverness-shire.

jockey c. 1. Waist-length jacket with standing collar, made of nylon, worn by jockeys for horse racing and indicating the stable, usually by two vivid colors bisected. Also called *racing silks* when combined with cap. 2. Rubber coat of same design, worn by jockeys when exercising to lose weight.

jump c. Thigh-length coat for casual wear. See *car coat*.

longuette c. Coats varying from below-the-knee length to maxi-length introduced in January, 1970, simultaneously in Paris and New York. Term was coined by the trade newspaper *Women's Wear Daily* to describe the radically longer coats, skirts, and dresses that made an abrupt change from the mini-skirts of the late 1960's.

mackinaw As long as a car coat, but in Mackinac county, Michigan, place of origin, it is called a *jacket*. See *mackinaw jacket* in *sport jackets* under *jackets*.

macintosh 1. Rubberized raincoat worn by sportsmen and especially by policemen and firemen. *Der.* Named after Charles Macintosh, who invented the treated fabric in 1823. 2. British slang for any raincoat; sometimes abbreviated *mac*.

mandarin c. Straight-lined coat with *Chinese neckline, q.v.*

maxi-c. Angle-length coat usually semi-fitted with large collar and revers, double-breasted closing, and a full skirt; worn in late 1960's, often over a midi- or mini-length skirt or dress.

midi-c. Mid-calf-length coat, sometimes high-waisted, with slightly flared skirt; maybe cut in the *Zhivago* style, *q.v.*, with stand-up collar, side closing, and hem trimmed with fur. Introduced in the late 1960's.

military c. Any coat that borrows details from military coats and jackets, *e.g.,* braid trim, epaulets, gold buttons, high-standing collar, etc., usually a fitted double-breasted coat with slightly flared skirt.

mini-c. Very short coat just long enough to cover a *mini-dress, q.v.,* under *dresses.*

morning c. Same as *cutaway,* above.

officer's c. Same as *guardsman coat, q.v.*

overcoat Man's coat, heavier than a topcoat and designed for very cold weather, often fur-lined and made in *balmacaan, chesterfield, Edwardian, q.q.v.* or other style.

pants c. Hip-length woman's coat designed to wear over pants.

pea c. See *sport jackets* under *jackets.*

peasant c. Long coat lavishly trimmed down front with embroidery and sometimes with fur borders and cuffs; fashionable in late 1960's.

pink c. Crimson hunting jacket styled like a man's one-button suit coat with peaked lapels, back vent, and black velvet collar; worn by men and women for fox-hunting. Also called *hunt coat.*

polo c. Double- or single-breasted camel, vicuña, or camel-color-wool coat, collared but buttonless and sashed; introduced in 1920's for men's spectator sports, for women in 1930's and perennial since.

pommel slicker Raincoat worn when riding horseback; similar to other raincoats but with long vent in back. Also called a *saddle coat.*

princess c. Woman's fitted coat cut in long panels with no seam at the waistline, flaring toward hem, usually single-breasted.

raglan c. Long, loose coat, often of waterproof fabric, that has wide sleeves cut in one with the shoulders with seams slanting from neck to underarm. *Der.* From coat designed for the Earl of *Raglan, q.v.,* who lost an arm in Crimean War, 1854, and needed an easier sleeve.

raincoat Any coat designed to be worn in the rain, whether completely *waterproof,* as those made of thin rubber or vinyl or of fabrics coated with rubber or vinyl, or made of *water-repellent* fabrics, treated to shed water easily. See *all-weather coat, fold-up raincoat, slicker,* and *trench coat.*

ranch c. Car coat *q.v.,* above, or jacket made in Western style, sometimes lined with or made of *shearling, q.v.,* under *leathers.*

redingote Slightly fitted coat matched to a dress to make an *ensemble, q.v;* in 1820's, called *pelisse robe, q.v.*

reefer Double-breasted fitted coat with large revers and flared skirt, *Der.* From British brass-buttoned naval coat. See *pea jacket* in *sport jackets* under *jackets.*

Regency c. Coat for man or woman, double-breasted, with wide lapels and high-rolled *Regency collar, q.v.,* and sometimes with large cuffs; man's coat has nipped waist and deep vent in back; inspired by coats of the *Regency* period, *q.v.*

riding c. Tailored, fitted jacket

worn for horseback riding, similar in cut to the *pink coat, q.v.,* but in other colors or plaids.

sack c. See *jackets.*

safari c. Same as *safari jacket* or *bush coat.* See in *sport jackets* under *jackets. Der.* East African Swahili *safara,* to travel.

shortie c. Short woman's coat, about finger-tip length, made in boxy, fitted or semi-fitted styles; worn in 1940's and 1950's.

show c. Longer style riding jacket, or suit coat, with hacking pockets, fitted waist, narrow lapels, three-button closing and inverted pleats at sides; worn for semi-formal showing of horses.

slicker Bright-yellow *oilskin, q.v.,* coat or similar coat of rubberized fabric in other colors, usually with clips fastening front; originally worn by sailors, often worn with *sou'wester hat, q.v.,* by fishermen and children.

sport c. See *jackets.*

stadium c. *Car coat, q.v.,* or three-quarter-length coat, made with *shearling* collar and *toggle* closing, *q.q.v.,* worn by sports spectators.

storm c. Heavy coat for men or women with water-repellent finish, sometimes with *shearling, q.v,* or pile-fabric lining and collar.

stroller c. A semi-formal man's suit jacket, similar to a *tuxedo, q.v,* with no satin on lapels.

suburban c. Same as *car coat, q.v.*

swagger c. Pyramid-shaped woman's coat with flared bias back, usually with *raglan sleeves, q.v.,* and large saucer-shaped buttons attached by fabric cord; popular in 1930's, revived in 1970's.

swallow-tailed c. Man's formal black suit coat, open to waist in front, cut away to back of knees, the long vent to waist in back giving the appearance of a swallow's tail; worn at night with braid-trimmed black trousers. Also called *tails* and *dress coat.*

sweater c. Knitted or *cardigan*-style, *q.v.,* coat.

tail c. See *swallow-tailed coat.*

tent c. Women's pyramidal-shaped coat, widely flared at hem; popular in 1930's and '40's, again in mid 1960's.

toggle c. Three-quarter-length *car coat, q.v.,* sometimes with hood, closed with loops of cord through which wooden or metal *toggles* are pulled; see *closings.* See also *duffel coat.*

topcoat Man's lightweight coat in any style, designed to wear over suit jacket. *See overcoat.*

topper coat. Women's hip-length coat, often with a flared silhouette; popular in early 1940's.

tow c. Three-quarter-length coat similar to a *toggle coat* or *duffel coat,* designed for winter sports.

trench c. Long, water-repellent cloth coat made in double-breasted style with epaulets, loose shoulder yoke, slotted pockets, and buckled belt; originally designed for military use in trenches of World War I, became classic all-purpose coat for men and women after 1940, aided by movie-spy image of stars Clark Gable and Humphrey Bogart and the personal choice of actresses Katharine Hepburn and Marlene Dietrich.

wrap-around c. Woman's coat made without buttons or fasteners in front, held together with long self-fabric sash. Also called *wrap coat.*

Zhivago c. Midi-length coat, lavishly trimmed with fur at neck, cuffs and hem, sometimes with frog closing: inspired by costumes for *Dr. Zhivago,* 1965 film of Boris Pasternak's novel about the Russian Revolution of 1917.

zip-off c. Long coat styled to be two or three lengths, achieved through placing zippers at *mini* and *midi* lengths; see *duo-length.*

coat dress Double- or single-breasted dress opening down the front like a coat. See *dresses.*

coated fabrics See *fabrics.*

coatee Short close-fitting coat, with short skirt, flaps, or coattails, fashionable in mid 18th century.

coating See *fabrics.*

coating velvet See *fabrics.*

coat of mail See *hauberk.*

coats 18th-century tailor's term for men's coat buttons. Also called *breasts.*

coat set Child's coat made with matching hat or matching pants, sold together.

coat shirt Shirt that buttons down front like a coat, introduced in 1890's for men, now the conventional shirt.

coat sweater See *sweaters.*

coat-style pajamas Two-piece pajamas with top that opens down front like a *jacket.* See *pajamas.*

coattail Portion of coat below the back waistline; especially the long back portions of a *swallow-tailed coat* or a *cutaway, q.q.v.*

cobalt blue Intense medium-blue color made from a cobalt compounds.

cobalt violet Brilliant violet, or purple, color made from cobalt compounds.

cobbler Shoemaker, a term first used in Middle Ages. Also called *cordwainer.*

cobbler's apron See *aprons.*

coburg See *fabrics.*

cocarde (co-card) French for *cockade, q.v.*

cochineal (koch-en-neel) Brilliant red dyestuff obtained from bodies of female insect, *coccos cacti,* used to dye wools in 17th-18th centuries.

cock Term used from end of 17th to early 19th century for turning up of hat brim and given various names for manner of turn-up. See *Denmark cock, Dettingen cock,* etc.

cockade 1. Ornamental *rosette* or *bow* of ribbon, usually flat around a center button; sometimes worn as a part of a uniform or badge of office,

e.g., tricolore cockade, red, white, and blue, worn on side of hat as patriotic symbol during French Revolution. Also called *cocarde.* 2. Feather trimming. See *feathers.*

cocked hat Man's hat of 18th century with wide stiff brim turned up to crown, e.g., tricorn, bicorn, q.q.v.

cockers 1. High boots, crudely made, worn by laborers, sailors, country people and shepherds from 14th to 16th centuries. 2. In 17th century and 18th century, term used for leggings buttoned or buckled at the side with straps under the instep; word still used today in North of England. Also called cokers and cocurs. See also okers.

cock feather See feathers.

cockle 1. Defect in fabrics that results in bumpiness or puckering in the finished goods. Der. From French coquille, shell. 2. Term for woman's curl, or ringlet, in 17th century.

cockle hat Hat trimmed with a scallop shell, worn by pilgrims returning from Spain during the crusades in the 9th to 12th centuries; the body of St. James is said to have been miraculously translated to the beach and found, covered with scallop shells, at the town now called Santiago (St. James) de Compostela. Cockle is English name for French coquille.

cockscomb spike Tall cone-shaped hairstyle worn by primitive people in Africa.

cocktail apron See aprons.

cocktail dress See dresses.

cocktail ring See ring.

coconut straw See straws.

cocottes (ko-kot) Courtesans or immoral women, sometimes connected with the stage, who set fashions in France from 1860's to World War I. Der. French, child's folded-paper chicken. Also see demi-mondaines.

cocurs See cockers.

cod Term used for a bag, or purse, from Medieval times to 16th century. See codpiece.

codovec (kod-o-vec) 17th century term for a man's castor or beaver hat, q.q.v.

codpiece Triangular flap at front of crotch of men's trunk hose, q.v., large enough for a pocket, and frequently padded and decorated; worn during 15th and 16th centuries, by early 17th century term applied to front fastening of breeches, q.v. Also called a brayette or cod placket.

Codrington Man's loose-fitting overcoat, single or double-breasted, resembling a chesterfield, q.v., worn in 1840's. Der. Named after Sir Edward Codrington, British admiral who led fleet to victory at Navarino in 1827.

coffer headdress Woman's headdress, usually worn over hair coiled in braids over the ears, in 12th and 13th centuries. Also called nebula headdress.

coggers Gaiters, q.v., of cloth or leather, buttoned up the outside of of the leg; worn by men during the 18th and early 19th century. Also see cockers.

coif (kwaf) 1. Short for coiffure, hairstyle. 2. v. To style or dress the hair. 3. White headdress worn by present-day nun under the veil. 4. Close-fitting cap (such as those worn in Brittany, France) of crisp linen or lace in various shapes to designate the region. 5. In 12th to 15th centuries, linen head-covering

9

• **8** Detail of the princess from "Saint Georges Terrassant le Dragon," Upper Rhine School, 15th century. See *crown, braid, belt, hanging sleeve.*

9 (above) Medieval French, 1395–1422. See *hennin, veil, fur, cross.*

10 (left) "Wife of Tommaso Portinari," by Hans Memling, 1472. See *collar, necklace, gown.*

10

11

13 (below) "Adoration of the Magi," illumination from the *Belles Heures of Jean de France, Duke of Berry*. French, about 1410–1413. See *cloak, fur.*

13

• **11** (above) English costume of the late Middle Ages, 1440–1460. See *bliaut.*

12 (below) Costume worn in battle during the Middle Ages, about 1349. See *armor, coutes, gorget.*

12

like baby's bonnet tied under chin, worn by the aged and the learned professions and by soldiers under metal helmets; in 16th through 18th centuries, an undercap worn mainly by women, sometimes embroidered, with curling sides called *cheeks-and-ears* or *round eared cap, q.v.* Also spelled *quoife* or *quafe.*

coif de mailles Hood of mail, worn by Norman war lords from late 11th century to mid 12th; later worn under helmet and, in 15th century, by ordinary soldiers.

coiffe Women's stiffened headdress worn in French provinces. See *coif.*

coiffette (kwah-fet) Iron or steel skullcap worn by soldiers during 14th century. Also called *pot-de-fer.*

coiffure (kwah-fure) French term used since 18th century for hairdressing or arrangement of hair. Note: *coiffeur* (m.) and *coiffeuse* (f.) are the hairdressers. See *hairstyles.*

coiffure à l'Agnès Sorel (ah-nyes sorel) Woman's hairstyle with ribbon bands in front, and knot of hair at back, worn in 1830's and '40's. *Der.* From hairdo of *Agnès Sorel, q.v.,* mistress of Charles VIII of France.

coiffure à la indépendance French hairstyle with a sailing-ship model perched on top of wavy locks and curls; worn in 1778 to honor Benjamin Franklin's appearance at the French court for negotiation of a treaty between the U.S. and France. Also called *Triumph of Liberty.*

coiffure à la Maintenon, (ah la man-ta-naw) Woman's coiffure of mid-18th century, hair parted in the center, curled and piled high, named

COIFFURE
À LA INDÉPENDANCE

after the *Marquise de Maintenon, q.v.,* second wife of Louis XIV of France.

coiffure à la mouton (ah la moo-ton) Short hairstyle fringed over forehead and crimped on sides. *Der.* French, sheep.

coiffure à la Ninon (kwaf-oor ah-la nee-nonh) Hairstyle with ringlet curls over the forehead, shoulder length curls at sides, frequently wired, back hair pulled into a knot. *Der.* From Ninon de Lenclos, a Parisian fashion leader and beauty, 1616–1705.

coiffure à la Sévigné (say-veen-yay) Women's hair parted in center, puffed out over the ears, hanging in waves and curls to the shoulders, and decorated with a bow at ear level; popular in 1650 and named after a witty correspondent and writer of the time, Marie, Marquise de Sévigné (1626–1696).

coiffure à la Titus Coiffure worn in late 18th century after the French Revolution that resembled the way a condemned man wore his hair, brushed forward over forehead. *Der.* From hairstyle of Roman Emperor Titus, A.D. 79–81.

coiffure à la zazzera Man's long hairstyle with ends curled under, originally worn by Romans and revived by Venetians in 15th century.

coiffure à l'enfant (ah lon-fon) Women's hairstyle bobbed short like a child's; worn in 1780's.

coiffure à l'hérisson (ah lair-ee-sonh) 18th century hairstyle, for women, short hair with loose curls in back and frizzled ends at front and sides; and, for men, same frizzy cut in front but with *catogan* or *pigtail*, *q.q.v.*, in back. *Der.* French, hedgehog.

coiffure en bouffons (on buff-on) Woman's hairstyle with tufts of crimped or curled hair arranged over the temples, the forehead covered with fringe of hair called *garcette:* worn in Louis XIII period.

coiffure en bourse (on boorce) Man's wig with hair pulled back and stuffed in a black silk bag tied at nape of neck; introduced in 1730. Also called a *bagwig, q.v. Der.* French, bag.

coiffure en cadenettes (on ka-de-net) 1. Hairstyle worn by men and women of Louis XIII period with two long locks, called *moustaches,* falling on either side of face, and wound with ribbons and tied with bows. 2. 18th century name for masculine hairstyle with two long locks pulled back and tied with a ribbon.

coiffure en raquette (on ra-ket) Women's hairstyle with hair brushed up, puffed over the temples, and supported by a wire hoop; worn in last quarter of 16th century. *Der.* French, racket, e.g., tennis.

coin de feu (kwan de fuh) Short padded coat made of silk, velvet or cashmere with high neck and wide braided sleeves, usually worn indoors over a home dress. *Der.* French, corner-by-the-fire or fireside.

coin dot See *dots* under *prints.*

coin necklace Necklace of coins representing wealth of married women in Eastern Mediterranean and North African countries, ancient Palestine, other countries.

coin purse Same as *change purse, q.v.,* under *handbags.*

coin silver Strong silver alloy containing 90 percent silver and 10 percent copper: used for jewelry; the only silver available to early American Colonists, obtained by melting down silver coins.

cointise (kwan-teez) 1. Cut-out decoration used on the *cyclas, q.v.,* or overgarment worn from 11th to 13th centuries and also the garment itself. 2. *Lappet* or *scarf* under the crest of helmet; worn in late 12th century. Also called *quaintise* and *quintise.*

coir Long, coarse reddish-brown fiber which comes from outer husks of the coconut, *cacos nicifera,* which is elastic and resistant to water; grown in the South Sea islands and Ceylon and used for straw called *sennit* braid, *q.v.* under *straws.*

coker See *cockers,* above.

Colbert embroidery See *embroideries*.

Colbertine lace See *laces*.

coleta Mexican term for short braided hairpiece worn pinned to back of head by bullfighter.

collar 1. Piece of fabric finishing or decorating neckline of clothing, may match or contrast, be flat, rolled, standing, draped, etc. 2. Separate piece of fabric, fur, leather, or other material which fits around the neck and is not attached to the garment. Evolved from the 16th century *ruff* and *falling band, q.q.v.*

COLLARS:

ROMAN COLLAR

CHINESE COLLAR

CONVERTIBLE COLLAR

COWL COLLAR

SHIRT COLLAR

DOG'S-EAR COLLAR

BERMUDA COLLAR

BUTTON-DOWN COLLAR

CHOIR-BOY COLLAR

BIB COLLAR

angled shawl c. Man's dinner-jacket collar with outer edge made with a peak, or angle, near the bottom.

ascot Long narrow scarf, or stock, attached in back to neck of blouse or shirt, the two ends brought around to the front, looped over in a half-knot. *Der.* Named after race course at Ascot Heath, England.

band c. 1. Narrow collar opening in front or back, cut in a straight strip and stitched to neckline so that it stands up against the neck; see *Chinese* and *Nehru* collars, below. 2. In 16th and 17th centuries, term was used for a wide ornamental col-

115

SHAWL COLLAR

SPREAD COLLAR

TURTLENECK COLLAR

lar or *ruff, q.v.;* contrast with *falling bands.*

Barrymore c. Shirt collar with long points in front, frequently worn with string tie, popularized by the actor John Barrymore in 1930's.

Ben Casey c. See *medic collar.*

Bermuda c. Small round woman's shirt collar that ends in right-angle corners in front; lies flat on the shirt; popular since 1940.

bib c. Flat oval or square on front of dress or blouse, fitting over dress and around neck like a child's bib. Also called *plasteron.*

bishop c. Large collar, rounded in front, extending almost to armholes.

bolster c. Large stuffed roll used around neckline.

bumper c. Large fur collar that extends to edges of shoulders when worn flat, becomes a rolled collar when ends are hooked in center front, extending almost to ears; popular on fabric coats of the late 1920's and early 1930's.

Buster Brown c. Medium-sized stiffly starched round white collar worn by comic strip character Buster Brown in early 1900's and widely copied for boys.

button-down c. Shirt collar with pointed ends fastened to shirt by small buttons; popular collar of 1950's and '60's for men and women.

Byron c. Collar with large points and not much roll, similar to *Barrymore* collar; named after English poet Lord Byron. Also called *Lord Byron collar* and *poet's collar.*

cape c. Large circular-cut collar that extends over shoulders.

cascade Circular-cut ruffle attached to neckline of blouse with a binding, and may extend to waist in diagonal line.

Cavalier c. Broad, flat collar, falling over shoulder, adorned with lace, similar to collars that were worn by Cavaliers, partisans of Charles I, in early 17th century. See *Cavalier.*

Chelsea c. Medium-sized flat collar with pointed ends which forms a V neckline in front; popular in late 1960s.

Chinese c. Standing-band collar that extends up on neck, not quite meeting at center front. Also called *mandarin* collar, *Nehru* collar and *Madame Chiang collar.*

choir-boy c. Fold-over collar, rounded ends in front, similar to *Peter Pan*

116

collar, q.v., only larger, worn over choir robes.

choker c. Tight *band* collar that stands up high on neck, almost to chin, and fastens in the back, often made of sheer material or lace, boned, and edged with a narrow ruffle; fashionable from 1890–1910 and revived in mid 1960's.

clerical c. Stiff white standing band collar worn by Catholic or Protestant clergy with suit or with liturgical robes; may be fastened in back (see *Roman collar*) or have a narrow opening in front; white collar is sometimes half covered by a similar black collar, which may be attached to the *cassock* or to a *rabat, q.q.v.* Also see *Geneva bands.*

convertible c. Rolled *shirt collar* that can be worn open as sport collar or fastened by a small concealed button and a loop.

Cossack c. High standing collar that closes on the side, frequently banded with embroidery. Also called *Zhivago collar* and *Russian collar.*

cowl c. Large draped collar that extends nearly to shoulders in circular style, frequently cut on the bias; popular in 1930's.

cowl drape Cowl collar that drapes to form a hood that can be pulled over head, inspired by a monk's habit.

dog c. 1. Collar that fits tightly around base of neck or higher, sometimes used with halter neckline. See *choker* collar, above. 2. Necklace which fits tightly around the neck. See *necklaces.*

dog's-ear c. Flat collar of medium size with long rounded ends, shape of a spaniel's ear. Also called *spaniel's-ear collar.*

Eton c. Stiffened detachable boy's collar similar to a man's shirt collar but twice as wide, with wide-spread points in front, worn by underclassmen at Eton College in England until 1967. Also see *Eton suit.*

fichu Originally a sheer fabric or lace triangular kerchief worn in late 18th century with very low neckline, reintroduced in 1968 as separate collar worn around neck, crossed in front and tied in back of waist.

funnel c. See *necklines.*

fused c. Collar of man's shirt made in two layers of fabric with adhesive between, making collar easier to iron and wrinkle-free.

Gladstone c. Man's starched band collar that stands high on neck, opens in front, with two small corners turned down under the chin: worn by some upperclassmen at Eton College until 1967. Also called *wing collar,* or *stick-up collar. Der.* Named for William Gladstone, Prime Minister of England in late 19th century.

half c. Collar that extends around back of neck, stopping at shoulder on each side.

hard c. Man's starched band collar with corners bent over, detachable and worn with patterned shirts or with evening clothes in the late 19th and early 20th century.

horseshoe c. Flat collar extending approximately $3/4$ to $7/8$ the distance around the neck with ends not quite meeting in center front.

Italian c. Collar cut in one piece

with front of blouse or shirt, then faced and turned back.

jabot 1. Standing band collar with hanging ruffle attached to front of collar. 2. Separate ruffle fastened to front of blouse.

Johnny c. Very small pointed collar for woman's or girl's shirt.

lapel Extension of the front-opening edge of a garment at the point where it joins the collar, folded back to show the facing, which is called the *revers;* cut in a variety of shapes and named for the shape formed with the collar, e.g. *notched, fish-mouth, clover-leaf,* etc.

mandarin c. Variant of *Chinese* collar, *q.v.* Named after *Chinese Mandarin robes, q.v.*

medic c. Standing-band collar on physicians' white laboratory jacket, side closing, fastened with single button, popularized by *Ben Casey* television show in 1961. Also called the *Ben Casey collar.*

middy c. Same as *sailor collar, q.v.*

military c. Standing collar, high in front and hooked either front or back, e.g., type used on cadet's uniform at U.S. Military Academy at West Point, N.Y.

moat c. Standing *ring* collar placed away from neck, sometimes extended far out on shoulders. Also called the *wedding-ring* or *wedding-band collar.*

mock-turtle c. Separate band stitched down to simulate a *turtleneck collar, q.v.*

Napoleonic or **Napoleon c.** Rolled-over collar that extends high at back of neck and around the ears.

Nehru c. Standing collar similar to *Chinese* collar but sometimes made with rounded ends in front, copied from the costume of Jawaharlal Nehru, prime minister of India 1947–64.

petal c. Collar made of a row of irregularly shaped pieces that look like petals of a flower.

Peter Pan c. Round flat collar with rounded ends in front, worn by children and copied from costumes worn in play *Peter Pan* by James M. Barrie.

Pierrot c. Double ruffle or *ruff* collar derived from costume of the comedy character in French pantomine called Pierrot (little Peter), especially the clown in opera *Pagliacci,* who wore a clown suit with this collar.

pin c. Shirt collar fitting high on neck, made with eyelet on each side of opening through which a special collar pin is inserted.

Pilgrim c. See *Puritan collar* below.

plastron Same as *bib collar, q.v.*

platter c. Medium-sized rounded collar with large rounded ends in front, lying flat on shoulders.

Puritan c. Wide flat white collar, or *falling band,* extending as far as shoulder seam, with points or right-angled ends in front, worn in early Colonial times, popular at various times to the present. Also called *Pilgrim collar. Der.* Unadorned version of the *Cavalier collar, q.v.*

rajah c. Similar to *Nehru collar, q.v.*

Regency c. Similar to *Napoleonic* collar but smaller, rolls up on neck in back, then turns over, extending about three-quarters of way around neck. See *Regency coat.*

revers (re-veer) Another name for lapel, actually the facing of the lapel, which folds back to show the reverse side or *revers.*

ring c. Stand-away band that circles the neck at a distance halfway to shoulder seam. Same as *wedding-band collar.*

rolled c. Collar extending upward from neckline and turning over, the roll higher at back than in front.

Roman c. Standing-band collar that fastens in back, worn by the clergy of the Roman Catholic Church. See *clerical collar.*

Russian c. See *Cossack collar.*

sailor c. Large square collar hanging in back, front tapers to a V with dickey inserted, trimmed with rows of braid and worn on middy blouses of seamen in the U.S. Navy; popular style since 1860's, especially for children. Also called *middy collar.*

separate c. Man's detachable shirt collar fastened with *collar button* or *stud, q.v.,* in front and *stud* in back, worn, late 19th early 20th centuries.

shawl c. Collar, cut in one piece or seamed in back, that follows the front opening of garment without separate *lapels;* may be narrow or broad, extends all the way to waistline on wrapped front; used on women's dresses and coats and men's *tuxedos, q.v.,* under *suits.* See *angled shawl collar* above.

shirt c. Turn-down collar used on a man's or a woman's shirt; specifically, a small collar fitting not too high on the neck, with medium spread points. Examples: *button-down, convertible, pin, tab, spread,* and *wing.*

spaniel's-ear c. See *dog's-ear collar.*

spread c. Man's shirt collar made with a wide division between points in front.

stand-away c. Women's collar that does not hug the neck, usually the *roll* type; popular in early 1960's.

stand-up c. See *band collar,* above.

stick-up c. See *Gladstone collar.*

stock Collar formed by a long scarf-like piece of fabric attached to blouse at center back, ends are looped once in a half knot in front. Also called *Ascot collar.*

surplice c. Flat collar fastened to a neckline that crosses and wraps around on a coat-style dress.

swallow-tail c. Tailored collar with extremely long narrow points in front, resembling swallow's tail.

tab c. Shirt collar fitting high on neck with small flap on either point which buttons or snaps across to other side of neckband to hold points down.

turn-down or **turn-over c.** Any collar that folds over on the garment or on itself, as contrasted with *standing-band* or *stand-up* type. See *falling bands.* Also see *rolled collar,* above.

turtleneck c. High band collar, usually knitted, that fits very closely on the neck and rolls over, sometimes twice; introduced in the 1860's, popular in the 1920's and 30's, and revived in the 1960's for men, women, and children.

turtleneck convertible c. Turtleneck collar with zipper down center front so collar may be worn high on neck or unzipped to a V.

tuxedo c. Collar that rolls over and extends down entire length of front opening in woman's jacket or coat, with no fasteners; borrowed from *shawl* collar of man's dinner jacket, so nicknamed in the 1920's after the country club at Tuxedo Park, New York.

Victorian c. See *choker collar.*

wedding-band c. See *ring collar.*

wing c. 1. Same as *Gladstone collar, q.v.* 2. Tailored shirt collar with spread points.

wrap c. Collar which has one end pulled around to side of neck where it buttons, worn in 1969–1970.

Zhivago c. High standing collar closing on the side, frequently bound with braid. Same as *Cossack collar,* and *Russian collar. Der.* Named for 1965 movie of Pasternak novel *Dr. Zhivago.*

collar and cuff set Women's separate collar and cuffs usually made of linen, lace, organdie, other sheer fabrics, often white, trimmed with lace, insertion embroidery, or tucks; popular from early 14th century until 1930's and used occasionally since.

collar button See *stud.*

collaret 1. Woman's tiny separate collar, specifically one made of lace, fur, or beads worn like an item of jewelry. 2. In Colonial America, a ruff of ribbon ending in a bow. 3. Ruching worn inside high standing collar of the 16th century. 4. Armor worn in the Middle Ages to protect the neck. Also spelled *collarette.*

collar necklace See *necklaces.*

collar pin See *pins.*

collar stay Narrow strip of plastic or metal inserted in point of man's collar from the underside, to insure a crisp, unwrinkled look.

collection Apparel-trade term for a grouping of merchandise offered to retail store buyers, originally used only for high-priced couture clothing offered to individual customers, now used as synonym for *line,* the trade term for the samples shown to buyers at the beginning of season.

Colleen Bawn cloak Woman's cloak of 1860's, made of white *grenadine, q.v.,* with large cape pulled up in

center back and caught with a rosette; named after a melodrama by Dion Boucicault.

college board Retail-store term for group of students, each from a different college, selected each year to advise prospective students in August on proper clothes to buy for campus wear.

college cap See *mortarboard.*

collegians Ankle-high boots worn by men in 1830's and '40's with notch on each side at tops that made them easy to slip on and off. Also called *Oxonians.*

colley westonward 16th century slang meaning worn awry or crooked, usually applied to the *mandilion jacket, q.v.,* which was worn without putting arms through sleeves and turned sideways so that one sleeve hung in front, the other in back. *Der.* From a Cheshire, England, saying for anything that goes wrong.

colobium Type of under tunic worn in ancient Rome under *himation* and, during the Middle Ages, as a liturgical garment called *shirte* by Anglo-Saxons; usually decorated with two vertical purple stripes.

colombe Pale dove-gray color. *Der.* French, dove.

Colombier, Janet See designers *appendix, France.*

Colonial shoe or **pump** See *shoes.*

Colonial tongue stiffened shoe tongue that extends up from vamp of Colonial pump, frequently trimmed with ornamental buckle.

Coloray Trademark owned by Courtauld's N.A. for spun-dyed viscose rayon staple yarn, used for knitted and woven fabrics.

comb Tool, often of tortoise shell, ivory, plastic, wood, or metal, with a row of narrow teeth, drawn through the hair or beard to arrange or untangle it. Combs of precious metals or those decorated with jewels are often placed in women's hair to hold it in place and as decorations, especially at sides of head, in back, or when hair is set in a twist; earliest combs are of late Stone Age.

combat boot See *boots.*

combed yarn See *yarns.*

combination Underwear in which two garments, chemise and drawers, are combined to make one, introduced with the *Jaeger underclothes* for men in 1862 and for women in 1877; other combinations of the 1890's in-

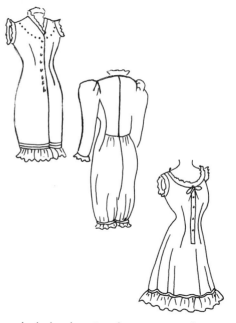

cluded chemise-drawers-pantaloons, pantaloon-petticoat and cami-knickers, introduced in 1920's. In 1920's, a *union suit, q.v.,* for women was called by this name.

combing Additional *carding, q.v.,* of fibers of wool and cotton that eliminates short fibers, as in fine cotton and worsteds. See also *combed yarn* under *yarns.*

combing jacket Woman's loose jacket, usually waist-length, worn in the bedroom when brushing hair or applying make-up, in late 19th century and early 20th century.

comb morion Type of helmet worn with armor by the Spanish conquistadors in 16th century. See *morion.*

comboys Full-length wrap-around skirt made of bright-colored printed fabric; worn by both men and women in Ceylon; named for the fabric, exported from England.

comedy mask Mask with corners of mouth turned up; worn in ancient Greek theater.

comforter Woolen scarf worn around the neck in cold weather, so named from 1840 on.

Comiso Trademark owned by Beaunit Fibers for a high-tenacity viscose rayon staple which has a silky hand.

commissionaire Middle-man who operates in foreign countries to buy merchandise for American retailers.

commode Late 17th and early 18th centuries term for a silk-covered wire frame used to support high *Fontanges headdress, q.v.*

commodore cap Flat-topped cap with a visor, fashionable for women for boating and sports, including bicycling, in 1890's. Similar to *yachting cap, q.v.,* under *caps.*

commodore dress Dress with nautical braid trim worn by girls and young ladies in early 1890's; typical dress might have a wide, braid-trimmed collar and gathered skirt with braid trim near the hem. Usually worn with a flat *sailor hat* or a *commodore hat, q.q.v.*

Communion dress See *dresses.*

compact Cosmetic container used to hold powder, rouge, or eye shadow and sometimes lipstick, made of metal or plastic with mirrored lid.

compass cloak Full circular cape worn by men in 16th and 17th centuries, a type of *French cloak, q.v.;* called a *half-compass cloak* when made in semi-circular shape.

competition stripes See *stripes* and *knit shirts* under *shirts.*

computer pattern Sewing pattern made to fit the individual; salesgirl in store takes customer's measurements, which are then sent to pattern company and fed into a computer to produce a custom-cut pattern for garment.

concierge See *hairstyles.*

cone Bobbin or yarn holder, of conical shape, used as a core on which yarn is wound in preparation for weaving. Also called *cone core.*

confetti yarn See *yarns.*

confidants Women's clusters of curls placed over the ears; worn in late 17th century.

congress gaiter Ankle-high shoe with leather or cloth top, an elastic gore inset on each side; popular in late

19th to early 20th century. Also called *congress boot.* Also see *Romeo slipper* and *Juliet slipper.*

Connolly, Sybil See *designers appendix, Ireland.*

considerations Lightweight *panniers, q.v.*, worn to extend sides of dresses in latter part of 18th century, eliminating need for petticoats.

constable Small cane with gold-plated top, carried by men in 1830's and 1840's. See *canes.*

construction boot See *boots.*

Continental hat Three-cornered hat with wide upturned brim, with one point placed in center front; worn by George Washington's Continental Army. Also called *tricorn.*

Continental heel See *heels.*

Continental pants See *pants.*

Continental stitch See *stitches.*

Continental suit See *suits.*

Continental system Yarn-making method. See *French system.*

continuous filament Man-made yarns made by pushing the spinning fluid through a nozzle, or spinerette, with tiny holes, producing strands of indefinite length.

contour belt See *belts.*

contour bra See *brassieres.*

contour clutch Wallet, similar to a *clutch purse, q.v.*, under *handbags*, but curved in on top edge, sometimes with attached leather carrying loop at one end. Also called *swinger* or *swinger clutch.*

control pantyhose Pantyhose with top section made of elastomeric yarn, *q.v.*, to give control similar to a girdle's. See *pantyhose.*

convent cloth See *fabrics.*

conversation bonnet Poke bonnet, *q.v.*, with rolled brim; one side extending beyond the cheek, the other side rolled back from face; worn in early 18th century.

convertible collar See *collars.*

convertible jumper Sleeveless dress worn with a sweater or blouse in daytime; for evening, worn without: in fashion in early 1950's.

convoy coat See *duffel* under *coats.*

cony, coney See *furs.*

coolie coat See *coats, q.v.*, under *furs.*

coolie hat See *hats.*

coonskin Same as *raccoon, q.v.*, under *furs.*

cop Yarn wound on a metal, wood, or paper spindle about six inches long, ready for insertion into the shuttle for weaving the filling of the fabric.

cope See *capes.*

Copenhagen blue A clear sky blue. Name sometimes shortened to *copen.*

copotain (cop-o-tan) Man's hat with high, conical, peaked crown and medium-sized brim, usually turned up at sides and back, made of beaver, felt or leather, sometimes with plume and jewel; very fashionable from mid 16th to mid 17th centuries. Also called *sugar-loaf hat, q.v.* Also spelled *copatain, copintan, coppintanke, copytank, coptank* or called *copped hat* or *cop.*

copped shoe Type of *piked shoe, q.v.*, worn by men in late 15th century.

copper toe See *toes of shoes.*

copyist Person who makes replicas of others' designs in the apparel trade, usually of high-priced dresses for a manufacturer of low-priced dresses.

coq feathers See *feathers*.

coral See *gems*.

corazza Man's shirt, buttoned down the back and tapered to fit the body, with close-fitting sleeves, usually made of cambric or cotton; worn in mid 19th century.

corbeau (kor-bo) Black with greenish reflections. *Der.* French, raven.

corded seam See *seams*.

cordé handbag See *handbags*.

cordeliere (cor-de-lyare) Long chain, often of gold, worn by women in the 16th century, which hung from the belt, or girdle, holding a cross, scissors, or other small items.

cording Trimming made by folding a soft rope-like cord into a strip of bias-cut fabric; used stitched into seam with rounded edge showing.

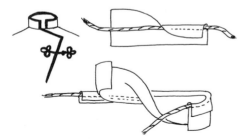

2. Full-rounded trimming used for frogs and loops, etc., made by pulling the cord through a seamed tube of bias fabric to cover cord.

cordonnet A heavier thread used in lace, usually for an outlining effect.

cordovan See *leathers*.

corduroy See *fabrics*.

cordwainer Term used in Middle Ages for shoemaker who learned his craft in Córdoba, Spain, and belonged to cordwainers' and cobblers' guild.

cord yarn See *yarns*.

core yarns See *yarns*.

Corfam Trademark owned by DuPont for leather-like, durable plastic material with some porosity, used for shoes and handbags, especially as a simulated patent leather, since introduction in early 1960's.

cork 1. Outer bark of oak, *quercus suber*, grown in Mediterranean countries; stripped, dried, boiled to remove sap and tannic acid, then used for fillers in shoes, for clogs, and for tropical hats and other items that require light weight, resilience, insulation against heat, and moisture resistance. 2. Man's *patten q.v.*, an overshoe of 15th century.

cork rump Bustle made in shape of a crescent and stuffed with cork; worn in late 18th century.

corkscrew curl See *curls*.

corkscrew yarn See *yarns*.

corned shoe Broad-toed shoe worn during first half of 16th century.

cornercap Cap with four, sometimes three corners, worn with academic and ecclesiastical costume during 16th and 17th centuries.

cornet 1. Ornamental band worn around head in 14th and 15th centuries, developing into a cap in 16th and 17th centuries; from 17th to 19th centuries, becoming a white day cap tied under chin or with side *lappets, q.v.* Also spelled *cornette.* 2. Square academic cap or *mortarboard*. 3. Woman's skirt of 1890's, cut straight and fitted in front, bias cut with small train in back; also called *French skirt*.

cornet sleeve Close-fitting sleeve ending in a flounce, trumpet-shaped.

cornflower blue Bright purple-blue of the cornflower or bachelor's button.

cornrowing See *hairstyles.*

coronation braid See *braids.*

coronation cloth See *fabrics.*

coronation robes 1. Garb worn for coronation by British king or queen in three layers: a red *cape* lined with white, an *ecclesiatical cope,* and a purple velvet *cloak* trimmed with ermine. 2. Robes worn by British nobility attending the coronation with trains of prescribed lengths according to rank, ermine trim; worn with various types of *coronets, q.v.,* according to rank. Also called *robes of state.*

coronet (kor-o-net) 1. Crown that denotes rank below that of sovereign. Nobility of Great Britain have seven different styles for prince of the blood, younger son, nephew, etc., duke, marquis, earl, viscount, and baron. 2. Band or wreath worn by women like a *tiara, q.v.,* on the head. 3. 14th-century term for open crown worn by nobility. 4. Originally a wreath of laurel or olive branches placed on head of deserving ancient Roman, particularly a warrior. Also spelled *coronal.*

corps (cor) 17th-century French term for *bodice, q.v.*

corps à baleine (cor ah bah-lenn) A *whalebone, q.v.,* bodice. See *corps piqué.*

corps piqué (cor pe-kay) 1. Quilted camisole with a *busk, q.v.,* of var-nished wood used as stiffening, first worn in 16th century in Spain, and later in France. 2. In 17th and 18th centuries, a tightly laced under-bodice, stiffened with whalebones, held on with shoulder straps. Same as French *corps á baleine,* whalebone bodice.

corsage (cor-sahge) 1. Small formal arrangement of flowers worn fastened to woman's shoulder or waist on special occasions or for formal events. 2. Term used in the 18th century and 19th century for a woman's *bodice, q.v.*

corsage à la Maintenon (cor-sahge ah la man-te-nah) Fitted bodice trimmed with bow knots down center front; named for Marquise de Maintenon, second wife of Louis XIV of France.

corsage en corset (cor-sahge on cor-seh) Tight-fitting evening bodice, cut in sections, with seams similar to those of a corset; worn in 1830's and '40's.

corse Tight-fitting under-bodice, of metal or leather with center front lacings, worn under tunic by men in 12th and 13th centuries. 2. *Baldrick, q.v.,* for carrying a bugle, used by men in 16th century. 3. Variant of word *corset, q.v.* in 14th and 15th centuries.

corselet 1. Woman's lightweight one-piece foundation. See *foundation garments.* 2. Tight-fitting waist-cincher belt, sometimes laced in front. See *belts.* 3. Originally a leather armor; later, in 16th century, metal-plate armor worn by pikemen, lighter than the *cuirass, q.v.* which was made of cast metal.

corset 1. In 11th century, a leather bodice stiffened with wood or metal; from 16th to 18th centuries,

1866 TO 1910

1927

a stiffened bodice called *whalebone, pettycoat badge* or *stays.* 2. Woman's gown laced up back and lined in fur, worn in 14th and 15th centuries. 3. Man's *surcoat, q.v.,* with or without sleeves worn in Middle Ages. 4. Woman's one-piece sleeveless, breast-to-hips garment, for shaping the figure, generally a heavily boned, rigid gar-

ment worn from 1820's to 1920's. Since 1940's, made of lighter-weight elasticized fabrics and called a *girdle* or *foundation garment, q.q.v.* Also see *Brummell bodice, corse, Cumberland corset, demicorset, stays,* and *swanbill corset.*

corset à la ninon Lightweight *corset* reaching to hips, laced up the back, designed to wear under *Empire, q.v.,* dresses; fashionable in second decade of 19th century.

corset batiste See *fabrics.*

corset cover See *camisole.*

corset frock Dress with bodice having three gores of white satin in front, lacing across the back, similar to *corset, q.v.;* worn in late 18th century.

Corsican necktie See *Napoleon necktie.*

corundum Common mineral, aluminum oxide; in certain rare, transparent colors it is a precious gem; blue, sapphire; red, ruby; purple, Oriental amethyst; yellow, Oriental topaz. Second only to diamond in hardness. See *gems.*

cosmonaut look Look of astronauts' clothes as interpreted by Parisian designers in 1965.

Cossack Pertaining to people inhabiting the Caucasus in southwestern Russia; men, particularly noted for their horsemanship, wore a distinctive costume including *Cossack hat, czerkeska* or *Cossack coat, q.q.v.,* full trousers, and boots. Contemporary fashions influenced by Cossack styles include *blouses, collars, hats, necklines, shirts,* and *pajamas, q.q.v.*

Cossacks Very full trousers pleated into a waistband and fastened at ankles with ribbon drawstrings; later, trousers narrowed with double straps under instep; worn by men from 1814 to about 1850, inspired by the Czar of Russia's entourage of *Cossacks,* see above, at the peace celebration of 1814.

costume 1. Dress, coat, or suit with coordinated accessories; an *ensemble, q.v.* 2. Fancy dress for masquerade parties, Halloween, costume balls and masked balls. 3. Dress which reflects a certain period in history. 4. Theatrical dress worn on stage. 5. Native dress worn for festivals and specific occasions. 6. In the 1860's term used for outdoor day dress or afternoon dress with a long train.

costume à la constitution Red, white, and blue striped—or flowered—dress of muslin or lawn worn with a vermillion-colored sash and helmet-shaped cap, symbolized the tricolore of the French Revolution and was worn by patriots.

costume jewelry Inexpensive jewelry not made of genuine gems or precious metals, worn both day and evening for its decorative effect to complete a costume. Introduction is credited to French couturiere Gabrielle Chanel, who showed imitation pearls, emeralds, rubies, for daytime in the 1920's, copies of her own real jewels.

côte de cheval French fabric characterized by a *warp*wise, *q.v.,* broken-rib effect; made in cotton, silk, or wool. *Der.* French *côte,* rib, and *cheval,* horse: probably so called because it was used for riding uniforms and habits.

cotehardi 1. Man's outergarment of 14th and 15th centuries, close-fitting with tight sleeves, shallow open neckline, bodice buttoned to waist and attached to full skirt of unpressed pleats. 2. Woman's close-fitting dress-like garment of same period, of rich fabric, laced up back or front, long tight sleeves and slits in sides of skirt, called *fritchets;* said to have been introduced by Anne, wife of Richard II of England. Also spelled *cote hardy* and *cote hardie.*

cothurnus Ancient Greek and Roman calf-high boot laced up the front, made of colored leather and decorated, with thick soles, sometimes of cork, if wearer wished to appear taller; worn by upper classes, huntsmen, and tragedians on stage in ancient Greece. Also called *buskin, q.v.* Also spelled *kothornus.*

cotillion (ko-til-yon) Originally the name for an underskirt, transferred to a country dance in mid 19th century, probably because the skirt was exposed during the vigorous activities of the dance. *Der.* French *cotillon,* petticoat and dance.

cotta Clerical *surplice, q.v.,* a full white short over-tunic, gathered onto a narrow rounded yoke, with long, full bell-shaped sleeves; worn by clergy over *cassock, q.v.* Similar to *cotte, q.v.*

cottage bonnet Straw bonnet fitting head closely with brim projecting beyond the cheeks; worn from 1808 to 1870's, early styles worn over a *foundling cap, q.v.,* and later styles

127

having upturned pleated brim with satin lining.

cottage cloak Woman's hooded cloak tied under chin, similar to those seen in pictures of the fairy-tale character Little Red Riding Hood; worn in 19th century.

cottage dress Morning dress with long sleeves; double cape collar cut in *Van Dyck points* over which was worn a *fichu collarette, q.q.v.;* and full-length skirt, decorated at hem with *rouleaux, q.v.,* and with border in a foliage design. Worn with long matching apron in early 1820's

cottage front Bodice with lacings in front for decorative effect; worn over a *habit shirt,* or *chemisette, q.q.v.* in early 19th century.

cotte Calf or ankle-length woman's tunic with sleeves cut in one with the garment; worn in 13th century. Also called *cote.*

cotton Soft white vegetable fiber from one-half to two inches long, which comes from the fluffy boll of the cotton plant, grown in Egypt, India, China and southern United States. American cottons include *acala, upland, peeler:* also *pima* and *Sea Island, q.q.v.*

cotton batting See *batting.*

cotton crepe See *fabrics.*

cotton flannel See *fabrics.*

cotton fleece 1. Fibers compressed into web-like sheet form called a *lap* used in making of cotton yarn; *carding, q.v.,* process changes this *lap* into a *sliver.* 2. Cotton fabric with a heavily napped surface.

cotton suitings See *fabrics.*

cotton velvet See *fabrics.*

cotton-yarn numbering system System used in United States and Great Britain for relative size of cotton yarns; lower numbers indicating heavier yarns and higher numbers indicate finer yarns. Also called *English yarn-numbering system.*

Coty American Fashion Critics Awards Annual awards—"Winnies," Hall of Fame, and Specials—given since 1942 for outstanding fashion design; judges are fashion editors of magazines and newspapers, broadcasters, and fashion retailers.

couching stitch See *stitches.*

counter Shoe-industry term for extra cup-shaped reinforcement placed at heel of shoe upper between outer upper and lining to add stiffness.

counter book See *pattern book.*

counter fillet Late 14th and early 15th centuries term for the *fillet,* or band, securing a woman's veil.

count of cloth Textile-industry term for number of *warp* and *filling* yarns, *q.q.v.,* in a square inch of fabric. Expressed by first writing number of *warps* then number of *fillings,* e.g., 72×64 would mean 72 warps and 64 fillings per square inch. Knit goods are counted in warpwise loops or *wales* and crosswise loops called *courses.*

count of yarn Textile-industry term expressed in numbers given for the size of yarns in relationship to their length and weight. Also called *yarn number.*

coupure Cashmere twill. See *fabrics.*

coureur (koor-er) Tight-fitting *caraco jacket, q.v.,* with short peplum or basques; worn by women during French Revolution.

Courrêges, André See *designers appendix, France;* and also *boots, glasses, helmets.*

course Textile-industry term for a crosswise or *filling*wise row of loops in knitting.

court dress Costume and items of apparel required to be worn for daily functions and cermonial occasion in the presence of ruling monarchs. Also see *court habit* and *coronation robes.*

courtepye *Surcoat, q.v.,* or very short overgarment made in a circle with round neckline, a high collar, slashed at the sides; frequently particolored or embroidered with gems; worn in 14th and 15th centuries.

court habit Term for men's clothing worn only at French court in 17th and 18th centuries; called *grand habit* for women.

court plasters Small black patches shaped like half-moons, stars, or hearts, etc., attached with adhesive to ladies' faces to emphasize charms or to hide smallpox scars; first appeared at end of 17th century and were carried in small jeweled, mirrored boxes at Court of Louis XIV. Also called *mouches, assassins, beauty spots* or *patches.*

court tie 1. British term for shoe designated for man's ceremonial *court dress, q.v.,* in England: a low cut *oxford, q.v.,* generally of patent leather. 2. Woman's laced *oxford* with two or three pairs of eyelets, made in *blucher style, q.v.,* worn in early 20th century.

coutenance Small muff carried in late 16th and early 17th centuries.

coutes (koot) Armor for the elbows worn over chain mail in early 13th century; also plate armor for elbows, in latter 14th century. *Der.* French, *coude,* elbow.

coutil Cotton twill. See *fabrics.*

couture 1. Most expensive Paris dress designers' establishments or houses, where clothes are made to order with several fittings, for private customers; the designs are shown in collections twice a year to foreign buyers. 2. Sometimes applied to highest-priced American designer collections, which are mass-produced, sold to department stores.

couture lace See *laces.*

couture group, New York See *New York Business Couture Group, Inc.*

couture society Fashion leaders, both American and international, including the designers themselves and women who can afford expensive couture clothes; called, by Rebecca Warfield in *Vogue* magazine in 1962, the Beautiful People, they can be seen at charity functions, balls, fashionable restaurants, etc.

couturier (koo-tu-ree-ay) Male French dress designer, e.g., Yves Saint Laurent, Hubert de Givenchy.

couturière (koo-tu-ree-ere) Female French designer, e.g., Gabrielle Chanel, Madame Grés.

coveralls One-piece work clothes. See *jumpsuits.*

coverchief Norman term for the Saxon head *rail,* or *veil,* a draped head covering made of different fabrics and colors, worn by women of all classes from medieval times to the 16th century. Also spelled *couverchief* and *couverchef.*

covered heel See *heels.*

covered yarn See *core yarn* under *yarns.*

covered zipper *Zipper, q.v.,* made with fabric tape covering teeth, so that it does not show when closed.

covert See *fabrics.*

cover-up See *sport set.*

cowboy styles See *belts, boots, hats,* and *shirts.*

cowhide See *cattlehide* under *leathers.*

Cowichan sweater See *sweaters.*

cowl Cape or mantle, with hood hanging over back and shoulders like a collar, worn by monastic orders. See *cowl collar,* under *collars.* Also see *necklines.*

cowl drape See *collars.*

coxcomb 1. Woman's upswept coiffure with hair brushed to the back and pinned to form a vertical row of ringlets down center back. 2. Cap trimmed with strip of notched red cloth formerly worn by licensed court jester. 3. A *fop;* a conceited foolish *dandy, q.q.v.*

C.P.O. jacket or **shirt** See *sport jackets,* under *jackets,* and *shirts.*

crab-back bathing suit Men's swimsuit with top cut out very wide at armholes and a second cutout near waistline; worn in 1920's.

Crahay, Jules François See *designers appendix, France.*

crakow (kra-ko) Long-toed shoe of soft material, either a separate shoe, or cut in one piece with the hose, introduced from Poland during reign of Richard II in England. During the 14th and 15th centuries, toes of shoes became so long they were stuffed and fastened by gold and silver chains to bracelets below the knees. *Der.* Named after Cracow, Poland. Also spelled *crackow, cracow,* and *crawcaw.* Later called *poulaine.*

crants Garland of flowers or *chaplet, q.v.,* made of gold and gems; worn by women from Medieval times to 18th century. Also called *craunce,* or *graundice.*

crapaud (cra-po) See *bagwig.*

crape A band worn for mourning. Also see *crepe* under *fabrics.*

crash See *fabrics.*

craunce See *crants.*

cravat (kra-vat) 1. See *ties.* 2. Neckwear of muslin or lace worn by courtiers of Louis XIV in 17th century, copies from Croat soldiers in King's service, replacing the *falling collar* and *ruffs, q.q.v.* See *scarf.*

cravate cocodes (kra-vat • ko-kod) Large bow-tied *cravat, q.v.,* worn by women about 1863 with a *habit shirt, q.v.,* which had a standing collar.

cravat strings Piece of colored ribbon worn on top of the *cravat, q.v.,* and tied in a bow under chin, later a ready-made bow placed behind the loosely tied cravat; worn by men in last half of 17th century.

Cravenette (krav-eh-net) Trademark for finishes used to make garments water repellent, used on raincoats and overcoats. *Der.* From Craven Street, in London, England.

crawcaw See *crakow.*

crawlers See *pants.*

Creed, Charles See *designers appendix, England.*

Creedmores See *shoes* and *oxfords.*

creepalong set Infant's or toddler's two-piece suit usually a knit shirt and overall-type pants. Also called *creepables* and *crawlers;* see *pants.*

creepers 1. One-piece infant's garment with long or short legs and with snaps or buttons at crotch; worn from 1920's to present. Sometimes called *creepalong* or *crawler.* 2. Small plates of metal set with spikes fastened over shoes by straps; worn when walking on ice and snow to prevent slipping.

creeping apron Infant's garment cut long and gathered at hem into a band through which a cord was

drawn. Could be pushed up above knees for a romper effect; worn in early 1900's.

Cremona cravat (kre-mo-nah kreh-vat) Plain ribbon cravat edged with gathers; introduced for men in 1702, after the battle of Cremona, Italy.

Creoles See *shoes.*

crepe See *fabrics.*

crepe-back satin See *fabrics.*

crêpe charmeuse (krepp shar-merz) See *fabrics.*

crêpe de chine (krepp deh sheen) See *fabrics.*

crêpe de laine (krepp deh lenn) See *fabrics.*

crêpe georgette (krepp jor-jet) See *fabrics.*

crêpe lisse (krepp lees) See *fabrics.*

crêpe marocaïn (krepp mar-o-kan) See *fabrics.*

crêpe meteor (krepp mee-teh-or) See *fabrics.*

Crepeset (krape-set) Trademark owned by American Enka Corp. for mono-filament textured yarn, used for tricot fabrics with a silk-like hand and crepe-textured surface; used for clothing, sleepwear, and lingerie. Trademark is licensed to manufacturer to put on finished product meeting producer's qualifications.

crepe-soled shoes See *shoes.*

crepe yarn See *yarns.*

creping (krape-ing) Achieving a crinkled effect in fabrics by using caustic soda and pressing with en-graved rollers as *plissé crepe, q.v.;* or by *S* and *Z twists, q.q.v.,* in the yarn; or by adjusting tension on alternate warp yarns to achieve a puckered effect, as *seersucker, q.v.*

crepon See *fabrics.*

crescent Motif copied from shape of moon in its first quarter. Also called a *lunette.*

Creslan 1. Trademark owned by Ameri-can Cyanamid for acrylic staple, filament, or tow. 2. A licensed mer-chandise term used on fabrics that come up to standards set by manu-facturer of the yarn.

Crete lace See *laces.*

cretonne See *fabrics.*

crève-coeur (krev kur) Term used at end of 17th century for curls at nape of woman's neck. *Der.* French, heartbreaker.

creves (krev-ay) See *slashing. Der.* French, slashes.

crew cut See *hairstyles.*

crewel work (kroo-el) See *embroideries.*

crewel yarn See *yarns.*

crew neckline See *sweaters* and *necklines.*

crew socks See *socks.*

criardes (kree-ards) Underskirt of gummed linen puffed out at the sides, forerunner of the *paniers, q.v. Der.* French, crying or scolding, because the petticoat creaked as the woman walked.

crimp 1. Natural or machine-made bending or waviness in a fiber making yarn resilient, less shiny, bulkier, and suitable for knitting. 2. To curl the hair with a hot iron. 3. To shape front of vamp and leg of a riding boot by a machine that uses heat and pressure.

crimp-set yarn See *yarns.*

crimson lake Bluish-red color.

crin Braid used in making hats and for stiffening skirts at the hem. Same as *horsehair braid, q.v.,* under *braids. Der.* French, horsehair.

criniere See *hairpieces.*

crinkle crepe Same as *plissé, q.v.,* under *fabrics.*

crinkle patent Man-made product of urethane or vinyl plastic resembling *patent leather, q.v.,* with a wrinkled finish, made backed with fabric in 54″ widths. Used for rainwear, active sportswear, handbags, etc. Urethane product is dry-cleanable and has very good resistance to abrasion and cold; vinyl products have slightly less glaze and are not dry-cleanable.

crinolette (krin-o-let) Smaller form of woman's *cage petticoat, q.v.,* with hoops only in back, made of steel half-hoops with *crinoline* or *horsehair, q.q.v.,* ruffles forming a *bustle* in the back, worn from late 1860's to early 1870's.

crinoline 1. Open-weave, heavily sized cotton fabric used for stiffening interfacings in inexpensive clothes and, in 19th century, for *petticoats* and *skirts, q.q.v.* 2. A petticoat made of crinoline or other stiffened fabric.

crinoline and tournure Stiffened petticoat with bustle added in back, for wear under dresses in late 1860's.

crinoline era Period from 1850–1870 when crinoline petticoats were at their height and Empress Eugénie of France was called Queen of the Crinoline.

crisp 1. 16th century term for a woman's *veil, q.v.* 2. 17th-century term for a *curl, q.v.,* of hair worn by a woman.

crispin 1. *Cape, q.v.,* with collar and armholes, worn by actresses waiting in the theater wings in early 19th century, later adopted for men, women, and children. 2. Man's evening *cloak, q.v.,* with full sleeves and padded, quilted lining; worn in late 1830's. 3. Woman's short *mantle, q.v.,* with close-fitting neck and small *pelerine* cape, q.v., sometimes with sleeves, made of bias satin, velvet, or cashmere, and often padded; worn in early 1840's.

crispine or **crispinette** See *caul.*

Criss-Cross girdle See *girdles.*

crochet (kro-shay) 1. Method of making a garment, fabric, braid, or lace with yarn and the use of one hooked needle, done by hand or by machinery. See *braids, laces.* 2. Term used from 14th to 17th century for a hook or fastener, e.g., a hook attached at woman's waist for suspending a pomander or a fastener on a shoe.

crochet hook Needle with one hooked end used for crocheting; usually made of metal, plastic, or in very large sizes of wood.

crochets and loops See *hooks and eyes.*

crocking Tendency of dye to rub off fabric or leather because of improper dye penetration, dyeing methods, or treatment after dyeing process.

crocodile See *leathers.*

Cromwell collar Wide turnover collar with front edges nearly meeting; worn by women in the 1880's *Der.* Named for Oliver Cromwell, Lord Protector of England, 1653–1658.

Cromwell shoes Women's shoe with large buckle-trimmed tongue, worn in late 1860's for croquet parties, reintroduced in 1888 with high-cut vamp and large bow trim for daytime wear.

crooked shoe Shoes cut specifically to fit left or right foot, first produced in volume about 1850, superseding shoes that were straight-cut and fit either foot.

crop-doublet Man's short-waisted doublet, popular about 1610.

cropping See *shearing.*

croquet boot (kro-kay) Woman's shoe of mid 1860's made of *Morocco leather, q.v.,* frequently trimmed with fancy toe-caps, laced with colored ribbons, and trimmed with tassels. *Der.* Named for the game of croquet, a fashionable pastime of this era.

cross 1. Motif of two bars intersecting at right angles, used in early Christian days and, in 12th century, by knights on their surcoats when undertaking pilgrimages to the holy land. 2. European term for *bias,* or *diagonal* cut, fabric cut "on the cross." 3. Item of jewelry, a simple or elaborately decorated cross motif worn as a pin or as a pendant on a necklace. See also *crusader's cross.* 4. (pl.) Fur term for small pieces of fur, such as paws and gills, sewn together to make a larger piece that is cross-shaped, done particularly to varieties of lamb.

cross-boarded Leather term for skins processed to make grain more pronounced by folding leather in one direction, pressing with a cork armboard and rolling, then folding in opposite direction and repeating.

crosscloth 1. Triangular kerchief worn by women with a *coif* or *caul, q.v.,* tied under chin or at back of head, frequently embroidered to match the coif; worn in 16th and 17th centuries. 2. A brow band worn in bed to prevent illness or as a beauty aid to remove wrinkles; worn by men and women from 16th to 18th centuries. Also called *forehead-cloth.* See also *frontlet.*

cross-dyed Term used to identify fabrics woven of two or more different fibers, such as acetate and rayon, immersed in one dyeing solution, which dyes fabric into a pattern by affecting the two fibers differently, frequently striped or checked.

cross fox See *fox* under *furs.*

cross gartering 1. Term used for binding or holding the *broc, q.v.,* of Anglo-Saxon, or *braie, q.v.,* of the French, close to leg by criss-crossing strips of leather around legs on top of pants. 2. From mid

16th to early 17th centuries— style of gartering hose by using a ribbon around leg below the knee, crossed in back, and tied with bow above front or side of knee, when stockings were worn over *canions, q.v.*

cross girdling Style of wearing the girdle, or sash, crossed at the chest and then wrapped around the waist, worn by ancient Greeks.

cross Persian lamb See *lamb* under *furs.*

cross stitch See *stitches, embroideries.*

crown 1. A garland or wreath worn on the head as an ornament or sign of honor, especially a circlet of precious metal and gems worn by kings and queens. 2. Bridal headpiece worn with veil. 3. Upper portion of a brilliant-cut faceted stone, e.g., a diamond. 4. Portion of hat covering top of head.

crown sable See *sable* under *furs.*

crowsfeet 1. Textile-industry term for wrinkles in finished fabric after it has been folded. 2. Wrinkles at corners of eyes.

cruches (kroosh) Late 17th century term for small curls worn on the forehead.

crusader hood Snug-fitting hood cut in one piece with a small shoulder cape, originally made of chain mail and copied for modern use in knits for winter sportswear.

crusader's cross See *necklaces.*

crushed leather Leather given a crinkled surface by hand boarding, machine boarding, or embossing to produce an imitation of a *boarded, q.v.,* finish. Also called *ecrasé* leather.

crushed vinyl Water-resistant or waterproof vinyl-coated fabric with crinkled effect, popular in 1960's for raincoats, handbags, and shoes. Also called *crinkle patent, q.v.*

crutch British for *crotch.*

crystal 1. See *gems.* 2. Beads or simulated gems of faceted glass, resembling rock crystal. 3. A flat film acetate continuous filament yarn which may be texturized. 4. Dress fabric, also called *crystalline.* See *fabrics.*

cuaran Knee-length boots of horsehide or cowhide held up by thongs; worn by Scottish Highlanders around 1500.

Cuban heel See *heels.*

Cubavera jacket See *sport jackets* under *jackets.*

cue 18th century term for the *queue,* the hanging tail of a wig, which first appeared for civilian wear about 1720.

cueitl Full-length wrap-around skirt made of colorful cotton or palm-leaf fabric, worn by Tehuan women of Mexico with a lace-trimmed sheer blouse over a heavier blouse and the *huipili, q.v.*

cue peruke (kyu per-uke) 18th century term for wig with hanging queue.

cuerpo See *querpo.*

cuff Finishing band of material, either made separately and attached or created by turning back an extension of the hem of a sleeve, trousers leg, wrist of a glove, or top of a boot, etc.

CUFFS:

barrel c. *Single cuff, q.v.,* on a tailored shirt.

double c. Same as *French cuff, q.v.*

fitted c. Wide band, shaped to fit the wrist and arm, usually fastened with buttons or zipper.

French c. Double-length stitched-on shirt cuff that folds back over itself and is fastened with *cuff link, q.v.,* through all four layers.

gauntlet c. Wide, turned-back cuff that slants away from the arm, flaring wide at top and tapered to wrist.

single c. Barrel-shaped cuff with rounded corners, stitched to shirt sleeve and closed with one small button matched to front shirt buttons.

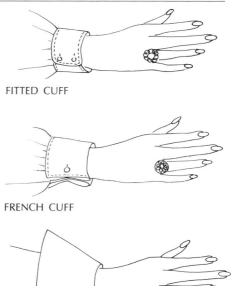

FITTED CUFF

FRENCH CUFF

GAUNTLET CUFF

cuff button 1. Small button or buttons usually of mother-of-pearl sewed on shirt cuff to fasten it; introduced in 19th century, used in lieu of *cuff links, q.v.* 2. Late 17th century—two metal disks connected by links used to replace earlier *cuff string.*

cuffed Describing shorts, pants, or sleeves with very wide hems turned back halfway to form a border called a *cuff;* on sleeves, *cuffs* may be separate pieces sewn to edges.

cuff link Decorative jewelry consisting of two buttons joined by a link or short chain; worn to close the *French cuff, q.v.,* of a shirt; may be metal, engraved or set with stones, or in wide variety of materials— worn originally by men and adopted by women. Also see *cuff button.*

cuff string String pulled through eyelets on cuff to fasten it, used in lieu of button in the 19th century. Also called *sleeve string.*

cuff-top girdle See *girdles.*

cuir (queer) 1. French word for leather. 2. Rich warm, yellowish-brown color.

cuirass (kew-rass) 1. Sleeveless leather thigh-length tunic worn as armor by ancient Greeks and Romans. 2. Armor consisting of breastplate and back plates of steel worn either under or over other garments from mid 14th to mid 17th centuries at first over a mail shirt and *jupel* and under a *tabard, q.q.v.,* later worn outside with metal *tassets, q.v.,* forming a skirt. Similar to *corselet* or *breastplate.* 3. Plain, close-fitting waist worn by women in early 1900's. *Der.* French, *cuirasse,* breastplate.

cuirasse bodice Extremely tight, boned women's daytime bodice extending down over hips to mold the body, frequently made in fabric different from the dress, with sleeves matched to the trim; worn in mid 1870's.

cuirasse tunic Tight-fitting tunic worn with the *cuirasse bodice, q.v.* by women in mid 1870's.

cuisse Piece of armor or padding shaped to protect the thigh; worn during Middle Ages.

cuit Completely degummed silk. Also spelled *cuite.* Also called *bright silk.*

culet (ku-lit) 1. Bottom facet of a brilliant-cut gem. 2. Piece of armor consisting of a skirt of articulated plate fastened to backplate to protect the loins; worn from mid 16th to mid 17th centuries.

culotte Garment that hangs like a skirt, but is actually pants, *i.e.,* a divided skirt. *Der.* French, knee breeches. See *dresses, pajamas, pants, pants-dresses, pants-skirts, skirts.* Also spelled *culottes.*

cultivated silk Term used in India and other countries of the Far East for silk fibers from cocoons raised in a scientific manner—the opposite of wild silk.

cultured pearl See *beads.*

Cumberland corset *Waist cincher* or *corset* stiffened with *whalebone* worn by English *dandies, q.q.v.,* during the Regency period, 1811–1820.

Cumberland hat Man's hat with eight-inch-high tapered crown and small brim turned up at the sides, worn in 1830's.

cummerbund 1. See *belts.* 2. Sash, worn by women, which hooks rather than ties. 3. Wide colorful sash worn on top of a wide leather belt, native dress of Albanian and Montenegrin men; used as a pocket for holding accessories, including a pistol. Also part of native dress in India and Turkestan. *Der.* Urdu, *kamarband,* loin-cloth.

Cupioni Trademark owned by American Bemberg Division of Beaunit Corp., for a nubby thick-and-thin cuprammonium rayon filament yarn, similar to *doupioni silk, q.v.*

cupola coat Dome-shaped petticoat made with *whalebone, q.v.,* or cane hoops, fashionable in England from 1710 to 1780.

curch 1. Untrimmed, close-fitting woman's cap worn in Colonial times in America. 2. Scarf-like woman's head covering; worn in Scotland. Also called a *kerchief or curchef.*

curing Process used on fabrics or garments previously treated with insolvent resins, placed in an oven with temperatures of 280 or above, which permanently sets fabric or garment so it will retain its shape after washing; labeled *durable press* when used on garments.

curl Hair twisted around in spiral fashion in short *ringlets* worn close to the head, long and *hanging,* or in horizontal *sausage* style, either tightly twisted or big and loose.

CURLS:

BARREL CURLS

GUICHE

SPIT
CURL

TENDRILS

barrel c. Full round large curls, frequently grouped at crown or back of the head.

bubble c. Very loose curl, backcombed slightly and turned under, appearing on head as series of rounded bumps.

bustle c. Curls worn at back of head, usually long and hanging.

corkscrew c. Free hanging curls which appear coiled, frequently lacquered to hold the shape.

finger c. Vertical hanging curl, similar to *corkscrew,* above, combed around the finger in a tight spiral cylinder.

Grecian c. Small curls around the face, copied from Napoleonic era, which was inspired by Greece.

guiche (gweesh) Few strands of hair made into a curl in front of ear. See also *reverse quiche.*

jumbo c. Very large curls similar to *barrel curls,* above.

kiss c. Same as *guiche.*

pannier c. Curls worn at sides of face or in front of ears.

pin c. Flat ringlet held against the head by a *bobby pin, q.v.,* a method of setting short hair; when pin is removed, curl may be kept intact or combed out into loose tendrils.

reverse guiche *Guiche, q.v.,* curled back toward the ear instead of forward.

ringlets Loose short curls that hang in dangling fashion.

sausage c. Tightly rolled horizontal curl; usually arranged in layers around sides and back of head from ear level to nape; popular in late 1930's and early 1940's.

spit c. Separate ringlets formed flat against the forehead or cheek often held in place by "spit"—setting lotion or lacquer; especially popular 1870–1880. Also see *guiche*.

tendrils Long loosely curled strands of hair worn hanging at forehead, sides, or nape of neck, popular with the *concierge hairstyle, q.v.*

curl yarn See *yarns*.

curricle coat or **cloak** (kur-eh-kul) 1. Woman's fitted full-length coat, with lapels but cut away in front from chest to waist, sloping to the back; worn in early 19th century, sometimes called *gig coat*. 2. Man's *box coat* or *driving coat, q.q.v.*, with one or more capes; worn in mid 19th century.

curricle dress Thigh-length, short-sleeved *over-tunic*, usually net, worn over full-length dress by women from 1790's to early 1800's.

curricle pelisse Term used in the 1820's for a woman's *pelisse, q.v.*, with three capes.

cushion cut See *gem cuts* under *gems*.

cushionet *Bustle* worn with the *farthingale, q.q.v.*, raising back of skirt higher than front, in late 16th century and early 17th century. Also called a *quizzionet*.

cushion headdress 19th-century term for large padded rolls worn as head-dresses by women in first half of the 15th century.

cushion pad Tiny bustle, stuffed with horsehair, worn in late 19th century.

cushion sole 1. Cork, felt, or foam rubber used under the insole of shoe as shock absorber for walking. 2. See *socks*.

custom designer Designer who creates an original garment that is executed by skilled seamstresses who drape the fabric on a *dummy, q.v.*, con-forming to the customer's special measurements; clothes also called custom-made or *made-to-measure*.

custom-made Describing garments made by tailor or couture house for the individual customer, following the coutrier's original design, either by fitting on a dressmaker's *dummy* built to the customer's measure-ments or by several fittings in per-son.

cut 1. Trade term used in ready-to-wear industry for cutting out fabric preparatory to sewing. 2. Manner in which a gem is faceted or cut. See *gem cuts*. 3. A length of *gray goods, q.v.*, approximately sixty yards long. Also called a *bolt*. 4. Knitting term used mainly in circular knitting for number of needles on machine in one inch of space.

cutaway coat, jacket See *coats*.

cutaway frock Man's suit coat, al-most knee-length, similar to a *frock coat, q.v.*, but cut away from waist-line to side seam in rounded curve; worn in 1890's and early 1900's.

cutaway sack Man's loose-fitting suit jacket reaching to hips, cut away in rounded lines in front to side seams; worn in 1890's and early 1900's.

cut-fingered gloves 1. Gloves slashed to show rings worn on fingers; worn in 16th century. 2. Women's gloves with tips of fingers cut off; worn in early 18th century.

cut-offs See *shorts*.

cutouts 1. Shoe term for tiny patterns shaped like diamonds, tear drops, squares, and other shapes, cutout

138

of the upper part of shoe to give open-air effect. Also called *perforations, q.v.* 2. Holes of different sizes and shapes cut from clothing, such as rounded section at sides of waist, or round section cut from center front of dress, popular in early 1960's.

cut-pile fabric Fabric made with a warp, a filling, and an extra yarn that is looped and cut to form pile, as in *corduroy, velvet,* and *velveteen, q.q.v.,* under *fabrics.*

cut-pile weave See *weaves.*

cut-steel beads See *beads.*

cut-steel buckle Popular buckle of early 20th century, made of polished steel with jewel-like facets, used on silk or moiré afternoon and evening shoes and on belts.

cutter Garment-production term for the person who cuts the fabric with an electric knife.

cutting-up trade Jargon used by textile industry for clothing manufacturers.

cut velvet See *fabrics.*

cut wig 18th-century term for a man's small plain wig without a queue.

cut work See *embroideries.*

cyclas 1. Rich, elaborate overgarment, sometimes fur or silk-lined, made of a large piece of cloth with round opening for head, worn in medieval times on ceremonial occasions by both men and women, e.g., at the coronation of Henry III of England, 13th century. 2. Sleeveless jumper-type garment worn over armor in early 14th century extended to waist in front, and to knees in back, and slashed up sides

and then laced similar to man's *dalmatic, q.v.* Also spelled *ciclaton. Der.* from Cyclades, a group of Greek islands.

cycling suit Any costume worn for bicycling in the late 19th century. For a small boy: jacket, similar to *patrol jacket, q.v.,* worn with tight knee pants. For women: *knickerbockers* or a *divided shirt* with

tailored or *Norfolk jacket, leggings,* and a straw *sailor* hat, *q.q.v.* For men: *knickerbockers* and *Norfolk jacket, q.q.v.* Also called a *cycling costume.*

cylinder printing See *roller print* under *prints.*

Czechoslovakian embroidery See *embroideries.*

czerkeska Calf-length coat worn by Caucasian Cossack Army. Distinctive feature was series of cartridge pleats on either side of chest; each pleat originally held one charge of gun powder. Also spelled *tjerkiska* and *cherkesska.*

D

D 1. Shoe size: Letter indicating a width; widths run from AAAAA to EEEEE with A's being the narrowest. 2. Pajama size: Men's size corresponding to 44–48 chest size. 185–210 pounds weight, or shirt sizes 16½–17. Also called "XL" or Extra Large. 3. Brassiere cup size: Letter indicating the largest sizes with sizes running AA, A, B, C, D, DD, with AA being the smallest.

Dacca muslin Handwoven fabric of fine cotton made locally by natives of Dacca, Pakistan; the yarn is so fine that ten yards of best quality fabric are reported to weigh only four ounces.

Daché, Lilly See *designers appendix, United States.*

Dacron (day-cron) Trademark owned by DuPont for approximately 46 types of filament yarns, staple, fabrics, and fiberfill, all given a type number and made for various end uses, with cotton for men's shirtings and with wool for coat and suit fabrics.

dagging Ornamental borders cut on garments in shapes of leaves, tongues, and scallops; originated about 1380, fashionable until the end of 15th century for hems of gowns, sleeves, and cape edge of the *chaperone, q.v.* Also called *castellated, cut work, dag, dagges, foliated, jags,* and *jagging.*

daharra (da-har-a) Wide Moroccan full-length robe made from rectangle of striped fabric sewed up sides, leaving openings for arms, and embroidered around neckline. Similar to *caftan, q.v.*

Dalí, Salvador (dah-*lee*) Spanish artist, one of leading exponents of Surrealism in painting, noted for his jewelry designs in fantastic shapes; his paintings influenced fashion display and advertising.

dalmatic (dal-ma-tic) Long, wide-sleeved, loose-fitting tunic, trimmed with two vertical stripes in front, open at the sides; worn as an ecclesiastical vestment by cardinals, abbots, and bishops, and as part of the coronation robes of Great Britain. *Der.* From *tunica dalmatica,* worn by Romans in 2nd century, starting in Dalmatia.

damaging-out Repair of tears or holes in fur pelts and garments.

damascene lace (dam-ah-seen) See *laces.*

damask See *fabrics.*

dance set Lingerie consisting of *brassiere* and wide, flaring, *step-in, q.q.v.,* panties; worn in the 1920's.

dandizette (dan-ee-set) Term used in early 19th century for a female *dandy, q.v.,* below, conspicuous for her *Grecian bend, q.v.* or the manner in which she walked.

dandy Term used from early 19th century on for a man excessively fond of and overly concerned with clothes, exemplified by *Beau Brummell, q.v.,* and *Compte d'Orsay,* who were great influences on men's fashions in England and France. Also called *beau* or, in excessive cases, *fop*.

dandy blouse See *blouses*.

dandy hat Woman's high-crowned, roll-brimmed hat decorated with jet embroidery, feathers, and a veil; introduced by New York milliner Sally Victor, in mid 1950's.

dandy shirt See *shirts*.

Danish trousers Pants worn by young boys in 1870's, calf-length and open at the hems. Also called *open-bottom trousers*.

darned lace See *laces*.

darning stitch See *stitches*.

dart Sewing term for V-shaped tuck used frequently on shoulders or at

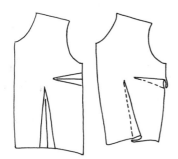

waist or in side seam under the arm to make garment conform to the body.

darya See *fabrics*.

dashiki African garment similar to collarless *kimono-sleeved, q.v.,* shirt, of bold native-print cotton; introduced in United States in late 1960's for general wear, particularly by Afro-Americans. Also see *dresses* and *blouses*.

Davies, Donald See *designers appendix, Ireland*.

Davy Crockett cap See *caps*.

death's head button 18th-century term for domed button covered with metal thread or mohair forming an X on top like the cross of the skull and cross-bones emblem.

De Barentzen, Patrick See *designers appendix, Italy*.

DeBevoise brassiere Sleeveless, low-necked waist similar to a *corset cover, q.v.,* reaching to waistline with a point in front, boned to support the bosom; patented by the De-

Bevoise Company in Newark, N.J., in early 1900's. Later models were the forerunners of the contemporary brassiere.

debutante slouch Posture fashionable for young sophisticated women in 1920's, shoulders drooped forward giving a flat-chested appearance.

decalcomania Process of transferring a picture or design from specially prepared paper to the skin. Fad of wearing designs of butterflies, flowers, etc., on legs and arms popular in the mid 1960's. Also see *tattoo*.

decating 1. Finishing process used on wool to set width and length and improve luster. 2. Finishing process on rayon and other man-made woven fabrics and knits to improve hand, color, and luster.

deccan hemp (dek-en) Vegetable fiber grown in Nigeria and India, used as substitute for hemp. Also spelled *decan*. Also called *ambari* or *kenaf*.

deck jacket See *sport jackets* under *jackets*.

deck pants See *pants*.

deck shoes. See *boating* under *shoes*.

décolletage (deh-coll-eh-tahzh) French noun meaning bare shoulders or outline of a low-cut neckline.

décolleté (deh-coll-eh-tay) French adjective for garment cut very low at neckline revealing shoulders, neck and back, sometimes part of bosom. See *brassieres*.

découpage The art of decorating items with cut-out pictures of paper or fabric, *e.g.*, handbags made from metal lunch boxes with cut-out pictures pasted to surfaces and shellacked; popular in mid and late 1960's. *Der.* French, cut out.

deerskin See *buckskin* under *leathers*.

deerstalker See *caps*.

de la Renta, Oscar See *designers appendix, United States*.

Delft blue Medium blue color, similar to color of pottery made in Delft, Holland.

Delhi work See *embroideries*.

demi-boot See *boots*.

demi-bra See *brassieres*.

demi brassard Armor worn in early 14th century consisting of a metal plate worn to protect the upper arm.

demi-circled farthingale Same as *French farthingale, q.v.*

demi coronal 16th-century term for a *tiara* or *half coronet, q.q.v.*

demi-corset Short corset worn by women in 1830's and '40's. See *corset*.

demi-gigot (demee jhee-go) Sleeve, tight from wrist to elbow but full at shoulder and upper arm, worn in the late 1820's, revived in early 1890's; shown again by young designers in England and Scandinavia in the early 1970's. *Der.* French, half leg-of-mutton.

demi jamb Armor consisting of a metal plate over front of leg from knee to ankle connected to the *solleret* or shoe, worn by knights and soldiers in the early 14th century.

demi-mondaines (demi-mon-dan) French term for mistresses of wealthy men, who were dressed by famous Parisian couturiers and greatly influenced fashion from the end of the Second Empire through the Edwardian era. Notorious demi-mondaines: La belle Otero, Polaire, Forzane, and Lantelme. *Der.* French, those of the half-world.

demi riding coat See *justaucorps*.

demi sleeve Full elbow-length sleeve worn by men in the 16th century. Also called *demi-maunch*.

demi vambrace Armor worn on front of forearm from elbow to the wrist.

démodé (day-mode-ay) French adjective meaning old fashioned, antiquated, passé, or out of style.

Demorest, Madame Operator of Demorest's Emporium of Fashion with showrooms and factory located at

Union Square, New York, where ladies came to select home-sewing patterns in the 1870's and '80's. Her husband published *Demorest Magazine* and *Demorest Fashions,* which was a profusely illustrated weekly newspaper.

denier (deh-nir or deh-nee-ay) International textile and hosiery system used for numbering silk and man-made filament yarns; the low numbers represent finer sizes and higher numbers the heavier yarns. *Der.* From old French coin, its weight used as measure of size and number of silk.

denim See *fabrics.*

Denmark cock Man's *tricorn, q.v.,* hat of late 18th century, made by turning up a brimmed hat in three sections, with the back higher than the front.

dentelle lace See *Dieppe point* under *laces.*

dentil Greek term for series of tooth-like scallops, used as a border.

de Rauch, Madeleine See *designers appendix, France.*

derby See *hats.*

Descat, Rose See *designers appendix, France.*

desert boot See *boots.*

deshabillé (deh-seh-beeyay) 1. French word for wrapper, dressing gown, or *negligee, q.v.* 2. Style of dressing with a loose, careless air, originating in 18th century Paris and London. Also see *banyan* and *morning dress.* Sometimes misspelled *dishabille.*

designer Person engaged in creating original garments in various fields of the fashion industry, some designers work in their own business setup, others are employed by manufacturers to develop collections of merchandise in ready-to-wear, couture, lingerie, millinery, footwear, accessories, and jewelry.

designer collections Retail-store term for a selection of clothes grouped by individual designers' names.

designer scarf See *signature scarf* under *scarfs.*

Dessés, Jean See *designers appendix, France.*

dettigen cock Man's *tricorn, q.v.,* hat, brim turned up equally in three sections; worn in 18th century.

development bundle system Garment-industry term for production of sewn garments in which the items move in units or bundles in organized manner from one operator to another.

devotional ring Bronze, gold, or ivory ring with ten spherical projections around the band used in Middle Ages for saying the creed.

dhoti (doh-tee) Man's garment worn in India, consisting of a length of cotton fabric draped around the body to form trousers or a *loin cloth, q.v.,* the fabric, sometimes with colored striped borders or Jacquard pattern, is approximately 3½ yards long, with width determined by the height of the wearer.

diadem 1. A crown. 2. Decorative headdress resembling a crown. 3. Ornamental headdress usually wider and higher toward the front, worn by Oriental kings, particularly in ancient Persia.

diadem bonnet Lace and velvet bonnet with brim forming a halo, made with two sets of bonnet strings— one tied under chignon in back, the other, trimmed with ruching, loosely tied under the chin; worn in late 1860's.

diadem cap *Bathing cap, q.v.,* usually of oiled silk, *q.v.,* shaped like a *shower cap, q.v.,* with a band and upstanding ruffle in front and ties under the chin; worn in 1870's.

diadem comb High, wide comb with ornamental top; worn like a tiara for evening by women in the 1830's.

Diadem mink See *mink* under *furs.*

Diaghilev, Sergei Pavlovich (dee-ah-geh-lef; 1872–1929) Russian aristocrat, avant-garde creator of the Ballets Russes, who produced *Cléopâtre,* 1909, and *Shéhérazade,* 1910, with costumes by *Leon Bakst, q.v.;* the brilliant colors and new concept of stage design started wave of Orientalism in Paris that affected whole couture, particularly the work of *Paul Poiret, q.v.,* and banished somber Victorian fashions.

diagonal weave See *twill weave.*

diamanté bands (dee-a-mont-ay) Fake jewels sewn on strips of fabric, used as trimming on dress or blouse. Also see *braids. Der.* French, set with diamonds.

diamanté headband Band of sparkling fake jewels worn around head, low on forehead; popular in Edwardian period from 1890–1910.

diamond See *gems.*

Diana Vernon hat Wide brimmed, shallow-crowned straw bonnet of the late 1870's; one side of the brim was turned up and trimmed with a rosette, wide streamers came from underside of brim to tie under the chin. Named for the heroine of *Rob Roy,* 1817 English novel by Sir Walter Scott. (Also called a *Diana Vernon bonnet.*)

dickey 1. Separate fill-in used inside woman's low neckline with or without an attached collar. 2. Man's false shirt front or turtleneck fill-in. 3. Shirt front with attached collar, worn over a flannel shirt by men in the 19th century, not considered proper attire for gentlemen. 4. *Pinafore, q.v.,* or *bib, q.v.,* for a child. 5. Late 18th- and early 19th-century term for under-petticoat worn by women. Also spelled *dicky* and *dickie.*

Dieppe point lace (dee-ep) See *laces.*

Dietrich, Marlene German actress and entertainer, considered supreme example of glamorous movie star and great fashion influence in the 1930's and 1940's; famous for her legs, arched plucked eyebrows, and screen wardrobe designed by Adrian with many clinging chiffons and feather boas; also credited with popularizing mannish slacks and *fedoras, q.v.,* for women.

dimayeh (dee-may-a) Long, striped coat with silken cord belt, native costume of men in Palestine, now Israel, usually striped in combinations of red and yellow or black, blue, and yellow.

dimensional stability Ability of fabric

to return to its original shape and size after wear, washing, or dry cleaning.

dimidje Full Turkish-style trousers of bright-colored silk; worn as native dress by women of Bosnia, part of Yugoslavia.

dimity Cord-striped or -checked cotton. See *fabrics*.

dink See *beanie* under *caps*.

dinner dress See *dresses*.

dinner jacket See *tuxedo* under *jackets*.

Dior, Christian See *designers appendix, France*.

dip Term used in 1890's and early 20th century for the point of a waistline that was lower in front than back.

dip belt *Contour* belt, *q.v.*, usually of stiffened fabric cut wider in the front with a pointed lower edge, fastened by strings attached to each end which came from back around to the front and tied under the belt; fashionable in late 19th and early 20th centuries.

dip dyeing Coloring by immersion in dye solution; see *dyeing*.

diploidon (dip-ploy-don) Mantle worn by ancient Greeks, made out of a square or oblong of fabric folded double, with the fold placed under the left arm, and fastened on the right shoulder; similar to *chlamys* and *himation, q.q.v.*

dip-top boots See *boots*.

Directoire bonnet (de-rek-twar) High-crowned bonnet fitting close over the ears with a high flaring front brim; worn in late 1870's.

Directoire coat 1. Man's single- or double-breasted, knee-length coat with wide peaked lapels, collar turned up high, worn over short waistcoat and with neckwear wrapped to the chin; worn in period 1795–1799, when a Directoire of five men ruled France's First Republic. 2. Revival in late 1880's of 18th century man's coat styles adapted for women. 3. Contemporary woman's coat, *maxi length, q.v.*, with fitted double-breasted high waist, wide lapels, and gauntlet cuffs; reminiscent of men's coats of Directoire period.

Directoire gown 1. Woman's high-waisted white muslin or calico long *chemise, q.v.*, sometimes transparent over flesh-colored tights; worn, with flat slippers and natural hair, in France in Directoire period, 1795–1799, in reaction to over-elaborate fashions of Louis XVI. 2. Slim coat-style dress with wide lapels, gauntlet-cuffed sleeve, high-sashed waist; worn by women in late 19th century, reminiscent of men's Directoire coat.

Directoire hat Similar to Directoire bonnet, without strings and with larger brim in front; worn in 1880's.

Directoire jacket Woman's waist-length jacket of late 19th century, similar to top of *Directoire coat, q.v.*

Directoire skirt Skirt cut in seven gores, the back four lined, stiffened, and fluted into *pipe-organ* or *godet pleats, q.q.v.*, the hem being four to six yards wide, front sometimes slashed to knee with pleat inserted at either side of center front gore; worn in 1890's.

DIRECTOIRE JACKET, 1889

DIRECTOIRE SKIRT, 1895

Directoire waistline See *waistlines.*

direct printing Method of making printed fabrics by placing colored design on white or light-colored ground with rollers. See *roller print* under *prints.*

dirndl (durn-del) See *coats, dresses, skirts, petticoats,* and *silhouettes.*

Di Sant' Angelo, Giorgio See *designers appendix, United States.*

discharge printing Method of printing a fabric in two or more colors by first immersing it in a dye of one

color, then imprinting it by using rollers with a chemical that removes the dye to produce a design, *e.g.,* white polka dots on a dark background; color may be added to the design by mixing the bleach with a dye not affected by it.

dishrag shirt Loosely knitted man's sport shirt with placket closing at neck; worn in 1930's, so-called for resemblance of knit to knitted dishrags of that period.

district check See *tartans.*

dittos Term for man's suit when same fabric is used for pants, jacket, vest, and sometimes the cap; worn in the 1850's.

divided skirt Wide trousers that hang like a skirt, introduced in England in 1882 by Lady Harberton for bicycling. Same as *pants-skirt* or *culottes, q.q.v.* Also see *skirts.*

djellaba (jel-a-ba) Moroccan man's garment worn for inclement weather consisting of three-quarter-length cloak with a hood; imported and copied for men and women in the late 1960's as informal *house* or *hostess gowns.* Also spelled *djellabah.* See *robes.*

djubba See *jubbah.*

dobby See *fabrics.*

dobby weave See *weaves.*

Dr. Denton's See *pajamas.*

Dr. Scholl exercise sandals See *sandals.*

Doctor's gown Black unclosed academic gown with wide bands of velvet down the front. The full sleeves are set in with cartridge pleats and have three bands of velvet. Worn

as part of academic costume by candidates for and holders of doctoral degrees.

Doctor's hood Black academic hood with colored band at neck to indicate type of degree. This velvet band

extends down the back and is rolled over to show the school's colors.

Square cut at hem and larger than Bachelor's and Master's hoods. See *academic hoods, colors.*

Doctor Zhivago See *Zhivago.*

doeskin 1. See *leathers.* 2. See *fabrics.*

Doeuillet, Georges See *designers appendix, France.*

dogaline Loose-fitting, straight-cut gown with very wide sleeves, lower edge turned up and fastened to shoulder, revealing sleeve of undergown; worn by men and women in Middle Ages and 16th century.

dog collar See *necklaces, necklines,* and *collars.*

dog's-ear collar Also called spaniel's-ear collar. See *collars.*

dollar-round toes See *toes of shoes.*

Dolley Madison hood Lace-trimmed opera hood somewhat resembling a *dust cap, q.v.,* with a deep ruffle of lace falling around the face and neck; worn toward back of head and held on with broad ribbon ties under chin; popular at end of 19th century.

Dolly Varden Type of woman's costume inspired by Charles Dickens' character Dolly Varden in *Barnaby Rudge,* consisting of a *polonaise* gown, *q.v.,* in chintz with flowered quilted underskirt, worn with wide straw hat trimmed with flowers and ribbon and tied under *chignon, q.v.;* popular in 1870's.

dolman (dole-man) 1. Woman's short mantle or full-length wrap that gave appearance of a cape from the back but sleeved in front; worn in 1870's through the 1880's, revived in early 20th century and returns frequently in coat collections. 2. Full-length outer robe worn in Turkey. *Der.*

DOM PEDRO SHOE, 1908

Turkish *dolaman,* to wind around. See *sleeves* and *sweaters.*

dolmanette Crocheted *dolman, q.v.,* woman's wrap fastened at neck with large bow of ribbon; worn in the 1890's.

domet flannel See *fabrics.*

dome umbrella See *bell umbrella.*

domino 1. Originally, a large hood worn by monks; later, a cloak with attached hood for men and women. 2. A large cloak, usually black, worn with a small mask for traditional carnival and masquerade costume; popular in early 18th century and revived at end of 19th century. 3. Small contemporary half-mask worn with masquerade costume.

Dom Pedro shoe Ankle-high man's heavy work shoe fastened with laces and one buckled strap over center of lacing; worn in early 1900's.

Donegal tweed See *fabrics.*

donnilette Variant of *douillette, q.v.*

don't mentions See *trousers.*

dopatta 1. Shawl or scarf worn draped around the shoulders as a part of native dress by men in India. 2. Fabric, spelled *dopota;* a fine grade of cotton muslin made in India and used there for veils and shawls.

dorelet (dor-a-let) Term used in Middle Ages for woman's *hair net q.v.,* ornamented with jewels. Also spelled *dorlet.*

doriah Cotton fabric in plain weave; bleached or dyed black or blue and used in Egypt for outer garments; also made in England for export to Saudi Arabia. Also spelled *doria* and *dooriah.*

dorino Outer garment worn on street by Bosnian women, a full garment covering the woman's body from head to calf of the leg, exposing striped hosiery and scarlet or blue slippers. Also spelled *dorina.*

dormeuse Ribbon-trimmed white cap with a puffed crown and falling *lappets, q.v.,* trimmed with lace, called *wings,* popularly known as *cheek wrappers;* worn in the house by women in second half of 18th century. Also spelled *dormouse.* Also called a *French nightcap.*

Dorothée Bis See *designers appendix, France.*

D'Orsay coat Man's overcoat of late 1830's—similar to a *pilot coat, q.v.,* but more fitted at waist—with darts, small collar, slashed or flapped pockets, plain sleeves trimmed with three or four buttons, and no pleats or hip buttons in the back. *Der.* Named for *Compte d'Orsay, q.v.,* a 19th century arbiter of fashion.

D'Orsay, Count See *Orsay, Compte d'*

D'Orsay habit-coat Fitted, man-tailored, three-quarter-length coat for women, somewhat resembling

man's cutaway style, double-breasted, with large revers; introduced in early 1880's.

D'Orsay pump See *shoes.*

D'Orsay slippers See *slippers.*

Dorset thread button Brass wire ring covered with cotton threads radiating from center to form a flat button, used on underwear from about 1700 to 1830.

dotted Swiss See *fabrics.*

dots See *earrings* and *prints.*

double-bar tricot See *tricot* in *knits.*

double-breasted Describing the front opening of a garment lapped over double and fastening with two rows of buttons; originally both rows were functional, now one row is usually decorative. Also called *d.b.,* British tailors' 19th-century slang. See *closings.*

double chignon Hairstyle with two large rolls of hair, one above the other, at the nape, sometimes using artificial hair; worn in 1860's.

double cloth See *fabrics* and *weaves.*

double cuff See *cuffs.*

double-girdled Describing the ancient Greek fashion of wearing a long narrow sash belt or two separate sashes, wound around waist and crossed over chest to adjust fullness of garment.

double knit See *knits.*

double ombré See *stripes.*

double-puffed sleeve See *sleeves.*

doubler Extra layer of soft fabric placed between the leather and the lining of shoe to make leather look plumper.

double ruffle Strip of fabric stitched in the center and gathered, forming a ruffle on either side of stitching.

double-running stitch See *stitches.*

double-satin ribbon Ribbon, *q.v.,* woven with satin face on both sides.

double-stitched seam See *topstitched* under *seams.*

doublet 1. Main garment for upper part of man's body worn from late 14th to mid 17th century, styled like a close-fitting jacket with various lengths of skirt showing *trunk hose* or *breeches, q.q.v.* See also *gambeson, jupon, pourpoint* and *peascod-bellied doublet.* 2. Part of woman's riding habit from 1650–1670. 3. Jewelry term for two pieces of material cemented together to form one large stone. 4. Jacket of Scots Highlander's costume.

double-zipper foundation See *foundation garments.*

Doucet, Jacques See *designers appendix, France.*

doupioni (doo-pe-own-e) Silk yarn reeled from double cocoons or two adjacent cocoons in which the silk is intertwined, the uneven yarn giving a decorative texture to *shantungs* and *pongees, q.q.v.* under *fabrics.* Also spelled *douppioni, dupion,* and *duppioni.*

doup weave See *weaves.*

down See *feathers.*

downhill pants See *pants.*

downy calves Extra padding woven into men's stockings to make calves appear more shapely, patented in 1788. Also see *false calves.*

dragon robe See *chi-fu.*

drape The hang or fall of fabric when made into a garment, an important quality to consider in designing: e.g. chiffon has soft drape, ottoman hangs stiffly.

draping 1. Fabric falling in folds in the garment; seen on statues of ancient Greece; most outstanding modern versions by Paris designer *Grés, q.v.* 2. Trade term for arranging and pinning muslin cloth over a dummy to conform to the design of the intended garment, after which muslin is removed from dummy, stitched at seams, tried on a model, altered, refitted on model, then cut apart for making the pattern.

drawers 1. Nineteenth-century term for *underpants* worn by men and women; used today for *thermal* type, *q.q.v.* Also see *panties.* 2. Underpants worn by men from 16th through 19th centuries, first in linen, footed or with stirrup straps under instep; later, any pants drawn on and called *trousers.* 3. Underpants worn by women in early 18th century consisting of two separate legs joined by waistband and, at end of 19th century, knitted or woven, trimmed with lace. Also see *combinations, knickers, pantalettes, pantaloons,* and *umbrella drawers.*

drawn work See *embroideries.*

drawstring Ribbon or cord inserted through a *heading, q.v.,* of fabric, pulled and tied to form a closing for neckline, pants, cuffs of sleeves, handbags. See also *blouses, shirts, shorts, necklines, waistlines,* etc.

Drécoll See *designers appendix, France.*

dress (noun) 1. Principal covering for a woman's body in the modern Western world, a skirted garment varied in weight according to temperatures, worn in public over undergarments and under a variety of wraps; before late 18th century called *gown* or *robe.* 2. (noun) Collective term for all clothing, e.g. the dress of Spain, of Eskimos, etc. Synonyms: apparel, clothes, costume, garment, habit, robe, uniform, vestments. 3. Man's full dress suit or formal clothes. 4. (verb) To put on formal clothing *e.g. dress* for dinner. 5. (verb) To arrange or set the hair. 6. (verb) To tan and finish hides for leather uses.

DRESSES:

BARE-MIDRIFF DRESS

SLIP-DRESS

CAFTAN

GRANNY DRESS

SKATING DRESS

A-line d. Dress style flaring gently from under arms to bottom of skirt, resembling the letter A, usually narrow shoulders and a high round neckline; similar to *shift, skimmer, q.q.v.,* and introduced in 1955 by Christian Dior.

Andean shift Native dress from Peru, made in straight-cut style of native fabrics and trimmed with embroidery; for sale in United States in late 1960's.

apron d. See *pinafore dress.*

asymmetric d. (a-sim-met-ric) Uses the principle of informal balance, rather than formal balance—may be draped to one side, have side closing, or cover only one shoulder;

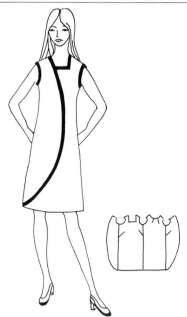

THREE-ARMHOLE DRESS

BATHROBE DRESS

SAFARI DRESS

TORSO DRESS

one version introduced in 1920's by Paris designer Vionnet, variations have been in vogue ever since the *toga, q.v.*

baby d. Woman's dress cut like a smock, with a high neckline and a yoke, similar to children's and infant's dresses of the 1930's; re-introduced in 1970 by designers of French ready-to-wear Emmanuelle Khanh, Jean Cacharel, etc. Also called *baby doll* or *smock dress.*

back-wrap d. Dress that closes in back, with a skirt wide enough to lap over to the sides; fastened with buttons and at waist by a sash.

ball gown See *evening dress.*

bare-midriff d. Fashion originating in tropical countries consisting of two-piece dress with top ending under the bust, baring the ribs, skirt starting at waistline or low-slung; introduced in the U.S. in the 1930's, revived in 1960's and 1970's following interest in East Indian fashions.

basic d. Dress simply cut with no ornamentation, usually black: jewelry, collars, and other accessories can be added to change the appearance; introduced in the 1930's, and worn through '40's and revived in 1973. Sometimes called "L.B.D." (little black dress).

bathrobe d. *Wrap-around* dress with *shawl* collar, *q.q.v.,* and no buttons, front lapped over and held in place with a sash; popular in mid 1960's.

beach d. Simple cover-up designed to be worn over a bathing suit, often in matching fabric. Also called *beach shift.*

bloomer d. Pants dress made like children's rompers with legs of wide pants gathered into bands at hems. See *pants dress.*

blouson (blue-sawn) Bloused-top dress with low waistline seam, a style introduced in 1920's and reintroduced in late 1950's. *Der.* French, a waist-length military battle jacket or lumber jacket.

bouffant d. (boo-fawn) Dress with tight-fitting bodice and full gathered, pleated, or ruffled skirt or a skirt like a bubble, a bell, or a cone that may be worn with hoops or petticoats. Popular from 1830's to 1880's and re-introduced by American designer Anne Fogarty in 1950's. *Der.* French, fluffy or puffy.

bra-shift Sleeveless *shift* with top of dress fitted to the figure like a *brassiere, q.q.v.;* an innovation of the mid 1960's.

bridal d. See *wedding dress.*

bridesmaid's d. Any type of dress worn by a bride's attendant at a wedding, selected by the bride. Dresses for bridesmaids are usually alike and harmonious in design with the wedding dress.

caftan Near East native full-length robe with embroidery around the neckline and front slit closing; introduced for Western women in dress lengths in same style as worn in Morocco in 1967. Also see *robes.*

cage d. Made in two layers, inner layer opaque and cut close to body, outer layer of sheer or latticed fabric hanging loosely; introduced in 1965 by French designer Yves Saint Laurent; similar to dresses designed by Spanish couturier Cristobal Balenciaga in Paris in the 1940's.

cardigan d. Coat-dress similar to long *cardigan sweater, q.v.,* usually unfitted, and buttoned down the front; worn in 1960's in *mini, midi,* and *maxi lengths, q.q.v.*

Carnaby shift Simple beltless dress made in fabrics of unusual color combinations, with a large white collar; named for Carnaby Street, in London, England, where the *Mod, q.v.,* fashions originated in 1960's.

chemise (shem-eez) Straight-cut dress with few darts and no waistline, introduced in 1957 by French designer Hubert de Givenchy, inspired by 1920's dresses. Also called *sack dress. Der.* French, shift or shirt.

cheongsam Contemporary Chinese dress with *mandarin collar, q.v.,* short sleeves, slit on one side of skirt 8″ to 10″ high but not more than 4″ or 5″ above the knee. Also known as the *Hong Kong sheath.*

Chinese or **mandarin d.** Straight-lined dress with slashes on side seams from hem to thigh, with *mandarin neckline, q.v.,* and closing that extends diagonally to the side seam, frequently fastened with frogs of braid or fabric; copied from traditional Chinese woman's dress and a basic style of dress since 1930 in the West. See *cheongsam.*

coat d. Dress fastened down front from neck to hem, like a coat, in double or single-breasted style, belted or unbelted; a classic since the 1930's.

cocktail d. Contemporary term for short evening dress with décolleté neckline, in luxury fabrics; suitable for formal late-afternoon parties, particularly popular in 1950's.

Communion d. White dress worn with short white veil by young girls receiving First Communion in the Roman Catholic Church.

culotte d. Dress with *divided skirt* or knee-length pants combined with blouse in one garment. Also called *culottes, pants-dress, pants-shift.*

dashiki Contemporary dress inspired by garment worn in central Africa, styled with straight lines similar to the chemise, with bell-shaped or kimono sleeves, and made of a distinctive African panel or border print; popular in America late 1960's and early 1970's.

dinner d. Evening dress, *q.v.,* suitable for a formal dinner, frequently made with long sleeves or accompanied by matching jacket and less décolleté than a dress worn for a late reception or for dancing.

dirndl (durn-del) Woman's dress usually of colorful floral print cotton with tight-fitting bodice attached to full gathered skirt, worn over short or long-sleeved white cotton blouse with lace trim and drawstring neckline and with matching solid-color apron. *Der.* From peasant style originating and still worn in Austrian and Bavarian Alps.

electric d. Novelty dress decorated with electric lights wired to a battery at the waïst, designed to be worn at discothèques in the late 1960's.

Empire d. (ahm-peer or em-pire) Dress with high waistline just under the bosom, defined by an inserted piece of fabric or a seam, derived from dress introduced by Empress Josephine during the First Empire in France from 1804 to 1814, with neckline low cut in front and back, small puffed sleeves, gathered ankle-length straight skirt, and a sash tied high; for court wear, a train usually hung from the shoulders.

ensemble Dress and coat designed to be worn together, either in matching or contrasting fabric.

Ethiopian shirt-d. Simple *shift, q.v.,* with slit at neckline trimmed with embroidery, imported from Ethiopia or made domestically in same style and introduced in late 1960's.

evening d. Any dress fashionable for wear at a formal evening party, usually long but varying with the styles; may be very ornate or bare.

flamenco d. Body-molded long dress made with a series of circular cut flounces starting at hips, widening at the hem, inspired by dresses worn by Spanish dancers of the flamenco. Similar to *rumba* dress.

flapper d. Very short-skirted, usually long-torso dress worn in the 1920's, when giddy young girls were called "flappers."

flip-chip d. Make-your-own dress of colored plastic chips or squares and connecting fasteners, put together in any pattern and similar to a *linked dress;* original was introduced in the late 1960's in Paris collection of designer Paco Rabanne.

foil d. Disposable dress made of aluminum foil, sometimes quilted, introduced in 1968 along with *paper dresses, q.v.,* for general wear.

graduation d. Traditional white dress suitable for wear, under an academic robe or without the robe, for school or college graduation ceremony.

granny d. Ankle-length dress in small *calico-print, q.v.,* cotton, with a high round neckline, short sleeves, high waistline, and slightly gathered skirt often ending in ruffled hem. Appeared simultaneously in early 1960's in California and on French Riviera as a beach dress and in London worn in town with old-fashioned shoes and *dog collar necklace, q.v.*

handkerchief d.1. Dress with peplum made from large square of fabric, like a handkerchief, with center opening for waist, ends hanging in points over skirt. 2. Dress with skirt made of several large printed handkerchiefs arranged diagonally to make pointed hemline. Both types popular in 1920's, especially in chiffon for evening dresses. 3. Dress with hemline cut to fall in points as if made of handkerchiefs.

harem d. Symmetrically or asymmetrically draped dress, falling in loose folds to the hem where it is turned under and fastened to a lining giving the hem a draped appearance; usually made of soft clinging fabric. An adaptation of Eastern dress introduced by Paris designers Paul Poiret and Drécoll, *q.q.v.,* in 1910; revived at intervals.

housedress Term used to describe simple inexpensive dresses made of washable fabrics, worn while doing household chores.

Indian d. 1. Dress of suede or buckskin with simple lines and fringed trimming, originally worn by American Indian squaws. 2. Modern interpretation of American Indian dress in leather, suede, or fabric, also called *Pocahontas dress.*

jacket d. See *suit dress.*

jiffy d. 1. Sew-it-yourself dress with limited number of pieces that can be stitched together in a short time. 2. Trademark for a dress, knit quickly on jumbo needles from a kit, or from separately purchased yarn.

Juliet d. Dress in medieval style with high waistline, puff-topped sleeves that loosely fit the lower arm, inspired by the third movie of Shakespeare's play *Romeo and Juliet,* made by Franco Zeffirelli in 1968.

jumper d. Sleeveless and collarless dress usually worn over contrasting blouse or sweater. See *jumper.*

kabuki d. Wrap-around dress, collarless, with *kimono sleeves, q.v.,* and held by a sash; copied from traditional dress of actors in Japanese popular kabuki theater, which is characterized by bizarre makeup and stylized acting.

kiltie d. Dress style adapted from the Scottish kilt: front of skirt plain with wrapped side closing, fastened with a safety pin, remainder of skirt knife-pleated; simple tailored top. Introduced in 1960's.

kimono d. Wrap-around collarless coat-dress held in place with a wide *obi, q.v.,* sash, made with *kimono sleeves, q.v.;* adapted from the classic Japanese kimono, first as a dressing robe and later as a dress in 1960's.

kurta Modern version of a straight-cut Hindu man's shirt which is elaborately trimmed around neck edges, sleeves, and hem with East Indian bead-work.

Lilly Trademark for a simple straight printed-cotton *shift, q.v.,* dress, designed and sold by Lilly Pulitzer of Palm Beach, Florida.

longuette Term for longer-length dresses of the 1970's, including any below-knee, above-ankle length, *Der.* Term coined by fashion-industry newspaper *Women's Wear Daily,* in January, 1970.

mandarin d. See *Chinese dress.*

maternity d. Dress designed for pregnant women, following the general style trends but made with more fullness in front.

maxi-d. Ankle-length dress worn for day or evening; introduced in 1969.

micro-d. Shorter version of the *mini-dress, q.v.,* reaching the top part of the thigh like a tunic blouse, introduced in 1966.

middy d. See *sailor dress.*

midi-d. Term for mid-calf length dress introduced in Paris in late 1960's, challenging the very short *mini-dress, q.v.*

midriff d. One-piece dress with wide inserted piece of fabric fitting snugly around rib-cage, attached to skirt at waistline. See *bare-midriff,* above.

mini-d. Dress with short skirt coming to mid-thigh or about six inches above the knee; first introduced in early 1960's by designer Mary Quant in England as part of the Mod fashions and became a mass fashion by end of 1960's.

molded d. Dress made with fabric that is heat set or molded to take on a sculptured geometrical form; introduced by Parisian couturier Pierre Cardin in fall of 1968.

monk's d. Dress styled like a monk's robe with *cowl* neck, *bell* sleeves, *q.q.v.,* cord belt confining fullness.

muumuu (moo moo) Loose, smock-like ankle-length dress in bold Hawaiian floral-printed fabric adapted from dresses worn on Pacific islands. *Der.* From the type of modest gown put on the natives by missionaries about one hundred years ago.

one-shoulder d. Any dress with only one sleeve and/or shoulder, baring the other shoulder and arm.

pants-d. Term introduced in 1967 for dress with skirt divided like trousers, accepted for school and business in late 1960's, longer version worn for evening. See *culotte*.

paper d. Dress made of soft paper (similar to a non-woven rayon fabric) and disposable instead of washable; introduced in 1968 for a brief popularity.

pearl d. Novelty dress adapted from Oriental fashion consisting of draped strands of pearls at top and long hanging strands for the skirt, worn over a body stocking; introduced by a jewelry firm, Richelieu Pearls, and designed by Bill Smith in 1969.

peasant d. 1. Native dress of farm women in many European countries consisting of snug bodice, gathered skirt, *puffed* sleeves, and *drawstring* neckline worn with a black laced-front *corselet* and *apron,* similar to *dirndl, q.q.v.* 2. Any dress cut along lines of European peasant dresses.

pinafore d. Dress with its own bib-top apron tied in back, popular for children. Also called *Alice in Wonderland* or *apron dress.*

polo-shirt d. See *T-shirt dress.*

poor-boy shift Knitted dress made in rib stitch, like an elongated *poor-boy sweater, q.v.*

poster d. Any dress imprinted with a blown-up photograph, a brief fad in the mid 1960's. Originally made of paper, later photographs printed on fabrics.

princess d. Dress cut with bodice and skirt all in one, fitted by seams from shoulder to hem with no belt or waist seam. The Empress Eugénie of France wore a princess-cut dress designed by *Worth, q.v.,* in the 1850's, and the style is now considered a classic cut.

rain d. Dress made of plastic or of fabric treated for water repellency; innovation of the 1960's.

rumba d. Ankle-length dress with a skirt consisting of a series of ruffles, style popularized by Brazilian Carmen Miranda in movies of the 1930's and '40's. *Der.* Named after the South American dance. Similar to *flamenco dress, q.v.*

Russian shirt-d. Dress with high neckline banded in braid and closed on the side, with slightly full sleeves gathered and banded at the wrist. Also called *Zhivago dress,* from clothes worn in 1965 movie of novel *Dr. Zhivago* by Boris Pasternak.

sack d. See *chemise.*

safari d. Tailored dress introduced in Paris by House of Dior in 1960's similar to *bush coat* or *safari jacket, q.q.v.* with convertible neckline, two bellows pockets on the chest and two on the skirt.

sailor d. Dress with *sailor collar* or *middy-blouse* effect, *q.q.v.,* trimmed with rows of braid in nautical style, very popular for boys and girls from 1860 to 1930 and for women from 1890 on. Also called *middy dress.*

sari (sah-ree) Principal garment of Hindu women, consisting of a length of silk or cotton, often delicately embroidered and banded in gold, wrapped about the waist and pleated at one side with loose end thrown over shoulder or head; worn over bust-length bodice with bare midriff. Adopted by Westerners, since early 1940's, with many variations. Also spelled *saree.*

sarong d. Dress with wrap-around skirt, a strapless top. *Der.* From native dress of Polynesian women, popularized by actress Dorothy Lamour in movies of 1930–40's.

see-through d. Sheer dress with bands of glitter at strategic places, usually worn with body stocking underneath; introduced by Paris designers Pierre Cardin and Yves Saint Laurent in 1966.

sheath Straight, narrow fitted dress, usually with no marked waistline but shaped to body by vertical darts, ease of skirt obtained by inverted pleats at sides or center back; popular in 1950's, early 1960's.

shift Straight-lined basic dress of 1960's, hanging away from body, similar to *chemise dress, q.v.,* of 1957 but slightly fitted by diagonal darts. Also see *skimmer* and *A-line.*

shirt-d. Straight dress cut like a man's shirt, buttoning down front, sometimes with hem slit and rounded at sides like tails of a man's shirt—a variation of classic coat dress.

shirtwaist d. Dress with top styled like a tailored shirt, usually buttoned from neck to waist, with either a full or straight skirt; introduced in the 1930's, very popular in 1940's and now a classic; shown by many designers in long versions for evening wear. See *shirt-dress,* above.

skating d. Close-fitting, long-sleeved bodice with brief hip-length skirt flaring from a natural waist, as worn by Norwegian skating star Sonja Henie in movies in 1930's; newer version with long torso and flared micro-skirt is worn by 1968 Olympics champion Peggy Fleming.

skimmer Name for *A-Line dress* or a *shift, q.q.v.,* that hangs away from the body.

slip-d. Simple bias-cut dress with fitted top, straps over shoulders, and no waistline, a revival in 1966 of bias-cut dress of the 1920's and '30's as worn by movie star Jean Harlow. Also see *bias cut.*

smock d. Dress with bodice and skirt cut in one piece and slightly gathered onto a high yoke, usually worn without a belt. Similar to the *baby dress, q.v.* Re-introduced in 1970 by designers of French ready-to-wear.

square-dance d. Pioneer American ankle-length dress usually of small-flowered print cotton, with puffed sleeves and wide, full, circular skirt, frequently ruffled at the hem; worn for square dancing.

squaw d. Full-skirted, minutely pleated dress, elaborately embroidered on long-sleeved bodice and in bands on skirt, may be similar to *square-dance dress, q.v.*

strapless d. Décolleté dress ending just at top of bosom, sometimes with sleeves attached under arms but without shoulders or straps; held in place by *boning, q.v.* or by shirring *elastic* thread or by using *stretch* fabric, *q.q.v.*

suit d. Term used in 1960's for a jacket and dress *ensemble, q.v.,* which resembles a tailored suit.

sundress Dress with a minimal top,

often with bathing-suit-style shoulder straps, designed for summer wear and sun bathing, introduced in the 1930's.

sweater d. Knitted dress styled like a long sweater, with or without knit-in waistline; e.g., *poor-boy shift* or *cardigan dress, q.q.v.;* introduced in 1940's and revived in the 1960's.

Swirl Trademark for a back-wrapped *housedress, q.v.*

tennis d. Short-skirted hip-length dress, usually white, with matching panties underneath, worn when playing tennis.

tent d. Pyramid-shaped dress with fullness starting at neckline and flaring to hem, sometimes *accordion pleated, q.v.* Introduced by Paris designer Pierre Cardin in 1967.

three-armhole d. A dress that wraps around the body one and a half times, so that one arm goes through two armholes, the other through one (see drawing, page 153).

thrift-shop d. Term used in the 1960's for second-hand dresses of the 1920's, '30's, and '40's found in American thrift shops, in Paris flea markets and in London's Portobello Road antique shops. Popular with young individualists on low budgets, sparked 1970's fashions for limp fabrics, muted-color prints, and old-fashioned trimmings.

torso d. Low-waistline dress with the fitted top extending well down over the hips; skirt may be gathered, pleated, or flared; popular in early 1940's, revived in 1970's.

toga d. Asymmetric dress or at-home robe styled with one shoulder bare, the other covered, reminiscent of Roman toga; an innovation of the 1960's.

trapeze d. Unconstructed dress, narrow shoulders, wide swing at hem; designed by Yves Saint Laurent for House of Dior in Paris in 1958.

T-shirt d. Simple knit dress styled like an elongated *T-shirt, q.v.,* innovation of late 1950's.

tunic d. Two-piece dress with a long *overblouse, q.v.,* worn over a separate narrow skirt or a one-piece dress designed to give this effect.

undershirt d. Simple knit dress similar to man's undershirt, introduced by Paris designer André Courrèges in 1969.

usha Long or mini-length dress imported from India made in native border-printed fabrics with high-waisted effect by means of elastic band below bust; popular in 1970's.

wedding d. Any dress worn for a wedding ceremony, traditionally long and of white satin, faille, or lace, with or without a train. Also called *bridal dress.*

weskit d. Tailored dress, usually full sleeved, combined with a vest.

wrap d. Dress fastened by wrapping half of a double front or back across to the opposite side and securing with a tie or by button.

dress clip Metal hook, attached at the waistline or belt, worn by women in the 1840's to lift the skirt when walking. Also see *dress holder.*

dress coat See *swallow-tailed* under *coats.*

dress elevator See *porte-jupe Pompadour.*

dress frock coat Man's double-breasted *cutaway frock* coat, exposing the shirt in front; worn from 1870 to 1890.

dress holder Elaborate device used for holding up skirt in the 1870's, made with two pendant chains and clips.

dress improver Polite term for *bustle, q.v.*, worn at intervals from 1840 to late 1890's.

dressing gown or **robe** See *robes.*

dressing sacque Short, loose hip-length woman's jacket worn in boudoir in late 19th, early 20th centuries. Also spelled *dressing sack.*

dress lounge jacket British term for man's semi-formal evening jacket from 1888 on. Originally worn only in absence of ladies, later called *dinner jacket, q.v.*

dressmaker Person who makes clothing for private customers from pattern to finished garment either by hand or by machine. From 1850 through 1920's, before ready-to-wear was plentiful, dressmakers often worked in customers' homes to prepare wardrobes.

dressmaker bathing suit See *swimsuits.*

dressmaker coat See *coats.*

dressmaker's brim Hat brim, usually on a fabric hat, that has closely spaced rows of machine stitching or stitched tucks around it.

dressmaker's form See *dummy.*

dressmaker suit See *suits.*

dress shirt See *shirts.*

dress suit Man's formal evening suit. See *full dress* under *suits.*

dress Stewart tartan See *tartans.*

dress Wellington Boot made with

fitted stocking reaching to the knee, attached to a shoe similar to an *evening slipper,* worn inside the dress trousers or *pantaloons, q.q.v.;* worn by men with evening clothes from 1830 to 1850.

drill Cotton twill. See *fabrics.*

drip-dry Describing fabric that needs no pressing after washing, achieved by weaving with man-made yarns and/or by giving a surface treatment with synthetic resins that resist wrinkles, *e.g. durable press, q.v.*

driving cape or **sac** See *Albert overcoat.*

driving gloves See *gloves.*

drop earrings See *earrings.*

drop-front Descriptive of pants that are fastened by two buttoned plackets on either side of the center front, allowing the front panel to drop down when unbuttoned; used frequently on *jodhpurs* or other *riding breeches, q.q.v.,* and in the past on U.S. Navy seaman's pants, *i.e., bell-bottoms.*

dropped shoulders See *shoulders.*

dropped skirt 1. Skirt set on a low waistline; also called a *torso skirt, q.v.* 2. Sewing term in late 19th and early 20th centuries for a skirt made separate from the lining, both attached to the same waist-seam.

dropped waistline See *waistlines.*

dropping See *letting out.*

druid 1. Term used for *cotton duck, q.v.*, in Great Britain and Australia. 2. United States term for *monk's cloth, q.v.*

druid's cloth See *monk's cloth* under *fabrics.*

drum farthingale Plate-like projection extending outward from waist from which woman's skirt drops straight to floor; worn in 16th to 18th centuries. Also called *tambour farthingale*.

drum major's hat See *shako* under *hats*.

Du Barry corsage (dew bar-ee) Bodice with a *stomacher*-shaped, *q.v.*, or wide *V-shaped* front, worn by women in the 1850's and 1860's, adapted from the style worn by Comtesse Du Barry (1746–1793), mistress of Louis XV of France. Also called *corsage à la Du Barry*.

Du Barry costume Style of dress worn by Marie Jeanne Bécu, Comtesse Du Barry (1746–1793), last mistress of Louis XV of France, consisting of a fitted bodice with low décolletage trimmed with lace ruching, elbow-length sleeves, and a full skirt.

Du Barry mantle *Dolman*-style, *q.v.*, wrap with smocked yoke front and back, fur collar, and large full cuffs, lavishly trimmed with ribbon bows and streamers at neck, below yoke, sleeves, and at center back; worn in early 1880's. *Der.* Named for Comtesse Du Barry, see above.

Du Barry sleeve Double puffed sleeve, one puff above elbow and another below it; worn in mid 1830's. *Der.* Named for Comtesse Du Barry, see above.

Dubinsky, David American labor leader active in the organization of the International Ladies Garment Workers Union and president from 1932 to 1966

duchess Late 17th-century term for knot or bow of ribbon worn as part of the *Fontanges, q.v.*, hairstyle.

duchesse See *fabrics*.

duchesse lace See *laces*.

duchesse pleat Term used in 1870's for back pleats of a skirt, usually four *box pleats, q.v.*, either side of center back placket or seam.

Duchess of Windsor The former Wallis Warfield Simpson, an American divorcee who married Edward VIII of England, causing his abdication and assumption of title of Duke of Windsor in 1936; world famous for her impeccable taste and conservative fashion leadership, usually dressed by French couture; her wedding gown, designed by *Mainbocher, q.v.* in Paris, became most copied dress in world, available at every price level.

duck See *fabrics*.

duckbills Broad-toed flat shoes worn in England from about 1490 to 1540, shown in paintings of Henry VIII.

duck-hunter Striped linen jacket worn by English waiters in 1840's.

ducks Trousers worn by men, late 19th century, made of *duck fabric, q.v.* Also see *white ducks* under *pants*.

duck's-foot fan Early folding fan that opened to one-fourth of a circle, made of alternate strips of mica and vellum with an ivory handle; introduced to France from Italy by Catherine de' Medici in mid 16th century.

ducktail haircut See *hairstyles*.

dude 1. American term at a Western ranch for someone from the city or the East Coast. 2. Term used in

1890's for a *dandy, q.v.,* an affected or fastidious man. 3. 1960's counter-culture slang for any man whether well-dressed or not.

dude jeans See *pants.*

dueling blouse or **shirt** See *blouses* and *shirts.*

duffel See *fabrics.*

duffel bag Large utility bag of heavy fabric with drawstring top used by men in the Armed Forces, widely copied as civilian travel bag or purse. See *handbags.*

duffel coat See *coats.*

Duke of Windsor (1894–1973) Briefly Edward VIII of England, married in 1936 to American Wallis Warfield Simpson, and known in international society as a fashion leader. As the Prince of Wales, he influenced men's fashion greatly in the 1920's and '30's, particularly the formal overcoat, derby, double-breasted suits, and *plus fours, q.v.*

dummy Dressmaking form in shape of human body on which the designer or home sewer drapes clothes before sewing.

dunce cap Tall conical cap, sometimes marked with a D, formerly worn in school by students who failed in their lessons. Sometimes wrongly called *fool's cap, q.v.*

dungaree See *fabrics.*

dungarees See *pants.*

dunstable Hat of plaited straw originally made in Dunstable, England.

duo-length coat See *coats.*

duplex printing Method of printing same design on both sides of fabric to simulate a yarn-dyed woven pattern, e.g., herringbone or checks.

duppioni See *doupioni.*

durable finish Fabric finish that should last during the normal life of a fabric, such as glazing on chintz and *durable press, q.v.,* below.

durable press Collective term for all finishes on garments and fabrics that need no pressing, even after repeated washings. Resins, fixed to garments or fabrics by a high-temperature curing oven, become an integral part of the fabric, giving it complete stabilization.

dust cap Cap made of handkerchief, or circular piece of fabric, hemmed on outer edge and gathered by elastic, worn by women for housework in early 20th century.

duster 1. Pongee-colored lightweight full-length coat worn when riding in an automobile in early 20th century to protect clothing from dust. Worn with *automobile veil, q.v.* 2. See *robes.* 3. See *coats.*

dust gown 16th century term for a *safeguard, q.v.,* or overskirt worn by women to protect the dress when riding horseback.

dust ruffle Ruffle inside of hem of full-length dress or petticoat to protect dress from becoming soiled when walking outdoors in late 19th and early 20th century. Also called *balayeuse* or *street sweeper.*

Dutch bob See *hairstyles.*

Dutch bonnet See *Dutch cap,* below.

Dutch-boy cap See *caps.*

Dutch-boy heels See *heels.*

Dutch breeches Long full trousers of dark-gray fabric pulled tight at the ankles, worn on the Dutch island of Marken.

Dutch cap Cap worn by women and girls in Volendam, Holland, made of lace or embroidered muslin fitted to the head with a slight peak at the crown and flaring wings at sides of face; made fashionable by *Irene Castle, q.v.,* famous ballroom dancer in 1920's. Sometimes used as bridal cap. Also called *Dutch bonnet.*

Dutch coat Man's jacket worn in late 14th and 15th centuries.

dutchess Misspelling for *duchess, q.v.*

Dutchman Triangular wedge placed between insole and outsole of shoe to improve posture of wearer, also used between layers of a built-up heel to adjust heel pitch.

Dutch waist Woman's bodice without a point in center front; worn with the *wheel farthingale, q.v.,* about 1580 to 1620.

duvetyn See *fabrics.*

Duvillier wig (doo-vee-yee-aye) Man's wig of early 18th century, dressed high on top of head with long, shoulder-length hair. Named after a French *perruquier* or wig maker. Also called *long Duvillier, falbala,* or *furbelow wig.*

dux collar Man's narrow standing collar with front corners turned down; worn in latter half of the 19th century.

dyed-in-the-wool Term for wool made of fibers dyed before yarn is spun. See *stock-dyeing, heather yarn,* and *gray flannel.*

dyeing 1. Impregnation of fibers, yarns, or fabrics with natural or synthetic coloring agents that are relatively permanent. 2. Coloring of furs by *dip dyeing, brush dyeing, blending,* or *tipping, q.q.v.* 3. Coloring of leathers by *dip dyeing* or *brush dyeing, q.q.v.*

dyes Color-producing substances, either natural or synthetic, that can be permanently impregnated into fibers, fabrics, furs, or leathers.

Dynacurl Trademark for fur-like fabric made of Dynel, *q.v.,* modacrylic fiber, the cotton backing cloth is woven and heatset, curled Dynel yarns are stitched to backing cloth with Schiffli machine giving appearance of Persian lamb fur.

Dynel Trademark owned by Union Carbide Co. for a modacrylic staple and tow. Three main varieties used for clothing and accessories, type 150 for wigs and hair pieces, type 180 for pile fabrics, type 183 for knitted pile and fur fabrics.

DROP EARRING

PIERCED-LOOK EARRINGS

CHANDELIER EARRING

E

E Shoe sizes: Letter indicating a width; widths run from AAAAA to EEEEE with A's being the narrowest and E's the widest.

earmuffs 1. Two disks of fur, felt, Orlon acrylic pile, or other warm fabric, fastened to a strap and tying under chin or on a springy metal band that fits over top of the head; worn to keep the ears warm in winter. 2. A pair of flaps on sides of a cap which may turn up, buttoned to top of cap, or down, unbuttoned, to cover the ears. 3. A woman's hairdo. See *hairstyles.*

earring Decorative ornament or jewel worn on or pendant from the ear, attached by *wire loops* or *posts* through pierced earlobes or held on by *screw* or *clip backs.* Worn now by women but historically worn by kings, nobles, and soldiers in Far Eastern countries; earrings were made to match necklaces, bracelets, and brooches after 1840 and were usually of genuine gold and gem stones. Contemporary styles range from simplest molded plastic through handcrafted metals and semi-precious stones to costly precious jewels. Some contemporary styles:

EARRINGS:

Art Déco e. Earring made in unusual geometrical forms, popularized in the late 1960's, copied from patterns of the 1920's shown in the 1925 Paris Exhibition of *Arts décoratifs.*

ball e. Earring in the shape of a round bead usually suspended from a tiny linked chain, made of gemstones, plastic, glass, or other material.

button e. Round flat earring like a button, made in various sizes, often of imitation pearls or plastic.

chandelier e. Long dangling oversized earring, made of metal or crystal beads hanging like crystals on a chandelier.

changeable e. Earring usually made with a selection of colored plastic disks that may be snapped into metal circlet; a 1960's fashion.

clip e. Earring that fastens to the ear by means of a spring clip that snaps against back of the ear to secure it; an innovation of the 1930's.

dots See *micro dots,* below.

drop e. Any earring in which the lower part swings free. See *pendant earring,* below.

gypsy e. Large *hoop* earring usually of brass or gold-colored metal, worn on pierced ear, inspired by plain brass circles worn by gypsies.

hoop e. See *gypsy earring,* above.

micro dots Very tiny earrings worn in pierced ears, the dot not much larger than the post to which it is fastened; popular in the late 1960's. Also called *posts* and *polka dots.*

165

mobile e. Delicate wire drop earring like small mobile sculpture with jewels or metal objects hanging from it, carefully balanced so it is constantly in motion.

pendant e. Same as *drop earring*, above, one of the earliest styles and popular for single genuine gemstones or pearls.

pierced-ear rings See *hoops, posts, and wires.*

pierced-look e. Screw-on earring designed for unpierced ear, with delicate band of metal coming under ear to front where it stops abruptly, giving appearance of passing through ear; popular in 1960's.

posts Basic earrings designed for pierced ears, similar to studs; ornament on front, post goes through ear and fastens with a screw-on or snap-on back.

screw e. Earring for unpierced ears, with screw behind the ear which can be tightened to hold it in place.

Wing-back e. Trademark for earring with patented attachment shaped to match convolutions inside the ear and inserted so as to be invisible while holding earring in place; designed by Judith McCann in early 1950's.

wires Earrings for pierced ears which have a thin wire, usually gold, that passes through the ear; usually dangling objects are attached to the wire or the wires may be worn separately.

ear string Black ribbon or strands of silk worn through pierced left ear by men during latter part of 16 century.

eartab See *earmuff.*

earthquake gown Warm woman's nightgown suitable for wear outdoors, made in England in 1750 in anticipation of third earthquake after two earlier quakes had taken place in London.

ease Factor taken into consideration when drafting a pattern, allowing extra measure at bust, hip, and waist so garment will be comfortable, not skin tight.

ecclesiastical vestments Garments worn by the clergy for religious services. See *alb, cassock, chasuble, chimere, cope, cotta, dalmatic, Geneva gown, miter, surplice,* and *stole.*

echantillon (eh-shawnt-e-yon) French word meaning sample, used for a swatch of fabric.

echarpe (eh-sharp) French word for scarf.

echelle (eh-shell) Decorative trim on front of woman's bodice, made with braid, lace, or ribbon bows arranged in ladder-like effect; popular from end of 17th century to end of 18th century. *Der.* French, ladder.

Eclipse tie Trade name for woman's shoe made with one pair of eyelets, usually with pointed tongue.

écrasé (eh-kras-eh) French term for creased or crushed leather.

edge 1. Shoe-industry term for part of shoe sole that is visible around outside of shoe to place where heel is attached, may be round, beveled, square, etc. 2. A late 15th- and early 16th-century term for an ornamental border, usually made by goldsmith, used on a headdress. Also called *neyge, age, oegge,* or *egge.*

edging Narrow decorative border of lace, embroidery, braid, or fringe, used for trimming on clothing, particularly at hem, sleeve and neck.

edozuma Japanese *kimono, g.v.,* worn only by married women, originally a pattern in the fabric on lower front from knees to hem, later word was transferred to garment decorated in this manner.

Edwardian 1. Period from 1901 to 1910 when Edward VII, son of Queen Victoria, was King of England, a period noted for men's fitted *frock* or suit coats, tall hats, and women's clothes in the *Gibson Girl* or *Merry Widow, q.q.v.,* style, with large decorative hats. 2. Middle 1960's revival of these styles for men's and women's *suits* and *jackets, q.q.v.*

Edwardian coat Man's high-waisted *frock coat, q.v.,* usually black, double-breasted, fitted and long to below knee, with high, notched satin-faced lapels showing sliver of *waistcoat* and stiff white collar; worn with high *silk hat* and *cane, q.q.v.,* in Edwardian period, 1901–1914. Also see *coats.*

eelskin masher trousers Very tight trousers worn in mid 1880's by *mashers,* or *dandies, q.q.v. Der.* Literally, as tight as an eel's skin.

eelskin sleeve Tight-fitting lace-trimmed sleeve worn by women in the 17th century.

eel skirt Woman's gored skirt cut on the bias fitting very snugly over the hips and flared slightly from the knees to hem; worn in late 1890's.

egge Variant of *edge, q.v.*

eggshell finish Dull finish given to fabric by running it between engraved rollers for a rough effect.

Egham, Staines, and Windsor Nickname used in early 19th century for *tricorn hat, q.v. Der.* From geographical location of three English towns that form triangle on map.

egret feathers (eg-ret) See *aigrette* under *feathers.*

Egyptian collar Wide flat necklace made in ancient Egypt of beads, shells, seeds, faience, and semi-precious stones in various colors, sometimes mounted in gold, or of papyrus or fabric with geometrical lotus designs embroidered in colored wool.

Egyptian styles Early costumes consisted of plain wraparound loin cloths called *shendyts,* and simple wrap dresses coming to below bust and held on with one or two straps; later costumes were more elaborate and made of sheer accordion-pleated fabric. See *Egyptian collar, Egyptian sandals, claft, utchat.*

Egyptian cotton High-quality long-staple, strong, lustrous cotton produced along the Nile River, staple averages one-eight to one and one-half inches. Imported to make threads, laces, and fine fabrics. Types include *Ashmouni, Maarad,* and *Sakellarides.*

Egyptian lace See *laces.*

Egyptian sandal Footwear worn by ancient Egyptians, fastened by a strap from between the toes almost to the ankle where it attaches to a strap over instep fastening to the sole, e.g., sandal found in King Tut's tomb made entirely of gold.

Egyptian wig 1. Long black wig with straight bangs and square cut at bottom, made on a framework that elevated it from the head, making a protection from the sun, often with intricate braiding interspersed with gold links; worn by ancient Egyptians. 2. Colored short wigs in layered style in blue or red worn in ancient Egypt.

eiderdown See *fabrics.*

eider yarn See *yarns.*

eighths Height of heels of shoes measured in eighths of an inch; hence a $^{16}/_8$-inch heel is a 2-inch heel; a $^4/_8$ heel is $^1/_2$ inch high, etc.

Eisenhower jacket World War II battle jacket, short, bloused to waistband, large patch pockets; worn by President Dwight D. Eisenhower when he was a general in the U.S. Army. See *battle jacket* in *sport jackets* under *jackets.*

Eisteddfod costume (a-steth-vo-di) Costume of Wales originating in 17th century, worn during Welsh national competitive song festivals, consisting of gown called *pais-a-gwn back, q.v.,* apron, square scarf, ruffled muslin cap tied on with ribbons under chin over which is worn a broad flat-brimmed polished beaver hat with tall tapered crown, and a large checked or plaid shawl or long circular cape with a hood.

eis wool See *yarns.*

elastic Stretchable tape woven originally with rubber yarn now made with *Lastex* (a trademarked rubber-core yarn) or *spandex* (man-made stretch yarn) yarn covered with cotton or nylon, used at waistlines of boxer shorts, half-slips, and panties and at sleeve hems or any other place where stretch is needed.

elastic bracelet See *bracelets.*

elasticity Ability of fabric or yarn to stretch and return to its original shape. See *hose.*

elasticized 1. Describing fabric made with natural or synthetic rubber yarns for stretchability, e.g., Lastex and spandex core yarns. 2. Use of stretch yarns on sewing machine to form rows of gathers for a top, waistline, or band at end of sleeves or neckline; very popular in early 1970's. 3. Use of *elastic, q.v.,* sewed to a garment or inserted through a tunnel of fabric at waistband of pants or skirts, hem of sleeves, and for waistbands of petticoats, panties, trunks, or pajamas.

elastic round hat Patented collapsible hat of 1812, which could be flattened and carried under the arm, forerunner of the *Gibus, q.v.*

elastic-sided boot Ankle-high boot, introduced for men and women about 1837, with India-rubber insert on each side, patented by James Dowie.

élastique See *fabrics.*

elastomer (e-las-to-mere) Textile term for a yarn with high stretch qualities made from natural rubber, segmented polyurethane, or other sythetic rubber material, used either covered or uncovered. See *elastomeric yarn* under *yarns.*

elbow cuff Turned-back cuff attached to woman's elbow-length sleeves, wide on outside of arm and fitting more closely at bend of elbow; worn early 18th century.

electric blue Brilliant greenish-blue color resembling the color of spark of electricity.

electric comb Electrically powered

vibrating comb for the hair that fluffs as it combs, producing a neat but not slick effect; introduced in the early 1970's.

electric dress See *dresses.*

electric mole Term used in early 20th century for *rabbit fur, q.v.,* prior to the Fur Labeling Act of 1938.

electric seal Incorrect terminology for *rabbit* that is sheared and then carved in ridges; correctly called *electric-processed rabbit.*

electric socks See *socks.*

electric vest See *vests.*

electrified lambskin Lambskins tanned with hair intact and given an electrical treatment that gives the hair a silky texture.

elephant-leg pants See *pants.*

elephant sleeve Large sleeve of early 1830's, usually made of sheer fabric; full at the shoulder, hanging down somewhat in the form of an elephant's ear and close-fitting at the wrist.

elevator shoes See *shoes.*

Elizabethan styles Garments and accessories worn during the reign of Elizabeth I of England, 1558–1603. Men's costume consists of *slashed* and *paned trunk hose* and *doublet, q.q.v.,* with slashed sleeves and variations of the *ruff, q.v.,* women's dress had barrel-shaped skirt, standing lace collar and slashed sleeves. Costume of this period also called *Shakespearean costume.*

elkside Misleading term for cattlehides finished to look like elk leather; should be labeled *elk-finished cowhide.*

elliptic collar (eh-lip-tic) Patented detachable man's collar with the front cut higher than the back, sometimes worn reversed, in the early 1850's.

EMBA mink See *mink* under *furs.*

embossed cotton See *fabrics.*

embossed crepe See *fabrics.*

embossing 1. Process using metal plates to impress a pattern, e.g., on leather, Corfam, or other plastic to imitate alligator, lizard, snakeskin, or turtle. See also *printed leather.* 2. Use of metal rollers to imprint a texture on fabrics, which gives a permanent finish on manmade fibers when heat set.

embroidery Fancy needle-work or trimming using colored yarn or *embroidery floss* (soft cotton or silk thread or metallic thread), usually done by hand, but may be made on a *Schiffli machine, q.v.* In primitive times, straws or grasses were used to embroider with a bone needle; gold embroidery was first made by Assyrians, copied by Egyptians, Greeks, and Romans and each country in Europe developed its own type of embroidery. Needlework has been a popular diversion for women since medieval times. *Canvas work* is embroidered on a special open-weave cotton or linen called *embroidery* or *Penelope canvas* by counting threads in each stitch to create the design; *crewel* or other embroidery done on *cloth* follows the design without regard for the number of threads of the cloth. Some types of embroidery are listed below; stitches may be found in the *stitches* category.

EMBROIDERIES:

aloe-thread e. Aloe fibers, such as agave, Ceylon bowstring hemp, and piteira, embroidered in a raised effect.

Anglo-Saxon e. Long surface stitches *couched* (see *stitches*) with metal or silk threads in an outline effect.

Appenzell e. (ap-en-tsell) Fine Swiss *drawn work, q.v.,* used chiefly on handkerchiefs and fine muslin, a cottage industry in Switzerland. *Der.* Named for town in Switzerland where it originated.

Arrasene e. (ar-a-seen) Embroidery with a velvet-like effect made by using Arrasene thread, made of silk or wool, resembling *chenille, q.v. Der.* From town of Arras, France.

arrowhead Triangular-shaped embroidery used at ends of pockets, pleats, or for decorative effect.

Ayrshire e. See *Madeira.*

back-stitch e. Outline embroidery similar to *Holbein work, q.v.,* but single faced instead of double. See *stitches.*

Beauvais e. (bo-vay) Tapestry-like embroidery, small stitches completely covering ground, done in many colors. *Der.* Named after the French city where it originated.

black work Embroidery done in black silk on white linen, fashionable from 1530's to 1630's, sometimes worked in an all-over continuous scroll design; used for collars, cuffs, smocks, and handkerchiefs.

bonnaz (bo-nahz) Machine embroidery, sometimes on canvas base cloth, with all types of designs possible as the operator can make the machine go in any direction; used on sweaters, dresses, hats, gloves, and handbags.

Breton work Peasant embroidery in colored silk and metallic threads made in floral and geometric designs, largely done in *chain stitch, q.v.* Also called *Brittany work.*

brocade e. Embroidery made by needlework done over designs of brocade fabric.

broderie anglaise (brod-e-ree onh-glaise) Eyelet embroidery, holes punched and re-embroidered, same as *Madeira, q.v.*

bullion e. (bool-yon) Embroidery done with gold wire or with gold or silver threads or cords; originated with the Phrygians.

Byzantine e. Appliqué work combined with decorative stitches done in the 19th century.

California e. 1. Leather stitching and braiding. 2. Primitive pre-Spanish embroidery made in California by Indians with fish-bone needles and animal substance for thread.

candlewick e. Tufts made with thick, loosely-twisted cotton yarn called *candlewicking* and a large needle, several stitches taken in same place making loops that are cut to form a fluffy tuft.

Cashmere work Rich, vari-colored embroidery done in India, with needlework covering almost entire surface, used for shawls.

chenille e. (shen-neel) Embroidery originating in France, using fine *chenille yarn, q.v.,* in flat stitches producing a soft, velvet-like surface on the pattern.

Chinese e. Single or double-faced embroidery worked in silk in complicated patterns either shaded or plain.

Colbert e. (col-bare) Embroidery made with colored threads outlining the designs and background covered with satin stitches.

crewel Coarse embroidery made with heavy colored yarns, usually a loosely twisted two-ply worsted, on a heavy plain-weave fabric, motifs such as leaves and flowers filled in with large stitches.

cross-stitch e. Embroidered pattern made with small X's on plain ground, usually done on *canvas* by counting threads.

cut work 1. Embroidery made by cutting designs out of fabric and embroidering the cut edges with *purl stitch, bars* frequently used to connect larger areas. 2. Term used in 16th century to refer to *dagging, q.v.,* or a *dagged border* of a garment, *e.g.,* motifs such as leaves, flames, scallops, etc.

Czechoslovakian e. Bright-colored cotton, silk, or wool threads used in geometric designs on linen, made by counting stitches or using a traced pattern.

Delhi work *Chain-* and *satin-stitch* embroidery made in India with metal and silk threads on satin or other fabrics.

drawn work Open-work embroidery made by removing some threads in each direction in the fabric and interlacing remaining yarns with embroidery stitches.

English e. See *Madeira.*

eyelet e. Holes punched out and embroidery worked around the hole, done by hand or on a *Schiffli machine, q.v.* see *Madeira embroidery.*

flame e. Embroidery done in zigzag patterns. See *Florentine embroidery.*

Florentine e. Embroidery done on canvas in zigzag patterns and in shaded colors, also called *flame stitch* from its effect.

Genoese e. Embroidery done by *buttonhole-stitching* over a cord on muslin or linen, then cutting fabric away from between parts of the design; formerly used for dress and undergarment trimmings.

grass e. American Indian embroidery using colored grasses as threads, usually done on skins.

gros point (groh pwanh) *Canvas* embroidery done with all-over *tapestry* or *tent stitches,* crossing canvas threads diagonally at each intersection; the same stitch in finer yarn on fine canvas is called *petit point.*

hardanger e. Needlework made in diamond or square patterns on coarse linen or open canvas, part of the material cut and threads pulled out between stitches to make designs; native to Norway.

hemstitching 1. Embroidery in which several parallel yarns are removed from the fabric and fine stitches used to catch groups of three or four cross threads at regular intervals giving an even open-work arrangement. 2. This embroidery done on table linens at the edge of the hem—holding and decorating at one time.

Holbein work (hole-bine) Delicate reversible outline embroidery done in *double-running stitch, q.v.,* using exact geometrical or conventional designs, popular for trimming in the 16th century and named after the painter Hans Holbein, 1465–1524, because it was so frequently painted by him. Also called *Rumanian embroidery* and *black work.*

huckaback e. *Darned* type of embroidery done on huckaback toweling by working the stitches between surface yarns of the toweling.

Hungarian point Zigzag designs done on canvas, same as *Florentine embroidery.*

inverted-T e. See *Mathilde.*

inverted-Y e. See *Mathilde.*

Japanese e. Elaborate embroidery worked with colored silk or metal threads in *satin stitch* forming an intricate design or scene, also includes padded shaded embroidery.

laid e. Cord or vellum overlaid with stitches to form embroidery. Also called *gimped embroidery.*

liquid e. Lines squeezed from a tube of special paint to outline designs on cloth, permanent and washable and resembling colored-thread embroidery.

Madeira e. (ma-deer-a) Eyelet embroidery, cut or punched and then overcast, with openings arranged in floral or conventional designs, done on fine lawn, linen, or longcloth. Also called *broderie anglaise, Ayrshire, English,* or *Swiss embroidery. Der.* From Island of Madeira where work was originally done by nuns.

Mathilde e. Wide vertical band of embroidery used on front of woman's dress about 1804–5; later a band added around hem of dress and the combination called an inverted T or inverted Y.

Mexican drawn work Removal of some yarns in both warp and filling of fabric, usually cotton, and securing the remainder by fine stitches giving a lacy effect.

Moravian work Type of cotton embroidery known from about 1850 as *broderie anglaise.* See *Madeira embroidery.*

needle point All-over wool embroidery worked on open canvas, with yarn in a variety of *tapestry* stitches either horizontally across the rows or diagonally, making it double-faced. Used for upholstery, slippers, and handbags. Regular sized stitches called *gros point, q.v.,* small stitches called *petit point, q.v.*

needle tapestry work Embroidery worked in a variety of small stitches on canvas to resemble woven tapestries.

net e. See *tulle embroidery.*

openwork Embroidery made by drawing, cutting, or pulling aside threads of fabric to form open spaces in the design.

petit point see *gros point* and *needle point,* above.

Philippine e. Hand-made embroidery done in dainty floral motifs on fine linen by native women in the Philippine Islands; used on lingerie and linens.

piqué e. (pee-kay) Embroidery worked on firm fabric with white thread using corded outlines and various filling stitches; used for children's garments.

pulled work See *punch work,* below.

punch or **punched work** Embroidery of open-work type made by pulling certain threads aside with a needle or stiletto and securing them with embroidery stitches. Also called *pulled work.*

raised e. Embroidery done in the *satin stitch* over *padding stitches* to give a raised effect in the design; used for monograms, scallops, etc., also called *stump work, q.v.*

rococo e. Type of embroidery made with very narrow ribbon, often called *China ribbon.*

Rumanian e. See *Holbein work.*

Russian e. 1. Embroidery done mainly in outline designs on Holland linen. 2. Cloth or canvas embroidered with wool, with background fabric cut away after embroidery is finished.

Schiffli e. A form of shuttle embroidery done by a machine that can embroider the entire width of fabric at one time, in elaborate or simple designs, eyelet or quilted, and in many colors simultaneously.

seed e. Type of German embroidery done with seeds for floral motifs and *chenille yarn* for stems and leaves, used for handbags.

shadow e. Embroidery worked with a *catch stitch* on the wrong side of transparent fabric.

Sicilian e. See *Spanish embroidery,* below.

Spanish e. 1. Muslin worked with *herringbone stitches.* 2. Lace-like embroidery made on muslin or cambric with braid and closely placed *buttonhole stitches.* Also called *Sicilian embroidery.*

stump work Embroidery in high relief due to much padding, sometimes with horsehair, and covered with *satin stitches;* the subjects are Biblical or allegorical scenes in grotesque shapes carried out with complicated stitchery.

Swiss e. See *Madeira embroidery.*

tambour work (tam-boor) Drumshaped frame used to hold embroidery which is done with a hooked needle and a stitch similar to the chain stitch; originally used in Eastern embroideries.

tulle e. Floss silk used on *tulle* fabric, *q.v.,* either by darning or by using embroidery stitches on a traced paper design; formerly used for trimming party dresses.

Tyrolean e. Bright colored yarn in reds, yellows, and blues worked in stylized floral designs on black felt or fabric.

Venetian ladder work Outline embroidery done with two parallel lines of *buttonhole stitches* connected with *cross stitches* at intervals in ladder style, used mainly for border work in conventional designs.

Yugoslavian e. Bright-colored wool used on coarse linen in geometical designs, done by counting threads, mainly in *cross stitch, double-purl, slanting,* or *satin stitch.*

emerald See *gems.*

emerald cut See *gem cuts* under *gems.*

emerizing Fabric passed through rollers covered with emery that brush a nap, producing a surface resembling *suede* or *chamois, q.v.*

empiecement Trimming effect with outer fabric cut away, and edges embroidered, to show a sheer fabric underneath; popular in late 19th century and early 20th century.

Empire bodice Dress bodice giving a short-waisted effect by arranging several silk scarfs around the waist and tying them on one side or in the back; popular in the late 1880's.

Empire bonnet Small outdoor bonnet shaped like a baby's cap; worn in 1860's. Also called *Empire cap.*

Empire coat Woman's three-quarter to full-length coat for traveling or evening wear made with a full skirt with large unpressed pleats attached to a high waistline; bodice cut somewhat like an *Eton jacket, q.v.,* with large lapels and a standing *Medici collar, q.v.;* worn in early 1900's.

Empire coiffure Style similar to that of French First Empire; hair curled in Greek manner around the face with a band of narrow ribbon wrapped three times around the head; back done in a large *chignon, q.v.,* with narrow ribbon wrapped around it several times ending in tiny bows at top of chignon; worn in 1860's.

Empire dress See *dresses.*

Empire house gown *Negligee, q.v.,* with high collar and tucked yoke crossed with ribbons tied in bow at center front; gown was floor length and fell in folds from yoke, sleeves three-quarter length, balloon-shaped and trimmed with large ruffle; worn in mid 1890's.

EMPIRE HOUSE GOWN, 1895

Empire jacket Square-yoked woman's jacket with *Medici collar,* large *box pleats* in front and back, and large *balloon sleeves, q.q.v.;* worn in mid 1890s. Also called a *box coat, q.v.*

Empire jupon (awm-peer zhu-pon) Gored petticoat, very full at the hem where two or three steel hoops were inserted, worn under the *Empire dress* of 1867 instead of the *cage petticoat, q.q.v.* Also called *Empire petticoat. Der.* Fashion of Second Empire of Napoleon III, 1852–1870.

Empire silhouette See *silhouettes.*

Empire skirt 1. Evening skirt, with *train,* set on waistband with gathers and finished with wide hem ruffle, with *steels* or *half hoops* inserted in back of skirt; worn in late 1880's and 1890's. 2. Daytime skirt with short *train* that had two panels, front and back, a triangular gore on each side; worn in the late 1880's and 1890's. 3. High-waisted skirt extending to just below the bust.

Empire stays Short *corset,* forerunner of the *brassiere, q.q.v.,* ending at high waistline, laced in back; for wear with high-waisted Empire dresses in the 1890's.

Empire styles Costumes worn during the First Empire in France, 1804–1815, under the reign of Napoleon I: men wore tight-fitting cashmere breeches, double-breasted jackets with high *Napoleon collars, q.v.,* and cravats or neck cloths; women wore high-waisted dresses with low square necklines front and back and tiny puffed sleeves, with *Spencer jackets, q.v.,* and bonnets. See *waistlines* and *dresses.*

Empress cloth Dress woolen. See *fabrics.*

Empress Eugénie hat See *Eugénie hat.*

Empress Josephine gown High-waisted dress with *surplice bodice, q.v.,* full sleeves, sash ends hanging from inserted belt, gathered skirt; worn in the 1890's with a *figaro jacket, q.v.,* inspired by dress of the First Empire in France.

Empress petticoat Evening petticoat substituted for the *cage petticoat, q.v.,* in mid 1860's, made in gores to fit tightly at the waist and spread to eight yards at the hem, forming a train a yard long; finished with a full gathered flounce beginning at the knees.

enameling duck See *fabrics.*

end 1. An individual *warp* yarn, *q.v.,* whether *single, ply,* or *cord.*

2. A fabric remnant or short piece of fabric.

end-and-end effect See *weaves.*

engageantes 1. French term for two or three tiers of lace or sheer-fabric ruffles used as cuffs on sleeves by some men during Louis XV period. 2. Detachable undersleeves of white fabric edged with lace or embroidery, worn by women from 1840's until about 1865.

engineer's boot See *boots.*

engineer's cap See *caps.*

engineer's cloth British term for blue *denim* and *dungaree fabrics, q.q.v.,* used for work clothes.

English bags See *plus fours* under *pants.*

English chain Form of *chatelaine, q.v.,* worn by women in the early 19th century, like a strand of twisted wire with attached watch, tweezer case, or other items.

English coat Woman's double-breasted three-quarter-length jacket somewhat like a *pea jacket, q.v.,* with lapels and flapped pockets; worn in 1890's.

English drape 1. Style used for man's single or double-breasted suit in 1930's and 1940's, distinguished by fullness at top of tapered sleeve, width through the chest, fitted waist, long jacket, trousers made with high-rise waistline and inverted pleats at side front. 2. Similar style adopted for women's suits in 1930's and 1940's.

English embroidery See *Madeira* under *embroideries.*

English farthingale Drum-shaped

ENGLISH DRAPE, 1930–40

farthingale worn with a *bourrelet* or *bum roll, q.q.v.,* around the waist, permitting the skirt to hang straight in a tub-like shape.

English hood Woman's headdress, usually made of black fabric, wired to form a peak or gable over the forehead, with long velvet *lappets, q.v.,* at sides and the back draped in thick folds over the shoulders; worn from 1500's–1540's. Also called *gable* or *pediment headdress,* by 19th-century writers.

English thumb See *Bolton thumb.*

English work See *Madeira* under *embroideries.*

English wrap Man's double-breasted *paletot sac,* similar to a loose chesterfield coat, *q.q.v.*

English walking jacket Woman's jacket in single-breasted style with lapels, unfitted in front and fitted at waistline in back, flaring to form a peplum, sleeves with large turned-back cuffs; worn in 1870's.

Enkalure Trademark owned by American Enka Co. for filament nylon yarn having a silky hand and taking prints well; trademark licensed for approved dresses and blouses.

Enkasheer 1. Trademark owned by American Enka Co. for nylon hosiery yarn with torque, excellent elasticity, good uniformity, and a soft hand, licensed for use on approved finished hosiery and panty-hose. 2. A nylon hosiery yarn made in the Netherlands.

ensemble (ahn-sahm-bl) 1. The entire costume, including accessories worn at one time. 2. More than one item of clothing designed and coordinated to be worn together. See *suit dress, dresses,* and *redingote.*

entari Ankle-length gown, with a rather full skirt and a sash at waistline, usually made of striped silk; worn particularly by Jewish men and women in Turkey, Palestine, Syria, and India in 19th century.

en tous cas (on too kah) Nickname for a parasol that could also be used as an umbrella, carried about 1870. *Der.* French phrase, in any case.

envelope combination Men's *undershirt* and *drawers* combined into one garment, type of loose-fitting *union suit, q.v.,* with open double fold in the back; worn in the 1920's and 1930's. Best-known trade name for this garment was *B.V.D., q.v.*

envelope handbag See *handbags.*

envelope pocket See *pockets.*

envelope sleeve See *sleeves.*

envoy hat See *hats.*

epaulet (ep-eh-let) 1. Ornamental shoulder trim used on military uniforms originally consisting of gold

braid looped to form fringe around the edge. 2. Loose band of fabric, sometimes fastened with a button, on uniform shoulders, also used on military-style civilian coats and jackets, e.g., *trench coats, q.v.* Also spelled *epaulette.* Also see *épauliers* and *shoulders.*

epaulet sleeve See *sleeves.*

épauliers (ep-eh-leer) Armor consisting of shoulder plates, first worn about 1300, larger in size than the *pauldrons, q.v.;* also called *epaulettes* and *shoulder caps.*

ephebi (ef-he-be) Military cape similar to the *chlamys, q.v.,* worn by Greek soldiers.

épinard (eh-pi-nar) Soft dark-green color. *Der.* French, spinach.

épingle See *fabrics.*

epitoga 1. Ancient Roman cloak worn over the toga, sometimes having bell-shaped sleeves. 2. Cloak of the 13th century similar to above but cut more like a robe, and worn as academic dress. 3. The medieval hood reduced to symbolic form as a part of academic and ceremonial robes. 4. A hood covering only the shoulders worn by French officials for ceremonial dress.

epomine hood See *epitoga,* above.

éponge See *fabrics.*

equestrian costume Term used for riding habits for women in 19th century.

equipage Same as *etui,* q.v.

eri A Japanese neckband.

eria Wild silk from Pakistan, East India, and Assam, uneven and coarse like *tussah* silk, *q.v.;* used for *spun silk.*

ermine See *furs.*

ermine cap See *lettice cap.*

erogenous-zone theory (e-roj-e-nus) Theory expounded by James Laver, noted English authority on historical costume, that emphasis in dress tends to shift from one erogenous zone of the body to another; e.g., when mini-skirts are worn, the legs are in focus; when plunging necklines are worn, the bosom or breasts get the attention. The cycle is about seven years between shifts of interest from zone to zone.

escallop See *scallop.*

escarelle (es-ka-rel) Pouch attached to a waist or hip belt, in the 14th and 15th centuries, into which a knife was frequently thrust.

esclavage Mid 18th-century term for a necklace composed of several rows of gold chain which fall in swags over the bosom. *Der.* French, *slave.*

Eskimo cloth See *fabrics.*

espadrille See *shoes.*

177

Esterel, Jacques See *designers appendix, France.*

Estevez, Louis See *designers appendix, United States.*

étamine See *fabrics.*

etched-out fabric See *burnt-out fabric* under *fabrics.*

Ethiopian shirt-dress See *dresses.*

Eton cap See *caps.*

Eton collar See *collars.*

Eton crop See *hairstyles.*

Eton jacket bodice Woman's fitted jacket of 1889 with large revers and flap pockets, worn with fancy double-breasted waistcoat with revers and large cravat.

Eton suit Uniform worn by junior schoolboys at Eton College, Eton, Buckinghamshire, England, from 1798 until 1967, consisting of a

waist-length square-cut jacket with wide lapels and small turned down collar worn with a white shirt with white starched collar, narrow dark tie, and single-breasted vest; jacket originally blue or red, becoming black in 1820 in mourning for George III, trousers usually grey.

Adaptation became a perennial dress-up suit for very young boys in U.S. and England from late 19th century through early 20th.

ethnic look Trend among young people in 1960's to clothing reflecting peasant styles or international origins, including many East Indian and African styles, as well as those adapted from American Indian clothes.

etui (a-twe) An ornamental case worn hanging from the waist by women in the 18th century, intended to hold thimble, scissors, and scent bottle. Also called *equipage.*

Eugenia, The Voluminous women's cape, usually black, of seven-eighths length, with second cape reaching to waist in back and shorter in front, both capes edged with fancy box-pleated ribbon; worn in 1860's.

Eugénie collarette Crocheted collar in two-tone yoke effect, pointed in center back and front, closed in center front with loops and buttons; worn in late 1860's.

Eugénie dress Full-skirted dress with tight fitting waist and skirt of three flounces, sleeves short or made in *pagoda* style, *q.v.;* worn in 1850's.

Eugénie, Empress (oo-jshe-ne; 1826–1920) Marie Eugénie de Montijo de Guzman, wife of Napoleon III and Empress of France (1852–1870), exerted great influence on fashion during the Age of Crinoline, with her constant desire for innovations; *Worth q.v.,* was her couturier and is credited with designing the first *princess dress, q.v.,* for the Empress.

Eugénie hat Small hat with brim rolled back on either side, worn tilted sideways and to the front, often trimmed with one long ostrich plume in the side roll; popular in the 1930's. *Der.* Named after *Empress Eugénie, q.v.*

Eugénie paletot 1. Tailored three-quarter-length woman's coat in unfitted double-breasted style with notched collar and bell sleeves made with false cuffs, side of cuff and rounded patch pocket trimmed with buttons; worn in 1860's. 2. Shorter length full sack-type jacket, collarless or with a small collar, closing at neck with one button.

Eugénie petticoat Petticoat worn in the early 1870's with semicircular steel *hoops* in the back and an attached *bustle, q.q.v.;* named for *Empress Eugénie, q.v.*

even checks See *checks.*

evening dress or **gown** A dress suitable for formal or semi-formal wear, usually long but changing with changing fashions. A *ball gown* is usually more elaborate and bare than a *dinner dress.* See *dresses.*

evening petticoat See *petticoats.*

evening slippers See *shoes.*

Everetts See *slippers.*

Everfast Trademark for fabrics of cotton, linen, or rayon sold as colorfast to washing and cleaning.

Everglaze Trademark controlled by Joseph Bancroft & Sons Co., applied to finishes on fabrics made of various fibers that come up to a certain standard, including polishing, taffe-tizing, embossing, and glazing to retain fabric's luster, shine, porosity, and resistance to spots, stains, wrinkles, and mildew through repeated washings or dry cleanings.

evil eye See *utchat.*

examining gown Simple wrap-around gown, or one slit up the back and fastened with ties, used by patients in doctors' offices, originally made in coarse muslin, now in disposable fabrics.

exercise clogs See *sandals.*

expandable bracelet See *bracelets.*

express stripes See *fabrics.*

extract printing See *discharge printing.*

extra large 1. Size range used along with *small, medium* and *large* for women's *sweaters, housecoats, nightgowns,* some *panties, girdles* and *panty girdles.* 2. Size for men's *sport shirts, sport jackets, sweaters,* and *robes.* 3. Size for some children's garments.

extruded latex Round *elastomeric yarn, q.v.,* made by forcing latex into a coagulating bath and drawing off solid round yarn.

eyelashes See *false eyelashes.*

eyelet 1. Circular metal ring, pressed through fabric or leather and cinched on garments or shoes, through which a lace is pulled; first used about 1830. See *blind eyelet.* 2. Punched holes, embroidered in fabrics for lacings or as decoration. See *eyelet batiste, eyelet organdy,* etc., under *fabrics.* Also see *buttonholes* and *embroideries.*

F

fabala Variant of *falbala, q.v.*

Fabiani, Alberto See *designers appendix, Italy.*

fabric Cloth made of textile yarns by weaving, knitting, lace construction, braiding, netting, felting, etc., also cloth made by *bonding, q.v.,* and non-woven methods. *Der.* Latin *fabrica,* workshop. See *weaves* category for individual weaves; *yarns* for yarn types; *fibers* are in main alphabetical listings.

FABRICS:

admiralty cloth Type of *melton* fabric used by British naval forces for officers' uniforms and coats, used in pea jackets and overcoats and in civilian outerwear.

airplane fabrics Group of strong fabrics usually made of *two-ply cotton yarns* tightly twisted: used for collars, cuffs, shirtings, and skiwear.

albatross 1. Fine, soft, lightweight *wool* fabric with pebbly napped surface, made in open plain weave in pale colors or black; used for dresses, negligees, and nun's habits. 2. A similar soft, napped fabric made of *cotton.*

Albert 1. *Cotton* fabrics made in the *twill weave,* usually dyed dark colors and finished with a high luster; used for pocketing and linings. 2. Lining fabric made in the *twill weave* with *alpaca* filling and a *cotton* warp; sometimes called Italian cloth.

Albert cloth Reversible overcoating fabric made by *double weave* construction with different patterns and colors on each side—not to be confused with *Albert.*

alma *Silk* fabric characterized by distinct diagonal *twill weave,* originally made in black or purple for mourning. *Der.* from Egyptian word meaning *mourner.*

alpaca fabric 1. Springy, shiny cloth made of silk, cotton, or wool with *alpaca* filling, usually black and resembling mohair, used for dresses and men's suitings; originated in England in 1838. Also called *brilliantine.* 2. *Rayon* and *acetate* imitation of this fabric often called *alpaca crepe.*

ancient madder Fabric with small foulard-type or paisley designs printed in England in dull red, green, blue, brown and yellow outlined with black; finished to give a suede-like hand. Often imitated.

antique satin Reversible rayon-and-acetate fabric with dull surface and satin back, characterized by slubs of yarn at intervals, used for evening wear, shoes, handbags, and suits.

antique taffeta Crisp *taffeta, q.v.,* of *doupioni silk* or man-made fibers with irregular slubs in imitation of 18th century fabrics; may be iridescent.

Argentine cloth Net-like *plain-weave* fabric, similar to glazed tarlatan; glazed to make it dustproof.

armozine Heavy French corded *silk,* generally black, used during 17th–18th centuries for waistcoats, dresses, mourning, etc. Also spelled *armazine, armozeen.*

armure (ar-moor) Classification of fabrics with pebbly surface sometimes using small motifs in repeat design, woven in variation of rib weave called *armure weave,* used for dresses and ties. *Der.* From French *armure,* armor; original fabric had linked pattern like chain mail. See *weaves.*

army cloth 1. Fabric used in army uniforms. 2. Gray woolen fabric of low grade made in Yorkshire, England, for export to Near East.

Austrian cloth Fine *woolen* or *worsted* fabric woven from highest grade merino wool, used for men's formal wear.

Avignon (ah-veen-yon) Lightweight *silk* taffeta lining fabric made in France.

backed cloth Any fabric woven with an extra warp or an extra filling, or both, making three or four yarns, frequently made in two-toned effect with different color on each side.

bagheera (ba-gee-ra) Fine *uncut velvet* with short, closely set loops.

Balbriggan Soft, lightweight tubular-knit cotton fabric made with plain stitch, sometimes slightly napped on the reverse side, used for intimate apparel, *e.g.,* pajamas. *Der.* Named for Balbriggan, Ireland, where term was first used for type of unbleached hosiery.

balloon cloth Strong, lightweight, *plain-woven cotton* fabric with high luster and high count, made of fine combed yarns; used originally in coated form for balloons, now also

in airplane manufacture; used uncoated for ski wear. See also *airplane fabrics.*

bannockburn 1. Napped *twilled wool* fabric similar to Cheviot used for coats and suits. 2. Originally, a twilled tweed fabric made with one single and one *2-ply yarn* of different colors. Named for Bannockburn, Scotland, where Scots defeated the English in 1314.

barathea (bar-a-thee-a) Closely woven silk, rayon, cotton, or wool fabric with *broken-rib weave* giving pebbly texture; used for neckties, dresses, uniforms.

barège (ba-rezh) Gauzy fabric used for veiling or dresses, made in a *leno weave* with a *worsted* filling and a warp of silk, cotton, or other fibers. *Der.* French town of Barèges in the Hautes-Pyrenees.

bark cloth Fabrics woven from fibers obtained from various trees in many countries, *e.g.,* cedar bark used by American Indians; paper mulberry, in Hawaii and South Pacific; wild fig tree, in Mozambique—soaked, beaten, and dyed or painted in designs; used for apparel, etc. See *tapa cloth.*

bark crepe Classification of rough textured *crepe* fabrics usually made with silk and rayon or other man-made fibers combined with *wool;* used for dresses and coats.

barley corn 1. Type of small-figured *basket weave* in geometric pattern. 2. Checked *cotton* fabric popular in 18th century for women's dresses. Also spelled *barlicorn.*

bathrobe cloth Heavyweight fabric,

heavily napped to give soft fuzzy hand, constructed with *backed cloth method, q.v.,* made of rayon, cotton, and nylon combinations and usually printed different colors each side to appear as woven double cloth; used for bathrobes. Also called *bathrobe blanketing, blanket, blanket cloth, cotton bathrobe flannel,* and *cotton blanket cloth.*

batiste Fine soft lightweight *cotton* in *plain weave,* bleached or printed and used for dresses and mens' shirts; also made in sheer wool similar to nun's veiling, in sheer silk like mull, and in spun rayon. *Der.* Named for French weaver Jean Baptiste. Also see *corset batiste.*

beach cloth Durable fabric of *cotton* or mixtures of cotton, mohair, and wool, used for sportswear, summer suitings, dresses, etc.

beaver cloth Heavy *wool* fabric with dense, curly, smooth sheared nap, woven in double-cloth construction with a *twill weave;* used for winter coats.

Bedford cord Medium to heavyweight *cotton* fabric characterized by heavy warpwise cords or stripes; ribs made by heavy yarn used as backing, or stuffing yarns, with carded single or two-ply yarns used in face. Popular for women's and men's summer suits, where word is shortened to *cord.* Also made in wool or a variety of man-made fibers. Lighter weights called *warp piqué.*

bengaline (ben-gal-leen) Heavyweight lustrous fabric with crosswise *ribbed* effect, made in many combinations of fibers, wool, cotton, rayon, or silk; frequently black and used for suits, coats, millinery, and ribbons.

beutanol (bew-ta-nol) Vinyl-coated fabric made of lawn, dyed and then treated with five coats of vinyl plastic. which make it waterproof, flame-resistant, and dustproof; used for raincoats.

birdseye 1. Absorbent fabric woven in *linen* or *cotton* on *dobby* loom in small diamond design with dot in center, used for baby's diapers. 2. Type of *piqué* woven with horizontal corded effect and small diamond design. 3. Clear-finished reversible *worsted* suiting woven in a two-tone diamond effect with small dot in center, used for men's and women's suits; also called *birdseye suiting.*

blazer cloths *Woolen* or *worsted* fabrics made in *satin weave* with woven or printed striped or in plain colors; used for sportswear and blazer jackets.

bobbinet Lacy net-like fabric originally made by hand but now *knitted* on bobbinet machine, made of cotton, silk, nylon, or rayon yarns, twisted so they form hexagonal-shaped mesh. Used for evening gowns, petticoats, and stiffening. Also called *net.*

Bolivia Velvety, light-to-heavyweight coating fabric made in *pile weave* with tufts running diagonally or vertically; usually of *wool,* sometimes with addition of mohair and alpaca fibers; used for coats and suits.

bombazine 1. Lightweight fabric made in *twill weave* with *silk* warp

183

and *worsted* filling; originally in a natural color, now usually dyed black and used for mourning. Also called *bombasin, bombasine,* and *bombazin.* 2. In rainwear, rubberized cloth, dyed solid colors or printed.

bouclé (boo-clay) Fabric characterized by a looped or nubbed surface, caused by using *bouclé yarn* in the filling, first made in 1880's. *Der.* French *bouclé,* buckled, curly, or looped. See *bouclé* yarn.

bourette silk (bur-et) Lightweight, rough textured *silk* woven in *twill weave* of *bourette yarn, q.v.,* used for suiting, dresses.

broadcloth 1. Originally, fabric made on a wide loom, more than 27 inches. 2. In the U.S., soft, closely woven, lustrous *cotton* or *cotton/ polyester,* in a *plain weave* with fine rib in the direction of the filling; used for shirts, dresses, undergarments, etc. 3. Similar fabric in rayon, called *Fuji, q.v.* 4. Soft, glossy napped *twill* or *plain-weave woolen* fabric used for suits, coats, and dresses.

brocade Fabric with raised design woven on *Jacquard* loom, usually a *satin-weave* pattern with background in *rib* or *plain weave;* made of all types of yarns including gold, silver, silk, cotton or man-made.

brocatelle Medium-weight *Jacquard* dress fabric with pattern in high relief giving blistered effect; silk, rayon, or acetate with cotton back.

buckram 1. Coarse, heavily sized fabric used for stiffening, similar to crinoline but heavier. 2. Fabric made of two layers of open-weave fabric glued together. 3. 16th century fabric, thought to be *linen* or *cotton,* used for hose and women's dresses. *Der.* Material made in Bokhara, South Russia.

buckskin cloth 1. Durable *woolen* or *worsted* napped fabric made in the buckskin weave, a variation of *satin weave.* See also *moleskin.* 2. Cream-colored fabric made in 19th century and used especially to imitate buckskin leather for riding breeches.

burlap Loosely constructed *plain-woven* fabric of *jute* or other coarse fibers, originally used for bags, sacks, etc., now used for draperies, handbags, belts, sportswear, etc. Also called *Hessian.*

burnt-out fabric Fabric or lace made on the *Jacquard* loom with two different yarns—lacy pattern produced when one of the sets of yarn is chemically dissolved. Also called *etched-out fabric* or *burnt-out print.*

butcher linen Heavyweight durable fabric made in *plain weave* used for summer suits and sportswear; originally made of *linen* for butchers' aprons, now made of *cotton* or *spun rayon* and properly called *butcher cloth;* used for slacks, suits, and sportswear.

Byrd cloth Trademark for high-count, medium-weight, wind-resistant reversible *cotton* fabric, woven very tightly in *twill weave;* may be given water-repellent treatment and used for ski wear, snow suits, parkas, and garments worn by aviators; fabric originally developed for Admiral Richard Byrd's Antarctic Navy Expedition.

cable net Mesh-like *cotton* fabric with large holes, made of heavy yarn.

cadet cloth Heavy bluish-gray *flannel, q.v.,* fabric used for overcoats and uniforms at military academies.

calico Low-count *cotton* fabric with small distinctive printed designs, usually flowers; printed first in England 1676. *Der.* Named for Calicut, India, where printed cloth first originated. See *prints.*

cambric Fine closely woven *cotton* fabric made with mercerized yarns and given a calendered finish; may also be made of *linen* and used for handkerchiefs. *Der.* From Cambrai, France.

camel suede *Cotton* fabric made in imitation of genuine camel hair, which should be labeled as made of cotton.

caniche (ka-neesh) A curly textured *wool* fabric similar to poodle cloth. *Der.* French, poodle.

Canton crepe Lightweight, rippled, textured *crepe* made of *silk* or *rayon* yarns; surface effect is achieved by yarns tightly twisted in both directions. *Der.* Yarn from Canton, China, called Canton silk.

Canton flannel Soft, fuzzy *cotton* fabric made in *twill weave,* with filling yarn twisted and brushed to form a heavy nap; used for nightgowns, robes, and pajamas. Similar to *flannelette, q.v.*

Canton silk *Silk* from yarn of southern China from small domesticated silk worms, weaker than Japanese silk but lustrous and of even diameter. *Der.* Named for Canton, China.

canvas Heavy, durable, utility fabric made from coarse, hard, twisted cotton yarns, sometimes sized; used for *coats, shoes,* and *handbags.* Also see *awning stripes* and *embroidery canvas.*

Carmelite cloth Loosely constructed, plain-woven *woolen* fabric, heavily fulled, used for habits by nuns of the Carmelite order of Roman Catholic church.

cashmere Any of the fabrics, often in fleece or flannel weaves; made from fine, soft downy wool undercoat of the cashmere goat, which is sometimes combined with sheep's wool for greater durability. Used for dresses and especially for coats.

cassimere Light to medium-weight lustrous *woolen* or *worsted* fabric made in *plain* or *twill weave* with hard-spun yarns, used for men's suits and trousers. Also called *cassimir* or *kerseymere* and frequently confused with *cashmere, q.v.*

cavalry twill Durable fabric of wool, cotton, spun rayon, or other manmade fibers in *twill weave* with pronounced diagonal wale, finished to give a hard surface; used for riding pants, suits, jackets, and coats.

challis (shall-e) Sheer worsted, cotton, rayon, or other fiber made in firm *plain weave,* frequently dyed and *printed* with small floral or geometrical designs; similar to *nun's veiling, q.v.;* used for dresses. Also spelled *challie.*

chambord (sham-bor) Dress fabric of wool, silk, and cotton, woven in *ribbed* effect, used in France for mourning garments.

chambray (*sham*-bray) Name given to a variety of lightweight, high-count yarn-dyed *cottons*, with silky hand, some iridescent, some woven with stripes, used for dresses, sportswear, and men's shirts; heavier weights are used for work shirts. *Der.* From Cambrai, France.

chamois cloth Soft *cotton* fabric, either *knit* or *woven*, made with fine soft nap in imitation of chamois-finished sheepskin. Should not be shortened to "chamois," as this refers to leather.

Charmeen Trademark for dress fabric made of fine *worsted* in steep *twill weave*.

charmeuse (shar-moez) Lightweight, smooth, semi-lustrous fabric with crepe back, made of cotton, silk, or man-made fibers dyed or printed and used for dresses. *Der.* French, charmer.

Charvet (shar-vay) Soft lustrous necktie fabric, woven with faint *herringbone* design. Named after the French firm specializing in men's neckties. Also called *Regence*.

cheesecloth Loosely constructed, non-durable net-like fabric made from coarse *cotton* yarns and used for interlinings in inexpensive coats and suits. If starched, called *theatrical gauze*. *Der.* From cloth used to wrap cheeses.

Cheviot (chev-e-eht) 1. Rugged harsh fabric with wiry nap, in *plain* or *twill* weave, originally made of *cheviot wool*, now all types of fibers used—wools, man-mades, re-used wool, cotton; used for sportswear. *Der.* Wool of hardy sheep native to Cheviot Hills on boundary between Scotland and England.

Cheviot shirtings 1. *Cotton* fabric made with heavy yarn in variety of *dobby* designs—striped or ribbed, blue or brown on a white ground. 2. British term for high quality fabric woven with combed yarns in medium count, plain or basket weave.

chiffon (sheef-ohn) Thin, transparent fabric of cotton, silk, rayon, or synthetics, made in *open weave* of *creped yarn*, dyed in solid colors or printed and used mainly for dresses, blouses, night wear, or scarves. *Der.* French, rag, or wisp.

chiffon taffeta Lightweight taffeta, soft and lustrous.

chiffon velvet Lightweight, soft velvet with a short thick pile made of silk, rayon, acetate or other man-made fibers. Also called *transparent velvet* and *wedding-ring velvet*.

China silk Soft-textured *silk* fabric in *plain weave* which may have slight imperfections, made in China as early as 1200 B.C. and used for linings for dresses, suits, and coats. Similar U.S. fabrics are also called *china silk*.

chinchilla cloth Thick, heavyweight coating fabric distinguished by curly surface nubs. 1. Woven as double cloth with *plain* back and *satin* front; extra filling yarns added to face of fabric are loosely floated over surface, then rubbed into curled tufts. 2. Similar fabric made by *knitting*, then brushing the surface yarns into nubs.

chino (chee-no) Durable *cotton*,

firmly woven with fine steep *twill,* made in a yellowish tan or khaki color, originally an English fabric purchased in China for the U.S. army in the Philippines in World War I and still used for summer uniforms in the U.S. army. In late 1950's adopted by men and boys for school and general wear, particularly for pants; and used for women's and children's sportswear.

chintz 1. *Cotton* fabric printed with floral or bird designs, with or without a shiny glazed finish; used for beachwear, and women's apparel as well as draperies and slipcovers. Trademarked Everglaze fabric is one example of shiny chintz. 2. Originally a stained or painted *cotton calico* from India. *Der.* From Hindu *chint,* spotted cloth.

Ciré Patented fabric given a brilliant, glossy finish by use of wax and hot calendering, especially successful in *acetate.*

ciselé velvet (seez-el-ay) English fabric, popular in 19th century, with raised velvet figures on a satin ground. *Der.* French, chiseled.

clays Distinctive type of *worsted* woven with *twill weave* and given a clear finish, introduced and popularized by J. T. Clay of Rastrick, Yorkshire, England; sometimes called *clay serge.*

coated fabrics Fabrics that are nonporous and waterproof through coating with various substances, e.g., lacquer, varnish, pyroxlin, polyethylene, and polyvinyl chloride; achieved by dipping, impregnating or by calendering with pressure. Used for raincoats.

coating 1. Any heavy fabric used for coats and overcoats. 2. Finishing process used on one or both sides of a fabric such as rubber, vinyl compounds, linseed oil, lacquer, or synthetic resins. 3. British term for heavy *twilled* fabrics with a lustrous finish or vertical *corded* fabrics made in a *satin* weave.

coating velvet Heavy cotton-backed velvet with closely woven silk or man-made-fiber pile.

Coburg Fabric woven in imitation of cashmere, made with *cotton* warp and *worsted* filling, piece-dyed or printed and used for dresses, introduced in England in 1840's after marriage of Queen Victoria. Also spelled *Cobourg. Der.* Named after Prince Albert of Saxe-Coburg, Gotha, Queen Victoria's consort.

convent cloth 1. Lightweight, black-dyed fabric used for nuns' habits, with *wool* warp and silk or rayon filling in a *crepe weave.* 2. Ribbed fabric in stripes, mixtures, solid colors.

corduroy Medium to heavy-weight *cotton* fabric with vertical cut-pile stripes, differentiated by size of cords as pin-wale, regular, or wide-wale corduroys. Used for coats, dresses, sportswear and now woven with polyester for better washability. *Der.* From *cord* plus obsolete *duroy,* a coarse woolen fabric, or from French *corde du roi* meaning king's cord.

coronation cloth Medium-weight suitings fabrics of *wool* and unfinished *worsted,* with warpwise single thread stripes about one inch apart made with *gold* or other *metallic yarns. Der.* First used at the coronation of King Edward VII of England in 1901.

corset batiste Heavy strong *cotton* or *rayon* fabric in *plain, Jacquard,* or *dobby* weave used to make brassieres, foundation garments, and girdles. Also may have elastic or elastomeric yarns combined with cotton for stretch fabrics. Term *batiste* is actually a misnomer.

cotton crepe 1. Crinkled-surface *cotton* fabric made with *crepe-twisted* yarns. 2. Less-permanent crinkled *cotton* produced by printing with caustic soda. Also called *plissé* or *plissé crepe.*

cotton flannel Soft *cotton* sheeting or twill, brushed to raise a nap on one or both sides, used for baby clothes, shirts, linings, and night-gowns. Also called *outing flannel, flannelette, Shaker flannel, Canton flannel.*

cotton suitings General term for wide variety of heavy weight *cotton* fabrics woven in patterns of other fabrics, e.g., tweeds, herringbones, stripes, checks, plaids, for summer suits and trousers.

cotton velvet Soft cotton pile fabric woven like *velvet, q.v.* Incorrect name for *velveteen, q.v.*

coupure *Cashmere* fabric made in *twill weave,* diagonally cut and used on the bias so the diagonal twill makes a lengthwise line. *Der.* French, crack or gash.

coutil (koo-teel) Durable, firm *cotton* made in herringbone *twill weave,* used for foundation garments and brassieres. Also called *coutille.*

covert Firm durable *worsted* or *cotton* fabric with a *diagonal twill,* produced by warp face weave, and characteristic mottled look, achieved in worsted by two colors in two-ply warp yarn, filling of the darker color and in cotton by a mock twist yarn in the warp, one ply dark, the other light. Used for men's suits and coats, work clothes, caps, uniforms and trousers. *Der. Covert* is a hiding place for game birds; the fabric used originally for field clothes.

crash Coarse, loosely woven fabric made in variety of weights, woven with irregular yarns giving it an uneven texture, made of cotton, cotton and linen, cotton and jute, and rayon staple fibers.

crepe (krape) 1. Fabric made with *crepe yarn, q.v.,* having a slight pebbly texture. 2. Wide variety of fabrics, cottons, silks, wools or synthetics, that have a crepe finish achieved by the weave or by embossing or application of chemicals. See specifics, e.g., *crepe-back satin, crepe georgette, alpaca crepe.* 3. Black or white *silk* fabric used for mourning clothes, usually spelled *crape. Der.* French *crêper,* to crinkle or frizz.

crepe-back satin Lightweight fabric with smooth lustrous finish on face and dull crepy appearance on back, made in *satin weave* with silk, rayon, or man-made fiber; used for dresses, blouses, lingerie. Also called *satin-back crepe* or *satin-faced crepe.*

crêpe charmeuse (krepp shar-merz) All *silk,* dull-luster, crepe-back satin with excellent draping qualities;

used for evening gowns, dresses, blouses, and linings. *Der.* French, charming crepe.

crêpe de chine (krepp deh sheen) Fine lightweight *silk* or *rayon* fabric with crepy texture made of highly twisted yarns, piece-dyed or printed; used for dresses and blouses. *Der.* French, Chinese crepe.

crêpe de laine (krepp deh lane) Slightly crinkled lightweight sheer piece-dyed *wool* fabric made with crepe-twisted yarn. *Der.* French, wool crepe.

crêpe georgette (krepp jor-jet) See *georgette.*

crêpe lisse (krepp lees) Lightweight *cotton* or *silk* pebbled fabric with slightly stiff lustrous finish, open weave. Der. French, glossy crepe.

crêpe marocain (krepp maro-kan) Heavy *silk* or *rayon* pebbled fabric with ribs caused by using coarser filling. Der. French, Moroccan crepe.

crêpe météor (krepp mee-teh-or) Soft lustrous *silk* crepe fabric made with a *satin* face and *twill* back.

crepon (krape-on) Heavy crepe fabric made in silk, rayon, cotton, wool or combinations with crepe effect in the warp by using different twists or some slacker warp threads or by a Jacquard weave with crepe effect; used for dresses.

cretonne (kreh-ton or kree-ton) Fabric made from various gray goods known more by its distinctive designs than its texture; includes: coarse *Osnaburg, print cloth, sheeting, fine sateen, dobby* figured goods, *rep,* and *twills* and made of

cotton, linen, man-made fibers and combinations of fibers with floral designs on colored ground. Similar to *chintz, q.v.,* but unglazed.

crinkle crepe See *plissé,* below.

cut velvet *Brocaded* fabric, woven on *Jacquard* loom, with pattern made by velvet pile on a sheer ground—such as chiffon, georgette, or voile; used for evening dresses. Also called *beaded velvet.*

crystal, crystalline Dress fabric with alternating fine and heavy *cords; silk* or *rayon* warp, *wool* fill.

damask (*dam*-ask) Jacquard-woven, *q.v.,* reversible fabric—linen, cotton, silk, etc.—with floral or geometric designs of high luster on a dull ground; used for evening wear. *Der.* Originally made of silk woven in China and introduced through Damascus into Europe.

darya Natural colored wild *silk* fabric made in India.

denim Sturdy *cotton* yarn-dyed fabric with warp-face *twill* in many variations of colors and in stripes and checks. Classic denim has indigo-blue face, gray or unbleached fill and is used for work clothes and jeans, and sportswear pants and jackets; popular in 1960's–'70's with young fad for wearing jeans and European interest in the American Western look. *Der.* French *serge de Nimes,* fabric made in Nimes, France. Also see *jean* and *dungaree.*

dimity *Cotton* fabrics characterized by *corded* warp-wise stripes made by addition of heavier cords spaced at regular intervals; finished in several ways, either soft or starched (as lawn or organdy), and used for dresses, blouses, children's dresses, and formerly for underwear and lingerie. *Der.* Greek *dimitos,* double thread.

dimity check Dimity, *q.v.,* that has heavy yarns at intervals both filling-wise and warp-wise, forming a *checked* design; popular in the 1920's and '30's for men's underwear.

dobby or **dobby cotton** Fabric, such as white-on-white broadcloth, woven with a small geometric pattern by a loom with a dobby attachment.

doeskin Woolen fabrics with a smooth, short-napped face, made in imitation of suede leather doeskin, in three weights, also made of rayon, or cotton; used for riding habits, uniforms, trousers, coating, suits, and sportswear. Should be called *doeskin fabric.*

domet flannel Soft napped medium-weight to heavy-weight fabric similar to *outing flannel, q.v.,* but with longer nap, made of cotton or cotton warp with cotton and wool filling. Also spelled *domett.*

Donegal tweed 1. Medium to heavy-weight handwoven tweed made in county of Donegal, Ireland. In *plain* or *twill weave,* or coarse *wool* yarns with single colored warp and blend of colors in the filling yarn. Used for coats, suits, skirts, trousers, and jackets. 2. Term for tweeds made from yarns spun and dyed in Donegal, Ireland, but woven in Yorkshire, England.

dotted Swiss Crisp, sheer cotton ornamented with evenly spaced dots of same color as ground or in contrast color, achieved originally by weaving and clipping, now also by adhesives as in *flock printing, q.v.* Popular for evening gowns, junior fashions, and children's dresses.

double cloth Heavy reversible fabric made of two complete fabrics often in contrasting colors usually fine *worsted* or *woolen,* woven at same time and connected by binder yarn; when binder yarns are released at edges of coat or cape to make felled seams, no lining is necessary. See *weaves.*

drill Durable *cotton* fabric in warp faced or *herringbone twill,* in medium or heavy weights, used in the gray or piece-dyed, e.g., khaki cloth. Similar to *denim, middy twill,* or *jean* fabrics and used for work and sports clothes and shoe linings.

duchesse (doo-shess) Lightweight glossy *satin-weave* fabric made of silk or rayon, dyed in solid colors. Also called *duchesse satin.*

duck Term for wide range of heavy *cotton* fabrics, closely woven in a *plain weave,* made in different weights. Lightweight duck is used for sportswear.

duffel 1. Heavy *woolen* fabric with a thick nap made in England in 18th century and used for overcoats. 2. Similar cloth, both domestic and imported, used in the U.S. *Der.* From a town in Belgium near Antwerp where fabric was first produced. Also spelled *duffle.*

dungaree Rugged *cotton twill* fabric,

usually blue, similar to denim, woven with colored filling and white warp—the reverse of denim. *Der.* From coarse cotton fabric woven in Dungri, a section of Bombay, India.

duvetyn (doo-veh-teen) Soft, napped fabric of wool, cotton, rayon or silk, with velvety finish. Used for dresses, coats, and sportswear. *Der.* French *duvet,* down of young birds.

eiderdown (i-der-down) Lightweight *knit* or *woven* fabric which is elastic and heavily napped on one or both sides, made of wool, cotton, or rayon or combinations of these fibers; used for robes, negligees. *Der.* From the under feathers or down of the eider duck.

élastique (aye-las-teek) 1. Fabric similar to *cavalry twill* of tightly twisted *worsted* yarn, made with steep twill weave and cords running diagonally; used for jodhpurs, riding habits, uniforms, and pants. Also called *tricotine.* 2. Overcoat fabric of the mid 19th century made of fine *merino* yarns.

embossed cotton Medium-weight *cotton* fabric with surface design impressed by steam-heated metal rollers, giving effect similar to *birdseye piqué, q.v.,* or other patterned weaves.

embossed crepe 1. Lightweight *cotton* fabric with crinkled surface made by running fabric through engraved rollers to give pebbly effect, which is not permanent. 2. Fabrics of *man-made fibers* given a perma-nent crepe effect by engraved rollers, e.g., *sculptured nylon, q.v.*

Empress cloth Woolen double-faced dress fabric with *twill face* and *ribbed back,* originally made with *cotton* warp and *worsted* filling, popularized by Empress Eugénie during the Second Empire Period.

enameling duck *Duck* fabric coated and used as oilcloth and imitation leather, e.g., tennis and basketball shoes, made in widths from 38 to 90 inches and in a variety of weights.

épingle (eh-pang-gl) Lustrous dress fabric with fine ribs running warpwise, may alternate in size or color; originally made in silk, now of fine worsted or man-made fibers. *Der.* French, pin.

éponge (eh-pongh) Soft, spongy fabric made in *plain weave* with plain warp and novelty filling. *Der.* French, sponge.

Eskimo cloth Heavy, napped overcoating fabric either dyed plain colors or woven in horizontal stripes, made in either *satin* or *twill* weave.

étamine Lightweight fabric with open weave of coarse, tightly twisted yarns, made in many different qualities and of various fibers and used for sportswear and sport jackets. *Der.* French, sieve; fabric originally used to sift flour.

express stripes Sturdy fabric, similar to denim, usually made in *twill weave* with twelve white warps alternating with twelve indigo-blue warps and a white or unbleached filling; used for sportswear and workclothes, originally worn by railroad workers.

eyelet batiste, eyelet organdy, eyelet linen, etc. Fabrics patterned along the border or in an all-over design with *eyelet embroidery, q.v.* under *embroideries;* originally fine hand work; now usually done by the *Schiffli* machine, *q.v.*

façonné velvet Pile fabric with pattern or design made by *burnt-out fabric method, q.v.*

faille (fie-yeh or file) Crisp *flat-ribbed* fabric with ribs made by use of heavier yarns in the *filling, q.v.;* originally of *silk,* now of silk or rayon with rayon/cotton filling; used for women's suits and dresses, robes, trimmings, hats.

faille crepe Smooth dull *crepe, q.v.,* with a fine face *rib* and a satin back, made of silk, rayon, acetate, or other man-made fibers; used for women's dresses.

faille taffeta A *taffeta, q.v.* below, with a pronounced cross *rib.*

fake fur A pile fabric that looks like fur, often made of Dynel modacrylic fiber, sometimes stenciled to imitate leopard, tiger, zebra, or giraffe. See *fur fabrics,* below.

farmer's satin Glossy durable lining fabric used for men's suits, made with *cotton* warp and worsted, rayon, or cotton filling, sometimes called *Italian cloth* or *Venetian cloth.*

fearnaught Heavy, shaggy British overcoating fabric similar to Cheviot, usually *shoddy* and reworked *wool* combined, which, when napped, gave a long hairy effect. Also spelled *fearnought.*

feather cloth 1. Soft novelty fabric made of wool yarn mixed with feathers. 2. Chicken or ostrich feathers, sewed to cloth before a garment is made; popular in 1960's for evening dresses, pants, jackets, stoles and shawls.

flannel Fine soft fabric made of *wool* or blend of wool and cotton or synthetics in tightly woven *twill* or *plain weave* and finished with a slightly napped finish; used for men's and women's suits, trousers, shirts. Rayon flannel or cotton *flannelette* used for women's and girl's dresses and nightgowns. *Der.* Middle English word *flanen,* sack cloth, or Welsh *gwlanen* or *gwlan,* wool.

flat crepe Soft, smooth, flat fabric of silk, rayon, or acetate with only a slight crinkle, achieved by creped or S- and Z-twisted yarns in the filling. Similar fabric, which does not use crepe-twisted yarns, is called *mock crepe.*

fleece Heavy wool coating fabric with an extremely soft napped finish completely concealing the weave, varying in thickness, the longer nap called *shag,* the shorter called *velour.* Also see *cotton fleece.*

fleece-backed fabric Soft *knit* fabric, with heavily napped surface on one side, used as linings in coats or for *sweat shirts, q.v.*

forestry cloth Fabric of olive-drab color, made in *twill weave* of cotton, wool, worsteds, and mixtures, used by the Forestry Service and the U.S. Army for uniforms, overcoats, shirts, and trousers.

foulard Soft lightweight silk, rayon, or acetate fabric made in *twill* *weave,* usually surface printed in small design, used for *scarfs, neckties, q.q.v.,* and dresses.

Frenchback Wool or cotton fabric with dull surface made with *twill weave* on right side and *satin weave* on reverse side, used for women's suits and trousers. Also called *Frenchback serge.* Also see *backed fabrics.*

French crepe *Silk* fabric with a flat, smooth surface woven of crep-twisted yarns and made in France; also similar fabrics made of rayon or other man-made fibers. See *lingerie crepe,* below.

French flannel Soft, slightly napped *wool* fabric, made in stripes, checks, or solid colors in *twill weave;* used for men's and women's dressing gowns, shirts, etc.

frieze Heavy rough *woolen* fabric with wiry surface, made in a variety of qualities and constructions including *double cloth, backed cloth,* and *plain* or *twill weaves, q.q.v.,* used for heavy outerwear, such as soldiers' overcoats. *Der.* First made in Friesland, Holland, in the 13th century. Also spelled *frise.*

fuji Dress or blouse fabric that combines *viscose rayon* or *acetate* dull filament warp with a *spun yarn* filling; formerly a trade name.

fuji silk Lightweight *silk* fabric made of *spun yarns,* not entirely degummed, in *plain weave;* originally made in Japan and used for underwear.

fur fabrics Woven or knitted fabrics, usually with a *pile weave,* made to resemble furs, e.g., stenciled with leopard or zebra markings or pressed in pattern to resemble *broadtail, q.v.,* or curled to resemble *Persian lamb, q.v.,* or sheared to resemble *mouton lamb* or *seal.*

gabardine Durable, closely woven fabric with definite diagonal ridges, made of wool, rayon, cotton, and other fibers; used for tailored suits, coats, pants, sportswear, riding breeches, etc. Also spelled *gaberdine, q.v.* See *twills.*

galatea 1. *Cotton warp sateen* or *jean, q.v.,* in solid colors and printed stripes; used for children's clothes, nurses' uniforms, etc. *Der.* Named for British man-of-war H.M.S. *Galatea.* 2. Even-striped blue and white *cotton* shirting fabric made in Great Britain.

gauze Net-like fabric used for trimmings and costumes made in *plain weave* of silk, cotton, rayon, and other man-made fibers.

georgette Fine sheer *silk* or *cotton* fabric made in *plain weave* with twisted yarns giving a crepy surface; used for dresses, evening gowns, blouses, and nightgowns. Also called *crepe georgette.*

gingham Yarn-dyed *cotton* fabric, checked in white with one color or plaid in several colors, sometimes in thin tissue weight called *zephyr gingham;* used for blouses, dresses, children's wear, etc. See *checks, plaids.*

gossamer (goss-a-mer) 1. Veiling fabric made of fine, sheer *silk.* 2. Lightweight fabric of cotton, silk, and wool, etc., treated with rubber composition to make it waterproof.

granite cloth Fabric, especially *wool,* firmly constructed with a pebbly surface produced by the weave, usually an irregular *satin* or *twill.*

grass cloth Hand-loomed fabrics of *ramie, flax, hemp,* etc. lustrous and loosely woven in *plain weave,* used for sportswear, blouses.

gray flannel *Flannel, q.v.,* that is dyed in the fiber rather than fabric piece in varying shades of gray, giving a slightly uneven coloring; the same effect also produced in other colors. The wide popularity of gray flannel as a man's suiting fabric among junior executives in the 1950's led to a novel by Sloan Wilson, *The Man in the Gray Flannel Suit,* in 1955. See *dyed-in-the-wool.*

grenadine Openwork *cotton* or *wool* fabric in which vertical warp threads are paired and twisted giving a firm texture; used for dresses and coats. *Der.* Named for Granada, Spain.

gros de Londres (grow de londreh) Lightweight *silk* or *rayon* fabric with flat ribs in varied, alternating sizes, used for dresses.

grosgrain (grow-grain) Fabric of silk, rayon, or cotton with rounded *ribs,* close together, running cross-wise; used for millinery, neckwear, and trimmings.

habutai (ha-boo-tie) Soft, lightweight, plain *silk* fabric woven in Japan on hand or power looms. Also spelled *habutae* and *habutaye.*

handkerchief lawn 1. Sheer combed-*cotton* fabric with borders woven in heavier yarns, used for women's and children's dresses, handkerchiefs, blouses, neckwear, etc. 2. Same type of fabric made of *linen,* called *handkerchief linen.*

Harris tweed *Woolen* fabric, hand woven only in islands of Outer Hebrides, off Scotland. Woven either from hand-spun or machine-spun yarns and marked with an orb for identification.

Hessian See *burlap.*

hickory stripes Fabric similar to *denim* made in blue and white stripes used for sportswear and work clothes. Also called *liberty stripes.*

himalaya 1. Variant of *cotton shantung, q.v.* 2. Austrian term for *wool* fabric with high brushed surface, similar to *zibelline, q.v.* Sometimes spelled *himalaja.*

hollow-cut velveteen Velveteen cut with wide ribs like corduroy. Also called *velvet cord.*

homespun Loosely woven fabric in simple weave, using coarse, uneven yarns, not too tightly twisted. Made of wool, spun rayon, wool blends, or man-made fibers; similar to homewoven tweeds in texture.

hopsacking Broad classification of fabrics made in loosely constructed *basket weave* of coarse *uneven yarns* —cotton, spun rayon, and man-made fibers—derived from type of *jute* sacks used by farmers.

illusion Fine *tulle, maline,* or *net, q.q.v.*

inauguration cloth Fabric made in U.S. in imitation of *coronation cloth, q.v.,* with single-thread stripes of red, white, and blue.

Indian dimity *Cotton* fabric with fine cords at intervals, finer than domestic dimity, made in India.

Indian Head Trademark for *cotton* fabric woven to imitate linen crash, introduced in 1831 by Nashua Manufacturing Co. and used for sportswear and children's clothing.

indienne French *cotton* fabric with a small design, or cotton fabric made with alternating warp-woven and floral-print stripes.

Irish linen Fine quality *linen* fabric woven from flax grown mainly in Northern Ireland; used for handkerchiefs and apparel.

Irish poplin 1. Irish fabric with slight rib made with *silk* warp and *woolen* filling. 2. Trademark once used in U.S. for similar fabric made entirely of *cotton*.

Irish tweed Variant of *Donegal tweeds, q.v.,* usually made in *twill weave* with white warp and colored filling. Used for suits, sportswear, and coats.

Italian cloth 1. Glossy *lining* fabric made in *twill* or *satin weave* in all cotton, or cotton with wool, usually dyed black. Also called *Albert, farmer's satin,* and *Venetian.* 2. Lining fabric used in uniforms of the U.S. Marine Corps, of combed *cotton,* dyed black or green.

jaconet Gray *cotton* goods made in variety of qualities, the best sheer finished for use in dresses and children's summer clothing; originally made in India. Also spelled *jaconet, jaconnette,* and *jaconnot.*

Janus cloth Reversible *worsted* fabric with different color on either side.

jean Warp-faced *cotton twill* fabric similar to but lighter than drill, may be printed or dyed in solid colors; used for sports and work clothes, uniforms, shoe linings, etc. Sometimes word is applied to *denim,* as in *blue jeans, q.q.v.*

jersey Fabric *knitted* in plain stitch of *wool, cotton,* or *man-made fibers,* in plain color, printed, or Jacquard-knitted patterns, etc.; used for dresses, coats, sportswear.

kanga Cotton fabric in bold prints, usually measuring 63" by 44", woven in Africa.

karakul cloth Heavyweight *pile* fabric, imitating caracul or astrakhan lamb; used for coats.

kasabeh Cloth woven from the *wool* of the sheep in Kashmir, made of fine mesh in *plain* weave in many qualities; used for shawls and veils. Also called *chaharbagh* or *chantahi.*

kasha 1. Light brown soft *cotton* flannel with napped face and iridescent back; used for lining coats, jackets, and hats. 2. Paris tradename for fine *wool* flannel in *twill weave* made of *vicuña, cashmere,* or *merino* wool. Also spelled *casha.*

kersey 1. Heavy durable *woolen* fabric with long lustrous nap, similar to melton and beaver cloth; used for uniforms and overcoats. 2. Fabric that originated in 11th century in English town of Kersey, made in wool or cotton and wool in *twill weave* of coarse yarns.

kerseymere Fabric made of fine quality *wool* in *twill weave* finished by napping. Similar to *cassimere.*

khaddar (kud-er) Handwoven *cotton* of coarse texture woven in India from native yarns, sometimes spelled *khada* and *khadi*.

khaki (kah-ki) Dull yellowish-brown *cotton* or wool uniform fabric, whether plain, serge, drill, or whipcord, used for its camouflage effect by armed forces of France, England, and U.S. since 1848; in World War I, a green tint was added. Khaki work pants and jackets adapted for sports by men and women in 1950's and 1960's. *Der.* Hindu, dust color.

laid fabric Type of non-woven fabric made with warp yarns and no filling yarns. Warps held together by latex rubber or other adhesives.

lawn Sheer, lightweight *cotton* fabric made in *plain weave* of fine combed yarns. May be dyed or printed and given a soft or starched finish; used mainly for handkerchiefs. *Der.* From fine linen fabric made in Laon, France. Also see *handkerchief lawn*.

leno Net-like transparent fabric made with the *leno weave, q.v.*

levantine 1. Glazed *cotton* fabric in *twill weave* used for linings, originally made of silk and imported into England from the Levant. 2. Early 19th century velvet.

limousine 1. Hairy, rough *woolen* fabric produced in England in late 19th century; thicker, heavier and coarser than Cheviot. 2. Striped *herringbone* fabric made in England, made of *worsted,* fulled and napped, sometimes with fancy loop yarn for added decoration.

linen cambric See *cambric,* above.

linen canvas 1. Firm *linen* fabric used as interfacing for collars and fronts of jackets and coats, contains no sizing and is shrinkproof to permit dry cleaning or washing. Also called *tailor's canvas.* 2. Openwork fabric used for embroidery purposes. Also called *Java canvas* and *Aida canvas.* See *embroidery.*

linen crash Fabric with an uneven textured effect woven in *plain weave,* usually with yarn-dyed yarns, particularly a white and black combination; popular for boys' knickers in the 1920's.

lingerie crepe Flat lightweight silky crepe originally made of crepe-twisted *silk* yarns in France and called French crepe; now made in rayon, acetate, nylon, and blends for slips and other lingerie. Also see *French crepe.*

linsey-woolsey Coarse loosely woven fabric in bright colors with *linen* warp and *wool* filling, with *cotton* sometimes substituted for the linen; popular in American Colonial times, came from England where it was first called *linsey. Der.* Named for Linsey, a village in Sussex, England.

loden cloth Thick, filled, water-repellent coatings and suitings woven by people of the Tyrol section of Austria of local *wool,* sometimes with the addition of *camel hair;* popular for winter sportswear, skiwear, and coats.

long cloth Lightweight, high count, *cotton* fabric woven in plain weave of slightly twisted combed yarns, similar to *nainsook, q.v.;* formerly used for infants and children's dresses and lingerie.

Lyons satin 1. Originally French *silk satin* with *twilled* back, used for linings. 2. Good quality satin with dull finish having *silk* back and *cotton* face, used for trimmings. *Der.* English name for the town of origin, Lyon, France.

Lyons velvet Velvet fabric with good body and erect pile; has excellent draping qualities and resistance to crushing. Originally made of *silk* with a silk pile in Lyons, France; now made of *rayon* with twill background weave and used for high quality millinery and dresses. *Der.* English name for Lyon, France.

Macclesfield silk Textile trade term for *silk* fabrics woven in Macclesfield, England; also applied in U.S. to other silks in small *dobby* patterns used for neckties, sometimes for dresses.

mackinaw or **Mackinac cloth** Heavy napped *wool* cloth similar in texture to blankets purchased by the Indians at remote trading post at Fort Mackinac, Michigan, from which original mackinaw coats were made; usually woven in *double-cloth* construction, with plaid on one side and a plain color or different plaid on other side. Today sometimes contains cotton or rayon mixtures.

mackinaw flannel Napped *woolen* fabric heavy in weight and soft in texture, usually dyed red or blue and used for sport shirts; named for Mackinac Island; see *sport jackets* under *jackets.*

Madras Fine *cotton,* hand-loomed in variety of striped, checked, or plaided patterns in the Madras section of India. Indian vegetable dyes bleed when washed, giving a soft blending to color; this effect sometimes called *bleeding Madras.* Simi-lar domestic fabrics are color-fast; Federal Trade Commission rules forbid their being sold as "Madras." Used for dresses and men's and women's sportswear. Heavier white-on-white versions used for foundation garments. *Der.* From city of Madras, India.

maline (ma-leen) 1. Extremely fine silk, rayon, nylon, or cotton *net* with hexagonal holes, used primarily for millinery. 2. A sturdy *plain-weave worsted* fabric. 3. See *laces.*

marble cloth British fabric made with several colored yarns used in the filling giving an iridescent effect.

marocain Fabric with wavy *ribbed* effect caused by using spiral filling yarns; may be in silk, wool, rayon, man-made fibers, or combinations of various fibers; used for dresses and women's suits.

marquisette (mar-kee-set) Fine, transparent, net-like fabric with good durability, in cotton, silk, and polyesters in *leno weave,* which prevents filling from slipping; used for evening gowns, cocktail dresses, and blouses.

Marseilles (mar-say) Reversible fabric in *Jacquard weave* with raised woven pattern, all white, or white with colored design, used for men's fancy vests. *Der.* Named for city in France where first manufactured.

matelassé (mat-lass-ay) Fabric with a "padded" effect, originally made in France of *silk* and quilted in the loom; now a double or compound fabric with raised designs produced by a *Jacquard* or *dobby* loom. Crepe and ordinary yarns are combined;

and, in finishing, the crepe yarns shrink to give a puckered or blistered effect. May be silk, cotton, wool, or man-made fibers. Rayon matelasse resembles *blister crepe, q.v.* Used for blouses, evening dresses and wraps, robes, etc. *Der.* French, padded.

melange suitings (may-lanzh) Fabrics of *wool* or fine *cashmere* yarns that have been printed with various colors before they are woven, giving a mixed-color effect.

Melrose Fabric of *silk* and *wool* in double *twill weave, q.v. Der.* Named for Melrose, Scotland, where it was first produced during 18th century.

melton Heavy, compact *woolen* cloth, with short lustrous nap; used for men's, women's and children's coats and snow suits and for army uniform coats; lighter weight is called *meltonette.*

merveilleux (mare-vay-yer) Lining fabric in *satin weave* with *twill back;* silk and cotton, all silk, or all rayon; used for linings in men's outer apparel. *Der.* French, marvelous.

metallic cloth Any type of fabric made with *metallic* yarns such as *Lurex* or *Mylar, q.q.v., woven* or *knitted,* some with Jacquard designs; used for blouses, dresses, and at-home wear, hose, etc.

mignonette Lustrous *circular-knit* rayon or *silk* fabric made with fine mesh; porous, elastic, and usually piece dyed, similar to but finer than *tricolette, q.v.*

millinery velvet Velvet with a crisp texture and short erect pile, similar to *Lyons velvet, q.v.,* but made in narrow widths for hats.

Mogador Tie fabric similar to *faille, q.v.,* with fine crosswise ribs, in striped patterns. *Der.* Named for Moroccan seaport town, Mogador, where natives wear similar colorful striped fabrics.

mohair Fabric made entirely of *mohair* obtained from the *angora* goat, or of mohair combined with other fibers; content must be declared. *Der.* Arabic *mukhayyar,* goat's-hair fabric.

mohair-pile f. Fabric woven as *double-cloth construction* with *mohair*-yarn pile, *cotton* back, and connecting mohair yarns which can be cut through to make two fabrics.

moiré Stiff, heavy ribbed fabric made of *rayon* or *acetate* and *cotton,* embossed to give a watered effect; used for evening dresses, skirts, coats.

moleskin Durable *cotton* fabric with suede-like nap, made in *satin weave* of coarse yarns; used for sportswear and work clothes. *Der.* From Arabian *molequin,* old fabric. Also see *buckskin* and *furs.*

momie cloth Classification of fabrics characterized by a crinkled or pebbly surface peculiar to crepes, the weave called *momie weave, q.v.*

monk's cloth A heavy, coarse cotton fabric in basket weave with loose construction, often in natural oatmeal color or dyed or woven in stripes or plaid; originally used for monks' robes.

Montagnac (mon-tan-yak) Soft, fine, high-quality fabric in *twill weave* with curly nap, made of *cashmere* frequently with *camel hair* or *vicuña* added, in Sedan, France; used for overcoats.

Moscow Heavyweight *woolen* overcoating fabric made in *plain weave* with shaggy nap, similar to *Shetland, q.v.*

mousseline de laine (moose-eh-lean de lenn) Lightweight *plain-weave worsted* dress fabric usually printed; first made in France in 1826, made in Massachusetts in 1840. *Der.* French, wool muslin.

mousseline de soie (moose-eh-lean de swah) Transparent, fine, lightweight *silk* or *rayon* fabric made in *plain weave* and given a stiff finish, but softer than organdy, used for formal dresses and millinery. *Der.* French, silk muslin.

Mozambique 1. Lightweight net-like fabric of combed *cotton* and *mohair* in plaids, checks, and openwork patterns. 2. *Woolen* fabric with nap raised in geometrical patterns of squares and dots.

muga silk Fawn or gold-colored wild *silk* from India of good quality, cultivated in Assam. *Der.* Assamese, light brown.

mull Soft, thin, *plain-weave* fabric in fine *cotton, silk,* etc., dyed in pale colors; popular in England, sometimes labelled China, Swiss, India, or French mull. Also called *mulmul.*

mummy cloth 1. Dull-finish crepe-like fabric of cotton or silk and wool, worn for mourning when dyed black. 2. Heavy *linen* or *cotton plain-weave* fabric used for embroidery work.

muslin *Plain-weave cotton* fabric, sheer to coarse, lustrous, washable, long wearing, the finer qualities dyed and printed and used for dresses, blouses, etc. A light, crinkled muslin

from India was popular in early 1970's. See *unbleached muslin,* below.

nacré velvet *Velvet, q.v.,* with an iridescent effect caused by using one color for background yarns, another color for the pile; used for evening wear.

nainsook Soft, lightweight *plain-weave cotton* fabric slightly heavier than *batiste, q.v.,* bleached, dyed or printed, sometimes given crisp glossy finish; used for infants' clothing and blouses.

nainsook checks *Plain-weave cotton* fabric divided by horizontal and vertical lines of *twill* or *satin* weave into checks; used for dresses and sportswear.

nakli daryai Handloomed *plain-weave cotton* fabric made in India in imitation of *darya silk, q.v.;* usually dyed light green or yellow.

nankeen 1. Durable brownish-yellow *cotton* fabric, originally handloomed in China. Also spelled *nankin.* 2. Rumanian term for *cotton* fabric of mixed white, pink, red, or yellow. See *Rajah* and *shantung.*

natte Loose *basket-weave silk,* or *rayon* fabric made with different colored yarns in the warp and filling. *Der.* French, mat or braid.

ninon Lightweight, crisp, transparent, *open plain-weave* fabric made of silk, nylon, polyester, etc.; used for blouses, dresses and lingerie.

Norfolk suiting *Woolen* or *worsted* fabric made in Norfolk, England, popular at time *Norfolk jacket, q.v.* was introduced in 1880's.

nun's veiling Sheer lightweight fabric woven in a *plain weave* of fine silk, cotton, or worsted yarns, usually dyed black for use by nuns or for mourning.

oatmeal 1. Heavy, rough-textured fabric with a flecked surface, made with crepe twisted yarn in *granite weave.* 2. Fabric with small repeat design woven in, producing a rough speckled effect.

oiled silk Translucent waterproof fabric made by giving linseed-oil treatment to lightweight *silk* fabric; formerly used for rainwear.

oilskin Sturdy bright-yellow opaque waterproof fabric made by coating *cotton* with linseed oil; used for raincoats worn by fishermen, sailors, children, etc. See *oiled silk.*

ondulé (on-dew-lay) Cotton, silk, or man-made fiber in *plain weave,* made with *wavy* effect on surface, either through texture of yarn or by technique of weaving. *Der.* French, wavy.

one-hundred-denier crepe Lightweight fabric with fine crinkled texture made of very fine *viscose rayon* yarn, similar in appearance to flat crepe.

organdy or **organdie** Sheer, high quality *cotton* fabric in open weave, made with permanent crispness, often white, sometimes printed or embroidered by *Schiffli machine, q.v.,* e.g., *eyelet organdy,* and used for dresses, aprons, collars and cuffs and millinery. Also see *organza* and *lawn.*

organza Lightweight, thin, wiry, transparent *rayon* fabric in *plain weave;* used for dresses, millinery, trimmings, neck-wear, blouses.

Osnaburg Medium-weight *plain-weave cotton* fabric, sometimes striped or checked, of coarse yarns, sometimes made partly of cotton waste; used for workshirts, overalls, tie linings, boot and shoe linings, etc. *Der.* Named for Osnaburg, Germany, where it was made of flax and tow, often striped in blue or brown.

ottoman Heavy luxurious fabric with broad flat crosswise *ribs* or *wales, q.v.,* made from silk, acetate, rayon, cotton, or wool, also knitted and called *ottoman knit;* used for coats, evening wear, suits, trimming.

outing flannel Light or medium-weight soft, fuzzy *cotton* fabric, made with lightly twisted yarns that are napped to conceal the *plain weave* completely; may be in yarn-dyed stripes, piece dyed, or printed and used for winter pajamas, nightshirts, and gowns.

oxford cloth 1. Man's shirting fabric made in *basket weave,* plain or with yarn-dyed stripes or small fancy designs. 2. *Woolen* fabric made of gray mixture yarns. See *Oxford gray.* Named for Oxford University in England by Scottish mill that first made it.

paddock Lightweight *worsted* coating fabric in *twill weave,* piece-dyed in shades of brown, with water-repellent finish; made in Great Britain.

Palm Beach Trademark for men's lightweight summer suiting fabric, originally made with a *cotton* warp and *mohair* filling, now made of blended yarns; named for Palm Beach, Florida.

Panama suiting Men's summer suiting fabric made of *cotton* and *worsted plain weave,* usually dyed in solid colors and wrinkle resistant.

panne satin Glossy, heavyweight dress satin made of all silk, fine cotton, acetate, rayon, or combination of acetate and rayon; the finish provided by very heavy roller pressure.

panne velvet Velvet that has pile flattened in one direction by heavy roller pressure giving a glossy appearance, sometimes with a pressed pattern and called *embossed velvet;* used for dresses, sportswear. *Der.* French, plush.

parachute cloth Lightweight, strong *silk* or *nylon* porous fabric originally used to make parachutes; sometimes used for bridal gowns because of shortage of fabrics during World War II.

Peau d'Ange (po de ahn-ghe) Trademark for *angel skin, q.v.*

peau de cygne (po de seen-yeh) Soft lustrous heavy *silk* fabric with crinkled effect made in *satin weave* with creped yarns. *Der.* French, swan skin.

peau de soie (po de swah) Heavyweight *satin* with a *fine ribbed* effect in the filling made of silk or man-made fibers, piece dyed and given a dull luster. Better grades are reversible; used for dresses, evening gowns, shoes, wedding dresses. *Der.* French, skin of silk.

pebble Cheviot Heavy nubbed fabric made in *twill weave* of *worsted, woolen,* etc.; used for overcoats and sport jackets.

Pellon Trademark, owned by Pellon Corp. of America, for non-woven fabric used for interlining and made by fusing natural fibers and man-made fibers; used as interlining in collars and facings, and for brassieres in women's swimsuits.

percale (per-kale) Plain, smooth lightweight fabric of *cotton,* sometimes blended with *polyester;* used for dresses, shirts, children's clothing and sheeting.

percaline (per-ka-leen) 1. Lustrous soft-finished *cotton* lining fabric, usually in dark colors, used for clothing and furs. 2. Lustrous *cotton* fabric with linen-like surface. Also called *cotton taffeta.*

Petersham (pee-ter-shem) 1. Narrow thick *cotton* fabric, slightly stiffened and used for belt linings and hat bands. 2. Heavy *woolen* overcoating made with nub yarns or a thick nap rubbed into small nubs. 3. Heavy, windproof navy-blue *woolen* used for seamen's overcoats in Britain.

pilot cloth Coarse, heavy navy-blue *woolen* fabric in *twill weave,* used for seamen's jacket called *pilot coat* or *pea jacket, q.q.v.*

pima cotton Fabric of fine-quality long-staple *cotton* raised in southern U.S.A. and in Mexico, a variety of American-Egyptian cotton developed in 1910; used in shirting, dress goods, etc. *Der.* Named for Pima County, Arizona, where cotton was developed; the county named for local Indians.

piqué or **pique** (pee-kay) Group of *double-woven* fabrics, usually *cotton,* with crosswise corded ribs or fancy weaves; e.g., 1. *pinwale piqué* with small ribs. 2. *Waffle piqué* with honeycomb weave. 3. *Birdseye piqué* with diamond pattern, etc.; used for women's and girls' dresses, sportswear, neckwear, etc. 4. The lighter weights of *Bedford cord, q.v.,* are called *warp piqué.*

plissé (plee-say) Lightweight *cotton* or *man-made fabric* with a puckered surface produced by a caustic-soda method; used for pajamas, nightgowns and children's clothing. Also known as *crinkle crepe* and *plissé crepe.*

plumetis Fine sheer fabric made in *wool* or *cotton* produced on a swivel loom with small feathery yarn tufts interspaced over the surface.

plush *Warp pile* fabric woven less closely than velvet with pile cut longer; made of cotton, wool, mohair, synthetic fibers, plain on multicolored; sometimes crushed or embossed to imitate furs and used for apparel, trimmings, and hats.

Poiret twill Trademark for a *worsted* piece-dyed fabric finer and smoother than gabardine; used for dresses and suits. Named after the French couturier *Paul Poiret, q.v.*

Polo Cloth Trademark for heavyweight coating fabric, usually in camel color, with soft thick nap on both sides, made of *wool* or *camel's hair* or a blend; used for *polo coats, q.v.,* and other overcoats.

pongee (pon-gee) Rough-textured light to medium-weight *silk,* originally made from Chinese wild silk in natural ecru color, with nubs and irregular cross ribs; used for dresses,

pajamas, linings, etc. *Der.* Chinese *pen-chi,* homewoven.

poodle cloth *Knitted* or *woven* fabric with curled nap over entire surface, similar to *astrakhan fabric, q.v.,* but with looser curls.

poplin Medium-weight durable *plain-weave* fabrics with fine *crosswise ribs* produced by using warp yarns finer than the filling, made of cotton, silk, wool or man-made combinations, used for sportswear, pants, shirts, dresses, etc., often given a water-resistant finish for raincoats.

poult de soie (pult de swa) *Silk* fabric in *plain weave* with a cross-rib created by heavier filling; made in solid colors, used for dresses.

prunella 1. Warp-faced *twill-weave* fabric. 2. *Worsted* fabric in *twill weave,* usually dyed dark purple or plum color and used for clergyman's clothes in 18th and 19th centuries. 3. Fabric, *worsted* or worsted warp and cotton filling, in a *satin weave,* used for shoe tops. *Der.* French, *prune,* plum.

Punjab silk Domestic imitations of *silk* fabrics from India made in checks, stripes, changeable effects, and Jacquard weaves.

Pussy Willow Trademark for *silk* fabric woven with a faint cross rib by more threads in warp than filling. Also called *Pussy Willow taffeta.*

Qiana Trademark of DuPont Co. for high quality *nylon* fabric with silky feel; used for women's and men's wear, especially dresses, shirts, robes. Also called *Fiber Y.*

queen's cloth Fine *cotton* shirting

bleached after weaving, made in Jamaica in West Indies.

radium Tightly woven crisp fabric of *silk* or *rayon* in *plain weave* with extra twist in the filling; used for dresses, blouses, linings. Sometimes called *radium taffeta*.

radzimir Fabric with a crosswise rib, usually a black lustrous *silk;* made in England and used for mourning. Also spelled *radsimer* or *rhadzimir*.

Rajah Trademark for horizontally slubbed fabric originally made in India and similar to *shantung,* or *pongee, q.q.v.;* usually made of *tussah* silk yarns, *q.v.,* and used for dresses, robes, suits, and ties.

ratiné (rat-in-ay) 1. Spongy, rough-feeling, nubby fabric loosely woven in a *plain weave* or *knitted* and made of curly, looped *ratiné yarn, q.v.,* of cotton or silk, rayon, worsted combinations. *Der.* French, frizzy.

rayon Generic name for artificial silk from 1927 on; man-made fibers derived from trees, cotton, woody plants first produced by Count Hilaire de Chardonet in 1889; now used for lingerie, dresses, shirts, etc. Also see *spun rayon* and *rayon staple.*

Reemay Trademark for *polyester* random filaments fused in sheeting form, used for interlining and disposable clothing.

Regence 1. Lustrous tie fabric with faint herringbone pattern same as *Charvet*. 2. 19th century English term for lustrous ribbed *silk* fabric.

rep Fabric with closely spaced, fine horizontal ribs, made in various fibers or combinations of fibers, originally in *silk* in 18th century France; now used for neckties and women's wear as well as upholstery. Also spelled *repp.*

ripple cloth 1. Dress fabric of coarse *wool* yarns made in *twill weave;* given a finish which raises a wavy nap. 2. Another name for *zibeline, q.v.*

romain Closely woven *satin* fabric made in France, used for dresses or linings.

Romaine Trademark for semi-sheer dull-luster fabric made of creped yarns, originally *silk,* now rayon and acetate. Also called *Romaine crepe.*

sailcloth Durable duck, *q.v.,* originally made of *cotton* or *cotton* and *linen,* frequently striped; used for sportswear. Also called *sail duck.*

Salisbury British white *wool flannel;* also called *Salisbury white.*

Sand Crepe Trademark for a fabric made of man-made fibers in a small *dobby* weave giving a sandy or frosty appearance.

sanglier *Plain-weave* dress fabric with rough, wiry surface made of tightly twisted worsted or mohair yarn. *Der.* French, wild boar.

sarcenet (sars-nit) British plain-weave *cotton* or *silk* lining fabric cloth with high luster. Also spelled *sarsenet* and *sarcenett.*

sateen Smooth, glossy, *cotton* fabric made in the *satin weave, q.v.;* used for dresses, linings, etc.

satin Smooth, lustrous, *silk* fabric woven with glossy face and dull back; with crepe back, called *crepe-back satin* or satin-backed crepe, with satin stripes and dobby designs, called *satin façonné;* finished with stiff texture, called *panne satin;* ribbed, called *ribbed satin;* dull surface with nubs and satin back, called *antique satin;* combined with velvet, called *satin-backed velvet.* Also made of rayon, acetate, nylon, or combinations of these yarns. *Der.* Name derived from Zaytoun, now Canton, China, from which fabrics were shipped in Middle Ages.

satin sultan 1. Glossy *silk* fabric made in India; used for dresses and lingerie. 2. Lustrous *worsted* fabric similar to *bengaline, q.v.*

seersucker *Cotton* fabric with permanent woven *crinkle stripes* obtained by releasing tension at intervals to produce alternating plain and puckered stripes; popular for summer suitings, children's wear, underwear, shirts, etc., either dyed or printed. Also made of man-made fibers or blends. *Der.* From Persian cloth *shirushakar,* literally, milk and sugar.

serge (surge) Fabric of wool, cotton, silk, or rayon, in *twill weave,* characterized by smooth diagonal wale; most popular as a navy-blue worsted suiting and used also for skirts, pants, etc. Silk serge is similar to *surah, q.v.*

Shaker flannel Soft, white plain weave cotton or wool fabric napped on both sides. *Der.* Said to have been first made in gray by Shakers, English religious sect that settled in U.S. first in upstate New York.

shal Plain-woven, handloomed fabric mostly *silk,* often with both vertical and horizontal stripes; made in Italy.

shalimar tweed Handwoven *wool* fabric made of handspun yarns in Kashmir in *herringbone-twill* weave.

shantung *Plain-weave silk* or man-made-fiber fabric with rough texture made by use of *uneven yarns* causing irregular slubs; dyed or printed and used for dresses, sportswear, shirts, etc. Originally made in Shantung province of China.

sharkskin 1. *Worsted* fabric with smooth finish, in *twill weave* with alternating black and white yarns to give greyed effect; used for men's suits. 2. Lightweight smooth *acetate* or *polyester basket-weave* fabric, often chalk white, used for women's sportswear and uniforms.

shot cloth Term for fabric made of silk, rayon or man-made fibers woven with yarns of different colors in warp and filling to achieve changeable appearance when held in the light.

Skinner's Satin Trademark for good quality satin in a variety of fibers; used especially for linings in coats and suits.

slipper satin Lustrous, stiff satin fabric made primarily of acetate, sometimes combined with rayon, silk, and cotton brocaded effect; used for formal gowns and shoes.

Spitalfields Fabrics with small geometric designs, made of *silk* in a variety of weaves or of other fibers, used for cravats and neckties. *Der.* From Spitalfields, England, a silk-weaving center in 16th century.

spun rayon Soft, medium-weight fabric made of *rayon* staple yarn in *twill* or *plain weave* with appearance of wool, may be yarn or piece-dyed or printed; used for dresses, men's sport shirts, children's wear, sportswear and pants.

suede cloth Woven or knitted *cotton* or *rayon* fabric imitating suede leather, having nap on one or both sides, heavier than *duvetyn, q.v.;* used for suits, coats, dresses, and sportswear.

Sunbak Trademark for a lining fabric with *viscose* warp and *worsted* filling; a *satin* face and *napped,* fleecy back.

surah Lightweight, *twill-weave* fabric of *silk* or *man-made* silky fibers woven in yarn-dyed plaids, printed, or dyed solid colors, similar to *foulard, q.v.,* but heavier; used for dresses, scarfs, neckties, blouses.

Swiss See *dotted Swiss,* above.

taffeta Crisp fabric with fine, smooth surface in *plain weave* or with small crosswise rib, made in silk, cotton, wool and man-made fibers. Produced in many qualities, called *antique, faille, moire, paper, shot cloth* and *tissue taffeta.*

tamis, tamese, tamise (ta-mee or tam-eez) 1. *Plain-weave worsted* fabric with a very smooth finish. 2. Sheer *worsted* dress fabric with satin stripe on plain woven ground. 3. Lightweight *wool* dress fabric with corded stripes. Also called *tamise rep.*

tapa cloth Fabric made from fibers of inner bark of paper mulberry tree, *Brousonnetia papyrifera,* of the tree *Pipturus albidus,* varying from a muslin-like to leathery, made by natives in Hawaiian Islands by beating bark to form web-like fabric; used for clothing by natives of Pacific Islands and eastern Asia. Also called *kapa* and *masi.* Also see *bark cloth.*

tarlatan Net-like transparent *cotton* fabric heavily sized, then dyed in solid colors; used for theatrical costumes. Also spelled *tareatane, tarletan,* or *tarlton.*

terry cloth Absorbent *cotton* fabric, *woven* or *knitted* in *pile weave* with uncut loops, solid colors or printed several colors or woven in Jacquard patterns; used for beachwear, bathrobes, sports shirts, etc.

Thibet cloth 1. Heavyweight *wool* dress or coat fabric with a soft smooth surface, made in *twill weave.* 2. *Goat's hair* fabric, similar to *camlet, q.v.;* also spelled *Tibet cloth.*

ticking Sturdy *cotton* fabric woven in close *satin* or *twill weave,* originally used for covering pillows and mattresses, now also used for sport clothes. See *stripes.*

tie silk Fabric of *silk* or *man-made fibers* used for men's neckties and scarves, usually distinguished by small geometric designs, woven in narrow widths.

tricolette 1. *Circular-knit* lustrous *rayon* or *silk* fabric made with fine mesh and gauge, which is porous, elastic, usually piece-dyed; used for underwear and dresses. Although sometimes called *mignonette,* this fabric is finer and made with a finer gauge. Tricolette, introduced in 1924, was the first knitted rayon fabric made. 2. Coarse *wool knit* fabric made in Great Britain.

tricot 1. Plain *warp-knitted* cloth

with fine vertical wales or face, cross ribs on back, made of silk or man-made fibers; "double warp" tricot is run resistant and is sometimes called *glove silk* or *charmeuse;* used for lingerie; dress tricot is called *jersey.*

tricotine Durable warp-faced fabric in a *twill weave* with double diagonal wales on surface, originally of *worsted,* now made of other fibers and blends; used for coats and suits. Also called *cavalry twill* and *elastique.*

triple sheer Lightweight *rayon* or *silk* fabric made with twisted yarn and tight weave, almost opaque, similar to *Bemberg fabric,* used for women's dresses and blouses.

tropical suiting Lightweight porous fabric made of many types of yarns, worsted, blends of wool or cotton and polyester, using fine yarns with a high twist; used for men's summer suits and coats.

tulle Fine sheer *net* fabric made of silk, nylon, or rayon with hexagonal holes; used unstarched for wedding veils and millinery, and starched for ballet costumes. *Der.* Named for French city of Tulle, where fabric was first produced by machine 1817. Sometimes called *illusion.*

tweed Rough textured, nubby fabrics made of coarse yarn-dyed *wool,* sometimes plaid or checked, in *plain, twill,* or *herringbone weave* and in various weights for coats, jackets, and suits; specialty of Scotland. *Der.* From Scottish word *tweel* meaning twill, also associated with Tweed river in Scotland.

unbleached muslin Coarse, heavily sized *cotton* utility fabric woven in a plain *weave* of natural yarns; used by dress designers to drape first pattern of a dress on dummy, also used for interfacing in suits and coats and popular for sportswear in 1970's. See *muslin,* above.

velours, velour (veh-loor) Soft thick *pile* fabric made in all cotton yarns, all wool yarns, or cotton warp and silk or mohair filling; used for coats and sportswear.

velvet Fabric, originally of *silk* but now also of man-made fibers, with short, soft, thick *pile surface* of looped warp yarns on plain or *twill-weave ground,* usually woven double and cut apart, and made in various weights and surface textures; used for dresses, coats, millinery and trimmings. Common velvet types: 1. *Bagheera* (bag-ee-ra): Fine, uncut, supple-pile velvet with rough, pebbly surface, practically uncrushable. 2. *Chiffon:* Lightweight, soft velvet with pressed pile, used for evening gowns, wraps, dresses, etc. 3. *Crushed:* Velvet processed to have irregular, bark-like surface. 4. *Lyons* (lee-on): Velvet with short, thick erect pile, backed by cotton, silk, etc., stiffer than usual velvets and used for dresses, coats and millinery. 5. *Mirror:* Velvet with shiny surface caused by pile pressed flat in various directions. 6. *Panne* (pan): Similar to *mirror velvet* with pile pressed in one direction.

velveteen *Cotton* or *rayon pile* fabric on *plain* or *twill* backing, woven singly, loops cut making soft velvety surface. See *plush.*

Viyella British trademark for lightweight flannel-like fabric, made of blended 50% *cotton* and 50% *wool,* in *twill weave* in several weights used for shirts, dresses, pajamas and underwear.

whipcord Medium to heavy-weight *worsted* fabric with a distinct diagonal wale caused by steep *twill weave,* giving a hard finish; used for men and women's suits and coats, riding habits and uniforms. Also called *artillery twill.* See *twill* under *weaves.*

windbreaker cloth Tightly woven fabrics with little porosity, which keep wind from penetrating to body, including some nylons, poplins, satin twills, and tightly woven plain weave cotton.

zephyr flannel *Flannel, q.v.,* made of silk-and-wool blended yarn.

zibeline Soft, lustrous *wool* fabric, often with hair fibers in filling, similar to *fleece, q.v.,* with long, silky waved nap pressed flat to give non-fuzzy surface; used for coats.

fabric count See *count of cloth.*

fabric finishes, basic The processes required to convert gray (or greige) goods into final fabric by mechanical or chemical means; these include shedding, singeing, brushing, beetling, mercerization, tentering, calendering, moiréing, pressing, embossing, crimping, glazing, polishing, napping, weighting, coating, sizing or dressing, and starching. See *special finishes,* below.

fabric finishes, special Treatments applied to fabrics to suit them to specific uses; these include shrinkage control, absorbancy control, crease resistance, flame resistance, anti-bacterial properties, mildew and rot prevention, moth- and water-repellency, wrinkle resistance, waterproofing, plastic coating, and durable press.

face 1. Right side of fabric with better appearance, as opposed to back, or reverse side; although some fabrics are reversible and may be used on both sides. 2. (pl.) Hair swept foreward to frame the face in a wind-blown effect; worn by *dandies, q.v.,* in the Directoire period.

face cone Long megaphone-type cone held over face while wig was powdered in 18th century.

face-finished fabric Textile-industry term applied to fabrics finished on right side or *face* of fabric, *e.g.,* Bolivia, chinchilla, bouclé, kersey, melton, etc.

facet In jewelry, small plane cut in gemstone to enhance its ability to reflect light; the more facets, the more brilliance.

facing 1. Sewing term for self-fabric lining used on curved or irregularly shaped area of garment, *e.g.,* neckline, lapels, collars, cuffs, or hem. 2. 12th century garments had turned-back sections or facings made of fur or a rich fabric to give appearance that entire garment was lined. Also see *parament.*

facing silk Term for fabrics of silk and rayon, such as heavy satin and grosgrain; used primarily for facing lapels of men's formal wear or as linings.

façonné (fa-so-nay) French term for figured fabrics with dobby-woven designs, usually small; term sometimes applied to Jacquard fabrics.

façonné velvet See *fabrics.*

facts See *fax.*

fad Short-lived fashion that becomes

suddenly extremely popular, remains so for a short period of time, and fades quickly.

fade-ometer Textile laboratory machine that tests amount of light fabric can take before color changes occur.

fading Loss of color in fabrics from exposure to light, from washing, dry cleaning, or from ordinary household fumes. See *fume fading.*

fagoting 1. Open-work embroidery done by drawing horizontal threads of a fabric and tying the vertical threads in hour-glass shaped bunches. 2. Method of joining two fabric edges together by means of embroidery stitches that gives a lacy effect. Also see *hem stitching,* and *fagoting stitch* under *stitches.* British spelling is *fagotting.*

faille Ribbed silk. See *fabrics.*

faille crepe Smooth, dull crepe. See *fabrics.*

faille taffeta Ribbed taffeta. See *fabrics.*

Fairchild, Edmund W. (1867–1949) Founder of *Menswear Magazine* originally called the *Chicago Herald Gazette* and *Chicago Apparel Gazette.* The business periodical was first published in 1896. Louis E., his brother, took over the financial management of the business. Founded *Daily News Record* in 1892, *Women's Wear Daily* in 1910, *Footwear News* in 1945, and other business periodicals. Retired in 1941 and sons Louis, Edgar and Edmund, Jr., took over the management of the business.

Fair Isle sweater See *sweaters.*

faja Broad brilliantly colored silk sash worn in Spain and Latin America by men as a part of their native dress.

fake fur Soft pile fabric made to imitate fur. See *fabrics.*

falbala French term for large gathered silk or lace ruffle used at hem of skirt or petticoat in second half of 18th century. Also called *furbelow, q.v.* Also spelled *fabala.*

falbala wig See *Duvillier wig.*

faldetta 1. Native headdress of Malta consisting of hood and cape in one piece, made of black silk, the hood stiffened with whalebone or cardboard to make an arched frame for face. 2. Waist-length colored taffeta women's mantle trimmed with wide lace ruffle; worn in 1850.

fall 1. See *hairpieces.* 2. A collar; same as *falling band, q.v.* 3. (plural) Term for the front opening of men's trousers from 1730 on; e.g., *whole falls* were flaps extending across front to side seams, *small* or *split falls* meant a central flap similar to that on sailor pants.

fal-lals Term for any trifling decoration on a garment or accessory, e.g., ribbons and bows, used from 17th century on.

falling band 1. Large flat turned-down collar attached to the shirt at first, later a separate garment, usually edged with lace and worn instead of

the *ruff, q.v.,* by men and women, e.g., Pilgrim's collar; worn from mid 16th century to mid 17th century. Also called a *fall* or a *falling collar.*

falling collar Variant of *falling band, q.v.*

falling ruff Unstarched *ruff, q.v.,* which fell around the neck in unregulated folds; worn by men in France during reign of Henry IV, 1589–1610, and called *fraise à la confusion;* worn in England from about 1615 to 1640 by men and women.

falling tucker Fabric fill-in hanging over front of low-cut bodice of gown; worn in late 18th century and early 19th century.

fall lift Late 1960's term for dome-shaped piece of wire mesh placed on head under hair to give height at top of head, frequently used when wearing a *hairpiece* called a *fall, q.v.*

false bosoms Term introduced in early 1800's for padding used to extend the bust.

false calves Padding inserted in men's stockings, to make legs more shapely; worn during 17th and 18th, and 19th centuries. Also called *downy calves.*

false doublet Jewelry-industry term for stone made from two pieces cemented at the girdle, genuine stone for the *crown* or top, and cheaper stone or glass for the *pavilion,* or bottom part.

false eyelashes Eyelashes made of animal hair or synthetic fibers attached to a narrow band that is fastened to the eyelid with adhesive; lashes may also be individually glued in place by a skilled technician.

false gown 18th-century woman's dress style borrowed from dresses worn by little girls in France, featuring a tight bodice, gathered skirt, and wide ribbon sash.

false hips Side hoops or *paniers, q.v.,* worn in England from the 1740's to 1760's. Also see *oblong hoops.*

false rump Same as *rump furbelow, q.v.*

false sleeves 14th century sleeve with a dangling streamer of fabric which hung to the ankle. Also called *hanging sleeves, q.v.*

falsies Bust pads, usually of foam rubber, inserted into brassiere to give a rounder appearance, originally made of lace ruffles and sometimes called *fluffy ruffles* or *gay deceivers;* height of popularity in 1950's when a large bosom was the desired shape.

fan A hand-held implement for creating a breeze; usually a wedge shape, pleated, and collapsible; or round, flat, and rigid, on a handle; made of hand-painted silk, paper, or carved ivory in early Egypt, China, and Japan and in the Western world made of paper, fabric, lace, tortoise shell, feathers, or woven palm. The fan was considered a weapon for coquetry with definite rules, from 17th through 19th centuries. See *duck's-foot fan,* or *folding fan.*

fanchon (fan-shon) Small lace-trimmed head scarf or the lace trimming on sides of an outdoor bonnet or day cap; worn in the 1800's.

fanchon cap Small indoor cap of tulle or lace with side pieces covering the ears; worn by women in 1840's to 1860's. See illustration, page 210.

fancies Term used from 1650 to 1670's for ribbon trimmings used on

FANCHON CAP

men's *petticoat breeches, q.v.,* or other types of open-legged breeches.

fan collar Standing collar shaped like opened fan, placed at back of neck; popular in Elizabethan age.

fancy dress See *costumes.*

fancy leather Industry term for leather having a natural grain of distinct pattern, e.g., alligator, lizard, and snakeskin, or embossed effects simulating reptile patterns or leathers given a decorative finish, such as gold and silver kid.

fancy work *Embroidery* or needlework. See *embroideries.*

fan hoop Hoop petticoat, cone-shaped but compressed front and back; worn in England in 1740's and 1750's.

fanny sweater See *sweaters.*

fanons Two decorative *lappets* attached to back of *miter, q.q.v.,* worn by Pope, which hang down over the shoulders; these may originally have been used to hold the miter on the head.

fan pleats See *sunburst* under *pleats.*

fantail hat *Tricorn* hat with wide brim cocked, *q.q.v.,* or turned up at the sides, tapered to a point in back,

worn, in last quarter of 18th century, by men and women for horseback riding.

fantail wig Man's wig of early 18th century with *queue* hanging loose in many small curls in back.

farmer's satin See *fabrics.*

farthingale Woman's coarse linen petticoat stretched over iron, wire, cane, bone, or whalebone into a cone-like shape; introduced in Spain in late 15th century and worn in France in 16th century. For other *farthingales* see *bum roll, drum farthingale, English farthingale, French farthingale, guard Infanta, Spanish farthingale,* and *wheel farthingale.*

farthingale sleeves Sleeves cut in *bishop, q.v.,* shape held out with wire, reeds or whalebone; worn in late 16th century and early 17 century by men and women.

fascinator Loosely crocheted shawl, oblong or triangular, worn over head

by women in 19th century, popular again in 1940's as replacement for hat. See *shawls.*

fashion Custom or style of dressing that prevails among any group of persons; the style for the present, which may last for a year or two or for a span of many years. In earlier times, a fashion could last fifty to one hundred years but changes in fashion occur rapidly in the 20th century.

fashion babies 17th and 18th-century term for dolls, sometimes life sized, dressed in latest Paris court fashions, and sent to England, Spain, and America to demonstrate the new modes, before printed fashion illustrations were available. Called *Pandoras, pedlar dolls* and *poupees de la rue de Saint Honore. E.g., Rose Bertin, q.v.,* made fashion babies for Marie Antoinette.

Fashion Group, The An international professional association of women executives in fashion manufacturing, marketing, retailing, communication, and education, founded in 1931 with Mary Brooks Picken as the first president; based in New York, the Group circulates information among its five thousand members by means of fashion shows, exhibits, speeches, and discussion panels—usually at breakfast or luncheon meetings.

fashion industry The production of all clothing and accessories for women, men, and children and all the related trades necessary to produce these items, considered one of the main industries in New York City.

fashion plate 1. Illustration depicting the prevailing or new styles in clothing and accessories. 2. Individual who consistently dresses in the current mode.

fashion promotion Sales promotion of fashion merchandise in a retail store, accomplished by newspaper and periodical advertising and by fashion shows.

fashion research 1. Conducting of fashion counts, consumer surveys, and the study of past performance of an item in order to forecast the demand for various types of fashion merchandise. 2. Study of historical costume to suggest ideas for contemporary styles.

fashion show Parade of fashions, on live models, usually on a runway or stage given by a retail store, a designer, or a manufacturer to promote fashion merchandise; frequently given to introduce the clothes for a new season, or as a benefit performance for charity. Same as *style show.* First fashion show with live models staged by *Vogue* magazine under Edna Woolman Chase in November, 1914, started the idea of fashion shows for charity which spread over the country.

fashion trend Direction in which styles, colors, and fabrics are moving, influenced by political events, movies, plays, social and sports events, etc.

fast-color Describing dyed fabric that will not fade when subjected to sunlight, washing, dry cleaning, perspiration, or atmospheric fumes.

fastener Small device used for closing on clothing and accessories, including *button, frog, gripper, hook and eye, lacer, snap, toggle,* and *zipper, q.q.v.,* some under *closings.*

fatas (fah-tus) Sheer silk or cotton veil, elaborately embroidered in gold and frequently made with gold fringed edge; formerly worn in Russia over an ornate headdress.

Fath, Jacques See *designers appendix, France.*

fatigue cap See *army cap* under *caps.*

fatigues See *pants.*

Fauntleroy, Lord Young boy's costume consisting of black velvet tunic with wide sash and knee pants, wide white lace collar and cuffs, black stockings and pumps, shoulder-length hair; a style inspired by popularity of book *Little Lord Fauntleroy* by Frances Hodgson Burnett published in 1886; worn by boys in U.S. for special occasions up to First World War, 1914.

fausse montre (foss mawn-tre) Term used at end of 18th century for a snuff box disguised as a watch. *Der.* French, false watch.

fausse Valenciennes See *Valenciennes* under *laces.*

Faust slippers See *Romeo* under *slippers.*

favourites 1. Late 16th- to early 17th-century term for women's curls worn near the temples. 2. First half of 19th century, man's small tuft of hair under the chin.

fax Term used from Middle Ages to early 17th century for hair on the head. Also called *facts* and *feax.*

fearnaught See *fabrics.*

fearnothing jacket Man's jacket similar to a waistcoat with sleeves; worn by sailors, sportsmen, laborers, and apprentices in the 18th and early 19th centuries; made of heavy woolen fabric called *fearnaught, fearnothing,* or *dreadnought.* See *fabrics.*

feather Individual units from a bird's plumage, consisting of a quill or hollow shaft surrounded by closely arranged parallel barbs usually tapering to the tip; used from earliest times as hair, necklace, or body ornaments, in fans or decorations on hats from 16th century on, e.g., plumes on *Gainsborough, Robin Hood* or *mousquetaire hats, q.q.v.* In late 1960's and 1970's whole dresses, pants, shawls, and jewelry were made of feathers.

FEATHERS:

aigrette Extremely long, delicate, white feathers with plume at the tip, from the egret, a long-legged wading bird, which became almost extinct from the excesses of fashion; it is now illegal in the U.S. to use these feathers on clothes. Also spelled *aigret* and *egret.*

Amazon plume Early term for an ostrich feather, generally taken from wing of the bird, with the tips of barbs curled so shaft is concealed.

bird-of-paradise f. Long feathers from native Australian bird, fluffy and with no barbules, in brilliant reds, blues, green; now illegal for use on clothes in U.S.A.

cockade Tuft of feathers used as trim, *e.g.,* hat trim of Italian *bersaglieri,* army riflemen.

cock f. Long curly feathers from tail of the rooster, often black with blue and green iridescent highlights.

coq f. French for *cock* or *chicken.*

down Basic term for soft fluffy feathers from ducks and geese, the first plumage of young birds or the under feathers of adults.

egret f. See *aigrette.*

grebe f. Feathers from waterfowl, similar to ducks, ivory flecked with brown, popular for millinery uses in early 20th century.

guinea f. (ginny) Small, flat feathers from the guinea hen characterized by black, white, and gray striated markings; popular in 1960's for pants and stoles.

jabiru Soft fuzzy plumage from a stork-like South American bird, the white, pale smoke-colored, and black-and-white feathers were popular for trimming on women's hats, muffs, and collars in early 20th century.

marabou Soft down-like feathers from tail and wing of a species of stork; made into trimming for hats, dresses, and negligees and used in 1960's for entire garments. Also spelled *marabout.*

osprey f. Feathers from the osprey or fish hawk, the breast feathers white, other feathers brown or gray-brown crossed by brown bars; used for trimmings on hats in early 20th century.

ostrich f. Long curly plume feathers from the ostrich, a native African bird, dyed all colors and used in 1960's for whole dress, cape, stole,

or pants; popular decoration on hats for men and women in time of the Cavaliers and Louis XIV and in Edwardian era for women.

paradise f. See *bird of paradise feathers.*

peacock f. Long thin dark feathers with brilliantly marked "eye" in greenish blue at the tip, from upper tail of peacock. Individual feathers became a fad of the *hippies,* carried in the hand, in the late 1960's.

pheasant f. 1. Long stiff tail feather from the domestic game bird, with striated markings of orange, black, and brown. 2. Small soft body feathers of same bird, sometimes used to cover hats or hat bands.

feather boa Long cylindrical scarf made of feathers; worn by women

in late 19th and early 20th centuries, revived in early 1970's. See *scarfs.*

feather boning Light boning. See *bones* and *stays.*

featherbrush skirt Daytime skirt of sheer material, with overlapping flounces below knees; worn 1890's.

feather cloth See *fabrics.*

feather cut See *hairstyles.*

feathering Applying extra dye delicately to guard hairs of fur, by means of a feather dipped in dye, to improve appearance of the fur.

feather stitch See *stitches.*

featherwork North American Indian robes, clothing, war bonnets, etc., made by sewing together feathers, weaving strips of feathers, or using single large feathers of birds such as turkey, hawk, quail, duck, blue jay, etc.; most prized feathers were those of the golden eagle used for war bonnets.

feax See *fax.*

Federal Trade Commission U.S. agency that investigates and enforces laws concerning fair competition and proper labeling of such items as furs, cosmetics, fabrics, etc.

fedora See *hats.*

feed bag See *handbags.*

felling Hemming down the edges of a seam. Also see *flat-felled seam* under *seams.*

felt 1. Non-woven fabric made by compressing wool, hair, and other fibers by steam heat into sheet form with no adhesives, leaving a hard smooth surface or a soft napped finish, e.g., best quality fur felt made of beaver and rabbit hair. Felt uses: hat *hoods, q.v.,* apparel, bags, slippers. Also see *fieltro, velours.* 2. (pl.) See *slippers.*

femoralia Short pants, or drawers, reaching from waist to knees, worn by Roman troops in northern climates; probably imported by Emperor Augustus from Gaul. Also called *feminalia* or *Roman leggings.*

fencing Sport using foils or épées for which special clothing is worn. See

sport jackets under *jackets* and *masks.* See also *dueling blouse* under *blouses.*

Feraud, Louis See *designer's appendix, France.*

fermail Term used in 15th century for buckles or pins used to hold *slashes* of the garments together as on sleeves or *doublets.* Also called *fers.* Also spelled *fermayll.*

Ferragamo, Salvatore See *designers appendix, Italy.*

Ferris waist Tradename for an item of underwear worn by young girls in the late 19th and early 20th centuries consisting of a straight sleeveless cotton vest extending over the hips with reinforced bands with buttons to hold underpants and petticoats, and elastic tabs with garters to hold up long stockings. Also called *pantywaist.*

ferroniere Narrow gold or jeweled brow band worn on the forehead with evening dress by women in the 1830's.

festooned 1. Term used for garlands of flowers, braid, or other decorative trimmings arranged in loops. 2. Term for draped skirt, popular from 1860's to early 1900's.

festul Veil made of an oblong red scarf decorated with embroidery hanging to the hips and sometimes held in place by a jeweled tiara; worn by Jewish women in Morocco.

feuille morte (fueheeyh mort) Dark grayish-brown color. *Der.* French dead leaf.

fez See *hats.*

fiber Basic filament or strand from which yarns are made, either such natural materials as cotton, wool, silk, or linen, which are short fibers; or such man-made products as rayon, acetate, glass, nylon, polyester, etc. made in long continuous filaments.

fiberfill Generic term for a material consisting of fluffy short synthetic fibers, which will wash without matting; frequently made of polyester and used for making quilted fabrics and padded brassieres.

fiberglass, Fiberglas See *yarns.*

fiber lace See *laces.*

Fiber Y See *Qiana* under *fabrics.*

fibranne Generic term for French viscose rayon staple.

fibula (plural *fibulae*) Pin or brooch used by the Greeks and Romans to secure garments, especially at the

shoulder, shaped like long straight *stiletto,* or hinged like *safety pin, q.q.v.* Also see *chiton.*

fichu 1. See *collars.* 2. Small triangular lace or fabric scarf worn knotted around the neck by women, with ends falling on the chest to fill in low neckline, worn in France from 1779 on; later, a large triangle of net edged in lace worn in early 19th century as a capelet. See *Antoinette, canezou, Charlotte Corday,* etc.

fichu lavallière Woman's shoulder scarf with sides not meeting in front, fastened with a button; worn late 1860's.

fichu menteur Scarf worn by women in late 18th century at neck of coat or low bodice, draped so it puffed out, increasing apparent size of bust.

fichu-pelerine Large cape or shawl-like covering for woman's shoulders, usually white, frequently with a double cape and turned-down collar, sometimes tied in front, the ends reaching to the knee; worn in 1830's and '40's.

fichu-robings Term used in 1820's for flat trimming used on the bodice of gown from shoulders to waist to give the effect of a *fichu, q.v.*

fieltro 16th century Spanish hooded cape made of *felt, q.v.,* in two layers—upper layer extended to the hips while second layer extended to below the knees; hood was cone-shaped standing away from the face. Worn particularly by men when riding horseback.

fiesta shirt See *shirts.*

Figaro jacket Variation of the *Zouave* or *bolero jacket, q.v.* with shoulder epaulets; worn by women in 1860's and again in 1890's.

fig leaf Small black silk apron worn by women in 1860's and 1870's.

figure improver Small *bustle, q.v.,* worn by women in the 1890's.

filament 1. See *fiber.* 2. Individual strand of continuous length of man-made fiber extruded through a single hole in the spinnerette in the manufacture of man-made yarns. Yarns may be *monofilament* or *multifilament, q.q.v.* under *yarns.*

filature Textile-industry term referring to a good grade of raw silk that has been reeled by machinery as opposed to hand-reeled silk, a product of cottage industry.

filet Net which is formed by knotting

threads at right angles. Also see *laces*.

filigree Ornamental metal work for jewelry or accessories made of fine silver, gold, or copper wire arranged in intricate manner or pierced metal open work similar to the above.

filled cloth Open-weave fabric which may have sizing, clay, or lead salts added after it is woven to improve appearance and give it more body, e.g., crinoline, silk with lead or tin salts added, wool fibers bulked with flocks, rayon weighted with chemical resins.

filled gold See *gold-filled*.

fillet 1. Narrow band tied around the hair, usually as a brow band. 2. In 13th to 19th centuries, a stiffened band of linen worn with the *barbette, q.v.,* or *fret, q.v.,* or both. 3. 19th-century evening *hairstyle* made by wrapping a satin band, embroidered with pearls, spirally around the head. 4. *Embroidery* thread made of fine raw silk fibers twisted together.

filleting Term used in 17th century for narrow tape used as trimming.

filling *Crosswise* yarn of a fabric which runs at right angles to the *selvage.* Also called *pick, woof,* or *weft.* Opposite of *warp,* the vertical yarns.

filling-backed fabric Fabric woven with two sets of soft, loosely twisted filling yarns and one set of fine warp yarns.

filling stitch See *stitches*.

filling-wise Textile-industry term meaning *across* the fabric or at right angles to the selvage. Also called *weft-* or *woof-wise.*

findings Sewing or trade term for all the smaller items and trimmings that complete a garment, e.g., buttons, hooks, bindings, lace, etc.

fineness 1. Term applied to the measurement of diameter of yarns or fibers. Also see *denier* and *count of yarn.* 2. Term used in reference to purity of gold. 3. Term used for sewing-machine stitches, meaning number of stitches to the inch.

finger curl See *curls*.

Finger-Free gloves See *gloves*.

fingering yarn See *yarns*.

fingernail shields Gold or jade devices worn to protect extraordinarily long fingernails by Chinese Mandarin women, the long nails indicating freedom from household chores.

finger wave See *hairstyles*.

finished width Measurement in inches across woven cloth after all operations have been completed, e.g., cottons usually are 36″ wide, wools 54″ and 60″, and knits 60″.

finnesko boot Boot of tanned reindeer hide with fur side out; worn in Arctic. Also spelled *finnsko.*

fins See *flippers*.

fire opal See *opal* under *gems*.

firmla Heavily embroidered vest extending to below the hips, worn indoors by the Berber women of Morocco and by women of Tunis over a linen shirt.

fish Term used in the first half of 19th century for dart cut off close to the seam on reverse side, used to reduce bulk and give better fit.

fishbone stitch See *stitches*.

fisher See *furs.*

fisherman's ring Gold ring used at investiture of Pope of the Roman Catholic Church, the figure of St. Peter in a fisherman's boat is engraved along with name of the Pope; ring is usually broken at Pope's death.

fisherman's sweater See *sweaters.*

fisherman's vest See *vests.*

fishing boots See *waders* under *boots.*

fishing pants See *waders* under *boots.*

fishmouth lapel Man's notched *lapel* resembling a fish's mouth, with corners of collar and lapel rounded at point where they join. See *lapel* under *collars.*

fishnet 1. Mesh fabric of cotton or elastromeric yarns with square-shaped holes made by knotting yarns together at right angles; used for beachwear, bathing suits, scarfs, and dress trimming. 2. Spandex knit fabric in open mesh design which is not knotted; used for *gloves, hose, swimsuits, sweaters.*

fishnet underwear Lightweight 100% cotton string yarn in net-like weave used for men's T-shirts and shorts, acts as an insulator protecting against zero temperatures and 90° heat; originally worn by Norwegian explorers and standard equipment in Norwegian Army. Now worn by Olympics athletes and by general public; a fad worn as outerwear like a T-shirt with jeans by young men in early 1970's.

fishtail setting See gem settings under *gems.*

fishwife dress *Blouson, q.v.,* dress with shawl collar, dickey insert, and full sleeves; double skirt gathered on at waistline with overskirt turned up revealing lining of contrasting fabric—sometimes polka dots to match collar, underskirt was made of a third fabric frequently striped to match dickey; made in imitation of dress worn by Portuguese fishermen's wives which have several petticoats; worn in early 1890's.

fitch See *furs.*

fitchet French term used from 13th to mid 16th century for vertical slit made in side front of the gown's skirt to enable woman to reach her pocket, which was located in an undergarment.

fitted Describing a garment that conforms closely to body lines. See *cuffs* and *sleeves.*

fitting Trade term for dressmaker's or tailor's session with customer for altering garment to fit her or his figure, pins used to designate changes in seams, hems usually marked with chalk; the price of dress or suit is varied by number of *fittings* given.

Fitzherbert hat Modified form of *balloon hat, q.v.,* with wide oval brim and low crown of puffed fabric; worn by women in mid 1780's.

fixing Textile term for process of steaming or hot washing, used to set dye in fabric or fiber.

flag blue Blue colors: both light, as found in the iris flower, or dark, as the blue of the American flag.

flake yarn See *yarns.*

flame embroidery See *embroideries.*

flamenco dress See *dresses.*

flame stitch See *stitches*.

Flammable Fabric Act Bill signed by President Eisenhower on June 30, 1953, and effective July 1, 1954, prohibiting certain flammable fabrics or clothing from importation or interstate commerce in the U.S.

flammeolum Small veil worn by ancient Roman brides.

flammeum Dark flame-colored full-length wedding veil worn by Roman brides, removed by bridegroom when couple reached new home.

flandan Late 17th-century term for a side flap, called *pinner* or *lappet*, *q.v.*, fastened to woman's day cap.

flannel See *fabrics*.

flannel petticoat Infant's and woman's winter petticoat worn for warmth under fancy petticoats from 1870's to early 1920's; usually made of wool flannel, sometimes of cashmere. Also called a *flannel skirt*.

flannels See *pants*.

flapper Term used to describe a young girl of 1920's wearing lipstick and make-up, bobbed hair, short skirts, and a long strand of pearls—the type pictured by cartoonist John Held, Jr., and described by F. Scott Fitzgerald in his novel *This Side of Paradise*.

flapper dress See *dresses*.

flap pockets See *pockets*.

flared-leg panties See *panties*

flares See *pants*.

flat crepe See *fabrics*.

flat-felled seam See *seams*.

flat heel See *heels*.

flat knit Knitted fabric made flat with selvages as contrasted to *circular knit*. See *knits*

flat lock seam See *seams*.

flat pleats See *pleats*.

flats or **flatties** See *shoes*.

flat stitch See *stitches*.

flat-top See *crew cut* under *hairstyles*.

flax fiber Vegetable or bast fiber from tissue between bark and woody core of a flax plant, which produces fibers 12 to 40 inches long; long fibers called *line linen*, shorter fibers called *tow*; grown in Europe, Russia and Egypt.

flea fur Fur scarf made of any small animal with head, tail, and paws attached, a jeweled muzzle and chain; worn by women during late 16th century. *Der.* From fact that fleas were attracted to it.

flea-market look The fashion for clothes made in the 1920's and 1930's found in the Flea Markets of Paris, London, and New York, worn by young hippies and girls with small budgets as reaction to Establishment dress in the 1960's and 1970's. See *thrift-shop dress*.

fleece 1. Wool, sheared from sheep, usually in one bundle. 2. See *fabrics*. 3. Sheepskin leather, or *shearling*, *q.v.*, tanned with wool left on, used for linings and collars.

fleece-backed fabric See *fabrics*.

fleshing 1. Processing the skin side of hides, by a machine with rollers fitted with sharp spiral knives, to remove excess skin and flesh, making hide appear even in thickness. 2. Hand process of smoothing reverse side of fur by scraping with a sharp knife.

fleur-de-lis See *prints*.

flexible bracelet See *bracelets*.

flight bag See *handbags*.

flight jacket See *sport jackets* under *jackets*.

flip See *hairstyles*.

flip-chip dress See *dresses*.

flippers Rubber extensions shaped like duck's webbed foot, which fit over feet and attach with straps around heels, worn for scuba diving, underwater swimming, and water sports. Also called *fins*.

flip-tie blouse See *blouses*.

float 1. *Filling* or *warp* yarn which extends over several rows without being interlaced. 2. In knitting, a yarn which extends for some distance across back of fabric without being interlaced.

floating pedestal wedge See *heels*.

floats See *boots*.

flocking 1. Adding weight to woolen fabrics by pressing short fibers into back of fabric. 2. Same as *flock printing, q.v.,* below.

flock printing Method of applying a design by first printing fabric with an adhesive and then causing minute pieces of cotton or rayon fibers to adhere to the design, e.g., flock-dotted Swiss. See *prints*.

flocked ribbon Ribbon given a pile-like surface by means of *flocking q.v.,* in an electrostatic process, rather than woven in a pile weave like *velvet ribbon, q.v.*

flokati See *slippers*.

floral print See *prints*.

Florentine embroidery See *embroideries* and *stitches*.

Florentine handbag See *handbags*.

Florentine neckline See *necklines*.

floss See *yarns*.

flotation jacket See *sport jackets* under *jackets*.

flounce Circular or bias-cut piece of material used on skirt of dress, usually at the hem, singly or in series of flounces, first introduced at end of 16th century; in 18th century and 19th centuries, called a *furbelow, q.v.*

flouncing Decorative lace or embroidered fabric, usually gathered at upper edge, used for trimming on dresses and slips. See *laces*.

flower bottle 1. Fresh flower in small bottle of water held in place under lapel by broad ribbon; worn by men in the 1860s. 2. Small pin-on water bottle used by women in 20th century for a single flower, such as an orchid.

flower-pot hat Man's hat with crown shaped like a truncated cone or upside-down flower pot and large turned-up brim; worn in 1830's. Also called *turf hat*.

flow-flow Term used in 1880's for bodice trimming consisting of a graduated cascade of ribbon loops.

fluffy ruffles See *falsies*.

flush setting See *channel setting* in *gem settings* under *gems*.

fluting Tiny pleats in sheer fabrics that give a corrugated effect; those in man-made fabrics may be permanently heat-set; a late 19th-century trimming popular again in 1960's and 1970. Also called *goffered* and *gaufre.*

flyaway jacket Very short jacket with a full back worn by women in the late 1940's and early 1950's.

fly fringe 18th-century term for fringe consisting of strands of silk floss knotted in clumps, used for trimming a gown.

fly front See *closings.*

flying-panel skirt See *skirts.*

fly shuttle Term for a device carrying the *filling* yarn across the *warps, q.q.v.,* when weaving; devised in 1738 by John Kay.

Foale & Tuffin See *designers appendix, England.*

foam-backed fabric Fabric with thin slice of foam, usually urethane or synthetic rubber, laminated or bonded to back by means of heat or adhesives, for insulation or to give stiffness.

fob See *watch fob* and *pins.*

fob or **watch pocket** Small horizontal *welt pocket, q.v.,* near waistband of man's pants, designed to hold pocket watch; popular from 17th century until the 1920's, when wristwatches began to be fashionable. See *pockets.*

fob ribbon Term used from 1740's to 1840's for ribbon attached to watch carried in the *fob pocket, q.v.;* ribbon end hanging outside of pocket held a fob, seals, or watch key; worn only with *breeches,* or *pantaloons, q.q.v.*

Fogarty, Anne See *designers appendix, United States.*

foil button Silk pasted on paper and glued to reverse side of glass button; patented in 1774.

foil dress See *dresses.*

folding fan Half- or quarter-circle fan pleated to close narrowly, called *duck's-foot fan, q.v.,* introduced to France in mid 16th century by Catherine de' Medici.

folding slipper See *Pullman slippers* under *slippers.*

fold-over clutch See *handbags.*

fold-up raincoat See *coats.*

folette (fall-et) Loose scarf, or *fichu, q.v.,* in triangular shape, of soft light-colored fabric, worn with ends tucked into neckline of bodice, during first half of 18th century.

foliated See *castellated* and *dagging.*

follow-me-lads Long ribbon streamers hanging from back of woman's straw hat; worn in 1850's and '60's.

folly bells Tiny bells suspended from chains, used to decorate belts, shoulder belts, or neckbands in 15th century.

Fontana, Sorelle See *designers appendix, Italy.*

Fontanges (fawn-tanjz) Woman's starched, pleated, lace-and-ribbon headdress placed on top of upswept hairstyle in late 17th and early 18th centuries; originated when Marie Angélique de Scoraille de Roussille, la duchesse de Fontanges, a favorite of Louis XIV, while out riding with the King about 1679, used her lace and jeweled garter to fasten back her hair. Also called *tower headdress,* and *high head;* compare with *commode.* Sometimes spelled *Fontange.*

fool's cap Jester's cap, or hooded cape, often trimmed with *folly bells, q.v.,* or tassels, usually in two colors, in twin peaks with bell on each tip. Mistakenly confused with *dunce cap, q.v.*

football jersey 1. Official jersey shirt with striped drop-shoulder sleeves and large identifying numerals on back, worn by football players. 2. Similar shirt worn as sportswear. See *knit shirts* under *shirts.*

footed pajamas See *pajamas.*

footing Term for trimming used on edges of garment, including elaborate ruffles, pleating, and arrangements of lace or net insertion and ribbon; widely used for women's dresses and undergarments in late 19th and early 20th centuries.

footlets See *socks.*

foot mantle 1. An outer, or extra woman's skirt, worn in American Colonial days, to keep dress clean when riding horseback. 2. An overskirt worn by country women when riding horseback in the 14th century. Also see *safeguard.* Also spelled *fote mantle.*

foot warmers See *bed socks* under *socks.*

fop Term used to describe a vain man preoccupied with the exquisiteness of his dress or showiness of his person, e.g., affected eccentricities such as the carrying of fans in the late 16th century and late 18th century. *Der.* From Middle English *foppe,* fool and *fobben,* to cheat. See also *dandy.*

forage cap 1. See *army caps* under *caps.* 2. Visor cap adapted from the military for small boys in 1st half of 19th century, made with circular felt crown, head band stiffened with cane, a tassel from center of crown, and sometimes japanned leather straps fitted under chin. 3. Small cap similar to a *kepi, q.v.,* formerly worn by soldiers in U.S. Army.

Ford Apparel industry slang for a style that has mass acceptance. *Der.* From the similarity to mass appeal of the inexpensive early Ford automobiles.

fore-and-aft cap See *deerstalker* under *caps.*

forehead cloth Same as *crosscloth, q.v.*

forepart 1. Term used from 16th century to early 17th century for an expensive decorative panel sewed to an underskirt of coarse fabric, the expensive fabric showing through the split skirt of the gown. 2. 19th century term for the part of a man's waistcoat extending across the chest.

foresleeve Sleeve covering the arm from wrist to elbow. Also see *half sleeve.*

forestry cloth See *fabrics.*

foretop Term used from 13th century to end of 18th century by men and women for the hair, or wig, just above the forehead, Also called *toupee, q.v.*

forks Same as *fourchettes, q.v.*

formal attire Clothes worn by men and women at formal social functions, e.g., a ball or a formal wedding. For items, see *ascot, black tie, cummerbund, cutaway coat, dinner jacket, evening dress* under *dresses, formal shirt* under *shirts, formal vest* under *vests, full dress, morning coat* under *coats, sack coat* under *jackets, swallow-tailed coat* or *tail coat* under *coats, tuxedo, white tie* under *ties,* and *wing collar* under *collars.*

Forquet, Federico See *designers appendix, Italy.*

Fortrel Trademark, owned by Celanese Corp. of America, for polyester fibers in many types for different uses; the name is licensed to manufacturers to use on finished products.

Fortuny, Mario See *designers appendix, Italy.*

Forty-Second Royal Highland Regiment tartan See *tartans.*

fotoz Headdress resembling a large off-the-face turban, worn by Jewish women in Turkey. It consists of an enormous cushion of parti-colored fabrics, ornamented with jewels and strings of pearls; worn with a large veil out of doors.

foulard See *fabrics* and *scarfs.*

foundation 1. Shortened form of term *foundation garment,* below. 2. Underskirt similar to a contemporary slip, attached to bodice at waistline seam along with outer skirt.

foundation garment Woman's undergarment combining *brassiere* and *girdle* in one piece to mold the figure; frequently has alternating stretch panels of elastic fabric such as Lastex or Lycra spandex and non-stretch panels, with straps over shoulders and attached hose supporters. Also called a *foundation, corselet,* or *all-in-one.*

FOUNDATION GARMENTS

boned f. Foundation garment that contains thin metal strips called *bones,* for stiffening, inserted under

FOUNDATION
GARMENT

cotton tapes, making a firm garment, so called because *"bones"* were originally made of *whalebone.*

bra-kini Minimal foundation garment composed of *brassiere* and *bikini panties, q.q.v.,* joined through midriff by see-through fabric.

double-zipper f. Easy-to-get-into foundation garment with one zipper extending from under arm to below waist, a second zipper on opposite side, extends upward from bottom of thigh to waistline.

laced f. Foundation closed by lacing through eyelets; an early method of fastening, still used in some support types of foundations.

panty f. Lightweight garment usually made of two-way stretch elastic, with a crotch.

torsolette *Brassiere* and *waist cincher* in one garment, frequently strapless, sometimes with attached *garters, q.q.v.;* popular in late 1940's and early '50's.

two-way-stretch f. Foundation made

entirely of elastic fabric such as Lycra spandex or Lastex that stretches both up and down and across.

foundling bonnet or **cap** Small soft-crowned, stiff-brimmed bonnet, usually made of plush and fastened with ties under chin; worn in 1880's.

fourchettes (foor-shet) Narrow pieces forming the sides of the fingers of gloves, ending in points at tips of fingers and joining the back to the front of the glove. Also called *forks.*

fouriaux (four-e-o) Silken sheaths worn over long braids by ladies of rank in 1st half of 12th century.

four-in-hand tie See *ties.*

fourragere (foor-ah-zher) Braided cord worn usually around left shoulder, as military award or decoration. Compare with *aiguilliette, q.v.*

fourreau (foor-o) Princess-style dress with no waistline seam, buttoned down front and usually worn with a peplum tied around the waist; popular about 1864. *Der.* French, scabbard.

fourreau skirt Gored skirt made without pleats at waistline; worn over a crinoline in the 1860's.

fourreau tunic Double-skirted dress with bodice and overskirt cut in one piece, worn as a tunic over underskirt in mid 19th century.

fox See *furs.*

foxing Shoe-industry term for extra fancy-cut piece of leather sewed on at the top of the back seam, for reinforcement and decoration.

frac French term for the English *frock coat q.v.,* made with turned-down collar and full skirt, without pockets;

worn by men in early 19th century. The jacket was cut away in front and had long narrow tails hanging in back, by mid 19th century.

fraise Embroidered muslin scarf folded across the chest and kept in place by an ornamental pin, worn by women in 1830's with a carriage dress.

frame 1. Metal top of handbag, around which the handbag is constructed; may be *square-bottom channel frame, side-channel frame,* or *inverted frame.* 2. Term used for machine used in yarn making.

framing Handbag-industry term for securing the frame to the handbag, material and lining are fitted into frame and secured permanently by machine.

France, point de See *laces.*

franchise Privilege granted to one retailer in an area or city by a wholesaler of manufacturer to sell manufacturer's entire line of merchandise exclusively.

frangipani Perfume from the flowers of the plumeria shrub, introduced during the reign of Louis XIII in the 16th century; made by an Italian nobleman, the Marquis Muzio Frangipani, and used to scent gloves.

frelan Late 17th-century term for woman's *bonnet* and *pinner q.q.v.,* worn together. Also called *freland* or *frelange.*

French antelope See *leathers.*

Frenchback See *fabrics.*

French back Back of dress made with three seams, one in center and one on either side curving into the armholes; fashionable in late 19th century and early 20th century, still used. See *side bodies*.

French beret See *beret* under *caps*.

French boa Tubular length of swansdown fabric, fur, or feathers, worn as a neckpiece by women from 1829 on; fashionable in 1890's, 1930's, and 1970's. See *scarfs*.

French bottoms 19th-century term for men's trousers flaring at the hems.

French bra See *brassieres*.

French cinch See *girdles*.

French corsage Woman's *basque* waist with wide tight-fitting *corselet* extending to middle of bust, *q.q.v.*; top and sleeves of contrasting fabric with boat-shaped neck and double-ruffled sleeves; worn in 1860's.

French cloak Long circular or semi-circular *cape, q.v.*, sometimes with a square flat collar or shoulder cape. See also *compass* and *half-compass cloak*.

French crepe See *fabrics*.

French cuff See *cuffs*.

French drawers 1. Flared, knee-length panties lavishly trimmed with lace, ruffles, and *insertion, q.v.*, at the hems, set on a band at waist with ties in back to adjust the size; with split crotch, called "open"; or with seam sewed, called "closed"; made of fine cambric, lawn, muslin, etc.; worn in late 1890's and early 1900's. 2. In the 1920's, similar garment, shorter and less frilly, called *French panties*.

French dress Little girl's dress, long waisted, usually with square or round neckline accented with a large *bertha, q.v.*; sleeves short, ruffled or puffed, or long in leg-of-mutton style; skirt full with wide

ribbon sash at waist. Usually made of lightweight fabrics and worn over a slip made in long-waisted style; worn in late 19th and early 20th centuries.

French-fall boots Leather boots with extravagantly wide tops crushed down to reveal elaborate lace *cannons, q.v.*; worn in 17th century. Also called *bucket-top boots*.

French farthingale Drum shaped skirt mounted on stiff frame with widened sides and slightly flattened front; worn in England from 1580 to 1620's. See *farthingale*.

French flannel See *fabrics*.

French frock Man's *frock coat, q.v.*, worn for full dress, usually trimmed with gold embroidered buttons; worn 1770–1800.

French gigot sleeves (zhee-go) Woman's sleeve, full at top, fitted at

forearm, sometimes with a point over back of hand; worn 1830–1900, popularized by actress Sarah Bernhardt. *Der.* French *gigot,* leg of lamb. Also called *leg-of-mutton sleeve, q.v.*

French gores Term used in early. 19th century for panels introduced into skirts to eliminate gathers at the waist. See *gore.*

French heel See *heels.*

French hood Woman's headdress consisting of a small bonnet over a stiffened frame worn at back of head with *ruching* trimmed, *q.v.,* front border curved forward to cover the ears, combined with two ornamental gold bands or *billiments, q.v.,* and a back flap that folded forward over head, projecting above forehead; fashionable in early 16th century.

French jacket See *pentenlair.*

French kid See *leathers.*

French knot See *stitches.*

French lace See *laces.*

French lock See *love lock.*

French nightcap See *dormeuse.*

French-opening vest Man's vest, cut low enough to reveal a large part of shirt front; worn in the 1840's.

French policeman's cape See *capes.*

French polonaise See *polonaise* and *Irish polonaise.*

French portrait buttons Buttons, worn about 1790, with profiles of famous people in light color mounted against a black silk background and surrounded with a rim of tin, e.g., profiles of Lafayette, Mirabeau, and Louis XVI.

French purse Wallet, folding to half the size of a dollar bill, designed to hold bills and change, with coin purse built in one end and slot inside through which to pull the bills.

French Revolution styles During the French Revolution in 1789, fashions changed immediately from elaborate to simple; powdered wigs, paniers, and costly fabrics disappeared and a careless, unkempt style prevailed, including muslin dresses, little underwear; and dress *à la constitution, q.v.,* became fashionable, the men copying the sober costume of the English country gentleman— tight breeches, cutaway coats, neck cloths, and boots.

French roll See *hairstyles.*

French ruff Extremely wide ruff, also called *cartwheel ruff, q.v.,* worn by men from late 16th to early 17th century.

French sailor cap or **hat** See *hats.*

French sailor dress Girl's long-waisted tailored dress with *blouson, q.v.,* effect, short pleated skirt, and *sailor collar, q.v.;* worn in early 20th century.

French seam 1. See *seams.* 2. Shoe seam which starts with a simple seam, or closed seam, restitched on either side of seam on outside, used for closing back of shoe.

French sleeves Detachable sleeves, worn by men in England in second half of 16th century.

French system One of three main systems for making worsted yarns, originated in Alsace and now used in Europe and United States; the process uses short fibers and resultant yarn is springier or loftier than other worsteds. Also called *Continental* and *Alsatian* system.

French twist See *hairstyles.*

French vest Man's high-buttoned vest of the 1860's, with lapels cut in one with the front but not turned over.

French wig Variant of *full-bottomed wig, q.v.*

fresh-water pearls See *beads.*

fret 1. Mesh *coif* or *skull cap, q.q.v,* made of metal or fabric worked in openwork design, worn by women in 13th to early 16th centuries. Also called *caul, crispine,* or *crispinette, q.q.v.* 2. An ornamental border of short right-angled straight lines; e.g., the *Greek key* design or *Grecian border.*

friar's cloth See *monk's cloth* under *fabrics.*

frieze See *fabrics.*

frileuse Woman's cape or *pelerine* wrap, *q.v.,* with a fitted back and loose sleeves, made of quilted satin or velvet and used indoors or at the theater during the late 1840's.

frill Term used since the 16th century for narrow piece of fabric or lace gathered to form a ruffle and attached as trimming on dress or blouse.

frilling Term used for ruffles of gathered stiff white muslin, worn at wrist and neck, specifically on widows' dresses of 1870's and 1880's.

fringe 1. Ornamental trim consisting of loose strands of thread, yarn, or beads, fastened to a band. 2. Fabric or leather slashed into narrow strands along the edge, used for trim.

fringed tongue Shoe tongue finished with saw-tooth edge at top or fringed. See *shawl tongue.*

frise See *frieze.*

frisette 1. 19th-century term for crimped fringe of hair, either real or false, worn on the forehead. 2. In 1860's, a sausage-shaped pad over which back hair was rolled.

frisk Small bustle worn by women in early 19th century to produce the *Grecian bend, q.v.,* posture.

frizze Frizzed or fuzzy-haired wig worn from 17th century on. Also called *frizz-wig.*

frizzy Describing hair in tight, kinky curls.

frock 1. Term used generally as synonym for woman's *dress, q.v.;* in 16th and 17th centuries, an informal gown; by 19th century, usually a dress of thin fabric; and in 20th century, usually a child's dress. 2. For men, from medieval times, a loose-fitting sleeved outer garment of coarse fabric, derived from a monk's *habit* and worn by farm workers or laborers. Also called *smock frock, q.v.* 3. For men, from 16th to end of 18th centuries, a loose-fitting jacket or *frocked jacket* or *undress* coat. Also see *French frock* and *frock coat, q.q.v.*

frock coat 1. Man's suit coat, close-fitting, single or double-breasted, and buttoned to waistline; with full skirt, flapped pockets, and vent in back and buttons at waistline; at first with a *Prussian collar, q.v.,* and no lapels. Worn with minor variations for many years and called *morning frock coat;* worn from end of 18th century throughout the 19th century when it extended to knees.

Also see *frac.* 2. Hip-length fitted tailored jacket worn by women in 1890's.

frocked jacket See *frock,* number 2.

frock great coat Man's coat similar in cut to a *frock coat* but usually longer, styled for outdoor wear without an undercoat; worn from 1830's. Also called *top frock.*

frock overcoat Boy's *overcoat, q.v.,* made with fitted lines, calf-length,

and frequently with a large *cape collar;* worn in late 1880's–'90's.

frog 1. Ornamental fastener made of *braid* or *fabric cording, q.q.v.,* used

for closing garments, especially military uniforms and some Chinese clothes. When introduced in West in 18th century called *Brandenburgs, q.v.* Also see *closings.* 2. See *leathers.*

frog button Braided button made in a spindle shape for use with frog fasteners. See *Brandenburgs.* Also called an *olivette.*

front 17th-century term for *hairpiece* consisting of a fringe of hair worn on the forehead.

frontayl or **frontel** See *frontlet.*

frontier pants See *pants.*

frontlet 1. Decorative brow band worn in medieval days under a *coverchief* or *veil,* also worn in 16th century with *coif, bonnet,* or *caul, q.q.v.,* and in 18th century called *forehead cloth* or *crosscloth.* 2. A brow band covered with face cream and worn at night to remove wrinkles.

frou-frou Fluffy trimmings such as ruffles, ribbons, and laces. *Der.* French, rustle or swish.

frou-frou dress Daytime dress with low-necked bodice, worn under a short muslin tunic with skirt cut away in front revealing a silk underskirt trimmed with many tiny pinked flounces; worn 1870.

frou-frou mantle Woman's shoulder cape or *pelerine, q.v.,* made of three rows of *ruching, q.v.,* closed with long streamer ties in front; worn in late 1890's. Also called *frou-frou cape.*

frouting 17th-century term for rubbing perfumed oil into a garment.

frouze Term used in late 17th and

early 18th centuries for curled *false hair* or *wig* worn to conceal baldness. Also called a *fruz.*

F.T.C. See *Federal Trade Commission.*

fuji See *fabrics.*

fuji silk See *fabrics.*

full-bottomed wig Extremely large man's wig with center part and small *sausage* curls all over and hanging in *lappets, q.q.v.,* on shoulders; worn from 1660 to early 18th century on formal occasions by lawyers and learned professional people only. Also called *full-bottom* or *French wig.*

full dress Term used to indicate formal attire—*formal evening dress* for women and *white tie* and *tails, q.q.v.,* for men. See *dresses, suits.*

full-fashioned hose Hose knit in flat pieces and seamed up the back, leaving *fashion marks* where knitting is increased or decreased. See *hose.*

full grain Grain side of leather. Same as *full top grain.*

fulling Finish applied to woolen and worsted fabrics to compress or shrink the fabric by use of heat, moisture, pressure, and friction, giving the appearance of felt.

full length See *lengths.*

full lining Finishing of the inside of the garment with a *complete lining, q.v.,* so that no seams of the outer fabric are showing; used mainly for coats and sometimes dresses.

full piqué seam Used on expensive kid gloves, all fingers are made by lapping one piece of leather over the other and stitching on the right side.

full skirt See *skirts.*

full top grain Leather-industry term for the side of the skin or hide from which the hair has been removed. See *full grain.*

fully let-out Fur-industry term for a fur coat with pelts cut so that one *let-out, q.v.,* strip goes from neck to hem of coat.

fume fading Fading of acetate fabrics caused by acid gases in the atmosphere.

fun furs Term popularized in 1965 for long-haired and unusual furs worked in an interesting manner into a coat or other garment suitable for sports or informal occasions.

funnel hat Brimless tall conical hat of felt or fabric worn by women in 1930's and '40's.

funnel neckline See *necklines.*

funnel sleeve See *pagoda sleeve* under *sleeves.*

fur (noun) 1. The *pelt* of an animal that has been tanned with the hair attached (as differentiated from leather, which is tanned without the hair); used for an item of wearing apparel or trimming 2. A *garment* made of fur.

Fur has been used since earliest times for clothing, preceding woven cloth; popular for trim and linings in the middle ages, with certain furs reserved for the nobility; popular in the latter half of the 19th century and early 20th century in sets of matching collar and cuffs and in full-length garments; during the 1930's, all types of furs were fashionable; during the 1940's, mink became the most generally used fur with the stole increasing in popularity; in the mid 'sixties, *"fun furs"*, *q.v.*, were introduced making a wide variety of low and medium-priced furs popular. Furs in retail stores must be labeled properly as to animal from which they come and country of origin as required by the Fur Labeling Act of 1938, amended in 1952.

In the early 1970's, a movement to save rare species, part of a broader national interest in ecology, had a conspicuous effect on the fur industry. Use in clothing of furs as leopard, jaguar, cheetah, and ocelot was frowned upon by many who sought to preserve these limited species. In some states legislation was passed prohibiting the sale of pelts from certain rare species.

FURS:

Alaskan seal See *fur seal.*

antelope Stiff flat hair similar to calf in beautiful soft brown color; rarely used for fur as the quantity is very limited.

badger Very stiff, bristle-like guard hairs and a soft silky fur fiber; pale-colored pelts are preferred, and best quality come from Western Canada. Used mainly for trimmings.

baum marten Medium-length brown guard hairs and yellow-brown fur fiber; resembles *sable,* but guard hairs are coarser, shorter, and not as lustrous. Best pelts come from Europe. Used primarily for jackets, scarfs, and trimmings. Fair to good durability; expensive.

beaver Rich velvety brown fur that, when sheared, reveals a wide silvery stripe down the center. Preferred color is blue-brown; some-times left natural or bleached beige for "blonde beaver." Most beaver is sheared and coarse guard hairs are plucked out. Peltries are large, requiring only five to seven used let-out for a coat. Best Qualities come from Canada, particularly the Laurentian Valley in Quebec, and the United States, including Alaska. *Der. Middle English bever,* brown.

broadtail lamb Flat fur with delicate moiré pattern and fragile skin; comes from stillborn Persian or caracul lambs or from lambs only a few days old; the hair is not fully developed and has not curled. Used for coats, jackets, suits, dresses. Durability is very low; expensive.

burunduki Usually small, lightweight, delicate skins with nine alternate stripes of white and black on a yellow or orangish background. Comes from a rodent native to Russia similar to the American chipmunk. Frequently imported in *plates, q.v.;* used only for linings and trimmings.

calf Flat, short, stiff-haired fur from young cattle; usually brown spotted with white; also may be black and white, all black, or brown. Used for trimmings and for handbags, belts, shoes, and vests.

caracul Lamb pelt with a moiré appearance—best peltries are flattest. Majority of skins are white and may be dyed; or may be rusty brown, dark brown, or black. Best quality comes from Russia; when from China, skins are called "Chinese lamb" or "Mongolian Lamb." Used for coats, jackets, trimmings. Durability is moderate. Also spelled *karakul.*

cheetah Flat fur from the cat family, with black spots on a tawny ground; hair is softer and lighter than *leopard.* Comes from Africa or Southern Asia. Used for coats, jackets, hats, etc. In short supply.

chinchilla Silky-haired fur with a very delicate skin; best quality has slaty blue fur fibers and guard hairs that are white and darker at the tips, center back is gray. Small rodent is native to the Andes Mountains in South America. Best skins were taken from ranch-raised animals beginning in the mid-1950's. Used for coats, jackets, hats, etc. Poor durability; very expensive.

Chinese dog Fur with long guard hairs and thick fur fiber used as trimming on inexpensive coats. Comes from Mongolia and Manchuria.

Chinese lamb See *caracul.*

civet cat Spotted fur characterized by elongated black marks against a dark gray background with a greenish cast. Not widely used.

cony Synonym for *rabbit* coming from the Latin word *cuniculers;* also spelled *coney.* The fur labeling act forbids the use of names other than "rabbit" for use in trade in the U.S.

ermine Pure white fur from weasel family with short guard hairs and silky, soft fur fiber. Best quality comes from the far north—Siberia, in particular. Light shades of brown occur further south. Fair durability; very expensive.

fisher Blue-brown to dark-brown color with long guard hairs and dense fur fiber. Used primarily for scarfs and jackets, usually in its natural state. Best quality pelts come from Labrador. Very good durability; fairly scarce and expensive.

fitch Yellow fur fiber and black guard hairs with a silky texture. Found in Europe. *White fitch,* another type, is found in Ural Mountains of southern Russia. Used for coats, jackets and trimmings. Durability is very good; relatively inexpensive.

fox Long lustrous guard hairs and deep dense fur fiber. There are four primary types of foxes and many miscellaneous types. Main groups are (a) *red fox*—includes *black, silver, platinum,* and *cross-fox* (yellowish with a black cross marking) as color phases; (b) *white fox*—with *blue fox* a color phase (c) *gray fox;* (d) *kit fox*—small buff-grey or (long-eared) grizzled grey animal. Found in every continent except South America and also raised for fur fibers. Used for coats, jackets, scarfs, muffs, jackets and trimmings.

fur seal Soft velvety fur from the genuine Alaska seal. All pelts are sheared and dyed either black or brown. Sealing is controlled by the United States Government with pelts coming from the Pribiloff Islands, off the coast of Alaska. Used for coats, jackets, hats, muffs. Durability is high. Expensive because of the limited quantity available.

guanaco Reddish-brown fur from camel family taken from the young animal or *guanaquito,* found in Argentina. Used for jackets and trimmings; not durable and inexpensive.

hair seal Stiff rather short-haired fur with a natural blue-black or blue-and-black mottled effect that may be dyed various other colors. Comes from two varieties of seals, the harp seal and the hooded seal, whose habitat is the North Atlantic.

hamster Small soft golden-brown pelts of rodent found in the Rhine River Valley and in Siberia. Similar in appearance to the American muskrat. Used most often for linings.

hare Soft, short-haired fur similar to rabbit but with more tendency to mat. Arctic hare from northern Europe and Asia has a long guard hair and is sometimes used to imitate the Arctic fox. Durability is low but higher than rabbit's.

Hudson seal Proper name is *Hudson seal-dyed muskrat.* See *muskrat.*

jaguar Flat spotted cat-family fur with dark rosette markings with two dots in centers against tawny background. Popular for coats and two-piece suits for women in the early 1960's. In comparatively short supply.

karakul See *caracul.*

kid Short-haired flat gray fur with a wavy pattern. The best peltries come from India and China. Fairly durable and inexpensive.

kolinsky Brownish fur with medium-length silky guard hair and slightly yellowish fur fiber. Best qualities come from Manchuria. Used primarily for scarves and trimmings and used in imitation of American and Canadian mink. Durability is fair.

lamb Many types of lamb are processed for fur, but three main types stand out; *Persian* lamb, *broadtail* lamb, and *caracul* lamb—differentiated by lustre, tightness of the fur curl. Other lamb variations include *Afghan, Astrakhan, Argentine, Bessarabian, borrego, Iranian, Kalgan, Soviet Union, India, China,* and *Southwest Africa. Crimean* lamb is called *crimmer* or krimmer. See *broadtail lamb, caracul lamb, mouton-processed lamb* and *Persian lamb,* in this section.

lapin The French word for *rabbit.* Not used in the United States except in a descriptive form, *i.e.,* lapin-processed rabbit.

leopard Spotted jungle-cat fur judged by (a) flatness; (b) contrast between spots and background; (c) shape of rosettes or spots. No fur fiber in the best qualities, and better qualities have shorter hair. Best quality comes from African Somaliland. Although leopard fur was used as early as Egyptian times, it was not popular for women's wear until after World War I. Good durability; very limited in supply and expensive.

lynx Long silky-haired delicately spotted fur. Colors vary from white, blue gray, pale gray, white, and brown. Best quality of white comes from the Hudson Bay area and Alaska. Peltries also come from other parts of Canada, Scandinavia, Siberia. Used for coats, jackets, trimming.

lynx cat Differs from lynx; darker in color, darker spots, shorter guard hairs; similar to the *American wild cat.* Best qualities come from Nova Scotia, other comes from Canada

231

and United States. Used mainly for trimmings.

marmot Fur with guard hair and fiber similar to *muskrat* and *mink*. Blue-black color is preferred and the peltries are dyed brown and frequently simulate mink. Marmot comes mainly from the Soviet Union, Manchuria, and China. Used mainly for coats, jackets, and trimmings for cloth coats; moderately priced.

marten Soft rich fur with fairly long guard hair and thick underfur, similar to *sable;* blue-black or brown colors preferred, but ranges to canary yellow. Best qualities found in eastern Canada and the Hudson Bay area. Incorrectly called the "Hudson Bay sable." Also see *baum marten* and *stone marten.*

mink Fur from weasel family with silky to coarse guard hairs and dense, soft fur fiber. Best qualities of the dark lustrous pelts give a blue reflection from the guard hairs. Best qualities of *wild mink* come from eastern Canada. Northeastern United States pelts rank second. *Vison* is name used in Europe for mink. Since the 1940's much mink, particularly in the United States and Scandinavia, is raised on *mink ranches.* Many variations in colors through breeding of new strains, or *mutations;* most mink is used in its natural color, but may be dyed. Good durability. In the 1930's, the mink coat became a status symbol. With the growth and popularity of the mink stole during the 1950's and the production of more pelts by fur farming, mink became available to the masses. Mink is usually made in *let-out style, q.v.,* for coats. In the 1960's mink also became fashionable worked *in-the-round, q.v.* In the mid-1960s patterned and patchwork minks were made of paws, gills, bellies, and sides pieced together to form "blankets" of *flowered, herringbone, plaid, tweed,* and *windowpane* patterns from which garments were cut. In the late 1960's and early 1970's hand-screened mink, painted, sheared, and tie-dyed mink gained an audience. Types of mink include: *China mink:* Yellowish mink found in China, dyed to imitate expensive North American mink. Also see *kolinsky,* under *furs. Jap or Japanese mink:* Muddy yellow-colored pelt from Japan which is always dyed in imitation of more expensive American mink. *Mutation mink:* Strains of mink developed scientifically by carefully mating the animals. Mutation colors range from a very dark brown to white, with grays, blues, and beiges in between. Marketed by large mink-rancher associations, the most prominent in the United States being Mutation Mink Breeders Association (EMBA), which has developed trademarks for its best merchandise, e.g. mink in these natural colors: Aeolian, taupe; Arcturus, lavender-beige; Argenta, gray; Autumn Haze, brown; Azurene, blue-gray; Cerulean, blue; Diadem, pale brown; Jasmine, white; Lutetia, gunmetal; Tourmaline, pale beige. The first mutation developed was very dark brown-black mink, sold under trademark names including *Black Diamond, Tyrian Glo,* and *Blackgama.*

mole Extremely soft gray fur, rather flat with a wavy appearance, very delicate skin. Best qualities come from Asia. Popular for jackets and trimmings in the early 1900's. Poor durability.

Mongolian lamb See *lamb.*

monkey Very long lustrous black fur with no fur fiber. Used for trimming and jackets, it comes primarily from the "colobus" monkey on the east and west coasts of Africa.

mouton-processed lamb Wooly fur with a dense pile. Made by shearing the merino sheep rather than a "hair" sheep. Used for coats, jackets, hats. Inexpensive, warm, and durable. See *lamb.*

muskrat Fur with long guard hairs and dense fur fiber, processed three different ways: (a) dyed and striped to resemble *mink* and *sable;* (b) sheared and dyed to imitate *Alaskan seal* and called *Hudson seal-dyed muskrat;* (c) left natural and finished to improve the coloring. Best qualities of northern muskrat, which is brown or black, are used for "Hudson seal" and come from the Great Lakes region in the United States. Southern pelts, which vary in color, are used for natural muskrat coats. Durability is moderate to high. Natural muskrat skins are split into five parts, each part used separately as "back coats," "golden sides coats," and "silver belly coats."

nutria Fur with a velvety appearance after long guard hairs have been plucked; color is from cinnamon brown to brown with gray stripes, and fur is similar to the *beaver* although not so thick, lustrous, and rich. Animal is a water rodent of northern Argentina, usually wild but some attempts at breeding made in 1950's. Used for coats, linings, and trimmings. Durability is moderate.

ocelot Spotted cat-family fur with elongated dark markings against a tan background. Flatter-haired peltries are the best qualities, come from Brazil and Mexico. Used mainly for coats and jackets. This durable fur is in short supply, relatively expensive.

opossum Long straight guard hairs and dense fur fiber which in the natural color is either black or gray; best qualities come from Australia, Tasmania, and the United States. Used for coats, linings, trimmings or dyed to imitate other furs such as *skunk* and *fitch;* moderately priced.

otter Relatively short-haired fur with silky, lustrous guard hair and dense fur fiber—the most durable fur for the weight and thickness, preferred color has blue-brown, black guard hairs and fur fiber slightly lighter with the base being gray to white color. Best qualities come from eastern Canada. Some otter is sheared and *plucked.*

Persian lamb Curly lustrous fur which is usually black but occasionally brown or white. Dark colors are always dyed to color the white skin. Quality is determined by the tightness of the "knuckle" curl and formation of interesting patterns called "flowers." Best quality comes from Bokara, Russia. Others come from Afghanistan, Southwest Africa, and

Iran. Popular for coats and trimmings. Durability is high. See *lamb.*

pony Short-haired flat fur with a wavy moiré appearance. Used in natural color, bleached, or dyed pale colors. Best quality comes from Poland and Russia. Durability good, but short bristly fur has a tendency to wear "bald."

rabbit Soft light fur in a variety of colors, used in natural state or can be dyed or processed: striped to imitate *muskrat,* sheared to imitate *beaver,* sheared and stenciled to resemble *leopard,* long hairs spotted to resemble *lynx.* Best qualities come from Australia and New Zealand. Must be labeled *rabbit.* Poor durability; inexpensive. See *cony,* above.

raccoon Long light-yellowish guard hair and dark-brown fur fiber. Lighter weight peltries from the southern part of the United States are used for coats. Northern United States provides heavy-skinned pelts used primarily for hats, trimmings. Popular for men's and women's coats in 1920's, revived in 1960's. See *sheared raccoon.*

sable Luxurious fur with lustrous, long silky guard hairs and soft, dense, fluffy fur fiber; preferred color, a blue-black-brown. Skins that are light brown in color are tipped and blended, called *natural sable,* others are dyed and called *dyed sable.* Used for coats or scarfs, with best quality, called *Russian crown sable,* coming from Siberia. Animal is also found in China, Korea, and Japan. Durability is good; in 1974, most expensive fur.

seal See *hair seal* and *fur seal.*

sea otter Light-to-very-dark-brown fur of a web-footed sea mammal of the otter family found on the North Pacific coast, with a rich, soft underfur and silver-tipped coarser outer hairs. Now very rare.

sheared raccoon Velvety-textured fur similar in appearance to *beaver,* but not as soft and silky and more cinnamon brown with lighter stripes. Raccoon is processed by plucking and shearing. Durable fur, much less expensive than beaver.

shearling Sheared *lamb, q.v.,* worked with the fur side in. See *leathers.*

skunk White-striped black fur with long guard hairs and thick fur fiber. Quality of the fur depends on ability of the fur fiber to remain black rather than take on a brownish or rust-colored appearance. For an all-black fur, peltries have white streaks removed and are dyed to darken the skin. Used extensively in the 1930's for jackets and coats; best qualities are from the Dakotas and Minnesota. Also found in Canada and South America. Better U.S. types have high durability.

snow leopard Long-haired grayish-white cat-family fur, much longer hair than that of other leopards. Comes from Himalaya mountains in Asia. Very scarce.

spotted cat Variety of spotted fur which comes from three main types of South American cat; the *chati* cat, the *marguay,* and *long-tailed cats.* Markings are more rounded than those of the *ocelot;* fur is less expensive.

squirrel Very soft gray or brown relatively short fur that takes dye readily and may be made any color or worked into a two-toned pattern. Best qualities come from Europe and Asia; used mainly for jackets, capes, and trimmings. Low durability, moderately priced.

stone marten Fur with brown guard hairs and grayish-white fur fiber judged for quality by the contrast of two colors. Best qualities come from Europe, particularly Russia; used primarily for scarfs.

wallaby Dark grey fur with long silky guard hair and thick fur fiber. Best quality comes from Tasmania, with peltries from Australia having shorter hair and not so adaptable for fur garments.

weasel Soft silky short guard hairs and silky fur fibers similar in texture to *ermine,* a close relative; color varies with the seasons—winter, white; spring, yellowish; summer, streaked with brown or gray. Brown all year in southerly climates.

wolf Long-haired fur with long silky guard hairs and dense fur fiber. Pale-colored skins are sometimes stenciled to imitate *lynx;* others are used in natural state or dyed brown, black, or gray. Quality depends on fluffiness and density of fur fiber that supports the long guard hairs. The best quality comes from the timber wolf of Canada. Used for coats, capes, jackets, trimmings, and scarfs.

wolverine Coarse fur with long brown guard hairs, dense gray fur fiber. Very durable; best qualities found in the Arctic regions, also found in the Rocky Mountains and Siberia. Used mainly for sportswear and trimming.

zebra Flat stiff fur of horse family, wide black irregularly shaped stripes against a light-colored background. Comes from Africa, used infrequently for coats. *Calf* is sometimes stenciled to imitate zebra.

furbelow 18th-century American term for skirt ruffle for woman's petticoat, also ruffles for skirts and scarves, usually made of same fabric or of lace, also used for whole gowns and aprons. English term *falbala, fabala;* French, *falbala.*

furbelow wig See *Duvillier wig.*

fur fabrics See *fabrics.*

fur farming Raising and scientific breeding of animals for their pelts; originated in the 1920's for the raising of silver foxes, later became a method of raising *ranch mink* and *mutation mink, q.q.v.*

fur felt Best grade of *felt, q.v.,* used for hats, made of fur fibers, especially from *beaver* and *rabbit.* Also see *beaver hat.*

fur fiber Short under-fur of animals such as *mink, muskrat,* and *fox,* supporting the guard hairs which are long and silky.

fur-fiber blends See *hair fibers.*

Fur Labeling Act Legislation passed by Congress on June 17, 1938, amended in 1952, in regard to labeling of fur items sold to consumers, designating that all furs must be labeled with correct name of animal, country of origin, and whether dyed, stenciled, *e.g., leopard-stenciled rabbit.*

fur lining *Lining, q̇.v.,* of a garment made of fur both for warmth and for fashion appeal. If the garment is meant to be reversible, the sleeves are lined, otherwise sleeves are not fur lined in order to reduce bulkiness. *Nutria* and *mink, q.q.v.,* are frequently used for fur linings.

fur scarf Neckpiece made of several skins of a small animal such as *mink,* or one large fox skin complete with head, tail and paws. Popular in 1930's in *red* or *silver fox.* In the late 1940's and early 1950's made of *mink, sable, fisher, kolinsky,* and *baum* or *stone marten;* a fashion revival in 1973.

fur seal See *furs.*

fur stole Term used in 20th century for waist-length fur cape with elongated ends in front, sometimes trimmed with tails of animals; formerly called a *fur boa, pelerine,* or *tippet, q.q.v.* Very popular in late 1940's and early '50's, especially in *mink.*

fused collar See *collars.*

fused fabric Non-woven fabric made up of more than one fiber, fused by heat; e.g., *Pellon,* used for interlinings, facing of men's shirt collars, etc.

fused ribbon Acetate ribbon, woven wide like piece goods and cut in strips with a hot knife that melts the edges to keep them from fraying.

fused seam See *seams.*

fustanella Knee-length, full, stiff accordion-pleated skirt worn by palace guards in Greece.

236

G

gabardine See *fabrics.* Also see *gaberdine.*

gabbia Italian term for hair accessory, often called a *rat,* consisting of a roll over which hair is wrapped for high round effect, e.g., in the *Belle Époque, q.v.,* manner. See *hairstyles. Der.* Italian, cage.

gaberdine (gab-er-deen) 1. Long, loose-fitting cloth overcoat, sometimes made of felt, with wide sleeves, sometimes belted, worn particularly by fashionable men in 16th century and by poor people until early 17th century. *Der.* Eastern *gaba,* coat. Also spelled *gabardine.*

gable bonnet or **hat** Woman's hat with front brim angled like a Gothic arch; worn in 1880's. See *English hood* and *Gothic.*

Gabrielle dress (ga-bree-el) Daytime dress with bodice and front of skirt cut in one piece; back made with two large box pleats on each side and one in center; worn in 1865.

Gabrielle sleeve 1. Type of sleeve used in *spencer jackets, q.v.* and dresses in 1820's and early 1830's; full to elbow, narrowed to wrist ending in deep cuff. 2. Sleeve composed of series of puffs extending from shoulder to wrist; worn in 1850's and 1860's.

Gabrielle waist Woman's fitted waist buttoned down center front, sometimes made with small fluted ruff and sleeves in a series of puffs; worn in 1870's.

GABRIELLE DRESS

Gainsborough hat See *hats.*

gaiter Cloth or leather covering for leg and ankle, buttoned or buckled at side, often held on by strap under foot; worn by men from early 19th century to early 20th century; also adopted by women in silk or stretch fabrics and revived in 1960's in vinyl, leather, or cloth. Also called *leggings.* See *spats, chaps.*

GABRIELLE WAIST

237

gaiter boots Buttoned or elastic-sided ankle-high leather shoes with cloth tops, fastened at sides, simulating low shoes worn with *spats, q.v.*

galage Variant of *galoche, q.v.*

Galanos, James See *designers appendix, United States.*

galatea See *fabrics.*

galatea fichu Large ruffled *fichu, q.v.,* with unpressed vertical pleats ending at center front waistline in a point, with two ruffles around the outside edge; worn in 1890's.

galatea hat Child's hat of Oriental plaited straw, with sailor crown and turned-up brim; worn in 1890's.

Galizine, Irene See *designers appendix, Italy.*

gallants Small ribbon bows worn in hair or on sleeve, bodice, or skirt in early 17th century

galligaskins (galli-gas-kins) *Trunk hose* similar to stuffed or *bombasted barrel hose, q.q.v.,* or close fitting like Venetian *gallicascoynes, q.v.* under Venetian; worn from 1570 to 1620 by men. Also called *gally gascoynes* and *gaskins.*

Gallo-Greek bodice Bodice style of 1820's: narrow flat trimming running diagonally from shoulders to waist in front and back.

galloon See *braid.*

gallose, galloshoe Variants *galoch, q.v.*

galosh 1. Waterproof ankle-high boot worn over shoe, fastening with a snap, buckle, or zipper. Also spelled *goloshe* and *golosh.* 2. Wooden platform elevating foot above street, worn from 14th to 17th centuries.

Also called *patten, q.v.* Also spelled *galoche, galage, galoss, galossian, galloses,* and *galloshes.* Also see *boots* and *closings.*

galuchat See *leathers.*

galungan Crown-shaped headdress with wing-shaped projections over the ears, worn—low on the forehead—by Bali temple dancers;

made of stenciled, colored, gilded leather and trimmed with fresh lotus flowers on top, metal rosettes and dangles in front of ears.

gambeson (gam-bee-son) Sleeveless leather or quilted fabric garment, worn under armor in Middle Ages, adapted as regular civilian garment in knee lengths, forerunner of *doublet, gippon,* or *pourpoint, q.q.v.* Also see *acton.*

gamin See *hairstyles.*

gamp 19th-century slang for umbrella. Named after Mrs. Sarah Gamp, character in Charles Dickens' 1843 novel *Martin Chuzzlewit.*

ganache (ga-nash) Tunic made of long rectangle of fabric with hole in center for head, sides sewn from hip to hem or left open, falling like cape over upper arms; worn as outergarment by men from 11th to 13th centuries. See *housse.*

ganges Leather embossed to imitate *snakeskin.*

gangster suit See *suits.*

Ganymede (gan-e-meed) See *sandals.*

Garbo hat See *hats.*

garcette (gar-cett) Fringe of hair over forehead; worn in Louis XIII period. See *coiffure en bouffons.*

garde-corps (gard cor) Full, unbelted tunic with hood and long full sleeves, frequently worn hanging with arms passed through slits above elbows; worn by men and women in 14th century England. Similar to *cyclas, q.v.*

garden hat 1. Woman's hat of muslin, with flat top cut in oval shape, with ruffles or long pieces hanging down to protect the wearer from the sun; frequently had ribbon

trim; worn in 1860's. 2. Large-brimmed floppy hat of horsehair or straw; worn in 1920's and '30's for afternoon teas and garden

parties. 3. Large-brimmed straw hat worn when gardening to protect face from the sun.

Garibaldi shirt, jacket (gar-ih-bawl-dee) 1. Red merino high-necked shirt, trimmed with black braid, bloused and belted, full sleeves gathered into wrist-band, small collar with black *cravat, epaulets* on shoulders, *q.q.v.* 2. Square-cut, waist-length jacket of red cashmere, trimmed with black braid. Both were ladies' garments inspired by clothes worn by Italian patriot Guiseppe Garibaldi and popular in late 19th century.

Garibaldi suit 1. Little boy's collarless suit consisting of a thigh-length overblouse with dropped shoulders, belted at waistline, and calf-length trousers; trimmed with binding or rickrack and buttons down center front around hem of blouse, at sleeves, and down sides of trou-

sers; worn in early 1860's. 2. Little girl's collarless two-piece dress with full blouse, sleeves set into dropped shoulders, and a full skirt; trimmed at neck, down front, around waist, wrists and hem with bands of leather or fabric and buttons; worn in early 1860's.

garland Wreath of flowers or foliage worn on the head as ornament or as an honor.

garnet See *gems.*

garniture 19th and early 20th centuries' term for trimmings, e.g., ruffles, lace, ribbons, bows.

garrison belt See *belts.*

garrison cap See *army caps* under *caps.*

garter, garters 1. Elastic supporters used to hold up hose, attached to *girdle* or to special *belt;* or buckled around calves of men's legs to hold socks; custom started in early 19th century. 2. Circle of elastic worn below knee to hold up hose or, covered with shirred ribbon and lace, for ornament. 3. Round elasticized band worn around sleeve to make it shorter. 4. Strips of fabric tied spirally around leg or buckled below knee, worn by men from medieval times through 18th century.

garter brief See *panties* and *girdles.*

gascon coat, gaskyn See *jupe, #3.*

gaskins See *galligaskins.*

gathering Drawing up fullness by tightening one thread in a row of stitching. See *shirring.*

gaucho (gow-cho) South American Spanish for horseman, indicates fashions inspired by South American cowboys. See *belts, hats,* and *pants.*

gaufré (go-freh) Raised surface effect produced by embossing patterns such as honeycomb or waffle on cotton. *Der.* French, crimped.

gauge (gage) Term used for measurement for fineness of knit in fabrics and hosiery. The *gauge* is the number of needles per inch of knitting; higher the number, finer the knit.

gauntlet 1. Armor of *mail, q.v.,* or plate, worn on the hand from 15th to 17th centuries. 2. See *gloves.*

gauntlet cuff See *cuffs.*

gauze See *fabrics* and *weaves.*

Gay '90's bathing suit See *swimsuits.*

Gaze, point de See *laces.*

gear British slang for clothes, popularized in 1960's by young people shopping on Carnaby Street and King's Road, London. Also called *threads* or *swinging gear.*

geisha (gay-sha or gee-sha) Japanese hostess trained in art of entertainment of men by singing and dancing, dressed in traditional Japanese headdress and kimono; fashions influenced by these clothes.

gem Precious or semi-precious mineral, cut and polished for use as ornamental jewelry or embroidered on clothing; worn since early times.

GEMS:

agate Translucent, microscopically crystallized *quartz* of the *chalcedony* type; may have parallel bands of color. See *moss agate.*

almandine Purplish-red *garnet, q.v.*

amber Semi-precious stone from fossil resin, clear or cloudy, in tones of pale yellow to deep red-brown, cut and polished in many shapes; most often used in bead necklaces. Found in Baltic sea, Sicily, and Burma.

amethyst Purple or violet-colored *quartz,* semi-precious stone popular in rings and necklaces.

aquamarine Semi-precious transparent stone from the mineral *beryl,* in blue-green, pale to deep; some of the best from South America.

beryl Mineral family of *emerald* and *aquamarine.*

bloodstone Semi-precious dark-green *quartz, q.v.,* spotted with red jasper; also called *heliotrope.*

cairngorm Scottish variety of *smoky quartz, q.v.*

carnelian See *chalcedony.*

cat's-eye Yellow-to-green-to-brown chrystoberyl, a relatively rare mineral, with needlelike inclusions that reflect a streak of light, resembling a cat's eye (chatoyancy); comes from Ceylon and Brazil.

chalcedony Microscopically crystallized translucent *quartz, q.v.,* with crystals often in parallel bands,˙ as in the type called *agate.* Also includes a red-brown variety called *carnelian* or *sard.* See *onyx.*

chrysolite See *peridot.*

coral Hard, translucent substance made up of skeletons of tiny marine animals called polyps, found in tropical seas; precious coral is red or pink, "grows" in branch-like formations that are used in jewelry, may also be cut into beads.

corundum Extremely hard mineral family, aluminum oxide, that includes precious gems *ruby* and *sapphire.*

crystal See *rock crystal.*

diamond Transparent, nearly pure carbon in crystalline form; one of the hardest substances known, with great brilliance; usually colorless, also blue, yellow, or brown. First found in India; now 95% come from South Africa; graded by color, weight, clarity and brilliance of faceting. See *gem cuts.* The diamond has been the symbol of wealth and luxury in fashion for hundreds of years and the "diamond look" is achieved in synthetics and artificial stones for costume jewelry and the decorative embroidery on gowns (see *rhinestones*). Individual diamonds are famous for historical and romantic reasons, such as *Cullinan:* 3,024.75 carats in the rough, the world's largest diamond, presented by government of the Transvaal to Edward VII in 1907, later cut in 105 stones, some now part of British crown jewels. *Hope:* 44.5 carats, most famous blue diamond, once belonging to Louis XIV, now in the Smithsonian Institution in Washington, D.C. *Koh-i-Noor:* 106.1 carats, oldest diamond of India, presented to Queen Victoria and now part of British crown jewels. *Krupp:* 33.1 carats, bought by actor Richard Burton in 1969 for $305,000 as gift for actress Elizabeth Taylor, then his wife. *Tiffany:* 128.5 carats, deep-yellow diamond cut with 90 facets, owned by Tiffany & Co., N.Y.

emerald Precious gem from mineral *beryl* in shades of deep to bright transparent green; best stones come from Colombia and Brazil. Name also applied to green *corundum.*

garnet Silicate minerals used as semi-precious gem stones, especially dark red color, very fashionable in late 19th century in sets of women's jewelry. A *cabochon*-cut, *q.v.*, garnet is sometimes called a *carbuncle* (French, little coal). Some others called *cinnamon stones.*

heliotrope See *bloodstone.*

Hope Star Trademark for synthetic — man-made — *star ruby* or *sapphire*. Synthetic gems are chemically identical to natural ones but less expensive because man-made.

hyacinth and **jacinth** See *zircon.*

jade Gem stone obtained from two minerals, *jadeite*, (true jade) and *hephrite*, colors varying from white to leaf- and deep-emerald green, clear or opaque; often carved for pendants, rings, and art objects. Found in South American, China, and other Eastern countries.

jasper Opaque, microscopically crystallized *quartz*, occurs in many colors — black, green, yellow, red, and in combination with other minerals; see *bloodstone.*

jet Black mineral *lignite*, which polishes to high luster, usually cut into tiny faceted beads; popular as trim on 19th century gowns.

lapis lazuli Translucent to opaque mineral in tones of blue from azure to brilliant deep purple-blue; comes from Afghanistan, Siberia, Chile.

Linde Star Trademark for synthetic *star ruby* or *sapphire*; chemically identical to natural stones but less expensive since man made.

marcasite Iron sulfide crystals, cut into tiny beads, polished to dark gray luster. Used in jewelry, handbag frames, etc.; popular in 1920's.

moonstone Opalescent gem variety of *feldspar*, usually *cabochon cut.*

moss agate Cyptocrystalline variety of *chalcedony quartz* that contains pigmented matter, usually dark in color, resembling moss or ferns. Also called *mocha stone.*

onyx Variety of *quartz* that consists of parallel bands of color, often black and white. One variety, layers of white *chalcedony* and red-brown *sard*, is called *sardonyx*. Used for *cameos* and rings.

opal Translucent *silica* capable of refracting light and reflecting it with a play of color. *Common opal* is whitish; *black opal* is dark green; *fire opal* has flame colors. Usually cut *cabochon, q.v.*

pearl Smooth lustrous vari-colored deposit in shape of small globe, formed around a worm or other foreign matter in shells of oysters, producing a valued gem stone, usually white, also yellow, black, pink, etc. *Oriental pearls* are grown naturally and retrieved by divers, the finest quality chiefly coming from Japan. *Cultured pearls* are obtained by artificially implanting irritants in oysters, to produce stones under controlled conditions at lower expense. Irregularly shaped pearls are called *baroque.*

peridot Transparent bottle-green to olive-green gem from Burma, Ceylon, Brazil. Also called *chrysolite.*

quartz Transparent or translucent crystalline mineral family including *agate, moss agate, rock crystal, ame-thyst, rose* and *smoky quartz, q.q.v.*

rock crystal Colorless, transparent variety of mineral *quartz,* often carved for beads.

rose quartz Coarsely crystallized translucent *quartz, q.v.,* in a rosy pink shade; rose quartz is rare, sometimes found in Maine, Brazil.

ruby Precious gem from mineral *corundum,* pigeon's-blood red the preferred color; stones with *aster-ism* called *star rubies.* Best quality come from Burma.

sapphire (saf-fire) Precious stone, one of pure forms of mineral *corun-dum,* transparent, in several colors, most typical in deep corn-flower blue and sometimes with inner *asterism, q.v.,* called *star sapphire.*

sardonyx See *onyx.*

smoky quartz Transparent crystal-line *quartz* in smoky yellow to dark brown or gray; national gem of Scotland. Also called *cairngorm.*

spinel Transparent to opaque miner-al largely composed of oxide of alu-minum, which when red closely resembles the ruby; softer and lighter in weight.

star ruby *Ruby* that shows a six-pointed star or *asterism* when cut *cabochon, q.v.*

star sapphire *Sapphire* that shows a six-pointed star or *asterism* when cut *cabochon, q.v.*

tiger's eye Variety of quartz that is *chatoyant* (changing color or luster like the eye of a cat), often *cabochon cut;* yellowish brown,

bluish, or red in color. Found in the southern part of South Africa.

topaz Transparent semi-precious mineral, *aluminum silicate,* in shades of yellow, found in Europe, North and South America, Ceylon, Japan. Name also applied to vellow *corundum* (called Oriental topaz) and to yellow *quartz.*

tourmaline Transparent green semi-precious stone; also in other colors: *achroite,* colorless; *rubellite,* rose-red; *siberite,* violet; *indicolite,* dark blue.

turquoise Semi-precious opaque mineral in sky-blue, greenish blue, or apple green, used rough or pol-ished for jewelry; often used set in silver by American Indians.

zircon Transparent gem that resem-bles diamond when white and bril-liant cut, also comes in smoky gray, yellow, orange, violet, and shades of blue—the best known.

gem cuts Methods of cutting gem stones to be set into gold and other metals as rings, bracelets, necklaces, tiaras, etc. Most common types are:

GEM CUTS:

baguette c. Small stones cut in narrow, convex oblong shape with facets. *Der.* French, rod.

brilliant c. Cutting of transparent stone, especially diamond or emer-ald, into 58 facets for maximum brilliance. First done by Vincent Peruzzi of Venice in time of Louis XIV.

cabochon c. Stone cut and polished

to convex circle or oval—not faceted. Used for translucent stones such as opals; for turquoises; always for star rubies and sapphires.

cushion c. Stone is cut rather flat with one or more rows of facets arranged around the *girdle.*

emerald c. Similar to *brilliant cut* with *table* and *facets* but basic shape is square or oblong.

marquise c. (mar-keez) Variation of *brilliant cut;* basic shape is oval with pointed ends. Introduced in time of Louis XV; named for his mistress Marquise de Pompadour.

pear c. Variation of *brilliant cut,* similar to *marquise cut* but with one pointed and one rounded end.

rose c. Simple faceted cut used for inexpensive gems.

square c. See *emerald cut,* above.

step c. See *cushion cut.*

gem setting Manner in which gemstone is mounted in article of jewelry. Either in *14K, 18K gold, gold-filled* or *platinum* for *precious* or *semi-precious stones* or in *gold washed* or *plated* metal for *costume jewelry, q.q.v.*

GEM SETTINGS:

channel s. Groove of metal holding stones. Also called *flush setting.*

fish-tail s. Series of scallops (like fish scales) holding stone in place.

flush s. See *channel setting,* above.

paste s. Stone is glued in place; method used for inexpensive stones.

pronged s. Stone held in place by narrow projecting pieces of metal.

square s. Four prongs forming corners for brilliant-cut or step-cut stones.

Tiffany s. High pronged setting for solitaire stone introduced by Tiffany & Co., New York jewelers, in 1870's and often imitated. In 1971 Tiffany introduced a modernized version of its famous ring.

Geneva bands Collar consisting of two short white linen tabs hanging down from neckline, worn mainly by clergy. Also called *short bands* and *bäffchen, q.q.v. Der.* Originated by Swiss Calvinist clergy in Geneva, Switzerland.

Geneva gown Black clerical gown worn by Calvinists and later by other Protestant clergy, similar to an

academic robe, q.v., often worn with two vertical white linen bands at neck called *Geneva bands, q.v.*

Geneva hat Wide-brimmed, low-crowned hat, worn in late 16th and early 17th century by Puritan ministers and others.

Genoa cloak See *Italian cloak.*

Genoese embroidery See *embroideries.*

George See *boots* and *hairstyles.*

georgette See *fabrics.*

German gown See *Brunswick gown.*

germantown Coarse woolen yarn, slackly twisted, usually four-ply, used for hand-knitted garments.

Gernreich, Rudi See *designers appendix, United States.*

gertrude Infant's slip with round neck, built up shoulders, and sometimes long in length; worn in early part of 20th century. Also called a *gertrude skirt.*

geta Japanese *clog,* raised about four inches by series of spikes or wedges of wood to keep feet off wet ground.

ghagra (gagra) Calf- to ankle-length red cotton skirt cut in a full style gathered in drawstring at waist, open down front; worn by women in India.

ghlîla North African vest, hip length with low neckline and short or long full sleeves; worn mostly by women, sometimes by men in a jacket style. In Morocco and Algeria, worn over a blouse and under the *djubba, q.v.*

Gibson Girl Style of dress inspired by the popular series of magazine sketches by Charles Dana Gibson in 1895–1910, consisting of high-necked tucked *shirtwaist* with leg-of-mutton *sleeves,* belted *wasp waist,* and long skirt fitted over hips, flared at hem; hair dressed in high *pompadour* and topped by flat, *straw sailor hat* banded in black, *q.q.v.* See *La Belle Époque* under *hairstyles.*

Gibus (jy-bus) Man's collapsible *opera* or *top* hat, *q.q.v.,* with sides containing metal springs that snapped open to hold it upright; named after Antoine Gibus, who invented the hat in 1823 and patented it in 1837. See *elastic round hat.*

gig Textile-industry term for machine used to raise nap on fabrics, usually a cylinder covered with wire brushes or *teasels, q.v.*

gig coat See *curricle coat.*

gigot sleeve See *French gigot sleeve.*

Gilbert, Irene See *designers appendix, Ireland.*

gilet (zhee-lay) 1. Term for *vest* or short *waistcoat, q.v.,* worn by men in the 1850's and 1860's. 2. Woman's lacy or frilly *plastron* or *vestee,*

q.q.v., worn from 2nd half of 19th century through early part of 20th.

gillie See *shoes.*

gills Colloquial term for upstanding points of men's shirt collars in 19th century. Also called *shirt gills.*

gimp 1. See *braids.* 2. Variant of *guimple* or *wimple, q.v.*

gingham See *fabrics.*

gingham check or **plaid** See *checks* or *plaids.*

gippon, gipon (jee-pon) Military garment of 14th century, variation of *gambeson, q.v.,* close-fitting, sleeveless, leather or padded, laced down front, extending to knees, sometimes belted and with long tight sleeves buttoned from wrist to elbow; forerunner of *doublet, q.v.* Also called *jupe, jupel.*

gipser Bag for alms, usually silk, worn by men in late Middle Ages. Also spelled *gipciere* and *gypsire.*

girdle 1. Undergarment worn by women and girls, designed to mold lower torso and sometimes legs; may be flexible two-way stretch or one-way stretch elastic with non-stretchable fabric panels; hip- to ankle-length, with or without hose supporters. 2. See *belts.* 3. Jewelry-industry term for circumference of largest portion of faceted stone.

GIRDLES:

Capri-length panty-g. Very long *panty-girdle, q.v.,* extending about four inches below knee.

Criss-Cross g. Trademark of Playtex Corp. for a girdle which has a lapped over front, with each side going diagonally to thigh—thus allowing for easier walking or sitting.

cuff-top g. Pull-on or zippered girdle that extends above waistline with

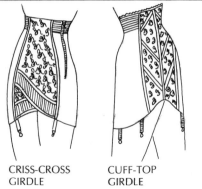

CRISS-CROSS GIRDLE   CUFF-TOP GIRDLE

wide band of elastic at top. Also called *high-rise* girdle.

French cinch Short girdle, designed to accentuate a small waist, starting at ribs, stopping above the hips; sometimes with attached long supporters for hose.

garter-brief Stretch panty or girdle offering light control, with detach-

able garters. Also called *stretch brief.*

guepiere (geh-pee-air) Short girdle to narrow the waist in hourglass shape, sometimes with attached garters; designed by Marcel Rochas, Paris couturier, in 1947. Also called *French cinch* or *waist-cincher.*

pants liner See *panties.*

panty-g. Girdle with closed crotch, resembling panties; in lengths from hip joint to ankle.

pull-on g. Girdle without zipper

PANTY-GIRDLE

PANTS LINER

or other opening, to be pulled on over the hips like panties.

Sarong Trademark for girdle with diagonal supporting panels criss-crossed over abdomen. See *Criss-Cross girdle*, above.

waist-cincher See *French cinch*, above.

zippered g. Girdle, usually one-way stretch, with zippered placket to aid in putting it on.

girdlestead Term used from Middle Ages to 17th century to indicate waistline of a garment.

Giudicelli, Tan See *designers appendix, France.*

Givenchy, Hubert de See *designers appendix, France.*

glacé (gla-say) Shiny finish applied to kid by using a glass roller; also called *glazed. Der.* French, frozen.

gladiator sandal See *sandals.*

Gladstone Man's double-breasted over-coat with short shoulder cape trimmed with border of *astrakhan, q.v.;* worn in 1870's. See *Ulster.*

Gladstone collar See *collars.*

glass Material made of silica, sand, limestone, and other chemicals, used in solid state for imitation gems in costume jewelry and melted and spun into *glass yarn, q.v.;* also used for lenses of *eyeglasses;* see *glasses,* below.

glasses Pair of lenses worn in front of eyes, set in frame of metal or plastic, usually with supports passing over ears; used to correct faulty vision or to shield eyes from glare of light, wind, or industrial hazards. First used in the 13th century, glasses became a fashionable accessory in the 1940's with the designing of the first plastic frames. Also called *eyeglasses, spectacles;* tinted lenses are called *sunglasses* or *shades.*

GLASSES:

Ben Franklin g. Small elliptical, octagonal, or square lenses with delicate metal frames, worn perched on the middle of the nose; a fad started in 1965, imitating the glasses, seen in paintings, worn by Benjamin Franklin, early U.S. statesman, in the 18th century. Also called *granny glasses.*

bifocals Glasses with lenses divided in parts for near vision and distance.

bug-eyed g. See *sunglasses.*

butterfly g. See *sunglasses.*

Courrèges g. Sun glasses introduced by French couturier André Cour-règes in 1966, made of opaque plastic encircling the face; narrow horizontal slits for tinted glass or plastic lenses.

GRANNY GLASSES

LORGNETTE

MONOCLE

PINCE-NEZ

CLIP-ON
SUNGLASSES

HALF GLASSES

PIXIE
GLASSES

WRAP-AROUND
GLASSES

goggles Protective glasses, usually with shatterproof lenses, in wide frames wrapped around temples, held on by strap around head; worn by auto racers, skiers, etc. Goggles for underwater swimming are watertight.

granny g. Variant of *Ben Franklin glasses, q.v.*

half g. Glasses for reading, with shallow lenses allowing wearer to look over top for distance viewing.

harlequin g. Glasses with diamond-shaped lenses; exaggerated form of *pixie glasses, q.v.*

horn rims or **horn-rimmed g.** Eyeglasses with heavy frames of dark horn or mottled brown plastic imitating horn; very popular in the

1940's and '50's. Often very similar to plastic *tortoise shell* frames, *q.v.* below.

lorgnette (lorn-yet) A pair of eyeglasses attached to a handle, or a pair of *opera glasses, q.v.* similarly mounted; usually hinged so glasses may be folded when not held up to the eyes. *Der.* French *lorgner,* to spy or peep.

monocle Man's single eyeglass worn only in one eye, usually suspended on ribbon around neck.

opera g. Binoculars (two small telescopes mounted for viewing with both eyes) used to provide close-up view at the opera or theater, usually a fashionable accessory, decorated with mother-of-pearl, gold, brocade, etc. Plain metal or leather-covered binoculars are called *sport glasses* or *field glasses;* used for games or hunting.

owl g. See *sunglasses.*

pince-nez (pants-nay) Eyeglasses without ear pieces, kept in place by a spring gripping the bridge of the nose. *Der.* French, nose-pincher.

pixie g. Lenses of conventional oval shape near nose but shaped to a point at temples, giving a tilted look to eyes.

Polaroid g. Trademark for special sunglass lenses coated with a substance that polarizes light, especially effective in cutting down glare.

rimless g. Lenses attached to metal nose piece and ear pieces but not outlined by the frame; popular from 1930's to 1940's, revived in 1960's.

shades Slang for *sunglasses, q.v.*

specs Slang for *spectacles.*

sunglasses Eyeglasses with dark-colored lenses to cut glare; invented about 1885, popularized by movie stars in Hollywood in 1930's and 1940's, prevalent fashion in 1960's and 1970's in various shapes and sizes, e.g., big round *owl* or *bug-eye, butterfly,* square. *Clip-on* sun lenses can be worn over corrective glasses.

tortoise-shell g. Glasses with frames made from tortoise shell or from plastic imitating tortoise shell, usually mottled brown. Heavy tortoise-shell frames became very popular in 1940's and '50's, replacing metal frames and rimless glasses worn earlier. Also called *horn rims.*

wrap-around g. Sun glasses made of one molded piece of plastic forming both lens frames and ear pieces without hinges at temples.

glass yarns See *yarns.*

glazed chintz See *chintz,* under *fabrics.*

glazed kid See *glacé.*

glen or **Glen Urquhart checks** See *plaids.*

Glengarry Scottish wool cap with lengthwise creased crown, collapsible; similar to *overseas cap, q.v.,* trimmed with ribbon cockade at side, banded with Stuart plaid ribbon (in memory of "bonnie Prince Charles") at edge, short ends loose at back. Worn since 1805. See *bluebonnet* and *caps.*

Glengarry cape Three-quarter-length cape with a tailored collar and single-breasted closing, with hood, sometimes plaid lined, attached

at neckline under the collar; worn by women in the 1890's. Also called *cawdor cape.*

glen plaid See *plaids.*

glocke (glokka) Medieval *poncho*-type outer garment made of *loden, q.q.v.,* fabric, with hole in center of large circle of fabric; still worn today, especially in mountainous Alpine regions of Europe. *Der.* German, bell.

gloria See *fabrics.*

Glospan Trademark owned by Globe Manufacturing Co. for *spandex* elastic yarn; used for knitted *stretch* fabrics.

glove Fitted covering for hand, with separate sheath for thumb and each finger, usually of leather, wool knit, stretch fabrics, or crochet, in lengths from wrist to upper arm. Worn for hundreds of years, gloves were a status symbol for gentry in 19th century, obligatory for formal dress and street wear until mid 1960's; worn more casually for warmth or specific sports in late 1960's and in 1970's. Seams varied from *full piqué* seams on fine kidskin to *whip-stitched, saddle-stitched, q.q.v.* (under *stitches*) on outside of heavy sports gloves. Also see *glove lengths.*

GLOVES AND MITTENS:

action g. Gloves with cut-outs on back of hand, or over knuckles,

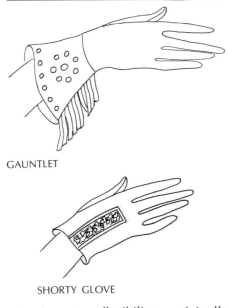

GAUNTLET

SHORTY GLOVE

to increase flexibility; originally used for sports such as golf or race driving, adopted for women's day-time wear in mid 1960's. Also called *cut-out gloves* or *racing gloves*.

driving g. Knitted gloves with leather palms for good grip on the steering wheel of car.

Finger-Free g. Trademark for gloves made with one long strip of material forming all the *fourchettes, q.v.,* between fingers; designed by Merry Hull, in 1938, for greater flexibility.

gauntlet Above-the-wrist glove with wide flaring cuff.

insulated g. Lined for protection against cold; lining may be fur, wool or acrylic knit, or—in mittens —fleece or bonded foam and fabric.

mitts Fingerless gloves, reaching above wrist, often of kid or sheer fabric and worn with bridal dresses, etc.; originally hand-covering in wool in Colonial America.

mittens Gloves with a thumb and one other compartment for rest of fingers, made of fur or leather or knitted; worn mainly by children and skiers for warmth.

mousquetaire g. (moos-keh-tare) Woman's long, loose glove, pull-on or with a buttoned slit at wrist; worn crushed down or with hand out of slit, remainder crushed up to elbow; often worn with formal evening dress.

opera g. Long-length glove, sometimes made without a thumb.

pull-ons Gloves without plackets or fastenings that slip easily over the hand.

shorty g. *Two-button* glove, see *glove lengths,* below.

slip-ons See *pull-ons* above.

table-cut g. *Tranks, q.v.* from which these gloves are cut are hand-pulled to determine the amount of stretch in the leather and then cut. Women's fine kid gloves are made in this manner to insure proper stretch but no bagginess.

glove band Ribbon or plaited horsehair band tied near elbow to keep a woman's glove in place; used from mid 17th to 18th centuries. Also called *glove string.*

glove lengths Measurement of length of glove is expressed in terms of *buttons; one button* equals one-half inch from the heel of the hand, or a wrist-length glove; *two-, four-, six-* and *eight-button* gloves are day-time gloves; *sixteen-button* gloves are for formal evening wear. System devised in France in centimeters.

glover's stitch See *whip stitch* and *saddle stitch* under *stitches.*

glove seams See *inseam, kid seam, lap seam,* and *outseam* under *seams.*

glove silk See *tricot* under *fabrics.*

glove string Variant of *glove band, q.v.*

goatee Small pointed *beard, q.v.,* similar to tuft of hair on a goat's chin.

goatskin See *leather.*

gobelin corselet Woman's belt in form of a *corselet, q.v.,* coming up high in front under the bust, having a

point in front, narrowing in back, trimmed with a ruffle of lace; worn in mid 1860's.

gobelin stitch (go-be-lan) See *stitches.*

gob hat See *hats.*

godet (go-day) Triangular piece, sometimes rounded at top, flaring at

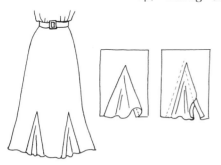

the base, set into a skirt, sleeve, etc. to give added fullness. See *gusset.*

godet pleat See *pleats.*

Godey's Lady's Book The first periodical for women, published by A. Godey from 1830 to 1898, edited by Sara Josepha Hale, 1837–1872; featured colored fashion sketches.

goffer (goff-er) 1. (verb) To press ridges or narrow pleats into a frill. 2. (noun) Headdress of white linen, fluted or *goffered* around face, worn in late 16th and early 17th centuries. *Der.* French *gaufrer,* to crimp. Also spelled *gauffer.*

goggles See *glasses.*

go-go watchband See *bracelets.*

gold Precious metal which in its pure state is too soft to be durable; it is usually made into alloys called *karat gold* or used for *plating* or *washing* jewelry items, *q.q.v.*

golden muskrat See *muskrat* under *furs.*

gold-filled or **rolled gold** Gold fused to a base metal and rolled in such a manner that the proportion of gold to base stays the same, *i.e.,* 1/10 18K means the gold used was 18 K (Karat) and that it represents 1/10 by weight of the object.

gold leaf Pure gold hammered so thin it takes 3,000,000 units to make a stack one inch high. Used for jewelry and gold leather.

gold-plated Describing jewelry with a thin surface of gold which is electrolytically plated to a base metal.

gold-washed Describing jewelry with a thin coating of gold applied to a base metal by dipping or washing it in a solution of gold.

gole Medieval term for cape part of the hood, which hung around the shoulders; also called the *golet*. See *chaperon*.

golf clothes By 1890's, golf was a sport enjoyed by both men and women. Men wore *knickers, a Norfolk jacket,* and a cap with a visor; by the 1920's they wore *plus fours* and a *sweater, q.q.v.* Women in the early days, wore a version of the *Norfolk jacket,* the *Glengarry cape, q.q.v.,* and sometimes shorter length skirts or *divided skirts;* in pre-World War I days, a *coat sweater* was worn; in the 1930's the *action-back dress* was introduced, *q.q.v.* Also see *caps* and *shoes.*

golf vest Man's knitted-wool single-breasted vest, braid-trimmed and made without collar, with three pockets, one each side plus watch pocket; worn in 1890's.

Goma, Michel See *designers appendix, France.*

gondolier's hat See hats.

gonel (gon-el) 14th century synonym for *gown, q.v.*

goose-bellied doublet See *peascod-bellied doublet.*

Gordian knot Decorative square knot used as trimming in the last half of 18th century, sometimes on bracelets, sometimes a length of false hair used as a chignon. *Der.* Named for Greek mythological founder of Phrygia (now Turkey) called *Gordius;* an oracle pronounced that he would be master of Asia until the knot he tied was undone; Alexander severed the knot with one blow of his sword.

gore 1. Skirt section, wider at hem than top, providing fullness and shaping waist without darts. A four-gore skirt has seams at sides, center front, and center back; six-gore has side-front and side-back seams as well as side seams, etc. There may be as many as twenty-four gores in a skirt. 2. Sewing term for triangular insert of fabric that creates fullness; used in skirts and bell-bottomed pants, particularly, also in gloves at wrist, to make flared cuff and facilitate opening. Also called *godet.*

gorge Men's tailoring term indicates seam where collar meets lapel, either high or low.

gorget (gorge-et) Term for variety of neck and shoulder coverings: 1. Armor worn on throat in Middle Ages. 2. Variant of *wimple, q.v.,* in 12th and 13th centuries. 3. Shoulder cape of the *chaperon, q.v.,* in 14th and 15th centuries. 4. Later, small neck *ruff, ruching* at edge of square neckline, or wide *falling collar, q.q.v.* 5. Chain with crescent-shaped ornament worn around the neck by officers in 1650–1700 as a badge of rank. 6. High collar worn by women in late 19th and early 20th centuries.

gossamer See *fabrics.*

Gothic General term for costume of Middle Ages when lines of architecture were reflected in design of headdresses and bodices, specifically pointed arches. See *English hood.*

Goulue, La See *hairstyles.*

gown 1. See *nightgown, robe.* 2. See *dress.* 3. Term used from 11th century on for woman's dress and for loose-fitting, wide-sleeved outer garment worn by judges, scholars, etc.

gown à la francaise (ah la frawn-saiz) "French gown": made with close-fitting bodice, front closing filled in with decorated *stomacher, q.v.,* two wide box pleats falling from shoulders to hem in back; fashionable in 18th century.

gown à la levantine (ah la levan-teen) "Levantine gown": comfortable dress of 1778, comparable to *negligee costume, q.v.,* made with *overskirt* and *bodice* in one piece fastened at the chest with a pin; skirt open down front over *underskirt, q.q.v.*

gown à l'anglaise (ah long-glaze) "English gown": dress without *paniers, q.v.,* the *bodice* shaped to long boned point in back, closed in front over *waistcoat,* the skirt slashed in front to show matching *petticoat, q.q.v.;* worn in late 18th century.

gown à la polonaise (ah la pole-o-naiz) "Polish gown": dress with unboned *bodice* and *overskirt* in one piece, low neckline, *sabot sleeves, q.q.v.,* and *overskirt* looped up by drawstrings into three big puffs; worn in last third of 18th century and revived in late 19th century.

gown à la turque (ah la toork) "Turkish gown": dress with a tight-pleated bodice, *turned-down collar, flared sleeves,* and draped belt knotted on one hip; a sensation about 1799 at the Palais Royal, Paris.

graduation dress See *dresses.*

grand assiette sleeve (grawn ass-ee-ette) Extra cap sleeve, crescent shape, extending over top curve of shoulder on the *doublet, q.v.,* of 14th and 15th centuries.

grand vair See *vair.*

granite cloth See *fabrics* and *weaves.*

granny Adjective used in mid 1960's for clothing and accessories reflecting era of wearers' grandmothers or actually great-grandmothers. See *boots, dresses, glasses,* and *granny gown* under *nightgowns.*

granny waist Fitted bodice with lace insert in front, large lace ruffle around a low neckline, and optional large lace ruffles falling over the arms from puffed sleeves; worn in 1890's, it was called by this name because the style was worn by grandmothers when they were young. Also called *1830 waist.*

grass cloth See *fabrics.*

grass embroidery See *embroideries.*

gray flannel See *fabrics.* Also see *dyed in the wool.*

gray fox See *fox* under *furs.*

gray goods Textile industry term used for unfinished fabrics as they come from the loom. Also called *greige goods.*

gray lawns Unfinished fine-yarn cloths made in various qualities to be converted into number of fabrics, including *organdy, batiste,* and *nainsook, q.q.v.,* under *fabrics.*

greatcoat See *coats.*

greave Metal-plate leg covering reaching from ankle to knee, similar to *gaiter, q.v.,* part of medieval armor. See *demi-jamb.*

grebe feathers See *feathers.*

Grecian bend Fashionable stance of woman, 1815–20, 1868–90; body tilted forward from a *wasp waist*, with *bustle, q.q.v.,* emphasizing the derrière.

Grecian border See *fret.*

Grecian curls 1. Hairstyle of 1860's with rows of *finger curls, q.v.,* hanging down the back from the nape of the neck; sometimes arranged in two rows, one shorter than the other. 2. See *curls.*

Grecian sandal See *sandals.*

Greek belt See *belts.*

Greek coiffure Woman's hairstyle with center part, hair braided and wrapped around the crown of the head, made to form three hanging loops in back and wound around the loops at nape of neck; worn in 1860's. Also called *coiffure à la grecque.*

Greek handbag See *handbags.*

Greek lace See *reticella* under *laces.*

Greek lounging cap See *lounging cap.*

green-aproned men London porters of 18th century distinguished by green aprons worn by members of trade.

greener-yallery, Grosvenor Gallery costume See *aesthetic dress.*

Greenway, Kate Popular English children's-book illustrator of late 19th century whose characters wore early 19th-century high-waisted, ankle-length dresses with ribbon sashes, *pantalettes* showing, and *mob caps* or *poke bonnets, q.q.v.;* these dresses were widely copied for children's wear through end of 19th century and are still an inspiration. See *Kate Greenaway styles.*

greige (grazh) Term used for raw silk reeled from cocoons.

greige goods Variant of *gray goods, q.v.*

grenadine 1. See *fabrics.* 2. Fine, strong hard twist *silk* yarn used in hosiery and lace.

Grès, Alix See *designers appendix, France.*

Griffe, Jacques See *designers appendix, France.*

grippers See *closings.*

grisaille (gree-zah-yeh) French term for pepper-and-salt effects or grayish mixtures in fabrics.

grommet (grom-it) Reinforced eyelet in garment through which a fastener may be passed.

gros de Londres See *fabrics.*

grosgrain See *fabrics* and *ribbons.*

gros point (gro pwanh) See *embroideries, stitches* and *laces.*

grow bag Another name for *baby bunting, q.v.*

guanaco See *furs.*

guanaquito See *guanaco* under *furs.*

guard Infanta *Farthingale, q.v.,* or frame under skirt, very wide at sides and flattened front and back; worn in Spain in 17th century, e.g. as in Velasquez' portrait of the Infanta.

guards 16th century term for decorative bands of rich fabrics, plain or embroidered, used to conceal garment seams.

guardsman coat See *coats.*

Gucci, Aldo See *designers appendix, Italy.*

Gucci loafers (goo-chee) See *shoes.*

guepiere See *girdles.*

guiche See *curls* and *hairpieces.*

guimpe dress Jumper-dress with *guimpe* or blouse under short-sleeved, low-necked dress; worn from 1880's to about 1915, first by children, later by older girls and women; sometimes took the form of a suspender-type jumper with blouse called *guanipe* underneath. Also called *guimpe costume.*

guimple Variant of *wimple, q.v.*

guinea feathers (ginny) See *feathers.*

guipure See *laces.*

guleron (goo-ler-on) Variant of *gorget, q.v.*

gum shoes Colloquial term for rubber overshoes or sneakers. The slang term *gumshoe* meaning a detective or private investigator alludes to the quiet tread of "sneakers."

gum twill Variant of *foulard, q.v.* under fabrics.

gun-club checks See *checks.*

gusset 1. Sewing term for diamond-shaped piece of fabric seamed at

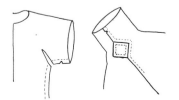

underarm of cut-on or *dolman* sleeve, to permit greater movement.

2. Triangular piece used in sides of handbag for wider opening and at sides of men's shirt-tails, sides of shoes, etc.

Guy, Maria See *designers appendix, France.*

gym bloomers Black sateen or navy-blue serge bloomers, bloused below knee, pleated into waistband; worn by women for gym classes from about 1900 to late 1920's, also worn for camping. See *Bloomer, Amelia.*

gym suit 1. Woman's gymnasium costume consisting of full-cut blouse, buttoned down the front, with small tailored collar and long full cuffed sleeves; front, collar and cuffs braid trimmed, with braid-trimmed calf-length skirt or bloomers with un-pressed pleats at the waist; worn from 1890's until early 20th century. 2. Costume worn today by schoolgirls in gymnasium; usually *shirt* and *shorts, q.q.v.,* in one piece, buttoning down the front, sometimes a *tunic* with separate *bloomers, q.q.v.*

gypsy look Colorful garments in bright shades, e.g., full skirts, blouses, boleros, shawls, head scarves, and hoop earrings—characteristic apparel of nomadic tribe in Europe. For contemporary adaptions, see *blouses, earrings, shawl,* and *bayadere* under *stripes.*

gypsy stripe See *stripes.*

H

haba Variant of *aba, q.v.*

haberdashery A store that sells men's apparel and furnishings.

habiliments (heh-bil-eh-ments) Clothing, garb, attire, or dress. *Der.* French *habillement,* clothing.

habit Characteristic costume of a calling, rank, or function, *e.g., clerical clothes, court dress* or *riding habit, q.q.v.*

habit à la française (ah-beet ah la fran-sayz) See *justaucorps.*

habit d'escalier (ha-bee des-kahl-yaye) Evening dress with overtunic or *half robe, q.v.,* and short sleeves slit open and rimmed with ribbons tied in ladder-like fashion, worn in late 18th and early 19th centuries.

habit-redingote Woman's dress made in *princess, q.v.* style with front closed from neck to knees, lower front of skirt cut away and rounded, revealing *underskirt;* worn in late 1870's.

habit shirt 1. Linen shirt with standing collar, ruffled at front and wrists; worn under vest as part of woman's *riding habit* in 18th and 19th cen-

turies. 2. Shirt worn as fill-in under low necklines in early 19th century. Also called *chemisette, q.v.*

habutai See *fabrics.*

hacking jacket or **coat** See *sport jackets* under *jackets.*

hacking pocket See *pockets.*

hacking scarf Long scarf, originally 72 inches, worn by four-in-hand coach drivers in Old England; popular at Oxford and Cambridge Universities in England in 1931 when it was worn by Prince of Wales, becoming a fad for U.S. college students in 1932.

hackled flax Flax fibers combed to remove short fibers and to straighten and separate before spinning.

haik (hike or hake) Voluminous wrap made of large oblong of fabric which covers entire head, face, and body; worn by Moslem women in northern Africa. Also spelled *haick. Der.* Arabic *hyak,* to weave.

haincelin (han-se-lin) Short *houppelande, q.v.,* with embroidery on only one sleeve. *Der.* Named after Charles VI's jester, Haincelin Coq.

hair band 1. Any piece of knitted or woven fabric worn around the head; or a metal or plastic U-shaped clip worn across the head from ear to ear. 2. In 15th to 17th century, *hair ribbon* or *fillet, q.q.v.*

haircut Trimming and shaping of hair with scissors or razor. See *hairstyles.*

hair fibers Animal fibers with silky hand, such as *mohair,* from angora goat; *alpaca,* from cashmere goat; *guanaco; llama; rabbit;* and *vicuña.*

hairline stripe See *stripes.*

hair net Fine *net, q.v.,* in a cap shape, worn over the hair to keep it in place; may be made of knotted human hair and nearly invisible; sometimes of chenille or gold or silver threads and worn as decoration.

hairpiece Added artificial or human hair used to conceal baldness or to enhance hair, arranged in various lengths and forms to attach to head by means of *combs,* elastic bands, *hair pins,* etc.; worn since 16th century and popular fashion accessory in 1960's and 1970's. Also called *postiche, transformation, toupee.* See *wig.*

HAIRPIECES:

chignon Extra bun or knot of hair, worn on back of head or at nape of neck; popular style in 1860's. Also worn in 1960's.

cluster curls Groups of false *ringlets* or *sausage* curls, *q.q.v.,* mounted on netting to be pinned in place as part of an elaborate coiffure.

criniere (cran-ee-yere) Hairpiece or wig of modacrylic yarns introduced by French designer André Courrèges in spring, 1969.

fall Long straight hair piece fastened to head with ribbon *hair band, q.v.,* or pinned in place, hanging down

over owner's hair, any length; fashionable in late 1960's and early 1970's.

guiches (geesh) Small curls at side of face in front of ears, glued in place. Also called *kiss curls* or *spit curls.*

postiche A hair piece. *Der.* French, false.

switch Long hank of hair which may be braided in a *plait* or twisted and worn as a *coronet* or made into a *chignon, q.q.v.*

toupee 1. Man's small partial *wig* used to cover baldness. 2. Curl of hair worn as topknot on *periwig* in 18th century.

transformation A *hair piece* or *wig.*

wig See *wig* in alphabetical listings.

hairpin A two-tined device, usually of tortoise shell, plastic, or metal, used to hold the hair in place, especially hair in a bun or knot. The classic hairpin is a wire, bent double with crimps half-way down each side to give flexibility. Pins of very fine wire tinted to match hair are called *invisible* hairpins. Decorated hairpins are worn as jewelry and may be of exotic materials or jeweled. Also see *bobby pins.*

hairpin lace See *laces.*

hair seal See *furs.*

hair sticks Long stiletto-like pieces of wood, plastic, metal, etc., worn for decorative effect, usually thrust through hair knotted at the back of the head.

hairstyle Manner in which hair is arranged. Also called *hairdo, coiffure, coif.*

HAIRSTYLES (also see CURLS):

abstract cut Straight short geometric haircut, often asymmetric, with one side of head different from other; introduced by English hairstylist Vidal Sassoon in mid 1960's.

Afro Style adopted by African-Americans in 1960's, with natural hair combed straight out from the

AFRO

BELLE ÉPOQUE

SASSOON

GAMIN

CORNROWS

EARMUFFS

UPSWEEP

FINGER WAVE

FLIP

head in a globular shape, the size varying with the length of the hair; many interesting variations. Also called *natural* hairstyle.

ape drape Longish bob, layered for shaggy look, with bangs and sideburns but cut to reveal the ears, tapering down back of neck in ragged point; innovation of late 1960's, similar to *shag.*

artichoke Short, layered hair, back-combed, but not too bouffant; popular in early 1960's.

bangs Hair combed forward over forehead and cut straight across, left smooth or waved. Called *fringe* in England.

Bardot Long hair, loosely curled and arranged in tousled disarray with loose tendrils around face, popularized by French movie star, *Brigitte Bardot, q.v.,* in 1959.

Beatle cut Man's hair worn full, with sideburns and well down the neck in back; first in revival of longer hair styles for men and introduced in the 1960's by the Beatles, avant-garde rock-music group from Liverpool, England. When asked in their movie *A Hard Day's Night* what he called his haircut, Beatle George Harrison replied, "I call it Arthur."

beehive High, exaggerated hair shape, achieved by *back-combing* into a rounded dome; first worn by

Teddy girls, q.v., in London in late 1950's, popular till mid 1960's.

Belle Époque Variant of *pòmpadour, q.v. Der.* Named for the period 1890-1910, called *La Belle Époque* in France.

bingle English term for very short haircut. *Der.* From *bob* and *shingle* combined.

bob Short, blunt-cut hair, forming a smooth cap, either with bangs or bared forehead, introduced in second decade of 20th century by Irene Castle, q.v. Also see *Buster Brown, gamin, Eaton crop.*

Boldini Variant of *pompadour hairstyle, q.v.* Named for Italian society painter Giovanni Boldini (1845–1931), who often painted women wearing this style.

bouffant Hair exaggeratedly puffed out by means of *teasing, back-combing,* and use of hair spray (lacquer or other fixative in an aerosol can); fashionable in early 1960's for medium-length and long hair.

boyish bob Short haircut for women similar to *Eton crop, q.v.*

brush cut See *crew cut,* below.

bubble curls See *curls.*

bubble cut See *beehive,* above.

bun Small roll of hair confined neatly by pins or net at top of head or at nape of neck. See *chignon.*

bustle curls See *curls.*

Buster Brown Straight short hairstyle with straight-across bangs over forehead, named for early 20th-century comic-strip character and popular for little boys. Also called *Dutch bob, q.v.*

Butch cut See *crew cut.*

chignon Large roll of hair twisted into circle or figure eight on back of head or at nape of neck, often enclosed in decorative net or held by fancy hair pins; classic style in 1860's and again in 1920's and '30's.

coif (kwaff) Originally a headdress; word now used to mean *coiffure* or *hairstyle.*

concierge Revival of *Gibson Girl look, q.v.,* of early 20th century with hair teased into bouffant *pompadour, q.v.* all the way around head with small bun at the crown, but with soft tendrils near the face. *Der.* Ironic name from French for caretaker of an apartment house; women *concierges* often wore this hairstyle, were not too neat. Also called *La Belle Époque, Boldini, the onion,* and *La Goulue,* see below.

corkscrew curls See *curls.*

cornrowing Hair braided in narrow rows, flat against the head, by adding more hair after each plait in the braid; derived from African styles; worn by Southern Blacks in 19th century, revived in early 1970's by fashionable Blacks.

crew cut Man's haircut closely cropped so that hair on crown of head stands erect. Originally worn by oarsmen to keep hair out of eyes, adopted by college men in 1940's and 1950's—when it was similar to Army haircuts. Also called *brush cut, Butch cut,* or *flat-top.*

curls See CURLS category.

ducktail haircut Short hairstyle combed to come to a point at nape of neck; worn by both men and women in the 1950's.

Dutch bob See *Buster Brown* hairstyle; same style worn by girls with back cut straight or shingled.

earmuffs Hair center parted, braided over each ear, and wound around in buns over the ears.

Eton crop Short boyish hair cut, shingled at sides and back, often side parted and with bangs brushed to one side, worn by boys at Eaton College in England and popular in U.S. in 1920's and again in late 1960's.

feather cut Short lightly curled woman's *bob*, cut in layers, popular in 1950's and 1960's.

finger wave Short hair set in flat waves by means of setting lotion and held until dry by *bobby pins, q.v.,* or sometimes by *combs;* popular in 1930's and revived in early 1970's. Also called *water wave.*

flat-top See *crew cut,* above.

flip Medium length woman's hairstyle with hair turned up on ends to form an incomplete curl, front often cut in bangs.

French roll or **twist** Upswept hairstyle with side and back hair combed and twisted in roll up the center back; popular in 1940's and classic style since.

gamin Short boyish cut with shingled back and sides and irregularly cut bangs; popular in 1940's. See *Eaton crop. Der.* French, street urchin.

George Long hair pulled back and secured at nape with a twist of hair, ribbon tie, or scarf; named for the wig seen in eighteenth-century portraits of U.S. President George Washington.

Gibson Girl Hair worn in high puffy *pompadour, q.v.,* with small *bun, q.v.,* on top of head; fashionable in 19th century and popularized by drawings of Charles Dana Gibson.

Goulue, La Variant of *pompadour, q.v.;* named for portrait of a music-hall performer called by this sobriquet (the glutton), painted by Henri Toulouse-Lautrec, late nineteenth-century French painter and lithographer.

Grecian curls See *curls.*

guiches See *curls* and *hair pieces.*

Irene Castle bob Short earlob-length hair brushed back off forehead, in loose waves, named after *Irene Castle, q.v.,* ballroom dancer who made bobbed hair fashionable prior to World War I.

ironed hair Long straight hair, achieved by placing hair on an ironing board and pressing with a warm iron to remove all waves; a fad with young girls in the late 1960's.

layered cut Woman's hair cut in graduated layers, similar to *shag, q.v.*

lion's tail See *queue.*

page-boy bob Straight hair with ends curled under at back and sides, shoulder length or shorter, very smooth; derived from hair of medieval pages and popular style of 1940's, revived in 1970's.

pannier curls See *curls.*

pigtails Hair worn in two side braids, sometimes with ribbon bow tied on ends; popular style for young girls for centuries.

pixie cut Variant of *gamin* and *urchin* hairstyles, *q.q.v.*

pompadour 1. Women's hair brushed up high and smooth from forehead and temples, *teased* or rolled over false stuffing and tucked into a small *bun* on top, *q.q.v.* Named for Marquise de Pompadour, mistress of Louis XV of France, and popular until early 20th century; revived in 1940's and 1960's. 2. Man's hair worn rather long and brushed straight up and back from forehead with no part.

pony tail Hair pulled to crown or center back of head and tied with a ribbon or elastic, ends left hanging loose like a horse's tail.

poodle cut All-over curled short hair like the dog's fur.

pouf Variant of *bouffant* hairstyle.

queue (kew) Long single braid of hair hanging in back, sometimes twined with colored cords and called *queue de lion* or lion's tail.

ringlets Another name for *curls.*

Romeo Modified *page-boy* cut with bangs falling to eyebrows, sides cut sloping backward to reveal the face as an oval, hair gently turned under in back.

Sassoon Short, straight boyish hairdo, combed forward from crown, cut in low bangs, shaped to points in front of ears and shingled in back to deep V; first *geometric cut, q.v.,* designed by English hairdresser Vidal Sassoon in 1963.

sausage curls See *curls.*

shag A hairstyle in which the hair is cut in layers—starting at the crown. The layers get progressively longer with those at the back and sides being longest, approximately five inches.

shingle Hair cut short in gradually tapering lengths, like shingles on a roof, in back and sometimes at sides, as in a man's short haircut, introduced for women in 1920's. See *Eton crop, gamin.*

topknot Hair twisted into a *knot* or *bun* at the crown of the head.

'twenties bob See *bob,* above.

upsweep Popular 1940's woman's hairstyle with medium-long hair brushed upward from the sides and nape and secured on top of the head in curls or a *pompadour, q.v.* Also called *updo.*

urchin Variant of *gamin hairstyle, q.v.*

Veronica Lake Long hair parted on side, heavier section hanging down almost covering one eye; popularized by movie star Veronica Lake in 1940's, revived after interest in late, late TV movies in 1960's.

wind-blown bob Popular 1930's woman's hairstyle, cut short and *shingled, q.v.,* so that hair fell softly about the face as if blown by the wind.

wing Medium-length hair with ends turned up in half-curl.

hakama (hak-e-ma) Stiff silk trousers, slashed up sides, giving effect of divided skirt, made by pleating fullness into stiff belt, six pleats in front and two in back, a belt with cords attached tied around the *obi;* formerly worn by Japanese men.

hakimono Variant of *zori* and *geta, q.q.v.*

Hale, Sarah Josepha (1788–1879) Editor from 1837 to 1877 of *Godey's Lady's Book,* first publication featuring women's fashion news.

half-apron See *aprons.*

half-bra See *demi-bra* under *brassieres.*

half-collar See *collars.*

half-compass cloak See *compass cloak.*

half dress Late 18th and 19th centuries term for daytime or informal evening dress. Also called *half-toilette* or *demi-toilette.*

half gaiters See *spats.*

half glasses See *glasses.*

half gown Variant of *half-robe.*

half handkerchief Neck or headscarf worn by women in 18th and early 19th centuries, made of decorative fabric in triangular shape. Also called *fanchon, q.v.*

half jack boots See *jockey* under *boots.*

half kirtle See *kirtle.*

half lining Lining of only part of the garment, e.g., front completely lined and only the shoulders lined in the back; frequently used in men's suits and topcoats.

half mask See *masks.*

half mourning Costume worn for a time following the period of deep mourning, usually consisting of black costume with touches of white, gray, or purple; worn until mid 19th century.

half robe Low-necked, short-sleeved, thigh-length tunic over long gown, fullness pulled in at waist by narrow ribbon; worn from late 18th century to early 19th century. Also called *half-gown* or *demi-habilliment.*

half shirt Man's short shirt with decorated panel down front; worn over plain or soiled shirt, 16th-18th

centuries. Also called *sham.*

half sizes Women's garments cut for a fully developed figure, shortwaisted in back, waist and hips full, height about 5′2″ to 5′3″; usually numbered 10½ to 24½.

half sleeves 1. Protective sleeves covering the undersleeves on forearms, held on by elastic garters and worn in first decade of 20th century. 2. Sleeves covering forearms made of richer material than rest of garment, attached by lacings; worn from late 14th to mid 17th centuries.

half slip See *slips.*

half socks See *socks.*

halo hat See *hats.*

Halston See *designers appendix, United States.*

halter Strap encircling the neck and supporting front of blouse or dress, leaving shoulders and back bare; often used on bathing suits; popular in 1930's and revived in early 1970's. See *necklines* and *tops.*

Hamburg lace See *laces.*

hamster See *furs.*

hand Qualities of fabric revealed through sense of touch, e.g., crisp or soft, smooth or rough.

handbag Accessory carried mainly by women to hold money, cosmetics, etc., in various shapes, e.g., barrel, basket, envelope, pouch, satchel, etc., with or without handles; made in leather, canvas, plastic, straw, etc. or woven wool, beaded or of tapestry or in hard or mesh metal. Handbags for men began to gain acceptance in late 1960's, early '70's. Also called *bag, pocketbook,* or *purse.*

HANDBAGS AND PURSES:

ACCORDION BAG

BARREL BAG

SADDLE BAGS

CHANEL BAG

LUNCH BOX BAG

TOTE BAG

SHOULDER BAG

SAFARI BAG

MAN'S BAG

accordion b. Bag with pleated sides, expandable like filing folder, closed at top, usually with handles.

Apache b. Slim, flat, oblong bag with shoulder strap, usually made of patchwork of different colored leathers finished with fringe at bottom, innovation of late 1960's to go with *Indian look, q.v.* Also called *hippie bag, Indian bag,* and *squaw bag.*

barrel b. Cylindrical bag, resembling

a barrel turned on its side, usually with a *zipper, q.v.,* closing and strap handles or shoulder strap.

basket b. A small basket used as a handbag, sometimes lined with fabric and often fitted with leather handles or hardware hinges and clasps; often chosen for summer wear.

beaded b. Any bag made of fabric covered with beading: 19th century up to 1920's, bags were made of tiny beads often in colors and woven in floral patterns or of jet or marcasite or seed pearls, especially for evening. In 1930's and '40's, daytime bags woven of larger wooden beads, often painted but usually in plain colors or two-color combinations, were popular. Present-day bags include both varieties, with larger beads usually made of plastic.

book b. Slim oblong bag, size of notebook, cinched around center with strap that forms loop handle; introduced in 1970's.

box b. Handbag with rigid frame, similar to small suitcase or lunch box, made in leather, metal, or vinyl.

briefcase Flat satchel with envelope flap fastened with a latch and a rigid handle on top originally used by lawyers to carry briefs; woman's handbag version has outside pocket for cosmetics, etc.

caravan b. See *safari bag.*

carpet b. Handbag, popular in late 1960's, made of patterned carpeting or heavy tapestry, usually in a large *satchel* style, derived from carpet valises popular for travel just after the Civil War and alluded to by the derisive term "Carpetbagger" for a non-native politician.

carryall *Tote bag, q.v.*

Chanel b. Soft-sided quilted-leather *envelope* with full side flap, gilt chains run through grommets at top corners, adjustable to wear over shoulder; introduced by French designer *Gabrielle Chanel, q.v.,* in 1956 and widely copied.

change purse Small purse that closes by a snap clasp on the rigid frame or by a zipper, usually carried inside handbag to hold coins; made in leather, clear plastic, or matched to the larger handbag. Also called a *coin purse.*

clutch b. Small handbag with no handle, carried in hand or under arm.

cordé b. Any type of handbag made out of a fabric composed of rows of *gimp* (see *braids*) stitched to a background fabric to make a pattern; popular style in the 1940's, still used.

duffel b. Large canvas bag with drawstring top or grommets at top that fold over a clasp, used originally by sailors and soldiers to transport gear, copied in smaller style for handbags or beach bags, sometimes with rectangular piece of fabric stitched on outside to form extra pockets.

envelope b. Long, narrow handbag, shape of a correspondence envelope, usually of *clutch* type without handle.

feed b. Cylindrical leather or canvas bag with flat round bottom and top handles; copied from horse's feed bag; popular in 1940's, forerunner of many open *tote* bags.

flight b. Soft canvas satchel with zippered top closing and two handles, copied from standard carryall issued by airlines to passengers. Similar to *safari* or *caravan bag.*

Florentine b. Fine leather handbag or coin purse, often black, tooled in gold and brilliant colors in elaborate designs, often fleur-de-lis motif.

fold-over clutch Small envelope bag open at the top and closed by folding over double, carried in the hand or under arm.

French purse Fold-over wallet for bills, one half of which incorporates *a change purse, q.v.,* with metal clasp closing at the top, which is actually one end of the wallet.

Greek b. Square wool open-top bag, hand-woven in Greek designs, trimmed around edge with cording that forms long loop handles.

hippie b. *Apache bag, q.v.*

Indian b. *Squaw bag* or *Apache bag, q.q.v.*

knapsack Canvas or leather, soft expandable army bag, usually square, reinforced by webbing straps that extend over shoulders when bag is worn on the back; also called *backpack* and widely used by hikers. Very popular with young people in 1960's and '70's, copied as a school bag and general carryall.

lunchbox b. Papier-mâché or metal box bag with domed lid, usually decorated with découpage: cut-out pictures lacquered on; copied from workman's metal lunch box and fashion fad in late 1960's.

man's b. Handbag, usually a *shoulder, q.v.,* style, carried by a man; a fashion gaining popularity in early 1970's as an outgrowth of wide use of attaché cases and camera bags by men.

mesh b. Tiny links of metal joined to make a flexible bag; popular in early 1900's in small size with sterling-silver top and chain, the metal frequently enameled in a floral design. In the 1940's, mesh bags were made with larger links, enameled white, and plastic frames.

minaudiere (min-ode-ee-air) Small, rigid metal evening bag to hold cosmetics, carried in hand or by short chain, in oval, oblong or square shapes, decorated by engraved designs or set with jewels; an expensive jeweler's product popularized by Cartier in New York. *Der.* French, *simperer.*

pouch Basic style of bag, made of soft leather or fabric gathered into a drawstring closing or shirred onto a rigid frame with handles.

saddle bags Pair of soft leather bags joined to central strap handle, copied from large bags thrown over horse's saddle to carry provisions.

safari b. Similar to *flight bag,* with two outside flapped pockets.

satchel Leather bag on a rigid flat bottom, sides sloped to close on metal frame hinged about half-way down bag; often fastened with extra snap locks and with metal reinforcements at corners and rigid curved handle. Similar to bags carried by doctors.

shoulder b. Handbag of any shape or size with a long strap or chain handle worn over the shoulder; some handles convertible for over-arm use by buckles, snaps, or doubling of chain.

signature b. Handbag of leather or canvas with designer's initials or signature stenciled in all-over repeat pattern, originating with Vuitton in Paris, later copied by Hermés, Saint Laurent, Mark Cross, etc. and considered a fashion Status Symbol.

squaw b. See *Apache bag.*

tote b. Utility bag, large enough to carry small packages, sometimes with inner zippered compartment for money, copied from shape of common paper shopping bag, with open top and two handles, sometimes with outside loop to hold umbrella.

vanity b. Stiff-framed bag in squared or oval shapes, usually fitted with large mirror and sometimes compact, comb, lipstick, etc.; made of leather, brocade or metal, usually carried with evening clothes. See *minaudiere.*

hand-blocked print See *prints.*

handcoverchief, hand cloth Variants of *handkerchief.*

hand fall Term for lace-trimmed, turned-back, flared starched *cuff, q.v.,* frequently made double; worn by men and women in 17th century, with *falling band, falling ruff, standing band, q.q.v.* Also called *hand cuff.*

handkerchief Square of linen, cotton, or silk, with plain rolled hem or decorative woven border or lace edge, used for wiping nose, face, or hands; often worn tucked into pocket, tied around neck, etc. as decoration. See *bandanna.*

handkerchief dress See dresses.

handkerchief lawn See *fabrics.*

hand-blocked print See *prints.*

hand-painted print See *prints.*

hand-screened print See *silk-screen print* under *prints.*

hand sleeve 16th-century term for lower part of sleeve.

hare See *furs.*

hang 1. Term used in clothing construction to describe how fabric

HANDKERCHIEF DRESS, 1882

drapes on the figure after it is sewn. 2. Term used for marking hem of skirt with pins or chalk for straightening, lengthening, shortening, *i.e., hanging* a hem.

hanger See *shoulder belt.*

hanging sleeve 15th-century term for slashed *oversleeve* that hung at sides, often embroidered.

hanseline (han-sa-lyn) Man's extremely short *doublet, q.v.,* fashionable in late 14th and early 15th centuries. Also called *paltock, q.v.* Also spelled *haslein, hense lynes,* and *henselyns.*

han-yeri Embroidered collar, worn by Japanese women, attached to the undergarment and worn pulled out over kimono at neck. See *shito-juban.*

haori (hah-o-ri) Loose, knee-length Japanese coat.

happi coat See *robes.*

happy face Stylized face made up of a yellow circle with black dots for eyes and nose and a single black line for mouth; used on *sweatshirts, buttons, jewelry, prints,* etc., in early 1970's.

Hardanger bonnet Native Norwegian cap, shaped to head like baby's bonnet, tied under chin; cut in three sections, alternate red and white, with black velvet edge and decorated with braid and colored beads in eight-pointed star designs.

Hardanger embroidery See *embroideries.*

hard collar See *collars.*

hard hat See *hats.*

hare See *furs.*

harem Adjective used for a draped dress with skirt made on a foundation, with hem turned up and attached to foundation making an irregular hemline, or for Turkish trousers. See *silhouettes, dresses, pants, skirts,* and *pajamas.*

harlequin Character in Italian comedy who wears costume of vari-colored diamond shaped patches on *tunic* and *tights,* a flaring brimmed black *bicorn* hat decorated with *pompons,* and a black *mask, q.q.v.;* term is applied to (1) pattern of lozenge-shaped checks in multi-color; (b) eyeglasses slanting up to corner peaks; (c) hat with brim wide at sides, cut straight across front and back. See *glasses.*

harlot Garment consisting of stockings and pants in one piece, tied to upper and outer garments by strings, worn by men in England in late 14th century. Also called *herlot.* See *points* and *trunk hose.*

Harlow, Jean Platinum-blond Hollywood movie actress of the 1930's, symbol of sexiness and associated with soft, bias-cut clothes worn over natural body; a fashion influence in the late 1960's. See *pants.*

Harris tweed See *fabrics.*

Hartnell, Norman See *designers appendix, England.*

Harvard crimson Deep cherry color with a violet cast, official color of Harvard University in Cambridge, Massachusetts.

haslein Variant of *hanseline, q.v*

hasp Decorative silver fastening, similar to hook and eye, used for fastening coats in 17th and 18th centuries.

hat Covering for head made of felt, fur, straw, etc., usually consisting of a crown and brim, designed for functional protection against weather or for ornament or as status symbol from 10th century on.

HATS:

Alpine h. Man's sport hat of coarse felt or rough tweed, with soft crown slanting to a lengthwise crease, narrow brim rolled up at sides and back, often trimmed with upright fur brush; copied from hats worn in mountains in Swiss Tyrol region. Also called *Tyrolean* hat.

beach h. Wide-brimmed hat of straw or fabric worn on the beach to shade the face.

beefeater's h. Distinctive hat worn by Yeomen of the Guard in England,

HARD HAT

PICTURE HAT

HARD HAT

HALO HAT

BEEFEATER'S HAT

MOUNTIE'S HAT

REX HARRISON HAT

consisting of a soft, high crown, pleated into headband, and narrow brim. Also see *beefeater's uniform.*

beret See *caps.*

bicycle-clip h. Tiny half-hat fastened over crown and side of head by piece of springy metal. *Der.* From clip worn around leg when riding a bicycle to keep trousers from catching in chain or wheel spokes.

boater Straw hat with flat oval crown, flat brim, and ribbon band; popular for men in 19th and early

SNAP-BRIM
HAT

SAILOR HAT

SAILOR HAT,
1898

20th centuries, originally worn for boating.

bobby's h. Tall version of *chukka hat, q.v.* worn by English policemen called *bobbies.*

bowler Man's hat of hard felt, with domed crown and narrow brim turned up at sides, usually black; worn originally by London business men or with formal riding habit. Similar to American *derby, q.v. Der.* From design of William Bowler in 1850's.

Breton Woman's off-the-face hat with medium-sized rolled-back brim, worn on back of head; copied from hats worn by peasants of Brittany, France.

bumper Hat with thick, tubular brim surrounding various style crowns.

busby Tall cylindrical black fur or feather military hat with cockade at top of center front, and bag-shaped drapery hanging from crown, draped to the back, worn by Hussars, etc., in British army.

bush h. Wide-brimmed man's felt hat, worn turned up sharply on one side; worn by Australian soldiers and in South Africa for safaris. Also called *caddie* or *caddy.*

caddie See *bush hat.*

canotier (kan-not-ee-ay) French variant of *sailor hat #2, q.v.*

cape h. Woman's half-hat made by attaching felt or fabric *capelet* to *bicycle clip* which crosses the head from ear to ear, letting capelet fall over back of head.

capeline (cap-leen) 1. Wide, floppy-brimmed hat with small round crown; worn since 1920's. 2. Hood with cape attached, worn by country women in 1860's.

cartwheel Woman's hat with extra-wide stiff brim, and low crown, frequently of straw

chukka h. Domed hat with small brim copied from hats worn by polo players, similar to English policeman's or *bobby's* hat.

clip h. Half-hat mounted on a spring-metal clip worn across the crown of the head; often used for a child's hat of fur. See *bicycle-clip hat,* above.

cloche (klosh) Deep-crowned hat with no or very narrow brim, fitting head closely, almost concealing all of short hair, worn pulled down almost to eyebrows; fashion of 1920's and again in 1960's. *Der.* French, bell.

coolie h. Wide, shady Chinese hat made of bamboo, palm leaves, or straw in many forms, e.g. mushroom-shaped with knob at top, bowl shaped, conical flare with peak in center, etc. Copied by Western world for summer and beach wear

Cossack h. Tall brimless hat of fur, worn crushed down at an angle by Russian horsemen and cavalrymen; copied for men's winter hat in U.S. and England in 1950's and 1960's.

cowboy h. Large wide-brimmed felt hat with high crown worn creased or standing up in cone shape, the brim rolled up on both sides, dipped in front, sometimes with hat band of leather and silver; worn in U.S. by Western cowboys to shade face and neck. Also called *ten-gallon hat.* See *Stetson, sombrero.*

derby 1. Man's stiff black or brown felt hat with narrow brim curved up at sides and high rounded crown; worn as semiformal hat by business

men, especially in England. 2. American name for English *bowler, q.v. Der.* Named for Earl of Derby and English horse race called the Derby, pronounced *darby* in England.

drum major's h. See *shako.*

envoy h. Man's winter hat, similar to *Cossack* hat, *q.v.,* with leather crown and fur or fabric edge; popular in late 1960's.

Eugénie (u-zhe-nee) Small hat with narrow brim turned up at sides trimmed with ostrich plume, worn tilted forward over eyes, plume trailing in back; name for Eugénie, Empress of France 1853–71.

fedora Man's soft felt hat with creased crown and curved brim. Named for *Fedora,* 1882 play by Sardou.

fez 1. Red felt hat shaped like truncated cone with long black silk tassel hanging from center of crown, worn by Turkish men until 1925; also worn in Syria, Palestine, Albania, etc. 2. Basic shape without tassel copied for women's hats in the West. *Der.* Named for town of Fez in Morocco.

French beret See *caps.*

French sailor h. Large navy-blue or white cotton *tam,* stitched to stiff navy-blue headband and trimmed with red *pompon* at center of *crown, q.q.v.;* originally worn by French seamen.

Gainsborough h. (gains-burro) Wide-brimmed felt hat turned up at one side, trimmed with mass of feather plumes, worn tilted over pompadour and shoulder curls, seen in portraits of women by 18th century English painter Thomas Gainsborough.

Garbo h. See *slouch* hat; a style often worn by movie actress *Greta Garbo, q.v.*

gaucho h. (gow-tcho) Wide-brimmed black felt hat with medium-high flat crown, fastened under chin with leather thong, worn tilted, originally by South American cowboys; adapted for women in late 1960's and worn with *gaucho pants, q.v.*

Gibus See *opera hat.*

gob h. See *sailor hat.*

golf h. See *golf cap* under *caps.*

gondolier's h. Man's medium-sized flat-brimmed, natural-color straw hat with shallow, flat crown, banded with narrow dark ribbon, long ends hanging in back; traditional headgear of Venetian boatmen and adopted by women as classic summer hat, especially in 1950's.

halo h. Hat with upturned brim forming circle around face; popular in 1940's; still worn by children.

hard h. Protective covering for the head made of metal or hard plastic in classic *pith helmet* shape or similar to a baseball *batter's cap, q.q.v.,* and held away from the head by inner straps or a foam lining to absorb impacts; worn by construction workers and others subject to hazards. In late 1960's, the term "hard hat" took on political connotations when U.S. construction workers expressed their sentiments against peace advocates.

high h. See *top hat.*

Homburg Man's hat of soft felt with narrow rolled brim and soft dented crown, worn from 1870's on, for formal daytime occasions; made fashionable by Edward VIII in the early 20th century and by British Prime Minister Anthony Eden in the 1940's. *Der.* From Homburg, Prussia.

leghorn h. Woman's wide, wavy-brimmed hat of natural-colored *leghorn straw, q.v.,* usually low-crowned, often wreathed in roses and with wide blue ribbons over crown and tied in bow under chin. Also called *picture hat* or *shepherdess hat, q.v.*

Mountie's h. Wide-brimmed felt hat with high crown dented into four sections meeting at small peak at top, worn by Canadian mounted police.

open-crown h. Women's hat with no crown; may be of the *halo* or *toque, q.q.v.,* type.

opera h. Man's tall black silk hat with collapsible crown worn, formerly, for full-dress occasions. Invented by Parisian Antoine Gibus in 1823 and also called *Gibus.*

padre h. (pa-dray) Shovel-shape black felt hat with long brim cut off squarely front and back, narrow sides turned up against crown. *Der.* From type of hat worn by Spanish priests in American Southwest.

Panama h. Hat made of fine, pale-colored straw, hand-woven in Ecuador and other Central and South American countries from the leaves of the jipijapa; named for the main distribution point, Panama City.

picture h. Wide-brimmed woman's hat. See *Gainsborough* or *leghorn* hat.

15

14

• **14** "Queen Elizabeth I" of England by an unknown British painter, 16th century. See *pearls, ruff, drop earrings, bombast.*

15 "Louis XIV" of France by Hyacinthe Rigaud,1659– 1743. See *metallic yarn, brocade, lace, fur, trunk hose.*

16 "The Fortune-Teller," Caravaggio, 1562– 1609. See *plume, gloves, ruff, cavalier hat, jerkin.*

16

• **17** (left) English costume of the Elizabethan Age, 1580–1590. See *doublet, fur, bombast.*

18 (above) "The Three Magi," German, 16th century. See *robe,* hat *brim.*

19 (below) During the reign of Charles IX, French. See *standing band, fan, beading.*

pillbox Classic round, brimless woman's hat like a box for pills, worn level or on back of head; introduced in late 1920's and worn since, usually untrimmed.

pith h. or **helmet** See *topee* below.

planter's h. Wide-brimmed white or natural hand-woven straw hat with high dented crown, banded in dark ribbon; worn by Southern gentlemen in the U.S. and popular for women in late 1960's.

polo h. See *chukka* hat.

pork-pie h. Classic snap-brim man's hat, flat on top with crease around edge of crown, made of fabric, straw or felt; worn in 1930's and copied for women in the 1940's.

profile h. Woman's hat with brim turned down sharply on one side, silhouetting the profile; popular in 1940's.

Puritan h. Black, stiff, tall, flat-crowned man's hat with medium wide straight brim, trimmed with wide black band and silver buckle in center front; worn by Puritan men in America in early 17th century.

Ranger's h. Hat worn by U.S. Forest Rangers similar to *Mountie's* hat, *q.v.*

Rex Harrison h. Man's snap-brim hat of wool tweed, with narrow brim, matching tweed band; popularized by actor Rex Harrison in his role as Henry Higgins in the movie version of the musical *My Fair Lady*, by Lerner and Loewe, in 1964.

roller Hat with close-fitting crown and narrow curved brim worn rolled up or with the front turned down; popular for women and girls in 1930's and 40's; revived in early 1970's.

sailor h. 1. *White duck* fabric hat with *gored crown* and parallel-stitched up-turned brim, worn on back of head or tilted forward by U.S. naval enlisted men. Also called *gob hat*. 2. Woman's or small boy's straight-brimmed straw hat with shallow flat crown, worn from 1820's on, popular in 1890's for sportwear and bicycling, sometimes with fictitious name of ship on ribbon band around crown. Also called *canotier*. 3. Flat navy-blue *beret, q.v.*, attached to ribbon band printed with name of battleship; formerly worn by U.S. Navy enlisted men, now replaced by the *gob hat,* above.

scarf h. Woman's soft fabric hat made by tying a scarf over a lining or base and sewing in place.

shako 1. Stiff cylindrical military hat with short front visor, trimmed with feather cockade at center front. 2. High fur hat worn by Russian officers, copied as winter hat for men and women in U.S., England, France, etc. See *Cossack,* above.

shepherdess h. See *leghorn* hat.

silk h. See *top hat.*

skimmer *Sailor* hat or *boater, q.q.v.,* with exaggeratedly shallow crown and wide brim.

slouch h. Soft-crowned felt hat with flexible brim usually worn down in front and at one side, originally worn by men but copied with wider brim for women, sometimes having single long pheasant feather trim. Also called *Garbo slouch* or *vagabond.*

snap-brim h. Hat, especially a man's, with a curled brim that can be turned down in front and up on back and sides.

sombrero Mexican hat with a high, tapered crown, sometimes dented, and wide upturned brim; worn by peons, made of straw, and by wealthier citizens, in felt, lavishly trimmed. See *cowboy hat.*

sou'wester, southwester Rain hat of *oilskin, q.v.,* cloth with dome-shaped sectional crown, parallel-stitched, turned-down brim longer in back to protect neck, usually bright yellow but also black and other colors. *Der.* From traditional deep-sea fisherman's hat with matching oilskin coat and pants.

Stetson Trade name for a man's hat manufacturer, maker of all kinds of hats, but often used generically to mean a wide-brimmed Western style hat, especially the *cowboy* or *ten-gallon* style.

swagger h. Informal sports hat, often felt, with medium-sized brim turned down in front; popular in 1930's and '40's for men and women.

ten-gallon h. See *cowboy hat.*

top h. Man's tall, flat-topped hat made of shiny black silk, with narrow brim rolled up at sides, sometimes collapsible; used only for formal wear. Also called *topper* or *high hat.* See *opera hat, plug hat, chimney-pot hat.*

topee or **topi** Hat, often made from the pith of the sola plant, with domed crown and turn-down brim, worn in tropical countries for protection against the heat of the sun.

Also called *pith hat* or *pith helmet.*

topper Nickname for *top hat, q.q.v.*

toque (toke) Soft, draped fabric hat without brim, fitting close to head, sometimes covered with flowers or made of tulle and worn with evening dress in 19th century; e.g., hat made made famous by Queen Mary, wife of George V of England.

trilby Man's soft felt hat with supple brim, inspired by George du Maurer's 1894 novel *Trilby,* dramatized by Paul Potter in 1895.

turban Adaption in West for women for daytime or evening hats of Eastern man's *turban, q.v.;* popular in 1930's revived in '70's.

Tyrolean h. See *Alpine hat.*

vagabond h. See *slouch hat.*

hatband Decoration, usually of ribbon, around the base of the crown of a hat. Men wear black hatbands for mourning.

hat cap 18th-century term for day cap worn under a hat, mainly by women. Also called *under cap*

hat fawr Distinctive hat, a part of the *eisteddfod* costume, *q.v.,* of Wales, made of polished *beaver* with a wide flat brim and extremely tall, tapered crown; copied for fancy dress as witch's hat.

hat pin See *pins.*

hauberk (ho-berk) Knee-length shirt of *mail,* with sleeves sometimes covering hands, split from waist down in front and back for convenience in riding horseback, worn as armor in 11th, 12th, and 13th centuries, over quilted *gambeson, q.v.* Sometimes called *coat of mail.* See *vambrace.*

haunseleyns (hon-se-len) Variant of *hanseline, q.v.*

hausse-cul See *bum roll.*

haut de chausses (oh de shos) See *trunkhose.*

haute couture (oht koo-toor) Top French designers of custom-made clothes. *Der.* French, highest quality dress-making Also see *Chambre Syndicale de la Parisienne.* Term sometimes applied to top designers in any country.

havelock Cloth covering for military cap, extending to shoulders in back, protecting neck from sun. Named for Sir Henry Havelock, British general in India.

havelock cap Cap and hood of waterproof fabric, worn by women for automobile riding in early 1900's; flat-topped cap with brim rolled down in front and up in back, worn over a tight-fitting hood exposing only the face. See drawing, page 14.

Hawaiian shirt See *shirts.*

headband 1. Strip of leather, cord, fabric, etc., bound around the head—horizontally, crossing the forehead, or from ear to ear—as an ornament or to keep hair in place; worn since ancient times. 2. Band at bottom edge of hat crown.

head cloth Medieval name for *kerchief, q.v.*

headdress A covering or decoration for the head. See *baizo, battant l'oeil, bourrelet, commode, fontanges, English hood, French hood,* etc.

heading 1. Small *hem* through which *elastic* is pulled. 2. Decorative borders woven on fabric shipped to Africa and the East from England, trademarked until 1882. 3. Beginning and ending of piece of fabric as it comes from loom. Also called *head end.*

head rail Kerchief, usually in colors, worn draped, starting on left side, over head and neck, then under chin and around back of neck and tied under chin, sometimes edged with lace and wired, worn by women in 16th and 17th centuries.

heather yarn See *yarns.*

heart breaker See *crève-coeur* and *love lock.*

heavy swell Term used in 1860's for gentleman dressed in ultra-fashionable style. Also called *rank swell.*

Hechter, Daniel See *designers appendix, France.*

hedgehog See *coiffere à l'hérisson.*

heel Part of shoe that lifts the foot under the heel, may be *flat, medium, mid,* or *high* and is measured in eighths of an inch, e.g. $16/8$ heel is 2 inches high; usually *built up* in layers of leather, or made of wood or plastic *covered* with leather or plastic; may be made of clear Lucite or metal, sculptured in oval or cube shapes. Inside edge of heel is called the *breast;* extra piece on bottom to give durability is called *heel lift.*

HEELS:

baby Louis h. See *Louis heel.*

ball h. Spherical heel of wood or Lucite; worn in 1960's.

bell-bottom h. *Chunky medium* heel, curved inward and then flaring at the bottom, an exaggerated version of a *Louis heel* and similar in shape

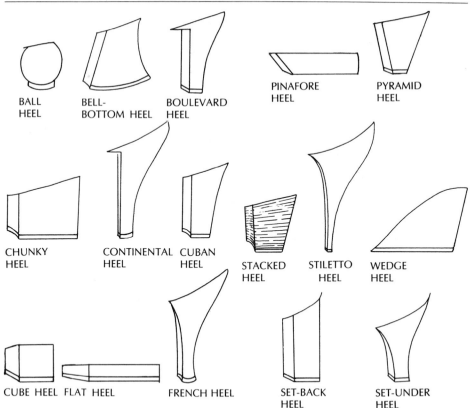

BALL HEEL

BELL-BOTTOM HEEL

BOULEVARD HEEL

PINAFORE HEEL

PYRAMID HEEL

CHUNKY HEEL

CONTINENTAL HEEL

CUBAN HEEL

STACKED HEEL

STILETTO HEEL

WEDGE HEEL

CUBE HEEL FLAT HEEL

FRENCH HEEL

SET-BACK HEEL

SET-UNDER HEEL

to *bell-bottom pants, q.q.v.;* popular in early 1970's.

block h. Straight heel similar to *Cuban heel* but set further back and approximately same width at top and base

boulevard h. Sturdy high heel, similar to *Cuban, q.v.,* with tapered sides and back and straight front, a flange where heel joins sole in front.

built-up h. See *stacked heel,* below.

chunky h. *High* or *medium* heel that is exaggeratedly wide; part of the *chunky shoe* fad of late 1960's and early 1970's.

Continental h. High narrow heel, straight in front with square corners and slightly curved in back, a slight edge extending forward where it joins the sole; exaggeratedly high and narrow version is called a *spike* heel.

covered h. Heel of wood or plastic covered with leather or another plastic, as opposed to a *stacked heel, q.v.,* below.

Cuban h. Medium to high, broad heel with slight curve in back, popular in 1930's and '40's.

cube h. Square-back heel of leather or Lucite.

Dutch-boy h. Low heel with medium-sized base, back slants slightly and inside edge is curved toward front where it joins the sole.

flat h. Low heel, usually less than an inch high.

floating pedestal wedge *Wedge heel* deeply carved out at back, so that heel of foot "floats" above in-curving pedestal.

French h. High heel that curves inward then flares slightly outward at base; popular during 1930's and 40's.

hooded h. Heel slanting into shank of shoe, usually covered in one piece with upper.

Louis h. Heel curved sharply inward around sides and back, then flared slightly at base, similar to heels worn in Louis XV period; low version called *baby Louis heel.*

museum h. Medium-sized heel with front and back curving inward and then outward to make a flared base. Also called *shepherdess heel.*

pinafore h. Flat leather heel made in one piece with the sole of the shoe in the same way that rubber heels and soles are joined on saddle oxfords.

pyramid h. Medium heel with squared base flaring toward the sole, like an inverted pyramid.

set-back h. Heel almost straight from top to bottom, set well back on the sole giving a faint pitch forward to the shoe.

set-under h. Heel, usually curved in at back and sides, set well under the foot, as in *Louis* style, giving a faint pitch backward to the shoe.

shepherdess h. See *museum heel.*

spike h. See *Continental heel.*

spool h. High rounded heel set back further than *Continental, q.v.,* heel.

stacked h. Heel built up of horizontal layers of leather. Also called *built-up* heel.

stiletto h. *Spike heel* ending in tiny round base, centered with rod of metal for strength; popular from 1950's until mid-1960's.

wedge h. Heel made in one piece with sole of shoe in various heights, introduced in 1930's and revived in 1970's.

Heim, Jacques See *designers appendix, France.*

heko-obi Soft sash worn by Japanese man over kimono for informal occasions, wrapped around waist three times and tied in loose bow.

Helanca Trademark owned by Heberlein & Co. for textured man-made yarn with considerable elasticity, used for knit and woven goods and hosiery; licensed on worldwide basis.

helmet 1. Historic protective head covering, deep rounded shape of metal or leather, worn by soldiers since Greek and Roman times, sometimes with moveable visor over face and decorated with embossing and plumes. 2. Contemporary protective head-gear worn by athletes, construction workers, astronauts, etc. See *hard hat, pith helmet,* and *topee* under *hats.* 3. Shape copied in felt for women's hats, especially popularized by Paris couturier André Courrèges in 1961. Also see *Pucci helmet* and *Saint Laurent helmet.*

hem Edge of garment, either at bottom of skirt or edge of sleeve or neckline, etc., finished in various ways, *e.g.,* folded and stitched, bound with tape, faced with bias, edged with ruffles, braid, cut in scallops, cut diagonally, etc. See *rolled hem;* also see *stitches.*

hemmer 1. Commercial machine for sewing hems. 2. Attachment for home sewing machine for hemming.

hemp The tough fiber of a tall Asiatic plant in the nettle family, *Cannabis sativa;* used in cordage, sailcloth.

hemstitch See *stitches, embroideries.*

Henley boater See *boater,* under *hats.*

Henley shirt See *knit shirts* under shirts; also see *necklines.*

hennin Woman's tall conical *head-dress,* worn tilted back with long, sheer veil hanging from tip down to

ground or caught up in drapery at waist; worn in the 15th century.

Henrietta jacket Loose three-quarter-length woman's jacket with large collar falling down over chest in front, frequently lined with quilted satin; worn in 1890's.

Henry II collar 1. Small, medium, or large collar standing up high on the neck in back and rolling over to form points in front, larger collars had a *shawl-collar, q.v.,* effect in front; worn by women in

1890's. 2. Medium-sized *ruff, q.v.,* with a large ribbon bow and ends in front; worn by women in 1890's.

Henry IV collar Standing collar around which are placed loops of ribbon forming a small *ruff, q.v.;* worn by women in 1890's.

hense lynes and **henselyns** (hens-lin) Variants of *hanseline, q.v.*

hercules braid See *braids.*

herlot See *harlot.*

Hermés See *designers appendix,* France.

hérisson See *coiffure à l'hérisson.*

herringbone Pattern made of short, slanting parallel lines adjacent to other rows slanting in reverse direction, creating a continuous V-shape design like the bones of a fish, used in tweeds, embroidery, and in working of fur skins, etc. See *stitches, weaves.*

Hessian See *burlap* under *fabrics.*

Hessian boot Man's black leather riding boot, calf-length in back, curved upward to below knee in front, ending in a point decorated with a tassel, often with narrow top border of another color; worn from 1790's to 1850's.

heuke *Veil* enveloping wearer to knees or ankles, sometimes with the top stiffened by wire and worn over head forming a cage; worn in Flanders in 16th and 17th centuries. Also called *hewke, heyke, hewk.*

heuse (huse) Mid-thigh leather riding boot with thick sole, fastened with buttons, buckles, or straps on outer side of leg, sometimes toe of foot left uncovered, similar to *gaiters, q.v.,* worn by men from 13th century to end of 15th century. Later called *houseau, housel* or *huseau.*

hickory stripes See *fabrics.*

high button shoe Shoe coming to ankle and above, closed to side of center front with a row of small *shoe but-*

tons; worn by both men and women from late 19th century through early 20th century.

high hat See *top hat* under *hats.*

Highland dress Traditional man's costume of Scottish Highlander, consisting of *kilt, plaid* over one shoulder fastened by *brooch,* scarlet

jacket, wide belt with *sporran* attached, feather bonnet or *Glengarry cap, q.q.v.,* plaid-top socks and

buttoned *gaiters* over shoes; costume forbidden by law between 1747–1782.

Highland suit Boy's suit of 1880's and early '90's consisting of jacket, kilts, Glengarry cap, and plaid socks,

copied from Scotch *Highland dress, q.v.* Also called a *Scotch suit.*

high-rise belt See *belts* and *waistlines.*

high-rise girdle See *cuff-top* under *girdles.*

high-rise pants See *pants.*

himalaya See *fabrics*

himation (hi-mah-she-on) Greek mantle, rectangular shawl, about 12 to 15 feet long, made of wool or linen, usually white with border, worn alone or over *chiton, q.v.,* by man and women; usually draped under right arm and over left shoulder, sometimes one end pulled over head. Also see *pallium.*

hip bags Slang term in 1883 for folds of skirt forming *paniers, q.v.,* at hips. Also called *curtain drapery* in U.S. and *pompadour* in England.

hip boot See *boots.*

HIMATION

hip buttons Term used from late 17th to end of 19th centuries for pair of buttons placed on either side of center back pleats in suit coat.

hip-hugger Contemporary term for *low-slung* pants, skirt, or belt, worn below normal waistline, resting on hip bones. Also see *belts, panties, pants, shorts,* and *skirts.*

Hiplets See *pantyhose.*

hippie Term coined in mid 1960's for young person who defied established customs, adapted unconventional mode of dress, e.g., long uncombed hair, aged blue jeans, miscellaneous tops, fringed jackets, strings of beads, symbolic pendants, pouches, bare feet and sandals; started a trend toward *ethnic* fashion and unusual mixtures of dress.

hip-rider bathing suit See *swimsuit.*

hipsters See *hip-huggers* under *pants.*

H-line Straight silhouette of dress marked by a low horizontal belt or seam; called H by Paris designer Christian Dior in 1957.

hobble skirt Woman's skirt rounded over hips, tapered to ankle so narrowly that walking is impeded;

fashion designed by Paris designer Paul Poiret, *q.v.,* about 1912. Later called *peg-top skirt.*

hogger, hoker Variants of *oker, q.v.*

Holbein stitch See *stitches.*

Holbein work See *embroideries.*

hollow-cut velveteen See *fabrics.*

holster pockets See *pockets.*

Homburg See *hats.*

homespun See *fabrics.*

honan *Wild silk* or *pongee, q.q.v.*

honeycomb See *stitches, weaves.*

Honiton gossamer skirt Lightweight summer *petticoat, q.v.,* made with strips of fabric attached to a waist belt, three circular ruffles attached to the bands starting at hip level; worn in 1850's.

Honiton lace See *laces.*

hood 1. Soft covering for the head, usually of fabric, shaped like a bonnet, squared, rounded, or peaked, fastened under chin and and often attached to cape or coat, sometimes of fabric lined with fur or all fur; worn for centuries. 2. Unblocked shape of *felt, q.v.,* before being made into a hat. See *academic hood, English hood, French hood.*

hooded heel See *heels.*

hook and eye See *closings.*

hoop bracelet See *bangle* under *bracelets.*

hoop earrings See *gypsy* under *earrings.*

hoops Framework of horizontal circular metal bands held together with vertical strips of tape or inserted through *headings* in *petticoat, q.q.v.* to hold skirt away from body; popular from 1850 to 1875, in various forms. See *crinoline.* Also see *bell hoop, fan hoop, farthingale, oblong hoop.*

hoop skirt See *skirts.*

Hoover apron See *aprons.*

Hope diamond See *diamonds* under *gems.*

Hope Star See *gems.*

hopsacking See *fabrics.*

hoqueton or **houqueton** Variants of *acton, q.v.*

horned headdress Wide headdress consisting of two horns extending horizontally at either side of face with a veil draped over, hanging down back; worn 1410–1420.

horn rims See *glasses.*

horsehair 1. Hair fiber obtained from a mane and tail of horse. 2. Fabric made from this fiber used in combination with mohair, linen, cotton, etc., in an openwork weave; used for interfacing in suits and coats, for stiffening, and in last half of 19th century for petticoats. See *braids* and *crinoline* under *petticoats.*

horsehide See *leathers.*

horseshoe Term for U-shape used as neckline or yoke on blouses, sweaters, dresses, etc. See *collars* and *necklines.*

hose, hosiery 1. Close-fitting knitted covering for foot and leg, *opaque* or transparent, called *sheer;* made of mercerized cotton, wool, nylon, Agilon for stretch, Cantrece for *texture,* Lycra spandex for *support, metallic* yarns, etc.; knitted in ribs, mesh, crocheted, or in Jacquard patterns; in *proportioned* sizes for various heights or in *one size* that *stretches* to fit all; with or without back *seams* or toe and heel *reinforcements* (no reinforcements called *sandal foot*); in all *colors;* sometimes decorated with embroidered *clocks* at ankles, lace inserts, printed or knitted stripes; held up by *garters* or *elastic tops.* Also called *stockings.* 2. For historical *hose* see *trunk hose, chausses.* Also see *full-fashioned hose, pantyhose, tights, socks,* and *support hose.*

hostess coat or **gown** See *robes.*

hot pants, HotPants See *shorts.*

hotoz Variant of *fotoz, q.v.*

hounds' ears Term used for large turned-back cuffs, with rounded corners, on men's coats; worn from 1660's to 1680's.

hound's-tooth or **houndstooth check**
See *checks.*

houppelande (hoop-land) 1. Man's voluminous outer robe, introduced by Richard II of England, with high *funnel*-shaped neckline, later V-shaped, sleeves long, full, *dagged, q.v.* at edge or *bagpipe-type, q.v.;* length varied from thigh-length to trailing on the ground when worn as ceremonial robe. 2. Woman's dress, worn throughout the 15th century, with fitted *bodice, V-neckline* with *revers* and *dickey* or scooped type, sleeves long and tight-fitting or voluminous with fur lining; frequently *trained* in back and so long in front skirt had to be lifted when walking.

hourglass silhouette Woman's silhouette, *q.v.,* with pulled-in waistline and emphasized hips and bosom; popular from 1890's through early 20th century. Also called *wasp waist.*

houseau (hoos-o) See *heuse.*

housecoat See *robes.*

housedress See *dresses.*

housel See *heuse.*

house slippers See *slippers.*

housse (oos) Man's *cloak* with wide short sleeves forming *cape,* put on over head, fastened with two little tabs at neck; worn during 14th century.

howling bags Slang term for men's *trousers* made of colorful patterned fabrics; worn in mid 19th century.

huarache (wa-*rach*-ee) See *sandals.*

Hubbard blouse Loose-fitting *tunic* blouse with ruffles at hem, sleeves, and neck, a cord *girdle* to pull in fullness at waist; worn by young girls in 1880's over *kilt-pleated, q.v.,* skirt.

huckaback embroidery See *embroideries.*

Hudson seal See *muskrat* under *furs.*

huipili (we-peel-li) Mexican Indian woman's headdress consisting of a white ruffled child's dress worn over head, with hem or neck ruf-

fles framing the face, rest hanging loose over shoulders. *Der.* Copied from dress of child rescued from shipwreck. Also spelled *huepil, hufa,* and *hupa.*

hug-me-tight See *vests*

huke Variant of *huque, q.v.*

Hulanicki, Barbara See *designers appendix, England.*

hula skirt Mid-calf length skirt made of long grasses fastened together at low waistline; worn by native Hawaiian women for hula dances.

Hungarian cord Heavy silk cord used as border on hem of skirt with train, fashionable in 1860's.

Hungarian suit Boy's *tunic-blouse* jacket with small *turned-down collar,* fastened on the side in double-breasted manner, narrow belt at waist, trimmed with *braid* down side front, on flapped pockets, on cuffs, around the hem; worn with matching full or fitted trousers to below the knee and *jockey boots,* in last half of 19th century.

Hungarian point See *embroideries.*

hunt breeches See *pants.*

hunt coat See *pink coat* under *coats.*

hunting calf English term for *reverse calf, q.v.* under *leathers.*

hunting cap See *caps.*

hunting jacket See *sport jackets* under *jackets.*

hunting necktie Man's broad, high necktie with three pleats on each side, angled toward center front, ends brought to front, tied, and hidden by coat; worn in 1820's.

hunting pink Fabric made for *riding coats* distinguished by its color, a crimson red.

hunting plaid See *plaids* and *tartans.*

hunting shirt See *shirts.*

hunting stock Man's long scarf, wrapped twice around neck and tied, worn instead of necktie for sports in 1890's.

hunting vest See *vests.*

hupa See *huipili.*

huque Flowing man's outergarment, generally calf-length, slashed up sides, fur-trimmed around edges, sometimes slashed up front and back for ease in riding horseback; worn throughout 15th century. Also called *huke.*

hurluberlu (her-loo-bare-loo) Woman's hairstyle with short curls encircling front of head, first worn by Madame de Montespan about 1670.

Hush Puppies See *shoes.*

husky sizes *Boys sizes, q.v.,* cut for a wide or plump child.

hussar boots Men's calf-length boots coming to a slight point in front, sometimes having turnover tops and iron soles; style borrowed from military and worn by men from 1800 to 1820.

hussar jacket Woman's short jacket fastened with frogs and trimmed with braid, worn over waistcoat, inspired by uniforms of English troops returning from campaign in Egypt; worn in 1880's.

hyacinth See *gems.*

I

Icelandic sweater See *sweaters.*

ice silk British term for loosely twisted silk yarn used for knitting.

ice wool See *eis wool* under *yarns.*

ichella Long cape fringed around hem, worn by Araucanian Indian women of Chile, fastened with distinctive brooch consisting of a large silver disk attached to a long pin.

I.D. bracelet, identification bracelet See *bracelets.*

igloo mitt Shaggy fur mitten, frequently with leather palm, worn for sportswear.

ihenga (ee-heng-a) Short, full skirt worn by Hindu women in India.

ihram (ee-rahm) Two-piece dress of white cotton consisting of wraparound skirt and shawl over left shoulder, worn by Moslem pilgrims to Mecca. *Der.* Arabic, forbid.

I.L.G.W.U. Abbreviation for *International Ladies' Garment Workers' Union, q.v.*

illusion See *fabrics.*

imbecile sleeve Very full balloon sleeve, set in at a dropped shoulder, gathered to narrow cuff at wrist; worn in the early to mid 1830's. *Der.* Named for sleeve of a strait-jacket used for the insane. Also called *sleeve à la folle.*

imitation gems Reproductions in colored glass or other inexpensive material of fine gem stones, distinguished from *synthetic gems, q.v.,* which, though man-made, are chemically identical to gems occurring in nature.

imitation leather Fabric—such as drill, sateen, or duck—coated with vinyl resin, rubber, pyroxlin, etc., to simulate calf, alligator, snakeskin, lizard, or other leathers.

imperial 1. Man's coat worn in 1840's similar to loose-fitting, fly-front *paletot* overcoat, *q.v.* 2. Small tuft of hair on man's chin, worn in 1st half of 17th century.

Imperial Skirt Patented cage-type *hoop, q.v.,* skirt with as many as 32 hoops hung on fabric strips to provide a flexible, lightweight crinoline; worn in late 1850's.

inauguration cloth See *fabrics.*

inchering 18th-century term for taking measurements of a person to make a garment.

incroyable (an-croy-ah-bl) Term used in France in the Directoire Period (1795–1803) for *dandy, q.v.*

incroyable bow Large bow of lace or *mousseline de soie, q.v.;* worn at neck by women in late 19th century, with revival of *Directoire costumes, q.v.*

incroyable coat Woman's coat of late 19th century, made with long coattails and wide lapels, worn with lace jabot waistcoat for afternoons, adapted from the *swallow-tailed coat, q.v.* under *coats.*

incrustation Set-in piece of embroidery or trimming on women's and children's garments.

Indian beadwork Tiny glass beads in various colors woven to make headbands, necklaces, and for trimmings, sometimes in shape of medallions, by various American Indian tribes; popular as part of the *ethnic, q.v.,* fashions of the 1960's. See *beads* and *belts.*

Indian blanket Originally, hand-woven blankets made by North American Indians in western United States, usually all wool, in tribal motifs; similar designs copied in machine-made fabrics.

Indian dimity See *fabrics.*

Indian dress See *dresses.*

Indian gown See *banyan.*

Indian handbag See *Apache* under *handbags.*

Indian Head See *fabrics.*

Indian headband Narrow band of leather, fabric, or beadwork placed low on the forehead, tied at side or back, sometimes with a feather in back, worn by American Indians; adopted by young people in the late 1960's for *Indian look, q.v.,* below.

Indian lamb See *lamb* under *furs.*

Indian look Late 1960's fashion influence, borrowed by young people from American Indians, for clothing and accessories. For items worn see under *beads, belts, dresses, shoes,* etc. Also see *Apache.*

Indian meditation shirt See *meditation* under *shirts.*

Indian moccasin See *shoes.*

Indian necklace See *necklaces.*

Indian necktie Muslin *cravat, q.v.,* worn by men from 1815 to 1830's, secured in front with a sliding ring. Also called a *maharatta.*

Indian nightgown See *banyan.*

Indian war bonnet Feathered head-dress worn by certain American Indian tribes, made by inserting large feathers into a leather brow band to give halo effect, with one or two tails in back with feathers attached, extending nearly to ground.

indienne See *fabrics.*

indigo 1. Blue dye made since earliest time from stems and leaves of wood plants; a similar dye now made from coal tar. 2. Deep violet-blue color of this dye.

indispensible Small handbag of silk or velvet, frequently square or diamond-shaped, fastened at top with drawstring forming cord handle; carried by women, 1800–1820. See *reticule.*

industrial zipper Large-sized zippers originally used for upholstery and industrial uses, adopted for decorative trim on clothing in mid 1960's.

inexpressibles Late 18th-century and early 19th-century polite term for men's *breeches* or *trousers, q.q.v.* Also called *ineffibles, don't mentions, nether integuments, unmentionables,* and *unwhisperables.*

infanta style Costume as shown in paintings of Velasquez of princesses of Philip IV of Spain, showing extremely wide *vertugale, q.v.,* used as inspiration for evening gowns by *Balenciaga, Givenchy,* and *Castillo—q.q.v.* under *designers appendix*—at various times in 1950's.

inflight coveralls See *space clothes.*

inlay Shoe-industry term for piece of leather, fabric, etc., placed underneath a cut-out layer of leather and stitched into place for decorative effect.

innerwear Variant of *underwear* or *lingerie.*

inseam The seam in a man's *trousers, q.v.,* from the crotch to the hem; leg length is measured by this *seam.*

insertion Trimming made in bands and set between pieces of fabric in garment; popular from 1890 to 1910, when bands of beading, embroidery, braid, or lace were often set in between rows of tucks and ruffles, particularly on white lawn dresses, blouses, petticoats, and drawers.

insole Part of inside of shoe on which sole of foot rests; usually covered by *sock lining, q.v.*

instita Flounce or narrow border on the lower edge of ancient Roman matron's robe, particularly the *stola, q.v.*

Institute Nacional de la Mode en le Vestir Association of Spanish couture designers located in Barcelona, Spain, which sponsors spring and fall showings preceding French showings.

insulated Describing a garment constructed to protect against cold. See *boots, gloves, sport jackets* under *jackets, thermal underwear, hug-me-tight* under *vests.*

intaglio (in-tal-yo) Method of cutting gems by engraving into the surface; compare with *cameo* carving.

intarsia See *knits.*

interfacing Canvas of linen, linen and hair, unbleached muslin, crinoline, Pellon, Armo, etc., inserted between the outside and the facing of a tailored garment to give body and shape.

interlining Loosely woven woolen or cotton fabric used between lining and outer fabric of coat of jacket to give added warmth and to retain shape. Compare *interfacing.*

interlock See *knits.*

International Ladies' Garment Workers' Union A semi-industrial union, founded in 1900, of United States' and Canadian needle-trades workers, an affiliate of the American Federation of Labor-Congress of Industrial Organizations, with 430,000 members. The union is famous for the militancy of its early organizational drives and its fight against sweatshop conditions; for its housing and educational and cultural programs for members; and for its medical services to members, including seven stories of the Union Health Center's twenty-five-story building in New York. David Dubinsky, elected president of the union in 1932, remained in office for thirty-four years and became a major figure in U.S. politics.

intimate apparel Department-store term for *lingerie, underwear.*

Inverness (*in*-ver-ness) 1. Man's loose-fitting overcoat with long removable cape, introduced in mid 19th century, a variation of *cape paletot;* sometimes, cape was divided in back or sleeves were omitted. 2. Man's full cape, usually long, of wool or worsted, close fitting at neck and falling loose from shoulders, often in plaid pattern. 3. See *coats. Der.* From county of Inverness-shire, Scotland.

inverted frame Handbag-industry term for type of frame, fabric or leather covered, that does not show at top of bag.

inverted leg-o'-mutton sleeve Woman's sleeve with tiny darts at shoulder, close-fitting at upper arm and

bouffant on lower arm, with tight-fitting cuff; worn in early 1900's. Compare *leg-of-mutton* under *sleeves*.

inverted pleats See *pleats*.

inverted-T or **-Y embroidery** See *Matilde* under *embroideries*.

invisible zipper See *zippers*.

Irene Castle bob See *hairstyles*.

Irene jacket Short, fitted, collarless woman's jacket cut away in front above waistline and sloping to below waistline in center back, lavishly trimmed with braid around neckline, on sleeves and in back; worn in late 1860's.

iridium (i-*rid*-i-em) Metal frequently alloyed with platinum to make a more durable metal, used in jewelry.

Irish crochet See *laces*.

Irish knit See *knits*.

Irish linen See *fabrics*.

Irish mantle Cloak or blanket of 15th century. See *bratt*.

Irish point lace See *Youghal* under *laces*.

Irish polonaise (poh-loh-nehze) Woman's dress of the late 18th century made with square-cut neckline, bodice buttoned to waist, fitted at back, elbow-length sleeves, a long gathered skirt caught up at waist by buttons or vertical cords into puffed sides, split in front to show shorter underskirt. Also called *Italian nightgown, French* or *Turkish polonaise*.

Irish poplin See *fabrics*.

Irish sweater See *fisherman's* under *sweaters*.

Irish tweed See *fabrics*.

ironed hair See *hairstyles*.

iron ring Finger ring worn by ancient Romans, the gold rings being reserved for badges of civil and military rank.

Isabeau bodice Woman's evening bodice ending at the waistline with a ribbon draped like a *postillion basque, q.v.,* in the back, low square neckline and short *puffed sleeves, q.v.,* trimmed with two ruffles of lace set on ribbon bands; worn in late 1860's. *Der.* Possibly named for Isabeau of Bavaria (1371–1435), consort of Charles VI of France.

Isabeau dress Daytime dress cut *princess style, q.v.,* trimmed down front with row of buttons or rosettes; worn in 1860's.

Isabeau sleeve Triangularly shaped sleeve with one point at the shoulder and widening to a full bottom; worn in the 1860's and used as an oversleeve with *engageantes* and on the *pardessus* and *Maintenon cloak, q.q.v.*

Isabella (The) Hip-length, collarless cape with slashes for arms and extra

capelets added at dropped shoulders to cover arms; worn in mid 1850's. *Der.* Named for Isabella I, queen of Spain (1451–1504), who gave help to Christopher Columbus in his voyage to the New World.

Isabella peasant bodice Close-fitting decorative *corselet, q.v.,* bodice decorated with long strands of beads hanging down from waistline; worn over a dress in early 1890's.

Isabella skirt Underskirt with three small *hoops, q.v.,* extending one-third of the distance from waist to

hem, remainder made with three widely spaced hoops with quilted fabric between; worn in late 1850's.

istle Mexican-grown fiber from leaves of various plants which is strong,

harsh, and stiff, substitute for *abaca* and *sisal.* Also used for hats and bags. Called *ixtle, Tampico fiber* or *Mexican fiber.*

Italian bodice *Corselet, q.v.,* bodice laced up the front with straps over shoulders, flat fitted collar, and embroidery in front; worn over a blouse in early 1870's.

Italian cloak Short hooded cloak worn by men in the 16th and 17th centuries. Also called *Spanish cloak* or *Genoa cloak.*

Italian cloth See *fabrics.*

Italian collar See *collars.*

Italian corsage Woman's low-cut *basque, q.v.,* bodice laced up the front and worn over a blouse;

sleeves of bodice were slashed and blouse was pulled through openings, peplum was made up of decorative tabs; worn in mid 1860's.

Italian farthingale See *wheel farthingale.*

Italian heel Shoe heel worn in last quarter of 18th century, curved inward at back, similar to *Louis heel q.v.,* having a wedge-shaped extension at top under the sole, nearly to ball of foot.

Italian hose See *Venetians.*

Italian nightgown See *Irish polonaise.*

ITMG See *space clothes.*

ivory 1. Hard, opaque substance, creamy white to pale yellow, from the tusks of elephants and other mammals; carved for fans and other ornaments for many centuries, very popular for jewelry in early 1970's. 2. Color of ivory—a creamy white.

Ivy League look Style originally worn by college men at Eastern colleges in the intercollegiate-sports Ivy League, *i.e.,* Brown, Columbia, Cornell, Dartmouth, Harvard, Pennsylvania, Princeton, Yale; suit jacket slim-cut with natural shoulders, narrow lapels, and skinny sleeves, pants also slim cut; popular look in 1940's and 1950's, often in medium-gray flannel. *Der.* The name was originally popular slang alluding to the old and ivy-covered buildings on these campuses; became an athletic reality in 1946, actual league formed 1954. Also see *shirts, pants,* and *suits.*

ixtle Variant of *istle, q.v.*

iznak Heavy gold chain worn as necklace, part of native dress in Palestine, now Israel.

J

jabiru feathers (jab-ih-roo) See *feathers.*

jabot (zha-*bo*) Ruffle of lace, embroidery, or sheer fabric in a *cascade, q.v.,* attached to front of dress or blouse or a made-up *cravat*-like neckpiece; popular in 19th century for men and women and for women in 1930's, '40's. See *blouses* and *collars.*

jack Padded tight-fitting military *doublet, q.v.,* worn from late 13th to late 15th centuries, sometimes made of 30 layers of fabric, worn over the *hauberk, q.v.,* also worn by civilians as a short jacket in rich fabrics.

jack boot 1. Man's heavy leather riding boot with square toes and heels and expanded bucket tops extended over knees; worn by cavalry and civilians from mid 17th to 18th century. 2. Light boots made of soft leather, sometimes laced or buttoned on outside; worn in 18th century.

jack chain Chain made of figure-eight links, joined at right angles, used as an ostentatious decoration by men in 17th century.

jacket Short coat, usually hip-length, opening down the front, worn over shirt or blouse with skirt or pants, by men, women, and children. Historically called a *jerkin, q.v.,* for men in 17th century; from mid 19th century to present worn by men as a suit with matching or contrasting pants and sometimes vest. Nineteenth-century women wore *Zouave jacket, dolman* and *tailor-made, q.q.v.* Following are types of contemporary jackets:

JACKETS:

bellboy or **bellhop j.** Waist-length jacket with standing collar, two rows of brass butons placed down front in V-style; originally worn by messenger boys, pages, and bellboys at hotels, now used mainly for band uniforms and occasionally adapted for women's and children's wear.

blouson (bloo-sohn) Jacket with a bloused effect at a normal or low waistline, either gathered into flat waistband or pulled in by drawstring. *Der.* French, blouse.

bolero Waist-length or above-the-waist jacket, usually collarless and often sleeveless, with rounded front corners and no fastenings; copied from the Spanish bullfighter's embroidered jacket and worn by women since late 19th century. *Der.* From name of Spanish dance.

box j. Any straight, unfitted jacket, waist-length or longer; popular in 1940's and 1950's as women's suit or dress jacket.

cardigan Front-closing jacket with no collar, usually buttoned; see *cardigan sweater.*

Chanel j. *Cardigan* (collarless) jacket with no fasteners, trimmed around neck and down front edges with braid, adapted from jackets designed by Gabrielle Chanel, the French couturiere, in 1930's. See *suits.*

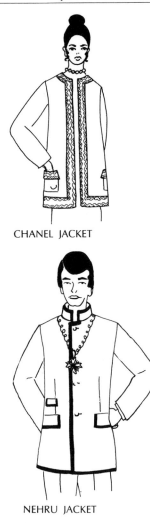

CHANEL JACKET

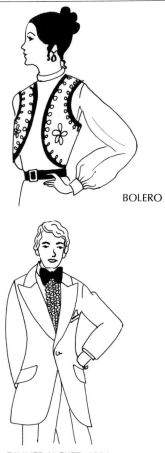

BOLERO

NEHRU JACKET

DINNER JACKET, 1971

Chinese j. 1. Hip-length jacket with standing *Chinese collar, q.v.,* fastened on a slant from center front to under right arm. 2. Quilted jacket fastened down front with *frogs, q.v.;* worn in winter. See *coolie coat.*

chubby Woman's straight-cut waist-to top-of-hip-length fur jacket, collarless, with wide, straight sleeves, made of long-haired fur; popular in late 1940's, revived in early 1970's.

cutaway j. See *cutaway coat.*

dinner j. Man's semi-formal suit coat; may be *tuxedo* style (see below) or Edwardian, *q.v.*

Edwardian j. Fitted jacket, double- or single-breasted, with some flare in back, side vents or center-back vent, frequently with *Napoleon* or *Regency* collar, *q.q.v.,* similar in cut to jackets of *Edwardian period, q.v.;* worn in 1960's.

Eton j. Waist-length to top-of-hip-length straight-cut jacket with collar and wide lapels, worn un-buttoned or with only top button closed; adapted from jackets worn by underclassmen at Eton College in England until 1967, popular for women in early 1890's and a perennial style for small boys. See *Eton suit.*

lounging j. See *smoking jacket.*

mandarin j. Jacket with *standing-band collar, q.v.,* copied from styles of *Chinese Mandarin costume, q.v.* See *Nehru jacket.*

man-tailored j. Woman's jacket tailored like a man's suit jacket in such fabrics as pin-stripes, tweeds, etc., introduced in 1890's and called a *tailor-made.*

mess j. 1. White waist-length fitted jacket with collar and wide revers, no buttons, back cut in three sections, tapered to a point; worn by restaurant bus boys and waiters. 2. A similar jacket worn as military summer semi-formal dinner jacket. *Der.* Middle English, portion of a meal, the Army term for military dining hall.

Nehru j. Man's single-breasted jacket, slightly fitted, with a standing band collar; introduced in late 1960's, adapted from type of coat worn by Indian maharajahs. *Der.* Jawaharlal Nehru, prime minister of India from 1947 to 1964.

rajah j. 1. For men: similar to *Nehru jacket, q.v.* 2. For women: usually tunic-length jacket with *Nehru collar, q.v.,* worn with pants. *Der.* shortened form of *maharajah.*

smoking j. 1. Man's jacket of velvet or other rich cloth, or with velvet or satin *shawl collar, q.v.,* buttonless, wrapped and tied with sash; worn at home for informal entertaining, introduced in 1850.

2. English version of American *tuxedo, q.v.,* short black semi-formal dinner jacket with satin lapels, called by French *"le smoking";* adapted for women by Paris designer *Yves Saint Laurent, q.v.,* in mid 1960's.

sport j. 1. Waist- or hip-length overcoat designed for specific active sports, e.g., flying, skiing, hunting, etc. made in sturdy materials such as poplin, duck, wool, buckskin, etc. 2. Short coat for casual wear copied from sport jackets worn by professional ball-players, cowboys, hunters, fencers, military, etc.; worn by both sexes, sometimes copied in luxury fabrics for women. 3. The term sport coat or jacket is also applied to a man's tailored hip-length coat, usually of wool tweed, worn with a shirt and tie or with a turtleneck shirt but with non-matching trousers (e.g. gray flannel) for daytime wear in place of a business suit. See category of contemporary types of sport jackets or coats at end of *jackets* section.

toreador j. Waist-length woman's jacket with *eqaulet, q.v.* shoulder trimming, frequently braid-trimmed, worn unfastened; based on jackets of bullfighters in Spain and Mexico. See *suit of lights.*

tuxedo j. Man's semi-formal evening jacket made in one-button style with *shawl collar q.v.,* collar usually faced with satin, faille, or other contrasting fabric; made in black or midnight-blue for winter, white for summer, also in other deep colors or plaids since 1950's. Also called *dinner jacket. Der.* Named after Tuxedo Park Country Club near Tuxedo Lake, New York, in late 1890's.

SPORT JACKETS OR COATS:

LUMBER JACKET

MACKINAW

SAFARI JACKET

SHEARLING JACKET

Afghanistan j. Jacket of *lambskin, q.v.,* tanned with hair left on, made with fur side in, giving a shaggy border around edge, sometimes embroidered on smooth side; popular late 1960's as part of trend to *ethnic* clothes.

battle j. Copies of waist-length Army jacket worn in World War II, having two breast pockets, fitted waistband, zippered fly front, and turn-down collar with revers. Also called *Eisenhower jacket.*

benchwarmer j. or **coat** Hooded knee-length jacket, slipped over head and zipped at neck, copied for young people from jackets worn by football players waiting on bench.

blazer Lightweight sport coat, semi-fitted, single-breasted with two or three patch pockets, often with embroidered emblem on left

294

chest, metal buttons; may also have school crest or other symbolic decoration; worn by schoolboys and schoolgirls as part of school uniforms and adopted by both men and women for casual wear. *Der.* From bold-colored, vertically striped jackets worn by British college students.

buckskin j. See *Western jacket.*

bush j. Jacket originally worn in Africa on hunting expeditions, made of khaki cotton with peaked lapels, single-breasted front, belt, and four large bellows pockets; made in all types of fabrics and worn by men, women, and children in mid and late 1960's. *Der.* From clothes worn on hunting trip into the African bush country. Also called *bush coat* or *safari jacket, q.v.*

C.P.O. j. Navy-blue shirt of lightweight wool worn by chief petty officer in U.S. Navy; buttoned front, patch pockets; adapted for civilian wear, sometimes in wool plaids, and worn open as a jacket over shirt or T-shirt by men and school boys and girls.

Cubavera j. Man's white cotton box jacket with four patch pockets, similar to *beer jacket* or *Norfolk jacket, q.q.v.;* worn with summer-weight slacks, introduced by Mal Marshall in Florida in 1946 and popular until 1950; revived in 1970's in double-knit fabrics.

deck j. Short, hooded, water-repellant jacket, sometimes with nylon pile lining, closed with zipper and knit-ribbed at wrists and neck; worn onboard sailboats and other craft.

Eisenhower j. See *battle jacket.*

fencing j. Close-fitting waist-length jacket, usually padded, with high standing collar, fastened diagonally to right side, a red heart embroidered on left chest; worn for sport of fencing and sometimes copied for general wear.

flight j. Waist-length jacket, sometimes made of leather, worn by commercial airline pilots; first worn as part of uniform by U.S. Army Air Corps pilots in World War II, adapted for sportswear in 1960's.

flotation j. Sleeveless jacket, worn by non-swimmers to enable them to float head up; made of water-repellent material with special padding or airlock interlining.

hacking j. Single-breasted, shaped jacket similar to man's suit coat, made with slanting flap pockets and center back vent; used for informal horseback riding and for general casual wear.

hunting j. Bright-red, fitted, single-breasted jacket with collar and lapels; worn by men and women with *riding pants, q.v.,* at formal hunt meets. See *pink coat* under *coats.*

insulated j. Lightweight jacket, usually made of tightly woven high count 70 denier nylon, frequently quilted, with padding of Dacron polyester fiberfill, usually made with zip front and rib-knit at neck and wrists and frequently given soil-resistant and water-repellent finishes.

judo j. Lightweight white cotton kimono-style jacket belted by sash and worn when engaging in sport of *judo* (see *judo clothes*), adapted for at-home wear by men and women. Also called *judo coat* and *karate coat.*

lumber j. Waist-length bloused jacket made of plaid wool, with rib-knitted band at waist and often at sleeves; originally worn by woodsmen in the lumbering trade, copied as winter sports jacket for men and children.

mackinaw Short, double-breasted coat of heavy wool blanket cloth, often in bold horizontal stripes; copied from coats improvised from blankets in 1811, when British officer was stranded with his men in Straits of Mackinac, between Lake Michigan and Lake Huron.

Norfolk j. Belted jacket with two box pleats from shoulders to hem, front and back, matching belt threaded through slots under pleats; worn by men for sport and travel since 1880's and associated with character Dr. Watson of Sir Arthur Conan Doyle's *Sherlock Holmes* stories; popular for young boys (see *Norfolk suit*) and revived in late 1960's for men and women.

parka j. Hip-length jacket with attached hood of windproof, water-repellent fabric, sometimes fur lined; worn by skiers, hunters, sportsmen, etc.; adapted from hooded fur jacket worn by Eskimos. See *parka.*

pea j. Copy of U.S. sailor's hip-length, straight, double-breasted navy-blue wool coat with notched lapels, vertical slash pockets, and vent in back; inspiration for coats designed by Yves Saint Laurent in Paris in 1960's and a classic coat style for men, women, and children. Also called *pea coat* or *pilot coat.*

reefer Semi-fitted navy-blue jacket, usually double-breasted, with collar and revers and brass buttons, often has shoulder tabs and two lower patch pockets.

sack j. or **coat** Unstructured single-breasted man's jacket with natural shoulder and no padding, usually straight-sided.

safari j. Jacket styled with single-breasted front, lapels, and four bellows pockets; designed in Paris by the House of Dior in 1967 and widely copied. See *bush jacket.*

shearling j. Jacket in a variety of casual shapes, made of a sheepskin tanned with wool attached; leather side is sueded, or buffed, and is used for the outside of the coat, with wooly side worn inside, collar has with wool side out. Also called *sheepskin jacket.*

sheepskin j. See *shearling,* above.

ski j. Windproof jacket; waist or hip length, belted or not; worn with *downhill pants, q.v.,* by skiers.

snorkel coat or **j.** Warm hooded *parka, q.v.,* with front-opening zipper extended up over the wearer's chin, giving the hood the look of a snorkel (a submarine's air-intake or exhaust tube); from hip- to knee-length, usually made of water-repellent nylon satin or taffeta, with *quilted* or *pile lining* and *fake-fur, q.v.,* edging around hood. Characterized by an inside *drawstring* waistline, knitted inner cuffs, a multiplicity of zippered and snapped pockets (including one for pencils on the sleeve), and a flap fastened with buttons and loops to keep snow out of the front zipper. Very popular in early 1970's for men, women, and children.

Western j. Waist-length jacket like those worn by American cowboys, in stout cloth or buckskin, with breast pockets, yoke, and sometimes having fringed leather on yoke, sleeves, and hem. Also called *wrangler* or *buckskin jacket.*

Windbreaker Trademark for warm nylon jacket, lightweight, zipped up front with close-fitting elastic waistband and cuffs, or drawstring waist, often with attached hood. Also called *Lindbergh jacket.*

wrangler's j. See *Western jacket,* above.

yachting coat Double-breasted four-button man's jacket with lapels and collar, usually in navy-blue woolen with brass buttons, similar to U.S. Naval uniforms with black braid instead of gold and yacht-club buttons instead of Navy ones; worn onboard boat by yacht-club members.

jacinth See *zircon* under *gems.*

jacket dress See *suit dress* under *dresses.*

jacket zipper See *separating* zipper under *zippers.*

Jack Tar 1. Man's trousers, close-fitting at knees, flaring widely around ankles, worn for yachting in 1880's. 2. Sailor suit with *bell-bottom, q.v.,* trousers, worn by small boys in 1880's and 1890's.

jaconet Sheer cotton. See *fabrics.*

Jacquard loom (jah-kard) A compli-cated loom that weaves an elaborate pattern, using various colored yarns —as in damask, brocade, and tapestry fabrics—by controlling each warp thread separately following a pattern on a punched card. Machine invented by Joseph Marie Jacquard in France, first exhibited in 1801.

Jacquard weave See *weaves* and *knits.*

jade See *gems.*

Jaeger underclothes (ya-ger) Type of wool *union suit, q.v.,* made with hygienic principles in mind, introduced for men and women by a German, Dr. Gustave Jaeger, in 1880's.

jagging, jags See *dagging.*

jaguar See *furs.*

Jamaicas See *shorts.*

jamb Armor for the leg; a *greave, q.v.* Also spelled *jambe.* See *demi jamb.*

jambeau (zham-bow) Leather armor worn to protect leg in 14th century. See *greave.*

James, Charles See *designers appendix, United States.*

jams See *swimsuits.*

Janus cloth See *fabrics.*

Japanese embroidery See *embroideries.*

Japanese kimono See *kimono.*

Japanese mink See *mink* under *furs.*

Japanese parasol Parasol or *umbrella, q.q.v.,* made of brightly colored glazed paper with bamboo ribs.

Japanese sandals See *zori* under *sandals.*

Japanese wrapper Woman's lounging robe made in wrap-around style with long wide sleeves and a square yoke, influenced by Japanese *kimono, q.v.;* worn in early 20th century.

jasey (jay-see) Man's wig of late 18th and 19th centuries, made of worsted jersey yarn, the word becoming a slang term for judge. Also spelled *jazey, jazy, jasy.*

jasmine gloves (jas-min) Same as *jessamy gloves, q.v.*

Jasmine mink See *mink* under *furs.*

jasper 1. See *gems.* 2. Fabric with salt-and-pepper effect made by using white and black yarns in opposite directions.

Java lizard See *lizard* under *leathers.*

Javanese batik See *batik.*

jazerant (jazz-er-ant) Armor consisting of a leather tunic covered with overlapping plates of leather, metal, or horn; worn in 14th century. Also spelled *jazeran, jazerine* and *jesseraunt.*

jazz garter Elaborate wide round-elastic garter covered with colored satin and sometimes trimmed with lace rosettes, worn for decorative effect with very short skirts in the late 1920's.

jean Cotton twill. See *fabrics.*

jeans See *blue jeans* under *pants.*

Jeanette Woman's necklace made of a narrow braid of hair or velvet with small heart or cross suspended from it; worn in mid 1830's.

jellaba Variant of *djellaba, q.v.*

jelly bag See *nightcap.*

jemmy Man's shooting coat styled like a many pocketed short *frock coat, q.v.;* worn in 19th century.

jemmy boot 18th-century term for man's lightweight riding boot, fashionable type of *jockey boot, q.v.*

jemmy frock Man's *frock coat, q.v.,* fashionable in mid 18th century.

Jenny See *designer's appendix, France.*

Jenny Lind cap Crocheted band crossing the crown of the head, down over ears, and around to the back where it fastened, sometimes made of scarlet and white wool; worn as a woman's *morning cap, q.v.,* in late 1840's and early 1850's. *Der.* Copied from style worn by Jenny Lind (1820–87), great coloratura soprano called the "Swedish Nightingale."

Jenny Lind dress *Hoop*-skirted, *q.v.,* dress of mid 19th century with three lace ruffles on skirt and off-the-shoulder neckline, copied from style of dress worn by Jenny Lind, singer known as the "Swedish Nightingale."

jerkin 1. Jacket similar to *doublet, q.v.,* with slightly longer skirt and sometimes with *hanging sleeves, q.v.;* worn 1450–1630. 2. Sleeveless jacket with *wings, q.v.* on shoulders; worn 16th–17th centuries. 3. Synonym for *vest, q.v.*

jersey 1. See *fabrics.* 2. Knit pullover shirt, often in bold horizontal colored stripes, worn by fishermen, sailors, and as sportswear by men since 1860 and later by women. See *knits* and *sweaters.* 3. Short, loose woman's coat made of knitted fabric; worn in early 20th century.

jessamy gloves Perfumed gloves given to bride and groom as wedding presents in 17th century, jasmine being most popular scent. Also called *jasmine gloves.*

jet See *gems.*

jewel 1. Precious stone that has been cut and polished; a *gem, q.v.* 2. Natural or synthetic precious stone used as a bearing in a watch.

jewel neckline See . *necklines.*

jewelry A purely decorative accessory such as bracelet, earring, necklace, pin, ring, etc., made of genuine or simulated stones and precious or plated metals. See *rings, pins, necklaces,* etc. Jewelry of less precious materials is called *costume jewelry.*

jibba (jib-eh) Arabic smock or long shirt-like garment. See *jubbah.*

jiffy dress See *dresses.*

jiffy-knit sweater See *sweaters.*

jigger button 19th-century term for button concealed under lapel on man's double-breasted coat.

jinken Generic Japanese term for rayon yarn of filament type.

jipijapa (he-pe-ha-pa) Palm-like plant of South America from which *panama* hats, *q.v.,* and braid are made. Also see *panama* under *straws.*

Joan cap Woman's small, close-fitting indoor cap, shaped like baby's bonnet, tied under chin; worn in mid 18th century. Also called *Quaker cap.*

Joan-of-Arc bodice Woman's tight bodice of the *cuirasse* type, *q.v.,* reaching to hips and covered with *jet* or steel beads, with tight-fitting sleeves and ruffles at wrists; worn in the mid 1870's.

jobba See *jubbah.*

Jocelyn mantle Knee-length, double-skirted, sleeveless woman's mantle made with three tiered capes trimmed with fringe; worn in early 1850's.

jockey boot 1. See *boots.* 2. Child's high boot often with cuff or collar of contrasting material trimmed with a tassel; worn in 19th century. 3. Man's below-the-knee boot with turned down top of softer and lighter-colored leather, loops on either side of top to aid in pulling on; worn from 1680's to end of 19th century. Also called *top boots, q.v.*

jockey silks Costume of race-horse rider, who wears a colorful shirt and cap to designate stable that owns his horse. Also see under *caps, coats, pants,* and *shirts.*

jockey waistcoat Straight-hanging men's *vest* or waistcoat, with a low standing collar (similar to *Chinese collar, q.v.*) leaving a gap under the chin when buttoned; worn in early 19th century and again in 1880's.

jodhpurs Riding breeches, wide and loose at hip, tight from knee to ankle. See *pants.* Also see *boots.* *Der.* From state of Jodhpur in northwest India.

jogging suit Suit worn for exercising by means of a slow type of running called "jogging," popularized in the mid 1960's; various types of suits are worn: 1. *Stretch knit jumpsuit* made of textured nylon; 2. *Sweatsuit type q.v.* 3. Suit consisting of a terry-cloth *zippered jacket,* cotton crew-necked sweater, and terry pants.

John L. bathing suit See *Gay '90's* under *swimsuits.*

Johnny collar A turned-down collar in various styles. See *collars.*

Johnson, Betsey See *designers appendix, United States.*

Joinville 1. Man's necktie made by

299

tying a narrow scarf, usually with fringed square-cut ends, in a bow; worn from mid 1840's to mid '50's. 2. Pre-tied man's necktie tied in a *sailor knot, q.v.;* narrow band around the neck, ends wide and cut straight across, usually trimmed with fringe; popular in 1890's. Sometimes tied in a four-in-hand manner, also called a *de Joinville teck.*

joobeh Variant of *jubbah, q.v.*

Joseph 1. Woman's green riding coat; worn in the mid 18th century. 2. Woman's outdoor wrap with loose sleeves, similar to Jewish man's long tunic; worn in early 19th century.

Josephine, Empress of France (1763–1814) Born in Martinique, Josephine entered Paris society as the wife of Viscount Alexandre Beauharnis, who was executed during the Revolution; she was a reigning social queen when Napoleon Bonaparte married her in a civil ceremony in 1796. In 1804, they were remarried in Notre Dame cathedral and crowned Emperor and Empress the next day. The styles favored by Josephine were widely copied in Europe and America, and her influence survives in the high-waisted dress known as *Empire.* In 1809

her marriage to the emperor was annulled and she retired to La Malmaison. For fashions, see *Empire styles, Empress Josephine gown.*

Josephine knot Ornamental knot used for trimmings, made by looping two ribbons in sailor's *carrick bend,* leaving the four ends of ribbon free.

journade (zhur-naad) Short circular jacket with large full sleeves or with sleeves long and slit; worn in 14th and 15th centuries for riding. Also spelled *jornade.*

juban Silk or cotton undershirt worn by Japanese. Man's *juban* is short, worn with cotton loincloth and black silk neckband called *eri.* Woman's *juban* is long, worn with *eri* of embroidered silk.

jubbah Ankle-length loose outer garment worn by men or women in the Near East; sometimes has wide sleeves, sometimes sleeveless, may be lined with fur or fastened down front by ties. Name occurs variously as *jubba, jibbah, jibba, jobba, gibbeh, djubba, djubbah, djubbeh, djebba;* and garment is found among Turks, Egyptians, Arabs, Moslems, and Hindus; in Morocco and Algiers the *djebba.* is a shorter, more shirt-like garment.

judo clothes Special clothes worn by participants in Japanese method of self-defense without weapons, now considered a sport: short kimono-cut jacket; white, brown, or black sash that denotes degree of skill; and loose, mid-calf-length trousers. Judo clothes were copied for casual wear for men and women in 1950's and 1960's. See *belts, sports jackets* under *jackets,* etc.

Jugoslavian embroidery See *Yugoslavian* under *embroideries.*

juive tunic (zweeve) Hip-length princess-style *overdress,* made with large armholes, *V-neck* front and back, and with *overskirt* forming a train in back; worn over regular dress as outdoor costume in mid 1870's. *Der.* French, Jewish.

Juliet Heroine of Shakespeare's drama *Romeo and Juliet.* For fashion influences, see *caps, dresses, sleeves,* and *slippers.*

jumbo curl See *curls.*

jump 1. Thigh-length 17th century soldier's coat, buttoned down front, with long sleeves and vent in back; adopted by civilians. Also called *jump-coat, jumpe.* See *coats.* 2. (plural) Unboned bodice worn by women for comfort or during pregnancy in the 18th century.

jumper 1. Women's and children's sleeveless garment, similar to a dress but usually beltless, worn over

a sleeved blouse; sometimes with *suspender straps,* or *bib front, q.q.v.,* or split at sides like sandwich board, or wrapped and tied or buttoned full length, etc. 2. British term for *pull-over sweater.* 3. British term for loose jacket-blouse worn to protect clothing. 4. Sailor's overblouse or *middy, q.v.*

jumper suit *Jumper* dress with matching jacket.

jumpshorts See *shorts.*

jumpsuit Combination *shirt* and *trousers* in one piece, zipped or buttoned up front from crotch to neck, worn during World War II for speedy dressing by parachute troops and other aviators and adopted by civilians during air raids, e.g. British Prime

Minister Winston Churchill's *siren suit;* similar to *coveralls* of mechanics, auto racers, sky divers, scuba divers, astronauts. When worn by

soldiers for work clothes, called *fatigues, q.v.*, under *pants*. Adapted for sports and leisure for men and women in 1960's and 1970's, especially for skiing, after-swim wear, and lounge wear.

jumpsuit pajamas One-piece sleeping garment. See *pajamas*.

jungle boots See boots.

jungle cloth Tightly woven cotton made for military use. See *Byrd cloth* under *fabrics*.

jungle print Print design of tropical foliage.

juni-hitoe Ancient type of *kimono, q.v.*, formerly worn by princesses and wives and daughters of court officials in Japan; later worn by imperial princesses at their weddings.

junior petite sizes Women's garments cut for adult, well-proportioned figure, about 5' to 5'1" tall. Usually numbered 3JP to 13JP.

junior sizes Women's garments cut for a well-proportioned adult figure, about 5'4" to 5'5" tall and shortwaisted. Usually numbered 5 to 15.

jupe (zhoop) 1. French term, from late 17th century on, for woman's skirt, sometimes in three layers: *modeste* on top, *friponne* in middle, and *secrete* underneath. 2. See *gippon*. 3. 16th and 17th century English term for woman's riding coat, covered by protective skirt or *safeguard, q.v.* Also called *gascon coat*. 4. Scottish woman's jacket or bodice. 5. (pl.) Stays or stiffeners.

jupel, jupon 1. See *gippon*. 2. Woman's *underskirt* that contrasted or matched fabric of bodice; worn between 1850 and 1870. Also see *Empire jupon*.

justaucorps (zhust-o-kor) 1. Man's loose-fitting short coat, usually to knee, worn over waistcoat, borrowed from military coat and worn from mid 17th to early 18th centuries in England and France. 2. Woman's riding coat styled like a man's *frock coat, q.v.*, worn from mid 17th through 18th centuries. Also called *chesticare, justacor, juste,* and *justico*.

jute A *bast, q.v.*, fiber obtained from the round-pod jute, *Corchorus capsularis*, or the long-pod jute, *Corchorus olitorius*; grown extensively in Pakistan and India. Used in coarse yarns for *buckrams, Hessians, q.q.v.*, etc.

K

kabaya (kay-bay-yah) Straight white jacket frequently trimmed with lace or embroidery; worn by Javanese women with the *sarong* and *slendang, q.q.v.*

kabuki costume (kah-boo-key) Clothes worn in popular stylized musical dance-theater in Japan, acted entirely by men: elaborate, exaggerated brocaded *kimono, q.v.*, wide jeweled belts, wigs, masklike face make-up. See *dresses* and *robes*.

kaffiyeh-agal (ka-fee-ya ah-gal) Headdress consisting of a large square of striped red and yellow cotton, folded diagonally and placed on head, tasseled corners hanging, held by a circlet of twisted cord called *agal, q.v.;* worn by desert tribesmen in Near East. Also spelled *kaffiyah, kaffieh* and *kuffieh*.

kafsh Low heelless slipper worn in Persia (now Iran).

kaftan Variant of *caftan, q.v.*

kaku-obi Stiff silk sash tied in a double knot worn over the kimono by Japanese men for formal occasions, replaced by the soft *heko-obi* for informal wear in the house.

kalasiris (kah-lah-seer-iss) Robe made of semi-transparent white linen, with belt knotted at waistline, the skirt sometimes pleated; worn by ancient Egyptians and Ionians in ancient Greece; also spelled *calasiris*.

kaleidoscope pattern Design multiplied by mirrors; used for prints.

Kalgan lamb Named for city in Inner Mongolia. See *lamb* under *furs*.

kall Variant of *caul, q.v.*

kalso See *sandals*.

kalyptra (ka-lip-tra) Sheer veil worn over head and face by women in ancient Greece.

kamarchin Gold embroidered silk or velvet *tunic, q.v.*, worn over the shirt by Persian men, length varied with importance of wearer; pockets (called *alkalouk*) on undergarment are reached through lengthwise slits on sides of garment.

kamelaukion (kam-e-law-ki-on) Brimless high flat-topped hat worn by clergy of the Eastern church.

kamik (kah-mick) Knee-high boot of smooth leather, elaborately decorated at top and down center front with beads, feathers, and colored leather in geometrical patterns; worn by Greenland Eskimo women.

kamis (ka-meece) Ankle-length white cotton shirt embroidered around neck and across front with red or white silk; worn by Arabian and Moroccan men.

kampskatcha slipper (kamp-skat-cha) Woman's shoe with pointed upturned toe, high vamp, and low curved heel, frequently made of Spanish leather and fur-lined; worn in late 18th century.

kandys (can-dis) *Caftan, q.v.*, with tight sleeves, worn by Byzantine emperors; Persian in origin.

Kanekalon Japanese trademark for modacrylic fibers used in wigs.

kanga See *fabrics*.

kangaroo See *leathers*.

kangaroo pocket Large puffy pocket. See *pockets*.

kapa 1. Black velvet pillbox hat with red silk crown, sometimes embroidered; part of native dress in Montenegro, worn by men and young girls until they are married. 2. Hand-woven fabric of Hawaiian Islands. Also called *tapa, q.v.*

kappel Skull cap with ear flaps, worn in Poland in 18th century. Also called *keppelche* or *yarmulka, q.v.*

Kaplan, Jacques See *designers appendix, United States*.

kapta Thigh-length, full-cut slip-on *tunic, q.v.*, with fullness pulled in with narrow sash, made of fur for winter; worn by Laplanders.

Karaca sweater See *sweaters*.

karakul cloth See *fabrics*.

karakul lamb See *caracul* under *furs*.

karate costume Clothes worn by participants in unarmed man-to-man combat developed on Okinawa during 17th century as means of self-defense, now a popular sport in Japan and U.S.A. For fashion influences, see *sport suits* and *pajamas*.

karcher Medieval *kerchief, q.v.*

kasa Straw hat, shaped like a deep basket, worn by Japanese men for traveling.

kasabeh Cashmere fabric; see *fabrics*.

kasha See *fabrics*.

Kate Greenaway styles Little girl's clothes influenced by those worn in illustrations by the late 19th-century English illustrator and watercolor painter *Kate Greenaway, q.v.*

Name is also the trademark of a line of girls dresses manufactured in the U.S.

kat-no Korean rain hat made of *oiled silk, q.v.*, or paper, like miniature half-folded parasol, worn to protect high horsehair hat worn over top-knots, and tied under chin.

kaveze (ka-veeze) Tall brimless hat, draped near base with plaid fabric, worn by Jewish people in Turkey from 18th century until end of 19th century. Similar to *tarboosh, q.v.*

Keds Trademark for *sneakers* and other rubber-soled shoes. See *shoes*.

keefieh Variant of *kaffiyeh, q.v.*

kelle Woman's *caul, q.v.* Also spelled *kall*.

Kellerman, Annette (1888–) Swim star of early 1900's who appeared in a one-piece bathing suit, considered very daring, which came to be called by her name and was worn by women in early 1920's; she was arrested in Boston for appearing on beach in her one-piece suit.

kemes, kemise, kemse Synonyms for *chemise, q.v.*, in England during the Middle Ages.

Kenyan tobe Wrap-around dress made of printed fabric with large border design, appears to be two large scarfs joined together; worn by women in Kenya, South Africa.

Kenzo, Takada See *designers appendix, France*.

kepi See *caps*.

keppelche Same as *kappel, q.v.*

kerche Untrimmed, close-fitting wom-

• **20** (above) English dress of the 1690's.
See *gown, metallic yarn, V neckline*.

21 French costume of the 16th century.
See (for man's attire) *armor*; (for woman's
attire) *slashing* and *puffed sleeve*.

22 Japanese teahouse maid, 18th century
woodcut by Kitagawa Utamaro.
See *kimono, obi, headdress*.

24 French uniforms, 1757–1790. See *coat, waistcoat, cravat, breeches.*

25 "George Washington," by Charles Willson Peale, American, 1741–1827.
See *uniform, buttons, epaulets, jabot, stock, vest, breeches.*

• **23** Afternoon dress, *Galerie des Modes,* French, 1778–87.
See *sausage curl, headdress, fichu.*

25

an's *cap* worn in Colonial America. Also called *curch*.

kercher Medieval variant of *kerchief, q.v.*

kerchief 1. See *scarfs*. 2. See *coverchief*. Also spelled *kercher, karcher,* and *kercheve*.

kersche Medieval variant of *kerchief*.

kersey See *fabrics*.

kerseymere Fine woolen fabric. See *fabrics*.

keswa el kbira Ceremonial velvet costume consisting of a wrap-around skirt, corselet and shawl; worn by Jewish women in Morocco in 19th century, and reserved for weddings and special occasions.

kevenhuller hat Man's *tricorn, q.v.,* hat cocked with front brim turned up higher than the back; worn from 1740 to 1760's. Also called *kevenhuller cock*.

keyhole neckline See *necklines*.

key pocket See *pockets*.

khaddar See *fabrics*.

khaki See *fabrics*.

khalak Large veil worn over the *tarboosh, q.v.* to make conical native headdress for Moslem women in Bethlehem, Palestine.

khalat (ka-lat) Long dark-colored wrap, once worn by Moslem women in Turkestan, that completely enveloped the person. Shaped like a coat, but worn like a cape with sleeves tied in back.

khalkhal (kal-kal) Large gold and silver ankle bracelets worn by Persian women.

Khanh, Emmanuelle See *designers appendix, France.*

khurkeh (ker-ka) A long linen dress, bloused over a figured belt, sleeves narrow at shoulder flaring to wrist, elaborately embroidered at top of dress and in bands on sleeves and skirt; worn by Palestinian women.

kick pleat See *pleats*.

kid, kidskin See *furs* and *leathers*.

kid gloves Gloves made of skins of young goats. See *gloves*.

kidney belt See *belts*.

kid seam A glove seam; see *lap seam* under *seams*.

kilt Man's knee-length, pleated, wrap-around skirt with plain front, made of *tartan, q.v.,* distinctive for each Scottish Highland clan. Worn by members of clan and army regiments; widely copied as basic skirt for women and children. See *pleats. Der.* From early 18th-century custom of cutting the ten-yard *plaid* into two parts, one pleated for skirt, the other length thrown over shoulder. See *Highland dress, dresses, pins, pleats, skirts, shoes,* etc.

kimono Loose, straight-cut cotton or silk robe with loose straight sleeves cut on or set in at right angles, made in various lengths and sashed at waist with an *obi, q.v.,* as traditional costume of Japan, either in dark colors for men or in bright colors and floral patterns for women. See *mofuku*. For variety of *obis,* see *kaku-obi* and *heko*-obi. Also see *robes, dresses.*

kimono flannel Same as *flannelette, q.v.,* under *fabrics.*

kimono sleeve See *sleeves.*

kip or **kipskin** Leather-industry term for pelts of young steers, cows, or horses that weigh between 15 and 27 pounds, as distinguished from *skin* or *hide* of older animals.

kirtle 1. Full-length sleeved garment worn by women from 10th through mid 16th centuries as basic garment over the *smock* and under the *gown;* worn by men as a knee-length *tunic, q.q.v.* 2. From mid 16th to mid 17th centuries, the *half-kirtle* became a *petticoat, q.v.* 3. Name for short jacket in 18th and 19th centuries. Synonym for *safeguard, q.v.*

kiss curl See *guiche* under *curls.*

kissing strings Term used for strings to tie the *mobcap, q.v.* under the chin in first half of 18th century. Also called *bridles.*

kiss-me-quick Popular name for tiny bonnet fashionable in late 1860's.

kit fox See *fox* under *furs.*

klaft Variant of *claft, q.v.*

Kleibacker, Charles See *designers appendix, United States.*

Klein, Anne See *designers appendix, United States.*

klompen Wooden shoes, toes turned up, hand-carved, sometimes with surface designs; worn in Netherlands.

knapsack See *handbags.*

knee breeches 1. Type of pants worn by men throughout 17th and 18th centuries, fitting the leg, blousing slightly to below the knee where they buttoned or buckled. Also called *gregues.* 2. Pants worn by boys as part of a suit or separately from end of 19th century until

1930's; buckled at knee, often of corduroy, and a fashion for young women in early 1970's. Also called *knee pants.* See *knickers* under *pants.*

knee-fringe Fringe of ribbons around bottom edge of open-style breeches, worn by men from 1670–75.

knee length See *lengths.*

knee pants See *knickers* under *pants* and *shorts.*

kneepiece 1. Upper part of *boot hose, q.v.* 2. Armor worn to protect the knee.

knee socks See *socks.*

kneestring Drawstring used in 17th and 18th centuries for tightening breeches below knee.

knee warmers Pair of knitted cuffs that slip on over legs to cover knees; worn under hose in winter.

knickerbockers 1. Baggy *knee breeches, q.v.,* worn by men and boys from 1860's on, cut fuller in the leg and longer than the standard pattern; named for a fictional character created by American writer Washington Irving: Dietrick Knickerbocker. 2. See *pants.*

knickers 1. Short form for *knickerbockers.* See *pants.* 2. English term for women's underpants coming to below the knee, made of flannel or longcloth and first worn in 1890. Name is used today in England for any type of women's underpants.

knife pleats See *pleats.*

knightly girdle Decorative belt made of sections of metal joined together and buckled around hips with ornamental buckle in front; worn only by nobility in Middle Ages.

knits or **knitting** Process of making fabric for wearing apparel by interlacing loops of yarn or thread in various stitches and textures. Uses: (1) For hosiery, since Queen Elizabeth I; (2) for garments since Lillie Langtry, actress, popularized *jersey* in late 1870's and Gabrielle Chanel made plain wool jersey fashionable in 1920's; (3) for underwear, since late 19th century; and (4) for sportswear and dresses after introduction of *double-knits* from Italy in 1950's and novelty patterns in manmade fibers since early 1960's. Types of knitting follow. Also see knit stitches illustration under *stitches.*

KNITS OR KNITTING:

Argyll or **argyle k.** Diamond-shaped knitted plaid with narrow overplaid in several colors, originally used for golf socks and sweaters, popular in early 1930's and again in late 1960's. *Der.* Argyll, a county in West Scotland.

circular k. Fabric knitted in tube form on a round knitting machine. *Hose, q.v.,* knitted in this way have no seams.

double k. Fabric knitted by interlocking loops in a double stitch (two needles per stitch) to form a fine-ribbed cloth of firm hand and reversible face.

flat k. Fabric knitted flat with selvages, in contrast to *circular knit,* above.

intarsia Decorative colored motifs knitted into a solid color fabric, giving an inlay effect.

interlock k. Tubular knitted fabric made on circular knitting machine by interknitting stitches, similar to *jersey* but front and back look alike.

Irish k. Hand-knit in traditional patterns usually including cables, bobbles, etc., done with large needles and natural wool yarns (oil not removed); used for Irish fishermen's bulky sweaters and imported to U.S. for general sportswear in 1950's and 1960's. Also, similar knits of manmade yarns imitating the Irish ones.

Jacquard k. Elaborate pattern carried out in several colors, done by special attachment on either flat or circular knitting machine, e.g., *argyle* knitting. See *Jacquard loom.*

jersey See *fabrics.*

mesh See *Milanese knit,* below.

Milanese k. Machine-made warp knit with diagonal yarns at intervals giving run-resistant openwork effect; used particularly for women's panties and micro-mesh hose.

ottoman ribbed k. Double-knit fabric with a pronounced wide crosswise rib, popular in late 1960's.

pile k. Knit with a velvety finish made either by raising a nap on loosely twisted yarn or shearing surface to make a true pile.

plated k. Reversible double-knit fabric knitted with two different colored yarns, one forming background on front and design on back, the other color in reverse, popular in mid and late 1960's with one side used for jacket, the other for skirt or pants.

raschel k. Type of *warp knitting* done with plain or Jacquard patterns in a lacy effect, which may be bonded to another knit for greater stability; popular in 1960's.

rib k. Knitting which has vertical ribs alternating on right and wrong side of fabric, providing elasticity.

run-resistant k. See *Milanese knit.*

single k. Knit fabric made on one set of needles; if *plain-knit* on front, *purled* on back. See *stitches.*

stretch k. Fabric made of *textured yarns* or *elastomeric yarns, q.q.v.,* with recovery ability, used for bras, girdles, foundations and hosiery.

tricot (tree-co) Machine-made *warp-knit* ribbed fabric of two types: *single-bar* or *single warp* and *two-bar* or *double warp,* impervious to runs and used for lingerie. *Der.* French, knit.

tubular k. See *circular knit,* above.

warp k. Machine-made knits in which each needle makes stitches of a different strand and yarns zig-zag from one needle to the next, as in *tricot* and *mesh, q.q.v.*

weft k. Simple hand- or machine-knit fabric with only one strand of yarn makes interlocking loops, each horizontal row joined to succeeding row.

knit shirt Sport shirt of knitted fabric, also called *jersey,* including *slip-ons,* which pull over head, and *cardigans,* which button; became popular in 1940's after public acceptance of convertible-neck fabric sport shirt and increased in popularity in 1950's and 1960's owing to improvements in knitting and spread of informal dress; originally worn for sports such as football and rowing, from 1860's on. See *shirts.*

knitting yarn Thread of cotton, silk, wool, or man-made fibers used for making knitted fabrics or garments either by hand or by machine; yarns include *baby, dress, fingering, Germantown, Shetland floss, sock, worsted, zephyr,* and *textured* or *stretch yarns, q.q.v.* See *yarns.*

knob toe See *toes of shoes.*

knockoff Clothing-industry slang for a design copied from a more expensive garment.

knot 1. Interlacing of threads, cords, ribbons, etc., joining them to fasten a garment or ends of a belt, etc. 2. Ornamental *bow* of ribbon, fabric, lace, etc. Also see *macramé knot, sailor knot.* For historical knots see *Josephine knot, love knots, lover's knot, mourning knot, shoulder knot.* 3. See *chignon* under *hairstyles.*

knot stitch See *French knot* under *stitches.*

knotted lace See *laces.*

knuckle curl Fur-industry term for tight natural curl in *Persian lamb.* See *furs.*

Kodel Trademark owned by Eastman Chemical Products, Inc., for various types of polyester filament, staple, yarn, tow, and fiberfill; used blended with woolens and worsteds to make durable-press fabrics for men's and women's suits and blended with rayon or cotton for dresses, blouses, shirts, sleepwear, sportswear.

kodpeased doublet See *peascod-bellied doublet.*

Koh-i-Noor diamond See *diamond* under *gems.*

kohl (coal) Black substance similar to lamp black, made from powdered antimony sulphide, used in ancient Egypt and the Near East by women for eye shadow and eyeliner; the look of kohl was revived in early 1970's for women's eye make-up, true kohl not sold legally in U.S.

kojah mink See *mutation mink.*

kolah (ko-la) Lambskin or cloth brimless hat, with tall tapered crown, wound with 20-yard strip of vari-colored fine muslin to make a turban; worn by Persian men at the time of Alexander the Great to cover heads shaved with exception of one remaining lock of hair.

kolbe (kol-be) Man's hairstyle, bobbed, with bangs in front and hair the same length at sides and back, usually above the ears; worn in mid 16th century. Also called *kolben-schmitt.*

kolinsky See furs.

kolpos Greek term for blousing of fabric at waistline of the *chiton, q.v.,* a second belt, worn at hips made a *double kolpos.*

kontush German and Nordic name for woman's gown, specifically *gown à la française, q.v.,* of the 18th century. Also spelled *con-touche.*

Korean dress See chi'ma.

koshimaki (kosh-e-ma-ki) Long petti-coat made of patterned crepe or wool worn by Japanese women over the *yumoji,* and under the *kimono, q.q.v.*

köteny (ko-ten-yee) Decorative apron worn by Hungarian women as part of native dress on festive occasions.

kothornos See *cothurnus.*

krepis (kray-pees) Man's sandal, toe-less, with sides and straps crossing in center front; worn in ancient Greece. Also called *crepida.*

krimmer See *lamb* under *furs.*

Krupp diamond See *diamonds* under *gems.*

k'sa Length of material, about six yards long, draped to form a gar-ment, worn by Moorish men in Morocco.

kufiyah (ku-fe-ya) Variant of *kaffiyeh, q.v.*

kulah (koo-lah) Red velvet brimless cap with gold-embroidered crown slightly peaked, fabric wound around the velvet part into a turban, and an *aigrette, q.v.,* sometimes added by royalty; part of native costume in states of Delhi and Pun-jab, India.

kulijah (koo-lee-jah) Overcoat with rolling collar, lapels, and pleats in back, made of camel's hair and lined in silk or fur; worn by Iranian (Per-sian) men.

kurta 1. See *dresses.* 2. Hip-length shirt, fastened on left side, with long sleeves buttoned at the wrist; worn by Moslems and some Hindu men in India. 3. Sleeveless shirt worn by Moslem women of southern India with the *angiya,* a short-sleeved bodice.

L

L Designation for size *large* in various ranges: women's *girdles, housecoats, nightgowns, panties, sweaters;* men's *pajamas, robes, sport jackets, sport shirts, sweaters;* some children's garments.

L-85 Law enacted during World War II by U.S. government, War Production Board, on March 8, 1942, restricting the use of fabric, limiting yardage: under 3 yards for a dress, jackets no longer than 25 inches, limits on sweep of hem, number of extra pockets, linings, etc.

lab coat Short for *laboratory coat, q.v.* Also see *smock.*

label 1. Small piece of cloth stitched to neck or facing of garment identifying manufacturer or fabric used in clothing, *e.g.,* ILGWU label, indicating garment was made under union conditions; custom of labeling started in early 19th century with men's tailored garments. 2. [pl.] 14th century term for two *lappets* of silk or fur that were part of the *hood* worn with *academic costume, q.q.v.*

La Belle Ferronnière (fehr-on-ee-air) Delicate chain worn as *brow band* with single jewel hanging in center of forehead; fashionable in late 15th century and revived in early 19th century. *Der.* Portrait of Beatrice d'Este by Leonardo da Vinci.

laboratory coat or **smock** Coat, usually with turn-down collar and revers, single-breasted, made of

white cotton, worn to protect street clothes while working in chemical or medical laboratory. See also *smock.*

lace Decorative openwork fabric, made by looping, braiding, interlacing, knitting, or twisting threads of cotton, silk, wool, nylon, etc. to form a pattern, with motifs sometimes joined by bars called *brides;* classified according to method as *needle-point* or *point* lace, *pillow* or *bobbin* lace and *tatting, q.q.v.* Lace making developed from embroidery in 15th century, was an important industry for centuries. Cities of Venice, Antwerp, and Brussels developed distinctive techniques and patterns. By early 19th century, John Heathcoat invented *bobbinet* machine and machine-made lace was used for *shawls, parasols, berthas, q.q.v.,* and trimmings. In 20th century, lace is used especially for lingerie trim, collars, cuffs, and wedding veils.

LACES:

Alencon l. (a-lonh-sohn) Fine handmade or machine-made *needle-point* lace with designs on sheer net ground outlined with cordonnet; first made in 1665 and called *point de France, q.v.,* later called *point d'Alençon. Der.* Town of Alençon in France.

all-over l. Term for wide laces with repeat pattern extending entire width of lace, purchased by the yard, cut, and used for clothing.

aloe l. *Tatting* and *bobbin lace* made of aloe—a term used loosely for agave, Ceylon bowstring, hemp and pitcairn—or other bast-like fibers, made in the Philippines and Italy.

Angleterre, point d' See *point d'Angleterre lace.*

antique l. Darned *bobbin* lace made by hand with heavy linen thread on knotted square net with large irregular or square openings. Also called *opus araneum* and *spider work.*

Antwerp l. Rare handmade *bobbin* lace similar to *Alençon* with a vase or basket effect in design. Also called *Antwerp pot lace* or *potten kant;* first made in 17th century. 2. All Belgian laces, including *Mechlin* and *Brussels, q.q.v.,* made before 17th century.

appliquéd l. Type of lace made by attaching previously made *bobbin* or *needle-point* handmade designs to machine-made mesh ground. Also called *point d'appliqué.*

araneum l. (a-ray-nee-um) See *antique* or *opus araneum lace.*

argentan l. (ahr-jen-tan) Flat-patterned French *needle-point* lace of *Alençon* type but with bolder designs, larger mesh background, and no cordonnets; popular for aprons, cravats, sleeve ruffles, and caps in 18th century. Also called *point d'Argentan* or *point de France.*

Armenian l. Handmade or machine-made *knotted* lace made in narrow widths with sawtooth edge.

baby l. Any narrow, fragile, dainty lace used to trim infants' garments, e.g., baby caps, baptismal gowns.

baby Irish l. Narrow fine *hand-crocheted* lace made in Ireland.

Battenberg l. Lace made by applying a coarse linen Battenberg tape to the design and connecting tape with decorative linen stitch made by hand or machine; similar to *Renaissance lace,* but coarser.

Bavarian l. Simple type of *torchon lace, q.v.*

Belgian l. Classification for *pillow* laces with machine-made grounds from Belgium, including *Antwerp, Valenciennes, Brussels,* and *Mechlin* laces. *q.q.v.*

Binche (bansh) Flemish *bobbin* lace similar to *Valenciennes,* with scroll floral patterns and snowflakes sprinkled on net ground; used for cuffs and fichus since 17th century. *Der.* Named for town of Binche, Belgium.

bisette (bee-set) Inexpensive narrow, coarse *bobbin* lace of *torchon* type, made in France since 17th century.

312

blonde Fine French *bobbin* lace with floral pattern on net ground, originally made of unbleached Chinese silk in Bayeux, Caen, and Chantilly; later bleached and dyed black or colors; fashionable at French court from mid 18th century to mid 19th century.

blonde de fil See *mignonette lace.*

bobbinet Mesh base for lace with hexagonal holes, made by hand or machine.

bobbin l. General category of hand-made lace made with small bobbins holding each yarn attached to a small pillow; paper design placed on pillow, pins inserted and yarns interlaced around pins to form pattern. Types include: *Brussels, binche, Cluny, duchesse, q.v.* Also called *pillow lace.*

Bohemian l. *Bobbin* lace characterized with tape-like designs on net ground; originally handmade in Bohemia from old Italian patterns.

bone l. *Bobbin* lace made by fastening threads to pillow by thin fish bones when pins were scarce in Elizabethan times. See *bobbin lace.*

bourdon (boor-dohn) Machine-made net lace, with cord outlining pattern and outer edge.

bretonne, breton 1. Lace made by embroidering on net, rather than weaving design, in imitation of *Alençon lace, q.v.* 2. Net fabric with larger holes than *Brussels net, q.v.*

bridal l. 1. Contemporary industry term for lace used to make a wedding dress, for trimming, or for the veil. 2. 16th and 17th centuries *reticella* type of lace worn by brides of France and Spain, the designs con-

sisting of heraldic devices, relating to owner. Also called *carnival lace.*

Bruges l. (broozh) *Bobbin* lace similar to *duchesse, q.v.,* but coarser. *Der.* Named for city of Bruges, Belgium.

Brussels l. *Needle-point* lace made with cords outlining designs made separately and appliquéd to fine net.

Brussels net Handmade *bobbinet,* made in Belgium, with hexagonal holes, two sides of holes braided, the other four sides twisted. Also called *filet de Bruxelles.*

Buckinghamshire l. Fine *bobbin* lace with simple pattern on a fine clear ground, worked all in one piece. *Der.* Named for Buckinghamshire, England, where it was first manufactured in 16th century. Also called *Buckingham lace.*

bullion Heavy lace made of silver or gold thread in a simple design.

burnt-out l. See *Plauen lace.*

carnival l. Also spelled carnaval. See *bridal lace.*

Carrickmacross l. (kar-ik-ma-cross) Two types of lace: 1. *guipure, q.v.,* type—design cut from fine cambric or lawn and embroidered with fine *needle-point* stitches and connected by *brides.* 2. *Appliqué, q.v.,* type—designs embroidered, then superimposed on machine net. *Der.* Made in or near Carrickmacross, Ireland, since 1820.

Chantilly l. (shahn-tee-yee) Delicate *bobbin* lace with hexagonal mesh ground and design of scrolls and flowers outlined in cardonnet; first used in early 18th century for shawls, for parasols in 19th century, and with scalloped edges for bridal gowns in 20th century. *Der.* From town of Chantilly, France.

chenille l. 18th century French *needle-point* lace with hexagonal mesh and designs outlined in *chenille yarn, q.v.*

Cluny l. 1. Coarse *bobbin* lace, similar to *torchon,* usually made of heavy ivory-colored linen thread in wheel or paddle designs; also machine-made in cotton.

Colbertine l. Coarse, rather inferior *needle-point* lace copied from *Venetian point lace, q.v.;* produced in France in 17th century under royal patronage when Colbert was prime minister. Sometimes spelled *Colberteen, Colbertan.*

couture l. Lace wide enough to be cut up for garments.

Crete l. Silk or linen *bobbin* lace usually made with geometrical designs on colored ground with colored chain stitch along the edge.

crocheted l. See *Irish crochet lace.*

Damascene l. Lace made with sprigs and braids of lace joined together by corded bars in imitation of *Honiton lace, q.v.*

darned l. Term applied to all *filet* type lace made by pulling out groups of warps and fillings from fabric and inserting stitches with a needle; background may also be reworked in buttonhole stitch.

dentelle de la vierge (donh-tell de la vee-airzh) See *Dieppe point.*

Dieppe point l. French *bobbin* lace similar to *Valenciennes* but simpler, made in 17th and 18th centuries; narrow variety called *poussin;* wider called *dentelle de la vierge. Der.*

Named after the town of Dieppe, France.

duchesse l. Type of *bobbin* lace characterized by floral designs and a tape effect made with fine thread and much raised work, giving an all-over effect with irregularly shaped spaces between designs. Frequently handed down from one generation to next for use on bridal dresses. Originally called *guipure de Bruges.*

Egyptian l. Knotted lace frequently made with beads placed between meshes.

fausse Valenciennes Imitation *Valenciennes lace, q.v.*

fiber l. Delicate lace made of banana and aloe fibers.

filet l. Hand-knotted lace with square holes frequently filled in with colored yarns in darning stitch; also imitated by machine. Also called *darned filet lace.*

filet de Bruxelles See *Brussels net.*

flouncing Lace wider than edging lace, used for ruffles or trimmings, with one straight edge, the other scalloped; usually made with one strong thread along straight edge that can be pulled to make gathers.

French l. Machine-made lace fabrics made in imitation of handmade French lace, e.g., 1. *lingerie* laces of the *Alençon, Chantilly, Valenciennes* types; 2. *Couture* laces used for garments, grouped into (a) *re-embroidered* lace, (b) *Chantilly* of the wider type, (c) *guipure* lace, (d) *veiling* and *tulle, q.q.v.*

Greek l. See *reticella lace.*

gros point Venetian *needle-point*

lace made in large designs with high relief work. Also called *gros point de Venise* and *point de Venise, q.v.*

guipure (gee-poor) 1. Heavy tape lace characterized by large showy patterns in *needle-point* or *bobbin* fashion over a coarse mesh ground. 2. Lace with designs, with or without bars, or brides, to hold pattern in place. 3. Early name for gold and silver lace.

guipure de Bruges See *duchesse lace.*

hairpin l. *Insertion*-type lace with a looped edge made by winding the thread around a *hairpin, q.v.,* and looping with a crochet hook.

Hamburg l. Heavy embroidered effect carried out on cambric or muslin fabric.

Honiton l. *Bobbin* lace, similar to *duchesse,* made in England, either motifs made first and appliquéd to machine-made net ground or lace with round heavy motifs made of fine braid joined together like *guipure, q.v. Der.* From town of Honiton, Devonshire, England, where lace was made since time of Queen Elizabeth I.

Irish crochet l. Handmade lace characterized by raised designs of roses, shamrocks, or other patterns set against a coarse diamond-shaped mesh with heavy scalloped edge; crocheted with a hook and a single thread; copied from *needle-point* lace of Spain and Venice and made in Ireland originally; popular for collars and cuffs in early 20th century.

Irish point l. See *Youghal lace.*

knotted l. Lace made by hand-tied knots to form a mesh-like pattern, e.g., *macramé* and *tatting, q.q.v.,* the main types.

lacis (lay-sis) Original term for square-mesh net that is darned or embroidered; a forerunner of lace.

Levers (leevers) Term applied to all laces made on Levers machine invented by John Levers in 1815 and used in factories, particularly in Nottingham, England, and in the United States.

Lille l. Fine *bobbin* lace of simple pattern outlined by heavy cordonnets on net background with hexagonal holes; similar to *Mechlin* lace. First made in 16th century. *Der. From town of Lille, France.*

Lyons l. *Malines* type of lace with pattern outlined in silk or mercerized cotton. Der. From English name for town of Lyon, France.

macramé l. One of the oldest types of handmade knotted lace, made of coarse thread in Italy; originally of Arabic origin, woven in geometrical patterns from selvage down. Revived popularity in early 1970's for belts, bags, etc. *Der.* From Turkish word *makrama* or *mahrama,* napkin or towel.

malines l. 1. Stiff *bobbin* lace with hexagonal mesh ground similar to *Mechlin* lace *q.v.* 2. General term for all Flemish lace before 1665. Also spelled *maline.*

Mechlin l. Fragile *bobbin* lace with ornamental designs outlined with shiny cordonnets and placed on a hexagonal net ground; used in Regency and Louis XV period; greatest vogue about mid 18th century. *Der.* Made in Mechlin, Belgium.

Medici l. (me-*dee*-chee) French *bobbin* lace, combining closed and open work, one edge finished in scallops, similar to but finer than *Cluny lace, q.v.* Also spelled *Médicis* in France. *Der.* Named for royal Italian family in power during 14th to 18th centuries.

mignonette l. (mee-yon-et) Narrow, light, fine, French *bobbin* lace made of linen thread and worked in small patterns on six-sided mesh ground that resembles *tulle, q.v.* Also called *blonde de fil.*

Milan l. Lace of *bobbin* type, originally made with flat, tapelike circular designs connected with *brides,* or bars; popular in 17th century and, earlier, made of gold, silver, and silk thread. Later, elaborate designs such as flowers, animals, and figures were used on a mesh ground and made in shaped pieces for collars. *Der.* Named for Milan, Italy. Also called *Milan point lace.*

needle-point l. Handmade lace made by outlining design with a single linen or cotton thread on parchment paper, holding it with tiny stitches to be cut away later, then working the background entirely with a needle.

Northamptonshire l. *Bobbin* lace with fine mesh ground imitating Flemish laces, similar to *Lille, Valenciennes,* and *Brussels laces, q.q.v.;* made in England in 17th and 18th centuries, and popular in United States in 19th century.

opus araneum See *antique lace.*

Orris l. (or-iss) 18th century lace of gold and silver. *Der.* Named for Arras, France. Also spelled *Orrice.*

passement French term used in 16th century for all types of lace, finally developed into *passementerie, q.v.*

pillow l. Same as *bobbin lace, q.v.;* made in two different ways: (a) motifs or designs made first then connected by *brides;* (b) made in one piece with same thread forming design and background.

Plauen l. Lace made by burned-out method, the design embroidered by *Schiffli q.v.,* machine, in a fiber different from the ground fiber, so when chemically treated, the ground dissolves, leaving lace. *Der.* From Plauen, Germany, where method was invented. Also called *Saint Gall* and *Saxony laces.*

point Shortened form for *needle-point* lace.

point d'Alençon See *Alençon* lace.

point d'Angleterre (pwanh donh-gla-tare) Fine handmade *Brussels bobbin lace* with pattern of floral, bird, or geometrical motifs worked separately and applied to handmade mesh; introduced into England from Belgium and used for collars, fichus, handkerchiefs, aprons, petticoats, fans, and to trim gloves in 17th century.

point d'Argentan See *Argentan lace.*

point de France *Needle-point* lace similar to *Venice* and *Milan* laces of same era, manufacture encouraged by French government under supervision of Colbert, who imported workers from Italy and started factory in 1665 at Alençon.

point de Gaze (pwanh de gahz) Belgian *needle-point* lace with flower designs appliquéd on fine *bobbin* net, later cut away under the designs.

point de Paris (pwanh de pa-ree) 1. Narrow *bobbin* lace with hexagonal mesh and flat design. 2. Machine-made lace similar to *val lace, q.v.,* with design outlined.

point de rose See *rose-point,* below.

point de Venise Type of Venetian *needle-point* lace made with padded, raised cordonnets, edges of designs trimmed with many picots; most sought after lace of 17th century Cavaliers. Also called *gros point de Venise.*

potten kant l. See *Antwerp lace.*

poussin l. (poo-sanh) See *Dieppe point lace.*

princesse l. (pranh-sess) Imitation of *duchesse, q.v.,* lace, done in a fine, delicate manner with machine-made designs joined together or applied to net ground.

punto Term for Italian laces of 16th century or applied to Spanish laces. *Der.* Italian, stitch.

Renaissance l. Heavy flat lace made with tape laid out in pattern and joined together in variety of stitches; first made in 17th century and revived in late 19th century for fancy work and called *Battenberg lace, q.v.*

reticella (ret-i-chella) First *needle-point* lace made by cutting out and pulling out threads and re-embroidering. Developed from cut-work and drawn work and done on linen; very fashionable in 16th century and widely imitated; still made in Italy. Also called *Greek lace, Greek point, Roman lace, Roman point* and *Venetian guipure.*

Roman l. See *reticella lace.*

rose-point l. *Venetian needle-point* similar to *Venetian point* but finer and with smaller motifs of flowers, foliage, and scrolls; more design repeats and connecting brides, or bars; padded with buttonhole edges and a heavy cordonnet. Also called *point de rose.*

Saint Gall l. A Term for Swiss laces and embroideries, specifically *Plauen lace, q.v. Der.* Named for Saint Gall, Switzerland.

Saxony l. See *Plauen lace. Der.* Named for Saxony, Germany.

shadow l. Machine-made lace that has flat surface and shadowy indistinct design.

Shetland l. *Bobbin* lace made of black or white Shetland wool, formerly used for baby covers and shawls.

Spanish l. 1. Lace with a flat design of roses connected with a *net* background, used for mantillas. 2. Coarse *pillow* lace made with gold and silver threads.

Spanish blonde Lace characterized by heavy pattern on fine net ground; made in Catalonia and Barcelona or frequently imported from France to Spain for use in mantillas, scarfs, and flounces.

spider work Coarse open *bobbin* lace, same as *antique lace, q.v.*

tambour See *embroideries.*

tatting *Knotted* lace, usually narrow, made by winding thread on small hand-held shuttle, the fingers making small loops and patterns; used for edging lingerie and handkerchiefs, etc.

torchon l. Coarse inexpensive *bobbin* lace made of cotton or linen in simple fan-like designs, produced in Europe and China. Also called *beggar's lace.*

val l. Short for *Valenciennes, q.v.;* this name usually applied to machine-made copies.

Valenciennes (va-lhan-see-en) Handmade French flat linen *bobbin* lace first made in time of Louis XIV; distinguished by small floral and bow designs made in one with the ground of square, diamond-shaped, or round mesh. *Der.* Named for Valenciennes, France.

Venetian l. Many types of laces from Venice including *cut work, drawn work, reticella, raised point, flat point,* etc.

Venetian point Heavy *needle-point* lace with floral sprays or foliage, or geometrical designs, made in high relief by buttonhole stitches with motifs connected with brides or bars and decorated with picots; originally made in Venice. Also called *Venetian raised point.*

Youghal l. Irish flat *needle-point* lace inspired by Italian laces, particularly *Venetian* types. *Der.* First made in Youghal, County Cork, Ireland. Also called *Irish point lace.*

laced closing Method of closing a garment by pulling a lacer, thong, ribbon, or chain through *eyelets, q.v.,* on either edge. Also see *foundation garments* and *closings.*

lacer or **lace** 1. Rounded or flattened string or thong, often with rein-

forced tips of metal or plastic, usually threaded through *eyelets* as a fastener. 2. Short form for *shoelace,* shoe fastener pulled through *eyelets, q.q.v.,* and tied; made of cotton, rayon, nylon, elastic, and leather. Also see *shoestring.*

lacerna Semi-circular cape fastened on right shoulder by a *fibula, q.v.,* worn by all ancient Romans during last century of the Republic; made in white, natural colors, or amythest and purple and decorated with gold.

lacet Term for a braid woven in various widths, frequently with looped edges, used for trimming and edging and sometimes combined with crochet work or tatting.

Lachasse See *designers appendix, England.*

lachet See *harlot.*

lacing studs See *button hooks.*

lacis See *laces.*

Lacoste See *knit shirts* under *shirts.*

lacquer (lak-er) 1. Orange-red color of lacquer used by Chinese. 2. Fingernail polish.

ladder braid See *braids.*

Lagerfeld, Karl See *designers appendix, France.*

La Goulue See *concierge* under *hairstyles.*

laid embroidery See *embroideries.*

laid fabric Non-woven material. See *fabrics.*

laid stitch See *stitches.*

laisse-tout-faire 1. See *tablier.* 2. 17th-century French term for a decorative apron without bib, made of silver or gold lace.

lamballe bonnet (lam-bahl) Saucer-shaped bonnet worn flat on head with sides pulled down slightly, tied under chin with large ribbon bow; some had lace *lappets,* others had small *veils* in back called *curtains, q.q.v.;* worn in mid 1860's.

lambskin See *leathers* and *furs.*

lame Armor composed of thin overlapping plates used for a piece such as a *gauntlet, q.v.*

lamé Textile made with metallic yarns woven to form either background or pattern, may be in Jacquard or rib weave. Popular evening dress and coat fabric in the 1930's and again in late 1960's. *Der.* French, spangled.

laminated 1. Made by a process permanently securing polyester foam to back of a fabric. 2. Layers of fabric bonded together with resins under heat and compression.

lampshade beads See *beads.*

Lancetti, Pino See *designers appendix, Italy.*

landrine Louis XIII boot with wide flared cuff reaching halfway up leg, top turned up for riding horseback. Also called *lazarine.*

langet 1. Term used for a *thong* or *lacer* used to fasten garments together in 15th century. Also see *points.* 2. Plume worn on a knight's helmet. 3. (plural) *langettes,* term for string of beads in 15th century.

Langtry Bustle Woman's patented, lightweight collapsible bustle, *q.v.,* made of a series of semicircular hoops fastened to a stay on either side; worn in late 1880's.

Langtry hood Detachable hood on woman's outdoor garment similar to an *academic hood, q.v.,* with a colored lining; worn in 1880's and named after actress Lillie Langtry.

Langtry, Lillie (1852–1929) Famous English actress and beauty born on the Isle of Jersey. Also called the Jersey Lily. Popularized the *jersey costume,* gave her name to many items of costume.

languti Loincloth worn in India.

languette (lang-get) Flat, tongue-shaped piece of cloth appliquéd as trimming on woman's cloak or skirt, either singly or in series; used in early 19th century. *Der.* French *langue,* tongue.

lantern sleeve See *sleeves.*

Lanvin, Jeanne See *designers appendix, France.*

lanyard Cord, usually braided in contrasting colors, used to suspend around neck or from belt an accessory such as a whistle or pocket knife.

lapel Turned-back front section of jacket, coat or shirt where it joins the collar, folding back to form a *revers, q.v.,* and cut in different shapes such as: *cloverleaf, semi-cloverleaf, fishmouth, L-shaped, notched, peaked,* and *semi-peaked.* See *collars.*

lapidary Person who specializes in cutting of gems other than diamonds. Same as a *gem cutter.*

lapin French term for *rabbit;* see *furs.*

lapis lazuli See *gems.*

la pliant (la plee-awnt) Invention of 1896 for holding out back of skirt by inserting steel strips, eliminating use of many petticoats. *Der.* French, folding.

lappets 1. Streamerlike side pieces

hanging down from the *miter, q.v.* Also see *fanon.* 2. 18th- and 19th-century term for drapery or long ribbon-like strips of fabric hanging at sides or back of an indoor head-dress, often lace trimmed.

lap seam See *seams.*

large Size used along with *small, medium* and *extra large* for these categories: women's sweaters, house-coats, nightgowns, some panties, girdles and panty girdles; men's sport shirts, sport jackets, sweaters and robes; children's gloves; girl's sweaters and pajamas; boy's paja-mas; knit shirts, robes and sport jackets.

Laroche, Guy See *designers appendix,* France.

last Carved wooden or molded plastic form on which a shoe is made, a right and left form for each pair in each size. *Combination last* has heel of narrower width than toe.

Lastex See *yarns.*

lasting 1. Shoe manufacturing process of attaching the shoe upper to the insole in three operations: side lasting, toe lasting, and heel lasting. 2. Durable fabric used mainly for shoe and bag linings, made of tightly twisted cotton or worsted yarns in twill weave.

lasting boots Term for late 19th century boots made with black cashmere uppers.

latch buckle Round, square, or oblong metal plates attached to each end of belt and closed over one another, a swivel from lower plate slips through a slot in upper plate and turns to fasten belt.

latchet Term used in Middle Ages for strap used to fasten a shoe.

lattice braid See *ladder* under *braids.*

lattice work Fabric or trimming made by stitching narrow bands of fabric in diamond-shaped or square design.

lavalière See *necklaces.*

lavender 1. Perfume of lavender, a fragrant European mint with a pale-purple flower. 2. A pale-purple color.

lawn Sheer lightweight cotton. See *fabrics.*

lawn-party dress Afternoon dress suitable for an outdoor reception; in 1890's, frequently with *choker* collar, *gored* full-length skirt, with *sash* at waist, *q.q.v.;* worn with floppy straw hat trimmed with flowers, ribbon, and veiling.

lawn-tennis apron Drab-colored bib apron with skirt pulled up on left side and draped at the hip, where there was a large patch pocket for holding tennis balls, another pocket placed low on the right side of front, bib and pockets decorated with embroidery; worn for tennis by women in 1880's.

lawn-tennis costume Woman's fitted jacket and long dress (some, a few inches above ankles) with bustle, sometimes embroidered with racquets and balls; worn as a suit by women for playing tennis in the 1880's. See *tennis dress* and *tennis shorts* for modern costumes.

layered 1. Adjective used in mid and late 1960's for garments of varying lengths, and with sleeves of varying lengths, worn one on top the other. 2. See *hairstyles.*

layette Garments and accessories collected by prospective mother for

LAWN-TENNIS COSTUME

use of a new baby; includes such items as *diapers, sacques, undershirts,* etc.; formerly included *pinning blankets,* and *gertrudes, q.v.*

lazy-daisy stitch See *stitches.*

lea 1. Measure for linen yarn which has been wet spun, based on 300 yards weighing one pound, *e.g.,* twelve *leas* make a *hank* and 16½ hanks or 200 leas make a *bundle.* 2. Also represents a unit of length for other fibers, *e.g.,* for *cotton* or *silk,* 120 yards equals a *lea;* for *worsted,* 80 yards equals a *lea.*

leading strings Term used in the 17th and 18th centuries for long narrow ribbons or strips of fabric attached to shoulders on children's dresses, used to guide the child when learning to walk, developed from *hanging sleeves* or *tippets, q.q.v.*

leaf English term for turned-down part of a *stand-fall* or *rolled collar, q.q.v.*

leather Skin or hide of an animal with hair removed, grain revealed by process of *tanning, q.v.;* usually dyed and finished by *glazing, buffing, embossing, sueding,* etc, *q.q.v.;* sometimes *split* into several layers. Leather has been used for shoes and clothing from primitive times, *e.g., buckskins, q.v.,* in Colonial America; now used extensively for all types of clothing including *coats, jackets, skirts, vests, pants, suits,* and trimming on fabric garments and sweaters.

LEATHERS:

alligator Leather from alligators, reptiles of an endangered species, with characteristic markings of blocks, rectangles, and circles with cross markings between: used for shoes, handbags, and belts. Law passed by Congress in 1970 prohibits use in United States.

alligator lizard Leather from a large lizard with markings like grains of rice and elongated blocks, similar to hides of small alligators. See *Lizigator.*

antelope Soft velvety leather made from antelope skins, usually sueded; used for fine shoes, bags, and jackets.

box calf Calf that has been *boarded, q.v.,* in two directions to give it squared markings on the grain side.

buckskin Deer or elk skins with the grain given a *sueded* finish, *q.v.,* similar to early skins cured by American Indians; second *splits* of deerskin must be called *split deerskin* or *split buckskin.*

Bucko calf Trade name for cattle

321

hides processed to look like *buck-skin* and used for shoe uppers.

cabretta Fine, smooth, tight-grained leather made from Brazilian sheep-skins; used mainly for women's dressy gloves.

calf or **calfskin** Supple, fine-grained, strong leather from skins of cattle a few days to a few weeks old; finished many ways—*glazed, sueded, boarded, embossed,* waxed, and made into *patent leather, q.q.v.;* used for shoes, handbags, belts, and wallets. Best qualities come from the U.S.

capeskin Light, flexible, fine-grained leather made from skin of the South African hair sheep and frequently shipped from Capetown, South Africa, hence the name.

carpincho Leather tanned from a water rodent. Often sold as pigskin and used mainly for sport gloves.

cattlehide Heavy leather, usually vegetable-tanned, from cow, bull, and steer hides. Used for *sole leather, q.v.,* below.

chamois skin Originally leather made from an Alpine goat or cham-ois; now undersplits of sheepskins which are oil dressed and *suede finished, q.v.,* are correctly called by this name.

cordovan Durable, almost com-pletely non-porous leather, made from sheepskin or horsehides and used for uppers of fine men's shoes; has characteristic waxy finish in black and reddish-brown colors. *Der.* Named for Córdoba, Spain, where tanning of leather was highly perfected under the Arabs.

cowhide See *cattlehide.*

crocodile Thick-skinned leather from a large water reptile, character-ized by black markings and scaly horny surface; hard to distinguish from alligator.

deerskin See *buckskin.*

doeskin Trade term for *sheepskin* and *lambskin* tanned by the alum or formaldehyde processes; when fin-ished white, often used for gloves; also tanned by *chamois* process, *q.v.,* and used for jackets, vests, etc.

French antelope lambskin Lamb-skins, tanned in France, that have been given a lustrous, sueded finish to make them look like *antelope* skin.

French kid Originally, *kidskin* im-ported from France, now means any alum- or vegetable-tanned kidskin resembling the original.

frog Leather with a distinctive grain and pattern made from the skin of a species of giant frog found in Brazil; limited in availability and used for women's accessories and trim. May be simulated by embossing other leathers and called *frog-grained leather.*

galuchat Leather made from tough outer layer of *sharkskin, q.v.,* used for handbags and novelty items.

glazed kidskin See *glacé.*

goatskin Leather made from the skin of the goat; used for gloves, shoe uppers, handbags, etc.

horsehide A durable, fine-grained leather from horses and colts, used flesh side up with grain used for inside surface of shoe uppers. Usu-ally imported. See also *cordovan leather.*

Java lizard Lizard skins with black, white and gray coloring; used for handbags, shoes and belts; imported from Java in Indonesia.

kangaroo Durable scuff-resistant leather made from kangaroo and wallaby hides, similar to *kidskin* in appearance; imported mainly from Australia.

kid or **kidskin** Leather made from young goat skins, used for women's shoe uppers, handbags, belts, and fine gloves.

lambskin Leather made from skin of a young sheep.

lizard Reptile leather with pattern like grains of rice; used for shoe uppers, handbags, and ornamental trim; often named for places of origin in India and Java.

Lizigator Tradename for imitation *alligator-lizard leather,* the pattern is embossed on *calfskin.*

mocha Fine *sueded, q.v.,* glove leather made from skins of blackhead or whitehead sheep from Somaliland and from Sudan and skins of Egyptian sheep. Used for women's fine gloves and shoes.

Moroccan leather Fancy *goatskins* with a pebbly grain, often dyed red; used for handbags, slippers, etc.; originally tanned in Morocco.

napa Glove leather from sheepskins or lambskins of domestic, New Zealand, or South American origin that have been tanned by chrome, alum, or combination methods.

ostrich Leather with a distinctive rosette pattern caused by removal of plumes from ostrich skin, used for fine shoes and handbags.

patent leather Leather processed on the grain side to form a bright hard surface, by degreasing, stretching on frames, and coating with paints and linseed oil, then alternately baking in the sun and rubbing with pumice stone. Plastic is used to make imitation patent leather.

peccary Leather processed from the skin of the wild boar of central and South America, used mainly for pigskin gloves.

pigskin Leather made from the skin of the pig with groups of three tiny holes caused by removing the bristles forming a distinctive pattern; genuine pigskins are rare, most *pigskin gloves* are made from *peccary* and *carpincho, q.q.v.*

pin seal High-grade skins from hair seal, with fine pebbly grain, imitated widely by embossing patterns on *calfskin, cowhide, goatskin,* and *sheepskin,* and then called *pin-grain calfskin,* etc.

python Leather processed from skin of a large non-poisonous snake with medium-sized scales and distinctive markings; comes in black and white, tan and white, and is sometimes dyed bright red, yellow, blue, other colors and used for handbags, shoes, and trimmings.

rawhide Leather in natural pale beige or yellowish color made from cattlehides not actually tanned but dehaired, limed, stuffed with oil and grease; used mainly for thongs.

reverse calf *Calfskin, q.v.,* finished with flesh side outside, grain side inside. Called *hunting calf* in England.

Russian calf Leather, tanned with

birch bark with distinctive odor, usually finished in brown and originally from Russia; the name now used for any similar brown calfskin.

saddle leather Natural tan leather, made from vegetable-tanned steerhides or cattlehides and used for tooled-leather handbags, belts, and saddles for horses. *California saddle leather* is made with native oak bark in the tanning process.

sealskin Leather made from genuine Alaska fur sealhides; rare, because the Alaska fur seal is protected by the U.S. government. Also see *pin seal.*

sharkskin Almost scuff-proof leather made from the skin of certain species of sharks; the outer armor, or shagreen, is removed before the skins are tanned; used for shoes, belts, handbags, wallets, and cigarette cases.

shearling Short-wooled skins of sheep or lambs, sheared before slaughter and tanned with the wool on; used for slippers; gloves, coats, jackets, etc. with the *sueded* flesh side out. Called *electrified shearling* when wool has been straightened by use of an electric comb.

sheepskin Leathers from sheephides, characterized by more than average sponginess and stretchability, small skins with fine grain called *lambskins;* frequently *sueded, q.v.,* and used for shoes, handbags, suede coats and jackets. Sheepskin tanned with wool left on is often used leather side out for *coats* and *sports jackets, q.v.*

snakeskin Diamond-patterned leather with overlapping scales, pro-

cessed from skin of a number of species of snakes, e.g., *diamond-backed* rattlesnake, *python, cobra, boas,* etc., from Java, Siam, Borneo, and India.

sole leather Heavy, stiff leather, usually *cattlehide, q.v.,* used for the soles and *built-up heels, q.v.,* of shoes.

steerhide Heavy leather from skins of castrated male cattle, usually used as *sole leather* for shoes or to make *saddle leather, q.q.v.*

suede Leather, usually *lambskin, doeskin,* or splits of *cowhide* (sometimes called *reverse calf, q.v.*) that has been buffed on the flesh side to raise a slight nap; sometimes done on grain side or on both sides of a split to cover small defects; used for gloves, jackets, vests, trimmings, etc.

vici kid Term used for all *glazed kid* (see *glacé*), formerly a trade name for a chrome tanning process developed by Augustus Schultz in 1880.

wallaby Leather made from the skins of small species of kangaroo family. Similar to *kangaroo leather* but sometimes finer grained.

leatherette Term formerly used for fabrics made in imitation of leather, correctly called *leatherette fabric.*

leathering Fur-industry term for using narrow strips of leather between strips of fur in order to make the fur less bulky and give it more graceful hang.

leather-palm gloves See *driving gloves* under *gloves.*

Leda cloth A wool *velvet,* see *fabrics.*

Lederhosen See *shorts.*

Leek button Metal edge surrounding a metal shell or mold of pasteboard, with a shank on the back; made at Leek, England, patented in 1842.

left-hand twill weave See *twill* under *weaves.*

left twist See *S-twist.*

legging 1. Covering for legs and ankle secured by stirrup strap under

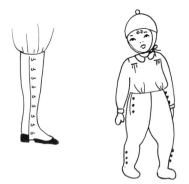

arch, may extend to knee or to waist; worn in 19th century in armed services and by civilian men, popular for children starting about 1920, and worn by women in suede, patent, and fabric in late 1960's. See *puttee.* 2. (pl.) Outer *pants* for children made with tight-fitting legs and usually matched to a coat making a *leggings set;* worn in cold weather.

leghorn 1. See *straws.* 2. Woman's hat of *leghorn straw.* See *hats.*

Legionnaire cap See *caps.*

leg-of-mutton or **leg-o'mutton sleeve** See *sleeves.*

Legroux, Germaine See *designers appendix, France.*

lei See *necklaces.*

Leicester Englishman's suit or lounge

jacket with *raglan sleeves, q.v.,* worn in mid 19th century.

leisure bra See *brassieres.*

Lelong, Lucien See *designers appendix, France.*

Lemmonier, Jeanne See *designers appendix, France.*

length Hem of coat, jacket, dress, or skirt in relation to total garment or total figure. The woman's skirt length was generally long for centuries, until the 1920's, has fluctuated ever since with the shortest appearing in late 1960's and early '70's.

LENGTHS:

ballerina l. Reaching to center of the calf of the leg or a little below, worn particularly by ballet dancers; popular for evening dresses in the late 1940's and 1950's.

boot l. See *midi,* below.

calf l. Hem of skirt, dress, or coat reaching below the knee, ending at the widest part of the calf or an inch beyond; compare with *midi* length, which is longer.

chapel-length train Skirt made with back cut longer, ending in short train of about one yard; popular for informal wedding dresses.

full l. Term indicating floor length. Most dresses were this length until early part of the 20th century.

knee l. Skirt or coat reaching to the middle of the knee cap or just to the top of the knee.

longuette Term coined in January, 1970, by clothing-industry trade paper *Woman's Wear Daily* to indicate skirts reaching from below knee to *maxi* length. *Der.* French-style diminuative for long.

MICRO LENGTH   MINI   KNEE   MIDI   MAXI
                LENGTH   LENGTH   LENGTH   LENGTH

matinee l. See *necklaces.*

maxi l. Hem of dress, skirt, or coat reaching the ankles or below and worn for daytime street wear in late 1960's.

micro l. To upper thigh, an exaggerated *mini, q.v.,* worn by ultra-Mod young girls in the late 1960's.

midi l. To the mid-calf of leg, so named in France when re-introduced in the late 1960's and popular in the fall of 1971, returning in 1974. Also called *longuette, q.v. Der.* French, midday, and name of region in Southern France.

mini l. Thigh-length dresses, skirts and coats, introduced in England in the early 1960's as part of Mod fashions, credit often going to Mary Quant, the English designer. In the late 1960's became an accepted fashion in the U.S.

nine-tenths l. Woman's coat one-tenth shorter than the dress or suit worn underneath.

opera l. See *necklaces.*

seven-eighths l. Woman's coat one-eighth shorter than the dress or suit it covers; popular for sport coats in the 1940's and 1950's.

three-quarter l. Woman's coat or jacket approximately three-quarters of the length of garment worn underneath; popular for jackets in the 1940's and 1950's.

waltz l. See *nightgowns.*

leno See *fabrics.*

leno weave See *weaves.*

leopard See *furs.*

leopard print Fabric, fur fabric, or rabbit-skin printed to resemble leopardskin.

leotard Form-fitting one-piece knitted garment, high or low neck, long or short sleeves, ending in brief panties; worn alone or over ankle-length *tights, q.v.,* as practice garment by dancers, acrobats, etc. *Der.* Named for Jules Leotard, 19th-century French aerial gymnast. See drawing opposite.

Leser, Tina See *designers appendix, United States.*

let-out See *letting-out,* below.

letter sweater See *sweaters.*

lettice Term used for *ermine* or

326

LEOTARD

miniver (white ermine or other white or gray fur) in 16th and 17th centuries. See *furs.*

lettice cap or **bonnet** 1. 16th-century term for woman's outdoor cap or bonnet of triangular shape that covered the ears, made of lettice, a fur resembling ermine. 2. In 16th and 17th centuries, man's night cap of lettice fur, supposed to induce sleep. Also called *ermine cap, miniver cap.*

lettice ruff Old spelling for lettuce, a ruff with flattened convolutions that looked like crinkled lettuce leaves. Also see *cabbage ruff.*

letting-in Fur-industry process of intricate cutting and resewing a fur skin to make it shorter and broader.

letting-out Fur-industry process of intricately cutting and sewing a fur skin to make it longer and narrower;

the pelt is cut down center back, slit into tiny diagonal pieces, and each piece dropped when joining to next pieces, thus making the pelt long enough that a skin may extend from neck to hem of the garment.

levantine See *fabrics.*

Levers See *laces.*

leviathan Soft woolen yarn used for embroidery and knitting.

Levi's See *pants.*

liars Wire framework that supported the *fichu, q.v.,* thus giving the effect of a larger bosom; worn during latter half of 18th century. Same as *menteurs* and *trompeurs.*

libas Knee-length or full-length full *trousers, q.v.,* worn by the Egyptian men as part of native dress.

Liberty 1. Trademark for a London fabric manufacturer which produces cotton prints called *Liberty prints, q.v.,* under *prints.* Also produces a *Liberty satin, Liberty lawn,* and some silk fabrics. 2. Liberty's, name of famous department store in London.

liberty cap Soft cap with close-fitting elongated crown, usually worn folded over. Worn by Roman slaves when freed, later adopted as a symbol of liberty in the U.S. and by French Revolutionists of the 1790's. Compare with *Phrygian cap.* Also called *bonnet rouge.*

lift The replaceable part on the bottom of the heel of the shoe, also called *heel lift.*

light jack boots See *jack boots* under *boots.*

Lille lace See *laces.*

Lilly See *dresses.*

lily Benjamin Colloquial term for man's white overcoat worn in first half of 19th century.

Limerick gloves Short or long *lambskin* gloves, made from very young or unborn lambs; worn by women during latter half of 19th century.

limousine 1. See *fabrics.* 2. Full-length circular woman's evening cape with shirring around neck so fullness falls in folds over the arms forming sleeves; worn in late 1880's.

Lindbergh jacket Waist-length heavy woolen or leather jacket with large pockets, lapels, and rolled collar; with waistband and cuffs made of stretchable rib-knit wool; type of jacket worn by Col. Charles A. Lindbergh, who made the first solo flight from New York to Paris across the Atlantic in 1927.

Linde Star See *gems.*

line See *collection.*

linecloths Pair of linen drawers worn by men in the 15th century.

line-for-line-copy American interpretation of Parisian or Italian couture garment, made expressly for American stores, often in fabric identical to original; copies are sold for lower prices.

linen 1. Fibers of the flax plant, either the short fibers called *tow* or the longer fibers called *line,* used to make linen yarn. 2. Fabric made of linen yarn in many qualities and many weights; cooler, stronger, and more absorbent than cotton; often given a crease-resistant finish.

See listings below and *handkerchief lawn* under *fabrics.*

linen cambric See *cambric* under *fabrics.*

linen canvas Firm linen interfacing q.v. See *fabrics.* Also see *embroidery.*

linen crash Textured linen. See *fabrics.*

line yarn Linen yarn made of longer fibers of flax plant as differentiated from *tow,* which uses the shorter fibers; used to make fine, silky linen fabrics.

lingerie (lan-zha-ree) Collective term for women's underwear including *slips, nightgowns, panties, brassieres,* etc., q.q.v. Sometimes called *intimate apparel* in trade. *Der.* French *linge,* linen fabric used for underwear from Middle Ages to 20th century. See *blouses.*

lingerie crepe Lightweight silky crepe. See *fabrics.*

lining Fabric, pile fabric, or fur used to finish inside of garment, the extra layer used for warmth or to retain shape of outer layer; fashion for stiff or limp garments fluctuates; e.g., linings strong in first quarter of 20th century and in 1950's, unlined garments prevalent in 1920's and 1930's and again in 1960's and early 1970's. See *half lining* and *zip-out lining.*

linsey-woolsey See *fabrics.*

lion's tail See *hairstyles.*

lipstick A crayon-like stick of lip coloring, usually in metal or plastic tube. Term sometimes used to describe a bright crimson red.

liquid embroidery See *embroideries.*

liripipe 1. Long pendant tail of the

chaperone, q.v., a hood worn from 13th through 15th centuries. 2. Part of a hood worn by graduates in 13th century. Also spelled *liripipium, lirapipe, liripoop.*

lisle Two-ply cotton yarn made of long staple fibers, combed, tightly twisted, and sometimes given further treatment to remove all short fuzzy fibers; used for knitwear, hosiery, and men's undershirts. *Der.* Early spelling of Lille, France.

lisle hosiery Socks and hose made of cotton *lisle, q.v.,* nearly as fine as silk, usually white, brown, or black; worn by men, women, and children throughout 19th and early 20th centuries, until replaced by silk in 1920's and nylon in 1940's.

list See *selvage.*

Littell, Deanna See *designers appendix, United States.*

little-boy shorts See *shorts.*

Little Lord Fauntleroy suit See *Fauntleroy.*

Little Women dress Child's dress made with plain, fitted, front-buttoned bodice, short or long plain sleeves, small turned-down collar with ribbon bow tie, and full-gathered skirt; inspired by dresses described in Louisa May Alcott's book *Little Women,* published in 1868.

livery Characteristic clothes or uniform worn by servants, now chiefly used in reference to chauffeurs' uniforms.

lizard, Lizigator See *leather.*

llama Fibers similar to *alpaca* obtained from an animal related to *camel,* native to high altitudes in Andes mountains of South America;

length of fiber from two to six inches, color ranges from white, gray, light brown to black; outer coat is coarse and under fiber is soft.

loafer See *shoes.*

locket See *necklaces.*

lockstitch *Chain* stitch, *q.v.,* used in attaching sole to upper in various types of shoe construction.

loden cloth Thick water-repellent woolen; see *fabrics.*

loft Term used to describe the resiliency of wool and man-made fibers that imitate wool, *e.g., Dynel modacrylic* and *Orlon acrylic.*

loincloth Garment wrapped around the lower torso worn by primitive people, American Indians, and ancient Egyptians; still used in some countries. Length may vary from very short to ankle-length. Also called a *breechcloth, lungi, q.q.v.*

long-bellied doublet See *peascodbellied doublet.*

long cloth See *fabrics.*

long clothes From latter half of 17th century, the dress of infants, replacing former *swaddling clothes, q.v.;* consisted of dress approximately three feet long, usually decorated with embroidery and worn with a matching petticoat; style still seen in the *christening dress* or *robe, q.v.*

long hood 18th-century term for a woman's hood similar to the *pug* or *short hood, q.v.;* sides made with long tabs to facilitate tying under chin.

long johns Slang term for *union suit* or *thermal underwear, q.q.v.*

long-line bra See *brassieres* and *slips*.

long lock See *love lock*.

long stocks or **long-stocked hose** Stockings attached at thigh to *trunk hose,* worn by men in 16th and 17th centuries. Also called *long stockings*.

long-torso Describing a garment with waistline placed near the widest part of the hips. See *silhouettes*.

longuette See *lengths*. Also see *coats* and *dresses*.

look A style of dress taken as a whole. See illustrations here and on next two pages.

UNISEX LOOK

WESTERN LOOK   INDIAN LOOK

loo mask Half mask hiding upper part of face, worn by women from mid 16th to early 18th century. Also spelled *lou*. Also see *loup* and *domino*.

loom-finished Industry term for fabric sold for end use just as it comes

MINI LOOK

330

FLAPPER
LOOK

GREEK BOY LOOK

KILTIE
LOOK

HIPPIE LOOK

GIBSON GIRL LOOK

from the loom without any further finishing processes.

loop-and-button closing See *closings.*

looped dress *Hoop*-skirted, *q.v.,* dress with skirt in two layers, outer layer gracefully looped up in five or six places by fabric tabs, *porte-jupe Pompadour, pages,* or *dress clips, q.q.v.,* to show the under-skirt; worn in the 1860's.

looped yarn See *bouclé* under *yarns.*

Lord Byron shirt See *shirts.*

Lord Fauntleroy suit See *Fauntleroy.*

lorgnette See *glasses.*

lorgnette chain Chain attached to round pin with a spring mechanism into which chain retracts; used to hold glasses in early 20th century.

lou See *loo.*

Louis XIV sleeve Woman's over-sleeve, flared as it descends from the shoulder, edged with fluting, worn with undersleeve or *engageantes, q.v.;* worn in 1850's.

Louis XV basque Woman's tailored jacket, worn open down center front revealing waistcoat or vest. Usually hip length with a standing collar and similar to *justaucorps, q.v.,* worn in mid 18th century by Louis XV of France; worn in 1890's.

Louis XV bodice Dress bodice with long point in front, cut away over hips, short peplum in back; several rows of *ruching, q.v.,* around neck forming a V-shaped trimming in front filled in with bows of ribbon; ruching also edging peplum and sleeves; worn in 1850's and '60's. *Der.* Similar to bodice worn by Marquise de Pompadour, mistress of Louis XV of France in mid 18th century.

Louis XV hat Woman's hat with large high crown, wide brim turned up on one side and fastened to crown with velvet bows, trimmed

elaborately with ostrich feathers; worn in mid 1870's. *Der.* Named for Louis XV of France, 1710–1774.

Louis XVI basque Woman's jacket-bodice fitted at the waistline and flaring over hips, with standing lace-edged *Medici collar, q.v.,* extended to two large lapels, moderate-sized *leg-of-mutton sleeves, q.v.,* with cuffs that fell down over the wrists; worn in late 1890's. *Der.* Named for Louis XVI of France, 1754–1793, who was guillotined during French Revolution.

Louis heel See *heels.*

Louis, Jean See *designers appendix, France.*

Louis Philippe costume Style of women's dress fashionable in 1830's and '40's, with sloped shoulders accentuated by *capes, berthas,* and ruffles: a fitted waistline, usually pointed in front; and wide, full skirt; usually worn with elaborate straw bonnet. *Der.* Named for Louis Philippe Robert, Duc d'Orleans and king of France from 1830–1848.

Louiseboulanger See *designers appendix, France.*

lounge suit English term for man's suit worn for informal occasions from 1860's on, consisting of *lounging jacket* (see #1, below), *vest,* and *trousers, q.q.v.,* of same fabric. Also see *suits.*

lounge wear Clothes designed to be worn primarily at home when relaxing or entertaining, may include *lounging pajamas* or *hostess robes.* See *robes, slippers,* and *pajamas.*

lounging cap Gentlemen's at-home cap in pillbox or dome shape with silk tassel fastened from center; worn during last half of 19th century. Also called *Greek lounging cap.* See drawing above.

LOUNGING CAP, 1857

lounging jacket 1. Man's suit jacket with rounded corners in front, flapped or slit pockets at sides, one breast pocket; sometimes with waistline seam, sometimes without seam; introduced about 1848 and worn from then on with modifications, forerunner of present-day suit jacket. 2. Contemporary man's jacket for at-home wear. See *smoking jacket* under *jackets.*

lounging robe Term used until 1920's for *housecoat, q.v.,* under *robes.*

LOUNGING ROBE, 1895

loup Black velvet mask worn during 16th century by fashionable women on the street or when riding to protect face from sun, rain, dust, and

333

eyes of passing men; when not being worn, mask hung from the belt by a string. See *loo* or *lou mask.*

love beads See *beads* and *necklaces.*

love knots 1. Decorative bows used in 16th century to tie across puffs in vertically slashed sleeves. 2. Ornamental knot of ribbon originally worn as love token.

love lock Long piece of curled hair brought forward from nape of neck and worn hanging over chest; worn from 1590 to 1650's by men and sometimes women. Also called a *Bourbon lock, French lock, long lock, heart breaker,* and *coiffure en cadenettes, q.q.v.*

love ribbon Gauze ribbon with narrow black and white satin stripes, formerly worn as a mourning band.

lover's knot Decorative knot made of intertwined loops of two cords, originally symbolized constancy of true love.

lower stocks Stockings made of silk or wool·cloth worn by men in 16th century, also called *bas de chausses,* worn with *upper stocks, q.v.,* called *haut de chausses.*

lozenge front Daytime dress bodice with front trimmed with strips of net, ribbon, etc., arranged in crisscross fashion to form a diamond-shaped pattern; similar to dresses worn by the Marquise de Maintenon, second wife of Louis XIV of France.

Lucille See *designers appendix, England.*

Lucite DuPont trademark for transparent acrylic plastic material used for handbags, sandals, shoe heels, and jewelry in 1960's and 1970's.

lumber jacket See *sport jackets* under jackets.

lumberman's over See *boots.*

Lunari hat See *balloon hat.*

lunchbox bag See *handbags.*

lungi 1. Short wrap-around skirt or loincloth, q.v., composed of single length of fabric worn by men of lower castes in India. 2. Fabric used for scarfs, turbans, and loincloths in India. Also spelled *longhee, loonghee, lungee, lungyi,* etc.

Lurex See *yarns.*

luster cloth British term for plain-weave fabrics made with shiny wool yarns in the filling (e.g., *mohair, alpaca* or other luster wools) and cotton in the warp, e.g. *brilliantine* and *Sicilian.* See *fabrics.*

lustering Any finish process that gives glossy appearance to yarn or fabric, produced by heat, steam, pressure, or calendering.

luster wool Natural glossy wool fibers from sheep of several types originally grown only in Great Britain including *Cheviot, Cotswell, Devon, Leicester, Lincoln,* and *Romney Marsh.*

Lutetia mink See *mink* under *furs.*

Lycra See *yarns.*

lynx See *furs.*

lynx cat See *furs.*

Lyons lace See *laces.*

Lyons loops Term used in 1865 for velvet straps used to pull up and loop the overskirt in three or four places, revealing underskirt.

Lyons satin See *fabrics.*

Lyons velvet See *fabrics.*

M

M Designation for size *medium* in various ranges: women's *girdles, housecoats, nightgowns, panties, sweaters;* men's *robes, sports jackets, sports shirts, sweaters;* some children's garments.

Macaroni Club Fashionable English men's club of George III's reign, founded in 1764 with membership of *dandies, q.v.,* based on their having made a trip to Italy; the members' style of dress developed by 1770's included the *Macaroni suit,* a thigh-length tight-fitting jacket, with sleeves so tight it was difficult to put the hands through the cuffs; very high, tight cravat; hose of different colors; shoes low-cut, with enormous buckles; very small tricorn hat, carried; and hugh nosegay of flowers on left shoulder. See *Macaroni collar* and *cravat.* Members were also called *bucks.*

Macaroni collar Dangerously tight high collar worn in the 1770's by English *dandies, q.v.,* who were members of the *Macaroni Club, q.v.*

Macaroni cravat Man's lace-edged muslin cravat, tied in a bow under the chin; worn in 1770's. Named for *Macaroni Club, q.v.*

Macclesfield silk Tie silk; see *fabrics.*

MacDonald tartan See *tartans.*

Macfarlane Man's overcoat with large cape and side slits to permit access to pockets of inner garment.

Macintosh 1. Loose-fitting, waterproof coat, made of patented India rubber cloth of olive drab or dark green, with proof straps over the seams; introduced in 1830's and named for the inventor, Charles Macintosh, who patented fabric in 1823. 2. English slang for various types of raincoats, often abbreviated to "Mac." Also see *coats.*

mackinaw or **Mackinac** See *sport jackets* under *jackets.*

mackinaw or **Mackinac cloth** Heavy double-faced woolen. See *fabrics.*

mackinaw flannel Heavy woolen flannel. See *fabrics.*

ma-coual 1. Wide-sleeved, short jacket made of fur in winter and of satin in other seasons, worn by Chinese gentleman over ankle-length silk robe. 2. Coat, knee-length or shorter, made with narrow standing collar and fastened under right arm, worn by Chinese women.

macramé knot Knot used in *macramé lace, q.v.* with two, three, four or more strands of cord tied in groups to form patterns. Craft used by sailors as a pastime, producing belts, ornaments, etc.; revived in early 1970's by young adults making neckwear, vests, belts, etc. Also see *belts.* Der. Turkish *maquramah.*

Mad Carpentier See *designers appendix, France.*

madder Natural dyestuff obtained from root of the Eurasian herbaceous perennial *rubis tinctoria,* used since ancient times to produce a rich red color on cotton and sometimes wool, now usually replaced by synthetic dyes. Also see *ancient madder* under *fabrics*.

made-to-measure See *custom-made* and *tailor-made*.

Madeira embroidery See *embroideries*.

Madras Hand-woven cotton from India. See *fabrics*.

Madras plaid See *plaids*.

Madras turban Turban worn by women in 2nd decade of the 20th century made of a blue and orange Indian handkerchief.

mafors Long narrow *veil* worn by women from 6th to 11th centuries, usually covered head and draped over shoulders.

magenta (mah-jen-tah) Reddish purple color, first chemical dye to be used for dress fabrics. *Der.* Named after Magenta, a town in northern Italy, where dyes to make the color were developed in 1860.

Magyar costume Hungarian native costume: man's shirt and woman's blouse of white linen lavishly embroidered, long aprons worn by both sexes; men also wear the felt or leather *szur, q.v.*, elaborately decorated.

maharatta tie (ma-ha-ra-ta) See *Indian necktie*.

maheutres (ma-hoy-treh) Term used in France from end of 14th century and in England from 1450 to 1480 for shoulder pads used as trim on sleeves of *gippon, q.v.* Also spelled *mahoitres*.

mail Early form of armor consisting of metal links sewn to foundation of leather in parallel rows, worn as armor by Normans and Saxons. Also called *chain mail*.

mail-coach necktie Man's large scarf, sometimes a cashmere shawl, loosely folded around shoulders and neck, tied in knot in front with ends falling over chest like a waterfall; worn as neckcloth in 1820's and 1830's. Also called *waterfall neckcloth*.

maillot (my-yo) See *swimsuits*.

Mainbocher See *designers appendix, United States*.

Maintenon coiffure (man-te-non) Woman's hairstyle with a long hanging curl at either side of face, tiny curls on the front of the head, and a *chignon, q.v.*, at the back of the neck; filmy lace decorated with foliage and flowers went over the crown of the head and hung down sides to shoulders in form of *lappets, q.v.*; the *Maintenon toupet, q.v.* could be worn to secure proper effect of curls on the forehead. Popular in the 1860's and named for the Marquise de Maintenon, *q.v.*

Maintenon cloak Woman's widesleeved, full, black velvet coat, sometimes embroidered and usually trimmed with wide pleated flounce covered with *guipure lace, q.v.*; worn in 1860's. Named for the Marquise de Maintenon, *q.v.*

Maintenon corsage Woman's evening dress bodice trimmed with ribbon bows down center front, in ladderlike effect, and lace ruffle at waist; worn in 1830's and early '40's. *Der.*

Named for the Marquise de Maintenon, *q.v.*

Maintenon, Marquise de Francoise d'Aubigne, (1635–1719), mistress and second wife to Louis XIV of France, married in 1685; a fashion influence in the following century.

Maintenon toupet Band of false curls attached to ribbon that tied at nape of neck; worn by women in 1860's pulled over the forehead so as to imitate the hairstyle worn by the Marquise de Maintenon, *q.v.*

Maison Callot See *Callot Soeurs* in *designers appendix, France.*

major wig Hairpiece consisting of a *toupee* with two *corkscrew curls* tied at the nape of neck to make a double *queue* in back, *q.q.v.*; originally a military style, but adopted by civilians and worn during latter half of 18th century.

majorette boot See *boots.*

Malabar 1. Cotton handkerchief from India printed with bright colors; named for Malabar district in India. 2. General term used for variety of printed cotton fabrics exported to East Africa from Great Britain and India.

malacca cane (ma-lak-a) Man's cane made from the mottled stem of the malacca palm; carried in 18th century. Also called *clouded cane.*

maline, malines See *fabrics* and *laces.*

Malmaison (mal-ma-zon) Pale rosy-pink color of a rose by this name grown at Malmaison, Napoleon's home where the Empress Josephine had a famous rose garden.

Maltese cross A cross with arms of equal length shaped like arrowheads pointing toward the center, the emblem of the Medieval Knights of Malta; used as a motif for jewelry—necklaces, pins, etc.

Mameluke sleeve (mama-luke) Full sleeve finished with a large cuff of thin fabric; used in daytime dresses of the late 1820's. *Der.* Named for the military group—once slaves called mamelukes—who ruled Egypt during Napoleon's campaign there in 1798.

Mameluke tunic See *tunic à la mameluke.*

Mameluke turban White satin woman's turban, *q.v.*, trimmed with one large ostrich feather, the front rolled back like a hat brim over a dome-shaped crown; worn in the early 19th century. *Der.* Named for Egyptian Mamelukes, see above.

mancheron 1. Late 15th-century half sleeve reaching from elbow to shoulder, lower part of sleeve called *brassard, q.v.*, two parts tied together by ribbons. 2. 16th century false sleeve attached only at shoulder and worn hanging down back. 3. 19th century very short oversleeve, similar to a large epaulette, worn by women, term gradually replaced by word *epaulet, q.v.*

manchette (mon-chet) Wrist ruffle of lace worn by women on afternoon dresses from 1830's to 1850's.

Manchu headdress (man-chew) Elaborate Chinese woman's headdress consisting of gold bar extending eight to ten inches above head, wound and decorated with flowers, wide ribbons, and wearer's own hair. Also called *black cloud head-dress.*

Mandarin floss hat or **tassel hat** Dome-shaped hat topped by a button that indicated the rank of the man or woman at the Chinese Mandarin court; from the button extended red silk floss which completely covered hat.

Mandarin hat 1. Chinese court hat with wide, flaring, up-turned brim and decorative button at crown, indicating rank of wearer; made of fur and satin for winter and decorated with a peacock feather. 2. Woman's black velvet *pork pie hat* of early 1860's, with feather trim over the back of the flat crown.

Mandarin headdress Tall, ornate head-dress studded with jewels, which stood away from the head, worn by Chinese Mandarin's wife before 1912.

Mandarin robes Costume worn by one of the nine ranks of officials of the Chinese empire during the Man-chu period from 1643 until 1912, the robe distinguished by patches of embroidery called *p'u-fu;* the costume used until 1912, when China became a republic. For de-scriptions of robes see *ch'ang-fu, ch'ao-fu,* and *chi-fu.* For modern adaptations of *mandarin* style, see *coats, collars, dresses, jackets, necklines,* and *sleeves.*

mandilion (man-dill-yun) Loose hip-length jacket with narrow long sleeves, worn by men from late 16th to early 17th centuries, often worn *colley westonward, q.v.,* or worn by soldiers around shoulders as a cape with sleeves hanging free; later worn, with short sleeves, some-times slit, for *livery, q.v.* Also called *mandeville.*

Mani-Hose See *pantyhose.*

Manila hemp See *abaca.*

man-made fiber Fibers made totally by chemical means as well as fibers made of regenerated cellulose. U.S. Textile Fibers Products Identifica-tion Act of 1960 states that these fibers must be labeled in accordance with generic groups as follows: *ace-tate, rayon, acrylic, azlon, glass, metallic, polyester, rubber, saran, spandex, vinal,* and *vinyon.* See in-dividual listings.

mannequin 1. A model of the human body used to display clothes in department stores, etc. 2. A woman whose job is wearing clothes in *fashion shows, q.v.* Also spelled *manikin.*

Manon robe Daytime dress with front cut in one piece from neck to hem, back with double *box pleat,* or *Watteau pleat, q.q.v.,* hanging from under collar to hem of skirt; worn in the 1860's. Named for Manon, heroine of 1733 book by Abbe Prevost.

mant 17th- or 18th-century term for *manteau* or *mantua, q.q.v.*

manta (man-teh) 1. In Chile and Cen-tral America, a woman's square shawl of thin fabric draped over head and shoulders, covering most of dress, made of silk or lace for highborn ladies and of alpaca and cashmere for other women; similar to the Spanish *mantilla.* Also called a *manto.* 2. Plaid wrap worn by men of Valencia, Spain. 3. Coarse *unbleached muslin, q.v.,* used in Mexico for items of clothing, sometimes shawls, or gray cotton sheeting made in Central America.

man-tailored Term usually applied to women's suits or coats, implying that garment is tailored similarly to a man's suit, coat, or shirt, as contrasted with tailoring of the softer variety as in *dressmaker suits, q.v.* Also see *jackets.*

manta suit Two-piece men's suit made out of *manta, q.v.,* worn in Mexico.

manteau (man-tow) 1. 16th century term for man's *French cloak,* or *compass cloak, q.q.v.* 2. Woman's gown. See *mantua.*

mantee Woman's coat worn open in front showing *stomacher* and *petticoat, q.q.v,* underneath; worn in 18th century.

mantelet, manteletta, mantelot, mantlet 1. Woman's scarf-shaped outer garment of fur, lace, or silk, worn around shoulders, crossed over chest, ends tied in back. 2. 19th-century woman's rounded shoulder cape with long ends tucked under belt in front, derived from the medieval short capes worn by men. 3. Sleeveless knee-length *ecclesiastical vestment, q.v.*

mantellone Purple ankle-length ecclesiastical mantle, worn over the *cassock, q.v.,* by lesser prelates of Papal court of the Roman Catholic Church.

mantilla 1. See *veils.* 2. *Shawl* or *veil* worn by Spanish women, usually of black lace, white lace worn for festive occasions; draped over head and sometimes over a high comb in hair and wrapped around neck, falling over shoulders. 3. Lightweight *shawl* of silk, velvet, or lace worn by women in 1840's, which hung long in back and had long ends in front. *Der.* Diminutive of Spanish *manta,* shawl.

mantle 1. Long, loose, sleeveless cloak, cape-like, worn from Middle Ages through 16th century by men and women; sometimes fastened by pin or clasp on one shoulder, or tied at neck; sometimes lined and called a *double mantle;* by 19th century, a name of a *cape, q.v.,* with or without sleeves. 2. Wrap for infants in 17th and 18th centuries. *Der.* Latin *mantellum,* cloak.

mantlet Matilde Type of shawl-like woman's garment trimmed with fringe or taffeta in front; worn in 1850's.

manto See *manta, manteau,* or *mantua.*

mantua (man-tu-a) Woman's *overdress* or gown worn over underskirt, with a loosely fitted, unboned bodice joined to overskirt with long train, split front exposed petticoat; worn on all social occasions from mid 17th century to mid 18th century. Also called *manteau, manto, manton* and *mantua gown.*

mantua maker 17th and 18th century term for tailor or dressmaker, either man or woman.

marabou See *feathers.*

marble cloth See *fabrics.*

marcasite (mar-ka-sight) See *gems.*

marcel Artificial wave put in woman's hair with heated curling irons, devised by Marcel of France in 1907 and popular in the 1920's.

Marguerite dress Dress with *stock neckline, q.v.,* full sleeves gathered into a wide cuff reaching halfway to elbow, full blouse gathered at neckline and full gathered skirt trimmed with bands of braid; contrasting low-necked, sleeveless peasant bodice, laced up the front and back over the dress; worn in early 1890's.

Marguerite girdle Stiff belt laced in back and wider in front, forming two points above and below waistline; or sometimes made with but-

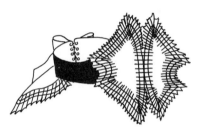

terfly arrangement in front and ruffle, peplum, or bow in back to give a *bustle, q.v.,* effect; popular in 1860's and worn at intervals since.

Marie Antoinette fichu See *Antoinette fichu.*

Marie Antoinette skirt Seven-*gored, q.v.,* skirt, three in front, four in back, with two back panels pleated in large *box pleats, q.v.,* and stitched down to hips, making a skirt four to six feet around the hem; popular style introduced in 1895. Named for Marie Antoinette (1755–93) wife of Louis XVI of France.

Marie sleeve Full sleeve tied at intervals to form several puffs; worn from about 1813 to mid 1820's and revived in the early 1870's and called the *Marie Antoinette sleeve.*

Marie Stuart bodice Tight-fitting, boned evening bodice ending in a deep point at waistline, worn in late 1820's; similar to bodice of dress worn by Mary Stuart Queen of Scots, in late 16th century.

Marie Stuart bonnet or **cap** Bonnet with heart-shaped crown or brim projecting over center of forehead, popular 1820–1870, frequently worn by

widows, a derivative of the *attifet, q.v.,* headdress worn by Mary Queen of Scots, in the late 16th century.

Marie Stuart hood Separate hood with peaked brim in front, extended over the

face; crown cut round, gathered at edge, and tied with ribbons under chin; lavishly trimmed with ruching, embroidery, braid, and ribbon; worn in 1860's.

Marimekko See *designers appendix, Finland.*

marin anglais bonnet Woman's bonnet worn on the back of head like a child's *sailor hat, q.v.,* trimmed with ribbon and feathers and tied under chin; worn in 1870's. *Der.* French, English sailor cap.

mariner's cuff Man's coat cuff of 2nd half of 18th century consisting of small turned back cuff decorated on outside with a curved flap, similar to a pocket flap and decorated with four buttons that matched those of the coat.

Marino Faliero sleeve Full *hanging sleeve, q.v.,* secured with ribbon band at elbow, popularized in early 1820's. *Der.* Called after drama of the same name by Lord Byron.

mark stitch See *stitches.*

marlota Spanish man's long coat with *hanging sleeves, q.v.,* similar in cut to a *caftan, q.v.;* worn only for tournaments and bullfights in late 16th century.

marlotte 16th-century woman's outer garment similar to short *mantle, q.v.,* open in front with back falling in folds, had short puffed sleeves and a standing collar or ruff.

marmot See *furs.*

marmotte bonnet Tiny bonnet with narrow front brim similar to *bibi bonnet, q.v.,* worn in early 1830's.

marmotte cap Triangular handkerchief placed on back of head and tied

under chin, worn indoors by women in early 1830's.

marocain See *fabrics.*

maroon Dark purple-brown-red color.

marquis (mar-kwiss or mar-kee) A three-cornered hat worn by women.

marquise (mar-keez) 1. See *gem cuts.* 2. Short lace-trimmed taffeta woman's *mantlet, q.v.,* with short sleeves, finished with a flounce below the waist in the back; worn in mid 1840's. Also called *marquise mantle.*

marquise bodice Evening bodice with low heart-shaped neckline forming two large scallops and trimmed with ruching or lace frill; fashionable in mid 1870's. Also called *bodice en coeur.*

marquisette Fine transparent fabric. See *fabrics.*

Marseilles See *fabrics.*

marten See *furs.*

Martha Washington fichu Large draped *fichu, q.v.,* extending to shoulders, with pointed ends con-

fined by a rosette of lace in front, two wide ruffles of lace extended around the edge; worn in mid 1890's, it was an adaptation of style worn by Martha Washington, wife of the first President of the United States in previous century.

Martha Washington waist V-necked blouse with *stock, q.v.,* inserted; *sur-*

plice front gathered at shoulder seams, draped to one side, and tied in back with a bow; sleeves varied from full double puff to single puff to elbow and fitted to wrist; worn during 1890's. *Der.* Named for wife of first U.S. President.

martingale See *belts.*

Marucelli, Germana See *designers appendix, Italy.*

Mary Janes See *shoes.*

Mary Stuart cap See *Marie Stuart bonnet.*

masher Term used for an elaborately dressed *dandy, q.v.,* of 1880's and 1890's. Also called *Piccadilly Johnny.*

masher collar Extremely high collar worn by ultra-fashionable men in 1880's and 1890's.

masher dust wrap Tight-fitting man's *Inverness coat, q.v.,* having large armholes with two separate capes over the shoulders, which did not meet in the back; worn in 1880's.

mask Covering for face used for various purposes: (1) disguise, as at fancy dress balls, *e.g., domino* or *loup, q.q.v.;* (2) for protection in active sports, *e.g.,* fencing, scuba

DOMINO
MASK

SKI
MASK

diving, football, hockey, skiing; (3) as protection against occupational hazards, *e.g.,* industrial or surgical masks. *Half mask* covers only the eyes. See *ski mask.*

Master's gown Black open-front gown with square yoke and long closed *hanging sleeves, q.v.,* with crescents cut out near hems (arms emerge through slits above elbows); full back and sleeves joined to yoke by car-

tridge pleats, q.v., worn with *Master's hood* and *mortarboard, q.q.v.,* by candidates for, holders of Master's degrees.

Master's hood Black cowl-drape three and one-half feet long in back with band of colored *velveteen* around edge, turned over in back to show lining color denoting institution granting degree; worn with *Master's gown, q.q.v.* Also see *academic hood.*

mat or **matt weave** Basket weave. See *weaves.*

matador hat (mat-ah-door) Hat shaped like top of bull's head—rounded over forehead with two projections like bull's horns, covered with black tufts of fabric and center of crown of embroidered velvet; worn by bullfighters in Spain and Mexico.

matelassé Puckered silk or wool fabric. See *fabrics.*

maternity blouse See *blouses.*

maternity dress See *dresses.*

Mathilde embroidery See *embroideries.*

Matilda 1. Term used in 19th century for velvet decoration around hem of women's skirt. 2. Term used in 1840's for a bouquet of flowers worn in hair.

matinee (mah-tin-aye) Another name for a *tea jacket, q.v.;* worn in 1890's and early 20th century.

matinee-length necklace See *necklaces.*

matinee skirt Woman's patented hoop-skirt, *q.v.* made by inserting 11 lightweight hoops into a petticoat,

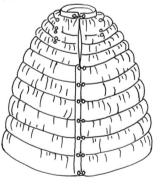

with total weight of 10 ounces; introduced in late 1850's.

matte finish (mat) 1. Textile-industry term for any dull finish. 2. Make-up that has no shine.

mattress-ticking stripe See *stripes.*

Maud Woman's fringed wrapper of plaid fabric, worn in mid 1850's.

mauve (mohv) Grayed lilac color.

maxi Word coined in 1968 for daytime skirt or coat reaching the ankles. See *coats, dresses, skirts, lengths, silhouettes.*

Maxwell, Vera See *designers appendix, United States.*

mazamet *Melton fabric, q.v.,* made in France.

mazarin hood (maz-a-rhan) Woman's *chaperon, q.v.,* or hood worn in last quarter of 17th century, named after Duchesse de Mazarin, niece of Cardinal Mazarin (1602–1661), Minister to Louis XIV.

McCardell, Claire See *designers appendix, United States.*

M-cut collar Man's coat collar with M-shaped notch at the *lapel;* worn in first half of 19th century for day

wear, continuing until 1870 for evening coats.

Mechlin lace (meck-lin) See *laces.*

Mecklenburg cap Turban-style indoor cap worn by women in 1760's, named after Charlotte of Mecklenburg, who married George III of England.

medallion 1. See *necklaces.* 2. See *prints.* 3. Shoe-industry term for ornamental pattern punched in leather in center of man's *wing-tip shoe, q.v.*

medic collar See *collars.*

Medici collar (meh-*dee*-chee) 1. Large standing fan-shaped collar, usually of net or lace, wired to stand up or roll away in back, sloping to join low, square neckline in front; worn by Maria de'Medici, (1573–1642), second wife of Henry IV of France, and reintroduced in 18th and 19th centuries. 2. Smaller woman's standing collar rolled over at top, sometimes nearly meeting in front; worn in 1890's.

Medici dress Trained *princess dress, q.v.,* of early 1870's with *tablier* front, *q.v.,* and short sleeves.

Medici lace See *laces.*

Medici sleeve Full sleeve, puffed to elbow and tight from there to wrist; worn by women in 1830's.

Medici vest Woman's fitted blouse with double-puffed sleeves ending in three fluted ruffles at elbow and V-neck trimmed with a single pleated ruffle, short *basque, q.v.,* below waistline with fullness in back; worn in mid 1870's.

medieval In a broad sense, usually refers to fashions of period A.D. 500 to 1450; same as Middle Ages.

meditation shirt See *shirts.*

medium Size range used along with *small, large* and *extra large* for these categories: women's sweaters, housecoats, nightgowns, some panties, girdles and panty girdles; men's sport shirts, sport jackets, sweaters and robes; children's gloves; girls' sweaters and pajamas; boy's pajamas, knit shirts, robes and sport jackets.

Medusa wig (meh-doo-sa) Woman's wig of early 19th century made of many hanging *corkscrew curls, q.v. Der.* From the Greek mythical Gorgan Medusa, with hair of coiled snakes, slain by Perseus.

melange suitings See *fabrics.*

melon sleeve See *sleeves.*

Melrose Scottish twill. See *fabrics.*

melton Heavy wool. See *fabrics.*

menteurs See *liars.*

mentonnière (mohn-ton-ee-ehr) 1. Protective armor for lower part of the face or chin, worn in tournaments in Middle Ages. 2. (pl.) *Lace* or *tulle, q.q.v.,* ruffles sewn to bonnet strings making frill under neck when tied; worn in 1820's and 1830's. Same as *chin stays.*

menu vair See *vair.*

Menzies tartan See *tartans.*

mercerized yarn Cotton yarn immersed in caustic soda to increase luster and dyeability, used for thread and for hosiery and fine cotton fabircs.

mercerizing Finishing process with caustic soda applied to cotton (or sometimes rayon) fabric or thread to make fibers more nearly parallel and to increase the luster. Named for John Mercer, calico printer in Lancashire, England, who developed the process in 1844 and patented it in 1850.

merino wool High-quality wool yarn made from fleece of merino sheep, which is short and fine, strong, resilient, and takes dyes well.

Merry Widow hat Very wide-brimmed hat, sometimes a yard across, frequently of velvet and ornately trimmed with ostrich plumes. *Der.*

Named for 1905 light opera, *The Merry Widow,* with music by Franz Lehar.

merveilleux 1. See *fabrics.* 2. Term used during French Revolution for a *fops* or *dandies, q.q.v.* Females who wore extreme clothes were called *merveilleuses. Der.* French, marvelous.

mesh 1. Metal links joined together to form a flat, flexible unit. See *chain mail, mesh belts, handbags,* etc. 2. Knitted or woven fabric in an open weave, such as *leno, q.v.,* producing a net or a screen-like effect. See *knits;* also see *hose.*

mess jacket 1. See *jackets.* 2. Waist-length jacket with standing collar worn by women in 1890's.

mest Turkish sock worn inside the *paboudj slipper, q.v.*

metallic cloth See *fabrics.*

metallic yarn See *yarns.*

meteor crepe See *crêpe meteor* under *fabrics.*

Metternich sack Woman's collarless, knee-length wrap of black velvet with three *box pleats, q.v.,* at center back, trimmed at neck, front, and shoulders with broad velvet ribbon embroidered with white cord; worn by women in mid 1860's. *Der.* Named for Prince von Metternich, Austrian statesman of the mid 19th century.

Mexican drawn work See *embroideries.*

Mexican wedding shirt See *shirts.*

Michael See *designers appendix, England.*

Micia See *designers appendix, Italy.*

micro Term used in fashion as a synonym for tiny or very short. See *lengths.* For various items see *earrings, dresses,* etc.

middy blouse See *blouses.*

middy braid See *braids.*

middy collar See *collars.*

middy dress See *dresses.*

middy suit Three-piece sailor suit for children in the mid 1890's. Boy's suit had waist-length jacket with large sailor collar, close-fitting collarless blouse, and short or

knee pants; girl's suit had hip-length jacket with sailor collar, leg-of-mutton sleeves, and unpressed-pleated skirt.

middy twill or **cloth** See *jean,* under *fabrics.*

mid heel See *medium* under *heels.*

midi (mee-dee) 1. Originally a French term for a skirt length coming to the mid-calf of leg, later applied to anything that length. For *midi* items see *coats, dresses, skirts, lengths, silhouettes,* etc. *Der.* French, midday.

midinette (mee-dee-net) French working girl or seamstress; a fashion influence. *Der.* French *midi,* midday.

midnight blue Very dark blue, almost

black; used for men's formal suits.

midriff style See *dresses* and *shirts.* Also see *bare-midriff* style.

mignonette See *fabrics.*

mignonette lace See *laces.*

Milan bonnet (mee-lan) Man's cap, usually black, with soft puffed crown, rolled-up brim sometimes slit on the side, trimmed with crimson satin lining pulled through slashes; worn in 16th century.

Milanese knit See *knits.*

Milan lace See *laces.*

Milan straw See *straws.*

military braid See *braid.*

military cap See *army caps* under *caps.*

military coat See *coats.*

military collar See *collars.*

military frock coat Frock coat, *q.v.,* with braid trim, a rolled collar, no lapels, no flaps on pockets; worn by men from early 19th century on.

military stock Man's made-up *neck-cloth, q.v.,* frequently of black corded silk edged with kidskin, stiffened with cardboard or leather, tied or buckled in back; worn in late 18th into 19th century.

military tunic Man's long tube-like coat with skirts lapped over in front; adopted by British army in 1855.

Milium Trademark for a finishing process in which aluminum particles are fixed to the reverse side of lining fabrics; aids in deflection of heat, helping to make garment warmer by retaining body heat.

milkmaid hat Garden type of straw hat, *q.v.,* with low crown and wide

drooping brim, tied under chin; popularized by Marie Antoinette (1755–93), wife of Louis XVI of France, when she played at farming on grounds of the palace at Versailles; worn until 1800 and revived in 1860's. Also called *bergère* or *shepherdess* hat, *q.v.,* under *hats.*

milkmaid skirt Double skirt, plain overskirt gathered and pulled up on one side by cord loop at waistband, revealing striped underskirt; worn in mid 19th century.

millefiore (meel-eh-fee-o-reh) Italian word describing tiny-flowered print. *Der.* Italian, thousand flowers.

millefleurs (meel-flhur) French name for a pattern of tiny flowers. *Der.* French, thousand flowers.

millinery Any covering for the head, specifically *hats, bonnets, caps, hoods,* and *veils* and, in 1970's, including *wigs, q.q.v.*

millinery velvet See *fabrics.*

minaudiere See *handbags.*

miner's cap See *caps.*

mini (minn-ee) 1. Originally a skirt length reaching to mid-thigh. See *lengths.* 2. Any fashion item that is tiny or short. See *coats, dresses, skirts, lengths,* and *silhouettes.*

minimal bra See *brassieres*

miniver 1. White or spotted gray and white fur used for linings and trimmings in the Middle Ages. 2. White fur, especially ermine, used to trim robes of state in various countries.

miniver cap Same as *lettice cap, q.v.*

mink See *furs.*

Minnie Mouse shoe Long-toed, strapped shoe worn by girls in England as a part of 1960's Mod styles, resembling those worn by the movie cartoon character drawn by Walt Disney in 1930's.

mino 1. Straw skirt and sometimes collar worn in Japan as protection from rain. 2. Straw raincoat made of long pieces of plaited straw leaving long fringe from knees down; shaped like a cone with square cut-window to see through; worn in rural Japan by children and adults.

misericord Man's dagger worn on right side as costume accessory in 14th and 15th centuries. Also spelled *misericorde. Der.* Named "pity-heart" because it was used to give the death stroke to a mortally wounded knight.

miser purse Small tubular silk purse closed at each end, with slit in center, and a moveable ring to keep money at one end or other, carried during latter half of 17th century. Also called a *stocking purse.*

misses sizes Women's garments cut for a well-proportioned adult figure, about 5'5" to 5'6" tall; usually numbered 6 to 18.

mistake hat Woman's hat with tall, flat-topped crown, front brim cut in blunt point and turned up, back brim turned down, worn on the back of the head; popular in the 1800's.

Mr. John See *designers appendix, United States.*

miter 1. Very tall ornamental head-dress worn by Catholic and Episcopal church dignitaries, has a large peak in front and back of outer part.

2. Judaism: high priest's official headdress with gold plate on front engraved "Holiness to the Lord." Mentioned in Ex. 28: 36–38. 3. Tall headdress worn by Assyrians with flaring top. 3. Woman's *fillet, q.v.,* worn in ancient Greece. 4. Name given by 19th-century writers to heart-shaped headdress worn in 15th century.

mitons Same as *moufles, q.v.*

mitts or **mittens** See *gloves.*

mitten sleeve Woman's tightly fitted sleeve of lace or net reaching to the wrist; worn in the early 1890's.

mitten-sleeve gown Infant's night-gown with drawstrings at the ends of the sleeves, to cover the hands to prevent scratching.

Mitzou See *designers appendix, Spain.*

mizz Foot covering of soft *cordovan leather, q.v.,* worn inside shoes by people in the near East, kept on at mosques and indoors when outer shoes are removed.

Moabite turban Woman's crepe turban, draped in many folds and trimmed with an *aigrette, q.v.,* on one side, worn tilted on side of head; popular in early 1830's.

moat collar See *collars.*

mobcap Woman's indoor cap of 18th and 19th centuries, made of white cambric or muslin with gathered crown and ruffled edge forming a bonnet, with side *lappets, q.v.,* called *kissing strings* or *bridles,* tying under chin. See *dust cap.*

mobile earrings See *earrings.*

moccasin Soft shoe made of one continuous piece of leather forming sole and most of the upper, a semielliptical piece inserted in vamp, copied from shoes of early American Indians. See *Indian* moccasin and *moccasin-toed shoe* under *shoes.*

mocha (mo-ka) Milk-chocolate brown.

mocha leather See *leathers.*

mockador Term used for handkerchief or child's bib in 15th century, also called *mocket, muckinder, moctour* or *moketer,* etc. in later centuries, up to early 19th century.

mock pockets See *pockets.*

mock seam Hosiery-industry term for seam sewed into circular-knit hose to give appearance of full-fashioned hose.

mock-turtleneck collar See *collars.*

mock-twist yarn Two colored yarns fed into the spinning frame at the same time to make fancy single yarn, resembling spiral twist in two-tone effect.

Mod English slang for a particular pseudo-Edwardian style adopted by the group of young men known as the Teddy boys and their girl friends about 1958; the Mods opposed the Rockers, who wore leather jackets, other motorcycle gear. Also see *Rocker look, Teddy boy,* and *Carnaby* look.

modacrylic Generic term for a man-made fiber made from acrylic resins, characterized by soft hand, warmth without bulk, resistance to moths and mildew, and high wrinkle recovery; used for sweaters, other knitwear, and fur fabrics.

mode French word for *fashion, q.v.*

model 1. American term for person who is paid to wear garment in a fashion show or a photograph. 2. French term for the garment itself.

modesty piece Piece of lace or lace-edged linen pinned to front of corset, covering the cleavage of the bosom, worn with décolleté bodices in 18th century.

modiste (mow-deest) French term for milliner; in English, a *modiste* is also a *dressmaker.*

mofuku kimono Mourning kimono worn in Japan, usually black silk although sometimes white with white crests; black accessories and black *zori, q.v.,* made of cloth are also worn.

Mogador Tie silk. See *fabrics.*

mohair 1. Hair of the angora goat. 2. Coarse, wiry yarn of mohair fibers popular for sweaters in the mid and late 1960's. 3. See *mohair* and *mohair pile* under *fabrics. Der.* Arabic *mukhayyar,* goat's hair fabric.

moiles Variant of *mules, q.v.*

moiré (mowahr-aye) 1. Fabric finish that achieves a wave-like watered effect by means of embossed, heated rollers. 2. Stiff, heavy, ribbed fabric with watered effect. See *fabrics. Der.* French, watered.

moiré pattern Fur term for appearance of Persian broadtail and American processed broadtail, flat furs with a wavy surface.

mokadour, moketer See *mockador.*

Moldavian mantle Full-length woman's mantle with long capes over the shoulders to form *elephant sleeves, q.v.;* worn in early 1850's.

molded dress See *dresses.*

molded felt Hat-industry term for

the felt *hood, q.v.,* made into hat shape by placing over a wooden block shaped like a head.

moleskin 1. Napped cotton cloth. See *fabrics.* 2. See *furs.*

Molyneux, Edward See *designers appendix, France.*

momie cloth Fabrics with a pebbled weave. See *fabrics* and *weaves.*

Mondrian dress Dress made of white fabric printed in colored rectangles and squares divided by black bands, inspired by Dutch painter Piet Mondrian's 1920's works and popular in mid 1960's.

money belt See *belts.*

Mongolian lamb See *furs.*

monkey See *furs.*

monkey jacket Short, fitted jacket made of heavy fabric like a waist-length *pilot coat, q.v.;* worn by sailors in rough weather from 1850's on — or any similar short jacket.

monk's belt See *belts.*

monk's cloth Heavy basket-weave cotton. See *fabrics.*

monk's dress See *dresses.*

monk's robe See *robes.*

monk-strap shoe See *shoes.*

Monmouth cap Man's knitted cap with high rounded crown, worn by soldiers, sailors, and others and listed as necessary item for new settlers in America; most common in 17th century and made at Monmouth and Bewdley in Worcestershire, England. Also called *Bewdley cap.*

Monmouth cock Broad-brimmed man's hat turned up or "cocked" in back, worn in second half of 17th century.

monocle See *glasses.*

monofilament yarn See *yarns.*

monogram 1. Marking by a single initial of person wearing the garment or the designer who created the garment. During the middle 1960's, the French couturier Cardin and the Italian designer Valentino used the "C" and "V" profusely on their creations. 2. A person's first or last initial worked into a design engraved on earrings, cuff links, a locket, etc. 3. Term misused to mean two or three initial letters of whole name grouped and embroidered on an item of clothing.

mono-kini See *swimsuits.*

Montagnac Napped cashmere coating. See *fabrics.*

Montague curls Woman's evening hairstyle with a fringe of crescent-shaped curls gummed to forehead; worn in late 1870's.

montero (mon-tar-o) Spanish hunting cap with round crown and ear flaps, worn from 17th century on. *Der.* Spanish *monte,* hill. Also called a *mountera,* and *mountie* cap in England.

Montespan corsage (mon-tes-pan) Tight-fitting woman's evening bodice with deep, square-cut neckline and pointed waistline in front; worn in early 1840's. *Der.* From Marquise de Montespan (1641–1707) mistress of Louis XIV of France.

Montespan hat Woman's small round velvet evening hat with brim turned up in front, trimmed with plume; worn in 1840's. *Der.* See above.

Montespan pleats Large, flat, double or triple *box pleats, q.v.,* used to join skirt to waistband; popular in 1840's. *Der.* See above.

Montespan sleeve Woman's puffed sleeve at upper arm with band at elbow and lace ruffle falling down from the band; worn in early 1830's.

Montgomery beret Military cap, a bit larger than the conventional Basque *beret* but set on a band like a Scots *tam-o'-shanter, q.q.v.,* decorated with regimental insignia; popularized by Field Marshall Bernard Law Montgomery, 1st Viscount Montgomery, commander of British ground forces in World War II.

mont-la-haut (mont-la-oh) Framework used to support the hair, same as *commode, q.v.*

montpensier mantle (mon-pon-see-ay) Woman's cape-like *mantle, q.v.,* long in back, with front ending in a point, slit up sides, leaving arms free; worn in 1840's.

moonstone See *gems.*

moppet 18th-century term for doll, dressed in France and sent to England to illustrate latest styles, from which women in England ordered ensembles.

Moravian work See *embroideries.*

Mori, Hanae See *designers appendix,* Japan.

morion Lightweight *helmet, q.v.,* with brim forming peaks front and back, turned down on sides, with high comb in center extending from front to back over crown of head;

popular in 16th century throughout Europe, and associated with Spanish conquistadors in Mexico.

morning cap Dainty cap of muslin, lace, tulle, and ribbon worn on the back of the head, indoors in the

morning, by women in last half of 19th century. Also called a *breakfast cap.*

morning coat See *cutaway* under *coats.*

morning dress 1. Term used in early 20th century for a *housedress, q.v.,* of inexpensive fabric. 2. Formal daytime apparel for men consisting of *striped pants, cutaway coat, ascot tie,* and sometimes *top hat, q.q.v.*

morning-glory skirt *Gored* skirt, *q.v.,* fitted through hips, then flared in trumpet fashion; worn in 1890's. Also called *serpentine skirt.*

morning gown 1. Long, loose dressing gown with a sash at the waist; worn indoors by men in early 19th century, similar to *banyan, q.v.* 2. Woman's dress, worn during 19th century, suitable for home or shopping.

morning robe 1. Type of *robe de*

chambre, q.v., worn in last half of 19th century by women. 2. See *morning dress,* 1.

Moroccan leather See *leathers.*

Moroccan slippers Leather slippers with turned-up toes; yellow worn by Moroccan men, red worn by women.

Morris bells Tiny bells attached to leather or ribbon trim worn for Morris dancing in Tudor England (16th century); bells were attached to ribbon-trimmed garters worn below knees, hat bands, sleeves, or special leggings.

mortarboard Academic headgear consisting of large, square black brim attached on top of a close cap, large tassel center of flat top hangs to right side before graduation, to left after; worn all over the U.S. today and since 14th century at universities such as Oxford and Cambridge in England. Also called *Oxford cap, cater cap.*

Morton, Digby See *designers appendix, England.*

moschettos (mos-ket-os) Pants similar to men's *pantaloons* of early 19th century but fitted to leg and worn over boots like *gaiters, q.q.v.*

Moscow Napped woolen. See *fabrics.*

Moscow wrapper Man's loose-fitting overcoat with *pagoda sleeves, fly-front, q.q.v.,* narrow turned-down collar of Astrakhan fur, and other fur trim; worn in late 19th century.

moss agate See *gems.*

Mother Hubbard Comfortable, plain *housedress* or *wrapper, q.q.v.,* fitted

only at its square yoke, used for morning wear at home in late 19th and early 20th century. *Der.* Named for nursery-rhyme character.

Mother Hubbard cloak Woman's or girl's three-quarter-length cloak of brocade, velvet, satin, or cashmere made with quilted lining, high collar tied at neckline, full sleeves often in dolman style, shirring over shoulders and sometimes back section draped over bustle and tied with ribbon bow; worn in 19th century.

mother-of-pearl Shiny, iridescent substance, lining of shell of pearl oyster, abalone, and other mollusks. Also called *nacre.* See *pearl buttons.*

motoring veil See *automobile veil.*

mouche (moosch) *Beauty spot, q.v.,* also called *court plaster* or *patch. Der.* French, fly or speck.

moufles 1. Fingerless gloves or mittens worn in Merovingian Period for hunting or working. 2. Late 14th century term for extensions of sleeves covering hand. Also called *mitons.*

moulds Men's *drawers* padded with horsehair and other fibers, worn under *bombasted* or *balloon* trousers in England in latter half of 16th century. Also spelled *mowlds.*

Mountie's hat See *hats.*

mourning 1. Clothes, usually black, worn for funeral or during mourning period after funeral, sometimes extended for one year. During 19th and early 20th centuries, deep mourning of black was worn for six months, followed by half mourning, with purple or lavender added, for six months. See *mourning crepe.*

mourning bonnet Any black bonnet worn to complete a mourning costume; specifically, in the 1870's and '80's, an off-the-face bonnet sometimes with a *Marie Stuart* peak, *q.v.,* made of black silk lavishly trimmed with ruching and ribbon, tied under the chin, and with veilling arranged over the face or left hanging down the back.

mourning crepe or **crape** Collective term for black fabrics, usually crepes, worn for funerals or for mourning.

mourning garland 17th-century term for a widow's hat band or garland of willow worn for mourning.

mourning jewelry Jet and black-enameled jewelry worn by women instead of regular jewelry during a mourning period, from mid 19th century through early 20th century.

mourning knot Term for armlet with attached bunch of black ribbons worn on left arm for mourning by men in 18th century.

mourning ribbons 17th-century term for black ribbon worn by men on the hat for mourning.

mourning ring Massive ring, frequently black, later blue enamel, sometimes with portrait of deceased, emblems, such legends as "be prepared to follow me," or hair of the departed plaited in a design; sometimes given to guests at funerals.

mourning scarf Scarf of lawn about 3½ yards long, presented along with hat bands to principal mourners at funerals in 17th and 18th centuries.

mourning tire 17th century term for *mourning veil, q.v.,* worn by women.

mourning veil See *veils.*

mousers See *boots.*

mousquetaire collar (moose-ke-tare) Medium-sized turned-down collar, usually linen, with the front ends pointed; fashionable for women about 1850.

mousquetaire cuff Deep, wide cuff, flaring above the wrist, copied from uniform of French musketeers, royal bodyguards in period of Louis XIII; worn on men's coats in 1870's.

mousquetaire gloves See *gloves.*

mousquetaire hat 1. Wide-brimmed hat usually trimmed with three ostrich plumes. *Der.* From hats worn by musketeers or royal bodyguards of Louis XIII in 17th century. Also called *Swedish hat.* 2. Brown mushroom-shaped woman's straw hat edged with black lace hanging from the brim; worn in late 1850's.

mousquetaire mantle Black velvet mantle with full sleeves and deep cuffs trimmed with braid, lined with quilted satin; worn by women in mid 19th century.

mousseline de laine Lightweight woolen. See *fabrics.*

mousseline de soie Transparent silk. See *fabrics.*

mouton-processed lamb See *furs.*

mowles, moyles Variants of *mules, q.v.*

Mozambique See *fabrics.*

mozetta See *capes.*

muckinder See *mockador.*

muff Warm tubular covering for the

hands, open at each end, frequently of fur or rich fabrics, usually round or oblong, in many sizes, sometimes with concealed inner pockets; carried by women as accessory matched to material of coat or trimming, and carried by men from 17th to 19th centuries. See *countenance, muffetees,* and *Roxburgh muff.*

muffetees 1. Pair of small wrist muffs worn for warmth or when playing cards to protect wrist ruffles by both men and women in 18th and 19th centuries. 2. Pair of small muffs worn for warmth in mid 18th century, closed at one end and sometimes with separate stall for thumb. 3. Coarse mittens of leather or wool knit, worn by old men in early 19th century.

muffin hat Man's fabric hat with round flat crown and narrow standing brim used for country wear; worn in 1860's.

muffler See *scarfs.*

muff's cloak Man's coat of late 16th and early 17th centuries. Same as *Dutch coat, q.v.*

muga silk See *fabrics.*

Muir, Jean See *designers appendix, England.*

mukluks (muk-luk) 1. Boots made in style similar to Indian moccasins, made of sealskin or walrus hide, reaching a little above ankle; worn by Alaskan Eskimos. 2. Also see *slippers* and *boots.*

mulberry silk Silk obtained from silkworms that are fed on leaves of mulberry tree.

mules Slippers that fit over toes but have no back or quarter; term used since 16th century. See *slippers.* Also spelled *moiles, moyles,* and *mowles.*

mull Thin soft cotton or silk. See *fabrics.*

Muller cut-down Man's hat of 1870's made like top hat with crown cut to half the height. *Der.* Named after English murderer whose hat led to his arrest in 1864.

mulmul Variant of *mull, q.v.*

multifilament yarn See *yarns.*

mummy cloth See *fabrics.*

museum heel See *heels.*

mushroom hat Woman's straw hat with a small round crown and downward-curved brim, shaped like a mushroom cap; trimmed with ribbons, flowers, and birds in 1830's; worn again in early 1900's and, usually in felt, in the 1930's and 1940's.

mushroom sleeve Woman's short sleeve, pleated into the armhole, the lower edge trimmed with lace; used in evening dresses of the 1890's.

musk apples, muskballs See *pommes de senteur.*

muskrat See *furs.*

muslin Plain-weave cotton. See *fabrics.*

muslin pattern Complete garment made in an inexpensive fabric, *e.g.,* muslin, usually draped on a dummy and, after muslin garment is finished, ripped apart to provide a pattern for actual dress, etc.; muslin patterns are sold by French couturiers to Seventh Avenue manufacturers. Process used for fur designing also. Also called a *toile*.

mutation mink See *mink*.

muumuu See *dresses*.

Mylar Trademark owned by DuPont for polyester film used laminated to either side of metallic foil to make non-tarnishable metallic yarns.

354

N

nabchet 16th-century slang term for *cap* or *hat*.

nacre (nah-creh) See *mother-of-pearl*.

nacré velvet See *fabrics*.

nailing Process used in making of fur garment which involves fastening strips of fur with thin nails to a board on which shape of garment is outlined.

nainsook Lightweight plain-weave cotton. See *fabrics*.

nainsook checks Lightweight cotton with woven checks. See *fabrics*.

nakli daryai Handloomed cotton from India. See *fabrics*.

nankeen Cotton cloth. See *fabrics*.

nap In fabrics, a fuzzy finish raised on cloth made of loosely twisted yarns by brushing the surface on one or both sides.

napa leather See *leather*.

nap finish Leather finish that *suedes, q.v.,* the grain side of the leather.

naphol dyes See *azoic dyes*.

napkin 16th and early 17-century term for handkerchief used for the nose.

napkin-cap Man's 18th-century house cap or plain *nightcap,* worn at home when wig was removed.

napkin hook Ornamental hook, attached to woman's waistband, used to suspend handkerchief; popular in 17th century.

Napoleon See *Bonaparte*.

Napoleon coat Woman's man-tailored hip-length jacket with standing *military* collar, full *leg-of-mutton* sleeves, and *military braid* trim

down front, fastened with large *Brandenburgs, q.q.v.;* worn in mid 1890's.

Napoleon collar See *collars*.

Napoleon necktie Man's medium-wide necktie of violet color, passed around neck, crossed over chest, and ends tied to suspenders or continued to tie in back; worn about 1818 and reported to have been copied from necktie worn by Napoleon on his return from Elba. Later called *Corsican tie*.

Napoleons Long military boots, reaching above knee in front, with piece cut out in back; named after Napoleon III; worn by civilians on horseback in 1850's.

napping See *nap*.

napron Term used in 14th and 1st half of 15th centuries for *apron*. Also called *appurn*.

Nast, Condé (1874–1942) Publisher of *Vanity Fair* from 1913 to 1936 and of *Vogue* magazine, including English and French *Vogues*, from 1909 to 1942; president of The Condé Nast Publications Inc. which also published the Vogue Pattern Book, *Glamour*, and *House and Garden* during his lifetime. Other CNP magazines were acquired later.

National Press Week Semiannual event when newspaper fashion editors across the country are invited to New York by the New York Couture Group, *q.v.*, to see collections of Seventh Avenue designers; idea originated with New York manufacturer Ben Reig in 1942.

natte Basket-weave silk or rayon. See *fabrics*.

natural bra See *brassieres*.

natural fibers Fibers that have animal, vegetable, or mineral origin as opposed to man-made chemicals, used to make yarn including *wool, linen, silk, cotton; jute, sisal, hemp* and *ramie; cashmere, mohair,* etc. For definitions see individual listings.

natural mink See *mink* under *furs*.

natural ranch mink See mink under *furs*.

natural shoulder See *shoulders*.

Naugahyde (naw-ga-hide) Trademark for fabric resembling leather, with vinyl resin coating on face and knitted back; knitting gives stretch; used for bags, shoes, etc.

Navajo American Indian tribe of Southwestern U.S. living in Arizona and New Mexico, noted for blankets woven in distinctive geometric de-signs and for handmade silver jewelry set with turquoise—a classic fashion in the West, popular all over the country in late 1960's and early '70's. In early '70's the tribe also provided *tie-dyed* and *block-printed muslins, q.q.v.*

Neapolitan bonnet (nee-a-poll-i-tan) *Leghorn, q.v.,* bonnet, trimmed with straw flowers, with matching ribbons attached at the crown and loosely tied at chest; worn early 19th century. *Der.* Named for Naples, Italy, originally old Roman town Neapolis.

Neapolitan hat Sheer, lacy, horsehair-braid conical hat made in Naples; later, any hat made of this braid.

nebula headdress Variant of *coffer headdress, q.v.*

neckatee Mid 18th century term for *neckerchief;* see *kerchief* under *scarfs.*

neck button Decorative button worn at neck of *doublet, q.v.,* held by loop on opposite side, revealing the fine shirt underneath; worn in 17th century.

neck-chain Decorative gilded-brass or gold chain worn by men from medieval times to mid 17th century; sometimes worn by travelers in Middle Ages, who used few links of it for money. Also called *jack chain, q.v.*

neckcloth General term from mid 17th to mid 19th century for any type of man's neckwear or *cravat* wrapped around neck; previously, a *neckerchief* for women. See *ties* and *scarfs.*

necked bonnet Lined or unlined cap with wide flap fitted around back of neck, worn by men in first half of 16th century.

neckerchief See *kerchief* and *scarfs.*

neckerchief slide Ring of metal, plastic, fabric-covered metal, etc., used to hold *neckerchief* in place; *e.g.,* those used by Boy Scouts or cowboys.

neck handkerchief Synonym in 18th and 19th centuries for *necktie* or *cravat, q.q.v.*

necklace Glass beads, jewels, gold links or other small ornaments connected by a string or chain and worn around neck in single or multiple strands of various lengths; a kind of personal adornment worn since earliest times in all cultures, often a symbol of wealth and social status or worn for religious or superstitious reasons (see *scarab* and *utchat*). Some contemporary styles:

NECKLACES:

Afro choker Necklace made of strands of springy metal wound around neck many times. *Der.* Copied from necklaces worn by Ubangi tribe in Africa. Also called *Ubangi necklace.*

beaded n. See *Indian necklace.*

bib n. Necklace fitting close to base of neck and extending over the chest in the shape of child's bib, sometimes made of linked metal looking like short triangular scarf, sometimes made of several irregular strands of beads or chains arranged like a fringe.

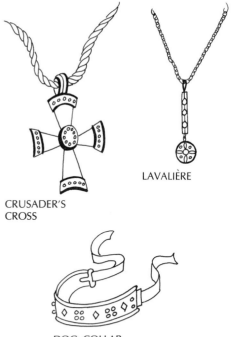

CRUSADER'S CROSS

LAVALIÈRE

DOG COLLAR

NECK RING

byzance Beads alternating with chain in long necklace with dangling ends similar to a rosary; created by Christian de Gasperi (nephew of former prime minister of Italy) and given this name by Pierre Cardin in 1968; popularized at St. Tropez, France.

choker Necklace fitting snugly

357

MEDALLION NECKLACE

around base of neck, may be one or more strands of beads, a suede or ribbon band, or a *dog collar, q.v.;* popular in 1930's and also in 1960's.

collar n. 1. Necklace shaped and fitted to neck like a collar, frequently of metal; popular in late 1960's. 2. Tiny beads interlaced to form separate collar.

crusader's cross Name given in 1960's to a large *Maltese cross, q.v.,* used as a pendant for necklace; also called *St. George cross.*

dog collar 1. Wide choker, similar to a dog's collar; often consisting of band of metal set with diamonds or rhinestones, popular in 1930's and again in 1960's; or of a band of colored suede or leather worn tightly around neck, popular in early 1970's.

hippie n. Beads, usually wooden or dyed seeds, strung on leather thongs; worn by *hippies, q.v.,* of both sexes in mid and late 1960's.

Indian n. 1. Long, flat necklace made with tiny glass beads of various colors, usually woven on small loom, made by American Indians or copied fron their patterns. 2. Necklace of tiny colored beads worked

in rope effect with American Indian motif as center pendant, also made by Indians or in their styles. Indian jewelry was popular in late 1960's and early 1970's.

lavalière Pendant, sometimes set with precious stones, worn as a necklace on a fine chain. *Der.* French, *lavallière,* a loosely-tied bow necktie named after Louise de la Vallière, mistress of Louis XIV of France.

lei Hawaiian garland of flowers or feathers, frequently orchids, worn around the neck; often presented to visitors on arrival in Hawaii.

locket Thin chain necklace with a gold or silver pendant opening to reveal picture of loved one or lock of hair; popular from mid 19th century to early 20th century.

love beads Simple strands of beads similar to *hippie necklace, q.v.,* worn by both male and female "flower people," a counter-culture youth movement of late 1960's.

matinee-length n. Bead necklace,, usually of pearls or simulated pearls, 30 to 35 inches long.

medallion n. Heavy chain necklace with large engraved disk as a pendant, worn by women during various eras and introduced for men in late 1960's, especially for wear with turtleneck shirts.

neck ring Single narrow band of springy metal worn as choker, sometimes with dangling ornament, snapping around the neck without a clasp; innovation of late 1960's.

opera-length n. Necklace of beads,

usually of pearls or simulated pearls, 48 to 128 inches long; usually worn wrapped twice around the neck; originated 1890's for wear to the opera or for other formal occasions.

pearls *Pearl beads, q.v., natural, cultured,* or *simulated, q.q.v.,* and all one size or graduated in size; usually strung on thread, often with a knot after each bead; made in a variety of lengths—see *choker, matinee, opera, rope*—and worn in single strands or combinations of strands. A classic fashion for many centuries.

pendant n. Ornament such as a locket, medallion, or single jewel suspended around neck from a chain, thong, or cord; worn since the Renaissance.

pop beads Plastic beads in various colors or simulating pearls, each with a round projection on side that fits into hole in next bead to form a chain; may be separated at any point to make necklace desired length. Original design, called Pop-pits, was widely copied in the early 1960's.

rope n. Extra-long beads, usually pearls, that may be wrapped around neck several times or worn long and knotted, very popular in 1920's and worn continuously since then.

rosary See *beads.*

St. George cross See *crusader's cross, above.*

sautoir (sow-twar) Pendant-type necklace with a dangling piece in front which may appear to be fringed at base. *Der.* French, wom-an's watch chain or a medal of honor worn around the neck.

throat belt Another name for *dog-collar* of 1960's.

Ubangi n. See *Afro choker,* above.

worry beads See *beads.*

neckline Shape of garment at or near the neck, or shape of top of garment above the bustline, varying in women's fashions from high, close band to low décolletage.

NECKLINES:

ascot n. High, round neckline with long scarf attached center back, brought around, and one end looped over other, ends hanging loosely; popular in late 1920's and in late 1960's. Also called *stock neckline.* Named for riding shirts worn in races on Ascot Heath in England.

band n. See *Chinese, mandarin,* and *Nehru* necklines.

bateau n. (bat-toe) Neckline cut in shallow curve across line of collar bones almost to tip of shoulders, the same across back of neck. *Der.* French, boat.

boat n. See *bateau.*

bow n. Strip of fabric attached around neckline, tied in a bow in front.

camisole n. Top of dress cut straight across above bust with straps over shoulders or cut in curve with built-up straps like a man's underwear. Also see *camisole.*

cardigan n. Plain, round, collarless neckline with center front opening, as on *cardigan sweaters.* See *Cardigan, 7th Earl of.*

SCOOP NECKLINE

DRAWSTRING
NECKLINE

V NECK WITH
DICKEY

NEHRU NECKLINE

Chanel n. (sha-nel) Collarless neckline similar to *cardigan* but with no fastening at front, frequently braid-trimmed; characteristic neckline of suits made by Gabrielle Chanel, French couturière. Also see *Chanel jacket,* under *jackets.*

Chinese n. Classic standing-band collar attached to garment, ends not quite meeting in front; adapted from Chinese *Mandarin court robes, q.v.*

choker n. Close band neckline rising to chin, sometimes vertically boned if in sheer fabrics, fastened in back; fashionable in blouses and evening gowns in Edwardian period (which was the first decade of 20th century), *e.g., Gibson Girl, q.v.,* shirtwaist, and revived in early 1970's.

Cossack n. Standing band, closing on one side, usually decorated with embroidery. *Der.* From shirts worn by Russian Cossacks.

cowl n. Bias-cut in one with garment or pieced on, falling in folds like a monk's *cowl, q.v.,* either in front or back or both; popular since Paris couturiere Vionnet introduced bias cutting in early 1920's.

crew n. Round neckline finished

360

with knit ribbing. *Der.* Named for neckline on crew-racing shirts.

dog-collar n. See *halter neckline.*

drawstring n. Neckline with cord threaded through a casing to be gathered and adjusted high or low, inspired by peasant styles; popular in late 1960's.

Florentine n. Wide neckline extending to shoulders, cut straight across front and back; inspired by Florentine paintings of Renaissance.

funnel n. High neckline cut in one with garment, made with shoulder seams slanted upward toward neck in shape of inverted funnel.

halter n. Sleeveless front of garment held by a strap around neck, leaving back and shoulders bare; may be gathered by a *drawstring* about neck, tied in a bow or held by a jeweled band as a *dog collar, q.v.*

Henley n. Round neckline with front placket opening, edged with ribbing. Named for crew-racing shirts worn at Henley, England.

horseshoe n. Scooped neckline, low in front, shaped like a horseshoe.

jewel n. High, round, faced neckline with no binding or collar, a simple background for jewels.

keyhole n. High round neckline with wedge-shaped or keyhole piece cut out at center front.

mandarin n. Same as *Chinese neckline, q.v.*

Nehru n. (nay-rue) Standing-band neckline similar to *Chinese* and *mandarin* necklines, sometimes with curved edges in front; popular in mid 1960's. *Der.* Named for Jawahar-lal Nehru, Prime Minister of India, 1947–64.

off-the-shoulder n. Neckline that falls below the shoulders but has sleeves or collar over arms.

one-shoulder n. Asymmetric neckline, starting under one arm and continuing diagonally over opposite shoulder leaving one shoulder bare: popular for evening dresses in 1940's and again late 1960's for swimsuits, evening dresses, and nightgowns. Also called *sling neckline.*

peasant n. See *drawstring neckline.*

rajah n. Variant of *Nehru neckline.*

scoop n. Low curved neckline, extending to shoulders or cut deep in front or back or both.

sling n. See *one-shoulder neckline.*

stock n. See *ascot neckline.*

strapless n. Boned or elastic bodice which requires no shoulders or straps; an innovation of the 1930's, popular for evening wear as well as sportswear, revived in 1970's.

surplice n. Neckline of wrap-around garment with one side lapping over other to form a V in center front.

sweetheart n. Low neckline with lower edge in front cut like top curves of a heart, revealing cleavage between breasts, sides cut straight up, back rounded; popular in 1930's, '40's, late 1950's and early 1960's.

tube n. Standing band of fabric extending upward from base of neck, similar to *turtleneck, q.v.,* but not turned over; innovation of late 1960's.

turtleneck See *turtleneck collar* under *collars.*

361

U n. Deeply scooped; see *horseshoe,* above.

V n. Cut down in front to a sharp point, like the letter V.

neckpiece *Boa* or *scarf, q.q.v.,* usually of fur.

neck ring See *necklaces.*

neck ruche Women's neckpiece of frilled mousseline pleated on ribbon or ruffled black tulle on silk foundation; very full, with long hanging streamers of silk or ribbon in front; worn in early 1900's.

neck stock Stiffly folded, made-up *cravat, q.v.,* buckled in back; worn by men in 18th and 19th centuries.

necktie or **tie** See *ties.*

necktie pin See *pins.*

neckwear Accessories worn around neck exclusive of jewelry, includes *neckties, scarfs,* and *collars.*

neck whisk 1. Small wired or stiffened fan-shaped man's sheer standing collar worn inside standing collar of the doublet in late 16th century. 2. Flat, round man's collar with pointed ends open in front; worn in Spain in 17th century.

needle Small, thin spike, usually of polished steel, with one end pointed and, at the other, an eye through which the thread is drawn for sewing; or a longer implement without an eye used for knitting or— when hooked at one end—for crocheting.

needle point, needle-point See embroideries, laces, stitches.

needle tapestry See *tapestry.*

needle toe See *toes of shoes.*

negligee costume (neh-glee-zheh) Informal costume, worn primarily in privacy of home or bedroom, usually a long easy robe of supple material, ranging from simple cotton to elaborately trimmed silk; worn by both men and women from 18th century through 19th century and developing into the *tea-gown, q.v.,* of early 20th century. Also see *banyan, robe, nightgown.* *Der.* French *négligée,* neglected, morning gown or wrapper.

negligee shirt Term used for a man's shirt, white or striped, with white stiff, separate collar and white cuffs; worn early 1900's to about 1925.

Nehru styles See *collars, necklines,* and *jackets.*

Nelson *Bustle, q.v.,* worn by women about 1819–20 to achieve the *Grecian bend, q.v.,* stance. Also called *frisk, q.v.*

net See *bobbinet.*

net embroidery See *tulle* under embroideries.

nether integuments See *unmentionables.*

nether stocks Same as *lower stocks, q.v.,* or stockings, worn by men and women in 16th century.

Newgate fringe Colloquial term in 19th century for men's short whiskers that formed a fringe around chin.

New Look Style introduced by couturier Christian Dior in Paris in 1947, characterized by almost ankle-length bouffant skirt, tiny waist, padded hips, sloping shoulder line, and fitted bodice—the extravagant opposite of restricted, short, skimpy woman's clothes worn—by law—during World War II.

Newmarket coat Man's long *tail coat,* single- or double-breasted, with front skirts cut away and rounded, often with flap pockets and cuffed sleeves; worn as a *riding coat* in 1880's and '90's. Also called Newmarket frock. *Der.* Named for racing center of Newmarket, England. See *cutaway* under *coats.*

Newmarket jacket Woman's close-fitting hip-length jacket with turned-down collar and silk-faced lapels, flapped pockets, and cuffed sleeves; frequently part of the "masculine" tailor-made fashion of 1890's.

Newmarket overcoat 1. Late 19th-century man's long single-breasted overcoat similar to a *frock overcoat, q.v.,* usually with velvet collar and cuffs and frequently made of *homespun, q.v.* 2. Late 19th-century woman's long single- or double-breasted winter coat with velvet collar, lapels, tight sleeves and cuffs, flapped pockets.

Newmarket top frock Man's overcoat of rough *Cheviot fabric, q.v.,* lower part lined with checked fabric, upper part with silk or satin; popular in 1895.

Newmarket vest Plaid or checked

NEWMARKET OVERCOAT, 1891

vest, buttoned high, worn by sportsmen in 1890's.

newsboy cap See *caps.*

New York Business Couture Group, Inc., The An organization of manufacturers of ready-to-wear clothing, serving as a trade council and mediating disputes between retailers and manufacturers; the promotional arm of this organization is called *The New York Couture Group* and is responsible for *National Press Week, q.v.*

neyge See *edge.*

niced See *nycette.*

nightcap 1. Plain washable cap worn in bed by men and women from 14th to 19th centuries, sometimes made like *stocking cap, q.v.,* of knitted silk with tassel on top. Also called a *jelly bag.* Also see *biggin.* 2. 18th century skullcap with upturned

NIGHTCAP, 1867

brim, worn indoors when wig was removed. 3. See *mobcap.*

night clothes See *nightgowns* and *nightshirts.*

night coif Woman's cap worn with *negligee costume, q.v.,* or in bed, frequently embroidered and usually worn with *forehead cloth, q.v.,* in 16th and 17th centuries.

nightgown 1. Contemporary word for loose garment worn by women and children for sleeping, usually of washable fabric in various lengths and weights, with or without sleeves, adapted to season; name sometimes shortened to *nightie.* 2. Also called *nightclothes, nightshirts,* and *nightshifts* when worn by men.

NIGHTGOWNS AND NIGHTSHIRTS:

baby doll Bouffant hip-length nightgown with short puffed sleeves, with matching bloomers; made of sheer fabrics; popular in 1940's and 50's.

granny gown High-necked, long sleeved, full-length gown with ruffle-trimmed yoke, no waistline seam, sometimes ruffled flounce at hem.

nightshift 1. Contemporary name for woman's simple nightgown. 2. Term used from 16th through 18th centuries for long shirt or *chemise, q.v.,* worn by men and women.

nightshirt Sleeping garment worn by both men and women, made like man's shirt, extending to calf of leg with hem rounded into slashes at side seams.

shortie Term for *mini-length* gown similar to *baby doll, q.v.*

sleep coat Woman's jacket-nightgown, cut like top of men's pajamas but usually to knee.

sleep shirt Variant of *nightshirt, q.v.*

toga n. Draped woman's gown designed to resemble a Roman *toga, q.v.,* sometimes with one shoulder exposed or with one or both sides split to waist or higher; worn 1960's.

waltz-length n. Mid-calf-length gown, popular in 1950's.

night-kercher 16th-century term for woman's *neckerchief* worn at night. See *kerchief* under *scarfs.*

night rail 1. Loose-fitting dress or robe made of plain drab fabric, worn in morning by women in Colonial America. 2. Woman's shoulder cape of lawn, silk, satin, or lace worn in 16th and 17th centuries, first as boudoir jacket, later for informal wear out-of-doors. Also spelled *night rayle.*

nightshift See *nightgowns, above.*

nightshirt See *nightgowns, above.*

nine-tenths coat See *lengths.*

ninon Transparent cloth. See *fabrics.*

Ninon coiffure Hairstyle with ringlet curls over the forehead, shoulder-lengths curls at sides, and back hair pulled into a knot; introduced in England in mid-17th century, style was later given this name after Anne de Lenclos (1620–1705), known as Ninon de Lenclos, a legendary courtesan and Parisian fashion leader.

non-woven fabric 1. Fabrics con-structed by means other than weaving, *e.g., braiding, knitting, felting, fusing, netting,* etc. 2. Fabrics made by interlocking or bonding of fibers by chemical, mechanical, thermal, or solvent methods and combinations. Methods include: *wet bonding, chemical bonding, spray bonding, extrusion bonding.*

Norell, Norman See *designers appendix, United States.*

Norfolk jacket See *sport jackets* under *jackets.*

Norfolk shirt Man's lounge jacket of rough tweed made with box pleat down center back and two pleats either side of front, collar and bands at wrists, styled like a shirt; worn in last half of 19th century and forerunner of *Norfok jacket, q.v.*

Norfolk suit 1. Little boy's suit with top styled like *Norfolk jacket* with two box pleats in front and back, belt at waist continuing under pleats; *knickerbocker* trousers to above knee, *Buster Brown collar, bow tie, q.q.v.,* and large off-the-face hat completed the costume; worn in early 1900's. 2. Man's suit with matching coat and pants, jacket styled in Norfolk manner, worn from about 1912 to about 1930. See *Norfolk jacket* in *sport jackets* under *jackets.*

Norfolk suiting See *fabrics.*

Normandie cape Lightweight, hip-length woman's cape with a yoke, ruffles extended down center front, around the hem, sometimes around

1914   1905

NORFOLK SUIT

yoke; standing collar or a double-tiered ruff; worn in late 1890's.

Northamptonshire lace See *laces.*

Norwegian morning cap Woman's cerise-and-white striped Shetland wool knitted kerchief-shaped head covering, ribbon tied under the chin and trimmed with bows over crown and back of the head; worn in 1860's. Also called *Norwegian morning bonnet.*

nouch See *ouch.*

novelty yarn Yarns made of more than one color or with a nub, a slub, a loop, or some other variation. See *bouclé, chenille, nub, slub,* and *ratine* under *yarns.*

nub yarn See *yarns.*

nude bra See *brassieres.*

numbered duck System of grading weights of *duck* fabric with numbers from 1 to 12. See *duck* under *fabrics.*

numeral shirt See *knit shirts* under *shirts*.

nun's habit Garments worn by nuns, women members of convents of the church, dating from Middle Ages, usually a covered-up ankle-length black dress, often with white collar, belted by long cord; head and neck wrapped in starched white cotton like a *wimple, q.v.,* shape varying with the convent, often covered by long black *veil;* many changes have been made in Roman Catholic nun's habits since 1965, such as simpler headdresses, shorter skirts, brown, navy, gray added to black, etc.

nun's veiling See *fabrics.*

Nureyev shirt See *shirts.*

nurse's cap See *caps.*

nurse's cape See *capes.*

nutria See *furs.*

nycette Late 15th and early 16th-century term for light scarf worn at neck. Also called *niced.*

nylon 1. Generic term for a man-made fiber made of long chain of synthetic polyamides extracted from coal and petroleum, introduced in 1939 by DuPont and later produced by other manufacturers; qualities include silky hand, strength, crease resistance, washability, and resistance to mildew and moths. Yarns used in knitted and woven fabrics for hosiery, dresses, gloves, nightgowns, shoes, etc. 2. Plural, synonymous with women's *hosiery.*

O

oatmeal See *fabrics.*

obi (o-bee) Sash approximately fifteen inches wide and four to six yards long, worn by Japanese brides and unmarried women on top of *kimono, q.v.,* folded lengthwise with fold toward hem, wrapped twice around waist and tied in flat butterfly bow in back. Sometimes spelled *obe.* See *heko-obi, kaku-obi* and *obiage.* Also see *belts.*

obiage (o-be-ege) Small pad that supports upper loop of *obi, q.v.,* or sash, worn over the kimono by Japanese women, held by silk cord tied in front.

obi hat Woman's hat with high flat-topped crown, narrow brim rolled up in front, with ribbons coming over crown and brim of hat and tied under chin, worn in early 19th century.

oblong hoops British term for *panniers, q.v.,* on women's gowns, projecting sideways over hips, flattened front and back, sometimes hinged to permit passage through narrow doorways. Also called *square hoops.*

ocelot See *furs.*

ocher, ochre (o-ker) Earthy yellow or reddish-yellow color of a clay containing iron ore.

octagonal hat Cap shaped like a *tam, q.v.,* made of wedges stitched together to form the crown. Sometimes made of two contrasting fabrics and usually trimmed with

two short hanging streamers; popular for girls and young women in mid 1890's.

octagon tie Made-up scarf or *cravat, q.v.,* with long wide piece of fabric folded to form an X in front, attached to narrow band fastening at back of neck with hook and eye; worn by men from 1860's on.

odhnis Head *veil* worn by women of India when *sari, q.v.,* is not pulled over head.

oegge Same as *edge, q.v.*

officer collar Fur band worn around neck in late 19th century.

officer's cap See *army service cap* under *caps.*

officer's cape See *capes.*

officer's coat See *coats.*

off the peg English expression for buying ready-made clothes from retail stores rather than custom-made clothing.

off-the-shoulder See *necklines.*

Ognibene-Zendman See *designers appendix, Italy.*

oiled silk Transparent waterproof silk. See *fabrics.*

oilet (oy-let) Term for *eyelet, q.v.,* used in 18th and 19th centuries.

oilskin Waterproof cotton. See *fabrics.*

oilskins Raincoats, jackets, hats, made of *oilskin, q.v.,* worn by fishermen and sailors and adapted for sportswear.

oker 16th–century term for boot worn by ploughmen. Also called *hogger, hoker,* or *cocker.*

old rose Dull rosy-pink color, with a grayish cast.

olefin Generic term for a man-made fiber made from petroleum by-products, used for women's knitted underwear and hosiery.

olive button Long oval-shaped, silk-covered button; worn from mid 18th century on.

Oliver, André See *designers appendix, France.*

olivette Oval-shaped button used with *Brandenburgs, q.v.,* same as *frog button.*

ombré (om-bray) Closely related tones of color shading from light to dark, either gradations of single color, e.g., pale pink to red, or as in rainbow; often used for silk chiffons. *Der.* French, shaded.

ondulé Wavy-surfaced. See *fabrics.*

one-hundred-denier crepe See *fabrics.*

one-piece pump See *pumps* under *shoes.*

one-piece bathing suit See *maillot* under *swimsuits.*

one-shoulder neckline See *necklines, dresses* and *toga* under *nightgowns.*

one-size bra See *stretch bra* under *brassieres.*

onyx See *gems.*

ooryzer Native helmet made of piece of gold fitted to head, worn under low cap by Frisian women in the Netherlands. Two caps worn underneath and lace cap placed over top toward back of head showing gold in front.

opal See *gems.*

opaque hose See *hose* and *pantyhose.*

open-back shoe See *sling-back* under *shoes.*

open-crown hat See *hats.*

open robe Term used in 19th century for dress with *overskirt* split in front revealing an ornamental *underskirt, q.q.v.,* fashionable mainly for daytime and evening wear in 1830's and 40's.

open-shank See *open-shank* under *sandals* and under *shoes.*

open-toed or **open-heeled shoe** See *shoes.*

open-welt seam See *seams.*

openwork Knitting, weaving, or embroidery in which threads are used in such a manner that holes in work give lacy effect. See *embroideries.*

opera cape See *capes.*

opera glasses See *glasses.*

opera glove See *gloves.*

opera hat See *hats.*

opera length See *necklaces.*

opera pump See *shoes.*

opera slipper See *slippers.*

opera wrap Term used in early 1900's for women's *opera cape, q.v.;* usually of elaborate fabric trimmed with fur or feathers; see drawing, opposite.

opossum See *furs.*

opus araneum See *antique* under *laces.*

oralia (o-ray-lee-a) Early Medieval term for *veil, q.v.;* by first quarter of 14th century, known as *cornalia* or *cornu.* Also spelled *orales. Der.* Latin, veil.

Orcel, Gilbert See *designers appendix, France.*

oreilles de chien (or-ray de she-en)

OPERA WRAP, 1900

Nickname for two long curls worn at either side of face by men from 1790–1800. *Der.* French, dog's ears.

organdy or **organdie** Stiff sheer cotton. See *fabrics*.

organza Crisp sheer rayon. See *fabrics*.

Oriental pearls See *pearl* under *gems* and *beads*.

Oriental stitch See *stitches*.

orle Variant of *ourle*, q.v.

Orlon Trademark owned by DuPont given to group of acrylic fibers known by various numbers and trademarks and designed for various end uses, e.g. Type 21 used for bulky knits, Type 27 used for fine-gauge knit sweaters; Orlon has soft hand similar to wool, good drapability,

and resistance to sunlight and gases. Used extensively for socks and sweaters.

O'Rossen See *designers appendix, France.*

orphrey (or-free) Y-shaped band of embroidery decorating the *chasuble, q.v.,* an ecclesiastical garment, extending from shoulders, meeting vertical stripe in center front or back. A medieval design copied in modern coats and dresses. Also spelled *orfray, orfrey, orfry.*

orrelet (or-let) Term used in latter half of 16th century for hanging side pieces of *woman's coif, q.v.,* that covered ears. Also called *cheeks and ears.* Also spelled *oreillett, oreillette* and *oriylet.*

orris or **orrice lace** See *laces.*

Orsay, Compte d' Compte Alfred Guillaume Gabriel (1801–1852). French society leader in Paris and London, in the time of William IV, a *dandy, q.v.,* or *arbiter elegantiarum* of fashion; described as a wit, a sculptor, and a conversationalist, he attempted to take *Beau Brummell's, q.v.,* place. See entries under *D'Orsay, shoes,* and *slippers.*

Osbaldiston tie (os-bald-stun) Necktie tied in front with a large barrel-shaped knot, worn by men in early 19th century. Also called *barrel-knot tie.*

Osnaburg Coarse cotton sheeting. See *fabrics.*

osprey See *feathers.*

ostrich See *feathers* and *leathers.*

otter See *furs.*

ottoman Lustrous ribbed cloth. See *fabrics*.

ottoman knit See *knits*.

ouch Term used from 13th to 15th centuries for a collection of jewels or a jeweled clasp or buckle. Also spelled *nouch*.

ourle Term used in 13th and 14th centuries for a fur border. Later spelled *orle*.

outing cloth See *outing flannel* under *fabrics*.

outing flannel Fuzzy-surfaced cotton. See *fabrics*.

outline stitch See *stitches*.

outseam See *seams*.

oval ruff Woman's large plain ruff, oval shaped rather than round, made

with large *pipe-organ pleats, q.v.;* worn about 1625–1650.

oval toe See *toes of shoes*.

overalls See *pants*.

overblouse See *blouses*.

overblouse bathing suit See *swimsuits*.

overboot Crocheted or fabric woman's boot worn over the shoes for warmth in carriages; worn in 1860's.

overcast See *seams* and *stitches*.

overcheck See *overplaid*.

overcoat See *coats*.

overdress 1. Term used in 1870's for a hip-length bodice worn with a separate skirt. Some were formal in style with low-cut neckline, peplum, and fancy decorative trim of lace and ribbons. 2. Transparent dress constructed with an attached opaque *underdress*. See *cage* under *dresses*.

overlapped seam See *seams*.

overlay In the shoe industry, a piece of leather or other material stitched on shoe in decorative manner, usually of contrasting color or a textured leather such as lizard, snakeskin, etc.

overplaid Textile design that combines a very large-scale crossbar with a regular-sized plaid, as in some Scottish *tartans, q.v.*

overprint See *prints*.

overseas cap See *army* under *caps*.

overshoe Waterproof fabric or rubber shoe, worn over other shoes in wet weather. See *Arctics* also *galoshes* under *boots*.

overskirt See *skirts*.

over-the-knee socks See *socks*.

owl glasses See *sunglasses* under *glasses*.

oxford See *shoes*.

Oxford bags See *pants*.

Oxford button-overs Men's shoes covering instep and closed with buttons instead of laces; worn in 1860's.

Oxford cap Same as *mortarboard, q.v.*

oxford cloth See *fabrics*.

Oxford coatee See *Oxonian jacket*.

Oxford gloves Perfumed gloves worn

from mid 16th to mid 17th centuries, scented with Earl of Oxford's favorite perfume.

Oxford-gray (or **grey**) **yarn** Mixture yarn, of wool or man-made fibers, approximately 5 to 20 per cent white fibers, the remainder black, mixed together to produce dark-gray mottled effect.

Oxford mixture See *Oxford-gray yarn,* above.

Oxford tie Straight, narrow necktie, worn in 1890's by men with informal lounge suit and by women with shirtwaist.

Oxonian boots Man's short black boots, often of patent leather, with wedge-shaped portion cut out of either side at top so they pull on easily; worn in 1830's and 1840's. Also called *Oxonians* or *collegians.*

Oxonian jacket Two- or three-button single-breasted tweed jacket with many pockets and a back shaped with three seams; worn by men in 1850's and again in 1960's. Also called *jumper* or *Oxford coatee.*

ozu aya Trade term in Japan for cotton *jean* fabric, *q.v.*

371

P

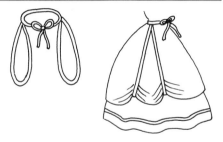

paboudj See *babuche.*

padding Any stuffing material used between two layers of fabric or leather to round out a section of clothing or an accessory, e.g. 1. Horsehair, in 16th century, for man's *busk* and for *bombasted hose, q.q.v.,* or, in latter part of 19th century, *false calves, q.v.* 2. In contemporary times, padding is used mostly for warmth, in the form of *quilting,* or for shaping in *brassieres, q.q.v.* See *shoulders.*

padding stitch See *stitches.*

paddock English coating. See *fabrics.*

paddock coat Man's long semi-fitted single- or double-breasted *overcoat* with fly-front closing, large pockets, and pleat-covered back vent: worn from end of 19th century on.

padre hat (pad-ray) See *hats.*

paejamas Pants worn by Moslem men in Persia and India, Either: (a) tight-fitting to ankles, or (b) very full at waist and knees and tight at lower leg, resembling cut of *jodhpurs, q.v. Der.* Hindu words *pae,* meaning leg, and *jamah,* meaning garment. See *pajamas.*

paenula (pie-new-la) Hooded *cape* or *poncho*-shaped, *q.q.v.,* garment worn by ancient Romans for traveling or inclement weather, made of heavy woolen fabric or leather. Also called *casula.*

page Belt with loop or clip on either side, used to loop up *overskirt, q.v.,* of dress; worn from 1850 to 1867.

page-boy bob See *hairstyles.*

pagne (panye) Tight wrap-around *skirt* or *loincloth* draped at right side, made of handwoven cotton in striped, chevron, or other designs; worn in Guinea and in the Belgian Congo and other parts of Africa.

pagoda sleeve 1. Man's coat sleeve with cuff reaching to elbow and tapered to wrist; worn in early 18th century. 2. Funnel-shaped woman's sleeve, flaring from elbow to wrist, showing the undersleeve, or *engageantes, q.v.,* sometimes slashed on outer seam nearly to the shoulder; worn from late 1840's to 1880's. Also called *funnel sleeve.* 3. See *sleeves.*

pagri East Indian turban divided into two types; (a) short—made from a strip of fabric 20 to 30 inches wide and from 6 to 9 yards long, (b) long—made from fabric 6 to 8 inches wide and varying from 10 to 50 yards long. The color, fabric designs, and method of wrapping are used to indicate rank, prestige, and other information about the wearer. Also called *pugree, puggree.*

pa-hom Length of fabric wound around the body with end thrown over left shoulder to form a dress, worn by Siamese women of lower classes.

pah-poosh Velvet slippers decorated with embroidery and with high heels studded with jewels; worn indoors by Persian women. See *papush.*

paille Yellowish straw color. *Der.* French, straw.

paillette (pai-yet) Spangle made of metal or plastic, usually a round disk larger than a sequin, used as trimming on evening clothes and bags. See *sequin. Der.* French, speck or spangle.

pais-a-gwn bach Welsh native dress consisting of tight-fitting *bodice,* an *overskirt* turned back to show striped *petticoat,* and full *apron;* worn as part of the *Eisteddfod costume, q.v. Der.* Welsh *pais,* country or people, and gwn, dress.

paisley print (paze-lee) See *prints.*

Paisley shawl Worsted shawl of fine quality, either large square or oblong, sometimes woven double with different pattern each side; very popular in 19th century.

pajamas or **pyjamas** 1. Sleeping or lounging garment, for men, women, or children, with pants legs joined to top in one piece or in two pieces; the top either tailored *coat style* buttoned-down front, back-buttoned *smock,* or *pullover;* the pants in various lengths and widths; worn also by women for beach and evening in variety of fabrics since 1920's. Also called *p.j's.* 2. Originally pants worn by men in Persia and India. *Der.* Hindu, *pae,* leg, and *jamah,* garment.

PAJAMAS:

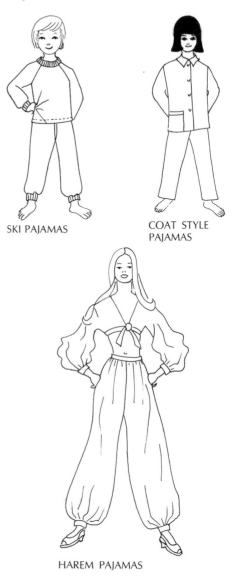

SKI PAJAMAS

COAT STYLE PAJAMAS

HAREM PAJAMAS

blanket sleepers Children's winter pajamas, two-piece or in one piece with front buttoned or zippered, made of napped fabric similar to that used for blankets.

bunny suit See *Dr. Denton.*

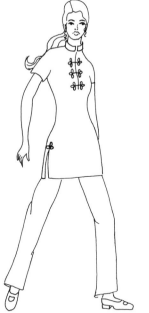

CHINESE PAJAMAS

Chinese p. Hip- or thigh-length jacket with side seams slashed to waist, *mandarin collar, q.v.,* closing — sometimes diagonal — with frogs; worn with straight-legged pants. Derived from work garments worn in China by men and women.

Cossack p. Pants plus tunic top closing at side front with standing-band collar; popular in 1930's and late 1960's.

culotte p. Floor-length pajamas with wide legs, resembling a long dress; worn for dining in mid and late 1960's and early 1970's. See *culotte.*

Dr. Denton Sleepers Tradename for one-piece knitted pajama with covered feet, buttoned down the front, with buttoned *drop seat, q.v.;* introduced in 1895, originally worn by children. Similar styles

are now produced for adults also and called *bunny suits.*

footed p. One- or two-piece child's sleeping garment with slipper-like coverings for the feet attached; soles often of non-skid plastics.

harem p. Very full trousers gathered at ankle, which may be paired with *tunic* or Oriental *bolero;* fashionable for at-home wear in late 1960's.

jumpsuit p. Fitted pajamas in one piece, usually buttoned or zippered up center front; similar to *bunny suit,* lacking feet.

karate p. Man's two-piece pajamas styled like a *karate costume, q.v.,* worn in late 1960's and early 1970's.

p.j.'s Abbreviation for *pajamas.*

ski p. Warm two-piece pajamas of cotton knit or cotton flannel with round-necked pullover top and full legs, rib-knit cuffs at wrists and ankles.

Pakistani vest See *vests.*

palatine, pallatine (pal-a-teen) 1. Woman's small fur or lace shoulder cape, sometimes hooded, introduced about 1676, formerly called *sable tippet.* 2. Woman's neck *tippet, q.v.,* with long ends reaching below waist and a quilted hood. Also called *Victorine, q.v.*

palazzo pajamas or **pants** See *pants.*

paletot (pal-e-toe or pal-tow) Term for variety of coat styles for men and women from 1830's to end of century. For women: 1. Close-fitting jacket with wide cuffed sleeves and *Watteau back, q.v.,* made in different material from

375

rest of costume: worn latter half of 19th century. Also called *yachting jacket, q.v.* 2. Three-quarter or long fitted princess coat with buttoned front, revers, hanging sleeves or circular capes, called *paletot-redingote* or *paletot mantle,* worn in late 19th century. For men: 1. short, loose overcoat, sometimes with side pleats or back vent. 2. Hip-length cape, single or double-breasted with armhole slits or cloak with three capes, called *paletot-cloak.* 3. Short straight coat, sometimes with collar or hood, called *paletot-sac.* All worn in mid 19th century.

palisade Wire framework worn by women to support the *Fontanges headdress, q.v.* from 1690 to 1710. Same as *commode, q.v.*

palla Shawl-like ancient Roman woman's garment resembling Greek *himation, q.v.,* made from rectangle of fabric, worn draped around body, sometimes with one end draped over head.

pallatine See *palatine.*

pallium Rectangular shawl worn by men in ancient Rome. See *stole* and *himation.*

Palm Beach See *fabrics.*

palmering Finish applied to taffetas, twills, and satins to give smooth hand by inserting fabric between two layers of felt and pressing with steam-heated roller.

Palmerston wrapper Man's single-breasted, loose-fitting sac overcoat with wide collar and lapels, sleeves full at wrists with no cuffs, pockets with side flaps; worn in mid 1850's. *Der.* Named after British statesman 3rd Viscount Palmerston, Henry John Temple, who was Prime Minister between 1855 and 1865.

palmetto Name used for a variety of fibers obtained from the cabbage-palm leaves, grown along south Atlantic coast, in the Bahamas, Cuba, and Mexico; used for hats and baskets.

paltock (pal-tock) Man's short outer jacket similar to the *doublet, q.v.,* to which the hose were fastened by means of *points, q.v.;* worn from 14th to mid 15th centuries. Also called *pourpoint, q.v.*

Pamela bonnet Straw bonnet, with small flat crown, U-shaped brim around face coming down over ears and ending in back, trimmed with ribbons and flowers; worn in mid 19th century. *Der.* Named after novel by Samuel Richardson called *Pamela: or Virtue Rewarded.* Also called *Pamela hat.*

panache (pa-nash) Plume or erect bunch of feathers worn on hat, originally on military helmets.

Panama hat See *hats.* Also see *Panama straw,* under *straw.*

Panama suiting Summer menswear suiting. See *fabrics.*

pancake beret See *caps.*

Pandoras Variant of *fashion babies, q.v.*

panel pants-dress Pants-dress with free-hanging panel front and back giving a skirt effect. See *pants-dress* under *dresses.*

panel print See *prints*.

panes Term used for series of vertical slashes in a garment, e.g., hose, doublet, or sleeves, with the contrasting lining pulled out through slashes; popular 1500 to 1650's.

panne satin Heavy dress satin. See *fabrics*.

panne velvet Velvet with flattened pile. See *fabrics*.

pannier crinoline Underskirt for extending the dress which combined a *cage crinoline petticoat* with a *bustle, q.q.v.,* worn in late 19th century. Also called *Thomson's pannier crinoline.*

pannier curls See *curls*.

PANNIER DRAPE, 1919

pannier drape (pan-yehr) 1. See *panniers*. 2. Puff formed over hip by looping up outerskirt, in late 1860's. 3. In 1880's, fullness or drapery on hips made by an extra piece of fabric attached to bodice or waistline draped over hips and remainder pulled to the back in *polonaise* style, *q.v.* 4. In World War I era, drapery over hips sometimes made in *tunic* effect sometimes cut as part of the dress to give *peg-top* look, *q.q.v.*

panniers or **paniers** (pan-ee-yay) Framework of wire, bone, cane, etc., used to expand a woman's skirt on either side at hips, popular in pre-Revolution France in various forms. *Der.* French, baskets—such as those carried on either side of a horse for provisions. 1. *Paniers anglais,* English style, (awn-glehze): hoop petticoat, either square or oblong. 2. *Paniers a bourrelet,* with cushion, (ah boor-e-lay): Hoop petticoat with thick roll at hem to make a flared skirt. 3. *Paniers à coudes,* at elbows (kood): Hoops extended wide at side and narrow from front to back to allow elbows to rest. 4. *Paniers en coupole,* domed (on ku-pole): Dome-shaped hoops. 5. *Paniers en gueridon,* table or pedestal (gehr-ee-don): Large round hoops fastened with strips of tape. For other types of *panniers* see *considérations, criardes, false hips, oblong hoops.*

pantalettes, pantalets 1. Women's and girls' underpants with long straight legs to or below the knee, ending in ruffles, tucks, or embroidery, usually showing below the dress for girls and worn from early 1800's to 1865; woman's version of *pantaloons, q.v.* See *pants.*

pantaloons (pant-a-loons) One kind of *trousers, q.v.* 1. Man's close-fitting garment for hips and legs, sometimes ending below calf or to ankles with strap under instep; worn starting after the French Revolution in late 18th century through 19th century. 2. Man's pants, tight-fitting to calf, loose from there to ankle, sometimes cut out over instep and called *pantaloon trousers.* See *breeches, trunk hose.* 3. Women's long, straight underpants; worn in first half of 19th century. Also called *drawers, pantalettes, q.q.v.*

panties Shortened name for women's and children's underpants: garments worn under outer clothing covering torso below the waist. See *drawers* and *pantyhose.*

PANTIES AND UNDERPANTS:

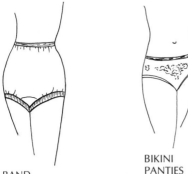

BAND BRIEFS

BIKINI PANTIES

band briefs Short panties finished at legs with knitted bands. Also called band-leg panties.

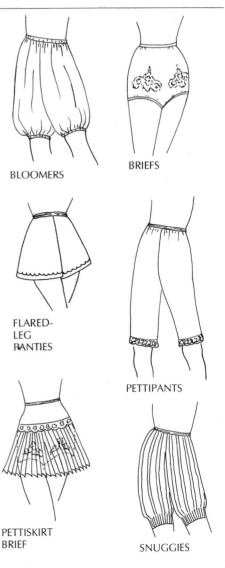

BLOOMERS

BRIEFS

FLARED-LEG PANTIES

PETTIPANTS

PETTISKIRT BRIEF

SNUGGIES

bikini p. Below-the-navel brief panties introduced in early 1960's, modeled after *bikini* bathing suit, *q.v.*

bloomers Full panty with thigh-length leg gathered into elastic, popular since 1920's for little girls, and worn by older women from 1930's to present. Named for Amelia Jenks Bloomer, early 19th century American dress reformer who wore full gathered pants instead of a skirt.

boxer p. Women's and children's loose-legged panties styled like men's boxer shorts. See *shorts.*

briefs 1. Woman's or girl's very short panties, sometimes of controlling stretch fabric with garters added. 2. Tight-fitting short knitted underpants worn by men and boys.

drawers Cotton-knit ankle or knee-length fitted underpants worn for warmth, introduced for men in 16th century and for women in early 19th century. Also see *umbrella drawers* and *tights.*

flared-leg p. Woman's short underpants with hemmed, unbanded legs, flared at the hip.

garter briefs Short panties with attached supporters to hold up stockings.

hip-huggers Low-slung panties starting at hip-bone level, to be worn with hip-hugger pants and bare-midriff dresses.

pants liner Tight-fitting control panties coming over the knee to the calf or the ankle, worn under pants for sleek fit.

petti-culotte Slip and panties combined in one garment having flared legs and inverted pleat in center front and back; frequently lace-trimmed.

pettipants Long, dress-length panties made of bright-colored or printed knits with ruffles and lace trimming; introduced in late 1950's.

pettiskirt brief Combination petticoat and short panties joined by elastic waistband. Also called pantyskirt when petticoat is combined with bloomers.

rumba p. Little girls' panties with several rows of ruffles across the seat.

Snuggies Knee-length or over-the-knee panties made of knitted cotton or wool; worn, for warmth, with matching tank-top undershirt.

step-ins Woman's bias-cut underpants with widely flared legs and narrow crotch; popular in 1920's and '30's.

tights 1. Underpants and stockings knit in one piece, worn originally by athletes, circus performers, dancers in late 19th century with *leotard, q.v.;* now worn by women and children in variety of textured cotton, nylon, or wool knits in many colors for all occasions. 2. A *leotard, q.v.,* with legs and sometimes feet added. Also see *pantyhose.*

pantile Term used for the *sugar-loaf hat, q.v.,* popular from 1640's to 1665 for men and women.

pantofle (pan-tof-l) 1. Slipper worn from 15th century to mid 17th century by men and women. 2. Overshoe, similar to a *patten, q.v.,* with a cork sole, worn in 16th century. Also spelled *pantables, pantacles,* etc. 3. Term used for bedroom slippers in Germany until 1930. *Der.* French *pantoufle,* slipper.

pants Garment enclosing hips and legs between waist and ankles, either form-fitting or loose; worn by men and women from ancient times but mostly by men through 19th century. Now a 20th-century universal garment for women and men, used for sleeping, sports, town wear, and evening. Men's pants are closed with a *fly, q.v.,* usually zippered; women's may have placket in front, side, or back, or be *pull-ons* with an elasticized waistline. Men's pants are sized by waist measure and *inseam, q.v.,* measure; women's are sized like dresses (see *juniors, misses,* etc.) often in proportioned lengths for several heights. Also called *trousers, slacks, shorts, breeches, pantaloons, knickerbockers, bloomers, q.q.v.* Also see *chaussembles, trunk hose,* and *braccae.*

PANTS AND TROUSERS:

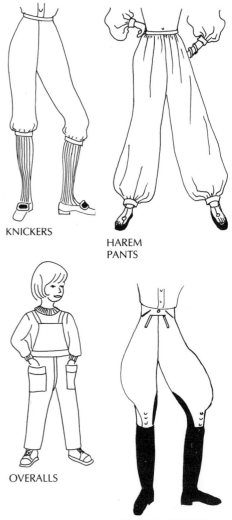

KNICKERS

HAREM PANTS

OVERALLS

RIDING BREECHES

HIP-HUGGERS

JODHPURS

bell-bottom trousers 1. Traditional white or navy-blue trousers worn by seamen in U.S. Navy, cut wide at the hem to facilitate rolling up for deck work; also see *sailor pants.* 2. Pants cut flared from knee down to give a bell shape at the hem; worn by young people in 1960's and early 1970's. Also called *flares, q.v.,* in late 1960's.

bloomers 1. See *panties.* 2. Black sateen full pleated pants gathered by elastic at knees; worn by wom-

380

PALAZZO
PANTS

SAILOR PANTS

WESTERN
PANTS

KNICKERS

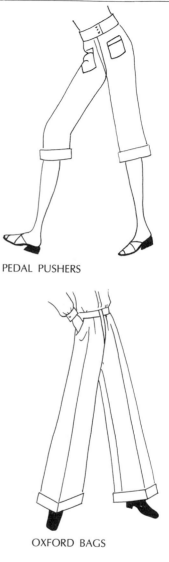

PEDAL PUSHERS

OXFORD BAGS

en from early 20th century to late 1920's as part of a gym suit. *Der.* From long gathered-above-ankle trousers designed by and named for *Amelia Jenks Bloomer, q.v.,* in 1851.

blue jeans 1. Ankle-length tight-fitting pants, made of *blue* or *indigo denim, q.v.,* with V-shaped hip yoke in back; front slash pockets, hip patch pockets; all seams *flat-felled,* usually with contrasting red-orange thread, and points of strain reinforced by copper rivets; originally work pants for cowboys and other laboring men, adopted by children and young people from

GAUCHO PANTS   FLARES   CULOTTES

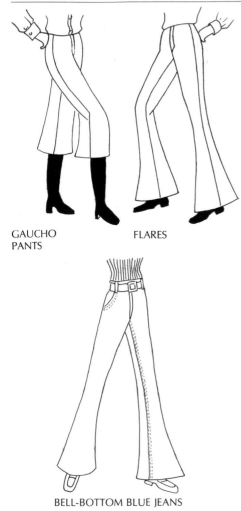

BELL-BOTTOM BLUE JEANS

1930's on; a fad with youth counter-culture in 1950's and—made with bell bottoms—into the 1970's. See *Levi's* and *Western pants.* 2. Same cut made in a wide variety of fabrics including striped denim, bleached or tie-dyed denim or muslin, printed fabrics, suede, corduroy, and velvet. *Der.* Named for *jean* fabric from which originally made.

Also called *dungarees, Levi's, q.q.v.,* and *dude jeans.*

boot p. Pants styled like riding breeches; worn with high boots by men and women in late 1960's and early 1970's.

breeches See *knickerbockers*

Capri p. Woman's tight-fitting pants with very narrow tapered legs, often with short slit at outside of ankle to aid in getting them over the feet; very popular in late 1950's in bright colors, prints, luxury fabrics. *Der.* Named for Italian resort island of Capri, where style first became popular.

chaps Leather or shearling covering for front part of legs, worn over pants for protection by cowboys, adapted in fur by women in late 1960's as novelty.

charro p. Wide Mexican-inspired pants in midi length, similar to *gaucho pants, q.v. Der.* From Mexican, rancher.

chinos Washable men's sport pants made of *chino cloth, q.v.,* a durable close-woven khaki-colored cotton fabric; popular in 1950's for sportswear and for school wear in early 1960's. *Der.* Adapted from Army summer uniforms made of fabric that originally was purchased in China before World War I.

choori-dars Pants with full-cut top and tight-fitting legs which are extra long and worn rumpled from knee down; worn in India.

CityPants Term coined by clothing-industry newspaper *Women's Wear Daily* in 1968 for women's trousers considered suitable for wear in town instead of at home or for sportswear.

clam diggers Snug-fitting calf-length pants, originating from cut-off *blue jeans, q.v.,* worn while wading to dig for clams and adopted for sportswear in 1950's.

Continental p. Men's narrow trousers made without the traditional set-on waistband or belt loops; front pockets placed horizontally, or curved, rather than in the side seam; style originating in Italy in mid 1950's.

coveralls See *jumpsuits.*

crawlers Long pants for infants and toddlers in sizes 1 to 3, made of durable fabrics, such as *corduroy,* and with *suspender* straps attached; often made in *overall* style, *q.q.v.*

cuffed trousers See *pre-cuffed trousers.*

culottes (koo-lots) 1. Women's pants of any length cut to look like a skirt, e.g., a divided skirt, worn from 1930's to 1940's and again in 1960's; sometimes cut in one with the top and called *culotte dress* or *culotte pajamas.* 2. Trousers that resembled a full skirt worn in 1660's and 1670's called *petticoat breeches, q.v. Der.* French from Latin *culus* meaning buttock, term first used for *breeches, etc.,* in reign of Henry III of France in late 16th century.

cut-offs See *shorts.*

deck p. Fitted pants ending just below the knee; worn by men, women and children particularly on boats in late 1950's and early '60's.

downhill p. Pants worn by skiers, closely fitted and tapered to the ankle, with straps under the arches of the feet to keep pants down inside the boots; often made of stretch fabrics.

dude jeans Similar to *Western pants, q.v.*

dungarees Sailors' work pants named for the coarse blue fabric from which they are made. See *blue jeans* and *fabrics.*

elephant-leg p. Long trousers with extremely full legs, sometimes cuffed, covering the shoes; introduced in late 1960's.

fatigues 1. Pants of tough blue-denim fabric, worn by United States army men for work details; also called *field pants.* 2. Coveralls for work worn by Army men and WACS during World War II; sometimes in olive drab or camouflage colors.

flannels Men's *trousers,* not part of a suit, made of *flannel, q.v.; white flannels* popular in early 20th century for sportswear and golf, continuing in popularity for resort wear, especially with a *blazer, q.v.,* and revived for city wear in early 1970's; gray flannels, in light and *Oxford-gray, q.v.,* shades, worn with tweed *sports coats, q.v.,* popular in 1950's.

flares *Bell-bottoms, q.v.,* with exaggeratedly wide bottoms, worn very long; popular in late 1960's, early '70's.

frontier pants See *Western pants.*

gaucho p. Wide calf-length women's pants, frequently of leather, copied from pants worn by Spanish as a part of Andalusian riding suit and adapted by South American cowboys; a fashion in the late 1960's. *Der.* South American word for cowboy.

harem knickers Knee-length bouffant *harem pants* similar to bloomers, introduced in late 1960's.

harem p. Bouffant pants gathered into bands at the ankles, copied from Near Eastern styles, popular at-home fashion of late 1960's. Also see *shalwar.*

Harlow p. Trousers wide from hips to hem, introduced in late 1960's and copied from slacks worn in 1930's by *Jean Harlow, q.v.*

hip-huggers Low-slung pants of any style starting below the normal waistline, usually with belt resting on hip-bones; popularized in mid 1960's. Also called *hipsters* and *low-slung pants.*

hipsters See *hip-huggers.*

hot pants, HotPants See *shorts.*

hunt breeches Riding breeches with *drop front, q.v.,* legs cut wide at thighs and hips and tight at knees; usually made in *canary* or tan *cavalry twill, q.v.,* with buckskin patches at inside of knee.

Ivy League p. Man's trousers with skinny legs, usually without cuffs, cut short at ankle; first worn by college men in the Ivy League, *q.v.,* and very popular for general wear in 1950's.

Jamaicas See *shorts.*

jeans 1. See *blue jeans.* 2. Originally, pants made of *jean* fabric, *q.v.;* worn by sailors since 1810.

jockey p. *Breeches* with *drop front, q.v.,* and *jodhpur*-type legs, tucked into boots; worn by jockeys in horse races.

jodhpurs Riding pants, with *drop-front* or zipper closing, that flare at thighs and have narrow straight-cut legs below knee, cuffs at ankles; similar to men's breeches worn in India and popular for men and women horseback riders since 1920's. *Der.* Jodhpur, city in India.

knee p. See *knickerbockers* and *breeches.*

knickerbockers Knee pants, cut full and held in just below the knee by a buckled strap or knitted cuff, derived from 1860's *knickerbockers* (see main listing) and popular for boys in the 1920's and '30's, especially in corduroy; revived for women in early 1970's, often in satin or velvet for evening. Also called *knickers.*

knickers Short name for *knickerbockers*.

leggings Sturdy long tight pants, often matching coat or jacket, held at ankles by knitted bands or straps under feet, sometimes with straps over shoulders; worn by children as part of *snowsuit* or *coat set, q.v.* See *leggings* in main alphabetical listings.

Levi's (lee-vize) Nickname given to work pants (see *blue jeans,* above) made by Levi Strauss & Co. in California for gold-prospecting miners in mid 19th century. Now term *Levi's* is part of trademark for pants and other work and sport clothes made by this firm.

mousers Leather *pantyhose, q.v.,* with attached chunky shoes, introduced by Mary Quant, English designer, in late 1968. See *boots.*

overalls Sturdy pants of jean fabric, white canvas, etc., with bib top and suspender straps crossing in back and fastened to bib with metal loops over metal buttons; traditionally worn by farmers, carpenters, house painters, etc.; now made in many fabrics for sports and leisure for men, women and children. Also called *bib-top pants* and *suspender pants.*

Oxford bags Men's long trousers with very wide cuffed legs, popular in the 1920's, beginning at Oxford University in England, and revived for men and women in early 1970's.

pajama p. See *pajamas.*

palazzo p. Woman's long, wide *pajamas* or *culottes, q.q.v.,* with voluminous flared legs or gathered at waist; worn for lounging or evening dress, popular in the late 1960's, early 1970's.

pedal pushers Below-the-knee, straight-cut women's pants, often with cuffs; popular during World War II for bicycling.

plus fours Full, baggy *knickers, q.v.,* popularized by Duke of Windsor in 1920's when he was Prince of Wales and worn by men, usually with patterned wool socks and brogues, for golfing and other sports. *Der.* When introduced, these knickers were 4 inches longer than usual length.

pre-cuffed trousers Full-length pants that are sold with the hems finished and the cuffs turned up, in contrast to those sold with the bottom edges of legs unfinished, to be hemmed and cuffed to suit the customer's own leg length. Men's trousers are more often sold unfinished than women's pants.

riding breeches Pants, full-cut at hips and thigh and tightly fitted below knee, sometimes of stretch fabric, some with zipper closure, others with buttoned drop-front; worn by men and women with high boots for horseback riding. Also called *canary breeches, hunt breeches, show breeches.* Also see *jodhpurs.*

rompers *Bloomers, q.v.,* cut in one piece with top of garment, popular for children in early 20th century, introduced for women in late 1960's.

sailor p. Traditional pants worn by seamen in U.S. Navy, with buttoned drop-front closing, lacing across back at waist, bell-bottom legs, in navy-blue wool or white cotton duck; also called *bell bottoms, q.v.;* may be modernized with straight legs and zippered fly-front closing.

shorts See *shorts.*

show breeches See *hunt breeches,* above.

ski p. Pants or leggings worn for skiing and other winter sports, the styles varying with the general trend in trousers legs from wide to tight-fitting, often with straps under feet. First introduced with jodhpur-type legs in the late 1920's; narrow styles in stretch fabrics appeared in 1950's.

stovepipe p. Tight-fitting pants with narrow legs, same width from knee down; worn by men from 1880 until 1920 and reintroduced in mid 1960's.

surfers Close-fitting pants extending to knee, popular in early 1960's, originating for beach wear and surfboard riding in California.

suspender p. See *overalls.*

sweat p. Pants of cotton knit with fleece backing to absorb moisture, worn by athletes while or after exercising. Also called *warm-up pants.*

tights See *panties* and *pantyhose.*

toreador p. Tight-fitting below-the-knee pants patterned after those worn by Spanish bullfighters, popular for women in late 1950's and early 1960's.

trousers Synonym for full-length pants, *q.v.*

waders See *boots.*

Western p. Low-waisted, slim-fitting pants of denim or garbardine, characterized by jeans-style tailoring, often with pockets opening at both top and side, producing right-angle front flaps that are buttoned at the corners; see *blue jeans.* Worn originally by Western American ranchers and cowboys; popular for general wear since mid 1960's. Also called *dude jeans* or *frontier pants.*

white ducks Slacks made of white *duck fabric, q.v.;* popular in 1920's and 30's for sportswear especially for men, revived for women in 1960's.

Wranglers Trademark for type of *Western pants* or *blue jeans, q.q.v.*

pants boot See *boots.*

pants coat See *coats.*

pants-dress See *dresses.*

pants-jumper Women's one-piece garment combining *jumper, q.v.,* with *culottes, q.v.;* worn over blouse.

pants liner See *panties.*

pants-skirt See *skirts.*

pants tops Blouses or sweaters designed to be worn with pants, often in the *overblouse* style, *q.v.*

panty See *panties.*

panty dress Girl's dress with matching bloomers, worn in the 1920's.

panty foundation garment See *foundation garments.*

panty girdle See *girdles.*

panty-girdle hose See *control* under *pantyhose.*

pantyhose Term introduced about 1963 for stockings and panties knit in one piece in textured and sheer nylon yarns such as Cantrece and Agilon, the panty portion of heavier yarn than the hose; first made in sizes *tall, medium,* and *petite,* later also in stretch yarns in one size; derived from *tights, q.v.* Pantyhose are now made in almost every variation available in regular stockings: sheer or opaque, reinforced or sandalfoot, ribbed or plain, colored, patterned, clocked, mesh, net, etc. A few special types:

PANTYHOSE:

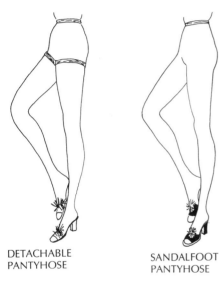

DETACHABLE PANTYHOSE

SANDALFOOT PANTYHOSE

CONTROL PANTYHOSE

bikini p. Pantyhose with below-the-navel top for wear with bare-midriff dresses or hip-hugger skirts or pants.

control p. Pantyhose with the panty portion knit of nylon combined with elastic yarn to give the control of a lightweight *girdle, q.v.*

detachable p. Three-piece pantyhose with patented bands on panties to attach replacement stockings.

Hiplets Pantyhose made in two pieces, a stocking for each leg with attached panty cut off diagonally from crotch to waist on opposite side; reversible, these "hiplets" could be interchanged and one half replaced when the stocking ran, without replacing the whole garment.

Mani-Hose Trademark for pantyhose for men made of stretch nylon, lower leg rib-knitted; introduced in 1970.

Patternskins Trademark for women's pantyhose made in bright-colored geometric designs of Jacquard knits by New York designer Giorgio di Sant'Angelo in early 1970's.

sandalfoot p. Sheer pantyhose with no reinforcements at toes or heels; may have opaque panty portion, or entire garment may be sheer.

support p. Pantyhose knit of entirely nylon combined with elastic yarn to produce a garment that gives support to the legs and relieves pressure on varicose veins.

tights See *panties.*

panty-skirt See *pettiskirt brief* under *panties.*

pantywaist Child's cotton undergarment consisting of fitted sleeveless top buttoned down front, with buttons around waistline to attach panties and *suspender garters;* worn from early 20th century to about 1930. Also called *underwaist;* see *Ferris waist.*

panty-slip See *petticoats.*

panung (pah-nung) 1. Length of fabric approximately three yards long and one yard wide, draped like an Indian *dhoti, q.v.,* to form loose-fitting trousers or skirt, worn by men and women in Thailand. *Der.* Siamese *pa,* cloth, and *nin,* one.

paper dress See *dresses.*

papier-mâché Lightweight material made of paste and sheets of tissue paper or bits of newspaper or of paper pulp molded with various binders; may be painted and shellacked. Used for jewelry, particularly bracelets, beads, pins in late 1960's. *Der.* French, chewed paper.

papillote comb Decorative tortoise shell comb, 3" to 4" long, used on either side of head to puff out hair; worn by women in late 1820's. *Der.* French *papilloner,* to flutter, *papillon,* butterfly.

papush Elaborately embroidered yellow or red flat leather sandal worn by Arabian men and women.

Paquin, Mme See *designers appendix,* France.

parachute cloth See *fabrics.*

parachute hat See *balloon hat.*

parachute sleeve Long full sleeve made without a cuff, the lower edge gathered to a lining cut shorter than the sleeve.

paradise feather See *bird-of-paradise* under *feathers.*

parament (pa-ra-ment) 1. Early term for *facing, q.v.* 2. Ornamental cuff at wrist, turned up over sleeve and stitched. Also spelled *parement.* 3. Trimming used on *gown à la française, q.v.,* usually a long decorated band, wider at hem. 4. Liturgical vestment.

parasol 1. Sun umbrella, sometimes made of fabrics matched to dresses and trimmed with ruffles, embroidery, etc., in various shapes, e.g., pagoda or dome, sometimes with folding handle; popular in 19th and early 20th century. 2. Japanese umbrella made of glazed waterproof paper and bamboo, in bright colors and printed with large decorative motifs, used to protect elaborate high headdresses; also carried by Burmese women and by men in royal ceremonies. Also called *sunshade. Der.* from Latin *parare,* to shield and *sol,* sun.

parasol skirt Skirt cut with many *gores, q.v.,* stitched in same manner as seams in a *parasol, q.v.;* worn by women in late 19th and early 20th centuries.

parchment calves Padding of parchment inside stockings to make legs shaplier; worn by men, latter half of 18th century. See *false calves.*

pardessus (par-de-soo) 1. French term for man's overcoat. *Der.* Literally "for on top." 2. General term used in second half of 19th century for woman's outdoor garment of half or

three-quarter length, made with sleeves and fitted at waistline, frequently with cape trimmed with lace or velvet. Also called *mantelet* and *paletot, q.q.v.* Also see *polonaise pardessus.*

pareu (pah-ray-oo) or **pareo** Rectangular piece of patterned cotton cloth worn wrapped as *skirt* or *loincloth, q.v.,* by natives on Tahiti and other Pacific islands; adaptations popular in U.S. as beach fashion in 1950's.

Paris, point de See *laces.*

parka 1. Hooded fur jacket worn by Eskimos, usually of flat fur with fluffy fur on hem and around hood, sometimes embroidered on yoke. 2. **See** *sport* jackets under *jackets.* *Der.* .*r*om Russian-Aleutian word meaning pelt. Sometimes spelled *parkah.*

Parnis, Mollie See *designers appendix, United States.*

parta Native headdress worn by unmarried girls in Hungary, consists of a halo-type hat trimmed with metallic lace and often studded with semiprecious stones.

parti-colored Bicolored garment divided vertically, each side a different color; popular from 12th century to 15th century for hose and clothing. Also called *pied.*

partlet 1. Decorative covering for upper part of chest and neck showing under low-cut *doublet, q.v.,* by men in first half of 16th century. 2. Fill-in for low-cut *bodice, q.v.,* worn by women from mid 16th throughout 17th centuries. Also called *chemisette* and *tucker.* Also spelled *patlet.*

parure (par-oor) Matched set of jewelry that may consist of a necklace, earrings, pin, bracelet, etc. *Der.* French, adornment.

passement See *laces.*

passementerie (pas-mehn-tree) Trimmings such as heavy embroideries, braid, tinsel, beads, lace, etc., used as edging through 19th century.

paste Highly reflective transparent types of flint glass, faceted or molded to make imitation gems; one variety called *strass,* named for Josef Strasser, a German jeweler. See *gem settings* under *gems.*

pasties See *brassieres.*

patch 1. Extra piece of fabric sewed or bonded by heat on a garment to mend a tear or for decorative effect. e.g., suede elbow patches on sweaters and knee patches on blue jeans. 2. Insignia sewed to sleeve of uniform to indicate rank. 3. In the 17th century, a decorative cutout shaped like moon, star, etc., applied to the face. Also called *beauty spot, q.v.* or *mouche* and originally used to cover scars of smallpox.

patch box Small box carried by women in 17th century to hold various types of decorative cutouts, called *patches, q.v.,* applied to face.

patchouli Oil used as fixative in perfumes, used in Oriental blends, made from Malaysian, Indian, and Indonesian plant leaves; very popular in 19th century.

patch pocket See *pockets.*

patchwork Small pieces of fabric, leather, or other material stitched together to make larger piece of fabric; used in Colonial America to convert worn-out garments into quilts or coverlets; revived in 1960's for clothes and interiors. Patchwork from the Appalachian Mountains of Kentucky was introduced by Paris couturier Yves Saint Laurent as a high fashion for dresses and skirts in early 1970's. Real patchwork, quilted or plain, and prints with a patchwork look became very popular at all levels of fashion for both men and women. Also see *prints.*

patent leather Leather with a shiny hard surface. See *leathers.*

patent plastic See *plastic patent.*

Paterson, Ronald See *designers appendix, England.*

patlet See *partlet.*

Patou, Jean See *designers appendix, France.*

patrol jacket 1. Men: Jacket of military cut made with five-button single-breasted closing and *Prussian collar q.v.;* worn in late 1870's with tight *knee pants* for bicycling. 2. Women: Hip-length jacket trimmed with military braid across front, standing collar, and tight-fitting sleeves finished with cuffs; worn in 1889.

patte Term for earliest form of *lapel, q.v.,* resembling a narrow collar with tabs, worn on *ganache, q.v.* in 13th-14th centuries. Also called *paw.*

pattens 1. Shoes fitted with iron blades for skating in Middle Ages. 2. Overshoes worn over regular shoes to raise feet out of mud, typically a wooden sole raised about 3 inches with bands of iron forming the walking surface, or wooden soles with top portion indented for the heel, secured by straps fitting over regular shoes; worn by men and women from 14th century to mid 19th century. Also called *clogs, q.v.* Also see *chopine.*

pattern book Large volume issued regularly (and updated) by the publisher of paper patterns for home sewing showing all of the designs available with details on fabric needed, etc.; available where patterns are sold for convenience of customers; also called *counter book.*

Patternskins See *pantyhose.*

pauldron Armor consisting of single large rigid shoulder plate lapping over armor at chest and back; worn in late 15th century. Also called *epauliere* and *shoulder cop.*

Paulette See *designers appendix, France.*

paultock Variant of *paltock, q.v.*

pavilion Jewelry-industry term for lower portion below the girdle of brilliant cut gem. Also called the *base.* See *gem cuts.*

paw See *patte.*

paw crosses Fur-industry term for small pieces of fur from paws, heads, tails left after cutting of garment and sewn into large crosses that are used to make less-expensive fur items. Same as *crosses.*

peace symbol Circle or oval enclosing a vertical staff with two bars projecting at about 60 degree angle down to left and right from center of staff; introduced in 1960's by opponents of U.S. involvement in war in Vietnam and used for rings, medallions, etc.

pea coat or **pea jacket** See *sport jackets* under *jackets.*

peacock feathers See *feathers.*

peaked lapel See *lapels.*

peaked shoe See *piked shoe.*

peanit straw See *straws.*

pear cut See *gem cuts.*

pearl See *beads, dresses, necklaces,* and *gems.*

pearl button Button made of *mother-of-pearl,* (called "smoked pearl" in darker shades), *q.v.,* the classic button for almost any use until the development of plastic buttons in the 1930's; pearl buttons are made from shells, sometimes called "ocean pearl," now imitated by plastic.

peasant blouse See *blouses.*

peasant bodice Women's *corselet, q.v.,* bodice laced up the front to bustline with straps extending over outermost edge of shoulder, worn over a blouse; popular in mid 1880's. See *necklines.*

peasant coat See *coats.*

peasant dress See *dresses.*

peasant skirt See *skirts.*

peascod-bellied doublet Man's *doublet, q.v.,* with a false front stuffed with cotton in a horn-shaped projection over waistline, introduced into France from Spain and popular from 1570 to 1600. *Der.* Said to be in imitation of the *cuirasse* to deflect bullets. Also called *bellied doublet, goose-belly doublet, kodpeased doublet,* and *long-bellied doublet.*

Peau d'Ange Trademark for *Angel Skin* fabrics. See *fabrics.*

peau de cygne Crepy silk satin. See *fabrics.*

peau de soie See *fabrics.*

pebble cheviot Nubbed coating. See *fabrics.*

pebbled finish An embossed leather finish similar to tiny cobblestones or pebbles, used on *Scotch-grained* leather, *q.v.*

pebble weave See *weaves.*

peccary See *leathers.*

pedal pushers See *pants.*

pediment headdress 19th-century term for the *gabled* or *peaked* hood worn in 16th century and called *English hood, q.v.*

pedlar dolls Variant of *fashion babies*, *q.v.*

Pedlar, Sylvia See *designers appendix, United States.*

Peds Trademark for *footlets*. See *socks*.

peek-a-boo waist Woman's waist made of eyelet embroidery; popular in early 20th century.

Peggy collar Rounded collar with scalloped ends similar to *Peter Pan collar, q.v.*

peg-top skirt Skirt made with fullness from waistline to hips, tapering narrowly to ankles, similar to the *hobble skirt, q.v.;* popular during World War I and revived at intervals. *Der.* Name borrowed from boy's cone-shaped spinning top.

peg-top sleeve Sleeve full at shoulder and tapered to wrist, modified form of *French gigot* or *leg-of-mutton sleeve, q.q.v.;* worn by men in mid 19th century.

peg-top trousers Men's trousers, wide and pleated at top, tapered on lower leg, fitting closely at ankles; popular from mid 19th century to early 20th century. Also called *Zouave trousers*.

peigne Josephine (pai-nyeh) Woman's high comb ornamented with small gilt balls; worn at the back of head for evening in mid 19th century.

peignoir (pai-nwar) 1. See *robes*. 2. Dress with unboned bodice, sometimes with *bishop sleeves, q.v.,* worn for informal morning wear from late 18th century on.

pelerine (pel-er-reen). 1. Woman's short shoulder cape of fur, velvet,

other fabrics, sometimes with long scarf ends crossed and tied around waist; worn from early 1740's through 1800's. 2. A muslin cape-collar trimmed with lace; worn from mid 18th through 19th centuries.

pelisse (pe-leese) 1. Long, loose cloak open in front with slits for arms, often lined and trimmed with fur, sometimes hooded; worn by both sexes in 18th century. 2. In 19th century, fitted three-quarter or long coat with one or more capes; by end of century, full-length and gathered from shoulders, sometimes with waist-length cape covering arms; called *pelisse mantle*. 3. Day dress fastened with ribbon bows or concealed hooks down front, called *pelisse-robe*. See *redingote*. 4. Infants' caped coat, usually of cream-colored cashmere, worn from 19th through early 20th centuries. Also spelled *pellice*.

Pellon Trademark for non-woven interfacing. See *fabrics*.

pembroke paletot Man's calf-length, long-waisted overcoat with wide lapels, double-breasted with eight buttons, easy fitting sleeves with turned-back cuffs, flapped side pockets and vertical breast pocket; worn in mid 1850's.

penannular brooch Pin used to fasten clothing from 11th through 13th

centuries: a moveable pin set on an incompleted ring.

pencil stripe See *stripes*.

pendant An ornament that hangs or dangles. See *earrings* and *necklaces*.

pendicle Term for single pendant earring worn by men in 17th century.

Penelope (peh-naell-o-pee) 1. British term for knitted jacket without sleeves. 2. Type of fine mesh canvas for needlework embroidery, named after the legendary Greek queen of Ithaca, the faithful wife of Odysseus, who did needlework to forestall suitors during his absence. See *embroidery*.

penny loafers See *shoes*.

pentes Distinctive skirt cut in two layers with the *overskirt* draped to reveal *underskirt* of alternate silk and velvet gores; worn in mid 1880's.

peplos Earliest form of Greek *chiton, q.v.,* worn in Homeric period by women, made of a rectangle of woolen fabric, sometimes heavily embroidered, wrapped around body and fastened on shoulder with a *fibula, q.v.,* or pin, tied by a rope belt at waist; sometimes, one breast was exposed and garment hung open on one side.

peplum Extension of bodice of dress that comes below waistline, sometimes pleated, sometimes flared; can be in one piece with bodice or cut separately and joined to bodice by a seam or attached to a belt. Popular in 1860's and 1930's.

peplum basque (bask) Woman's dress with peplum attached to belt, usually short in front with long hanging ends at sides; worn in 1860's.

peplum bodice Bodice of evening dress cut with long side panels draped to form *panniers, q.v.,* at hips; worn in late 1870's.

peplum dolman *Dolman, q.v.,* with long points hanging at the sides; worn by women in the early 1870's.

peplum rotonde Woman's waist-length circular cloak, made with back vent and fringed border; worn in the early 1870's.

percale Plain lightweight cotton. See *fabrics*.

percaline See *fabrics*.

perdita chemise English term for daytime dress made with close-fitting bodice, V-neck with large falling collar, and long tight sleeves; fastened with buttons or ribbon ties down front; sash at waist tied with long ends in back; worn in early 1780's.

perforations Small holes punched through leather of shoe to achieve decorative effect; used particularly for *spectator pumps* and *brogues*, *q.q.v.* under *shoes.* Also called *perfs* in shoe-trade slang.

perfume cone Small cone of perfumed wax worn on top of head by ancient Egyptians during parties and dinners; the cone melted, giving off a pleasant scent.

peridot See *gems.*

periwig A wig, specifically an extremely large powdered wig with raised peaks on top and long hanging loose curls, as worn by Louis XIV of France. Also called *peruke.*

permanent press See *durable press.*

permanent wave Waves or curls that last until hair is cut off, created either by heated rollers or by means of chemicals. First *machine* wave, introduced in beauty shops about 1909, required electrical wiring to each roller to heat it; in 1930's new *machineless* wave used chemicals to heat the rollers; in the early '40's, the first *cold wave,* in which chemicals curled the hair without heating it, was introduced. The cold wave made *home permanents* possible. In 1960's a soft version called a *body wave* gave hair more stiffness for non-curly coiffures. Name usually shortened to *permanent;* in English slang, called *perm.*

perruque à l'enfant Man's wig with tiny curls over most of the head, larger horizontal curls above ears and neck, and long *queue, q.v.,* hanging down in back; worn in 1780's. Also called *perruque naissante.*

perruquier (perook-kee-ay) Term used for a person who arranged and set wigs in the 18th century.

Persian lamb See *furs.*

Persians Leather-industry term for hair-sheep leather tanned in India.

Pertegaz, Manuel See *designers appendix, Spain.*

peruke See *periwig.*

Peruvian hat Term for woman's rain hat made from plaited palm leaves, worn in early 19th century.

petal collar See *collars.*

petenlair Separate bodice extended to thigh length, with fitted stomacher front and full back, elbow-length sleeves; combined with petticoat to make a dress; worn by women from mid 1740's to 1770's. Also spelled *pet-en-l'air.* Also called *French jacket.*

Peter Pan collar See *collars.*

Peter Pan hat Small hat with brim extended in front and turned up in back, a conical crown trimmed with long feather; named after hat worn by actress Maude Adams in 1905 playing Peter Pan in James M. Barrie's play by the same name.

Petersham See *fabrics.*

Petersham, Viscount Charles (1790–1851) Fashionable figure from Regency period to 1850, something between an eccentric and a true dandy, for whom various men's clothes and fabrics were named. Also see *Petersham, Petersham frock coat,* and *Petersham Cossacks.*

Petersham Cossacks Cossack, *q.v.,* trousers cut wide at ankles, spreading out over foot, pulled in with drawstring above ankle making a flounce; worn by men in 1817–18.

Also called *Petersham trousers. Der.* Named for *Viscount Charles Petersham, q.v.*

Petersham frock coat or **greatcoat** 1. *Frock coat, q.v.,* with velvet collar, lapels, and cuffs and slanted flapped pockets on hips. 2. Man's *overcoat, q.v.,* with short shoulder cape. Both worn in 1830's. *Der.* Named for *Viscount Charles Petersham, q.v.*

Petersham trousers See *Petersham Cossacks.*

Peter Thomson dress Schoolgirl's one-piece dress with *middy collar* and *box pleats* from yoke to hem, worn as uniform by many school children in early 20th century; named for designer Peter Thomson, who was once a naval tailor.

petit casaque (pe-tee ca-sack) French name used in 1870's for *polonaise dress, q.v.*

petite 1. Size range for women who are below average height, usually numbered from 6 to 12. Junior petite sizes for short-waisted women run from 5 to 11. 2. Smallest size, along with *small, medium,* and *large,* for pantyhose, body suits, nightgowns, etc.

petit point See *embroideries* and *stitches.*

petits bonshommes (peh-tee bunzum) Bands of fabric—like bracelets with several ruffles, often of lace—used to edge sleeves of *gown à la française, q.v.,* from early 1720's on.

pettibockers Ankle-length silk-jersey *pantaloons, q.v.,* worn as underwear by women in early 20th century.

petticoat 1. Man's *undershirt* worn under *doublet* in 16th and 17th centuries and called *petti-cotte. Der.* Middle English *pety,* small, and *cote,* coat. 2. Short coat worn by men in 18th century, called *waistcoat.* 3. Woman's *underskirt,* usually shorter than outer skirt, in various widths to match silhouette of dress, plain or trimmed with tucks, lace etc., at hem; a fashion since 16th century, when garment was called a *kirtle, q.v.*

PETTICOATS:

CRINOLINE

crinoline 1. Stiffened petticoat intended to hold out *bouffant, q.v.,* skirt, may be stiff nylon, either plain or ruffled. 2. Underskirt, worn in 1840's and 1850's, made of fabric called *crinoline, q.v.,* or of fabric made of *horsehair.* 3. Term applied to any underskirt, even hoops, that support a full skirt. See *hoops.*

dirndl p. (durn-dul) Petticoat fitting smoothly over hips releasing gathered fullness below, sometimes with

DIRNDL PETTICOAT

EVENING PETTICOAT   PETTICULOTTE

tiers of ruffles. *Der.* From Austrian Tyrol full-skirted peasant costume.

evening p. Ankle-length *half-slip, q.v.,* with slash at center front or at both sides to aid in walking.

hoop p. Full-length petticoat consisting of series of circular metal bands held by vertical tapes, making skirt flexible to permit seating; introduced in 1860's and worn in intervals since. See *cage, cage-americaine, cage petticoat. Empire jupon* and *Empress petticoat.*

panty-slip Short petticoat with panties attached at waistband.

petticulotte Short petticoat and panties combined into one garment. See *culotte.*

petticoat bodice 1. Petticoat joined by waistline seam to sleeveless bodice; worn from about 1815 until 1890. 2. In 1890, a type of *corset cover.* See *camisole.*

petticoat breeches Wide-legged *cullottes, q.v.,* fashionable for men in England in latter half of 17th century, pleated to waistband, full to knees and trimmed with ribbon loops. Also called *Rhinegraves.*

pettipants See *panties.*

pettiskirt brief See *panties.*

petti-slip See slips.

pheasant feathers See *feathers.*

Philippine embroidery See *embroideries.*

Phrygian cap (frij-i-an) Cap with high rounded peak curving forward, with hanging side *lappets, q.v.,* sometimes made of leather; worn in ancient Greece from 9th to 12th centuries and copied in 18th century on. Also called *Phrygian bonnet.*

physical wig Short wig, brushed back from forehead and bushing out at sides and in back of head; worn by professional men during latter half of 18th century, replacing *full bottomed wig, q.v.*

Piccadilly See *pickadil.*

Piccadilly collar Man's detachable high-wing collar fastening to the shirt with a stud in front and back; worn in the 1860's. By 1895, collar

PHYSICAL WIG, 1755-56

was cut to allow for the band of a scarf to pass through it. Also see *pickadil.*

pickadevant Also *pick-a-devant* and *pick devant.* Variants of *piqué devant, q.v.*

pickadil 1. Standing collar with scalloped edge. 2. Notched edges on sleeve, bodice front, and neck openings; worn in late 16th through 17th centuries. 3. Stiffened band to hold ruff up in back; 17th century. Also spelled *piccadill, pickardil* or *Piccadilly. Der.* From Piccadilly, fashionable street in London built in late 16th century.

picot (pee-ko) 1. A row of small loops woven along selvage of fabric or ribbon or a part of the edge design of lace. 2. Machine-made edge on fabrics produced by cutting through center of hemstitching, each edge

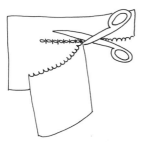

becoming a *picot edge.* 3. Run-resistant loops on edge of welt in hosiery. See *hemstitch* under *stitches.*

picture hat See *Gainsborough* under *hats.*

pied (pide) Piebald. See *parti-colored.*

pied hose Hose, similar to *tights, q.v.,* with each leg a different color. Also called *pales.* See *parti-colored.*

pierced-ear rings See *earrings.*

pierced-look earrings See *earrings.*

Pierpont collar (peer-pont) Man's collar ending in sharp points extended over tie, worn in 1840's and '50's. Also called *pinpoint collar.*

Pierrot bodice (pee-ehr-o) Close-fitting, low-necked bodice extending to slightly below the waist, worn with a matching flounced skirt in latter part of 18th century.

Pierrot cape Woman's three-quarter-length cloak with additional shoulder cape and satin ruff at neckline. Also see *Pierrot collar.*

Pierrot costume Clown suit worn by the comedy character in French pantomime called Pierrot (Little Peter) and interpreted by the Italian clown Pagliacci in Leoncavallo's opera; face is whitened, the suit loose and baggy, usually white or with diamond-shaped *harlequin checks, q.v.* of color, and with large buttons or pompons on the jacket front (see drawing, page 398). Also see *collars.*

pigeon-wings Man's hairstyle or wig with single or double horizontal curls over the ears, smooth top and sides; worn from 1750's to 1760's.

PIERROT COSTUME

Wig also called *pigeon-winged toupee* or *aile de pigeon.*

pigmented yarn See *yarns.*

pigskin See *leathers.*

pigtail See *hairstyles.*

pigtail wig Wig with a *queue, q.v.,* interwoven with black ribbon, tied with black ribbon bow at nape of neck and smaller bow at end; worn by men in 18th century.

Piguet, Robert See *designers appendix, France.*

piked shoe Long-toed shoe worn in late 14th century and early 15th century and again from 1460 to 1480. Also called *peaked shoe.* See *crakow.*

pilch 1. Close fitting fur-lined outer gown worn by men and women from 14th to 16th centuries in winter; still worn by clergy in drafty churches. Also called *pelisson.* 2. English term for baby's knitted diaper cover.

pile knit See *knits.*

pileolus Skullcap worn by Catholic priests and Pope under the *miter* and *tiara, q.q.v.* Also spelled *pilleolus.*

pileus (pil-ee-us) 1. Ancient Roman skullcap worn at games and festivals. 2. Felt brimless cap with peak folded over, similar to *Phrygian* or *liberty cap, q.q.v.,* worn by freed Roman slaves. Also spelled pilleus. Also see *pilos.*

pile weave See *weaves.*

Pilgrim collar See *collars.*

pillbox hat See *hats.*

pilling Tendency of woven fabrics and knits, especially wools, nylons, and acrylics, to form surface nubs or bunches of fibers resulting from rubbing in normal wear and in washing; pilling is caused by loosely twisted yarn fibers unwinding and interlocking with each other.

pillow lace See *laces.*

pillow-slip dress Straight-cut *chemise, q.v.,* dress, usually short, made with short *kimono* sleeves; popular in early 1920's.

pilos (pi-los) Conical cap worn by Greek peasants or fishermen, derived from those worn by ancient Greeks and Romans; similar to *pileus, q.v.*

pilot cloth Navy-blue woolen. See *fabrics.*

pilot coat See *pea jacket,* in *sport jackets* under *jackets.*

pima cotton See *fabrics.*

pin 1. Small fastener, used to join two parts of clothing together, consisting of a straight, pointed metal shaft and a blunt head; used in France and England in present form since 14th century, when pins were scarce and sold only once a year. 2. Ornamental piece of jewelry with pin fastener attached to back, made in many metals with real or fake gems. Also called *brooch.* Also see *fibula.*

PINS OR BROOCHES:

bar drop p. Long narrow pin with *pendants, q.v.,* attached.

bar p. 1. Long, narrow pin secured by back fastener same length as pin; fashionable in early 20th century in platinum and diamonds.

brooch Synonym for *pin.*

cameo p. Single, double, or triple facial silhouettes carved in bas-relief in onyx or other layered gem, top layer often white against black or orange background, mounted in gold or silver pin setting. Also see *Wedgwood cameo.*

chatelaine p. Pin worn on the lapel or chest with hook on back to secure a watch, etc.; or two decorative pins joined by a chain. See *fob pin.* Der. Keys worn at the waist on a chain by medieval mistress of the castle or *chatelaine.*

clip Ornament similar to a pin but with spring clasp on back that snaps closed over the edge of fabric; popular in 1930's and '40's.

collar p. Pin fastened, through eyelets embroidered in points of man's shirt collar, underneath tie to hold points down on either side of tie; popular in 1940's and '50's.

fob p. A pin designed to hold a woman's watch on shoulder or at waist.

hat p. Straight pin from three to twelve inches long with bead or jewel as head, used by women to secure their hats in late 19th through early 20th centuries, becoming less common after hair was bobbed in 1920's.

kilt p. See *safety pin.*

necktie p. See *stick pin.*

safety p. A pin bent back on itself to form a spring with a clasp to cover the point. Gold or silver safety pins are often used to hold *kilts,*

q.v., in place and were a popular jewelry fashion, with or without *chains* or *medallions, q.v.,* in the 1940's and early '50's.

scarf p. Variant of *necktie pin* or *stick pin, q.q.v.*

stick p. Straight pin with ornamental head worn by man to secure a *four-in-hand necktie, q.v.,* popular from late 19th century to 1930's. See *tie tacks* and *tie pins.*

tie p. Pin used to hold *four-in-hand necktie, q.v.,* in place, sometimes resembling a gold *safety pin, q.v.,* or having additional ornament or insignia. See *stick pin.*

pinafore Sleeveless garment like an *apron, q.v.,* worn over dress as protection against soil, usually open in back and tied with a sash at waist, often with bib top and ruffled shoulder straps crossed in back; worn by women and children, now adapted for summer evening and sports dresses. See *dresses* and *swimsuits.*

pinafore heel See *heels.*

pince-nez See *glasses.*

pinchbeck Alloy, composed of five parts copper and one part zinc, used for pins and buckles cast with surface design and then plated with thin layer of silver or gold and frequently set with colored glass or *paste, q.v.,* gems. *Der.* From invention of Christopher Pinchbeck, London watchmaker, about 1700.

pincheck See *checks.*

pin collar See *collars.*

pin curl 1. See *curls.* 2. Term in 1840's to '60's for curl pinned on to underneath side of bonnet.

pin dot See *dots* under *prints.*

pin fitting See *fitting.*

pink coat See *coats.*

pinked seam See *seams.*

pinking 1. Unhemmed border of fabric cut with saw-tooth edge to prevent raveling by using special *pinking scissors* or shears that have sawtooth blades. 2. Decorative effect made by cutting short slits to form a pattern in shoes or garments, in late 15th–17th centuries. Also called *pouncing.*

pinner Term for *lappet, q.v.,* of wo-

man's indoor cap, frequently worn pinned up and, by extension, term for cap itself in 17th to mid 18th century. Also 17th-century term for *tucker, q.v.*

pin-on curls See *cluster curls* under *hairpieces.*

pin-point collar See *Pierpont collar.*

pin seal See *leathers.*

pinson Lightweight indoor slipper, often furred; worn from end of 14th century to 16th century by men and women. Also called *pinsnet* or *pump.*

pin stripe See *stripes.*

pinwale Narrow rib in *corduroy* (see *fabrics*). Also written *pin wale.*

Pipart, Gérard See *designers appendix, France.*

pipe-organ pleats See *godet* under *pleats.*

pipes Small rolls of pipe clay heated and used to tighten curls of man's wig in 17th and 18th centuries. Also see *roulettes.*

piping Narrow piece of bias-cut fabric folded over edge of, or folded and stitched into seam between edge and facing of, matching or contrast-

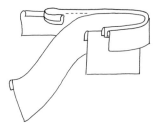

ing garment to form decorative trim, e.g., navy-blue blazer with white piping on revers and pockets. See *piped* under *buttonholes, pockets,* and *seams.* Also see *cording.*

pipkin Woman's small hat with flat crown pleated into narrow brim, usually trimmed with narrow jeweled band and feathers; worn about latter half of 16th century. Also called *taffeta pipkin.*

piqué, pique Firm cotton with ribbed or fancy weave. See *fabrics.*

piqué devant Short, pointed beard worn by men, from 1570's to 1600, with a moustache. Also called *pickadevant.*

piqué embroidery See *embroideries.*

piqué seam See *seams.*

piqué weave See *weaves.*

pith helmet See *topee* under *hats.*

pixie glasses See *glasses.*

pixie hairstyle See *gamin* under *hairstyles.*

pizazz (pih-zazz) Word coined in 1930's to express the quality of audaciousness or daring; credited by the fashion magazine *Harper's Bazaar* to students at Harvard University.

p.j.'s Abbreviation for *pajamas, q.v.*

p.k. seam See *piqué* under *seams.*

plackard 1. Chest piece or *stomacher, q.v.,* used to fill in gap made by open neckline of man's *doublet, q.v.,* in late 15th to mid 16th centuries. 2. Front panel of woman's open-sided *surcoat, q.v.,* often trimmed with fur and embroidery, from mid 14th to early 16th centuries. Also spelled *placcard, placart* and *placcate.*

placket Word used since the 16th century for slit at neck, side, front, back, or wrist in dress, blouse, pants, or

skirt to facilitate putting garment on and off; fastened in early times by lacings, buttons, or hooks and eyes, since 1930's also by *zippers, q.v.*

plaid 1. Common term for *tartan, q.v.,* pattern, woven of various colored yarns in stripes of different widths running at right angles, making blocks; derived from Scottish fabrics woven to designate different clans. 2. Traditional Scottish garment consisting of long length of tartan wool, worn pleated around waist as a skirt with one end thrown over shoulder; eventually the long *plaid* was cut in two, the upper scarf still called a *plaid,* the lower skirt a *kilt, q.v.* See *tartans.*

PLAIDS:

Argyll or **argyle** Knitting or wool fabric pattern of vari-colored diamond shapes with narrow overplaid superimposed; copied from *tartan* of Duke of Argyll and Clan Campbell of Argyll, Scotland.

blanket p. Very large plaid with dark ground colors and lighter overstripes; used originally in woolen and cotton blankets.

gingham p. Yarn-dyed pattern in a plain weave with stripes of three or more colors crossing each other, usually of lightweight cotton. Two-color ginghams are usually called *checks, q.v.,* also see *fabrics.*

glen p. See *Glen Urquhart,* below.

Glen Urquhart or **Glenurquhart p.** Woven design which pairs small checks with larger checks in a combination of subdued color and white; used particularly for men's worsted suits. Also called *glen plaid* or *glen check.* Named for Glen Urquhart, a valley in Inverness-shire, Scotland.

hunting p. Everyday version of a Scottish clan's *tartan, q.v.,* in subdued colors to blend with landscape, in contrast to *dress plaid* worn on ceremonial occasions.

Madras p. (mad-dres) East Indian woven cotton in multi-color crossbar patterns that bleed after washing giving a blurred effect. See *fabrics.*

Tattersall p. Plaid consisting of narrow lines in two alternating colors, crossed to form checked design on a plain light-colored ground, often red and black lines on white ground. *Der.* Named for London horse market using such horse blankets. Also called *Tattersall check.*

windowpane p. Fine cross stripes, widely spaced making design like multipaned window; popular in wool for women's coats and suits in 1960's and for knits in 1970's. Also called *windowpane checks.*

plain stitch See *stitches.*

plain weave See *weaves.*

plait (plate) 1. A *braid, q.v.,* of hair. See *switch* under *hairpieces.* 2. (verb) To weave three or more strands into

a single strip or *braid,* e.g., bands of straw for hats or ribbons for trimming. 3. Variant of *pleat, q.v.*

planter's hat See *hats.*

plastic patent Simulated or imitation *patent leather* made from a vinyl compound, very durable and will not split or crack like genuine patent. May have a crushed surface (often called *crushed vinyl*) or be imprinted with a design such as alligator, snakeskin, etc. Used for shoes and handbags and in lighter weights for jackets, coats, and trimmings; popular in 1960's and '70's.

plastron 1. Front center portion set into a woman's dress, usually made of a contrasting fabric for a decorative effect; used in the 19th century and early 20th century. Formerly called the *plackard* and *stomacher, q.v. Der.* French, breastplate. 2. See *collars.* 3. Iron breastplate worn as as armor between *hauberk* and *gambeson, q.q.v.*

plated As applied to jewelry—e.g., *gold-plated*—a thin film of precious metal applied to an inexpensive base, usually by electrolysis.

plated knit See *knits.*

plated yarn see *yarns.*

plates Small pieces of fur joined together to make larger unit, e.g., *Persian lamb plates* made from paws and gills that are left over from other garments.

platform sole Mid-sole of shoe, often made of cork or sponge rubber, raising the foot off ground on a platform varying in height from ¼ to 3 inches; popular in 1930's and 1940's for women's shoes, reintroduced in late 1960's by Roger Vivier in Paris and popular in U.S. in early '70's. See *shoes*.

platinum 1. Rare white metal used for mounting jewels, usually alloyed with 10% iridium to increase hardness. 2. Very pale silvery blond; popular shade of hair in 1930's and 1940's.

platter collar See *collars*.

Plauen lace See *laces*.

pleat 1. (noun) Fold of cloth or other material, turned on itself and stitched at one end, pressed or unpressed, released for fullness below; used for *skirts* or *trimmings* in various forms. 2. (verb) To set in folds. 3. (verb) Spelled *plait* or *plat* when referring to weaving a braid of hair or ribbons.

PLEATS:

accordion p. Narrow pressed-in pleats, similar to the folds of the bellows of an accordion, often edge-stitched.

bias p. Pressed in pleats in fabric cut on the diagonal, usually stitched part way down.

box p. Double pleat formed by two facing folds meeting in center underneath the pleat.

cartridge p. Small rounded pleats used for trim, copied from cartridge loops on military belts.

cluster p. Pressed or unpressed pleats made in groups with several pleats on top of one another making one unit, usually having box pleat on top with other pleats underneath it.

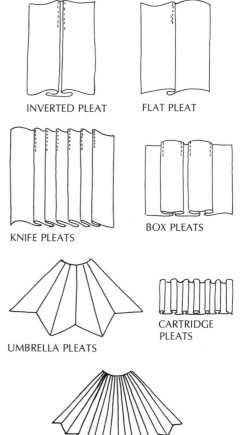

INVERTED PLEAT FLAT PLEAT

KNIFE PLEATS BOX PLEATS

UMBRELLA PLEATS CARTRIDGE PLEATS

SUNBURST PLEATS

fan p. See *sunburst pleats*.

flat p. Simple pleat formed by single fold of fabric.

godet p. Gored skirt pressed on the inside where gores are stitched, forming pleats that hang in a series of rolls; popular in 1890's. Also called *pipe-organ pleats*.

inverted p. Reversed *box pleat* with folds meeting on top of pleat.

kick p. Single *flat pleat* or one *in-*

verted *pleat* at center back of skirt to make walking easier.

kilt p. Flat pleat covering half of next pleat, all folded in same direction as in Scottish *kilt, q.v.*

knife p. Narrow sharply pressed flat pleats going in same direction.

pipe-organ p. See *godet pleat.*

sunburst p. Pressed-in pleats similar to *accordion* style, narrow at the top and wider at hem giving flare to skirt or sleeve; first used about 1880. Also called *fan pleats.*

umbrella p. Wide folds, similar to *sunburst* pleats, often created by seams, as in the segments of an umbrella top.

Watteau p. Box pleats hanging free from back shoulder yoke to hem of dress or dressing gown. Named for 18th century French painter who often depicted women wearing this style.

plissé Puckered cotton cloth. See *fabrics.*

plucked otter See *otter* under *furs.*

plucking Fur-industry term for the process of removing some of the longer guard hairs which may mar the beauty of the peltry.

Pluderhose German and Swiss unpadded *trunk hose, q.v.,* characterized by broad slashes with loose silk linings protruding; worn by men in late 16th century. Also see *almain hose.*

plug hat American term for *top hat, .q.v.,* worn by men from 1830's on. Same as *chimney-pot hat, q.v.*

plug oxford See *oxfords* under *shoes.*

plumet petticoat Narrow, back-buttoned petticoat with ruffles forming bustle at back and, continuing to

form a detachable train; worn in late 1870's.

plumetis Tufted sheer cotton or wool. See *fabrics.*

plummet Term used in 17th century for *pendant earring, q.v.* Also see *pendicle.*

plumpers Hemispheres of cork used by women inside mouth to make cheeks look rounder; worn from late 17th century to early 19th century.

plunge bra See *brassieres.*

plus fours See *pants.*

plush Warp-pile fabric of various fibers. See *fabrics.*

ply 1. See *yarns.* 2. Layers in fabric, referred to by number, joined to form one fabric; e.g. two-ply cloth.

pocket 1. Since the 16th century, a small flat pouch, for carrying handkerchief, money, etc., sewn on interior of garment with access through outside slit; an outgrowth of earlier 15th-century fashion, continuing into the 19th century, for pouches attached to belts or concealed in folds of skirt. 2. Pouch formed by a piece of material stitched to outside of a garment with top edge open, sometimes with opening covered by a flap. Many variations according to use, either functional or decorative.

POCKETS:

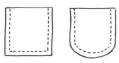

PATCH POCKETS

RAILWAY POCKET
(see page 419)

angled p. See *hacking pocket.*

bellows p. Outside pocket made with center *box pleat* or *inverted pleat* that expands when pocket is used; characteristic of *bush jacket* and *safari dress* and *jacket, q.q.v.*

bound p. Interior pocket with slit finished like a bound buttonhole on outside providing access to inner concealed pocket. Also called *slit* or *slot pocket.*

envelope p. Outside pocket with flap and pleated sides, expanding like an envelope in use.

flap p. Pocket with separate piece of material covering the opening; may be bound, welt, or patch pocket.

fob p. A small pocket in the front of a man's trousers, usually of the *slot* or *welt* style, used to carry a watch; also called a watch *pocket.*

hacking p. Flapped pocket placed on an angle, used on jackets and coats, especially on *hacking jacket, q.v.* in *sport jackets* under *jackets.*

holster p. Novelty pocket shaped like gun holster; used on sportswear.

kangaroo p. 1. Extra-large pocket placed on center front of garment, such as an apron, frequently with buttoned flap closing. 2. Any extra-large pocket.

key p. Small patch pocket sewn inside of larger right-front pocket in jeans-style pants, just large enough for a key or a few coins.

mock p. Flap sewed on outside of garment to suggest a real pocket.

patch p. Pocket sewn on outside of garment, either plain or with a flap.

piped p. See *bound pocket,* above.

safari p. See *bellows pocket.*

seam p. Interior pocket inserted in a seam: (a) placed in a side seam of garment, e.g., a trouser pocket; (b) placed in topstitched seam in side-front of garment, e.g., in front panel of skirt.

slash p. See *bound pocket.*

slit p. See *bound pocket.*

405

slot p. See *bound pocket.*

vest p. *Welt* pocket on side chest of waistcoat or vest, originally used to carry a pocket watch. In the Louis XV period, men carried two watches; so a pocket was made on either side of garment. Also called a *waistcoat* or *watch pocket.*

waistcoat p. See *vest pocket.*

watch p. See *vest* and *fob pockets.*

welt p. *Slot* pocket finished with wide binding on the lower edge that extends upward to cover the slit; frequently used as chest pockets on men's coats, called *bosom pockets.*

pocketbook Synonym for *handbag, q.v.*

pocket handkerchief 1. See *handkerchief.* 2. From 16th to mid 19th centuries, handkerchiefs carried for display; often made of fine lace, silk, or linen.

pocket watch See *watches.*

poet's collar See *Bryon* under *collars.*

poet's shirt See *Lord Byron* under *shirts.*

point d'esprit (pwan des-pree) 1. Netlike machine-made fabric of cotton or nylon mesh with regularly spaced raised dots, used for evening gowns and veiling; first made in France in 1834. 2. Open stitch used in *guipure lace* with loops forming a pattern on a mesh ground. 3. Sheer stockings knitted with a dotted pattern.

pointing Glove-industry term for ornamental stitching on back of glove, same as *silking.*

Point l'Abbé coif Woman's high-crowned cap of voile or lace, with long streamers tied under right side of chin; worn in fishing village of Point l'Abbé on Brittany coast of France.

point lace Shortened *French* form for *needle-point lace.* For varieties, see *point de . . . Alençon, Angleterre, Espagne,* etc., under *laces.*

point noué French lacemakers' term for *buttonhole* stitch, *q.v.,* the basis of all needle-point lace.

points Cords with metal tips used to fasten garments together from 14th to mid 17th centuries, e.g. *hose* tied to *trunk breeches, q.v., trunkhose* attached to *doublet.* Also spelled *poynts.*

Poiret, Paul See *designers appendix, France.*

Poiret twill Trademark for dress worsted. See *fabrics.*

poison ring 1. Finger ring designed to hold a dose of poison, worn from Roman period through the 17th century. Made in Roman times with the setting a mere shell and the poison behind it. Cesare Borgia's ring, dated

1503 and still in existence, has a small sliding panel which opened into a small cavity in which poison was placed. 2. Novelty item of the late 1960's sometimes used to contain perfume. See *rings.*

poke Large pouch used as pocket in late 16th and early 17th centuries; word still used for a bag in Southern U.S.

poke bonnet Bonnet with wide brim slanting forward from small crown to frame face in shadow; worn throughout 19th century. Also called *poking bonnet.*

poking sticks Term used in 16th century for heated bone, wood, or metal sticks used to set pleats of ruff.

Polaroid glasses See *glasses.*

Polish boot Woman's high front-laced boot decorated with colored heels and tassels; worn in 1860's.

Polish greatcoat Full-length tight-fitting men's coat, with collar, cuffs, and lapels of Russian lambskin, closed with *frog, q.v.,* fasteners; worn with evening dress in early 19th century.

Polish jacket Woman's waist-length jacket made with revers and collar; sleeves wide at wrist, squared off and slit to elbow on inside seam; usually made of cashmere lined with quilted satin; worn outdoors informally in mid 1840's.

Polish mantle Knee-length cloak made of satin edged with fur, with attached cape; worn in mid 1840's.

Polish toque Woman's hat somewhat similar to *pillbox, q.v.,* trimmed in front with foliage and in back with a large bunch of velvet ribbon loops; worn in mid 1860's.

polka 1. Woman's short outdoor jacket with full sleeves, made of cashmere or velvet lined with silk; worn in mid 1840's. Variety of *casaweck, q.v.* 2. Woman's knitted close-fitting jacket. 3. Woman's French cap of cream-colored tulle with crocheted edges, appliquéd

with lace floral designs, wide lappets covering ears and tied under chin.

polka dot See *dots* under *prints.*

polo belt See *belts.*

Polo Cloth Trademark for heavy coat. wool. See *fabrics.*

polo coat See *coats.*

polo collar Man's white starched collar with points sloping towards shoulders, standing or turned down; worn in late 1880's.

polo dress See *dresses.*

polo hat See *chukka* under *hats.*

polonaise (po-lo-nehz) A garment in the Polish manner: 1. Woman's ankle-length dress with fitted un-boned bodice, low neckline, and

tight elbow-length sleeves with ruffled edge; the overskirt cut away in front, draped up by drawstrings over hips revealing elaborate underskirt; worn in 18th century. Also called *gown à la polonaise* or *Pompadour polonaise* in late 19th century. 2. Woman's fitted jacket, buttoned in front, cut away over skirt, sometimes with cape, called *polonaise pardessus* in mid 19th century. 3. Man's frock coat, in late 18th century. 4. Man's blue military coat, in early 19th century. *Der.* French, Polish—feminine form of adjective.

polo shirt See *knit shirts* under *shirts*. See *dresses*.

polyester Generic name for man-made fibers made of ethylene glycol and terephthalic acid, having the following qualities: shrinkproof, wrinkle-and-moth resistant. Yarns are knitted or woven, often in blended fabrics with cotton or rayon. See *Dacron, Kodel, Fortrel,* and *Vycron.*

pomander See *pommes de senteur.*

pommel slicker See *coats.*

pommes de senteur (pum de sawn-tehr) Small balls of gold or silver filigree set with precious stones used to hold scent, carried or hung from belt in Middle Ages. Also called *apples, musk balls* or *pomander. Der.* French, perfumed apples.

pompadour 1. See *hairstyles.* 2. Woman's drawstring handbag, usually velvet or lace, of 18th century, named after Marquise de Pompadour, mistress of Louis XV of France. 3. See *pompon.*

Pompadour bodice Name for bodice of *polonaise,* 1., *q.v.*

Pompadour polonaise Variant of *gown à la polonaise, q.v.*

Pompadour sleeve Adaptation in 1830's and '40's of elbow-length sleeve edged with ruffle worn by the Marquise de Pompadour, mistress of Louis XV of France.

Pompeian silk sash Wide black silk belt woven with allegorical figures, usually worn by women with a white summer jacket and bodice and colored skirt in 1860's.

Pompey See *physical wig.*

pompon 1. Round ball of cut ends of yarn used as trimming. 2. Hair or cap ornament composed of feathers, tinsel, butterflies, etc. worn in center part of hair by women from 1740's to 1760's, originally called *pompadour.* 3. Same as *top knot, q.v.,* under *hairstyles.*

poncho (pon-cho) 1. Blanket-like cloak with slit in center for head,

worn originally by South American cowboys, usually waterproof; sometimes knitted or woven in bold Indian designs. *Der.* from Spanish-American version of Araucamion word *pontho,* name for a woolen fabric. Also called *ruana, q.v.,* in Colombia. 2. Oblong of waterproof fabric with center slit for head, used as rain garment or flat as tarpaulin or similar strip of terry cloth used as combination beach wrap and mat. 3. Blanket that goes over head and buttons under arms to form sleeves, insulated against cold or heat, developed for NASA space program in 1960's and called *space blanket.* 4. Men's and women's loose cape-like cloak with wide full sleeves, worn in mid 19th century. 4. Poncho-like garments in many materials including suede, knits; popular with young people of both sexes in 1960's and '70's.

pongee Lightweight wild silk. See *fabrics.*

pony See *furs.*

ponyet 1. *Doublet* sleeve on lower part of arm, frequently of different fabric from upper sleeve, worn from 14th to 16th century. Also called *poynet.* 2. Long pin with decorative head worn by men in 17th century. Also called *little bodkin.*

pony tail See *hairstyles.*

poodle cloth Curly-napped fabric. See *fabrics.*

poodle cut See *hairstyles.*

poor-boy Descriptive term used in mid 1960's referring to type of shrunken, casual clothing influenced by that worn by newsboys in early 20th century. See *dresses*

and *sweaters* and *newsboy* under *caps.*

pop beads See *beads* or *necklaces.*

poplin Firm, cross-ribbed fabric. See *fabrics.*

Poppits See *beads.*

porcupine headdress Hairstyle with short hair standing up like bristles; worn at end of 18th century. Also called *porc-epic.*

pork-pie hat See *hats.*

port cannons See *cannons.*

porte-jupe Pompadour (port zhupe pom-pa-door) Belt worn under dress in 1860's, made with eight suspen-

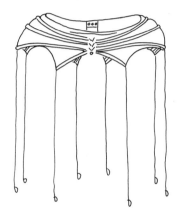

ders for looping up outer skirt when walking; also called *dress elevator.*

Porter, Thea See *designers appendix, England.*

posh British slang term meaning rich or luxurious, derived from the acronym for preferred quarters on ships sailing between Britain and India: Port Out, Starboard Home— *i.e.* the shady side of the ship.

postboy hat Woman's small straw hat with high flat crown and narrow brim sloping down all around, trimmed with plume in front and worn perched on top of head, popular at end of 19th century.

poster dress See *dresses.*

postiches See *hairpieces.*

postillion (poce-till-yun) 1. Hat with tall tapered crown and narrow brim, usually beaver, worn by women, sometimes with flowing scarf tied round base of crown, for riding. 2. Dress bodice extended below back waistline, usually with pleats or ruffles that flare outwards; worn by women in latter half of 19th century. Also called *postillion basque. Der.* From clothes worn by postillions, men on horseback accompanying carriages.

postillion coat Fitted greatcoat with *pannier* flap pockets, high *Regency collar,* and broad *revers, q.q.v.*

postillion corsage Tight-fitting jacket-top with long sleeves and high neck, back with a series of double box pleats, one over the other to form

fullness over hips, or with long tabs over the bustle in back; usually worn with contrasting skirt in 1880's. Also spelled *postilion corsage.*

posts 1. See *brassieres.* 2. See *earrings.*

pot derby Colloquial term for *derby* or *bowler,* see under *hats.*

pot hat See *chimney-pot hat.*

potholder vest See *vests.*

potten kant lace See *Antwerp* under *laces.*

Potter, Clare See *designers appendix, United States.*

potting See *decating.*

pouch 1. See *handbags.* 2. Bag, or purse, suspended from gentlemen's belt, often with dagger thrust through, worn from 12th to early 16th centuries.

pouf See *hairstyles.*

pouf au sentiment (poof o sont-eh-mont) Extravagantly high hairstyle elaborately ornamented with flowers and other objects worked over framework of gauze; worn by women in 18th century before French Revolution, *e.g.,* Marie Antoinette.

poulaine (poo-lan) French term for shoe in England called *piked shoe* or *crakow, q.q.v.* Also spelled *poulain* and *pullayne.*

poult de soie Cross-ribbed dress silk. See *fabrics.*

pouncet-box Another name for *dry-scent box,* or *pomander, q.v.,* carried during late 16th century.

pouncing See *pinking.*

pourpoint French term for the stuffed and quilted *doublet* or *jack-*

et worn by men from 14th century to 17th century and formerly called *paltock* or *gippon, q.q.v.* Also see *doublet* and *gambeson.*

poussin lace See *Dieppe point* under *laces.*

powder blue Pale gray-blue.

powdering jacket or **gown** A loose wrap put on by men in 18th century to protect clothing while the wig was powdered. Also see *face cone.*

poynts Variant of *points, q.v.*

prayer veil See *veils.*

pre-cuffed trousers See *pants.*

Premet See *designers appendix, France.*

première main(prem-ee-er man) French term for head of workroom in French couture house. *Der.* French, first hand.

prêt-à-porter (preh ah portay) French adjective for ready-to-wear clothes; literally, ready to be carried.

pre-walkers Infants' shoes with very soft soles, worn before child begins to walk.

Prince Albert coat 1. Double-breasted, long *frock coat, q.v.,* with flat collar, usually of velvet; worn for formal weddings, funerals, etc., until about 1920. 2. Adaptation of this coat for women, a double-breasted, fitted knee-length coat with turn-down collar and revers, flared skirt seamed at waistline, with two unpressed pleats with button trim at center back; worn in late 1890's. *Der.* Named for Prince Albert of Saxe-Coburg-Gotha, consort of England's Queen Victoria.

Prince of Wales jacket Man's jacket, similar to reefer, cut in double-breasted style with three sets of buttons; worn in late 1860's and named for future Edward VII of England.

Prince of Wales shoe See *oxfords* under *shoes.*

Prince Rupert Woman's full-length fitted coat of velvet or plush, worn with a blouse and skirt, in late 19th century.

princess chemise Woman's undergarment with *corset cover* and *petticoat, q.q.v,* made in one piece with no waistline seam, sometimes lavishly trimmed with lace at neckline, armholes, and hem; worn in late 19th and early 20th centuries.

princesse lace See *laces.*

princess style Basic cut for women's clothing characterized by continuous vertical panels, shaped to body through torso without waistline seam; used in dresses, coats, underslips, etc., from mid 19th century on, especially in late 1930's and 1940's. Also called by French form, *princesse.* See *dresses, coats, slips, silhouettes, waistlines.*

Princeton orange Brilliant orange color, official color of Princeton University.

print Design reproduced on fabric in color either by mechanical means or by hand, in *repeat patterns* or *all-over designs.* Also see *direct printing* and *discharge printing;* hand printing methods include *batik, tie dye, silk screen,* and *hand-blocked prints, q.q.v.,* below.

411

PRINTS:

all-over p. Pattern covering entire fabric, repeats not obvious.

abstract p. Stylized designs of a non-naturalistic type, e.g., geometric pattern.

African p. Bold geometrical designs frequently carried out in browns, blacks, and whites.

American Indian p. Bold geometrical designs from North American or Mexican Indian sources, carried out in bright colors, popular in late 1960's. Also called *Navajo* or *Aztec prints.*

Art Déco p. Small, geometrical prints frequently outlined in black inspired from a decorative-art exhibit in Paris 1925, reintroduced in the late 1960's and used for fabrics and knits for dresses, sweaters, etc.

Art Nouveau p. Flowing prints of stylized leaves, flowers, and intertwined vines popular in late 1960's, inspired by early 20th-century French art movement.

Aztec p. Designs based on Mexican Indian geometrical motifs in bright colors usually banded in black, popular in late 1960's.

bandanna p. Designs, usually in black or white on a red or navy-blue background, in imitation of *bandanna handkerchiefs, q.v.*

batik p. Designs, usually in dark blue, rust, black or yellow, copied from Indonesian technique of painting with wax before dyeing. See *batik* under *fabrics.*

block p. See *hand-blocked print.*

bookbinder p. Designs copied from multi-colored abstract swirled and wood grain designs on end papers of expensively bound books.

border p. Print designed so that one selvage forms a distinct border which is used at the hem of a dress or shirt or worked into the garment in some other way.

burnt-out p. Design made by printing with chemical on fabric woven of two different types of fibers; the printing dissolves one of the fibers to form the pattern.

calico p. Small repeat print usually of sprigs of flowers on colored ground—red, blue, yellow or black; popular since mid 19th century in America.

discharge p. Method of printing fabrics with color-destroying chemicals to bleach out a design, leaving it white against colored ground; colored design on contrast color ground can be produced by adding a bleach-resistant dye to the bleach itself.

dots Circles used as a pattern, in regular rows or a random arrangement; e.g., *coin dot,* larger than a dime; *pin dot,* as small as the head of a pin—up to 1/16 inch; *polka dot,* any dot larger than a pin dot.

duplex p. Fabric with same design printed on both sides to imitate a woven pattern.

fleur-de-lis French stylized lily design, used in heraldry and part of the coat-of-arms of France's former royal family; often employed in a formal repeat design.

flocked p. Design made by applying

glue to lightweight fabric such as organdy, and dusting with tiny fibers that adhere to form a pattern; frequently used to make *border prints* or *flock-dotted Swiss, q.q.v.*

floral p. Any design using flowers in either a natural or stylized manner, e.g., a daisy, a rose, or sprigs of flowers together in a repeat design.

hand-blocked p. Pattern made by cutting design on wood or linoleum blocks, one for each color in the print, inking the blocks, then printing colors individually with hand press.

hand-painted p. A contradiction in terms, not a print at all but a pattern painted directly on fabric; a technique used by American Indians and revived in early 1970's by New York designer Halston and others.

hand-screened p. See *silk-screen print,* below.

Liberty p. Trademark of Liberty, London, for wide range of printed fabrics, best known are small multicolored floral designs on cotton or silk.

medallion p. Repeat round or oval design sometimes connected with realistic swags of foliage.

overprint Print on fabric already dyed.

paisley p. All-over design of stylized flowers, pears, leaves, *etc.,* usually in rich reds, beige, gold tones in imitation of classic Paisley shawls. See *Paisley shawl.*

panel p. A large design intended to be used in one length, without repeat, for each dress.

patchwork p. Fabric actually made by sewing together small patches of several prints or a print designed to mimic this effect.

Pucci p. A series of distinctive prints designed by Italian designer Emilio Pucci, *q.v.,* the earliest ones using heraldic patterns and motifs from medieval banners in brilliant colors on white ground. The designer incorporates his signature in the designs, usually printed on silk jersey. Pucci's prints have been widely imitated on Ban-lon jersey.

resist p. Same process as in *batik* (see *fabrics*), but using chemicals instead of wax to keep dye from pattern.

roller p. Use of engraved copper cylinders to produce a colored design, with as many as sixteen separate rollers, one for each color.

screen p. See *silk-screen print.*

shadow p. Design formed by printing the warp yarns before weaving fabric. See *warp printing.*

silk-screen p. Pattern blocked out on silk screen laid over flat fabric, color squeezed through mesh, each color using a separate screen; usually done by hand or a small machine.

stenciled p. Design made by using cardboard or metal cut-outs over fabric, spraying or printing over them, the covered portions resisting color.

tie-dyed p. Handmade primitive print, made by folding fabric and tying at intervals, then immersing in dye and unfolding to reveal irregular motifs; method originated in Dutch East Indies; popular as a handicraft in U.S. in late 1960's, and early 1970's; used on denim pants, knit shirts, dresses and even furs and imitated commercially by other methods. Called *banada* in India.

wallpaper p. Tiny floral stripes alternating with plain colored stripes, frequently in pastel colors, in imitation of 19th century wallpaper.

warp p. Design put on warp yarns before fabric is woven, producing watered effect and fuzzy edges.

Priscilla apron Young girl's apron with full skirt shirred into waistband and bib, *q.v.*, extended around neck in broad, lace-trimmed, *sailor-collar, q.v.*, effect, straps from shoulder blades to waistband in back; frequently made of *dotted Swiss, nainsook,* or *lightweight muslin;* worn in late 1890's.

profile hat See *hats.*

promenade or **walking costume** Terms

used in last half of 19th century for clothes suitable for walking, shopping, etc. as contrasted with *carriage clothes* for riding.

promenade skirt Underskirt with steel

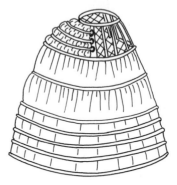

hoops set into muslin; worn in late 1850's.

pronged setting See *gem settings* under *gems.*

proportioned hose See *hose.*

proportioned pants See *pants.*

prunella See *fabrics.*

Prussian collar Man's narrow coat collar, standing, with ends nearly meeting in front, or turned down; worn in 19th century.

Psyche knot (si-kee) Copy of Greek hairstyle for women; hair pulled back and twisted to form a knot at back of head. Named for Greek mythological maiden, the lover of Cupid, made immortal by Jupiter.

Pucci, Emilio See *prints,* also see *designers appendix, Italy.*

Pucci helmet Clear plastic bubble to protect the head and face from rain, designed by Italian *Emilio Pucci, q.v.,* as part of uniform for stewardesses of Braniff International airline in 1965.

PUCCI HELMET

pudding-basin cut Bowl-shaped hairstyle for men consisting of hair combed from crown of head into bangs in front; fashionable in England, France and Italy in 15th century.

p'u-fang Patch of embroidery in gold and bright colors sewn to front and back of Chinese *Mandarin court robe, q.v.,* indicating rank of wearer, *e.g.,* circle indicated princely rank, square patch worn by lesser officials of the imperial court. Also see *p'u-fu.*

puff 1. (verb) To make full, particularly in a *sleeve, q.v.* 2. 19th-century term for a V-shaped *gore, q.v.,* of thin fabric that filled in space at back of waistband of men's trousers, lacing used to close gap and fabric pulled out through laces.

p'u-fu Three-quarter-length coat of purple-black silk, worn in China during imperial period from 1644 to 1912, interesting during Ch'ing dynasty because of embroidered patches, or *p'u-fang, q.v.*

pug hood Woman's soft hood with pleats radiating from back where it fitted the head, with or without attached cape, usually black with colored turned-back lining, tied under chin with matching ribbons;

worn in 18th century. Same as *short hood.*

pugree, puggree 1. See *pagri.* 2. Scarf tied around a hat or sun helmet with ends hanging down the back; worn for protection from sun, particularly in India.

Pulitzer, Lilly See *Lilly* under *dresses.* Also see *designers appendix, United States.*

pull English abbreviation for *pullover sweater.*

pullayne Variant of *poulaine, q.v.*

pullback Skirt with the fullness drawn to the back and draped; fashionable in 1880's.

pulled work See *punch work* under *embroideries.*

pullings out Decorative effect used from 16th through mid 17th centuries made by drawing out colored lining fabric through slashes in the outer garment, *e.g.,* the doublet, trunk hose or sleeves. Also called *puffs.* Also see *panes.*

Pullman slipper See *slippers.*

pull-on See *girdles, gloves,* and *pants.*

pullover A garment without full-length opening, can be pulled over the head; especially a *pullover* sweater as opposed to a *cardigan, q.q.v.* under *sweaters.* Also called *pull.* Also see *knit shirts* under *shirts.*

pultney cap Woman's heart-shaped indoor cap, wired peak over forehead; worn in mid 18th century.

pumps See *shoes.*

punched Shoe- or leather-industry term for leather perforated for decorative effect.

punch work See *embroideries.*

Punjab silk Fancy silks imitating Indian cloth. See *fabrics.*

punto lace See *laces.*

Puritan collar See *collars.*

Puritan hat See *hats.*

purse Synonym for *handbag, q.v.*

push-up bra See *brassieres.*

pussy-cat bow Large bow of stiff fabric placed at high neckline of dress, blouse, or coat.

Pussy Willow Trademark for a silk taffeta. See *fabrics.*

puttees 1. World War I U.S. Army leggings consisting of long strip of khaki-colored wool fabric, about four inches wide, wrapped around leg from ankle to knee. 2. U.S. Army leggings made of shaped pieces of fabric or leather, usually closed with buckles, similar to *gaiters.* See *leggings, chaps.*

PUTTEES, 1927

PVC Initials for polyvinyl chloride, a plastic material used for children's shoe soles, also British and French term for man-made fiber of this product used for apparel and lingerie.

pyjamas English variant of *pajamas, q.v.*

pyramid coat Tent-shaped woman's coat with narrow shoulders and wide at hem; worn in late 1940's and early 1950's.

pyramid heel See *heels.*

python See *leathers.*

Q

Qiana Trademark for a nylon. *See fabrics.*

quafe See *coif.*

quaftan See *caftan.*

quail-pipe boot Man's high, soft leather boot worn wrinkled down on the legs; fashionable in late 16th and early 17th centuries.

quaintise Variant of *cointise, q.v.*

Quaker bonnet Small, close-fitting, undecorated woman's bonnet with a puffed crown, made in same fabric as the dress (often gray), and worn over a ruffled white muslin cap; prescribed for women of Quaker faith by the Society of Friends.

Quaker cap See *Joan cap.*

Quaker hat Hat with large, slightly rolled brim, low crown, and no ornament; worn by Quaker men.

Quant, Mary See *designers appendix, England.*

quarter Back portion of shoe upper, covering the sides and back of the foot.

quartered cap Boy's cap with flat, circular crown divided into four segments, attached to stiff band, with or without a visor; worn from mid 18th to mid 19th centuries.

quartz See *gems.*

quatrefoil Geometrical four-leaf design derived from heraldry; popular for printed fabrics.

queen's cloth Jamaican cotton. See *fabrics.*

querpo (kwer-po) 17th century term for a man without cloak or jacket. *Der.* From Spanish *cuerpo,* body.

queue (kew) See *hairstyles.*

queue de lion (ker de le-ohn) See *queue* under *hairstyles.*

queue-peruke (ker pear-ook) Man's small wig with fluffed or curled sides and long ends tied back with black bow to make a *queue, q.v.,* under *hairstyles.*

quill 1. Long stiff shaft of a feather with many thin projections called barbs; used as ladies' hat trim, especially in 1940's. 2. Bobbin used in weaving to hold filling yarn.

quill work Decorative designs made on fabric and leather by North American Indians using porcupine quills.

quilling 1. Trimming made of narrow fluted fabric. 2. Process of winding filling yarns on bobbins or *quills.*

quilting Technique of joining together layers of fabrics, sometimes with *batting, q.v.,* or other filling between, by hand or machine topstitching in criss-cross lines, in diamonds or in other patterns, to provide added bulk or warmth, *e.g.,* quilted petticoats worn as underskirts in 18th and 19th centuries, patchwork bed quilts popular in 19th and 20th centuries. Used for *robes, raincoats, sports jackets, handbags, linings,* etc.

quirk Small triangular insert placed in glove at base of each finger and at thumb; used to give a close fit yet permit flexibility.

quissionet See *cushionet.*

quizzing glass *Monocle, q.v.,* a single eyeglass, suspended from neck chain or fixed in head of cane; worn by dandies and women in 18th and early 19th centuries.

quoif (kwaf) See *coif.*

quoton, qutum, qutn Arabic word for *cotton.*

R

Rabanne, Paco See *designers appendix, France.*

rabat 1. Black *dickey* or *shirtfront* to which the white *clerical collar, q.q.v.,* is attached; worn with suits or with liturgical robes by Catholic and Protestant clergy. 2. *Falling collar* of linen and lace, worn over man's *doublet, q.q.v.,* in 17th century.

rabato (rah-bah-toe) 1. White collar wired to stand up at back of neck, worn with low-cut neckline by women from late 16th century to mid 17th century. 2. 17th-century term for a support of wire, wood, etc., used for the ruff. Also spelled *rebato.* Also called a *supportasse* or *underpropper.*

rabbit See *furs.*

raccoon See *furs.*

race Textile-industry term for floating yarns in *pile weave, q.v.,* that are cut after weaving and brushed up to make pile, e.g. the pile on velvets.

racing shoe See *shoes.*

radium Silk or rayon taffeta. See *fabrics.*

radzimir Ribbed silk. See *fabrics.*

raffia See *straws.*

Raglan, Lord (1788–1855) Fitzroy James Henry Somerset, British General in Crimean War, after losing an arm in charge of a light-cavalry brigade in 1854, had coat designed with special sleeve, later called *raglan sleeve, q.v.*

raglan boot Thigh-length, soft, black leather boot worn by men for hunting in late 1850's; named after *Lord Raglan, q.v.*

raglan coat See *coats.*

raglan sleeve See *sleeves* and *shoulders.*

rail 1. A loose garment; in the 17th and 18th centuries, a *nightgown, q.v.,* also applied to gown worn at home in morning. See *night rail.* 2. Folded *neckerchief* worn like shawl around neck by women from late 15th to late 17th centuries. See *head rail.* Also spelled *rayle.*

railroad trousers Term for men's trousers with stripes, horizontal or vertical; worn from late 1830's to 1850.

railway pocket Flat bag with side opening tied on with tape around waist, reached by slit in skirt; worn by women under dress when traveling, from 1850's. (See drawing, page 405)

railway stitch See *chain* under *stitches.*

raiment Archaic or poetic term for clothing.

rain bonnet See *bonnets.*

rain boot See *boots.*

raincoat Topcoat of waterproof or water-repellent material worn by men and women in various styles, single- or double-breasted, belted or loose, knee to ankle length; contemporary versions: *reversible* or with removable fur or wool *linings,* quilted, laminated, plain or patterned, folded in small case, made of bonded wool, silk, plastic, canvas, etc.; often used as utility garment or all-weather coat. See *macintosh, slicker, pommel slicker,* and *trench coat* under *coats.*

419

rainwear Waterproofed or water-repellent coat, cape, hat, or other accessory. See *boots, coats, dresses.*

raised embroidery See *embroideries.*

Rajah Trademark for a slubbed silk. See *fabrics.*

rajah collar See *Nehru* under *collars* and *necklines.*

rajah jacket See *jackets.*

ramie Strong soft fiber from inner bark of ramie plant, imported from China; used for dress goods, hats, etc. Also called *rhea* or *China grass.*

Ramillies wig Man's wig puffed at sides with long, tapered, single- or double-braided *queue, q.v.,* tied with black ribbon at nape or looped up and fastened; worn in 18th century. *Der.* Named for English victory over French in Ramillies, Belgium, in 1706. Also spelled *Ramilet, Ramille.*

ranch coat See *coats.*

ranch mink See *mink* under *furs.*

ranelagh mob Woman's cap consisting of a *kerchief, q.v.,* with two long ends tied under chin, pulled back and pinned or left to hang down; worn in 1760's.

Ranger's hat See *hats.*

Raphael body Woman's fitted *bodice, q.v.,* with a low square neckline, frequently worn with a high-necked *chemisette* underneath, matching skirt; worn from late 1850's through 1860's.

rapolin (rap-o-lin) Swiss millinery braid having uneven surface, made in triple rows.

raschel knit See *knits.*

rat Sausage-shaped padded roll of hair or felt worn by women under natural hair to create high *pompadour* effect in early 20th century. See *pompadour* under *hairstyles.*

ratcatcher See *shirts.*

ratine See *fabrics.*

ratiné yarn See *yarns.*

rationals Popular name for full pleated serge bloomers worn by women for bicycling in 1890's.

rat-tail braid See *braids.*

rat-tail comb Fine hair comb with half of length having teeth; other half, a long pointed end for shaping curls.

rattan 1. Flat reed-like stem from tropical palm woven to form *basket handbags, q.v.,* and other items. 2. Man's *cane, q.v.,* made from East Indian palm; carried in 17th and 18th centuries.

rawhide See *leathers.*

raw silk Silk fiber reeled from cocoon while still containing the gum or sericin; wound into reels for sale, it may have two filaments and be called *bave* or one filament and called *brin.*

rayon Man-made fiber resembling silk. See *fabrics.*

rayon staple Uniform short *rayon, q.v.,* fibers, usually one to five inches in length, manufactured directly or by cutting filaments into short lengths; spun into yarns similar to cotton and wool.

ready-to-wear Apparel that is mass produced in standard sizes. Records of ready-to-wear industry tabulated in U.S. in Census of 1860 and included *hoop skirts, cloaks,* and *mantillas;* from 1890 on, *shirtwaists* and *wrappers* were added and, after 1930, *dresses.* Also abbreviated *RTW.*

Reboux, Caroline See *designers appendix, France.*

rebozo (re-bow-zo) 1. *Veil* or *scarf* worn over head by Spanish or Mexican women in place of lace *mantilla, q.q.v.* 2. *Shawl,* similar to a *poncho, q.q.v.,* worn by South American Indians.

rebras (ray-bras) 13th and 17th-century term used when garment or accessory was turned back to reveal lining, e.g., *revers* of coat, upturned *brim* on hat, *cuff* of glove.

Récamier, Madame Jeanne Françoise Julie Adelaide (1777–1849); famous beauty of Napoleonic era, painted by David and Gérard, her mode of dress and hairstyles widely imitated.

Récamier hairstyle (ray-cahm-ee-ay) Hair arranged with *chignon, q.v.,* high on back of head, with curls at neck; worn in 1870's and 1880's after hairstyle worn by *Madame Récamier, q.v.* above.

reclaimed wool Term required by U.S. Wool Labeling Act of 1939 to be used when referring to *reprocessed* and *reused wool, q.v.*

Redfern, Charles Poynter See *designers appendix, France.*

red fox See *furs.*

redingote (red-in-gote) 1. Man's long full *overcoat* with overlapping front skirts, wide collar; worn for horseback riding in mid 18th century.

2. Woman's semi-fitted *coat-dress,* open above waistcoat; worn during 19th century. Also called *pelisse-robe, q.v.* by 1840's. In 1890's, an *ensemble* of dress and coat. 3. Woman's *semi-fitted coat,* often matched to a dress, and worn as an ensemble; popular in 1940's–'50's. See *coats.*

reefer Short, double-breasted, semi-fitted jacket or *short coat,* usually dark blue, with three or four pairs of buttons, low collar and lapels, vents on side seams; worn by men from 1860 on and from 1890's by men and women as an overcoat. See *coats.* Also see *pilot coat, pea jacket,* and *yachting jacket* in *sport jackets* under *jackets.*

reel 1. Revolving frame used for winding skeins of yarns. 2. Frame used for winding raw silk from the cocoon. 3. Linen yarn measure consisting of 72,000 yards.

Reemay Trademark for a non-woven interlining. See *fabrics.*

regard rings Rings worn in 16th century set with stones with names having initials spelling out such words as L-O-V-E or name of the beloved.

regatta shirt Man's *cambric* or *oxford-striped* shirt with plain front; informal summer wear in 1840's.

Regence Tie silk. See *fabrics.*

Regency coat Man's short-waisted coat, cut away to show waistcoat, with knee-length tails, high rolling *Napoleonic* or *Regency collar, q.q.v.,* revealing close-wrapped cravat; worn by *dandies* like *Beau Brummell, q.v.* during English Regency, 1811–1820. Also see *coats.*

Regency collar See *collars.*

421

Regency costumes 1. French period during regency of Philip, duc de Orleans, 1715–1723; characterized by lightweight dresses with *basque bodices, sabot sleeves,* enormous *panniers, q.q.v.* 2. English period during the regency of the Prince of Wales; from 1811–1820, noted for fashions of the *dandies* and *Beau Brummell, q.q.v.*

regimental stripe See *stripes.*

Regny, Jane See *designers appendix, France.*

regular The ordinary size range as opposed to special sizes; e.g. *regular* boys as opposed to *slim* or *husky.*

regular twist See *Z-twist.*

Renaissance lace See *laces.*

rengue Cloth made in the Philippines of pineapple fiber.

rep Ribbed silk. See *fabrics.*

rep stitch See *stitches.*

rerebrace Plate armor worn on the upper arm; an upper *cannon* or *vambrace, q.q.v.*

resist dyeing Piece-dyeing process in which some of the yarns are chemically treated, resulting in two-toned fabric as treated yarns remain undyed while other, untreated, yarns take the dye. Also see *resist printing.*

resist printing Method of printing fabric by first printing design on fabric with chemical paste that will not take dye and then dying the fabric; when chemical is removed, design is left white against colored background.

reticella lace (reh-tee-chella) See *laces.*

reticulation (re-ti-cu-lay-shun) Decorative *netting* holding hair on either side of face, worn with *horned headdress* by women in 15th century. See *caul.*

reticule (ret-ih-kewl) Woman's small *drawstring purse* made of satin, mesh, velvet, red morocco leather,

etc., from late 18th to early 20th century. Also called *indispensible* and *ridicule.*

reused wool Wool that has been previously made into a garment, worn, and discarded; collected, cleaned, and reduced to a fibrous state; after some new fibers are added it is respun into yarn, woven into fabric, and again made into a garment. Reused wool is composed of short fibers and generally has a harsh feel or *hand, q.v.* The Wool Labeling Act of 1939 requires that such wool be labeled properly.

revers See *collars.*

reverse calf See *leathers.*

reverse guiches See *curls.*

reverse twist See *S-twist.*

reversible Any garment constructed so that it may be worn inside out;

tweed-and-poplin reversible rain-coats were very popular in 1940's.

Reykjavik sweater See *sweaters.*

rhadzimir Variant of *radzimir, q.v.* under *fabrics.*

rhea Indian name for *ramie, q.v.*

Rhinegraves See *petticoat breeches.*

rhinestone A colorless transparent artificial gem made of glass or *paste, q.v.,* usually cut like a diamond and used widely in costume jewelry, buttons, etc. *Der.* Originally made in Strasbourg, France, on the Rhine river.

Rhodes, Zandra See *designers appendix, England.*

rhodium White-colored metal in the platinum group, used for plating jewelry.

rib 1. Textile-industry term for *corded* effect in fabrics caused by weave or by use of heavier yarns, *e.g.* as in piqué, ottoman, faille, etc. 2. Individual strip of metal that forms part of frame of umbrella, *e.g.,* usually are seven to sixteen ribs in an umbrella. See *rib knit* under *knits.*

ribbon 1. Long narrow strip of silk, cotton, rayon, etc., woven with *selvages, q.v.,* on both sides, or of acetate woven and then sliced into narrow strips by heated knives that fuse the edges, in various widths; used mainly for trimming and for tying hair and made in a variety of weaves: cross-ribbed, called *grosgrain;* with looped edges, called *picot;* cut-pile surface, or *velvet* (sometimes satin-backed); *satin* (vary narrow pink or blue satin is called *baby ribbon, q.v.*). Also called *riband* from 14th to 16th century.

rib-tickler Term used to describe short *top, sweater,* or *shirt* that just reaches to rib-cage; similar to *bare-midriff top, q.v.*

rib velvet See *corduroy* under *fabrics.*

rib weave See *weaves.*

Ricci, Nina See *designers appendix, France.*

rice braid See *braids.*

rickrack See *braid.*

ridicule See *reticule.*

riding boots See *boots.*

riding breeches See *pants.*

riding coat 1. See *coats.* 2. Man's suit coat with skirt slanting from waist to thigh-length in back; worn from 1825 to 1870's. Also called *New-market coat, morning coat, q.q.v.*

riding-coat dress Dress cut in coat style with buttons down front, large collar and lapels, long tight sleeves, and skirt with slight train; worn in last quarter of 18th century.

riding habit Men's and women's costume for horseback riding, usually consisting of *jacket, breeches* or *jodhpurs, q.v., stock-*tied shirt, *cap* or *hard hat, boots;* varying in degrees of formality from hunt-club regulation colors to casual *hacking jackets, q.v.,* and long trousers. See under *jackets, pants, pink coat.* For historical riding habits see *justaucorps, Brunswick,* and *Joseph.*

riding pants See *riding breeches* and *jodhpurs,* under *pants.*

riding skirt Calf-length wrap-around skirt, worn by women who rode side-saddle in late 19th and early 20th centuries.

riding smalls Man's *riding breeches* of light-colored *doeskin, q.q.v.,* made with wide hips but tight from knees down; worn from 1814 to 1835.

riding stock See *stock* under *ties.*

riding suit See *riding habit.*

rimless glasses See *glasses.*

ring Circlet, usually of metal, plain or ornamented in many designs with incised pattern or set with precious or fake stones, worn on *fingers* or *toes* since early times as symbol of rank, seal of faith, or ornament. Commonest types: *wedding bands,* traditionally gold, worn on third finger, left hand; *engagement ring,* usually a diamond *solitaire* (a ring with a single stone); *signet ring* with intaglio-cut stone with ·crest or initial; *cocktail* or *dinner* ring usually *cluster* of stones in *dome* shape; and special colored gems indicating birth months or sentimental meanings. *Watches* are sometimes mounted on rings.

ring and pin See *annular* and *penannular brooches.*

ring bracelet See *bracelets.*

ring buckle Two rings on one end of belt through which opposite belt end threads—first through both, then back through one—and pulls tight. Also called *cinch buckle.*

ring collar See *collars.*

ringlets See *curls.*

ring scarf See *scarfs.*

ring watch A timepiece mounted on a *ring, q.v.,* and worn on the finger.

ripple cape Woman's short ruffled cape extended beyond the shoulder by shirring three layers of fabric or lace onto a yoke, trimmed with ribbon; worn in 1890's.

ripple cloth See *fabrics.*

ripple skirt *Gored* skirt, *q.v.,* sometimes with as many as eleven gores, fitting snugly over hips but flared at hem to a width of six yards or

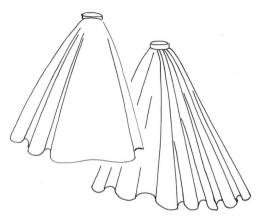

more; lined with *horsehair, q.v.,* stiffening and pressed to hang in rounded *pipe-organ pleats, q.v.;* worn in 1890's.

rise Men's tailoring term for distance from crotch to top of waistband in pants, e.g., hip-hugger pants have low rise.

robe 1. French word for *dress;* in the 18th and 19th centuries, applied to a variety of women's gowns with overskirts or back panels. See *robe à l'anglaise* and *robe redingote.* 2. Full-length ceremonial garment worn by men and women to indicate rank: academic gown, clerical gown, judge's robe, coronation robes, etc. 3. Loose garment with sleeves, sometimes belted, usually long but may be hip or knee-length and in such materials as quilted silk, terry cloth, brushed nylon, fake fur, etc.; worn informally as housecoat over night-clothes, as hostess coat or as a cover-up over bathing suit.

ROBES AND HOUSECOATS:

BRUNCH COAT

SHAVE COAT

BATHROBE

bathrobe Wrap-around robe usually with long sleeves, shawl collar, and sash; popular for both sexes in terry cloth or plaid wool or *bathrobe cloth, q.v.;* worn at home or as cover-up on beach.

beach r. Any coat-like garment worn at the beach or swimming pool to protect the bathing-suit wearer from the sun or to dry off after swimming; often made of *terry cloth, q.v.*

beach toga Full-length sleeved tunic with side seams slashed to waist, worn over swimsuits.

bed jacket Waist-length jacket, usually fastened down front and made of lightweight material, sometimes quilted, lined, or lacy knit, in pastel colors, often trimmed with *lace* or *marabou, q.v.,* as in the 1920's and 1930's; worn while sitting up in bed.

brunch coat Knee- or mid-calf-length front-buttoned robe, often in printed cotton, worn in the daytime at home; popular in 1950's. Also called *duster* or *breakfast coat. Der.* Named for meal combining breakfast and lunch.

425

caftan 1. Moroccan- or Mid-Eastern-inspired garment like a long full dress with slit neckline decorated with embroidery, long bell-shaped sleeves; introduced for at-home wear for men and women in mid 1960's. Also spelled *kaftan.*

djellaba Loose garment, sometimes hooded, derived from Moroccan man's cloak; worn by women as a *housecoat* or *hostess robe,* popular in 1960's along with the *caftan, q.v.*

dressing gown Loose robe worn informally by men and women since end of 18th century, usually in plain or patterned silk, frequently lined, with shawl collar, wrapped and tied with tasseled sash; more a host or hostess garment than utilitarian robe.

duster See *brunch coat.*

happi coat Hip-length jacket made in *kimono, q.v.,* style of brightly printed fabric, copied from knee-length jackets worn by Japanese laborers, frequently with printed medallion on back in imitation of original Japanese jackets which had symbol of employer on the back; used in U.S. as beach coats in 1950's–'60's. Also spelled *happie.*

hostess r. Full-length robe fastening in front, frequently with zipper, in elaborate fabrics; worn for entertaining at home. Also called *hostess gown, hostess coat.*

housecoat Informal robe worn at home. See *brunch coat* and *lounging robe.*

kabuki r. Similar to *happi coat, q.v.,* inspired by costumes of Japanese *kabuki* theater.

kimono (ki-mo-no) Long, loose, collarless outer garment with front opening, the characteristic *surplice* neckline band extending to hem and with wide straight sleeves set at right angle to body, held closed by wrapping wide sash or *obi, q.v.;* typical national Japanese garment copied by Westerners for at-home and beach wear in printed silk and cottons or terry cloth.

lounging r. Term applied to any woman's robe, often a long one, worn informally in the house for relaxation; *housecoat* or *brunch coat* usually suggests a garment more suitable for housework or morning meals.

monk's r. Full-length, flowing robe with bell sleeves, frequently with a hooded *cowl neckline, q.v.,* and rope belt; inspired by a monk's habit.

negligee (neg-le-zhay) Flowing, informal woman's robe of delicate fabric with trim of lace, ruffles, etc.; often worn with a matching nightgown.

peignoir See *negligee. Der.* French, garment worn when combing the hair.

shave coat Man's knee-length wrap-around bathrobe, frequently matched to pajamas.

sleep coat See *nightgowns.*

wrapper 1. Any robe made in wrap-around style. 2. Early 19th-century term for women's *housedress, q.v.,* one of first items made by garment industry in mass production.

robe à l'anglaise *Sack*-back dress with *box pleats, q.q.v.,* stitched from neck down to waist; worn in 1770's.

robe de chambre French term for *dressing gown, q.v.,* under *robes.*

robe gironnee Loose-fitting dress with *pipe-organ pleats, q.v.,* at waistline; worn in 15th century.

robe redingote Dress with collar and lapels on bodice, skirt opening in front over an *underskirt;* worn in 1830's and 40's. See *redingote.*

Robespierre collar (robes-pee-air) Man's coat collar coming up high at back of neck and then turned down with *jabot, q.v.,* showing in front, similar to *Regency collar, q.v.,* on a double-breasted coat. *Der.* Named for Maximillian Francois Marie Isadore de Robespierre, French lawyer and Revolutionist, executed in 1794.

robin front 19th century term for bodice with trimming from shoulder to waist, forming a deep-V point.

robings See *robins.*

Robin Hood hat Hat with high peaked crown, brim turned up in back, down in front; trimmed with one long feather. *Der.* From hat worn by legendary English outlaw of the 12th century.

robins Wide flat trimmings around neck and down front of woman's bodice, sometimes continued down sides of open overskirt; used in 18th and 19th centuries. Also called *robings.*

roccelo See *Roquelaure.*

Rochas, Marcel See *designers appendix, France.*

rock crystal See *gems.*

Rocker look Tough look of British young men in late 1950's, mixture of storm trooper and motorcyclist costume with crash helmet, tight jeans or drain-pipe trousers, black leather jacket, and knee-length boots or short boots with high heels. Also see *Mod.*

rocklo See *Roquelaure.*

rococo embroidery See *embroideries.*

roculo See *Roquelaure.*

Rodriguez, Pedro See *designers appendix, Spain.*

roll 1. 15th-century term for the circular pad made when converting the man's *chaperon, q.v.,* into a hat. 2. 16th and 17th century term for pad used to raise the front hair up from forehead. Also called *rowle.* 3. See *bourrelet.*

rolled collar See *collars.*

rolled gold Gold fused to a base metal then rolled in such a manner that the percentage of each metal stays the same. Sheets of gold are $\frac{1}{30}$ to $\frac{1}{40}$ and are thinner than sheets used for *gold filled, q.v.* Used instead of *karat gold, q.v.,* for less expensive and costume jewelry.

rolled hem Narrow *hem, q.v.,* usually made by rolling the cut edge of garment between the fingers to form a neat, tight edge and sewing invis-

ibly by hand; used principally on *scarves* and on *bias-cut ruffles* or *flounces, q.q.v.*

roller See *hats.*

roller print See *prints.*

roll farthingale Tub-shaped skirt, supported by means of *bum roll, q.v.,* tied around the waist.

roll sleeve See *sleeves.*

rollups Men's stockings pulled up over knee of breeches and folded over in wide band; worn in late 17th

to mid 18th centuries. Also called *rollers, roll-up stockings, rolling stockings* or *hose.*

romain French satin. See *fabrics.*

Romaine Trademark for a sheer crepe. See *fabrics.*

Roman collar See *collars.*

Roman costume See *toga, tunica, palla,* and *stola.*

Roman lace See *reticella* under *laces.*

Roman stripes See *stripes.*

Romany stripe See *bayadere* under *stripes.*

Romeo hairstyle See *hairstyles.*

Romeos See *slippers.*

rompers See *pants.*

rope necklace See *necklaces.*

Roquelaure (roke-lowr) Man's knee-length to full-length heavy *overcoat,* often fur-trimmed and lined with bright-colored silk, usually made with cape collar and back vent for riding horseback; worn in 18th century. *Der.* From Antoine Gastone Jean-Baptiste, le duc de Roquelaure (1656–1783), minister of wardrobe under Louis XV. Also called *roculo, roccelo,* and *rocklo.*

rosary See *beads.*

rose beads See *beads.*

Rosebery collar Man's detachable collar of white linen 3″ high in back, with rounded points in front; worn in mid 1890's. *Der.* Named for 5th Earl of Rosebery, British statesman, author; Prime Minister, 1894–95.

rose cut See *gem cuts.*

rosehube See *Rosenkäpli.*

Rosenadel Two-pronged, curved, ornamental hat pin used by Schwyz women of Switzerland to hold the *Rosenkäpli, q.v.*

Rosenkäpli Native *lace cap* worn by Schwyz women in Switzerland. Cap shaped like two open, upstanding fans dipping down in the front to show the raised central portion, decorated with flowers, under which long braids of hair are coiled.

rose-point lace See *laces.*

rose quartz See *gems.*

Roser, Maud See *designers appendix, France.*

rosette 1. Ornament arranged like a rose, usually ribbon arranged in standing loops or flattened into a formal pattern; used to trim shoes in 17th century and used today on dresses and hats. 2. Spotted marking on leopard fur, resembling a paw mark. 3. Mark left on ostrich skin when quill is removed.

rotonde Woman's short or three-quarter length circular *cape* of

lace or of same material as dress; very fashionable in 1850's and '60's.

rouche Variant of *ruche*. See *ruching*.

Rouff, Maggy See *designers appendix, France.*

Rough Rider shirt Khaki shirt, buttoned down the front, with standing collar, breast pockets with flaps, and epaulets; similar to shirts worn by Theodore Roosevelt and Leonard Wood and their volunteer cavalry regiment in Cuba during Spanish-American War in 1898.

rouleau (roo-low) Tubular-shaped trimming stitched in at regular intervals to make puffs of fabric; used around hems of women's skirts in 19th century. Also called *rollio*.

roulettes See *pipes.*

round dress or **skirt** Term used in 18th to mid 19th centuries for full-length dress cut without a train and with closed skirt. Also called *round gown* or *closed robe* or *gown.*

round-eared cap Woman's white cambric or lace indoor *cap,* curving around face, finished with ruffle, shallow back pulled together with drawstring revealing hair, sometimes with side *lappets* pinned up or tied loosely under chin; worn in mid 18th century.

round hat Term used for hat that began to replace the *tricorn, q.v.,* in 1770's.

round hose *Trunk hose, q.v.,* worn from 1550's to 1610, which were padded in an onion-shaped style. See *bombast.*

round knitting Hand-knit method, using four small, straight needles or a flexible needle with points at either end, for knitting socks, skirts, etc., without seams.

roundlet 1. 17th-century term used to describe the *roll,* of the 15th-century *chaperon, q.q.v.* 2. Man's small round hat of the 18th century with attached streamer for carrying it over shoulder.

round seam See *seams.*

rowle See *roll.*

Roxalane bodice Term used from late 1820's on for low-necked bodice trimmed with wide pleated folds meeting at an angle at the waistline, where bodice was boned to hold them in place.

Roxalane sleeve Bouffant sleeve, worn from the late 1820's on, made by tying a fringed band around a full sleeve above elbow, dividing it into two puffs.

Roxburgh muff Woman's muff made of *swansdown, q.v.,* fabric sometimes gathered and trimmed with bands of white satin; popular in second decade of 19th century.

Roy, Hippolyte See *designers appendix, France.*

royal blue Bright purplish blue.

Royal George stock Man's black velvet *stock, q.v.,* made with satin over the velvet at base of neck and tied in bow in front; worn in 1820's and 1830's.

Royal Stewart tartan See *tartans.*

RTW Abbreviation for *ready-to-wear* clothing industry; first shops appeared in Paris in 1792.

ruana Colombian scarf-wrap. See *poncho.*

rubber boot See *boots.*

rubbers See *shoes.*

rubber yarns See *yarns.*

Rubens hat High-crowned woman's hat with brim turned up on one side, sometimes trimmed with feather and bow; worn in 1870's and '80's. Named for hats painted by Flemish master Peter Paul Rubens, 1577–1640.

ruby See *gems.*

Ruby Keeler shoe See *shoes.*

ruching Trimming made by pleating a strip of lace, ribbon, net, muslin, etc., and stitching through the center. Also spelled *rouche* or *ruche.*

ruff 1. Pleated stiff white collar of varying widths, usually edged in lace, projecting from neckline like a wheel; worn by men and women

in 16th and 17th centuries, supported underneath by *rabato, supportasse,* or *underpropper, q.q.v.;* sometimes made in *flat pleats* or *pipe-organ pleats, q.q.v.* See *falling ruff, Betsie ruff, cherusse, whisk.* 2. Narrower versions of collar used at wrist.

ruffle Strip of cloth, lace, ribbon, etc., *gathered, q.v.,* along one edge or cut in a curve to produce a ripple; used to trim neckline, wrist, hem of a garment, etc. Also called *flounce.*

rumal See *kasabeh* under *fabrics.*

Rumanian embroidery See *embroideries.*

Rumanian stitch See *stitches.*

rumba dress See *dresses.*

rumba panties See *panties.*

rumba sleeve See *sleeves.*

rump furbelow Stuffed pad forming a *bustle, q.v.,* worn in the late 18th century. Also called *rump, false rump* and *cork rump.*

running stitch See *stitches.*

run-resistant knit See *knits.*

Russell, Lillian (1861–1922) American singer and actress, noted for her spectacular costumes with narrow waists, full bosom and hips, and for her large hats; a fashion ideal of the turn of the century.

Russian blouse See *blouses.*

Russian blouse-waist Woman's blouse, full in back and front and gathered into a band at neck and waist, sleeves full at shoulder to below elbow, gathered into wide cuff; worn in 1890's.

Russian braid Same as *soutache braid, q.v.,* under *braids.*

Russian calf See *leathers.*

Russian collar See *collars.*

Russian embroidery See *embroideries.*

Russian-style dress Two-piece dress with knee-length *tunic* over full-length skirt, high *Russian neckline, q.v.,* and embroidery trim around neck, cuffs, down side of blouse front, and around the hem; worn in 1890's. Also see *Russian shirt dress* under *dresses.*

Rykiel, Sonia See *designers appendix, France.*

S

S Designation for size *small* in various ranges; women's girdles, housecoats, nightgowns, panties, robes, etc.; men's pajamas, sport shirts, sport jackets; sweaters, robes, etc.; some children's garments.

S.A. 1. Abbreviation for *Seventh Avenue, q.v.,* New York City garment district, coined by trade newspaper *Women's Wear Daily.* 2. 1940's term for sex appeal, as exemplified by Lana Turner, the movie "sweater girl."

sabaton Broad-toed armor strapped over top of foot; also called *bear paw* or *duckbill solleret;* worn mid 16th century. Also spelled *sabatayne.*

sable See *furs.*

sabot (sa-bo) 1. Shoe carved from one piece of wood, worn by peasants in France, Belgium, Spain, Portugal and part of Dutch national costume. 2. *Clog shoe, q.v.,* with thick wood sole with closed leather vamp or leather bands across instep, open heel. See *sabot-strap* under *shoes.*

sabot sleeve 1. Sleeve, tight-fitting to elbow then flared, trimmed with ruffles, used in *gown à la polonaise, q.v.* 2. Sleeve with single or double puff above elbow; used on women's dresses from late 1820's to 1840's. Also called *Victoria sleeve.*

sabot-strap shoe See *shoes.*

sack coat 1. Man's above-the-knee, loose-fitting overcoat with sleeves wide at wrist, optional pockets, sometimes with narrow velvet collar, lapels, and cuffs; worn in second half of 19th century. 2. See *jackets.*

sack dress See *chemise* under *dresses.*

sack suit See *suits.*

sacque or **sack** 1. Loose-backed woman's gown with wide *box pleats, q.v.,* hanging from back neck band, front of gown semi-fitted; popular in England and France from 16th through 18th centuries. Also called *Adrienne, sac, sack gown.* See *robe à l'anglaise.* 2. Child's or woman's short, loose jacket, with full sleeves, edged in lace or marabou, tied in front; worn at home or, fur-trimmed, on the street.

saddle Extra piece of leather sewed over instep of oxford shoe, usually of contrasting color or texture, such as black or brown on white shoes. Also see *oxfords* under *shoes.*

saddle bag See *handbags.*

saddle coat See *pommel slicker* under *coats.*

saddle leather See *leathers.*

saddle seam See *seams.*

saddle shoe See *oxfords* under *shoes.*

saddle shoulder See *sleeves.*

saddle stitch See *stitches.*

safari clothes Garments adapted from or similar to the *bush jackets, q.v.,* worn in South Africa by hunters on safari. See *handbags, belts, coats, dresses, sport jackets* under *jackets, bellows* under *pockets,* and *shirts.*

safeguard 1. *Overskirt* worn by women when riding horseback to protect regular skirts from soil, term used from 16th to 18th centuries. Also called *foot mantle, q.v.,* and *seg-*

gard. 2. Man's colored apron worn by bakers and tradesmen from 16th to 18th centuries. 3. Swathing band for infant, early 18th century.

safety pin Elliptical pin with covered head to sheath the point; introduced from Denmark, late 1870's. See *pins*.

saffron Bright orange-yellow color; the dye obtained from the stigmas of the saffron plant.

Sag-No-Mor Trademark owned by Wyner Division of Ames Textile Co. for a textile finish used on knitted fabrics to make them more shape retentive with less tendency to become baggy with wear.

sailcloth Durable cotton duck. See *fabrics*.

sailor blouse See *middy* under *blouses*.

sailor cap or **hat** See *hats*.

sailor collar See *collars*.

sailor dress See *dresses*.

sailor pants See *pants*.

sailor scarf See *scarfs*.

sailor shorts See *shorts*.

sailor's reef knot Common double knot or square knot used on sailor ties in U.S. Navy; fashionable for men's neckties in 1890's.

sailor suit 1. Boy's suit inspired by French and English sailors' uniforms consisting of *middy blouse* with braid-trimmed collar, square in back, plus baggy *knickerbockers*, or *Danish trousers*; introduced in early 1860's. 2. Girls' two-piece dress with similar middy blouse and pleated skirt; popular until 1930's and worn at intervals since.

sailor tie See *ties*.

1891   1906

SAILOR SUIT

St.-Cyr, Claude See *designers appendix, France*.

St. Gall See *laces*.

St. George cross See *crusader's cross* under *necklaces*.

Saint Laurent, Yves See *designers appendix, France*.

Saint Laurent helmet Bowl-shaped, cuffed hat with earlaps; designed in

Paris by *Yves Saint Laurent* in 1966. See *designers appendix, France*.

salett Helmet worn by medieval Germans, French, and English, usually cast in one piece in pot-like shape flaring somewhat at neck in front and sometimes in back, covering

entire face with small slit to see through, sometimes with moveable visor; worn in 15th century. Also spelled *celata, salade, salet, sallet.*

Salisbury See *fabrics.*

salon dresses Retail-trade term for expensive dresses by well-known designers sold in a special room in department store; not hung on view but brought out by sales-people.

salt-box pocket Term used in 1790's for men's narrow, rectangular, flapped waistcoat pocket.

salvar Woman's long full pants gathered at ankles, sometimes held at waist by a *cummerbund, q.v.,* or draped scarf; worn in India, Turkey, Albania, and Persia. Called *harmen pants* in U.S. and England. In 1890, Persian ruler Nair-ne-Din ordered substitution of skirts for *salvar* after seeing the ballet in Paris. Also spelled *chalwar, salwar,* or *shalwar.*

Salvation Army bonnet High-crowned black straw bonnet with short front brim raised off forehead showing pale-blue lining, dark-blue ribbon around crown and tied under chin; worn by women of Salvation Army, a religious and charitable organization.

Sam Browne belt See *belts.*

samite Rich, heavy silk brocaded fabric used in Middle Ages for robes of state.

sampot Length of colored silk, wrapped about waist and draped to form trousers, worn by men and women in southern Cambodia as part of national dress.

sandal Shoe consisting of sole held on to foot by thongs or straps over or between toes or wrapped around ankle and leg; a foot covering dating from ancient times, standard in desert and tropical dress of Far East and adopted by Westerners for beach, street, and evening wear in many varieties of lacings and heel heights. The term *sandal* is sometimes extended to any shoe with an open shank or one that leaves a large part of the foot bare. Descriptions of contemporary sandals follow.

SANDALS:

T-STRAP SANDAL

THONG SANDAL

clogs Thick wooden or cork soles fastened to foot by various strap arrangements, popular for beach-wear in late 1930's and for street in late 1960's and '70's. Also see *shoes.*

Dr. Scholl exercise s. Trademark for wooden sandal with sole shaped to fit foot and special carving underneath the ball of the foot for gripping when walking; has only one strap over front of foot, buckled to adjust the size, and an outer sole of ridged rubber. Worn in late 1960's and early 1970's. Action of foot on carved sole when walking provides healthful exercise for the muscles.

Ganymede s. Open sandal derived from ancient Greek style, with vertical straps coming from the sole up the legs, crossed at intervals by straps around the leg; introduced in 1960's to wear with mini-dresses. *Der.* Named for the beautiful boy who was the cupbearer of the gods in Greek mythology.

geta Japanese sandals elevated by means of wooden blocks under the sole, fastened to foot by two straps meeting between first and second toes, curved to fasten at sides of sole; popular step-in beach shoe.

gladiator s. Flat sandal with several wide cross straps holding sole to foot, and one wide strap around ankle, introduced in late 1960's and copied from ancient Roman sandals.

huarache (wah-*rah*-chee) Mexican sandal consisting of closely woven leather thongs forming vamp, with sling back and flat heel, popular casual shoe in the United States for all ages and both sexes.

kalso Danish open sandal with *platform sole, q.v.,* carved from laminated mahogany, finished with rubber walking sole and held with two wide straps, one over instep and one around heel.

open-shank s. High-, medium-, or low-heeled sandal shaped like a *D'Orsay pump, q.v.,* with a strap around the ankle or over the instep; frequently heelless and toeless; popular in 1930's, '40's, and '60's.

thong s. Flat, often heelless sandal held to the foot by narrow strips of leather coming up between first and second toes and attached at either side. Popular for beach wear.

T-strap s. Sandal with a strap coming up from the vamp to join second strap across the instep, forming a T; may have high or low heel; popular since early 1900's.

V-strap s. Sandal with a strap around the heel, attached to sole by vertical straps at sides, then meeting at center front of vamp, forming a V.

zori Woven straw sandal from Japan consisting of a flat sole fastened to the foot by two straps meeting between first and second toes and fastened to sides of the sole; copied inexpensively in rubber with sponge-rubber soles for beach and swimming pool.

sandal-foot hose Stockings with no foot reinforcements. See *hose* and *pantyhose.*

Sand Crepe Trademark for a frosty rayon. See *fabrics.*

sandwich-board jumper See *jumpers.*

Sanforized Trademark owned by Cluett, Peabody & Co., licensed for use on fabrics, that insures the residual shrinkage will not be more than 1%.

sanglier Rough dress worsted. See *fabrics.*

sans-culottes (sahn koo-lot) Nickname for those opposing the monarchy during the French Revolution, *i.e.* those who wore *trousers* (common people) instead of *breeches, q.v.,* (aristocrats). *Der.* French, literally, without breeches.

santon Colored silk *cravat* and small *ruff, q.q.v.,* worn together by women in 1820's. Also called a *sautoir*.

sapphire See *gems.*

saradi Sleeveless waistcoat worn over *anga, q.v.,* by Mohammedan men of India.

sarafan Dress formerly worn by women in Russia consisting of a full pleated skirt gathered to a short-sleeved bodice with either high round or low square neckline.

saran Generic term for man-made fibers derived from vinylidene chloride, the raw materials being salt water and petroleum. Qualities; resistant to moth, mildew, weather, and chemicals. Not used in fabric form for ready-to-wear.

sarape See *serape.*

sarcenet British cotton lining. See *fabrics.*

Sardina, Adolpho See *Adolpho* in *designers appendix, United States.*

Sardinian sac Loose-fitting single-breasted man's *overcoat* made with square-cut collar, no lapels, and full bell-shaped sleeves; worn flung over shoulders, secured by cord and tassel in front, in mid 19th century.

sari (sah-ree) 1. Woman's outer garment consisting of long length of cotton or silk wrapped around the waist and pleated at the side to form skirt, one end thrown over shoulder or covering head; worn mostly in India and Pakistan. 2. Fabric used for such garments, often of silk interwoven with gold and bordered in floral designs; adopted by Western women for evening wear in traditional form

or cut and sewn to Western patterns. Also spelled *saree.* See *dresses.*

sarmah Same as *carma, q.v.*

Sarmi, Fernandino See *designers appendix, United States.*

sarong (seh-rong) Long straight wrap-around skirt made of a tube of bright-colored batik-printed fabric with deep fold in front, held on by scarf around waist; worn by men and women of the Malay Archipelago. Adapted as a beach style and popularized by actress Dorothy Lamour in movies of the 1930's and 1940's. Also see *swimsuits, dresses, girdles, skirts.*

sash See *belts.*

sash ring Large ring on a chain suspended from belt at hip so over-

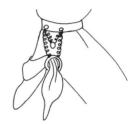

skirt could be pulled through to drape the skirt; worn in late 1860's.

Sassoon hairstyle See *hairstyles.*

satchel See *handbags.*

sateen Cotton satin. See *fabrics.*

satin See *fabrics.*

satin-back crepe or **velvet** See *satin* under *fabrics.*

satin-backed ribbon See *ribbon.*

satin stitch See *stitches.*

satin stripe See *stripes.*

satin sultan See *fabrics.*

satin weave See *weaves.*

sausage curl See *curls.*

sautoir 1. See *necklaces.* 2. See *santon.*

Savile Row Street in London West End where many of finest men's custom tailoring shops are located, catering to wealthy internationals, stressing quality and conservatism since Henry Poole & Co. opened in 1843.

Saxony 1. Superior merino wool from Saxony, Germany. 2. Type of fine knitting yarn. 3. Men's overcoating fabric made in England originally of woolen or worsted yarns from Saxony, Germany; now applied to flannels and fine, clear-finished woolen fabrics similar to Saxony wools.

Saxony lace See *Plauen* under *laces.*

saya Bright-colored skirt with train worn with the *camisa* blouse *q.v.,* by the women of Philippines.

Scaasi, Arnold See *designers appendix, United States.*

scabilonians Men's *underpants* worn in latter half of 16th century. Also called *scavilones.*

scaling hose *Trunk hose* similar to *Venetians, q.q.v.,* popular in latter half of 16th century. Also called *scalings.*

scallop 1. The shell of a mollusk used in ornamentation. See *cockle hat.* 2. One of series of curves or circle

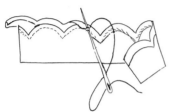

segments (like one edge of the scal-

lop shell) forming an ornamental edge on cloth, lace, etc.

scalpette (scal-pet) Term used in late 19th century for woman's hairpiece composed of extra curls attached to invisible net worn on top of head.

scarab A beetle regarded as the symbol of immortality by the ancient Egyptians and stylized in fabric designs or carved from gem stones with inscriptions on the undersides. Semi-precious carved scarabs are still used in *rings* and *bracelets, q.q.v.,* were especially popular in the U.S. in the late 1940's.

Scarborough ulster Caped and hooded man's *ulster, q.v.,* without sleeves; worn in early 1890's.

scarf 1. Rectangular or triangular piece of fabric in a variety of fibers, colors, and patterns, worn around neck or over head for warmth or adornment; in contemporary times, worn by men inside coat or shirt collar and by women around head or neck tied in many ways. 2. Man's wide *cravat* or long *sash* worn diagonally on military uniform. Also see *baldrick, tucker.*

SCARFS OR SCARVES:

Apache s. Man's small square or triangular scarf introduced in late 1960's for wear instead of necktie, worn knotted or pulled through a *slide, q.v.* Named for French slang for gangster or thug, especially as depicted by French nightclub dancers; the French word taken from the American Indian tribe, thought to be very fierce.

ascot Oblong scarf worn loosely

MUFFLER

BOA

tied, with broad ends hanging down flat on each other; derived from type of scarf worn at Ascot race course in England.

babushka Triangular-shaped scarf or square folded diagonally, worn draped over head and tied under chin in manner of Russian peasant woman. *Der.* Russian, grandmother; a wearer of such a scarf.

bandanna Large square cotton handkerchief, either red or blue with distinctive black or white design; worn, in late 19th century and early 20th century, tied around the head or neck by workmen, later adopted for wear with sports clothes. *Der.* Hindu, *bandhnu,* referring to method of putting design on cloth.

boa Woman's long tubular scarf (snake shaped) usually made of feathers or fur; in 1890's, made of lynx, fox, sable and worn with matching muff; revived in late 1920's and again in early 1970's, especially in fur, ostrich feathers, or marabou.

designer s. See *signature scarfs.*

foulard s. Scarf of silk twill, often with small designs on plain ground, originally imported from India.

kerchief Scarf worn as head or neck covering usually a square folded into triangle, crossed ends fastened on chest. Also called *neckerchief.* Also spelled *kerchner, kercheve, karcher.* See *coverchief, fichu.*

mantilla See *veils.*

muffler 1. Long, narrow scarf, usually knitted or of plaid or plain colored loosely woven wool, worn by men and young people from 19th century on for winter warmth; also a similar scarf of white silk worn with men's formal evening clothes from 1920's to 1950's. 2. Square of fabric, folded diagonally, worn over chin, mouth and nose as disguise in 16th and 17th centuries. See *chin cloak.*

ring s. Oblong scarf with ends stitched together to form a circle;

439

worn with jewelry to form a collar on a dress, popular in early 1950's.

sailor s. Square neckerchief folded diagonally, worn under sailor collar and slipped through loop on front of blouse or tied in a knot. Also called *sailor tie.*

signature s. Pure-silk scarf with couturier's name printed in one corner; a fashion started in Paris in 1960's by Balenciaga, Dior, etc. and spread to Italy and U.S. as status symbol for most prestigious designers. Also called *designer scarf.*

stock 1. Long, narrow scarf wrapped once around neck, ends lapped over loosely in a single knot; worn by men instead of necktie with *riding habit, q.v.,* or for informal occasions. 2. Man's stiffened high white neckcloth, buckled at back; worn from mid 18th century to end of 19th century. Also see *ascot, hunting stock, military stock, Royal George stock,* and *solitaire.*

scarf hat See *hats* and *caps.*

scarf pin See *pins.*

scarf slide Round ring, of metal, wood, plastic, etc., used to hold corners of square scarf in place. Also called *neckerchief slide.*

scavilones Variant of *scabilonians, q.v.*

Schiaparelli, Elsa See *designers appendix, France.*

Schiffli embroidery (shif-lee) See *embroideries.*

Schoen, Mila See *designers appendix, Italy.*

Scholl exercise sandals See *Dr. Scholl* under *sandals.*

school sweater See *sweaters.*

Schuberth, Emilio See *designers appendix, Italy.*

scissoring See *slashing.*

scoop bonnet Bonnet with wide stiff brim, shaped like flour scoop, attached to soft crown; popular in 1840's.

scoop neckline See *necklines.*

Scotch fingering Soft, fluffy knitting yarn made in Scotland of native wool.

Scotch finish Textile-industry term for finish applied to woolens on which nap is sheared short.

Scotchgard Trademark owned by Minnesota Mining & Manufacturing Co. for finish applied to fabrics and garments making them stain resistant.

Scotch-grain Describing leather finished by embossing a pebbly pattern on calfskin or cowhide.

Scotch plaid See *plaids* and *tartans.*

Scotch tweed See *tweed* under *fabrics.*

Scott, Ken See *designers appendix, Italy.*

Scottish Highlander costume See *Highlander.*

Scout cap See *caps.*

scratch wig Man's *bob wig,* made with one long hanging curl, covering only back of head, arranged with the natural hair brushed over top of wig; worn in second half of 18th century. Also called *scratch bob.*

screen print See *silk-screen printing.*

screw earrings See *earrings.*

scuba suit See *sport suits* and *wet suit.*

scuffs See *slippers.*

scye See *armseye.*

Sea Island cotton Excellent grade of long staple cotton raised in hot, humid climates; originally brought from the West Indies to islands off the coast of southeastern U.S.

seal or **sealskin** See *Alaskan fur seal* and *hair seal* under *furs;* see *leathers.*

seam Two edges of fabric or leather joined by sewing in a variety of stitches, sometime incorporating *bias binding, cording, piping,* etc., *q.q.v.*

SEAMS:

CORDED SEAM

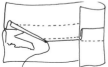

FLAT-FELLED SEAM

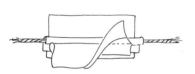

FRENCH SEAM

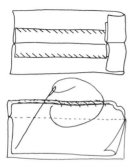

OVERCAST SEAMS

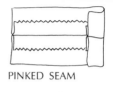

PINKED SEAM

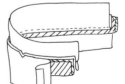

PIPED SEAM

PIPED SEAM

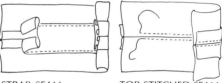

STRAP SEAM   TOP-STITCHED SEAM

corded s. Plain seam with cord inside bias binding inserted in seam before basting so that covered cord appears as decoration along the seam.

double-stitched s. See *top-stitched* seam.

fell s. See *flat-felled* seam, below.

flat-felled s. Two edges of fabric, joined and stitched on right side, one edge then cut close to seam, other edge folded over cut edge and both pressed flat, then top-stitched; showing two rows of stitching on outside. Also called *fell seam.*

flat lock s. Edges of material joined together with zigzag stitching over raw edges.

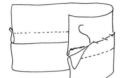

WELT SEAM: SINGLE STITCHED

WELT SEAM: DOUBLE STITCHED

French s. Seam first stitched on right side of garment, trimmed, then stitched on inside of garment, covering raw edges; used on transparent or raveling fabrics.

fused s. Seam made in plastics by heating edges to be joined.

inseam 1. Inner seam of pants leg from crotch to hem; length of men's pants is measured by this seam. 2. Seam used on the inside of a glove.

kid s. Lap or piqué seam.

lap s. 1. Edges of fabric lapped one across the other and stitched without edges being turned under, seam used on firmly woven fabrics which do not fray. 2. Simplest seam used on shoe uppers; one edge of leather placed on top of another and top stitched. Also used for gloves.

open-welt s. See *tucked seam,* below.

outseam A glove seam stitched by hand or machine with wrong sides together, leaving the edges exposed; used on sport gloves such as pigskin and sometimes on cotton.

overcast s. Plain seam pressed open on wrong side, raw edges finished by overcast stitches to prevent raveling.

overlapped s. See *lap seam,* above.

pinked s. Plain seam pressed open on wrong side, finished by trimming raw edges with a pinking shears to make saw-toothed edges that prevent raveling.

piped s. Seam decorated by inserting piece of bias binding between two layers of fabric before stitching. Similar to a *corded seam, q.v.*

piqué s. See *lap seam;* used for gloves and also written P.K.

saddle s. Hand or machine-stitched seam used on shoes, two raw edges of leather standing up on outside, as on moccasin vamps; same as *outseam,* above.

slot s. Plain seam basted and pressed open, an additional strip of fabric placed underneath, then stitched on outside at equal distance on either side of seam before basting is removed.

strap s. Plain seam stitched with wrong sides together, pressed open, and covered on right side by bias tape that is stitched on either edge.

top-stitched s. Plain seam pressed open and stitched on either side of seam on right side of garment or pressed to one side and stitched on that side. Also called *double-stitched seam.*

tucked s. Seam finished with tucks stitched about $\frac{1}{4}$" to 1" from either side of seam and pressed to meet

442

above seaming. Also called *open-welt seam*.

welded s. See *fused seam*.

welt s. Plain seam stitched on wrong side, one edge trimmed, both pressed in same direction, and top-stitched to catch wider edge.

seam binding Narrow tape woven on the straight, used at hems of garments to cover raw edge and stitched into seams on wrong side to prevent stretching; sometimes used to bind cut edges of raveling seams.

seamed hose See *hose*.

seamless hose See *hose*.

seamless knit See *circular* under *knits*.

seam pocket See *pockets*.

seamstress Same as *dressmaker, q.v.*

seam tape See *seam binding*.

sea otter See *otter* under *furs*.

seed embroidery See *embroideries*.

seed pearls See *beads*.

seed stitch See *stitches*.

seersucker Cotton with woven crinkled stripes. See *fabrics*.

see-through Fashion category started by American designer Rudi Gernreich in 1964, with sheer blouses over bare skin; later developed by French couturiers Pierre Cardin and Yves Saint Laurent with sequinned chiffon dress over *body stocking, q.v.*, in 1966, transparent blouse in 1968; became man's fashion with voile shirts in late '60's — part of a general trend to nudity.

seggard See *safeguard*.

selham See *burnoose*.

selvage Term used since 14th century for narrow tightly woven band on either edge of fabric parallel to the warp that prevents fabric from raveling; originally called *self-edge*. Also spelled *selvedge*. Also called *list* and *listing*.

semi-formal suit See *tuxedo* under *suits*.

semi-precious gems Gems too plentiful to be considered rare, e.g. topaz, garnet, tourmaline, spinel, zircon, opal, amethyst, quartz. See *gems*.

sempstress bonnet Woman's bonnet with long, wide ribbons crossing under chin and brought up to top of crown where they tied in a bow; worn in French Empire period.

sennit braid See *braids* and *straws*.

senorita Woman's waist-length, bolero-style jacket with three-quarter-length or full-length sleeves, lavishly trimmed with braid, fringe, buttons, or lace, worn over a blouse with full sleeves; popular in mid 1860's. Also called a *Spanish jacket*.

separate collar See *collars*.

separates Clothes, mostly sportswear, intended to be worn together; jacket, blouse, and skirt or pants not sold as a *suit* are *separates*.

sequin Small shiny disk of metal or plastic in silver, gold, or metallic color, pierced in the center and sewn onto garments in decorative designs or all over a thin fabric in plain colors or patterns; often used for evening dresses or sweaters; popular for day wear in early 1970's. See *suit of lights*.

serape (se-*rah*-pee) Woolen blanket, folded lengthwise like a wide scarf, worn by Mexican peasants over one shoulder or wrapped around body. Also spelled *sarape* or *zerape*.

serge Twill with a diagonal wale. See *fabrics*.

serpentine skirt See *morning-glory skirt*.

serul Long, full, Turkish-type trousers worn by women in Northern Africa. Also spelled *serual*.

service cap See *army* under *caps*.

set-back heel See *heels*.

set-in waistline See *waistlines*.

setting See *gem settings* under *gems*.

set-under heel See *heels*.

seven-eighths coat See *lengths*.

Seventh Avenue Nickname for garment district of New York City, roughly from 40th Street to 34th Street and from Avenue of the Americas (6th) to 9th Avenue, where much of American ready-to-wear is produced. Abbreviated *S.A.*

sew To join together by *stitches, q.v.*

sewing machine Machine for stitching invented in late 18th century, patented by Thimonnier in France in 1830, improved on and patented by several others, most widely known by I.M. Singer in mid 19th century; responsible for rapid growth of ready-to-wear garment industry.

shades Slang term for dark sunglasses. See *glasses*.

shadow Term used from end of 16th century to mid 17th century for separate piece of linen edged with lace or velvet, used inside hood over forehead as a shield against the sun.

shadow embroidery See *embroideries*.

shadow lace See *laces*.

shadow-panel slip See *slips*.

shadow print See *prints*.

shadow stripe See *stripes*.

shag See *hairstyles*.

shagreen (sha-green) 1. Rawhide with a rough, granular surface. 2. Sharkskin, buffed to smooth hard surface, showing pattern of tiny circles, often dyed bright green; popular for vanity and cigarette cases in 1920's. 3. Fabric treated to produce a pebbly surface resembling polished sharkskin.

Shaker flannel See *fabrics*.

Shakespeare collar 1. Standing collar of medium width, flared away from face, made of a curved, pleated strip of stiffened lawn; similar to those shown in portraits of 16th century dramatist William Shakespeare. 2. Small collar with points turned down in front, worn by men from the 1860's on. 3. Similar collar with longer points, sometimes trimmed with *lace* and *insertion, q.q.v.,* worn by women in mid 1860's.

Shakespeare vest Man's single- or double-breasted vest with narrow lapels and a turned-down, notched collar; fashionable in mid 1870's.

shako (shay-ko) See *hats*.

shal 1. See *fabrics*. 2. Indian term for *chadder, q.v.* made with small figured borders.

shalimar tweed Handwoven Indian wool. See *fabrics*.

sham See *half shirt*.

shamew See *chamarre*.

shamiya (sham-i-ya) Headscarf of

red, white, or green worn in Bulgaria by married women knotted under chin and by single girls knotted at back of head.

shank 1. The narrow part of the shoe under the arch of the foot between the heel and the ball of the foot. 2. The narrow strip of metal inserted under arch of shoe between insole and outsole to give strength to the arch.

shank button See *button.*

shantung Slubbed silk. See *fabrics.*

shantung straw See *baku* under *straws.*

shapka Brimless hat, ranging up to two feet tall and two feet across, with peaked or creased crown, made of fur: caracul, Persian lamb, etc.; traditional hat worn by Russian Tatar horsemen. Also called *Cossack hat, q.v.* under *hats.*

sharkskin See *fabrics* and *leathers.*

shatweh Palestinian women's conical *fez*-like, *q.v.,* hat, stiff and hard with a hollow top for carrying things on the head, made of elaborately striped fabric and trimmed with beads and embroidery and two rows of coins on front; worn with veil.

shave coat See *robes.*

Shaver, Dorothy President of Lord and Taylor, a specialty store in New York, from 1946 to 1959. One of first women to hold such a position; a backer of American designers during World War II, when French couture was in eclipse, thus an important person in the development of clothes design in the U.S.

shawl Decorative or utilitarian wrap; oblong, square, or triangular and often fringed; worn around shoulders or over head, from early times, especially in Far East, Persia, Pakistan, India, etc. and in Europe by *gypsies* and country people; became high fashion in 18th and 19th centuries when *Paisley* and *Cashmere shawls, q.q.v.* were imported to Europe from India; and popular off

and on in the U.S. in 20th century, especially in early 1970's when authentic *Spanish* embroidered shawls, crocheted *fascinators,* Mexican *rebozos* and lace *mantillas, q.q.v.* were part of so-called *ethnic* dress: fashions that reflected native dress of other countries.

shawl collar See *collars.*

shawl tongue Extra-long tongue on an *oxford shoe, q.v.,* folded over the lacing; sometimes with decorative fringed end and perforated; made fashionable when Prince of Wales wore such a shoe with kilts in Scotland in mid 1920's. Sometimes called *kiltie shoe, q.v.*

shawl waistcoat Man's vest with *shawl collar, q.v.,* sometimes made of a shawl fabric; worn in the 19th century.

sheared raccoon See *furs.*

shearing 1. Process used on such furs as beaver, lamb, muskrat, raccoon, and seal: all hairs cut to same length, giving velvety appearance. 2. Textile process of clipping nap of fabric to desired length.

shearling See *leathers.* Also see *sport jackets* under *jackets.*

sheath See *dresses* and *silhouettes.*

sheepskin See *leathers* and *sport jackets* under *jackets.*

shell See *blouses, shirts, shoes, sweaters,* and *tops.*

shell lining 1. Lining for only part of a coat or jacket, similar to a *half-lining, q.v.* 2. See *zip-out lining.*

shell pump See *shoes.*

shell stitch See *stitches.*

shendyt Ancient Egyptian loin cloth, sometimes pleated in front, attached to narrow belt.

shepherdess hat See *hats.*

shepherdess heel See *museum* under *heels.*

shepherd's check or **plaid** See *checks.*

sheriff tie See *ties.*

Scherrer, Jean-Louis See *designers appendix, France.*

sherte Chief male *undergarment* worn by men from 12th to 18th century, forerunner of modern shirt, usually called *chemise, q.v.,* until 14th century. Also called *camise.*

shetland 1. Soft suiting fabric made of fine soft wool in gray, brown, black, or white from Shetland sheep of Scotland; usually woven in herringbone weave. 2. Fabric, shawl, or sweater knit from Shetland wool. 3. Knitting yarn of Shetland wool. Also see *sweaters.*

Shetland lace See *laces.*

shift 1. See *dresses* and *silhouettes.* 2. *Undergarment* worn in 18th century by women; called a *chemise, q.v.,* in late 18th–19th centuries.

shillelagh See *cane.*

shingle See *hairstyles.*

shirring Three or more rows of *gathers, q.v.,* made by small running stitches in parallel lines; used to pro-

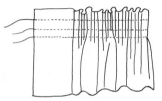

duce fullness on gloves, swimsuits, skirts, sleeves, etc.

shirt 1. In Middle Ages, garment pulled over head to wear next to skin; later, band collar, frills, and embroidery added. 2. Garment for upper part of body, typically having collar (tailored, convertible, turtleneck, etc.), sleeves, front opening, and—often—one breast pocket; basic part of man's or boy's costume, worn tucked into pants; later adopted by women in 19th century and called *shirt-waist, q.v.* in early 20th century. See also *bosom shirt, Garabaldi blouse, regatta shirt.* 3. Contemporary garments for both sexes designed for special sports, *e.g. hunt-*

ing, fencing, polo, riding, tennis, etc.; sometimes designed to hang outside pants or button at back or sides; made in many fabrics both utilitarian and decorative. Following are popular styles.

SHIRTS

BODY SHIRT

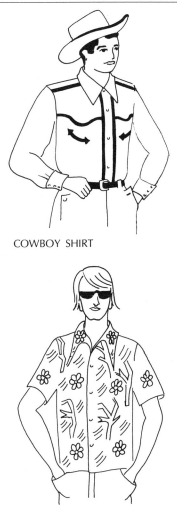

COWBOY SHIRT

HAWAIIAN SHIRT

Afghanistan wedding tunic 18th-century-style velvet tunic-blouse, lavishly decorated with gold embroidery; worn in early 1970's by men in U.S. in both the original and copied styles.

aloha s. See *Hawaiian shirt.*

barong *Overblouse, q.v.,* shirt made from sheer white fabric, frequently trimmed with fine embroidery; worn by men in the Philippines.

Ben Casey s. Nickname for white shirt-jacket with standing-band collar and shoulder closing; worn by members of medical profession. *Der.* Named for television series *Ben Casey,* popular in early 1960's.

body s. 1. Man's shirt well fitted by shaping of side seams to conform to body lines; introduced in early 1960's. Also called *tapered shirt.* 2. Long shirt with rounded tails worn by girls over short shorts in 1960's. 3. Woman's *leotard* or shirt-panties combination, often with a snap crotch; introduced in 1960's in stretch fabrics; adapted in a variety of styles and fabrics by seaming

447

shirt to stretch panties below the waistline.

bush s. See *safari shirt.*

button-down s. See *Ivy League,* below.

calypso s. Tailored-collar or V-neckline shirt with lower parts of front panels tied together to show bare midriff.

cavu s. Long-sleeved man's sport shirt with single pocket on the left and pointed collar, closing diagonally from under collar almost to right side seam; popular from 1940 to 1950.

Cossack s. 1. Russian-type shirt with standing collar, neck placket placed to one side; often with braid trimming at neck, down front, and at cuffs. 2. Similar style with turtleneck called turtleneck Cossack shirt Same as *Zhivago shirt, Cossack blouse,* and *Russian blouse, q.q.v.*

cowboy s. Long-sleeved shirt with front pockets, front yoke, pointed back yoke above center pleat, often with *grippers, q.v.,* instead of buttons, convertible collar worn with neckerchief or string tie; often of denim, twill, or gabardine. Also called *Western shirt. Der.* From Western U.S. cowboys' shirts designed for hard wear; now a classic for sportswear.

C.P.O. s. Tailored shirt of navy-blue wool, with two breast pockets, worn by Chief Petty Officers in U.S. Navy; adopted, sometimes in plaid fabrics, for wear by teenagers and children in late 1960's and worn unbuttoned over another garment as a jacket. *Der.* From abbreviation for Chief Petty Officer.

dandy s. Shirt with lace or self ruffles down front and at cuffs; popular in late 1960's for women and worn with dinner suits in evening by men. *Der.* From shirts worn by Beau Brummell, *q.v.* and other 18th- and 19th-century dandies.

drawstring s. Hip-length shirt with drawstring at bottom giving a bloused effect, designed to be worn over a bathing suit and frequently made of terry cloth or cotton knit; popular in 1940's and '50's.

dress s. Same as *formal shirt, q.v.*

dueling s. Full-sleeved white shirt of *slipon* type, with pointed collar or long *stock, q.v.,* tied around neck, frequently laced placket in front; similar to shirts worn in dueling scenes in swashbuckling 1940's movies starring Errol Flynn.

fiesta s. Man's white cotton sport shirt trimmed with a wide band of eyelet embroidery down either side of front; popularized in Acapulco, Mexico, in late 1960's. Also see *Mexican wedding shirt* below.

formal s. Man's shirt worn with *tuxedo* or *cutaway, q.q.v.;* formerly white with stiff pleated-bosom front, now may be blue and/or have ruffles or pleats down front and at wrist.

Hawaiian s. Man's sport shirt printed with colorful Hawaiian floral designs, made with convertible collar and worn outside of trousers; introduced in 1940's. Also called *aloha shirt.*

27

27 The style of 1834.
See *bateau neckline,
handkerchief, French gigot
sleeve, bonnet, bow, drop
earrings, walking stick, boots,
top hat.*

28 The seaside dress, 1826.
See *parasol, balloon
sleeve, ruffles.*

26

28

• **26** The fashions of
London and Paris in 1843.
See *cape, fichu, taffeta,
satin ribbon, lace, poke bonnet.*

29

32

30

• **29** (top left) Hairstyle of 1872.
See *curls, bows, locket, U neckline.*

30 (left) Promenade dresses, French, 1872.
See *bustle, cuff, braid, scallop,
pannier drape, parasol.*

31 (below) Clothes for afternoon wear, 1899.
See *Breton hat, choker collar, leghorn hat, frock,
boots, Gibson Girl shirtwaist, barrel cuff.*

32 (above) Men's attire, France, 1854.
See *cape, watch chain, bow tie, weskit, closings,
coachman's coat, top hat.*

33 (top right) Hairstyle and jewlery, 1872. See
love lock, necklace, off-shoulder neckline, earrings.

34 (top, far right) Dressing gown, French, 1922.
See *robe, trousers, neck scarf.*

31

33

34

35   (below left) Dresses by Marie Marielle,
French, 1928. See *cloche,*
pleats, plastron, silhouettes.

36   (below right) The St. Moritz look,
French, 1925. See cloche, box pleats,
V necklines, appliqué.

36

35

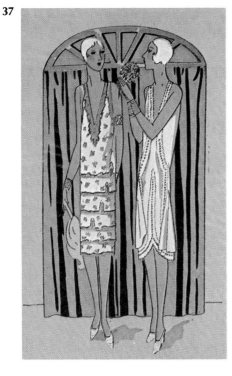

39 Hat by Rose Descat, French, 1932. See *felt, brim, choker,* and *designers appendix, France.*

40 Afternoon dress and evening dress by Mutine, French, 1927. See *V neckline, 'twenties silhouette, button earrings, bangle bracelet.*

40

• **37** Dresses by Brialix, 1927. See *georgette, tiers, satin, rhinestones, cuff bracelet.*

38 Gown by Beer, French, 1932. See *headband, train, camisole neckline,* and *designers appendix, France.*

hunting s. Bright-red wool shirt worn by hunters, visible for long distances in woods.

Ivy League s. Traditional oxford-cloth or chambray shirt with *buttoned-down collar, q.v.,* and back yoke; popular with college men in early 1950's and adopted by girls and younger boys. *Der.* Named for group of seven eastern men's colleges with sports teams competing in The Ivy League; title alludes to ivy-covered centuries-old buildings.

jockey s. Woman's shirt with contrasting colored inserts, similar to *jockey silks, q.v.* Introduced as sportswear in late 1960's after first woman was admitted as a professional jockey.

knit s. See separate category, below.

Lord Byron s. Shirt with full sleeves, long pointed collar, open at neck to a V; popular in 1920's and late 1960's. Also called *poet's shirt* and named for the 6th Baron Byron, early 19th-century English poet.

meditation s. Loose, open-sleeved, pull-over tunic blouse, usually of India printed cotton or in solid colors banded with embroidery around slit neck, across shoulders and at hem; part of 1970's *ethnic look, q.v.;* inspired by Eastern gurus.

Mexican wedding s. Tailored shirt of crisp white fabric usually with wide bands of embroidery down either side of front and on collar, inspired by shirts worn by Mexican peasant grooms and popular in Acapulco, Mexico, for men and women in late 1960's.

midriff s. Shirt for women cut to just below bustline, revealing ribcage, often improvised from a conventional shirt by tying the tails in a knot under bosom.

nightshirt See *nightgowns.*

Nureyev s. Shirt with long full sleeves gathered in bands at wrists and a low round neckline finished with bias binding; popularized in late 1960's by Rudolf Nureyev, Bolshoi ballet star who defected from his native Russia to the West in 1961. Similar to *Tom Jones shirt, q.v.* below.

polo s. See *knit shirts,* below.

ratcatcher s. Tailored shirt that has detachable self-fabric collar with long ends to lap or tie in front; worn by men or women with informal riding habit. *Der.* From informal hunt shirt worn at English rat hunts, when foxes are out of season.

safari s. See *bush jacket* under *jackets.*

stock s. Man's or woman's shirt with self-fabric scarf attached at neckline, ends flipped over once or wrapped and tied. See *stock* under *scarfs.*

tapered s. See *body shirt,* above.

Tom Jones s. Pullover shirt made with *stock tie,* yoke, full body, and full sleeves gathered into dropped shoulder and at wrist into ruffled band, inspired by shirts worn in movie made in 1963 of Henry Fielding's 18th-century English novel *Tom Jones.* See *sleeves.*

T-shirt See *knit shirts,* below.

449

Western dress s. Western shirt that is elaborately decorated with fringe, embroidery, beads, etc.; worn by cowboys for important rodeos.

Western s. See *cowboy shirt* above.

Zhivago s. Same as *Cossack shirt, q.v.* inspired by shirts worn in movie made in 1965 of Russian Boris Pasternak's novel *Dr. Zhivago,* set in Revolutionary Russia.

KNIT SHIRTS:

WALLACE BEERY SHIRT

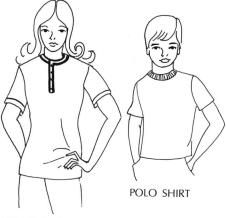

POLO SHIRT

HENLEY SHIRT

FOOTBALL SHIRT

A shirt See *athletic shirt,* below.

athletic s. 1. Sleeveless shirt with large armholes and scooped neckline, worn for track and active team sports, copied for men and women in 1960's and early '70's; also called *tank top* or *A shirt.* 2. Man's *undershirt* of similar style.

cardigan s. Identical to *cardigan sweater, q.v.,* but usually in lighter weight knits.

chukka s. See *polo shirt.*

competition-striped s. Sport shirt designed in two-color combinations of white with wide colored stripes similar to those worn on football, hockey, and other sports uniforms.

football jersey or **s.** Knit shirt with round neck, long or short sleeves set on dropped shoulders, large numerals printed on front and back, copied from shirts worn by football players and popular for children and teenagers in 1960's. Also called *numeral shirt.*

450

SWEATSHIRT

ATHLETIC SHIRT

Henley s. Lightweight knit shirt with buttoned placket at neckline, usually striped at placket and around ribbed neck, copied from shirt worn originally by rowers in crew races at Henley, England; popular in early 1960's for men, women, and children.

Lacoste s. Trademark for a knit sport shirt marked with a tiny alligator symbol on the left front to indicate (even when shirt is folded in drawer) that it has a long tail in back and won't pull out of trousers.

numeral s. See *football shirt.*

polo s. *Pullover* knit shirt in plain colors or stripes, copied from the white, short-sleeved, *crew-neck, q.v.,* shirts worn by polo players, popular for sportwear since 1930's for all ages of men and women. Also called *chukka shirt.*

pullover Any light knit shirt with no full-length placket or fastening.

shell Sleeveless knit *pullover* shirt worn by women as a blouse.

skivvy Knit shirt, copy of undershirt worn by sailors, made with bound neckline and tiny placket opening in front.

sweatshirt Long-sleeved fleece-backed cotton-knit pullover or zipped-front shirt with ribbed crew or turtleneck, cuffs, and waistband, sometimes with attached hood; originally worn for exercise or warming up for active sports but adopted as a school fad, with cartoon pictures printed on front or name of college or club printed on back, and for general sports wear.

tank top See *A shirt.*

T-shirt Basic knit pull-on shirt with round neck and sleeves set in at right angles forming a T, worn as a man's undershirt in plain white or, in colors or in stripes, with long or short sleeves, as sportswear by men, women and children.

Wallace Beery s. *Skivvy* often worn by film actor Wallace Beery in his 1930's films made with actress Marie Dressler; popularized as a sport shirt in early 1960's, when Beery's old films were being shown on television.

shirt collar See *collars.*

shirt-drawers Men's combination undershirt and underpants; worn 1890's.

shirt-dress See *dresses.*

shirt front Term used from 1860's on for a man's false shirt or *bosom,* which had a complete front but tapered into a band in back, buttoning in center back of collar.

shirt gills See *gills.*

Shirtmaker Trademark of Best & Co., New York specialty store, for tailored shirt-dress, popular in 1940's and 1950's.

shirt sleeve See *sleeves.*

shirtwaist Term originating in 1890's for women's blouses styled like men's shirts: buttoned down front, with tailored collar, and sometimes worn with a black tie; or a woman's

blouse with a high choker collar and back-buttoned—one of first items in the ready-to-wear industry. After 1920, term *blouse* more common.

shirtwaist dress See *dresses.*

shitagi (shi-taag-e) Inner *kimono* with attached collar that folds over

top of outer *kimono, q.v.,* worn by Japanese men.

shito-juban (shee-to-joo-ban) Short undergarment with attached collar called *han-yeri, q.v.,* that folds over top of *kimono;* worn by Japanese women.

shoddy *Reused wool, q.v.* In British terminology *shoddy* has longer fibers than *mungo.*

shoe Outer covering for foot, consisting of *sole, vamp, quarter* and *shank, q.q.v.* (*i.e.,* part under foot, over toe and instep, around heel and sides, and under arch) made of leather, canvas, vinyl, suede, patent, etc., with low to high heels, in various heights from shallow slipper to above ankle; for conventional wear or special sports, e.g., baseball, bowling, golf, etc. See *boots, sandals, slippers.* Following are contemporary types:

SHOES

alpargata (ahl-par-gah-ta) Spanish shoe with rope sole and canvas upper; laces threaded through top edge of shoe, crossed and tied around ankle; adapted for bathing and sportswear, as was the French *espadrille, q.v.*

ankle-strap s. Shoe fastened by a strap buckled around the ankle; either a *bracelet strap,* passing through a loop at back of shoe; or two straps, one on either side, crossing in front or back of foot and buckled around ankle.

baby dolls Low-heeled shoes with wide rounded toes, similar to *Mary Jane shoe, q.v.,* sometimes with straps around ankles; popular for women in late 1940's, revived '60's.

ballerina s. Soft, low kid shoe with

SABOT-STRAP SHOE

COLONIAL, 1902

COLONIAL SHOE, 1970

OPEN-SHANK SHOES

BASKETBALL SHOE

SLING PUMP

MARY JANE

SPECTATOR SHOE

WALKING SHOE, 1940

WEDGIE

GOLF SHOE

KILTIE SHOE

thin sole and flat heel, sometimes with drawstring throat; inspired by shoe worn by ballet dancers and popular in 1940's for school girls. See *ballet slipper.*

basketball s. High-topped rubber-soled canvas shoe of the *sneaker,*

q.v., type with lacings to toe and extra rubber reinforcements at ankles; worn for basketball and other sports and by young people for general casual wear.

453

LOAFER

MOCCASIN-TOED SHOE

PLATFORM
SHOE, 1973

RUBY KEELER SHOE

SNEAKER

SADDLE OXFORD

blucher See *oxfords,* below.

boating s. Canvas shoe similar to *tennis shoe, q.v.,* but made with a special non-skid rubber sole for walking on slippery decks. Also called *deck shoes.* See *Sperry-Top-siders.*

bowling s. Soft, supple shoes of oxford or other type with cushioned insole for comfort; made with hard rubber soles and heels with a leather tip on the sole of the right shoe (or left, for lefthanded bowlers).

brogan Man's heavy work shoe, usually ankle-high, frequently made in *blucher, q.v.* style with lacing.

broques See *oxfords,* below.

chain loafer Moccasin-toed slip-on shoe with low or medium heel, trimmed with metal links over in-step; popular in mid and late 1960's. See *Gucci .loafer.*

chunky s. Shoes of all types made in exaggeratedly heavy shapes with bulbous toes and massive heels, often with very thick platform soles; a fad with young people in late 1960's, early 1970's.

clogs Shoes made with thick soles of wood or cork, held on by broad straps or leather or canvas vamp; popular in 1930's and—in Swedish variations—in late 1960's and early 1970's. Also see *sandals, sabots.*

Colonial s. Medium-heeled slip-on shoe with stiffened tongue over instep, frequently decorated with large ornamental buckle; worn in the 17th and 18th centuries in U.S. and revived often.

Creedmore Calf-high laced work boot with two buckled straps at top; popular during last part of 19th and early 20th centuries.

creole s. Heavy work shoe with

454

elastic side gores worn by men in early 20th century.

creped-soled s. Shoes made with creped rubber soles and heels. Originally worn for sportswear, they were so comfortable that they were adopted for everyday wear particularly by men and school children, fashionable in all heel heights for women in early 1970's.

deck s. See *boating shoe.*

D'Orsay s. Pump with closed heel and toe, cut down to the sole at the sides leaving shank bare; often with high heel and popular in 1940's as evening shoe or at-home shoe.

Elevators Man's shoes with extra wedges inside the heels to give the wearer added height; popular in 1940's and '50's when men's shoes had only very flat heels.

espadrille French canvas shoe with rope sole, the toe and vamp cut in one piece and seamed to quarter at sides; may have lacings around throat wrapped around ankle. See *alpargata.*

evening slipper Delicate shoe worn with evening clothes; woman's styles include *pumps* or *sandals* in gold or silver kid or rich fabrics, man's style is usually a patent-leather *pump, q.q.v.*

flat or **flatties** Any shoes with broad low heels worn by children and women for school or general wear.

galoshes See *boots.*

gillie See *oxfords,* below.

golf s. Study oxford suitable for golf course; woman's style is often a *kiltie shoe* or a *spectator oxford;*

man's usually the *spectator oxford* style in white with another color; both have *spikes, q.q.v.,* in the sole for better traction.

Gucci loafer Most popular of the fine shoes sold by Italian firm Gucci in U.S. beginning in early 1960's: a slip-on with modified moccasin toe and distinctive gold-metal harness hardware decoration across vamp; men's shoes with low heels, women's with a medium heel; widely copied throughout the 1960's and early 1970's.

Hush Puppies Tradename for casual oxford or slip-on shoes with sueded leather uppers and crepe soles, popular for men and women and children.

Indian moccasin Soft-soled heelless shoe made by American Indians in which the leather sole continues up around foot, forming toe and quarter, and hand-stitched onto an oval vamp, often decorated with bead embroidery or fringe; upper edge of shoe often folded over, with a thong threaded through and tied in front over vamp.

Keds Trademark of U.S. Rubber Company for rubber-soled shoes. See *sneakers.*

kiltie s. Shoe with a shawl or fringed tongue folded over front of shoe, covering the lacings underneath; adapted from Scottish golf shoe. Also see *shawl tongue.*

loafers Slip-on shoes with moccasin-toe construction and slotted straps stitched across vamps and sometimes decorated with metal *chains* or with *tassel*-tied bows; popular with sportsmen and a fad with college girls in 1940's, now a classic fashion for adults and children. See *penny loafers*.

Mary Jane Child's low-heeled slipper made of patent leather with blunt toe and one strap over instep buttoned or buckled at center or side; popular since early 20th century; named for shoes worn by character Mary Jane in comic strip *Buster Brown*, *q.v.*

moccasin-toed s. Shoe construction based on the *Indian moccasin*, *q.v.* in which the upper starts under sole of foot and forms the quarter and toe stitched to an oval vamp; hard soles, sometimes of rubber, are added to produce a more durable shoe than the soft Indian moccasin.

monk-strap s. Closed shoe with wide buckled strap over tongue at instep rather than lacings; popular for women in 1940's and for men during World War II when this style way favored by U.S. Army Air Corps officers; revived in late 1960's and early 1970's.

open-back or **open-heel s.** See *slingback shoe*, below.

open-shank s. Women's shoe with closed toe and heel portions but open on sides down to sole; sometimes with side straps connecting vamp and quarter. See *D'Orsay pump*.

open-toed s. Women's shoe with the toe section cut out; popular in the 1940's and worn intermittently since.

opera pump Plain, undecorated woman's pump on medium to high heel, cut from a single piece of leather or fabric; basic style during 1940's and 1950's, revived in 1970's.

overshoes See *Arctics* and *galoshes* under *boots*.

oxfords See separate section, below.

penny loafers *Loafers*, *q.v.* with a slash in the strap across each vamp into which a coin is sometimes inserted.

platform s. Shoe with thick mid-sole, usually made of cork and covered, that makes the wearer appear taller; popular for women in 1940's and revived by Paris designer Yves Saint Laurent in 1960's; worn by men in 1970's.

pumps 1. Closed slip-on shoe with low-cut rounded or sometimes V-shaped throat and medium to high heels, often in solid color leathers or fabrics with no applied decoration, sometimes made from one piece of leather; varied toe shapes, sometimes with open toe or open *(sling, q.v.)* heel; classic for women for day and evening from 1930's on, also worn by men with flat bow for evening. 2. Historical term, since middle of 16th century, for a soft flat Spanish-leather shoe with thin soles, worn by men and women.

racing s. Sport shoe with crepe or rubber sole, upper made of two or three colors of contrasting leather. Sometimes laced to the toe and sometimes styled like a regular oxford. Inspired by the *track shoes* worn by athletes, which sometime have contrasting stripes of colored leather on the sides of the shoe.

rubbers Low-cut rubber shoes to pull over regular shoes for protection against water; sometimes with *sling back, q.v.,* and called *toe rubbers.*

Ruby Keeler s. Low-heeled *pump* tied across instep with ribbon bow similar to *tap shoes, q.v.,* popular for teenagers in early 1970's. *Der.* Named after tap dancer Ruby Keeler, popular star of 1930's films, who made a stage comeback on Broadway in 1971 in a revival of the 1917 musical *No, No Nanette.*

sabot-strap s. A woman's *pump* with a wide strap across the instep or a man's *oxford* fastened by a wide strap instead of lacing *q.q.v.* See *sabot* and *monk-strap shoe.*

saddle s. See *oxfords,* below.

sandals See separate category, *sandals.*

shells Very low-cut pumps for women, with shallow sides, set on low or flat heels; usually of very soft leather. Also called *skimmers.*

side-gore s. Slip-on shoes with triangular insertions of elastic at sides.

sling-back s. Any shoe with an open back and a strap around the heel of the foot to hold it in place; may be *pump* or *sandal* style.

sling pump *Pump* with open back, held on heel by slender strap, sometimes buckled at side. Also called *sling-back pump.*

slip-on Shoe with no fastenings—laces, buttons, or buckles—that slips on the foot easily.

sneakers See *oxfords,* below.

Space Shoes Side-laced leather oxfords custom-made over castings of the wearer's own feet, with moving space for every toe, thick crepe soles and low wedge heels for comfort. Introduced in 1938 by Mr. and Mrs. Alan Murray; high cost made shoes status symbol for men and women.

spectator s. Pump or oxford in two-toned leather, usually black or brown on white, the darker trim on toe, quarter, and top band often perforated in designs, often with a stacked-leather heel; popular spectator sports or golf shoe for women and (oxfords) for men from 1920's to 1940's; revived in 1970's.

step-in s. See *slip-on shoe.*

stocking-s. Shoe covered with knitted fabric and attached to a long stocking, introduced in late 1960's by shoe designer Beth Levine.

tap s. Any shoe worn by a tap dancer; has metal plates at tip of toe and back edge of heel to increase sound; man's style usually a patent-leather *pump* or *oxford;* women's, usually patent-leather *pump* with ribbon instep tie. See *Ruby Keeler shoe.*

tennis s. See *sneakers* under *oxfords.*

T-strap s. See *sandals.*

walking s. Any comfortable shoe with a relatively low heel, sometimes with a cushion or crepe sole; worn more for comfort than style.

wedgies Shoes with wedge-shaped heels completely joined to soles under arches, made in all styles and heights; popular for women in late 1940's, revived for women and worn by men in 1970's.

457

wing-tip s. *Oxford* or *spectator pump, q.q.v.,* with appliquéd leather on the toe, reinforcing and decorating the tip, shaped like spread bird's wings and edged with perforations.

winkle pickers British slang for exaggeratedly pointed shoes worn by Teddy Boys, *q.v.* in early 1950's. *Der.* From suggestion that the pointed toes can dig out snails or periwinkles from sand.

OXFORDS:

Balmoral or **bal o.** Basic style of oxford with a tongue under the lacing cut in separate piece from vamp of shoe and joined to it with stitching; quarters meeting and stitched under the vamp below the tongue. *Der.* Named for Balmoral Castle in Scotland in early 1850's.

blucher bal Modified *blucher* oxford with vamp stitched over quarter at sides, but not stitched over tongue.

blucher o. (bloo-cher or bloo-ker) Man's shoe or half boot with quarters projecting forward to the throat of vamp and vamp in one piece with tongue under the lacing. *Der.* Named after Field-Marshal von Blücher, commander of Prussian forces at battle of Waterloo, Napoleon's final defeat in 1815.

brogues Men's heavy oxfords, usually with wing tips (full, half, or quarter brogue, depending on length of wing tip) decorated with heavy perforations and pinkings called *broguings,* frequently worn for golf but also for city wear. *Der.* From coarse heelless shoe of untanned hide with hair left on worn by men in Ireland and Scottish highlands.

Creedmore oxford Heavy *blucher oxford, q.v.,* worn by workmen.

gillies Laced shoes, usually without a tongue, a rounded lacer pulled through leather loops instead of eyelets and often with ends fastened around ankle. Sometimes called *Prince of Wales* shoe when worn by men; popular for women also in 1920's and revived in early 1970's. Sometimes spelled *ghillies.* Named for Scottish farm workers.

plug or **plugged o.** Low laced shoe cut with vamp and quarters in one piece and a separate lace stay, e.g., *saddle oxfords, q.v.*

Prince of Wales shoe See *gillie.*

saddle o. Sport or school *plugged oxford,* see above, with plain, rounded toe, usually made of white buck calf with brown or black smooth-leather section or saddle, across laced portion; often rubber soled. Basic style since 1920's, very popular in the 1940's, revived in exaggerated colors and shapes in early 1970's.

sneakers Canvas or very soft leather oxfords with rubber soles, used for gym, tennis, and general sportswear; often white but also in colors. Also called *tennis shoes.*

Sperry-Topsider Trademark of Uniroyal Inc. for shoes with a specially designed rubber sole that provides good traction on a wet boat deck; often in *sneaker* style, *q.v.,* with canvas upper.

Theo tie An open-throated, tongueless shoe; ribbon or cord lacings.

wing-tip o. Laced shoe decorated at toe with wing-shaped overlay perforations; may be two-toned, with overlay at heels as well (or wing may extend around sides to meet at back seam). Popular in black and white for golf in 1920's, revived in late 1960's and early 1970's. Two-toned wing-tip oxford is also called a *spectator shoe*. See *brogues,* above.

shoe button Tiny round domed button, often with a metal stud in the center, with metal shank on back, used with buttonholes to close shoes or to fasten straps of shoes.

shoe duck Firm heavyweight *duck* fabric used to make shoe linings or shoe uppers including tennis shoes, basketball shoes, deck shoes, various slip-on styles.

shoe horn Term used since the 16th century for a curved device made of metal or horn used behind the heel to aid in pulling on tight shoes. Also called a *showing horn*.

shoelace See *shoestring,* and *ties.*

shoe roses Large ornamental rosettes of lace or ribbon, frequently jeweled, used by men and women to

trim shoes in 17th century and sometimes used on garters and hat bands.

shoestrings Lacers for tying shoes, at first not acceptable to society, some invitations stating that shoe buckles were required, but fashionable by the end of 17th century.

shoestring tie Extremely narrow necktie, tied in bow in front or fastened by pulling ends through small ring; worn by men in 19th century. Also see *Byron tie.*

shooting coat Term used from 1860's to 1880's for *morning coat, q.v.*

shop coat See *smock.*

short Woman's size group for various *proportioned* garments along with *average* and *tall.* Abbreviated *S.*

short bands Collar consisting of two narrow white linen bands hanging in front, fastened by strings around neck tied in back; worn in 16th and 17th centuries by clergymen, barristers and collegians. Also called *Geneva bands, q.v.,* or *bands.*

short hood See *pug hood.*

shortie, shorty See *coats, nightgowns, gloves,* and *socks.*

shorts Brief trousers, usually mid-thigh to knee-length, originally worn by athletes, adopted by men as under pants, then as summer sportswear; worn by women for active sports since 1930's and as part of pants suits in 1960's and early 1970's. Also see *drawers, trunks.*

SHORTS:

Bermuda s. Just-above-the-knee shorts that fit close to leg, first worn with knee socks as street wear by men on the island of Bermuda; introduced in U.S. in early 1950's as sportswear for women, later adopted by men for summer casual wear both in country and in town. Also called *walking shorts.*

BERMUDA
SHORTS

CUT-OFFS

HOT PANTS

boxer s. Shorts with elastic in a casing around waist, similar to those worn by prize fighters; worn as men's underwear and children and women's play clothes.

CityShorts Women's tailored shorts worn instead of skirt with matching jacket for town wear. *Der.* Term coined in 1969 by fashion-industry newspaper *Women's Wear Daily.*

cut-offs Full-length pants, often *blue jeans, q.v.,* cut off above knee and fringed; fad among the teenagers in early 1960's.

drawstring s. Pull-on shorts fastened with a drawstring at the top, similar to short pajama pants; introduced in late 1960's. See *boxer shorts* and *jams.*

hip huggers Low-slung shorts, resting on hips rather than at waistline.

hot pants, HotPants Slang term given a new meaning and spelling by fashion-industry newspaper *Women's Wear Daily,* in early 1971 to describe women's short shorts, made of luxury fabrics and leather, worn with colored tights and fancy tops, as evening wear and on city streets.

Jamaica s. Shorts ending at mid-thigh, shorter than Bermuda length, but not short-short. *Der.* Named for shorts worn in resort areas on island of Jamaica.

jumpshorts Jumpsuit with legs reaching knee or above, worn in late 1960's, similar to style worn in 1930's and '40's called *playsuit.*

Lederhosen Leather shorts, usually made with bib top, originally a Tyrolean style, adopted for American children and young people in late 1960's.

little-boy s. Short-length shorts made with turned back cuffs; popular in early 1960's for sportswear and bathing suits.

sailor s. Shorts that fasten up back with lacings and made with square buttoned flap closing in front like *sailor pants, q.v.*

Skort Tradename for shorts combined with mini-skirt.

460

tennis s. Conservative type of shorts, traditionally white, worn by men, women, and children for playing tennis and general sportswear. Colored shorts were promoted in the late 1960's, but white was still first choice on the courts. Originally women players wore skirts but when length of skirts got longer in the 1930's, Senorita de Alvares played in a below-the-knee divided skirt in 1931; and in 1933 Alice Marble appeared in the above-the-knee shorts.

trunks Men's brief, loose shorts worn (originally over *tights, q.v.*) for swimming, boxing, track, etc., and for *underwear* since the late 18th century.

walking s. See *Bermuda shorts.*

Western s. Shorts styled like *dungarees* with zipper fly in front, patch pockets on hips, and tight-fitting legs; popular for men, women, and children in late 1960's.

shot cloth See *fabrics.*

shotten-bellied doublet Man's *doublet* worn from mid 16th to early 17th centuries, made with a short front. See *peascod bellied doublet.*

shoulder Area of garment cut to fit over shoulder in various ways, e.g., in one piece with upper sleeve, in sections joined to yoke and collar, etc.

SHOULDERS:

drop or **dropped s.** Shoulder of garment extended over upper arm making a lowered sleeve seam. Popular in women's dresses in mid 19th century, at intervals in 20th century.

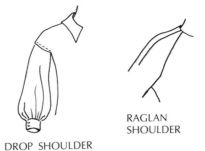

RAGLAN SHOULDER

DROP SHOULDER

epaulet Wide, flat band extending along top of shoulder to sleeve seam, frequently trimmed with braid and borrowed from military uniforms.

natural s. Follows body lines with sleeve set in at natural armhole without padding; fashionable for men's suits in 1950's and 1960's.

padded s. Pads sewn inside garment to make shoulders appear broader; introduced for women in 1930's by Schiaparelli, inspired by the *gambeson, q.v.;* revived in the early 1970's. Also popular for men in exaggerated form in the 1930's and early '40's.

raglan s. Smooth, rounded shoulder cut in one with sleeve and set in by diagonal seams in front and back from under arm to neck; may have dart at neckline. Variation called *saddle shoulder;* see *sleeves.* Also see *Raglan.*

shoulder bag See *handbags.*

shoulder belt Sword belt worn diagonally from right shoulder to left hip by men in 17th century and formerly called *baldrick, q.v.* Also called *hanger.*

shoulder dart V-shaped dart, *q.v.*, from mid shoulder seam to bust or from shoulder seam to shoulder blade in back.

shoulder heads English term for shoulder straps of low-cut dress, used from 17th century on.

shoulder knot 1. Ribbon loops, sometimes jeweled, worn by men on right shoulder from 1660 to 1700. 2. 18th century decoration used on footman's livery. 3. One of a pair of detachable flaps decorated with braided metallic cord insignia, worn on the shoulders by commissioned and warrant officers of the U.S. armed forces to designate rank. Also called *shoulder loop* or *shoulder strap*.

shoulder wing Projection at shoulder attached at armhole seam like a wing covering the *points, q.v.,* by which the sleeves were fastened to the armholes; worn from 1545 to 1640 by both men and women.

show coat See *coats*.

showing horn See *shoe horn*.

shrink See *sweaters*.

shrug See *sweaters*.

Sicilian bodice Evening-dress *bodice* with square décolletage and four knee-length panels attached, two in front, two in back, giving *tunic* effect; fashionable in the 1860's.

Sicilian embroidery See *Spanish* under *embroideries*.

side 15th to 16th centuries' term for *long*, e.g., *side gown* or long gown.

side bodies In tailoring, the two side pieces in a three- or four-piece back of garment; seams that join these side panels to center back piece (or pieces) curve outward at the shoulder blades, ending in sleeve seams; construction gives better fit and flexibility than one- or two-piece back.

side-gore shoe See *shoes*.

side leather Cattlehides too large to process in one piece, cut down center back into two parts, each part called a *side;* used for sole leather or for shoe uppers and belts.

sideless surcoat Full-length, pull-over woman's garment with boat-shaped neckline and huge armholes extending to below hips showing *kirtle, q.v.,* and jeweled belt underneath; worn from mid 14th to early 15th centuries. Also called *sideless gown*.

side placket Placket placed under arm in the side seam of a dress or blouse, originally fastened with *snaps, q.v.,* later by a special *zipper, q.v.,* that is closed at top and bottom; from 1930's to 1950's most dresses had this type of opening; replaced in '50's by long back zippers extending from neckline to the hips.

signature bag See *handbags*.

signet ring See *rings*.

silhouette Contour of a costume seen as a flat two-dimensional *design,* e.g., straight and narrow, straight front and bustle back, small top with bell skirt, etc.; changes occur almost yearly in modern times but more slowly in earlier centuries. *Der.* From an outlined profile style of portrait named for French

Minister of finance in 1759, Étienne de Silhouette, who had evanescent career; something incomplete.

SILHOUETTES:

A-LINE

MAXI

MINI

A-line Garment shaped away from the body, flared from under arms to hem of skirt like the letter A, usually with narrow shoulders in sleeveless or short-sleeved style; one of most prevalent silhouettes worn during 1960's, originated by Paris designer Christian Dior in late 1950's.

asymmetric Silhouette using the principle of informal balance rather than formal balance with each side of the garment giving a different sillhouette. Used for *dresses, coats, blouses, nightgowns,* and *swimsuits;* particularly the *toga* or one-shoulder style in the 1960's.

463

MIDI

TENT

baby or **baby-doll** Garment bouffant from neckline or with a shoulder yoke and an undefined waistline; gives an outline similar to children's and infant's dresses of the 1930's. Used for dresses and nightgowns particularly in the 1960's.

blouson (blue-sahn) Bloused effect at the waistline, often below the natural waist, in various types of dresses, jackets, shirts and blouses.

bouffant (boo-fawn) Full skirted dress shape, usually combining fitted bodice and close waist with skirt gathered into bell or cone supported by means of hoops, ruffles, or stiff under-petticoats. See also *bubble* and *dirndl*.

bubble Bouffant shape that balloons from cinched waist and curves in again at hem, giving a rounded contour; popular for evening dresses in 1950's.

bustle Straight front with fullness over hips drawn to the back giving a bulging effect in rear; worn in 1880's.

chemise See *shift,* below.

dirndl Modified bouffant silhouette, the skirt gathered at waistline, adapted from Tyrolean peasant dresses; worn in 1940's and 1950's.

Empire (em-pire or om-peer) High-waisted garment with waistline directly under bust, skirt hanging straight and narrow; popular in dresses and nightgowns. *Der.* From style worn by Empress Josephine during First Empire in France, 1804 to 1815.

harem Far Eastern woman's costume shape, consisting of loosely draped skirt or full pants gathered in at ankle, first popularized in the West by Paris designer *Paul Poiret, q.v.,* in early 20th century.

hour-glass Woman's dress shape: full busted, pinched in at waist above full curving hips; height of fashion from 1890's to early 1900's; popularized by *Lillian Russell q.v.*

long-torso Closely fitted silhouette to a low waistline; skirt in circular, pleated, or straight style. Also called *torso* shape.

maxi Ankle-length silhouette introduced in the late 1960's particularly for coats and skirts, usually a semi-fitted or princess silhouette.

midi Variety of silhouettes distinguished by length which is mid-calf; introduced in mid 1960's with *Doctor Zhivago look, q.v.*

mini Variety of silhouettes defined by the length of the skirt which reaches to mid-thigh. Top usually conforms to body lines, the skirt may be flared, long torso, or dirndl type. Introduced in England in early 1960's, the mini shape became one of the most popular silhouettes in the late 1960's.

princess Semi-fitted dress or coat vertically seamed, with no waistline seam, flared slightly at hem; popular for day wear in 1940's and for evening and wedding dresses since.

sheath Narrow shape, with hemline below the knee, fitted closely to the figure—usually by darts at the shoulders and bust and vertical darts at waist but no waistline seam —and closed by a long zipper from

neckline to hips in back; usually collarless, often sleeveless. Very popular in mid 1950's, replaced slowly by the "unshaped shape" of the *chemise,* when hemlines rose above the knee in early 1960's.

shift or **chemise** Straight-line unfitted garment, beltless, often sleeveless; basic style of woman's dress in early 1960's.

tent Pyramidal silhouette with fullness starting at neckline and flaring to hem, popular for coats in 1940's and revived in mid 1960's for dresses and coats.

tiered Silhouette composed of series of flounces; worn in 1930's, e.g., rumba skirt.

torso See *long-torso,* above.

trapeze Shape created for House of Dior in Paris by Yves Saint Laurent in 1958; narrow shoulders, unfitted waist, flare to hem.

trumpet Long fitted-torso dress, flared out from mid-thigh to hem in shape of inverted lily or trumpet; popular in 1920's, l930's, and 1960's.

'twenties Straight-hanging dress, short to knees, sometimes bloused on top, with belt line around hips or lower; "flapper" look of 1920's.

wasp-waist See *hourglass,* above.

silk Fiber from larvae of insects produced when spinning their cocoons, specifically fiber from cocoon of the silk worm, primarily grown in Japan and China; notable for its resiliency, elasticity, and strength. Also see *doupioni, raw silk, spun silk, tussah.*

silk hat See *top hat* under *hats.*

465

silking Glove-industry term for the ornamental stitching on back of glove; also called *pointing*.

silk-screen printing Method of printing designs on fabric by blocking out motifs for each color on separate silk or man-made fabric screens that are laid over the flat fabric, color brushed through by hand or machine; used for small amounts of fabric. Also see *screen prints* under *prints*.

silk stocking Hosiery knit of silk yarn, first pair said to have been worn by Queen Elizabeth I; in early 1900's hosiery was made of heavy pre-dyed silk yarns and cotton tops, sold for $12.50 per pair; after World War I, perfection of machinery plus the use of gum silk in knitting and then dyeing produced hose which were much sheerer—and lower in price. Very popular until 1940's when replaced by nylon. In early 1900's term "Silk Stocking District" coined for a high-rent Congressional district on New York's East Side.

silver fox See *fox* under *furs*.

simar (si-mar) 1. Woman's loose-fitting jacket with side pieces, or skirts, extending to knee, sometimes worn over petticoat to make dress; worn in 17th and 18th centuries. Also spelled *samarre*. 2. Clerical robe worn particularly by prelates of the Catholic church, similar to full-length *cassock, q.v.*, but having short button-on false sleeves and a shoulder cape that does not fasten in front; worn at home or on the street, but not worn for high church services; made of white wool for the Pope, black wool with scarlet trimmings for Cardinals, black wool with amaranth red or of black with purple trim for Penitential or mourning days for Bishops, made of ash-gray wool for Franciscians; worn by seminarians without the false sleeves (thus indicating inferior dignity). Italian spelling is *zimarra*. 3. Robe worn by chancellors and magistrates in Italy; takes its name from full-length long-sleeved robe worn by senators of Venice in 14th and 15th centuries. Also spelled *simarra*. 4. *Simarre:* French justice's robe.

Simonetta See *designers appendix, Italy*.

Simpson, Adele See *designers appendix, United States*.

simulated gems or **pearls** Copies of pearls or precious gems made of *paste, q.v.,* or other inexpensive materials; sometimes confused with *synthetic gems,* which are man-made but chemically identical with natural gems. See *beads*.

single-bar tricot See *tricot* under *knits*.

single-breasted See *closings*.

single cuff See *cuffs*.

single knit See *knits*.

siphonia (sy-fo-ni-a) Weatherproof overcoat thin enough to be rolled and carried; worn by men in 1850's and 1860's.

sisal, sisol or **sissal straw** See *straws*.

sissy shirt See *blouses*.

sizing 1. Measurements of body used as guide for cutting garments to fit a variety of body types. 2. Non-permanent finishing process applied particularly to cotton fabrics to increase weight, crispness, and luster by means of starch, gelatin, oil, wax.

skating dress or **skirt** See *dresses* and *skirts*.

skein 1. Unit by which knitting yarn is sold, usually comes packaged in loosely coiled form. Also called a *hank*. 2. Originally the form in which silk and other yarns were sent from spinning plant to weaving plant; now yarn is frequently delivered in *tubes, cones, warps, cakes*.

skeleton skirt Another name used for the *cage crinoline, q.v.,* in 1850's.

skeleton suit Boy's suit consisting of tight jacket decorated with two rows of buttons extending over shoulders, ankle-length trousers buttoned to jacket at waist; worn from 1790 to 1830.

skeleton waterproof Woman's full-length front-buttoned raincoat with large armholes, instead of sleeves, covered by a hip-length circular cape; worn in 1890's.

ski boot See *boots*.

ski cloth Variant of *mackinaw cloth, q.v.,* under *fabrics*.

ski jacket See *jackets*.

skimmer See *dresses, hats,* and *shells* under *shoes*.

ski mask A knitted hat that covers the entire face, with holes for eyes, nose, and mouth (see drawing on page 342); worn for warmth while skiing and, in 1974, as disguises by otherwise nude runners while "streaking." See *streaker*.

Skinner's Satin See *fabrics*.

skin socks Socks made by Greenland Eskimos, of hides with fur inside.

SKELETON
WATERPROOF

ski pajamas See *pajamas*.

ski pants See *pants*.

skirt 1. Lower part of dress from waist to hem. 2. Separate garment starting at waist, mid-thigh to floor length, worn with blouses, sweaters, jackets; may be plain seamed, pleated, or cut on bias, circular, or gored, in various silhouettes. See *pleats, suits*. 3. Lower part of man's coat or jacket, term used since Middle Ages for slashed panels of *doublet, q.v.* Contemporary skirts follow.

SKIRTS:

bell s. Skirt flared widely from a narrow waist, forming a bell shape.

broomstick s. Full skirt of lightweight cotton, often a *calico print, q.v.,* that, after washing, is folded

SKORT

WRAP
SKIRT

CULOTTE

tightly around a broomstick and tied with string; when dry, skirt shows vertical wrinkles like tiny pleats; popular in 1940's, especially for square dancing; similar to *squaw skirt, q.v.,* below.

bubble s. Skirt gathered to small waistline, ballooning out and tapered in at hem; popular in 1950's. Also called *tulip skirt.*

circular s. Skirt made of a complete circle of fabric with smaller circle (and placket) cut in center for waistline, or a skirt made of two or four large segments of circles giving a small waist and very wide hemline.

crinoline Underskirt made of stiffened fabric, which holds out the main skirt; used in 1850's before hoop skirts were invented and popular again under dresses from 1940's to 1950's.

culotte Skirt divided into two sections for legs, so that it is actually a pair of pants but looks like a skirt when not in motion. Also called

culottes. Der. French, *culotte,* knee breeches; *des culottes,* trousers.

dirndl Skirt, full and gathered into band at waist, popular in 1940's and 50's. Copied from Tyrolean peasant skirts.

divided s. Pants constructed to look like a skirt when not in motion; first worn in England by Lady Harberton for bicycle riding in early 1880's, still popular for sportswear. Also called *culotte* or *culottes, q.v.*

flying-panel s. Free-hanging section or sections joined at the waist forming a partial *overskirt* on a dress or separate skirt.

full s. A skirt that is gathered or flared so that hem is much wider than hipline.

harem s. Draped skirt with hem gathered and turned up, fastened to lining, worn in the Near East and introduced to the West by Paris designer Paul Poiret in 1912.

468

hip-hugger s. Any skirt that rides low on hips below the natural waistline, usually belted; popular in 1960's.

hoop s. Full *bell skirt, q.v.,* held out by a *crinoline* or *hoops, q.q.v.,* fashionable in mid 19th century.

kilt s. Traditional Scottish *knife pleated* wrapped skirt of *tartan wools, q.q.v.,* just mid-knee length, with flat front wrapped to side, edge often fringed, and held by leather straps at top and large brooch near hem. See *kilt.*

maxi-s. Term used for ankle-length daytime skirt, popular with young women in late 1960's as reaction against *mini-skirts, q.v.,* below.

midi-s. Skirt with hem half-way between ankle and knee, below the widest part of the calf; introduced by designers in 1967 as a reaction to very short *mini-skirt, q.v.,* below.

mini-s. Term used for extremely short skirt, any length from 4″ to 12″ above the knee; popular for day and evening in the 1960's, credited to London designer Mary Quant.

overskirt An extra skirt or drapery shorter than the skirt itself and often looped up or split at sides, front, or back; or an entire skirt of a sheer fabric constructed over a more opaque *underskirt.*

pants-s. Variant of *culotte* or *divided skirt, q.v.,* popular 1960's.

peasant s. Full gathered skirt, often trimmed with bright-colored embroidered bands, copying native costume of European peasants.

sarong (sah-rong) Wrapped skirt, usually of bold floral-print cotton, used as beach cover-up, copied from Indonesian native dress, popularized by actress Dorothy Lamour in movies of 1940's.

skating s. Very short, full circular skirt; first popular in late 1930's after movies by Norwegian-American ice-skater Sonja Henie.

Skort *Mini-skirt* with *shorts* combined in one trademarked garment. Also called *scooter skirt,* late 1960's.

slit s. Straight-lined skirt with one or more slashes from hem to knee or thigh in front, sides, or back; sometimes in the form of an overskirt with brief shorts underneath.

squaw s. Full skirt, finely pleated, sometimes with embroidered bands and ruffle hem, originally worn by American Indians and popular for square dances in 1940's and 1950's.

sunburst-pleated s. *Circular skirt, q.v.,* pressed into *accordion pleats,* narrowed toward the waistline in a sunburst pattern.

swing s. Flared skirt, circular or cut in gores, fitted at hips with a wide flare at the hem; popular in the late 1930's and at intervals since.

torso s. Skirt with fitted yoke to hips, flared or gathered below; popular in late 1930's, early '40's.

trumpet s. Straight-lined skirt with one large circular flounce at the hem, flaring like an inverted trumpet.

tulip s. See *bubble skirt,* above.

tunic s. Two-tiered skirt with shorter *overskirt,* q.v.

underskirt Simple, basic skirt over which an *overskirt,* q.v., or drapery hangs; also a term for a woman's *slip* or *petticoat,* q.q.v.

wrap s. A skirt open from waist to hem, wrapped around the body and fastened by buttons or ties, usually lapped across the front or back.

skirt supporter Patented elliptical metal *hoop,* q.v., with two moon-shaped wire metal cages inserted within the hoop, one on either side. Fitted over woman's petticoat just below the waistline to hold out a full skirt; worn in late 1850's.

ski suit Two-piece pants suit or jumpsuit worn for skiing, usually of water-repellent poplin or nylon; jackets lightweight, close fitting, often quilted; originally in dark colors or plaids, now may be in bright colors, florals, or stripes. Women's ski pants copied from men's in late 1920's were gathered into knitted ankle bands, later became tight and straight in stretch fabrics, strapped under foot. See *downhill* under *pants* and *ski jacket* under *jackets.*

ski sweater See *sweaters.*

skivvy shirt See *knit shirts* under *shirts.*

Skort See *skirts* or *shorts.*

skullcap See *caps.*

skunk See *furs.*

slacks See *pants* and *trousers. Slacks* is usually applied to loose-cut casual pants, not part of a suit.

slammerkin Loose-fitting, unboned morning gown, q.v., worn without hoops by women from 1730 to 1770. Also called *trollopee.*

slap shoe Woman's shoe of the 17th century styled like *mule,* q.v., usually with high heel.

slashed sleeve See *Spanish sleeve.*

slashing 15th- and 16th-century term for vertical slits in garments that enabled the contrasting lining to be pulled through; used on doublets, sleeves, and hose. Also called *scissoring, chique-tades,* and *creves.* See *panes.*

slash pocket See *pockets.*

slave bracelet See *bracelets.*

sleep bonnet See *bonnets.*

sleep bra See *leisure* under *brassieres.*

sleep coat or **shirt** See *nightgowns.*

sleepwear Department-store term for *nightgowns, pajamas,* and *robes.*

sleeve Part of garment that covers all or part of arm, either cut in one with top of garment or set into armhole or joined by raglan seams, etc.; can be tucked, puffed, pleated, ruffled, or tailored, etc. Some types of sleeves:

SLEEVES:

balloon s. Very large *puff* sleeve extending to elbow, set into a regular armhole, frequently made of organdie; popular in 1890's and since for evening and wedding dresses.

barrel s. Sleeve that fits at armhole and at wrist but is full at the elbow, similar to *lantern sleeve,* q.v., below.

batwing s. Long sleeve cut with

PUFFED SLEEVE

BELL SLEEVE

BATWING SLEEVE

FITTED SLEEVE

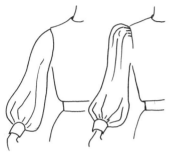

BISHOP SLEEVE

KIMONO SLEEVE

BRACELET SLEEVE

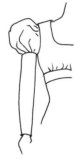

JULIET SLEEVE

deep armhole almost to waist, tight at wrist, giving wing-like appearance when arm is extended.

bell s. Sleeve narrow at the top and set into normal armhole and flared at lower edge like a bell.

beret s. Short sleeve, often used on evening dresses, made from two circles of fabric, seamed at outer edges, with holes cut in centers for armhole and arm, lined to stand out stiffly; popular in early 19th

century and again in 1930's. Also called *melon sleeve, q.v.*

bishop s. Full sleeve set into normal armhole and gathered into band at wrist.

bracelet s. Three-quarter-length fitted, cuffless sleeve allowing bracelet to show.

butterfly s. Wide flaring sleeve, set in smoothly at armhole, extending to elbow or wrist, giving cape effect.

471

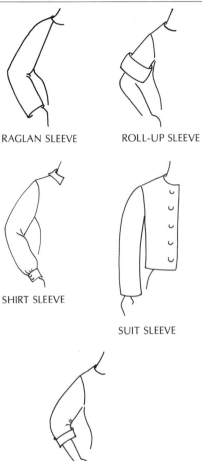

RAGLAN SLEEVE   ROLL-UP SLEEVE

SHIRT SLEEVE

SUIT SLEEVE

THREE-QUARTER SLEEVE

cap s. Small sleeve just covering top of arm, not continuing under arm.

dolman s. Sleeve cut all-in-one with shoulder, making wide top, sometimes similar to *batwing, q.v.,* above.

double-puffed s. Full sleeve with band around arm that divides it into two puffs; in 1960's, a bracelet sometimes worn around upper arm over full sleeve to give same effect.

envelope s. Sleeve made with tri-angular pleats at the shoulders.

epaulet s. Yoke across the top of shoulder cut in one piece with the sleeve.

fitted s. Narrow sleeve set into small armhole, fitted all the way to wrist.

funnel s. See *pagoda sleeve,* below.

Juliet s. Long sleeve with short puffed top, fitted below. *Der.* Named after heroine of William Shakespeare's drama *Romeo and Juliet.*

kimono s. Wide straight sleeve set in at right angle to garment or cut in one, like sleeve of a Japanese kimono. See *kimono.*

lantern s. Sleeve in two sections, narrow at shoulder and wrist, wid-ened at mid-arm by a seam, forming a lantern shape.

leg-of-mutton s. Woman's sleeve, wide and rounded at the shoulder, tapering to a snug fit on lower arm, the shape of a leg of mutton; fash-ionable last half of 19th century, periodically revived in small or exag-gerated size. Also called *leg o'mut-ton* and *gigot sleeve;* see *French gigot sleeve.*

mandarin s. See *kimono sleeve,* above.

melon s. 1. Short globular sleeve made by joining two "doughnuts" of fabric at outer edges, the arm passing through central holes, some-times lined to extend shape in smooth curves; popular in 1930's and '40's. 2. Similar sleeve, short or elbow length, attached to a nar-row transparent sleeve to wrist.

pagoda s. Funnel-shaped sleeve with flared wrist ruffling over a puffed undersleeve; named for the shape, similar to a Far Eastern temple's flaring roof.

puff or **puffed s.** Short sleeve *gathered, q.v.,* either at the armhole or at the *cuff* or *band* or both, producing a rounded shape; popular in 1920's and '30's and still used for baby's and children's wear; revived in late 1960's.

raglan s. Sleeve that extends to neckline, set in by seams slanting from underarm front and back. See *Lord Raglan* and *raglan* under *coats.*

roll or **roll-up s.** Sleeve, approximately elbow length, finished only with a narrow hem, designed to be folded—or *rolled*—up at least twice in lieu of a cuff; popular for women's tailored shirts in 1950's-'60's, an outgrowth of earlier fad for wearing long sleeves folded up in this manner.

rumba s. *Barrel sleeve, q.v.,* covered with rows of small horizontal ruffles. *Der.* From shirts worn by men dancing South American rumba.

saddle s. Variation of *raglan sleeve, q.v.,* in which shoulder portion forms a straight band cut in one piece with the sleeve and seamed to front and back parallel to shoulder instead of at an angle as in *raglan* style. See *epaulet sleeve,* above.

shirt s. Tailored wrist-length sleeve with *flat-felled* seams, set smoothly into the armhole; sometimes has one or two small unpressed pleats where it joins the cuff; basic sleeve for men's shirts since late 19th century; may have *barrel* or *French cuff, q.q.v.* Women's may have band cuff.

suit s. Long straight sleeve made in two pieces with vertical seams at either side of underarm.

three-quarter s. Sleeve ending between elbow and wrist.

Tom Jones s. Full sleeve, gathered into cuff or ruffle, used on men's shirts, sometimes set into dropped shoulder. *Der.* Named for style of shirts worn in 18th century, popularized by 1963 movie of Henry Fielding's 1749 novel *Tom Jones.*

trumpet s. Variant of *bell sleeve, q.v.,* above.

sleeve à la folle See *imbecile sleeve.*

sleeve bracelet See *bracelets.*

sleeve button See *cuff button.*

sleeve hand 17th-century term for opening in sleeve through which hand is thrust.

sleeve string See *cuff string.*

sleeve tongs Ornamental metal tongs used to position large sleeves inside coat sleeves when dressing; used in mid 1890's.

sleevings See *slivings.*

slendang (slen-dahng) Cotton scarf of brightly colored woven pattern with fancy headings and fringed ends, manufactured in England and exported to the East, particularly Java, Siam, and Philippines. Also called *pahom.*

slicker See *coats.*

slide See *scarf slide.*

slide bracelet See *bracelets.*

slide fastener See *zipper.*

sling-back shoe See *shoes.*

sling-duster English term for coat with

dolman sleeves, q.v., frequently made of black and white checked silk and worn by women in mid 1880's.

sling neckline See *necklines.*

sling pump See *shoes.*

sling sleeve Sleeve cut in one with upper part of garment like a cape, frequently with attached horizontal piece of fabric, similar to a sling, to rest the arm in; worn in mid 1880's.

slip 1. Woman's undergarment matching length of dress, acting as a lining, may be cut across top of bust with thin straps or shaped in U with *built-up* straps; may be cut on bias for close fit, cut in gores to flare, or be cut straight; often lace trimmed. 2. Woman's undergarment combining *brassiere* and *petticoat, q.v.*

SLIPS:

blouse-s. Combination slip and blouse with top cut like a blouse and lower part serving as a slip under the skirt.

bra-s. Slip with a fitted top. One garment replaces two—the brassiere and the slip. Popularized in 1960's, earlier version of this garment was called the *bandeau slip.* Also see *longline bra-slip.*

built-up s. Slip with U neckline and deep armholes, forming wide straps, *i.e.* a *tank top.*

camisole s. Slip with a lace or embroidered top to be worn under a sheer blouse; often cut straight across neck, wide straps. Also see *camisole.*

half-s. Another name for *petticoat, q.v.*

CAMISOLE SLIP

STRAPLESS BRA-SLIP

long-line bra-s. A *long-line brassiere, q.v.,* attached to a *petticoat* or *half-slip.*

petti-s. Same as *half-slip* or *petticoat, q.v.*

princess s. Slip made in fitted panels from top to hem having no waistline seam, may be flared or straight cut; called *princess petticoat* in mid 19th century.

shadow-panel s. Slip made with an extra layer of fabric in the panel in front or back to diffuse the light when worn under a sheer dress or skirt.

snip-bottom s. Slip finished with three rows of hem-stitching around bottom, one or more rows may be cut off to adjust length.

strapless s. Slip baring shoulders, designed for wear under *strapless* *dress* or *top;* held up by *elasticized shirring* or by *boning, q.q.v.;* popular in 1940's, revived in early 1970's.

suit s. Slip with white top and dark skirt, to be worn with suit with sheer or white blouse.

slip-blouse See *blouse-slip* under *slips,* above, and *blouses.*

slip-dress See *dresses.*

slip-on Term referring to clothing that pulls on without use of extra slashes or plackets. See *blouses, gloves, shoes,* and *sweaters.*

slip-over See *slip-on,* above.

slipper Flexible-soled shoe, often low-cut and flat-heeled, usually worn indoors and put on and off easily. Also called *house slippers.*

SLIPPERS:

OPERA SLIPPER

SCUFF

acrobatic s. Soft open-shank shoe of sueded splits of leather, high vamp has T-strap connected by elastic to quarter; worn by dancers and gymnasts and popular for sports wear in 1960's.

after-ski s. Warm socks with lightweight soles attached. Also called *aprés-ski slippers, slipper-socks.* See *mukluks,* below.

ROMEO SLIPPER

ballet s. Soft kid slipper with drawstring throat, the upper pulled under to form part of sole, sometimes with padded toe, called *toe shoes;* worn by ballet dancers and, often in modified form, for women's wear in 1940's. Also see under *shoes.*

bootee 1. High-cut bedroom slipper edged with fur or fake fur. 2. Infant's fabric or knitted shoe. 3. Type of sock worn by astronauts in flight; see *space clothes.*

boudoir s. Early 20-th century term usually referring to slippers without backs, made in fancy fabrics, sometimes trimmed with *marabou, q.v.* See *mules,* below.

carpet s. 19th-century informal slip-on house slipper made of carpeting, cut pump style with a standing rounded tongue cut in one piece with toe; soft padded leather sole and flat heel made in one piece. Style still made in other fabrics and in felt. See *felts,* below.

D'Orsay s. Pump-shaped open-shank slipper cut down to the sole at either side; women's styles have heels of varying heights; men's have flat heels.

evening s. Delicate shoe worn with evening clothes; man's style is usually a *patent-leather pump, q.q.v.*

Everett s. Man's house slipper with

low back and high tongue curving over instep.

Faust s. See Romeo slipper.

felts Soft indoor slippers made in the same style as *carpet slippers* (see above) but of felt, sometimes with felt sole and heel; often trimmed with felt *overlays—pinked* and *perforated, q.q.v.*

flokati Hand-crafted Greek slipper-sock in above-ankle length, made of fuzzy wool in bright colors and used as *after-ski slipper, q.v.,* above.

Juliet s. Woman's slipper with a high front and back and V-shaped elastic gores at the sides.

mukluk s. Slipper-sock with knitted sock top attached to lightweight leather sole, with *moccasin, q.v.,* construction. See *mukluks.*

mule High-heeled slipper with vamp but no back, often made in fancy leathers and fabrics. Term used since 16th-century for slipper without a quarter. Also spelled *moile, moyle,* and *mowle.*

opera s. Man's bedroom slipper similar to *D'Orsay, q.v.,* slipper but front and back sections overlap at shank.

Pullman s. Man's lightweight glove-leather flat slipper that folds into small envelope for traveling; also made in patterned stretch fabrics for women. *Der.* Named for railroad sleeping cars designed by George Pullman and Ben Field in 1858–9 and owned since 1864 by Pullman Palace Car Co.

Romeo s. Man's pull-on, boot-type slipper with elastic side gores.

scuff Open-back, sometimes open-toe, slippers with flat heel. May be of fur, shaggy fabric, lightweight kid, terry cloth, or other fabrics.

slipper satin See *fabrics.*

slipper-sock See *mukluk* under *slippers,* above.

slip-shoe Man's *mule, q.v.,* with flat heel that produced a shuffling step from which came word *slipshod;* worn from 16th to mid 18th century.

slip stitch See *stitches.*

slit Slashed opening in front of garment used from 13th century on to facilitate entry; also, at back of jacket, called *vent, q.v.* Also see under *pockets* and *skirts.*

slivings Knee-length breeches similar to contemporary *Bermuda shorts, q.v.,* worn by men in late 16th and early 17th centuries. Also see *slops.* Also called *slivers, slives* and *sleevings.*

sloper Basic flat pattern used in apparel manufacture which may be adjusted to change style of the garment; method used by mass-production manufacturers.

Sloppy Joe See *sweaters.*

slops 1. Knee-length unpadded *trunk hose, q.v.,* worn during late 16th century. Also see *small slops.* 2. Term used until late 18th century for sailors' trousers, carried in a sea chest, or *slop chest.* 3. 17th- to 19th-century term for ready-made clothes and also the bedding and supplies sold to seamen; stores were known as *slop shops.*

slot pocket See *bound* under *pockets.*

slot seam See *seams.*

slouch hat See *hats.*

slub yarn See *yarns.*

small Size used along with *medium, large* and *extra large* for women's sweaters, housecoats, nightgowns, some panties, girdles, and panty girdles; men's sport shirts, sport jackets, sweaters, and robes; girls' sweaters and pajamas; boys' pajamas, knit shirts, robes, and sport jackets. Abbreviated *S.*

smallclothes Polite term for men's *breeches, q.v.,* from 1770 to mid 19th century.

small falls See *falls* and *spair.*

small slops Trunk hose with open legs reaching just to knees, similar to modern *Bermuda shorts, q.v.,* but fuller at top; required for Cambridge University students in England from 1585 to about 1610.

smock 1. Utility garment with sleeves, fastened down front or back, meant to protect clothes while wearer engages in labor. 2. Garment worn next to skin by women from 11th century to end of 18th century.

smock blouse Child's dress, the top bloused below the waistline by gathering with a ribbon pulled through insertion; knee-length skirt sometimes consisted of two ruffles; worn in 1880's.

smock dress See *dresses.*

smock frock 1. 18th- and 19th-century term for man's knee-length loose-fitting, homespun gown worn by farmers; sometimes with a sailor collar, or yoke, usually shirred in various patterns indicating the locality. Also called *smock.* 2. In

1880's, a women's garment cut like a farmer's smock, called *aesthetic dress, q.v.*

smocking Decorative needlework used to hold gathered cloth together in honeycombed pattern, the stitches catching alternate folds in elaborate designs; used especially on infants' and childrens' yokes and on waists and sleeves of dresses in early 20th century, revived in early 1970's. See *stitches.*

smock top See *tops.*

smoking cap See *lounging cap.*

smoking jacket See *jackets.*

smoky quartz See *gems.*

snail button Covered button ornamented with French knots (see *stitches*); used on men's coats and waistcoats in 18th century.

snake bracelet See *bracelets.*

snakes 17th-century term for *love locks, q.v.*

snakeskin See *leathers.*

snap-brim hat See *hats.*

snap fastener See *closings.*

sneaker See *shoes.*

sneaker sock See *socks.*

snip-bottom slip See *slips.*

snood Mesh cap worn by women to confine the hair, usually over back of head or to enclose only the *chignon, q.v.,* and often made of chenille crochet or metallic cord decorated with pearls, as in 15th and

16th centuries; popular in 1940's attached to back of hat or to replace for hat. See *Juliet* under *caps*.

snorkel coat or **jacket** See *sport jackets* under *jackets*.

snow leopard See *furs*.

snowsuit Two-piece or one-piece outer garment of warm fabric or quilting; zipped up front and part-way on legs, usually with hood and rib-knit at cuffs and ankles; worn by infants up to two years.

Snuggies See *panties*.

socks Knitted covering for foot and lower part of leg, made of wool, silk, cotton, Orlon, Agilon, etc., in various lengths from ankle to above knee, in plain rib, cable stitch, Argyll, etc., for both sexes; knee-length socks were high fashion for women in 1960's and 1970's with mini-skirts, hot pants, and other shorts.

SOCKS:

ankle s. Sock that just covers the ankle bone, either pulled straight up or when cuff is folded over; also called *anklet*.

Argyll or **argyle s.** Sock knitted by hand or machine with main body in diamond plaid pattern of several colors. See *plaids*.

bed s. Wool-knit sock worn when sleeping to keep the foot warm; often hand-knit in a variety of fancy stitches. Also called *foot warmer*.

bobby s. Ankle sock, usually with turned-down cuff, worn by children and popular with teenagers during 1940's and 1950's, so universal that young girls were called *bobby soxers*.

crew s. Heavy sock extending to lower calf, foot knit in plain stitch, upper part with rib stitch; originally white and worn for rowing and other sports, now made in colors, especially for men and boys.

cushion-sole s. Sock worn for active sports, knit with a special sole that keeps the foot from blistering— often a layer of cotton-and-stretch-nylon terry cloth; frequently given a special finish to help protect the foot from fungus, bacteria, and odor.

electric s. Heavyweight knee-high sock, usually made of a combination of fibers, with a specially designed heating element operated by a battery held on by strap around the leg; worn by spectators at winter sports events.

footlets Very low-cut socks, usually lightweight, not visible above pumps or other shoes, keep feet comfortable while maintaining bare-leg look in summer. See *Peds*.

half s. A mid-calf sock, sometimes cuffed, taller than an *ankle sock* or *anklet* but shorter than a *knee sock, q.q.v.*; popular for children in 1920's and '30's.

knee s. Sock that reaches just below the knee; popularized by boys wearing *knickers, q.v.*, in early 1900's and worn by girls in 1920's and 1930's, predating *ankle socks, q.v.* Worn by all children from 1940's on; adopted by teenagers and adult women in the 1960's for wear with the mini-skirt and shown by French designer André Courrêges with his collection in 1965. Also called *knee-high socks*. Traditional socks worn with *Scotch kilts, q.v.*

over-the-knee s. Sock or stocking with an elastic top that reaches

above the knee, holds the stocking up without a garter.

Peds Trademark of the first widely available *footlets, q.v.,* above; available in a number of fibers and styles.

short or **shortie s.** See *ankle sock,* above.

sneaker s. Type of *footlets* which are shaped higher in front to conform to laced instep of the sneaker. Worn instead of socks for the bare-legged look. Also called *snuggies.*

sweat s. *Crew sock,* sometimes with a *cushion sole, q.q.v.,* made with a combination of fibers, *e.g.,* 50% wool, 30% rayon and 10% cotton, worn for active sports and exercise. Originally made of coarse white cotton yarns that stretched out of shape easily but were used instead of wool because of absorption and washability; blends now make these socks more shape retentive.

sock boot English term for *slipper socks, q.v.*

sock lining Sole-shaped piece of leather or fabric covering shoe *insole, q.v.*

sock suspenders British term for men's garters, introduced in 1895 to hold up calf-length socks.

soft goods Retail-trade term for fashion and textile merchandise such as dresses, lingerie, coats, etc., opposite of hard lines, *e.g.,* home appliances, hardware, furniture, etc.

sole Bottom part of the shoe, under the foot; usually in three parts—*out-sole, mid-sole,* and *innersole.*

solea (pl. *soleae*) Simple form of *sandal* worn by ancient Romans consisting of wooden sole held on with thongs; later, from 12th century on, leather or cloth slippers strapped to foot and called *solers.*

soleil (so-lay-ee) 1. Lustrous fabric with rib finer than *ottoman, q.v.,* closely woven of cotton or worsted, used for dresses and suits. 2. Soft, silky felt used in millinery.

sole leather See *leathers.*

soler See *solea.*

solitaire 1. See *ring.* 2. Necktie worn with man's bag-wig from 1730's to 1770's, tied in various ways, *e.g.,* bow under chin; pinned in place, or loosely knotted with free ends. 3. Narrow colored scarf worn by women in mid 1830's, loosely tied with ends hanging to knees, usually worn with white dress.

solleret Piece of medieval armor consisting of joined pieces of iron designed to protect the foot. Also spelled *soleret* and *solaret*. Also see *sabaton*.

solution-dyed See *yarns*.

sombrero See *hats*.

sombrero Córdobes (som-bray-yo cor-do-base) Spanish riding hat with wide brim and high, flat-topped crown, worn tilted forward and fastened under chin with ribbon; named for town of Córdoba, Spain.

sontag (sonn-tag) Woman's cape, often knitted or crocheted, with ends crossed in front; worn in the

1850's for warmth under a cloak. Named for German opera singer Henriette Sontag.

Sorel, Agnès Mistress of Charles VII of France (ruler from 1444–40), called "La Dame de Beauté" (Lady of Beauty), wore jewel-studded robes, made the king a waistcoat embroidered with pearls and precious stones, was the first commoner to wear diamonds; acted as a model for the financier and merchant Jacques Couer who brought linen, silken gowns, sables, pearls, etc. from the Orient; painted by Fouquet. See *Agnès Sorel coiffure*, *corsage*, and *dress*.

sorquenie Woman's *tunic* fitted tightly over bust; worn from 13th century to 19th century. Also spelled *soucanie*.

sortie de bal (sor-tee-de-bal) Woman's evening *cloak* with attached hood made of silk or cashmere, lined with quilted fabric; worn from 1850's to 1870's.

soufflé (soo-flay) Textile-industry term used to describe fabrics with puffed surface; *e.g., matelassé, q.v.*

soulette (soo-let) Early 17th-century term for leather band crossed over instep and under arch of foot to hold *patten, q.v.,* to the shoe. Also spelled *solette*.

soutache (soo-tash) See *braid*.

soutane See *cassock*.

Southern Colonel tie See *string* under *ties*.

sou'wester or **southwester** See *hats*.

space blanket See *poncho*.

space boot See *space clothes*, below.

space clothes Garments designed to meet special needs of astronauts, which are flexible, durable, abrasion and flame resistant.

SPACE CLOTHES:

BIGS Acronym for *biological isolation garments, q.v.,* below

biological isolation garments Clothes worn by astronauts after splashdown from moon journey, designed to keep possible germs inside, consisting of jumpsuit zipped up front with hood and mask attached.

bootee Sock-like covering for foot made of Teflon-coated Beta cloth with non-skid sole finished with 3 ½-inch disk of Astro-Velcro.

inflight coveralls Two-piece utility suit worn inside capsule while traveling.

ITMG Acronym for *integrated thermal micrometroid garment;* see *space suit,* below.

integrated thermal micrometroid garment See *space suit,* below.

space boot Boot made of layers of special cloth, durable and flame resistant, for walking on moon surface.

space suit Suit made of 20 layers of fabric, outer layer of Teflon-coated Beta cloth, with accordion-like joints and attached gloves and shoes, designed to withstand high temperatures, first worn by Schirra, Eisele, and Cunningham in manned Apollo flight and for moon landing, July 20, 1969.

space-dyed yarn Yarns that are dyed various colors at intervals, producing a random design when woven.

spaier Medieval term for vertical slash in garment, similar to *slit,* used to reach pocket on inner garment.

spair Term used from 1840's on for closing on men's trousers. Also called *falls, q.v.*

spandex Generic term for man-made fibers, composed largely of segmented polyurethane, that are stretchable, lightweight, and resistant to body acids, used primarily for girdles, foundations and brassieres. See also *elastomeric yarn, Lycra,* and *Vyrene.*

spangle A *sequin* or *paillette, q.q.v.*

spaniel's-ear collar See *collars.*

Spanish blonde lace See *laces.*

Spanish breeches Narrow, high-waisted, below-the-knee breeches, loose at bottom, trimmed with rosettes buttons, hooked to doublet lining and similar to *small slops, q.v.,* but longer; worn by men in latter half of 17th century. Also called *Spanish hose.*

Spanish cape See *capa.*

Spanish comb Comb with ornamental top, sometimes five inches high, worn at crown of head to support a *mantilla, q.v.,* or separately for decorative effect.

Spanish embroidery See *embroideries.*

Spanish farthingale *Underskirt* in dome shape, made either with graduated *hoops* of wood, wire, etc., or with one hoop at bottom; worn in England last half of 16th century.

Spanish flounce Deep gathered ruffle joined to hem of short skirt worn in late 19th century and early 20th century.

Spanish hose See *Spanish breeches,* above.

Spanish jacket See *senorita.*

Spanish kettledrums English colloquial term for *trunk hose, q.v.,* particularly *round hose type, q.v.,* worn in third quarter of 16th century.

Spanish lace See *laces.*

Spanish shawl See *shawls.*

Spanish sleeve Puffed sleeve with vertical slashes revealing colored silk lining; worn by women, 1807–1820 and in late 1850's. Also called a *slashed sleeve.*

sparterie See *straws*.

spats Short cloth or leather *gaiters, q.v.*, reaching over ankles, buttoned at sides and held on by straps under insteps; first worn by military, later

adopted by civilian men to wear with *morning coat, q.v.*, in white, tan, or gray. Also worn by women from 1914–1920. See *spatterdashes*, below.

spatterdashes High leggings made of leather, canvas, etc. reaching to knee, fastened down outside of leg

by buttons, buckles, etc.; worn by men in latter half of 18th century.

spectacles or **specs** See *glasses*.

spectator pump See *shoes*.

speed lacing Closing on boot consisting of metal hooks replacing eyelets for upper part of lacing; used particularly on skating boots.

Spencer 1. Man's waist-length, double-breasted *jacket* with rolled collar and cuffed sleeves. *Der.* Named for 2nd Earl of Spencer (1758–1834), who accidentally burned off tails

of *frock coat, q.v.*, and preferred shorter style. 2. Woman's waist-length *jacket* with shawl collar, often fur-trimmed, sleeveless or with long sleeves covering hands, sometimes collarless; worn late 18th century to early 19th century. 3. Sleeveless knitted *jacket* worn by elderly women in late 19th century. 4. Woman's *blouse* with a band at the waistline; worn in 1860's and 1890's. Also called a *Spencer waist*.

Spencer cloak Woman's cloak of embroidered net with elbow-length sleeves; worn in early 19th century.

Spencerette Woman's fitted jacket with low-cut neckline edged with lace; worn at end of Empire Period, about 1814. See *Spencer*, above.

spere Late 16th- and 17th-century term for *placket, q.v.* Also spelled *speyer*.

spider work See *laces*.

spike heel See *heels*.

spike tail Slang term for man's *swallow-tailed coat, q.v.*

spindle 1. Tapered rod used to hold bobbin when winding yarn. 2. Yarn unit of measurement: for cotton, 18 hanks, or 15,120 yards; for linen, 48 cuts, or 14,400 yards. Generally spelled *spyndle* for yarn measurement.

spinel (spe-nel) See *gems*.

spinneret Textile-industry term for nozzle with holes through which man-made liquids are pressed to form filaments.

spinning 1. Process of twisting natural fibers together to form a yarn. 2. For man-made fibers, the extrustion of the solution into a coagulation bath to form fibers.

Spitalfields Tie silk. See *fabrics.*

spit-boot Man's boot combining *shoe* and *gaiter, q.v.,* closing down outside of leg with interlocking fasteners, the last fastener was an iron spike or spit that fastened through an iron socket; worn from 18th to mid 19th centuries in northern England.

spit curls See *curls.*

splinter-hat See *splynter-hat.*

split One of several layers or *cuts* sliced from thick cattle hide, with grade of leather determined by the split: *top-grain* is the smooth fur side of the skin; other splits have a rough surface, called *deep-buff, split slab,* etc.; popular for sportwear in 1960's and '70's.

split falls See *falls.*

splynter-hat 16th-century term for hat made of braided split pieces of straw, rather than whole rounded stalks.

spool heel See *heels.*

spoon back Term used in mid 1880's for circular folds of drapery formed at back by the overskirt of a walking dress.

spoon bonnet Small-crowned bonnet with brim narrow at sides, projecting upward above forehead in elliptical shape; worn in early 1860's.

sporran (spor-an) Scottish leather or fur pouch worn suspended from belt in front of *kilt, q.v.,* part of Highlander's traditional dress; copied as woman's handbag in early 1970's.

sport cap See *caps.*

sport coat or **jacket** See *jackets.*

sport set Trade term for two or more items of sportswear made to match or contrast and sold as a set, most commonly: bathing suit with cover-up, top with shorts or skirt, twin sweaters and skirt, child's bloomers with pinafore, etc.

sport suit Clothing designed to be worn for specific sports, e.g., a suit used for fencing, riding, racing, scuba-diving, etc. For descriptions

see *swimsuits, riding habit, jogging suit, judo costume, jumpsuits, karate costume, wet suit,* and *sports jacket* under *jackets.*

sportswear Term popularized in the 1930's for casual tailored clothing: sweaters, skirts, blouses, shorts, shirtdresses; etc.

spotted cat See *furs.*

spread collar See *collars.*

spring-bottom trousers Trousers that flare at ankles; worn in 1870–'80's.

spring bracelet See *bracelets.*

spun-dye See *solution-dyed.*

spun rayon See *fabrics.*

spun rayon yarn Yarn made from rayon staple, *q.v.*

spun silk 1. Rough-textured silk fabric made from short fibers spun into uneven yarns. 2. Silk yarn made from short length fibers secured from silk wastes in two main grades, *schappe* and *bourette, q.v.*

spun yarn Textile-industry term for man-made fibers of controlled length that are spun into yarn in a manner similar to that used for cotton and wool yarns, giving a mat finish and a soft hand.

spyndle See *spindle.*

square cut See *gem cuts.*

square-dance dress See *dresses.*

square setting See *gem settings* under *gems.*

square toe See *toes.*

squaw Clothes influenced by those worn by North American Indian women. See *blouses; boots; dresses, handbags,* and *skirts,* etc.

squirrel See *furs.*

stacked heel See *heels.*

stadium boot See *boots.*

stadium coat See *coats.*

standard ranch mink See *mink* under *furs.*

stand-away collar See *collars.*

stand-fall collar 19th-century term for *rolled,* or *turn-over collar, q.v.,* under *collars.*

standing band 1. Standing white collar usually of starched or wired linen; worn in 16th and 17th centuries by men and women. Also see opposites: *band* and *falling band.* 2. See *collars.*

staple Trade term for short natural or man-made fibers long enough to be spun into yarns.

starcher Man's starched *cravat, q.v.,* of 19th century.

star ruby See *gems.*

star sapphire See *gems.*

startup High shoe, reaching above ankle, frequently laced or buckled, made of untanned leather; worn by country men and American Colonists in late 17th and early 18th centuries. Also called *startop, styrtop, stertop,* and *bagging shoe.*

Stavropoulos, George See *designers appendix, United States*

stay, stays 1. (pl.) 19th-century term for *corset, q.v.* 2. Sewing term for strip of bone (now usually thin metal or plastic) inserted in seam to flatten woman's foundation garment or to stiffen fabric belts, strapless bodices, corners of shirt collars, etc. 3. Piece of fabric stitched under pleats or gathers to hold fullness.

stay hook Small ornamental hook to hold watch, attached to bodice, worn in 18th century. Also called *breasthook* or *crochet.*

stay stitching Machine stitching just beyond the seam line done on pieces of the garment before seaming to keep them from stretching out of shape during construction, especially on bias or curved edges.

steeple headdress See *hennin.*

steerhide See *leathers.*

Steinkirk Long, lace-edged *cravat, q.v.,* loosely knotted under the chin with the ends pulled through buttonhole, pinned to side, or left hanging; worn by men from 1692 to 1730. *Der.* From the Battle of Steinkirk, in 1692, when soldiers were surprised into battle, with cravats untied.

stem stitch See *outline* under *stitches.*

stenciled print See *prints.*

stenciling Applying dye to fur or fabric by painting through a cutout stencil; e.g., used to make pony fur or Dynel pile fabric look like leopard. In late 1960's and early 1970's applied to sheared mink and all kinds of fur and fur fabrics to simulate giraffe, tiger, leopard, jaguar, zebra, etc.

step cut See *gem cuts* under *gems.*

step-ins See *panties.*

step-in shoe See slip-on under *shoes.*

Stetson See *hats.*

Stewart, dress tartan See *tartans.*

Stewart, hunting tartan See *tartans.*

stick pin See *pins.*

stick-up collar See *Gladstone collar,* under *collars.*

Stiebel, Victor See *designers appendix, England.*

stiletto (stil-let-o) 1. Narrow, pointed stick used in ancient Greece as a hairpin. 2. Pointed instrument similar to a large needle, used to punch holes in embroidery. 3. See *heels.*

stirrup hose Stockings with no foot, fitted with strap under arch of foot, laced through eyelets at top to connect with breeches; worn over finer stockings for protection when riding. Also called *boot hose, q.v.,* and *stirrup stockings.*

stitch 1. Single complete movement through fabric or other material of a threaded needle that produces a pattern of threads in many variations, used in joining of two pieces of fabric, or as trim on garments and accessories. 2. Movement of needle or hook to complete a loop or particular set of loops in the process of knitting or crocheting.

STITCHES, SEWING AND EMBROIDERY:

arrowhead s. Embroidery consisting of two stitches slanted to form an arrow, used singly or filled in as in *satin stitch, q.v.,* often as reinforcement at top of a pleat.

Aubusson s. Needle-point half-stitch, worked diagonally over intersection of vertical and horizontal threads, only on *penelope, q.v.,* canvas, giving look of *rep silk, q.v.* Also called *rep stitch.*

back s. Hand sewing in which needle inserted from right to left, then

485

thread brought back to right and re-inserted to emerge a stitch to the left; as process is repeated stitches touch each other on top (like machine stitches), are doubled over each other on the back.

bargello s. Straight vertical stitches worked in a rising and falling pattern across canvas forming peaks and valleys; the next row exactly meeting the first. Also called *flame, Florentine,* or *zigzag stitch.*

basket s. Embroidery stitch resembling series of overlapped cross-stitches used to fill in backgrounds.

basket-weave s. Needle-point stitch in which a series of diagonal stitches is used to fill background of canvas.

basting Loose running stitches, often alternating long and short, used to hold sections of garment together before machine stitching.

blanket s. Embroidery stitch that looks like a series of connected U's, used to finish edges.

blind s. See *slip stitch.*

brick s. *Blanket stitch, q.v.,* used on flat fabric in continuous rows to resemble brick wall. Also called *brickwork.*

bullion See *French knot.*

bundle Embroidery stitch resembling small bow knot, made by taking three or four long loose stitches side by side, then placing a small stitch across at the center, drawing them together.

buttonhole s. Embroidery stitch similar to *blanket stitch q.v.,* worked close together and with an extra purl at the edge; used for *worked buttonholes, q.v.* Also called *close stitch.*

Byzantine s. Slanting embroidery stitch, worked on canvas over three or four vertical and horizontal threads in diagonal zigzag stripes; good background-filler.

cable s. 1. Embroidery stitch similar to *chain stitch, q.v.,* but with extra stitch connecting links. 2. Hand-knitting stitch that produces a vertical cable pattern by crossing groups of "knit" stitches over each other.

catch s. Loose stitch like a series of X's crossed near their tops, used for bulky hems and for pleats in linings, etc. Also called *cat stitch.*

cat s. See *catch stitch,* above.

chain s. 1. Embroidery stitch making connected loops that form a chain on the front. 2. Sewing-machine stitch done with a single thread, forming a chain on the back; easy to rip out, used for hems and shoes. 3. Basic *crochet stitch.*

close s. See *buttonhole stitch,* above.

Continental s. Small stitch worked on canvas covering areas with diagonal lines; used to fill in needle-point backgrounds. Also called *tent stitch.*

couching *Overcast, q.v.,* stitches at regular intervals fastening down a heavier strand of thread that outlines a design.

cross s. Basic embroidery stitch with one thread crossed over the other to form an X; used for cloth embroidery, with one row of slanted stitches worked first, then cross-bars added by reversing the direction; also done on canvas in needle-tapestry work, where each cross is completed before next is begun.

darning Vertical stitches woven through horizontal stitches in a one-to-one checkerboard pattern, resembling plain-weave cloth; used for mending holes or as an embroidery stitch.

double running s. Tiny *running stitch, q.v.,* worked and then reversed so that new stitches fill spaces and make pattern similar to sewing-machine stitch. Also called *two-sided stitch, Holbein stitch,* and *Italian stitch.*

fagoting (fa-got-ing) 1. Open seam stitch similar to single *feather stitch, q.v.,* used to join two edges of fabric. 2. See *hem-stitching* and *picot.*

feather s. Decorative stitch which looks like a double row of V's branching out first to one side then the other in continuous line.

filling s. Any type of embroidery stitch used to fill in part of an outlined design.

fishbone s. Embroidery stitch like backbone of fish, made with series of *blanket stitches, q.v.,* stitches worked to right and left, branching from unmarked center line: similar to *feather stitch, q.v.,* but worked closer togetther.

flame s. See *Florentine* and *bargello* stitch.

flat s. Embroidery stitch worked in the same way as *fishbone stitch,* above, with shorter stitches and more overlapping.

Florentine s. Variant of *bargello, q.v.*

French knot Embroidery stitch made by twisting thread around needle three to five times and putting needle back through same point, making a small nub. Also called *bullion stitch.*

gobelin s. (go-be-lan) Canvas needlepoint stitch worked vertically over two horizontal threads from left to right straight across canvas.

gros point (grow-pawn) Large needlepoint stitch worked diagonally over two rows on canvas. See *petit point.*

hemming Long loose slanting stitch placed through hem and caught to garment with very small stitch.

hemstitch Ornamental stitch made by drawing out several parallel threads, then tying together groups of vertical threads at regular intervals making hourglass shapes, used as border on blouses, handkerchiefs, etc. See *picot* and *fagoting.*

herringbone s. Continuous overlapped V stitches in solid rows giving a tweed effect, based on the *catch-stitch, q.v.*

Holbein s. See *double-running stitch.*

honeycomb Variant of *brick work, q.v.*

laid s. See *couching.*

lazy daisy s. Single *chain stitch, q.v.,* used in embroidery, with extra stitch added at outer edge to hold loop in place to form petal. Also called *detached chain stitch.*

mark s. See *tailor's tacks.*

Oriental s. Series of long straight stitches placed side by side with each stitch intersected in center by short diagonal stitch. Also called *Rumanian stitch.*

outline s. *Back stitch, q.v.,* done in reverse, so that overlapping stitches are on front; used to outline stems, leafs, etc. in embroidery.

overcasting 1. By hand: diagonal edging stitch that enters the fabric always from the same side and goes around raw edge to keep it from fraying. 2. By machine: a similar finish for raw edges made by a special sewing-machine attachment.

padding s. 1. *Running stitch, q.v.,* used, sometimes in rows, to provide a base for embroidery stitches such as *satin stich, q.v.,* worked on top. 2. Diagonal rows of *basting stitch, q.v.,* used in tailoring to augment interfacing and hold it in place.

petit point Tiny diagonal stitches worked on canvas over only one pair of the background yarns. See *gros point.*

picot stitching See *hemstitching.*

plain s. Simple *running stitch, q.v.,* below.

railway s. See *chain stitch.*

rep s. See *Aubusson stitch.*

Rumanian s. See *Oriental stitch.*

running s. Very tiny even stitches with spaces between equaling visible stitches. Used for seams, tucking, gathering, and quilting.

saddle s. Small running stitch in contrasting or heavy thread, frequently used for trim on coats, sport dresses, and gloves.

satin s. Embroidery stitch with straight, usually long, stitches worked very close together, either vertically or slanted, to fill in large area, such as leaf or flower.

seed s. 1. Embroidery stitch consisting of tiny individual *back stitches, q.v,,* worked at random to fill background. 2. A *knitting stitch* made by alternating *knit* and *purl* stitches.

shell s. 1. Stitch taken at intervals on a tuck to produce scalloped effect. 2. A *crochet, q.v.,* stitch.

slip s. Small, almost invisible stitches with connecting thread hidden under fabric; used to join an edge to a single layer, e.g., a hem or facing.

smocking s. Embroidery stitches that gather the fabric into folds forming a complex diamond pattern combined with folds like *cartridge pleats, q.v.;* popular in place of plain *shirring, q.v.,* on baby's and girl's dresses and coats, also used on adult clothes. See drawing, page 477.

stem s. See *outline stitch,* above.

tailor's tacks Large stitches taken through two thicknesses of fabric with a loop left between the layers which are later cut apart, leaving tufts in each piece; used for guide marks in tailoring. Also called *marking stitch.*

tent s. See *Continental stitch.*

whip s. Short *overcast stitch, q.v.,* used over rolled or raw edges, especially on glove seams.

stock See *collars, scarfs, shirts,* and *ties.* Also see *flip-tie* under *blouses* and *necklines.*

stock-dyed See *yarns.*

stocking See *hose.*

stocking bodice Knitted or shirred elastic tube, pulled over woman's torso as *strapless top* to wear with pants, shorts, or an evening skirt; popular in the 1940's, revived in late 1960's.

stocking boot See *boots.*

stocking cap See *caps.*

stocking purse Small tubular purse shaped like a stocking closed at each end, but slit in center to provide entry, often crocheted in

elaborate designs; carried by both men and women in latter half of 17th century and also in mid 19th century. Also called *miser purse.*

stocking shoe See *shoes.*

stocks Men's *hose,* like modern *tights, q.v.,* upper part called *upper stocks,* lower part called *nether stocks,* and finally synonym for *stockings;* worn from 15th to 17th century. Also see *trunk hose.*

stola (stow-la) Long, belted outer garment, usually woolen; worn by early Roman matrons and resembling *Doric chiton* (see *chiton*) of ancient Greeks.

stole 1. Long wide scarf, often fringed at ends, made of fabric, knit, or fur, and worn as woman's wrap since 19th century; especially a short fur cape with long ends in front, popular in 1940's and 1950's instead of jacket. 2. Long, wide scarf matched in fabric to woman's dress, popular with bare-top dress in 1950's, especially in evening. 3. Part of ecclesiastical vestments derived from early Greek *pallium,* worn over the *cotta, q.v.,* by clergymen.

stomacher 1. Heavily embroidered or jeweled V-shaped panel over chest, extending down to point over stomach, held in place by *busks, q.v.;* part of men's and women's court dress of 15th and 16th centuries; acted as *dickey* under man's *doublet, q.q.v.* 2. Same type of inserted front panel made of shirred fabric; used on women's dresses in first half of 19th century. Also see *cottage front, ribbon front,* or *waistcoat bosom.*

stone marten See *furs.*

storm boot See *boots.*

storm coat See *coats.*

stovepipe hat Man's black silk dress hat with high crown, flat on top, like tall hat worn by Abraham Lincoln. See *plug hat.*

stovepipe pants See *pants.*

strapless Woman's garments that bare shoulders. See *brassieres, dresses, necklines, slips,* and *tops.*

strapped trousers Trousers with one or two straps under instep, worn by men last half of 19th century.

strap seam See *seams.*

strass See *paste.*

straw Material made by braiding or weaving natural fibers from stalks, leaves, grasses, etc., to make hat bodies, handbags, shoes, and belts.

STRAWS:

baku Fine lightweight, dull-finished straw made from fibers of buri palm, found in the Philippines. *Shantung baku* is fine and given glazed finish.

ballibuntl 1. Fine, lightweight glossy straw, similar to *baku, q.v.,* woven of buntal fibers from stems of unopened talipot palm leaves from the Philippines. Also spelled *balibuntal.* 2. Smooth lightweight dull straw also called *Bangkok straw.*

Bangkok s. See *ballibuntl.*

chip s. Wood, straw, etc. cut in fine strips for hats or baskets, particularly for women's *chip bonnets,* in the 19th century.

coconut s. Braided straw, usually tan or light brown, made from coconut-palm leaves. Also called *coco straw.*

Leghorn s. Fine, smooth straw braid plaited with thirteen strands, made from upper part of wheat stalks grown near Leghorn, a town in Tuscany, Italy.

Milan s. Plaited straw using seven strands in each braid, made from lower part of wheat stalk, called pedal straw, grown near the city of Milan, in Tuscany, Italy.

Panama Fine, durable hat body handwoven under water from young leaves of jipijapa, palm-like plant cultivated in Equador.

peanit s. Inexpensive exotic straw imported from Java.

raffia Fiber from species of Madagascar palm used for making hats, bags, embroidery, etc.

sennit Braided rough straw, grass, or leaves used for men's hats in Japan and China.

shantung baku See *baku.*

sisal (sy-sal) Finely woven, smooth straw with linen finish, made from Philippine sisal hemp shipped to China. *Der.* Named after Sisal, port in Yucatán, Mexico. Also spelled *sisol* and *sissol.*

sparterie Straw fabric made of esparto grass from North Africa, cheap enough to use for experimental shapes in millinery designs.

toyo Hat body material made of cellophane-coated rice paper, produced in Japan, Okinawa, and Formosa; of fine quality and woven like Panama.

Tuscan s. Straw braid, made of Tuscany wheat, similar to Milan but with eleven strands in each braid.

streaker One taking part in the winter of 1973–74 in a fad for running across a college campus or other public place nude except for shoes and possibly hat; "classic" college streaker's costume consisted of knit *ski mask, q.v.,* and *tennis shoes.*

street sweeper See *dust ruffle.*

stretch knit See *knits.*

stretch fabrics Fabrics of great flexibility that return to shape after pulling, knitted or woven with *crimp-set yarns* or *elastomeric yarns* like *Lastex* or *spandex, q.q.v.,* used for sportswear or foundation garments. See *brassieres, hose, tops.*

stretch top See *tops.*

stretch wig See *wig.*

stretch yarns See *crimp-set* and *elastomeric* under *yarns.*

string tie See *ties.*

stripes 1. Bands of color or texture of varying widths, making a design in a fabric, either printed or woven in; may go with warp, filling, or be diagonal. 2. Narrow bands of braid or colored ribbon applied to fabric in rows, all over or as border trim.

STRIPES:

awning s. Wide even bands of one or more bright colors and white, woven or printed on coarse *canvas, q.v.,* for window awnings, copied in ligher fabrics for garments.

bayadere s. (bah-yah-deer) Horizontal stripes of varying widths in brilliant colors, reds, greens, blues, and gold. Also called *gypsy* or *Romany stripes. Der.* Named for Hindu dancing girl.

blazer s. Inch-wide bands of one or several colors alternating with white. *Der.* From *blazer jacket, q.v.*

candy s. Narrow bands of red on white background, imitating peppermint candy sticks.

chalk s. Narrow lines of white, widely spaced, frequently used on gray, navy, or black flannel; classic for men's business suits.

competition s. Brightly colored single or cluster stripes across front of garment, borrowed from competitive-sports uniforms, e.g., football jerseys.

double ombré s. Stripes of two colors shaded from light to dark, usually run horizontally, either printed or woven.

gypsy s. See *bayadere stripes.*

hairline s. See *pin stripe.*

mattress-ticking s. See *ticking stripes.*

pencil s. Vertical stripe as wide as a pencil line, with wider stripes of background color between.

pin s. Very narrow—width of a straight pin—woven or printed vertical stripes, placed close together, either white stripes on dark ground or vice versa. Same as *hairline stripe.*

regimental s. Wide even colored stripes on plain dark background, used for men's tie fabrics, taken from insigniae on British military uniforms in which colors of stripes identify the regiments.

Roman s. Horizontal stripes varied in size and grouped together with no contrast background.

Romany s. See *bayadere stripes.*

satin s. Satin-weave stripe alternating with bands of plain fabric.

shadow s. Indistinct, narrow stripes, all in tones of one color family, woven vertically, e.g., navy, light blue, and grey blue used together.

ticking s. Narrow woven dark-blue stripes, sometimes spaced in pairs, on white ground, often in a twill weave, originally a heavy fabric used to cover mattresses, now used for sport clothes and copied in lighter weights and other colors for clothing.

stroller 1. See *coats*. 2. Casual, mannish felt hat, worn by women for town and spectator sports in 1930's and 1940's.

stud Small, ornamental button, mounted on short post with a smaller button-like end, inserted through eyelet to fasten shirt fronts, cuffs, or neckbands; used since late 18th century. Also called *collar button*.

stump work See *embroideries*.

styrtop See *startup*.

S-twist Yarn twisted so that, when held vertically, the spirals slope in the direction of the center of a letter S: from upper left to lower right.

suba Sleeveless short sheepskin coat with leather side out, heavily ornamented with leather applique; worn by Hungarian men.

suburban coat See *coats*.

suede See *leathers*.

suede cloth See *fabrics*.

sugar-loaf hat Man's and woman's high tapered-crown hat with broad brim; worn in mid 17th century. *Der.* Crown is in shape formerly used for loaf sugar.

suit Costume for men and women, consisting of jacket (also called *suit coat* or *coat*), pants or skirt, sometimes a vest; conventional attire for men's business and evening wear; for women, day or evening, in many fabrics, jackets in varied styles. See *blazer, cardigan, Nehru,* etc., under *jackets* and *sport jackets*.

SUITS:

business s. Man's suit, conservative in style, color, suitable for daytime wear in an office; so called and cut to distinguish it from a *sport suit,* which may be made of plaids and brighter colors. May be *single* or *double-breasted* and in *one, two,* or *three-button* style, *q.q.v.*

Chanel s. Popular woman's suit by Paris designer *Gabrielle Chanel, q.v.,* in late 1950's, consisting of collarless cardigan jacket and knee-length skirt in colorful tweeds; jacket usually trimmed with fancy *braid* down front and on sleeves, breast pockets; worn with coordinated blouse. Style was widely copied and still worn in 1970's.

Continental s. Man's suit with natural shoulder line, easy fitting jacket; narrow, tapered trousers with no belt, pockets in trousers slanted from waistline to side seams; style originating in Italy in 1950's.

dress s. See *full dress,* below.

dressmaker s. Woman's suit that is made with soft lines and fine details, as by a dressmaker, contrasted to tailor-made styles that have the sharply defined lines of a man's suit made by a tailor.

Edwardian s. Man's suit with close-fitting finger-tip-length jacket, with high notched lapels, and narrow stove-pipe pants; copied from styles of 1900–1911 reign of Edward VII and popular in exaggerated form with London *Teddy Boys, q.v.,* in late 1950's and in velvet for women in late 1960's and early 1970's.

Eton s. Young boy's dress-up suit adapted from uniform formerly worn by schoolboys at Eton College in England; see *Eton suit* in alphabetical listings.

formal s. See *tuxedo* and *full-dress suit,* below.

full-dress s. Man's formal suit consisting of *swallow-tailed coat* and matching trousers, frequently trimmed with satin lapels and satin

stripes down side of pants; worn with formal shirt, white vest, and white tie. Also called *white tie and tails.*

gangster s. Single or double-breasted, wide-shouldered suit with wide lapels, inspired by movie *Bonnie and Clyde* in 1967, usually black or gray pin-striped flannel; re-creation of 1930's man's fashion.

Ivy League s. Man's suit with natural shoulders, narrow lapels, three-button closing, and narrow trousers; popular in 1950's, spreading from the seven Eastern college campuses in the Ivy League as reaction against exaggeratedly wide padded shoulders of the 1940's.

lounge s. Man's business suit, also known as a sack suit, with double or single breasted jacket in a soft fabric. Originally called a lounge suit because today's business suit is much more informal than the cutaway coats, morning suits and striped trousers considered correct daytime dress prior to World War I.

sack s. Man's daytime suit; single-breasted unstructured jacket with

natural unpadded shoulders, usually straight-sided.

semi-formal s. Man's *dinner suit:* Edwardian style, *q.v.,* popular in early 1970's, or *tuxedo,* see below.

tuxedo s. Man's semi-formal finger-tip-length jacket and pants, with satin or faille lapels and side stripes on pants; black or midnight blue in winter, white jacket with dark pants in summer; sometimes other colors or plaids in 1960's. Worn with *cummerbund, q.v.,* and black bow tie. Also abbreviated *tux,* or called *black tie.* See *tuxedo* in main listings.

walking s. 1. Woman's three-quarter-length coat, sometimes fur-trimmed, and straight skirt; usually made in tweed. 2. Woman's suit worn in 1901 with skirt just brushing the ground. 3. Man's knee-length outer coat with matching pants; introduced in late 1960's.

suit dress See *dresses.*

suit of knots Term used for set of matching bows used to trim a dress and to wear in hair, from 17th to the mid 18th century.

suit of lights Working costume of banderilleros and matadors for Spanish and Mexican bullfights, consisting of waist-length, long-sleeved, heavily embroidered jacket, open in front, trimmed with elaborate epaulets, worn with tight-fitting below-the-knee pants. Also called *suit of sequins* and *traje de luces.* Also see *matador's hat.*

suit of ruffs Term for matching neck and wrist ruffs, worn by men and women from 1560 to 1640.

suit of sequins See *suit of lights.*

suit slip See *slips.*

suit vest See *vests.*

sultana scarf Scarf worn in mid 1850's over *canezou jacket, q.v.,* tied below waistline, long hanging ends.

sultana sleeve Full *hanging sleeve,* slit open down outside, sometimes fastened with ribbons around upper and forearms; also called *sultan sleeve.*

sultane dress *Princess, q.v.,* daytime dress with scarf elaborately draped to one side; worn in late 19th century.

sultane jacket Very short, sleeveless *bolero*-type woman's jacket coming just below shoulder blades; worn in late 1880's. See *Zouave jacket.*

Sunbak See *fabrics.*

sunbonnet Woman's summer head-covering made of cotton fabric with crown gathered to a large brim, often with a flap at back of neck, tied under chin, designed to protect the face and neck from the sun; popular in U.S. from Colonial days through early 20th century and still made for children. See *bonnets.*

sunburst pleats See *pleats.*

Sunday clothes Term used in 19th century and early 20th century for clothing kept especially for church and special occasions, as opposed to *work clothes.* Also called *Sunday best.*

sundress See *dresses.*

sunglasses See *glasses.*

sun hat See *beach hat* under *hats.*

sunray skirt Variant of *sunburst-pleated skirt, q.v.*

sunshade See *parasol*.

sun suit Rompers or shorts with bib top and straps crossing in back, worn by small children in summer.

super tunic Variant of *surcoat* or *sideless surcoat, q.q.v.*

Supima Trademark for *pima* cotton, *q.v.*, grown in southwestern U.S.

supportasse Wire framework, used to tilt enormous starched ruffs up in back. Also called *underpropper*. The *rabato, q.v.*, was similar.

Supphose Trademark for *support hose, q.v.*, for men and women.

support hose or **socks.** Stockings or socks for men or women knit of stretch nylon combined with elastic yarns to provide support to the muscles and veins of the legs; an innovation of the 1950's, may be quite sheer, more attractive in appearance than the elastic stockings formerly worn for this purpose. See *support pantyhose*.

surrah Silk twill. See *fabrics*.

surcoat 1. Man's outer garment, usually knee-length with wide sleeves, worn over *armor* by knights or over *tunic* or *cote, q.q.v.*, in Middle Ages. 2. Woman's long, loose outer garment with full tubular or bell-shaped sleeves, worn over *kirtle, q.v.*, in Middle Ages. Also called *super tunic*. See *sideless surcoat*.

surfers See *pants*.

surpied See *soulette*.

surplice 1. Loose white overblouse, either waist or knee-length, gathered to flat yoke, with full open sleeves; worn by clergy and choir singers and copied for children's wear,

blouses and nightgowns. See *cotta*. 2. Garment that overlaps diagonally in front making V neckline, sometimes wrapped and fastened in back. See *collars* and *necklines*.

surtout (ser-too) 1. Contemporary French and English term for man's *cloak* or *overcoat. Der.* French, literally *overall*. 2. 17th century term for *Brandenburg overcoat, q.v.,* 3. 18th century term for *wrap-rascal, q.v.*, under *wrapper*. Also called *surtout greatcoat* in 19th century.

suspenders 1. Detachable straps of elasticized fabric passed over shoulders and clipped or buttoned to trousers or skirts front and back, same as British *braces, q.v.* 2. British term for woman's stocking garters attached to corset. 3. Shoulder straps on bodice or bib front. See *jumpers* and *overalls*.

Suzy See *designers appendix, France*.

Svend See *designers appendix, France*.

swaddling clothes Term used from earliest times to end of 18th century for narrow strips of fabric wrapped around infant in place of clothing. See *long clothes.* Also called *sweath-bands* and *swadding bands.*

swagger coat See *coats.*

swagger hat See *hats.*

swagger stick Short stick, usually leather covered and shaped somewhat like a baton, sometimes carried by Army officers.

swallow-tailed coat See *coats.*

swallow-tail collar See *collars.*

swanbill corset Back-laced woman's corset with long metal bone in front, curving out over lower abdomen; worn in mid 1870's.

swan's down 1. Soft underfeathers of swans, used to trim negligees, dresses, cloaks, especially in late 19th century and early 20th century. 2. Same as *Canton flannel, q.v.,* under *fabrics.* Also spelled *swansdown.*

sweat band Band, usually made of sheepskin leather, around the inside of a man's hat where crown joins the brim to protect hat from sweat.

sweater Garment for upper part of body *knit* by hand or machine or *crocheted,* with any length sleeve, neckline varied from scoop to crew to turtleneck, in cardigan, coat, blazer, pullover or wrapped style; various lengths from bolero to tunic; in such yarns as wool, mohair, shetland, cashmere, various man-made fibers, chenille, bouclé, or ribbon; plain or in patterns. Called *jersey, q.v.,* in mid 19th century, now a classic garment for all occasions, glamorized with embroidery and beads for women's evening wear in 1940's. Some contemporary styles:

SWEATERS:

Aran Isle s. Pullover with round or V-neck, knit in traditional Irish designs, including raised *cable knit, q.v.,* interlaced vertical diamond-shaped patterns. *Der.* Named for island off coast of Ireland where sweaters of this type were originally made. See *fisherman's sweater,* below.

Argyll or **argyle s.** Jacquard-knit using several colors to make diamond-shaped design, often matched to socks; popular in 1920's and '30's and revived in late 1960's. See *plaids.*

award s. See *letter sweater.*

beaded s. Woman's sweater with decorative *beading, q.v.,* sometimes of *seed pearls;* often worn for evening in 1940's to 1950's.

cardigan Coat-like sweater buttoning in center front with collarless neckline. *Der.* Named after *7th Earl of Cardigan, q.v.,* who needed an extra layer of warmth for his uniform during Crimean War.

cashmere s. Sweater in any style knitted of yarn spun from the hair of the cashmere goat; extremely soft and luxurious, usually imported from England or Scotland.

coat s. Any sweater that opens down the front like a coat or jacket; may be a collarless, buttoned *cardigan, q.v.,* or have a shawl collar, zipper front, or other variations.

Cowichan s. American Indian pattern, black on white or gray back-

CARDIGAN

COAT SWEATER

DOLMAN SWEATER

FISHERMAN'S SWEATER

ground, made by Indians on Vancouver Island, B.C.; popular in late 1940's and early 1950's, revived in early 1970's.

crew s. *Pullover* sweater with a round rib-knit neck, named after those worn by college rowing teams or *crews*.

dolman s. Sweater with *dolman sleeves, q.v.* under *sleeves*.

Fair Isle s. Sweaters, both *pullovers* and *cardigans,* imported from Fair Isle off the coast of Scotland, characterized by soft *heather yarns,*

q.v., and bright-colored knit-in traditional patterns forming round yokes or cuffs; name also applied to sweaters imitating this style.

fanny s. Woman's sweater long enough to cover the buttocks or "fanny"; popular in 1973.

fisherman's s. Bulky hand knit of natural-color water-repellent wool in characteristic patterns including wide *cable stripes, q.v., bobbles, seed stitch,* etc., imported from Ire-

CREW SWEATER

land; popular in early 1960's and widely imitated in man-made yarns.

Icelandic s. Bulky hand knit of natural-color water-repellent wool from heath sheep, with brown, black, gray, and white designs on yoke, imported from Iceland and copied from beaded collars of Eskimos. Also called *Reykjavik sweater.*

jiffy-knit s. Sweater hand-knit of bulky yarn on very large needles; popular in late 1960's.

Karaca s. *Turtleneck pullover* sweater with elaborate Turkish embroidered panel down center front and lines of embroidery down sleeves; imported from Black Sea area.

letter s. Bulky shawl-collared *coat sweater* with *service stripes, q.v.,* on upper sleeves and school letter on right front chest; given to varsity sports team members in high schools and colleges; now copied for general sportswear. Also called *award* or *school sweater.*

poor-boy s. Tight fitting, almost shrunken ribbed-knit pullover with round or turtleneck; popular in mid 1960's.

pullover Sweater with *round, crew,* or *V-neck,* pulled on over the head, as contrasted with a *cardigan* or *coat sweater, q.q.v.,* which opens down the front. Also called *pull-on* or *slip-on.*

Reykjavik s. See *Icelandic sweater. Der.* Capital of Iceland.

school s. See *letter sweater,* above.

shell Sleeveless, collarless pullover sweater, usually solid color, worn with woman's suit instead of blouse; popular in 1950's.

shetland s. Originally, a sweater knit of fine *worsted* yarn from the Shetland Islands off the coast of Scotland, usually made in classic style, in a medium-sized *stockinette stitch;* by extension, name now used for same type and knit of sweater made in man-made yarns.

shrink Short, narrow, sleeveless sweater in wool washed to shrink, a fad fashion in early 1970's for women and children. Also called *Heidi shrink, q.v.,* after heroine of 19th-century children's book, *Heidi,* by Johanna Spyri, popularized by 1937 movie starring Shirley Temple, shown in '70's on television.

shrug Shawl and sweater combined, wrapped across back like a shawl, with edges drawn together at ends to form brief sleeves.

ski s. Heavy *pullover* with pattern in two or more colors, which make it thicker, worn for warmth when skiing. Also see *Icelandic sweater.*

slip-on See *pullover,* above.

tennis s. Man's or woman's *pull-on, q.v.,* long-sleeved sweater with a V-neck, often *cable-knit, q.v.,* usually white and trimmed with narrow bands of maroon and navy blue at neck and wrists.

turtleneck or turtlenecked s. A *pullover* sweater with a very high rib-knit *band collar* that folds over twice to form a flattened roll around the neck; *mock-turtle* neck may fold only once or be knitted double to give turtleneck effect without folding.

tuxedo s. *Coat* style with no buttons, with collar that rolls around neck and down each side of front.

undershirt s. *Pullover* with *tank top, q.v.,* similar to man's undershirt, sometimes tunic length; popular in early 1970's.

vest s. Sleeveless coat style, double- or single-breasted with V neck. Also called *sweater vest, q.v.*

sweater blouse See *blouses.*

sweater coat See *coats.*

sweater dress See *dresses.*

sweater girl 1940's slang for shapely film stars who wore tight pullovers to emphasize the bosom; e.g., Lana Turner.

sweater vest See *vest* under *sweaters,* above.

sweath-band See *swaddling clothes.*

sweat pants See *pants.*

sweatshirt See *knit shirts* under *shirts.*

sweatshop Slang term for turn-of-the-century clothes-manufacturing plant, where workers were paid low wages and worked long hours under unfavorable conditions.

sweat sock See *socks.*

Swedish clogs See *sandals.*

sweet coffers Term used in Elizabethan times for boxes used by women to hold cosmetics.

sweetheart neckline See *necklines.*

swinging gear See *gear.*

swimbra See *brassieres.*

swimsuits See *bathing suits;* modern styles listed below.

SWIMSUITS OR BATHING SUITS:

apron s. 1. *Bikini, q.v.,* swimsuit with extra apron front fastened on to brassiere by *Velcro, q.v.,* or snaps. Same as *pinafore swimsuit.*

bikini 1. Woman's brief two-piece swimsuit with tiny brassiere top and brief pants cut below navel, narrow at sides; designed by Jacques Heim and introduced in Paris, 1946, at the Piscine Molitar, coincident with the explosion of first atomic bomb in island of Bikini in the Pacific. Named for its shock value and a sensation on Riviera· beaches; not accepted on U.S. public beaches till early 1960's. 2. Man's very brief swim trunks.

boxer shorts Men's *trunks* with loose legs and elastic waistband.

boy shorts Womans suit without skirt panel, legs like short shorts.

cabaña set Men's and boy's swimsuit trunks and jacket cut in same fabric.

dressmaker s. Woman's print or plain fabric one-piece swimsuit with attached skirt and dressy trimmings, usually worn by mature figures.

Gay '90's s. Two-piece, horizontal-striped knitted suit with knee-length narrow pants and tank top: worn in

BIKINI

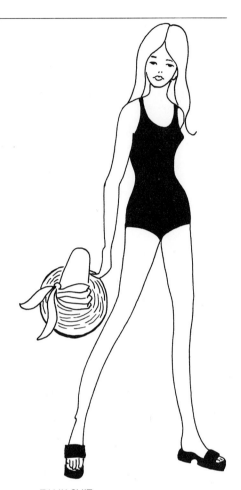

TANK SUIT

late 1960's imitating men's jersey suits of 1890's. Sometimes called *John L. suit* after late-19th-century prizefighter John L. Sullivan.

hip-rider s. Two-piece swimsuit with low-slung pants or skirt, showing the navel; innovation in the 1960's.

jams Men's swim trunks with mid-thigh leg, in printed or striped fabric, looking like cut-off pajamas, with lacing in center front or a drawstring at waist.

John L. s. See *Gay '90's* suit.

maillot (my-yo) Classic one-piece knitted or jersey swimsuit without skirt, form-fitting and usually backless, sometimes with detachable strap tied around neck or buttoned to back of suit, popular since 1930's. *Der.* French *maillot,* tight garment.

mono-kini Woman's topless swimsuit consisting only of brief panties cut below the navel; the name is a misnomer based on *bikini, q.v.,* in which the *bi* does not mean *two* (as *mono* means *one*) but is part of a

500

geographical name—the Pacific island Bikini, where the first atomic bomb was exploded by the U.S.

overblouse s. Woman's two-piece bathing suit with brief *trunks, q.v.,* and a separate blouse, often with a *tank-top* neckline, *q.v.,* and unfitted waist, gathered over the hips by a *drawstring* or *elastic, q.q.v;* kind to less-than-perfect figures.

pinafore s. See *apron* suit.

sarong s. *Dressmaker, q.v.,* swimsuit with round-cornered wrap skirt draped to one side.

tank s. Classic *maillot, q.v.,* swimsuit without skirt, with scooped neck and built-up straps, originally meant for indoor pool or "tank."

topless s. Spectacular swimsuit that starts below bust or at waist, held up by two straps from the back meeting in a V in center front; introduced by American designer Rudi Gernreich in 1964; forbidden on most U.S. beaches, started topless-waitress style in California nightclubs.

trunks Man's shorts for swimming, in lengths from very short to knee, also worn for surfing.

swing skirt See *skirts.*

Swirl See *dresses.*

Swiss See *dotted Swiss* under *fabrics.*

Swiss belt Broad woman's belt, pointed at center top and bottom sometimes laced up front in *corselet* style; popular in 19th century. Also called *Swiss girdle.*

Swiss bodice Sleeveless velvet bodice with *Swiss belt, q.v.,* worn over sleeved blouse in late 1860's.

SWISS BODICE

Swiss embroidery See *Madeira* under *embroideries.*

switch See *hairpieces.*

swivel strap Narrow strap on woman's pump that goes across instep and buckles on opposite side.

sword Weapon of various types, typically with a long straight or slightly curved blade, sharp on one or both sides, with an ornamental handle; fashionable man's accessory from 16th century to end of 18th century.

syglaton See *cyclas.*

synthetic fiber Man-made fibers including *acrylic, nylon, polyester, vinyl,* etc., *q.q.v.*

synthetic gem A gem chemically identical to those found in nature but man-made in the laboratory. See *gems.*

szur White felt full-length Hungarian man's coat with large lapels and broad collar, lavishly decorated with embroidery and appliqué in flower motifs; worn like a cape fastened with a leather strap across chest.

T

T Designation for *tall* category in a number of proportioned size ranges.

tab 1. An extra flap, strap, or loop of fabric, used with buttonhole, buckle, or snap to close coats, collars, sleeve cuffs, etc. See *closings*. 2. (pl.) 19th-century term for loose-hanging piece of fabric with a border of squared or rounded projections, forming a peplum or used as trimming. See *vandykes* and *turret bodice*.

tabard 1. Short heavy *cape* of coarse cloth worn out-of-doors in 19th century by men and women. 2. *Tunic* with loose front and back panels and short winglike sleeves, sometimes with heraldic coat-of-arms embroidered on back; worn by knights over armor from 13th to 16th centuries. See *garnache*.

tabbed closing See *closings*.

tabby weave See *weaves*.

tab collar See *collars*.

tabi Ankle-length white woven-cotton socks with separate division for big toe; worn by Japanese indoors and, with *zori, q.v.,* out of doors.

tablecloth check See *checks*.

table-cut gloves See *gloves*

tablier (tab-lee-ay) Skirt with decorated free-hanging panel in front, suggesting an apron; fashionable from 1850's to 1870's.

tack To sew together lightly with invisible stitches or to join by sewing loosely at just one point.

taffeta Crisp silk. See *fabrics*.

taffeta pipkin See *pipkin*.

Taglioni (tah-gyee-oh-nee) Man's fitted *greatcoat,* usually double-breasted, with wide turned-back lapels, large flat collar and cuffs of satin or velvet, back vent, and slit pockets, edges bound with twill fabric; worn in mid 19th century. *Der.* Named after Italian ballet master Filippo Taglioni (1777–1871).

Taglioni frock coat Man's single-breasted *frock coat* with short full skirts, broad collar, one large cape, slashed or flapped pockets, and back vent, with no pleats; sworn in mid 19th century. *Der.* See above.

tail coat See *swallow-tailed coat* under *coats*.

tailleur (ty-yer) French name for tailored costume—a suit.

tailoring Process of cutting, fitting, and finishing a garment to conform to the body by means of darts, linings, pressing, etc. as in a man's suit or coat; same techniques applied to women's suits, slacks, shirts, with simple clear lines, no fancy details. Garments are called *custom-made* or *tailor-made* when garment is made to order for an individual in a special shop, e.g., as at tailoring establishments in *Savile Row,* London, *q.v.* The antonym of *tailored* for a woman's garment is *dressmaker.* See *tailored* under *buttonholes*.

tailor-made 1. Garment made specifically for one individual by tailor; customer's measurements taken, several fittings necessary. Also called *custom-made* or *custom-tailored.* 2. In the late 19th century, a woman's costume for morning or country wear, usually a jacket and skirt, made by a tailor rather than a dressmaker; introduced by *Redfern, q.v.,* in late 1870's.

tailor's ham Pillow, shaped like a ham, used in pressing shoulders and other rounded surfaces in tailored garments.

tailor's tack See *stitches.*

tails See *full-dress* under *suits.*

talaria (ta-lay-ree-a) Winged sandals, as seen in representations of Roman god Mercury and Greek god Hermes.

Talbot, Suzanne See *designers appendix, France.*

tall Size designation used for woman's stockings and pantyhose and for proportioned skirts and pants. Abbreviated T.

Tallien redingote (tal-ee-en red-in-goat) Outdoor coat created by French couturier *Worth, q.v.,* in 1867, matched to dress or made of black silk, with heart-shaped neckline, full back, trimmed with sash tied with large bow in back, ends falling down each side, ending in bows. Named for Thérésa Tallien, Princess de Chimay, a fashionable woman who is said to have owned 30 wigs of different colors.

Talleyrand collar (tal-i-ranh) Collar standing up at back and turned over, similar to *Robespierre collar, q.v. Der.* Named after French statesman *Charles Maurice de Talleyrand-Perigord,* active in politics from 1775 to 1815.

Talma 1. Woman's long *cape* or *cloak,* frequently hooded, worn in

early 19th century; in 1860's sometimes had pleats to a little below waistline in back giving a fitted appearance. 2. Woman's hip-length *cape* of embroidered satin, lace, or velvet with fringe at hem; used as an outer garment in 1850's to mid 1870's. 3. In 1890's, a woman's full-length *coat* with loose sleeves and lace cape or deep velvet collar. *Der.* Named for Francois Joseph Talma (1763–1826), a French tragic actor of Consulate and Empire period. Also called *Talma mantle.*

tam See *tam-o'-shanter* under *caps.*

tambour work See *embroideries.*

tambour farthingale See *drum farthingale.*

tamein Wrapped garment worn by women of Burma, made of a length of cotton or silk, 4½ feet by 5 feet, woven in two pieces in different patterns; wrapped around bust and secured by twisting the ends. Also spelled *tamehn* and *thamein.*

tamis See *fabrics.*

tam-o'-shanter See *caps.*

tank suit See *swimsuits.*

tank top See *tops, knit shirts* under *shirts,* and *built-up* under *slips.*

tanning The process of making leather from hides; methods include vegetable tanning with tannin, mineral tanning with chrome or alum, and artificial methods. See *buckskin tannage.*

tantoor Bridal headdress formerly worn in Druse sect in Syria; a spike about a yard high was fixed in position

on top of the bride's head by the bridegroom and worn thereafter, night and day; style indicated home district of husband. Also spelled *tantoura.*

tanzen Padded jacket worn as dressing gown by Japanese. Also called *dotera.*

tapa cloth Bark cloth. See *fabrics.*

tapered shirt See *body shirt* under *shirts.*

tapestry Heavy handwoven fabric, or one resembling it, with colored pictorial design, in cotton, silk, wool and other fibers; originally

a wall hanging; now used for shoes and handbags.

tap shoe See *shoes.*

tarboosh, tarbush (tar-boosh) Flat topped, brimless felt cap like a truncated cone, usually red with black tassel from center of crown, similar to the *fez, q.v.,* sometimes worn under a turban. *Der.* From Arabic word meaning *sweating cap.* See *Bethlehem headdress.*

tarlatan See *fabrics.*

tartan Combination of bars or *stripes* in various widths and colors, crossed at right angles to form distinctive patterns, identifications of various Scottish clans; used for *kilts* and *plaids, q.q.v.,* and widely copied for classic suits, coats and sportswear for men, women, and children. Some well-known tartans are described below.

TARTANS:

Balmoral Wearing of this tartan is reserved in Scotland to the use of the British Royal Family; it was designed for Queen Victoria by the Prince Consort, Albert; the colors are red, blue, and black.

Black Watch See *Forty-Second Royal Highland Regiment.*

Bruce The clan founder was Sir Robert de Brus, a Norman Knight who came to England with William the Conquerer; colors: on a red field, groups of four green crossbars of varying widths and very narrow overplaid between them—white alternating with yellow.

Buchanan The name in Gaelic means Son of the Canon and the clan traces its origin to a son of a king of Ulster in the 11th century; the tartan is one very frequently copied or paraphrased in other fabrics; wide bars of green, red, and yellow alternating, with separating bands and narrow overplaids of yellow and black.

Cameron The Clan Cameron is thought to be of pure Celtic ancestry; the tartan is similar to *Bruce, q.v.,* but the four green crossbars grouped on the red ground are of equal width and narrow overplaid between them is all yellow.

Forty-Second Royal Highland Regiment (The Black Watch) During the Scottish risings, Highland troops were sent to serve in the English armies; six of these companies were absorbed in 1739 as the 42nd Regiment of the line; the six had chosen the Campbell tartan, and its somber hues in contrast with the scarlet of the English uniforms gave them their name, The Black Watch. The plaid consists of alternating groups of blue and green bars separated by black bars of varying widths.

MacDonald One of the oldest and most powerful of the clans; their founder freed his countrymen from the Danes and Norwegians in the 12th century; the tartan alternates groups of bars of varying widths of blue with groups of green, the center bars separated by very narrow red bands and the groups separated by black.

Menzies The name of this Gaelic-speaking clan is pronounced "Mingies" and was originally spelled *Mengues;* the tartan of grouped white bars of varying widths on a brilliant red ground is frequently copied; the clan also uses an identical pattern in black and white, which is very popular also.

Royal Stewart The tartan of the Scottish Royal Family; see *dress Stewart* and *hunting Stewart,* below. The Royal Stewart tartan is worn by the pipers of such regiments as the Royal Archers and the Royal Scots. Colors: on a red ground, groups of matched pairs of color bars in varying widths, with green, blue, and black reading from the center out; between them, narrow overplaids of white, yellow, and black.

Stewart dress The name, also spelled *Stuart, Steward* and *Stubbard,* comes from the Lord High Steward of Scotland, the title held by the family for two centuries before they came to the throne; this tartan was a favorite of Queen Victoria and is also called *Victorian tartan;* the colors, on a white ground, are almost identical to those of the Royal Stewart tartan, with red bars replacing the white ground at the center of each group, so that red, green, black, and blue form the sequence with wide bars of the white ground between the groups and narrow overplaids of yellow, white, and black.

Stewart, hunting A special hunting tartan is not unusual among the more important Scottish families, the colors were chosen to harmonize more closely with the landscape during the hunt; the colors of the hunting Stewart are alternating groups of black and blue bars of varying widths on a green ground; narrow overplaids of red and yellow alternating between the groups.

tassel Bundle of threads, bound at one end, hung singly or in groups as ornament on belts, hats, shawls, other garment.

Tasell, Gustave See *designers appendix, United States.*

tassel-tie loafers See *loafers* under *shoes.*

tasset Armor for the upper thigh, made either of a single plate or of several narrow flexible plates joined together by rivets. Also called *tace* and *tasse.* Also see *tuille.*

tatas See *leading strings.*

tattersall Pattern of narrow dark lines crossed to form squares on solid light-colored ground, commonest in white with red and black overcheck; called *tattersall check* or *plaid, q.q.v.,* and used for vests, sportshirts, coats, etc. *Der.* Named for 18th century English horseman Richard Tattersall and bright horse blankets worn at his horse market in London.

tattersall vest See *vests.*

tatting See *laces.*

tattoo (tat-oo) 1. Permanent design made on skin by process of pricking and ingraining indelible pigment; of Polynesian origin and practiced in aboriginal tribes, adopted by Western world and popular with sailors. 2. Fashion fad in early 1970's of decorating body with transfer designs of ships, hearts, etc., imitating those tattooed on sailors' skins; also

similar patterns printed on T shirts and dresses.

taupe (tope) Brownish-gray color with a purple cast.

tchamir (cha-meer) Moroccan *overblouse* with heavily embroidered round neckline and slit center front, in black with white embroidery and white with multi-colored embroidery; popular in U.S. in 1960's for both men and women.

tchapan (cha-pan) Man's long loose outer robe with full sleeves, made of quilted silk or cotton fabric striped red, orange, and green; worn in Turkestan.

tea-cozy cap See *caps.*

tea gown 1. Loose-fitting long gown in pale colors, usually of thin wool or silk, trimmed with ruffles and lace down front opening and on sleeves; worn without corsets as an informal

hostess gown in late 19th century and early 20th century. See *peignoir.* 2. Term *tea gown* used in 1920's and 30's for semi-formal dress suitable for afternoon tea or garden party.

tea jacket Loose informal jacket or bodice with close-fitting back, sometimes with tight sleeves and loose-

hanging front, profusely trimmed with lace; worn by women from 1880's to replace the tailor-made bodice of the dress for afternoon tea. Also called *matinee.*

teardrop bra See *brassieres.*

teasel Dried burr of plant called *Dipsacaceus,* used in England to brush up nap of woolen fabrics. See *gig.*

teddy Abbreviated undergarment combining *chemise* and *drawers, q.q.v.,* with loose legs or a chemise with a strap between legs. Often used in the plural *teddies;* Also called *envelope chemise.* See *panties.*

teddybear coat Bulky coat of natural-colored alpaca-pile fabric;

worn by men, women, and children in 1920's. Named after the Teddy bear, children's toy of early 20th century named for President Theodore Roosevelt.

Teddy boy styles Tough young men's fashions appearing in London in early 1950's consisting of exaggerated *Edwardian, q.v.,* jackets, high stiff collars, tight pants, pointed-toe shoes, called *winkle pickers, q.v.,* long hair, and no hats, starting trend to individual style of dress, a protest against the Establishment. Also see *Rockers. Der.* Teddy is nickname for Edward.

Teddy girl styles British girls' fashion fad in early 1950's, counterpart of Teddy boys', consisting of short tight skirts, high-heeled pointed shoes, and high *beehive* hairstyles, *q.v.,* forerunners of the new wave of youth-created fashion. See *Carnaby Street.*

teen bra See *brassieres.*

tee-shirt Variant of *T shirt, q.v.*

templar cloak Loose-fitting man's robe wide enough to be worn without putting arms through sleeves; worn in 1840's. Also see *caban.*

templers Ornamental *nets* or *bosses, q.v.,* worn at sides of face to conceal the hair, sometimes connected by band above forehead, sometimes part of headdress; worn by women in first half of 15th century. Also called *templettes,* or *temples.*

tendrils See *curls.*

ten-gallon hat See *hats.*

tennis clothes See *dresses, sneakers* under *shoes, shorts,* and *sweaters.*

tennis costume See *lawn-tennis costume.*

tent coat See *coats.*

tent dress See *dresses, silhouettes.*

tent stitch See *Continental* under *stitches.*

terai hat Riding hat of fur or felt, shaped like a *derby, q.v.,* with large brim, with red lining and metal vent through crown, made of two hats sewed together at edges of brims; worn by English women in tropical climates; introduced in the 1880's.

Teresa Variant of *Therese, q.v.*

terno Grand-occasion dress worn by Filipino women in Hawaii, frequently elaborately embroidered or beaded, with flared sleeves shaped to stand up from shoulder; skirt, high-waisted and slim cut.

terry cloth Cotton with uncut pile. See *fabrics* and *weaves.*

Terylene British and Canadian trademark for polyester of both filament and staple types, first developed in 1941.

tete de mouton Woman's short curly wig; worn in Paris from 1730 to about 1755. *Der.* French, sheep's head.

tethered studs Men's evening jewelry consisting of three ornamental shirt *studs, q.v.,* joined with small chains; fashionable in 1830's and '40's.

textured yarn See *yarns.*

T.F.P.I.A. Textile Fiber Products Identification Act; Federal law enacted in setting labeling requirements.

thamein Variant of *tamein, q.v.*

Theo tie See *oxfords* under *shoes.*

Therese (ter-eece) Large *hood,* held out with wire, designed to go over tall bonnets and hairstyles; worn in France from mid 1770's to end 1780's, later with an attached shoulder cape. Also spelled *Teresa.*

thermal underwear Long-sleeved, long-legged undershirt and pants or one-piece *union suit, q.v.,* made of knitted cotton or cotton-and-wool mesh, which retains body heat by trapping air; worn for winter sports.

Thibet cloth See *fabrics.*

thong Narrow strip of rawhide or other leather used for a lacer or braided into a belt or wound around foot and leg as a fastening for sandals. See *belts* and *sandals.*

thong-toe hose See *tabi.*

thread Yarn twisted tightly enough for use with needle or the sewing machine, in various fibers and strength.

thread count See *count of cloth.*

three decker Term used in late 1880's for man's or woman's triple-caped *ulster, q.v.* Also see *carrick.*

threads British slang term of young trendy people in 1960's for *Mod* clothes on *Carnaby St., q.q.v.,* London. See *gear.*

three-armhole dress See *dresses.*

three-quarter See *collars, lengths,* and *sleeves.*

three-seamer British tailoring term for man's jacket with center back seam and two side seams, contrasted with coat having *side bodies, q.v.,* and five seams.

three-storeys-and-a-basement Amusing name given to woman's hat with very high crown; worn during mid 1880's.

thrift shop Secondhand clothing or fur store; in the 1960's, a popular source of fashion of 1920's, 1930's and 1940's. See *dresses.*

throat belt See *necklaces.*

thrum 1. Short tufts of wool, left on loom after fabric is cut away, knitted into workmen's caps in 18th century America and England. 2. Long-napped felt hat worn in 16th century.

tiara (tee-ar-a) 1. Curved band, often of metal set with jewels or of flowers, worn on top of woman's head from ear to ear, giving effect of a crown; sometimes used to hold a wedding veil. 2. The Pope's triple crown. 3. An ancient Persian headdress. Also see *diadem* and *coronet.*

Tibet cloth See *Thibet cloth* under *fabrics.*

ticking See *fabrics.*

ticking stripes See *stripes.*

tie, necktie Long narrow band of fabric worn around neck, usually under turned-down collar, tied in bow or in knot with ends hanging down; a fashion for men since early 19th century, replacing wide *cravat, q.v.,* and adopted by women in late 19th century to wear with shirt-waists; widths change, e.g., extremely wide in 1930's and early 1970's, narrow in 1940's and '50's.

TIES OR NECKTIES:

ascot 1. Wide necktie worn looped over with ends crossed diagonally and held in place by scarf pin, vest or jacket; introduced in 1876 in

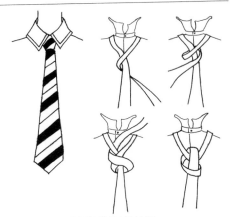

HOW TO TIE FOUR-IN-HAND

BLACK TIE

form of self-tied and made-up necktie, similar to *octagon tie, q.v.* 2. Scarf looped under the chin. *Der.* Named for celebrated race course at Ascot Heath in Berkshire, England. See *scarfs.*

black t. Man's black *bow tie* worn with *dinner jacket* or *tuxedo, q.q.v.,* at semiformal occasions.

boater t. Man's *four-in-hand tie, q.v.,* with extra-large knot, shorter than average, usually having square-cut ends; introduced in late 1960's from England.

bolo t. Thin cord tie held by metal *slide, q.v.*

bow t. Man's narrow tie, square cut or with shaped ends, tied in a bow under the chin. See *black tie* and *white tie*.

clip-on t. Tie, either knotted like a *four-in-hand, q.v.,* or a *bow tie,* that is permanently tied and fastened to the collarband by a metal clip.

cravat 1. Folded scarf, replacing a *necktie,* worn around neck and crossed to tuck inside neckline. 2. Wide muslin or silk *neckcloth,* with ends tied in knot in center front, worn with starched collar from 1660 to end of 19th century with *morning coat, q.v.,* under coats. Also see *stock,* below.

four-in-hand t. Most common contemporary man's necktie, long and of varying widths, tied around neck under collar, tied in a smooth flat knot (see drawing, opposite) with two overlapped ends hanging to waist; worn since 1890's with business suits and sports coats; adopted by women in early 1970's.

sailor t. Large square *scarf* of black silk folded diagonally, worn under square *sailor collar, q.v.,* tied in knot or pulled through strap on front of middy blouse; formerly worn by U.S. Naval enlisted men, adopted by women and children in late 19th century to wear with *middy blouse, q.v.,* under *blouses.*

sheriff t. British variant of *string tie, q.v.,* below.

shoelace or **shoestring t.** Variant of *string tie, q.v.,* below.

Southern Colonel t. Variant of string tie, q.v.

stock 1. Long, wide cotton or silk *scarf* worn around neck, usually inside collar, lapped over once,

broad ends hanging loose or tucked into neckline of shirt, sweater, or jacket; popular for men's informal summer evening wear and for sports. 2. Similar tie matched to shirt fabric, worn lapped and pinned, instead of collar, with formal riding habit.

string t. Narrow black tie worn in a bow, typical of 19th-century American Westerners and Southern gentlemen. Also called *Southern Colonel* or *shoelace tie.*

white t. 1. Man's white silk *bow tie* worn for formal occasions with full-dress *swallow-tailed coat;* e.g., "white tie" invitation signifies full-dress suit for man and formal evening dress for woman.

Windsor t. 1. Black silk bias-cut scarf tied in loose floppy bow, associated with artists since late 19th century. 2. Man's *four-in-hand, q.v.,* tied with oversized knot called *Windsor knot.*

tie bars See *brides.*

tie clasp or **clip** Jewelry consisting of a decorative metal bar, bent double, that slides over a man's tie and behind his shirt front placket, clipping the tie in place; may also have a spring-clip back.

tied closing See *closings.*

tie dyeing Hand method of coloring a fabric by first dyeing the background color, then tying strings tightly around puffs of fabric and dipping in a second color to get two-color designs, repeating to add more colors. A technique originating in Indonesia and popular in the 1920's for scarves, etc., revived in

1960's for blue jeans, T-shirts, dresses, furs. See *prints*.

tie shoe See *oxfords* under *shoes*.

tie pin See *pins*.

tiers Several layers of ruffles or bias-cut sections, placed one above the other and overlapping, used mainly on skirts or on full sleeves or pants. See *silhouettes*.

tie silk Narrow silk fabric used for neckties. See *fabrics*.

tie tack Small ornament on a sharp-pointed back worn pierced through two ends of a man's necktie to hold them together; fastened with a clasp on the back.

Tiffany setting See *gem settings*.

Tiffeau, Jacques See *designers appendix, United States*.

tiger's eye See *gems*.

tights 1. See *pantyhose* and *panties*. 2. Skin-tight men's *trousers*, usually white or light-colored, cut to give unbroken line from chest to ankle, molded to body like second skin, secured by braces (suspenders) over shoulders; an exaggerated fashion worn after French Revolution in late 18th century. See *Macaroni*.

tika or **tikka** Mark painted on center of forehead by East Indian women, originally of caste significance, now ornamental. Also called *tilak* or *caste mark*.

tilbury hat Man's small hat with high tapered flat-topped crown and narrow rounded brim; worn in 1830's.

tile Colloquial term for a high stiff hat—shaped like a roof tile.

tile red Red-orange color similar to brick, the color of clay roof tiles.

tilak Variant of *tika, q.v.*

Tinling, Teddy See *designers appendix, England*.

tippet Streamer hanging from sleeve of the *cotehardi, q.v.;* a white streamer worn around arm and hanging from elbow in Middle Ages.

2. See *liripipe*. 3. Shoulder cape of fur or cloth worn by women from 16th century on. See *palatine*.

tipping Fur-dyeing process in which only the tips of the guard hairs are colored.

tissue Descriptive of lightweight, semi-transparent fabric, e.g., *tissue gingham, tissue taffeta*.

Titus coiffure or **wig** See *coiffure à la Titus*.

Tiziani See *designers appendix, Italy*.

Toby ruff Woman's ruff, made of two or three layers of frills, tied at throat with ribbon; worn in 1890's.

toca White cotton headcloth worn over red cap by Jews and Moors in Algeria.

toddlers Size range from 1 to 4 for very young children.

toe Front portion of shoe, covering the toes, the shape varied in contemporary designs—pointed, rounded, squared—according to changing fashion and historically varied from one exaggeration to another, e.g., *duck-billed toes* of Henry VIII or *poulaines, q.v.*

TOES OF SHOES:

bulldog t. Bulbous toe; popular on man's buttoned ankle-high shoe before World War I.

copper t. Term for metal cap placed on children's shoes at turn of century to keep them from wearing out.

dollar-round t. Old shoe-trade term for toe of shoe on which shape matched rounded edge of silver dollar.

knot t. Exaggerated form of *bulldog toe,* popular in early 1970's.

needle t. Long narrow extremely pointed toe. See *winkle picker* under *shoes.*

oval t. Woman's shoe toe, narrower than a *round* toe but not an extreme *point.*

walled t. Deep toe cap with vertical edge at least ¾ inch high.

toe-ankle chain See *bracelets.*

toe ring See *rings.*

toe rubbers See *rubbers* under *shoes.*

toe shoes or **slippers** See *ballet* under *slippers.*

tog, togs 1. (pl.) Slang for clothing, especially fancy garments. 2. (s.) Medieval term for coat, shortened form of *toga.*

toga 1. Outer garment, consisting of large rectangle of cloth, cotton, wool, or silk, either all white or royal purple, often rounded at corners and decorated along one end, worn draped about the body by ancient Romans; basic pattern adapted in contemporary designs for *dresses, nightgowns, robes, q.q.v.* 2. Large rectangle of printed cotton, pinned on one shoulder and draped under opposite arm, worn today in African countries.

toggle Rod-shaped button, usually wood, attached by rope loop on one side of garment opening, fastened by passing through similar rope loop or *frog, q.v.,* on opposite side; used mainly on sport coats. See *coats* and *closings.*

toile (twal) 1. French word for *cloth.* 2. French term for *muslin* pattern, *q.v.,* for a garment. 3. Lace-makers term for *pattern* of lace as distinguished from the *background.*

toilet, toilette (twa-let) 1. Late 19th-century term for a woman's entire costume; e.g., *afternoon toilette.* 2. Process of a woman's dressing, combing her hair, applying her make-up; term used especially in 19th century and early 20th century. 3. Name used in 18th century for loose *wrapper* worn by women while having hair arranged.

Tom Jones shirt See *shirts.*

Tom Jones sleeve See *sleeves.*

tongue Part of *oxford shoe, q.v.,* under the lacing; sometimes with an ornamental flap, fringed or perforated, that hangs over lacing of shoe, called *shawl tongue, q.v.*

tonlet Flaring skirt of metal plates or of solid metal, sometimes fluted with deep vertical folds, worn as armor in 16th century. Also called *lamboy, jamboy,* or *base.*

top 1. See *toupee* under *hairpieces.* 2. Button with decorative face made of fabric, metal, or glass and metal shank on the back. 3. See *boot-hose tops.* 4. Garment that covers upper part of body, such as pullover *sweater, T-shirt,* or *blouse, q.q.v.;* just covering breasts or reaching to waist or hips; worn with skirts, pants, or shorts. Some contemporary styles:

TOPS FOR WOMEN:

bare t. 1. Strapless knit top extending from waist to above bust. 2. Strapless evening bodice tightly fitted and boned

bare-midriff t. Top cropped below bust, baring rib cage; may have *halter* or *tank* neckline. See *choli.*

bib t. Bare-back top, just covering front of body, like top of *overalls, q.v.,* under *pants.*

bikini t. Brief top of minimum of fabric, covering just breasts and tieing in back. See *bikini* under *swimsuits.*

halter t. Bodice with front supported by tie or strap around the neck, leaving back bare.

shell Sleeveless, collarless blouse with back closing; worn with suits.

smock t. Full *overblouse* with full sleeves, similar to a *smock, q.v.*

strapless t. See *bare top,* above.

stretch t. Close-fitting blouse made of stretchy knit fabric, see *body suit.*

tank t. Similar to man's *undershirt* with U neckline and deep arm holes, shaped toward shoulder to form narrow straps; named for *tank suit, q.v.,* under *swimsuits.*

topaz See *gems.*

top boot Variant of *jockey boots, q.v.*

topcoat See *coats.*

topee or **topi** See *hats.*

top frock Man's overcoat cut like a *frock coat, q.v.,* but longer, usually double-breasted and intended to be worn without an undercoat; worn from 1830 on.

top grain Leather-industry term for first *split, q.v.,* from grain side of leather. Used in shoes and handbags.

top hat See *hats.*

topknot See *hairstyles.*

topless bathing suit See *swimsuits.*

top lifts See *lifts.*

topper 1. See *hats.* 2. See *coats.*

Top Siders See *Sperry-Topsiders* in *oxfords* under *shoes.*

top-stitched seam See *seams.*

toque See *hats.*

toquet (tow-ket) Woman's small draped evening hat of satin or velvet with small turned-up brim in front, trimmed with ostrich feather, worn on back of head; popular in 1840's.

torchon lace See *laces.*

torque Twisted metal collar or necklace worn by ancient Teutons, Gauls, Britons, etc.

torque yarn See *yarns.*

toreador clothes See *suit of lights, jackets,* and *pants.*

torsade *Coronet* of pleated velvet or tulle with long *lappets, q.v.v.;* worn for evening by women in mid 19th century.

torso blouse See *blouses.*

torso dress See *dresses* and *silhouettes.*

torsolette See *foundation garments.*

torso skirt See *skirts.*

tortoise shell 1. Mottled yellowish to brown substance from horny shells of turtles used for ornamental combs, jewelry, buckles, eyeglass frames, etc. 2. Pattern taken from tortoise shell, popular in printed fabrics, plastic eyeglass frames, etc.

tote 1. See *handbags.* 2. (pl. Cap.) See *boots.*

toupee (too-pay) See *hairpieces.* Also called *toupet, foretop,* and *top.*

toupet Maintenon Semi-circle of curls attached to ribbon; worn over top of head and at sides of face by women in mid 1860's.

tourmaline See *gems.*

Tourmaline mink See *mink* under *furs.*

tournure corset Laced *foundation garment, q.v.,* with straps over shoulders and hip-length underskirt of stiff fabric intended to hold out the skirt; worn in late 1850's over the *chemise, q.v.*

tournure and petticoat *Bustle* combined with *petticoat, q.q.v.;* some

TOURNURE AND PETTICOAT, C. 1875

TOURNURE, 1872

made all in one piece, some with buttons and buttonholes at hip-level so that *tournure* or *bustle* could be used separately; worn from about 1875 to 1885.

tow 1. Tangled, broken flax fiber less than 10 inches long, as distinguished from *line,* flax fiber more than 10 inches long. 2. Bundles of continuous man-made fiber filaments without a definite twist; the form in which most man-made fibers are cut into *staple, q.v.*

tow coat See *coats.*

tower False curls worn by women above the forehead, usually with the *Fontanges headdress, q.v.,* from 1670's to 1710. In French, called *tour.*

toyo See *straws.*

trad English slang for *traditional* or Establishment dress. Also see *Mod.*

Trafalgar turban English woman's evening turban of 1800's, embroidered with Admiral Nelson's name. *Der.* Named for British naval victory near Cape Trafalgar, off Spanish coast, in 1805.

train Elongated back portion of woman's skirt that lies on the floor and is pulled along behind wearer; worn for formal evenings, especially in late 19th and early 20th centuries, and traditionally part of bridal gowns; dates from Middle Ages when length of train, worn only at court, indicated rank.

traje charro Mexican riding costume consisting of ruffled shirt, short jacket, ankle-length fitted trousers, and elaborately trimmed large *sombrero;* front of jacket and side seams of trousers trimmed with silver or gold buttons.

traje de corto Traditional Andalusian crimson waist-length riding jacket, with a black collar and lavishly trimmed with black braid around lapels, slit pockets, and sleeves; disks with hanging fringe decorate the buttonless front.

traje de luces Spanish for *suit of lights,* *q.v.*

trank Rectangle of leather from which a glove is cut.

transformation Term used in early 20th century for a natural-looking wig or hairpiece worn by women.

trapeze See *dresses* and *silhouettes.*

trapunto Type of quilting in which design is outlined by stitching and then stuffed from the back of fabric to achieve a raised effect.

traveling wig See *campaign wig.*

trench coat See *coats.*

trencher cap Same as *mortarboard,* *q.v.* Also called *trencher.*

trencher hat Woman's silk hat with triangular brim coming to point above forehead; worn in first decade of the 19th century.

Trevira Trademark for West Germany polyester fiber licensed for approved knitted or woven fabrics.

trews (trooz) Narrow tartan (plaid) trousers worn in Scotland; originally, breeches and hose in one piece worn by Highlanders.

triacetate Man-made fiber made from regenerated cellulose, used particularly for knits that are easily washed and dried and need little pressing.

tricolette See *fabrics.*

tricorn Basic hat style, originating in 1690 and worn through 18th century, consisting of a crown with a rather large brim, worn buttoned up to form three corners or unbuttoned to make a large brimmed hat. Originally *tricorn* was a man's hat but was later worn by women for horseback riding. Also see *Continental hat, Kevenhuller hat,* and *bully-cocked hat.* Also spelled *tricorne.*

tricot See *fabrics.*

tricotine See *fabrics.*

tricot knit See *knits.*

Trigére, Pauline See *designers appendix, Italy.*

trilby Soft black man's felt hat with

indented crown and *slouch* brim; worn in Great Britain since mid 1890's. *Der.* Named after 1895 play *Trilby,* featuring Beerbohm Tree as Svengali and adapted from an 1894 novel by George du Maurier.

triple sheer Lightweight rayon. See *fabrics.*

trollopee See *slammerkin.*

trompeurs See *liars.*

trooper cap See *caps.*

tropical suiting Lightweight menswear fabric. See *fabrics.*

trousers (trow-zers) Early 19th-century replacement for *breeches, q.v.,* a long, loose garment, covering each leg separately; worn in 1814 by George IV, considered shocking and called *unmentionables, nether integuments,* etc. See *pants.*

trouser skirt 1. Tailored skirt split at side front to reveal matching bloomers attached at waistline; worn from 1910 to 1920 by dress reformers.

trouses (trouz) 1. *Underpants* worn by Englishmen under the *trunk hose* in 16th and 17th centuries. Also spelled *trowses.* 2. French *tights* similar to *gregues;* worn by pages and knights of king's order in 17th century.

trowses Variant of *trouses, q.v.*

trumpet See *silhouettes, skirts,* and *sleeves.*

trunk hose 1. *Breeches* and *hose* made in one piece, the upper part often padded or slashed; worn by men in 16th and 17th centuries. 2. When separated, upper half called *bombasted breeches, round hose, trunk*

slops, trunk breeches, upper stocks, and *Venetians, q.q.v.;* lower half called *nether stocks* or *lower stocks, q.q.v.*

trunks 1. Men's *shorts,* loose legged, gathered at waist; worn from 19th century on for boxing and other sports, sometimes over full-length *tights, q.v.* 2. See *trunk hose.* 3. See *swimsuits.* 4. See *panties.*

trunk sleeve See *cannon sleeves.*

truss 1. (verb) To tie up. Term "to truss the points" meant to fasten *hose* to *trunk hose* and *doublet* by means of *lacers* which ended in decorative metal tips, called *aglets, q.q.v.* 2. See *Venetians.*

tsarouchia (sar-ooch-ee-a) Pointed shoes with upturned toes decorated with pompons, formerly worn by Greek palace guards. Also see *fustanella.*

T-shirt Man's *undershirt* with short sleeves, at right angles, and high round neck forming a T shape, usually in white cotton knit; adapted for sportswear by men, women, and children. Also spelled *tee-shirt.* See *knit shirts* under *shirts,* and *dresses.*

T-strap See *sandals.*

tube neckline See *necklines.*

tubular fabrics See *knits.*

tuck Narrow pleat in fabric of even width, usually stitched in place; used for decorative effects on blouses, dresses, children's and baby dresses. See *seams.*

tucker 1. Narrow strip or frill of plain or lace-trimmed fabric used by women, in 17th and 18th centuries, to fill in low décolletage. Also called _pinner_ or _falling tucker_ when it hung down over bodice. See _partlet_ or _chemisette_.

Tudor cape Woman's short circular cape, usually embroidered, made with pointed _yoke_ front and back, an _epaulet_ on each shoulder, and velvet _Medici collar, q.q.v.;_ worn in 1890's.

tuft Variant of _tassel;_ a cluster of threads or fibers, fixed together at one end.

tulip skirt See _bubble_ under _skirts._

tulle Transparent net. See _fabrics._

tulle embroidery See _embroideries._

tunic, tunica 1. Straight, loose-fitting _basic garment,_ knee-length, with full sleeves, worn in ancient Greece and Rome and for centuries a full-length outer or undergarment for all classes, elaborately decorated for emperors, etc. 2. Long, plain, close-fitting _military jacket._ 3. Short loose skirted garment worn in 19th and 20th centuries by women and girls

for athletics, often called _gym tunic._ 4. _Overblouse_ of sheer, decorated fabrics, used as upper part of long evening gowns, first shown by designer Worth in Paris, 1868, later in 1890's and up to 1914. 5. Thigh-length sleeved or sleeveless _overblouse,_ usually slightly fitted and beltless, worn over skirt, slacks or alone as short dress; popular in 1940's, revived in 1960's. See _dresses._

tunic à la mameluke Woman's knee-length tunic with long sleeves; fashionable at beginning of 19th century, later called _tunique à la juive;_ inspired by Napoleon's Egyptian campaign, 1798. _Der._ Mamelukes were originally slaves brought to Egypt in 19th century, later trained as soldiers; many who were freed rose to high rank and from 1250 to 1517 Egypt was ruled by Mameluke sultans.

tunic à la romaine Full-length, high-waisted, long-sleeved tunic of gauze or lawn; worn in late 18th century.

tunic skirt See _skirts._

turban 1. Man's headdress of Muslim origin, consisting of long scarf of linen, cotton, or silk wound around the head, sometimes with one loose end hanging, or decorated with jewel in center front; sometimes wrapped around _fez, q.v.,_ which shows through at crown. 2. See _hats._ Also see _pagri._

Turkey bonnet Term used in the 15th and 16th centuries for man's or woman's cylindrical hat without a brim, introduced from the East, woman's style like inverted flower pot with veil from crown passing under chin. Also called _Turkey hat._

Turkey gown 1. Black velvet gown bordered with lynx, with 77 gold and black-enamel buttons, made for Henry VIII of England. 2. Long gown open and fastened in front, each long narrow sleeve slit above elbow so arm could pass through, remainder of sleeve hanging, worn from early 17th century on and becoming pattern for clergy's gowns.

Turkey red Brilliant red produced in cotton by madder, alizarin, or synthetic dyes, originally imported from Turkey.

turn-down or **turn-over collar** See *collars.*

turn-ups British term for men's *cuffed trousers,* first worn in House of Commons in 1893.

turquoise See *gems.*

turret bodice Bodice with *peplum, q.v.,* cut in squared *tabs* below waistline; popular in early 1880's.

turtleneck See *collars, necklines, sweaters.*

turumagi Korean man's wrap-around *overcoat* extending to lower calf of leg, worn wrapped to right and fastened by tying attached fabric into bow with one loop on right breast, made of grass cloth or calico for lower classes and of white silk for upper classes.

Tuscan straw See *straws.*

tussah Rough brown silk. See *fabrics* and *yarns.*

tutu Ballet dancer's costume—designed in 1832 by Eugene Lami for Maria Taglioni, a great Italian ballerina of the romantic period—consisting of a tight-fitting *bodice* leaving the shoulders bare, a *bell-shaped* sheer white gathered skirt reaching midway between knee and ankle; worn with pale-pink *tights* and pale-pink satin *ballet slippers, q.q.v.*

tuxedo 1. Man's *dinner jacket,* usually black, with satin or grosgrain shawl collar; for semi-formal evening occasions. 2. Semi-formal *evening suit* with jacket, black trousers with stripes down sides, white shirt, and black bow tie. *Der.* Style advocated by Frank G. Griswald, at Tuxedo Park, N.Y., in early 20th century, who suggested copying Prince of Wales' velvet smoking jacket for semi-formal wear. Also called *dinner jacket* or *dress lounge.* See *sweaters.*

tweed See *fabrics.*

tweeds Men's country or sports suits made of *tweed, q.v.,* or other informal fabrics, antonym of *business suits.*

'twenties bob See *bob* under *hairstyles.*

'twenties silhouette See *silhouettes.*

twill Broad term for *twill*-weave fabrics, often sturdy cotton, made with distinct diagonal rib on surface; includes *denim, garbardine, surah, tricotine,* and *whipcord, q.q.v.,* under *fabrics.*

twill weave See *weaves.*

two-bar tricot See *knits.*

two-ply 1. Yarn made by combining two lightly twisted single yarns into one yarn, making it stronger. 2. Fabric consisting of two layers, woven or bonded together.

two-way-stretch foundation See *foundation garments.*

tye 1. Term for man's tied-back wig in 18th century. 2. (pl.) American term for girls' apron in late 19th century.

Tyrian purple Red-purple color originally obtained from shellfish found off shores of Tyre and reserved for royalty in Biblical times.

Tyrolean (tee-roll-ee-an) Type of dress worn by natives of Austrian Tyrol region, including *dirndl skirts, q.v.,* embroidered vests, and aprons worn by women; *Lederhosen, knee socks,* feather-trimmed felt *Alpine hats, q.q.v.,* worn by men. Also see *embroideries.*

U

ugly English term for collapsible brim worn over bonnet as a sunshade when traveling or to protect weak eyes. Made of series of cane half-

hoops covered with silk; when not in use, folded up over the hat, like a *calash, q.v.;* worn from late 1840's to mid 1860's.

Ukrainian peasant blouse White cotton blouse with full, puffed sleeves and narrow standing-band collar, embroidery in vivid-color geometric designs on upper sleeves and around shoulders, extending down front in narrow bands; worn by peasant women in Russian Ukraine.

ulster 1. Man's heavy overcoat, single or double-breasted, with belt and detachable hood; introduced in late 1860's. 2. Loose ankle-length coat with attached cape—sometimes two or three layers—or half-cape, with fly-front and a ticket pocket on left sleeve above cuff; worn by men and women in late 19th century. Also see *Albert, Gladstone,*

and *carrick.* 3. Heavy wool overcoating fabric with long pressed nap, made in Belfast, Ulster County, Ireland.

ultramarine Rich deep blue-purple color made from powdered lapis-lazuli, or made chemically to reproduce this color.

ultrasonic sewing Sewing done by special machines using ultrasonic sound waves that fuse, or weld, fabrics together without the use of needle and thread; in early 1970's possible for most synthetic fabrics but most often used on double-knit polyesters. Advantages: eliminates use of needles and thread, eliminates seam slippage.

umbrella Portable, collapsible circular canopy, mounted on central rod, the framework of radiating spokes covered with cloth or plastic, carried by hand to protect against rain and sun, came into general use in Europe in late 18th century; at various times regarded as stigma of poverty, sign of stinginess or of effeminancy, or—by Quakers—as snobbish and worldly. Also see *parasol.*

umbrella brim Brim of woman's hat set in *accordion pleats, q.v.,* opened out to resemble an umbrella.

umbrella drawers Women's full, bell-shaped drawers, trimmed with *tucks, insertion* and *lace, q.q.v.,* gathered to waistband; worn in late 19th century and early 20th century.

umbrella pleats See *pleats.*

unbleached muslin Plain-weave natural cotton. See *fabrics.*

underarm dart See *dart.*

under cap 1. Woman's indoor cap usually shaped like a *coif, q.v.;* worn under outdoor hat from 16th to mid 19th centuries. 2. Indoor cap, like a *skullcap, q.v.;* worn under hat by elderly men in 16th century.

underground fashion Type of casual, sometimes *ethnic,* inexpensive dress adopted by young people, the so-called "hippies," starting in California in the 1950's. Usually characterized by *jeans* worn with miscellaneous *T-shirts* or *peasant blouses, q.q.v.,* or by nostalgic secondhand early 1920's to 1940's dresses, all intended to be anti-Establishment. *Rags,* an underground fashion magazine edited in San Francisco and New York from 1970–71, was founded by Mary Peacock and Daphne Davis.

under petticoat Term for white cambric or flannel skirt worn under dress skirt or under hoops from 16th through 18th centuries.

underpropper See *rabato.*

undershirt 1. Man's knitted shirt, usually white cotton, with U neckline continued into *built-up straps* or with short sleeves and *crew neckline;* worn underneath outer shirt or sweater. See *T-shirt.* 2. Woman's knitted undervest, usually of cotton or cotton and wool, shaped like man's undershirt. 3. Infants' knitted wool or cotton shirt, in four styles: double-breasted, fastened with *grippers, q.v.;* high-necked *cardigan, q.v.,* usually with long sleeves; *pullover, q.v.,* similar to man's undershirt; sleeved *pullover* with lapped shoulders that stretch to permit easy passage over head.

undershirt dress See *dresses.*

undershirt sweater See *sweaters.*

underskirt A *petticoat, slip,* or *half slip, q.q.v.* Also see *skirts.*

under sleeve See *engageantes.*

undervest British term for *undershirt, q.v.*

522

underwaist See *pantywaist.*

under waistcoat Man's short sleeveless waistcoat, introduced in 1790; fashionable between 1825–1840 to wear one over another in contrasting fabrics. Survives in men's formal wear as waistcoat with *white slip, q.v.*

underwear 1. Women's *lingerie,* e.g., *panties, slips, brassieres,* etc. 2. Men's *A-shirts, T-shirts, shorts, trunks,* or *thermal shirts* and *pants* worn beneath outer clothes. 3. Infants' *vests* and *panties.*

undress Ordinary or unceremonial dress for man or woman; term used in 18th and 19th centuries. Also see *negligee costume.*

U-neck See *necklines.*

Ungaro, Emmanuel See *designers appendix, France.*

uniform Distinctive clothing worn by all members of a group to denote common activity, e.g., the military, students, policemen, firemen, nurses, clergymen, those engaged in sports, etc.; parts of these uniforms freely borrowed as fashion ideas for sportswear, millinery, shoes, etc.

union suit One-piece knitted undergarment buttoned up center front, with long legs, short or long sleeves, a drop seat, worn for warmth; copied from the *Jaeger suit, q.v.,* introduced in 1880's, worn by all ages until 1940's, now mainly used under ski or other winter-sports' clothing. Long-legged underwear is often nicknamed *long johns* or long-handled underwear. See *thermal underwear.*

Uniply Trademark for fabric-to-fabric foam bonding of woven fabrics made from man-made fibers and blends; dyeing, finishing, and bonding are all done by one manufacturer, producing a dry-cleanable fabric.

unisex fashions Style introduced in late 1960's for identical fashions in shirts, pants, jackets, etc., worn by both men and women; often grouped in one shop.

university coat See *angle-fronted coat.*

university vest Double-breasted *waistcoat* made with sides cut away from lowest button, fashionable with *university coat, q.v.,* in early 1870's.

unmentionables or **unwhisperables** See *trousers.*

upper Shoe-industry term for all parts of shoe above the *sole, q.v.*

upper garment English term used from 17th century for outer garments such as a *cloak, cassock,* or *gown,* which indicated dress of a gentleman; without upper garment, gentleman was said to be *in querpo, q.v.*

upper stocks See *trunk hose.*

upsweep See *hairstyles.*

urchin cut See *hairstyles.*

usha See *dresses.*

utchat Sacred eye of Egyptians, worn as pendant on necklaces to ward off evil.

V

vagabond See *slouch* under hats.

vair Name for highly prized fur worn by kings and magistrates in 13th and 14th centuries, used for linings and trimmings.

Valenciennes lace See *laces.*

Valentina See *designers appendix, United States.*

Valentino, Garavani See *designers appendix, Italy.*

val lace See *laces.*

vallancy (va-lan-si) Extremely large wig, shading the face; worn in 18th century.

Valois hat *Velvet* or *beaver, q.q.v.,* hat with brim of equal width all around; worn by men or women from 1814–1835.

Valois, Rose See *designers appendix, France.*

vambrace 1. *Armor* consisting of metal plate worn on forearm, under the *hauberk, q.v.,* or over it, in early 13th century. 2. Later, plate armor for entire arm, made up of upper and lower *cannons* and *coute, q.q.v.,* for the elbow.

vamp Term for front part of shoe covering toes and instep, so called since 15th century. Formerly called *vamprey.*

Van Dyck, vandyke Name given to various collars and trims, as illustrated in men's portraits by early 17th century Flemish Sir Anthony Van Dyck, who painted English court of Charles I. 1. Saw-tooth lace or fabric borders. 2. Large, flat linen collar with serrated border or saw-tooth lace, called Van Dyck points; Also a small crocheted collar with seven or more deep points, worn by women in 1860's. 3. 17th century ruff edge with points or sawtooth lace. 4. Lace-bordered handkerchief. 5. Small pointed beard.

vanity 1. Small metal or plastic case carried in women's handbag containing face powder, sometimes rouge or other cosmetic. 2. See *handbags.*

varens Woman's short outdoor jacket with loose sleeves, made of cashmere or velvet and silk-lined, variation of *casaweck* and *polka, q.q.v.;* worn in late 1840's.

vareuse (va-reuz) Rough woolen *overblouse,* or jacket, similar to *pea jacket, q.v.,* worn by French sailors onboard ship, copied as woman's easy swinging-back topper in 1950's.

varsity sweater See *letter* under *sweaters.*

Vassar blouse Woman's blouse similar to a *peasant blouse, q.v.* made with a *drawstring* neckline and up-standing ruffle, sleeve bouffant and either three-quarter length or full length ending in a ruffle, sometimes decorated with embroidery, with ribbon suspender straps, or with clusters of bows on the shoulders; worn in 1890's. See drawing, next page.

vasquine See *basquine.*

veil Piece of light transparent fabric such as net, lace, tulle, etc., worn by women over head or face for ornament or concealment, in vari-

VASSAR BLOUSE

ous lengths, attached to hat and worn tightly over face or loosely hanging from brim in 20th century; long and enveloping in ancient times; traditional in white for brides, black for mourning. See *coverchief, crisp, goffer, hennin, kalyptra.* Modern types listed below.

VEILS:

bird cage Dome of stiff wide-mesh veiling, pinned to crown of head, covering face and ears, worn in place of hat, especially in 1950's.

bridal v. Traditionally, length of white net, lace, tulle, or silk illu-

sion, reaching to waist, hips, ankles, or floor; worn over face during wedding, turned back after ceremony.

chapel v. Small circle of lace or tulle, frequently edged with ruffle, worn by women over top of head while inside a church. Also called *chapel cap.*

mantilla Large oblong (or triangular) fine lace veil, usually in rose pattern, black or white, worn wrapped over head, crossed under chin and one end thrown over shoulder, frequently worn to church instead of a hat in Spain and South America; popularized in U.S. in early 1960's by President's wife, Mrs. John F. Kennedy, now Mrs. Aristotle Onassis.

mourning v. Semi-sheer black veil to the shoulders, usually circular, sometimes edged with wide band of black fabric, worn under or over hat at funerals or during period of mourning.

prayer v. Small triangular veil similar to a *mantilla,* worn instead of hat for church services.

veiling Sheer net used for veils.

Velcro See *closings.*

velours, velour (veh-loor) 1. Soft pile fabric. See *fabrics.* 2. Velvet-like felt used for hats. 3. French word for velvet. See *plush.*

velvet Cut-pile fabric. See *fabrics.*

velveteen See *fabrics.*

vendeuse (von-derz) French term for saleswoman employed at couture houses in Paris.

Venet, Philippe See *designers appendix, France.*

Venetian 1. Lining fabric of wool or

worsted in *satin weave*. 2. (pl.) Men's pants or breeches, worn from late 16th to early 17th centuries in form of pear-shaped *trunk hose, q.v.,* fastened below knee by garter-ribbons; when voluminous throughout, called *Venetian slops* or, when tightly fitted, called *Venetian galligascoines or galligaskins.* Also called *trusses.*

Venetian cloak Woman's black satin cloak with collar, cape, and wide hanging sleeves; worn in late 1820's.

Venetian lace See *laces.*

Venetian ladder work See *embroideries.*

Venetian point lace See *laces.*

Venetian sleeve Full sleeve fitting into armhole, slashed nearly to shoulder, worn in late 1850's by women over puffed *engageantes, q.q.v.*

Veneziani, Jole See *designers appendix, Italy.*

Venise, point de See *laces.*

vent Term used since 15th century to indicate vertical slit in garment, usually from hem upward, used in coats, jackets, shirts and suit coats.

ventail Armor for lower part of face on 16th century helmet; if face guard is made in three pieces, *ventail* is middle piece.

Vera See *designers appendix, United States.*

verdigris Brilliant blue-green color similar to color of deposit seen on copper, brass, or bronze that has been exposed to the atmosphere.

Verel Trademark of Eastman Chemical Products, Inc. for a modacrylic fiber used for high-bulk knit apparel and

for pile fabrics which are flame resistant; sometimes finished, dyed and printed to look like *hair seal* and *herringbone mink, q.q.v.,* etc.

vermilion Brilliant red-orange color. Also called *Chinese red.*

Veronese cuirasse (ver-o-naiz-e cure-ass) Jersey bodice laced up back; fashionable in 1880's. *Der.* See *Veronese dress.*

Veronese dress Daytime dress with knee-length *princess*-type woolen *tunic* ending in deep points over silk *underskirt* with large *box pleats* around hem; worn in 1880's. Named for Paolo Veronese, 16th century Venetian painter born in Verona, Italy, whose paintings inspired the style.

Veronica Lake hairstyle See *hairstyles.*

vertically worked Fur skins which are first *let out, q.v.,* and then sewn together so that each skin runs from top of garment to hem.

vertugale (var-tu-gal-leh) Spanish hoops or *farthingale, q.v.* Also see *Infanta style.*

vest 1. Historically, from late 17th through 18th centuries, man's knee-length coat with short sleeves, sashed at waist, worn under *surcoat* or *justaucorps, q.q.v.* 2. Short, close-fitting, sleeveless garment, buttoning in front, typically worn by men over shirt and under jacket of business suit, either matched or contrasted to fabric of suit. Also called *waistcoat, weskit, veston, vestee.* 3. Woman's sleeveless, collarless, short, fitted outer garment, fastened in front or hanging open, matched to skirt, pants, or coat, sometimes extending to knees as substitute for jacket. 4. See *undershirt*. Also see *bolero* and *Zouave jacket*.

VESTS:

Afghanistan v. Vest made of curly lamb tanned and worn with smooth, embroidered, skin side outside showing edges of curly lamb, copied from vests worn by natives in Afghanistan; *ethnic* fashion popular in late 1960's.

electric v. Vest with a lining that reflects 80% of body's heat; special built-in electric heating system, operated by batteries, is located at the center of the lower back, batteries concealed in left pocket.

fisherman's v. Sportsman's vest similar to *hunting vest, q.v.,* including pockets for flies and other fishing gear, a rod holder, and a storage compartment in the back of the garment.

formal v. Man's *formal daytime* single- or double-breasted *waistcoat* to match *cutaway* coat or a double-breasted waistcoat of pearl-gray or fawn-colored woolen *doeskin, q.q.v.; formal evening* waistcoat is single- or double-breasted, made of white *piqué, q.v.,* with or without revers, and worn with *swallow-tailed* coat.

hug-me-tight Knitted or quilted vest with V-neck, buttoned down front, usually worn by older people under coats for extra warmth.

hunting v. Sportsman's vest of cotton duck fabric, front-buttoned, with large rubber-lined game pocket, worn over *hunting shirt, q.v.*

FISHERMAN'S VEST

PAKISTANI VEST

jerkin 1. Man's sleeved jacket worn over *doublet, q.v.,* sometimes laced or buttoned up front, sometimes sleeveless with shoulder wings; worn in late 15th through 16th centuries. 2. Contemporary close-fitting sleeveless *jacket* reaching to waist, often of leather. 3. Variant of *waistcoat* or *vest, q.q.v.*

Pakistani v. Fitted vest with long, gold-braided shawl collar, fastened

SWEATER-VEST

in front with invisible hooks, elaborately trimmed around edges with wide gilt braid, mirrors, and tassels, originally called Pakistani wedding vest; part of fad for *ethnic* fashions in late 1960's.

pot-holder v. Vest sewn together of bright-colored crocheted squares made in the "granny" pattern often used for pot holders; popular with young people in late 1960's.

suit v. Vest made to match a particular suit; for men, usually of matching fabric or, also for women, of a fabric co-ordinated with the jacket and pants or skirt.

sweater-v. Sleeveless sweater shaped like a vest, usually with a V neckline and often buttoned down the front.

tattersall v. Man's vest in small checked fabric, single-breasted with six buttons, no collar, and four flapped pockets; first worn by sportsmen in 1890's. See *tattersall.*

waistcoat, weskit Other names for *vests.*

vestee Woman's decorative front, half of a *vest, q.v.,* attached around neck and by ties around waist; worn under a jacket. Also called *chemisette.*

vesting Fabrics used for men's vests, such as fancy *silks, Jacquards, Bedford cord, piqués* and *dobby-figured* fabrics, *q.q.v.,* under *fabrics.*

veston Variant of *vest, q.v.*

vest pocket See *pockets.*

vici kid See *leathers.*

Victor, Sally See *designers appendix, United States.*

Victorian collar See *choker* under *collars.*

Victorian fashion Woman's way of dressing, generally sober by day, influenced by long reign of England's Queen Victoria, 1837–1901. Many garments were named after the queen. Typical: wide hoop skirts, basques, berthas, bustles, shawls and poke bonnets. Also called Victorian: double-breasted, knee-length mantle with wide sleeves, flat collar or shoulder cape short in front and to the waist in back; small shoulder cape edged in fur and tied with neck ribbons, also called *palatine royal, q.v.*

Victorine See *palatine #2.*

vicuña Hair fiber from the vicuña, species of llama, extremely soft with colors ranging from golden chestnut to deep fawn; marketed exclusively by Peruvian government.

Vionnet, Madeleine See *designers appendix, France.*

vinaigrette Small metal perfume container made by jewelers, sometimes attached to outside of mesh handbags in early 20th century.

vinal Generic term for man-made polyvinyl-alcohol fibers; fabrics are used for gloves, raincoats, and umbrellas.

vinyl Non-porous plastic, tough, flexible, shiny, elastic, can be transparent; used for fabric coating and to produce materials resembling leather; used for *boots, capes, gloves, raincoats, shoes,* etc.

vinyon 1. Generic name for man-made vinyl resin fiber; originally manufactured in both *staple* and *continuous* filaments, *q.q.v.,* now made only in the former. Several fibers originally made under "Vinyon N" trademark differ from the above fiber and are no longer known by this name; one of them is now known as Dynel. 2. Vinyon HH is a trademark for polyvinyl chloride fiber with little or no elasticity.

V-neck See *necklines.*

violin bodice Long *tunic* bodice, reaching below hips, *princess* style, with violin-shaped dark fabric insert in back, worn over dress in 1870's.

virago sleeve Puffed sleeve with many slashes, tied at intervals to the elbow; worn by women in first half of 17th century.

viscose rayon Type of rayon fiber made from regenerated cellulose, produced in large quantities and suitable for many uses in clothing manufacture.

visite (vee-zeet) General term for woman's loose cape-like outdoor garment, worn in last half of 19th century. See *pelerine, mantle, cloak.*

visiting dress Term used throughout the 19th century for woman's costume worn especially for making calls in the afternoon; also called *visiting costume* and *visiting toilette.*

vison See *mink* under *furs.*

visor Cuffed stiff shade, attached to a headband or to front of a cap, protecting eyes from sun. *Der.* From ancient armor's moveable part of helmet, covering the face.

Viyella Trademark for British wool-cotton flannel. See *fabrics.*

voile Sheer cotton. See *fabrics.*

voilette Variant of *veil, q.v.*

Volendam cap Variant of *Dutch cap.*

V-strap See *sandals.*

V-throat See *pumps* under *shoes.*

Vuitton, Louis See *designers appendix, France.*

Vycron Trademark of Beaunit Fibers (Division of Beaunit Corp.) for polyester staple, filament yarn, and tow, sometimes used for knitwear.

Vyrene Trademark of Uniroyal Inc. for a monofilament extruded *spandex* yarn which is available in *core-spun, bare,* or *covered* types; in knit and woven fabrics, used for foundations, girdles, swimwear.

W

wad Variant of *woad, q.v.*

wadded hem Hem that has been padded with wide band of *cording, q.v.,* used in 1820's and used occasionally in contemporary dresses and robes.

waders See *boots.*

waffle weave See *honeycomb* under *weaves.*

waist 1. Term used for narrowest part of torso. Also called *waistline, q.v.* 2. Term for *blouse* or *shirtwaist,* used from 1890 to the 1920's.

waistband Band of fabric, usually faced and interfaced; seamed to waistline of skirt or pants and buttoned or fastened along with the *placket, q.v.,* to hold garment firmly around waist; also a set-in belt in a dress.

waist-cincher See *French cinch* under *girdles.*

waistcoat 1. In 16th to 19th centuries, man's *under-doublet,* sleeved, waist-length, quilted; knee-length and often heavily embroidered in 18th century; double-breasted in 19th century. See *petticoat, justaucorps, vest.* 2. Similar garment worn with riding habit by women in latter half of 18th century and as complement to tailor-made suit in late 19th century.

waistcoat-bosom dress *Dress* buttoned down front, made with a long *stomacher, q.v.,* showing in front; worn in early 19th century.

waistcoat paletot Woman's knee-length *coat* in tailored style buttoned only at neckline with hip-length waistcoat showing in front; worn in 1880's.

waistcoat pocket See *vest* under *pockets.*

waistline Place where belt or seam is placed joining top to skirt, usually at normal line of waist.

WAISTLINES:

cinched or **corselet w.** Narrow curved waist produced by a *waist-cincher* or *guepiere, q.q.v.,* under *girdles.*

Directoire w. Variant of *Empire waistline,* below.

drawstring w. Waistline with a cord or belt drawn through a *casing, heading,* or *beading, q.q.v.,* gathering the fullness in when tied in a bow or knot.

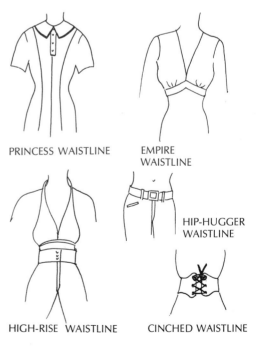

PRINCESS WAISTLINE   EMPIRE WAISTLINE

HIP-HUGGER WAISTLINE

HIGH-RISE WAISTLINE   CINCHED WAISTLINE

dropped w. Belt or waistline seam placed below the natural waistline, as in *torso* styles, *q.v.*

Empire w. High-waisted effect with seam placed directly under bust; used from late 18th century to 1820's during Empire and Directoire periods in France, popular ever since for women's dresses, coats, lingerie.

high-rise w. Pants or skirt with a very wide waistband extended from the natural waistline upward; popular in early 1970's as a reaction to *hip-hugger, q.v.,* styles of the 1960's.

hip-hugger w. Waistband of skirt, pants, or shorts that falls below the natural waistline, resting on the hip-bones; derived from Western jeans, popular in 1960's.

princess w. Fitted waistline with no seam, garment cut in panels from neck to hem and fitted by vertical seams, worn by Empress Eugénie in 1860's and popular since.

set-in w. Horizontal panel of fabric used at waistline of dress, fitted between top and skirt, making two seams, one at normal waistline and one higher.

waist nipper Variant of *waist cincher* or *guepiere, q.q.v.,* under *girdles.*

wale Textile term for woven ridge in fabric running vertically in *Bedford cord, corduroy,* etc., crosswise in *faille,* diagonally in *twill* such as *gabardine, q.q.v.,* under *fabrics.*

walking dress See *promenade dress.*

walking shoe See *shoes.*

walking shorts See *Bermuda* under *shorts.*

walking stick See *cane.*

walking suit See *suits.*

wallaby See *furs* and *leathers.*

Wallace Beery shirt See *knit shirts* under *shirts.*

walled toe See *toes of shoes.*

wallet Accessory used to carry paper money, credit cards, and photographs, some times with change purse attached, or space for checkbook and note pad. Originally used only by men; now also used by women and children.

wallpaper print See *prints.*

walrus mustache Mustache with long drooping ends hanging at either side of the mouth, similar to tusks of a walrus.

waltz-length gown See *nightgowns.*

wamus (wah-muss) Heavy outdoor jacket or cardigan of coarse cloth, buttoned at collar and wrist, worn in U.S. Also spelled *wammus,* or *wampus.*

wampum belt See *Indian* under *belts.*

wardrobe 1. All clothing of an individual. 2. 15th century term for room where clothing was kept. 3. From 19th century on, piece of furniture used to contain clothing, also called *armoire.*

warm See *British warm.*

warm-up suit *Jumpsuit* or two-piece suit of quilted or napped fabric worn by athletes and skiers while warming up or while resting to avoid cooling too quickly. See *sweatshirt* under *shirts* and *sweat pants* under *pants.*

warp Basic weaving term for yarns in fabric that run parallel to selvage.

warp-backed fabric See *backed cloth* under *fabrics.*

warp beam Roller of warp yarn placed on loom for weaving.

warp-faced fabric Fabric with more *warp, q.v.,* yarns, than *crosswise* yarns showing on surface of fabric, *e.g., slipper satin.*

warp knit See *knits.*

warp piqué The lighter weights of *Bedford cord, q.v.* See *weaves.* Also see *piqué* under *fabrics.*

warp print See *prints.*

warp printing Method of making design on fabric by printing the *warp,* or vertical yarns before the *filling,* or crosswise, yarns are woven, giving an indistinct design; used for cretonne fabric and silk ribbons.

wash-and-wear See *durable press.*

washed gold Thin coating of gold applied to a base metal by dipping or washing it in a solution of gold salts.

wasp waist See *silhouettes.*

watch Decorative timepiece carried in *pocket,* pinned on *bodice,* hung on a *necklace* or worn on a *band* on *wrist,* fashionable accessory since 16th century; wrist watch developed after World War I, in 1920's, worn with novelty straps and face designs in 1960's and early 1970's; now considered costume

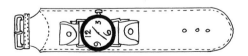

jewelry; many technical developments in recent decades, *e.g.,* self-winding, waterproof, shock-resisting watches and watches powered by electric cells or with faces read digitally instead of dials.

watch bracelet See *bracelets.*

watch cap See *caps.*

watch chain A decorative chain attached to a man's pocket watch; when watch is worn in vest pocket, chain may be pulled through vest buttonhole and end tucked into pocket on opposite side; often embellished with seals or emblems.

watch coat Short coat worn by sailors on watch; see *pea coat.*

watch fob Short chain, ribbon, or charm, frequently engraved with initials, attached to man's pocket watch and named for the trouser pocket in which the watch is carried, called a *fob, q.v.*

watch pocket See *vest* under *pockets.*

watch ring See *ring.*

waterfall back Skirt worn over bustle, made with series of cascading puffs down center back, fullness held in place with series of drawstrings inside dress; popular in mid 1880's.

waterfall neckcloth See *mail-coach necktie.*

waterproof Describing clothing, usually of rubber, plastic, or heavily-coated fabric, that cannot be penetrated by water, especially boots and coats. See *water resistant* or *repellent,* below.

water resistant or **water repellent** Describing clothing of fabric or leather treated to shed water easily and dry quickly but not entirely *waterproof, q.v.*

Watteau (wat-toe) Term used to describe the type of early 18th century woman's dress depicted by French painter Jean Antoine Watteau (1684–1721). Principal elements: 1. Dress with fitted bodice, low-cut neckline edged with ruffled lace, fastened up front with ribbon bows, loose back with wide *box pleats, q.v.,* hanging from high shoulder yoke to the ground: called *Wateau sacque* or *polonaise.* 2. Any garment, *coat, robe,* etc. with wide box pleats forming a loose back, either short or long. 3. Shallow-crowned straw hat, tilted forward, brim turned up in back with flowers filled in behind, often tied under chin with wide ribbons. See *pleats, open robe.*

wearing sleeves 17th-century term for sleeves worn on the arms as compared to sleeves which hung down the back. See *hanging sleeves.*

weasel See *furs.*

weaves Manner in which the vertical, or *warp,* and horizontal, or *filling,* yarns are inter-woven to make a fabric, achieved on a loom, either by hand or machinery.

WEAVES:

armure w. Filling-rib weave which produces a pebbled effect similar to scales on chain mail.

backed w. Fabric made with an extra warp or filling or both to provide extra thickness, sometimes of two colors, a different color showing on each side, sometimes one side printed; used for *bathrobe cloth, q.v.*

basket w. Variation of *plain weave,* made by weaving two or more fillings over and under same number of warps to produce checkerboard effect.

cut-pile w. See *velvet weave.*

diagonal w. See *twill weave.*

dobby w. Weave forming small repeated geometric patterns done on plain loom with dobby attachment, which controls the harnesses handling series of threads; e.g., *diaper cloth* and *white-on-white broadcloth.*

double cloth Weave which uses five sets of yarns interlacing to form two layers of fabric; if cut apart, two separate fabrics result; used for wools with different colors on

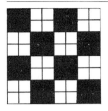

BASKET WEAVE

PLAIN WEAVE

LEFT-HAND TWILL
WEAVE

HERRINGBONE
WEAVE

SATIN WEAVE

each side or in plaid and plain combinations.

doup See *leno weave.*

end-and-end effect Men's-shirting weave with a fine colored yarn alternating with white in the warp and white or all-color filling, producing a pin stripe; or the alternation used in both directions, producing a pin check.

gauze See *leno weave.*

granite w. Weave characterized by pebbly effect somewhat similar to crepe. See *granite cloth* under *fabrics.* Also called *momie weave* and *pebble weave.*

herringbone w. Chevron pattern produced in fabric by using *twill weave*

for several rows in one direction, then reversing. Also called *broken twill weave.*

honeycomb w. Weave which forms series of recessed squares, similar in appearance to a waffle, made on the dobby loom, e.g., *cotton waffle cloth, q.v.* Also called *waffle weave.*

Jacquard w. Elaborate pattern woven on Jacquard loom where each warp yarn is controlled separately by use of a pattern on a punched card; background may be plain, rib, satin, or sateen, with design usually in *satin weave, q.v.,* e.g., *brocades* and *damasks, q.v.*

leno w. Open weave with two warps locking around each filling in figure-eight design, e.g., *marquisette, q.v.* Also called *doup* and *gauze weave.*

momie w. See *granite weave.*

pebble w. See *granite weave.*

pile w. Weave with loops in either warp or filling producing thick, soft surface; loops may be *left whole* as in *terry cloth, q.v.,* or *cut,* as in *velvet, q.v.*

plain w. *Filling* yarn goes over one *warp,* then under one warp, *q.q.v.;* second row alternates, in a checkerboard pattern.

rib Variation of *plain weave* in which lengthwise or crosswise wales are formed by using heavier yarn or by interlacing, e.g., *faille* or *dimity, q.q.v.,* under *fabrics.*

satin Irregular weave in which warp or filling yarns predominate, with many more yarns in the set that form the face, intersections staggered to produce a smooth, lustrous surface.

tabby w. Old term for the *plain weave, q.v.*

terry w. Weave of uncut pile made with extra loops on surface, used in *terry cloth, q.v.* Also called *uncut pile weave.*

twill w. Basic weave, characterized by diagonal ribs, produced by staggering the points of intersection of warp and fill, generally upward from left to right (called *right twill* or *right-hand twill; left twill* or *left-hand twill* goes from lower right to upper left) making a firm, durable fabric as in *denim, ticking, serge, gabardine, q.q.v.,* under *fabrics;* popular for men's wear.

waffle w. See *honeycomb.*

warp piqué w. Weave with pronounced vertical ribs similar to *Bedford cord, q.v.,* produced by two-ply yarns in face and heavy single backing.

webbing Very strong, closely woven, narrow fabric of cotton, jute, hemp, nylon, etc., in a variety of weaves used for belts, straps, and waistbands.

webbed belt See *belts.*

wedding band See *rings.*

wedding-band collar See *collars.*

wedding dress See *dresses.*

wedding garter Decorative garter, usually blue satin trimmed with lace, worn by brides, traditionally given away at reception to an unmarried man; the custom derived from 16th to 18th centuries practice, in which young men wore pieces of bride's garter in their hats.

wedding veil See *veils.*

wedge heel See *heels.*

wedgie See *shoes.*

Wedgwood cameo Decorative plaque similar to a carved-gem *cameo, q.v.,* but molded instead from pottery clay by the Wedgwood firm in England, often in the soft blue and white coloring characteristic of one pattern of Wedgwood pottery.

weed Term for a *garment,* from medieval times through 16th century; now, especially, *widow's weeds,* meaning *mourning clothes, q.v.* Also spelled *wede* and *weyd.*

weepers 1. Muslin armbands or hat bands, worn by mourners in 18th and 19th centuries, usually black but sometimes white if deceased was young girl. 2. Name for ostrich feathers, worn in late 19th century.

weft Cross yarns in weaving; opposite of *warp.* See *filling.*

weft knit See *knits.*

Weinberg, Chester See *designers appendix, United States.*

welded seam See *fused* under *seams.*

Wellington styles Man's fashions of early 19th century, named for first Duke of Wellington, British military hero who defeated Napoleon in the battle of Waterloo in 1815, consisting of single-breasted overcoat, buttoned to waist, with full skirt to knees no waistline seam but center back vent, side pleats and hip buttons; worn with narrow pantaloons with slits from ankle to calf, closed with buttons; worn also with boots, tall flared-top beaver hat, and sometimes a cape. See *Wellington* under *boots*.

welt 1. Narrow piece of leather stitched to shoe *upper, q.v., lining,* and *insole* before being attached to *outsole;* seam to outsole is concealed. 2. Term used since 16th century for a border around edge of garment, either for decorative purposes or for strengthening.

welt pocket See *pockets*.

welt seam See *seams*.

weskit Variant of *waistcoat, q.v.* Also see *dresses*.

Western Describing clothes worn in western part of U.S. by cowboys and sportsmen and styles inspired by these clothes. See *jackets, pants, shorts,* and *cowboy* under *shirts, hats, boots*.

wet look Shiny, glossy vinyl, Ciré, or other shiny materials, popular in late 1960's for sport jackets, mini-skirts, pants and beach wear.

wet suit 1. Three-piece suit made of black rubber backed with nylon, consisting of skin-tight *pants,* leotard jacket, and *hood* shaped to fit closely over head with Plexiglas window for eyes; fastened by zippers at center front, down each arm and leg; often worn with flippers on feet; used for underwater sports and scuba diving. 2. Long-sleeved one-piece black rubber suit, with knee-length pants, zipped in front; worn for surfing.

weyd See *weed*.

whalebone Pliable, horn-like strips, called *baleen,* from upper jaw of certain whales; used for stiffening garments since Middle Ages,

e.g., whalebone *stays, q.v.,* used in waist of woman's dress in 16th and 17th centuries, forerunner of *corset*.

wheel farthingale Drum-shaped *farthingale, q.v.,* produced by wearing of wheel-shaped piece of whalebone to extend skirt outward at waist, permitting it to fall straight in drum shape; worn from 1580 to 1620's. Also called *Catherine-wheel farthingale,* and *Italian farthingale*.

whipcord Hard-finish twill. See *fabrics*.

whip stitch See *stitches*.

whisk Wide, flat, lace-trimmed, or plain collar like *falling band, q.v.,* worn by women from about 1625; standing lace collar called *standing whisk*.

white belt See *judo* under *belts*.

white ducks See *pants*.

white flannels See *flannels* under *pants*.

white fox See *fox* under *furs*.

white mink See *mink* under *furs*.

white slip Narrow border of white piqué along front edges of man's waistcoat, correctly worn only with *morning coat, q.v.,* fashion introduced by Prince of Wales in 1888. Also see *under waistcoat*.

white tie Brief designation of men's *full evening dress;* compare *black tie*. See *ties*.

whittle Large white shawl, usually made of Welsh flannel; worn by country women from 17th century on.

wide-awake 19th-century name for man's broad-brimmed, low-crowned *hat* of felt or fabric; used for country wear.

widow's peak 1. Term for hairline forming a point in center of forehead. 2. Small cap wired in heart-shaped form with peak in center of forehead, originally worn by Catherine de' Medici as a widow's bonnet and much worn by Mary Queen of Scots. Also see *Marie Stuart bonnet.*

widow's weeds See *weed.*

wig 1. Contemporary type of false hair, human or artificial, mounted on elastic net cap or foundation of bands (called *capless*) stretched over head to conceal natural hair and styled in conventional cuts and colors or in fancy arrangements and colors as fashion fad, popular since mid '60's. 2. Historically, false hair worn from early Egyptian times and becoming a status symbol of royalty and upper classes through 18th century; considered a secret device to conceal baldness in 19th and early 20th centuries; openly worn by both men and women as a fashion in late 1960's and early 1970's. For historical wigs see *aile de pigeon, bagwig, bob-wig, campaign, categan, Duvillier, physical, scratch* and *Titus* wigs.

wild mink See *mink* under *furs.*

wild silk Silk filaments from cocoons fed on uncultivated mulberry, oak, or castor-oil plant leaves, producing silk poorer in color, less even in texture, firmer and less elastic than *cultivated silk.* See *tussah.*

William Penn hat See *hats.*

willow grain See *boarded finish.*

wimple 1. Piece of linen or silk draped around woman's throat and pinned to the hair above the ears, worn in late 12th to mid 14th centuries and still part of some nuns' habits. 2. Gauze veil worn with evening dress in early 19th century. Also called *guimp, guimple, gwimple.* Also see *barbe.*

wind-blown bob See *hairstyles.*

wind bonnet See *bonnets.*

Windbreaker See *sport jackets.*

windbreaker cloth See *fabrics.*

windowpane See *checks* and *plaids.*

Windsor knot or **tie** See *ties.*

Wing-back earrings See *earrings.*

wing collar See *collars.*

wing hairstyle See *hairstyles*

wings Term used from mid 16th to mid 17th centuries for decorative pieces projecting upward from shoulders of *doublet* or dress, sometimes in shape of padded rolls or crescents.

wing tip Decorative leather cap sewn to toe of shoe, curving, often with center point, and perforated in patterns. See *wing-tip oxfords* under *shoes.*

winkle pickers See *shoes.*

winkers Men's collars with extremely high points reaching nearly to eyes, worn from 1816 to 1820.

wired bra See *brassieres.*

wires See *earrings.*

woad Natural pale-blue color prepared by fermenting leaves of woad plant. Also called *wad.*

wolf See *furs.*

wolverine See *furs.*

women's sizes Women's garments in sizes for heavier figure than *misses* range; even-number bust sizes 38–50.

woof Variant of *weft* or *filling*, *q.v.*

wool, woolen, woollen Fiber from fleece of the sheep, angora or cashmere goat, alpaca, vicuña, or camel, sometimes blended with other fibers and spun into yarn that is either woven or knitted into soft, warm, slightly fuzzy fabrics for coats, suits, sweaters, etc., e.g., *wool broadcloth, wool crepe, q.q.v.*

Wool Labeling Act Law passed by Congress in 1939 stating that *reprocessed wool, reused wool, q.q.v,* and *virgin wool* products must be labeled for the consumer.

work apron See *aprons.*

work clothes Sturdy pants, overalls, coveralls, jackets, etc., usually of denim, drill, chino, or duck, and shirts, often matching or of blue chambray; worn by laboring man on the job and adopted by young people for casual wear in the 1960's.

worked buttonholes See *buttonholes.*

worked in the round Method of joining fur skins together horizontally so that skins continue around coat or garment.

worry beads See *beads.*

worsted Smooth wool yarn made with longer than average fibers, carded several times, combed to eliminate short fibers and twisted so tightly there are few fuzzy fibers, used for woven or knitted fabrics giving smooth, crisp hand for suits and coats, e.g. *gabardine, serge, q.v.*

Worth, Charles Frederick See *designers appendix, France.*

woven stripe Pattern created in the weaving of the fabric either by different-colored yarns or by varying the weave, as opposed to a *printed stripe.* See *stripes.*

W.P.B. War Production Board. See *L-85*

Wragge, B. H. See *designers appendix, United States.*

Wrangler Term used in the West for a cowhand, now a trademark for a brand of Western pants, jackets, etc. See *pants.* See also *wrangler's* or *Western jacket* in *sport jackets* under *jackets.*

wrap 1. Loose outergarment, open down front, draped around body in various ways, may be coat or dress with no buttons, or Far Eastern unconstructed garment, e.g., Indian *dhoti, q.v.* 2. Shortened term for wrap-around. See below.

wrap-around Garment lapped and closed with sash. See *wrap* under *blouses, closings, coats, collars, dresses, skirts,* etc.

wrap-around glasses See *glasses.*

wrap cuff links Cuff links made with extra band extending around outside of cuff connecting the two parts.

wrapper 1. Woman's *dressing gown* worn in 18th-century boudoir which developed into woman's *negligee, q.v.,* in early 20th century. See *robes.* 2. Mid 19th century man's loose-fitting *overcoat,* thigh-length, which sometimes did not button, made with shawl collar. Also called *wrap-rascal.*

wrist band, belt, strap Strip of fabric, usually faced, seamed to the lower edge of a sleeve and fastened around the wrist; see *cuff.* Also see *bracelets.*

wrist watch See *watches.*

Y

yachting cap See *caps*.

yachting coat or **jacket** 1. See *sport jackets* under *jackets*. 2. Woman's hip-length jacket, single- or double-breasted with large buttons and loose sleeves; worn from 1860's to 1880's. Also called short *paletot*, *q.v.*

Yankee neckcloth See *American neckcloth*.

yard Unit of fabric measure used in the United States, comprising thirty-six inches or three feet, equivalent to .9144 meter.

yard goods Fabric sold by the yard at retail stores for sewing; also called *piece goods*.

yarmulka Skullcap used by Orthodox Jewish men for day wear and especially in the synagogue; may be fabric, embroidered, beaded, crocheted, etc.; also worn by other Jews for special occasions and religious services.

yarn A strand of fibers twisted together used for weaving or knitting; two basic types: (a) staple yarn, made from twisted short parallel fibers of cotton or wool or man-made fibers cut in short lengths, and (b) man-made yarn, comprised of fine strands of continuous length twisted together. Some types of yarn follow.

YARNS:

bouclé yarn A rough, curly, knotted yarn made with two fine foundation threads twisted along with a thicker, hard-twisted yarn that is delivered at a quicker rate than the foundation threads and is twisted with the former group in the opposite direction at half the number of turns. When woven, the bouclé yarn is often alternated with plain yarns. *Der.* French, buckled or curled.

bourette y. Fancy yarn made of various fibers including silk, worsted, or mohair with nubs of a different color formed when yarn is carded.

chenille y. (sheh-neel) Yarn with fuzzy pile protruding on all sides; used for fabric for bathrobes, etc. *Der.* French, caterpillar. See *fabrics* and *robes*.

confetti y. Knitting yarn spun with a vari-color speckled effect; completed garment has a tweedy appearance.

cord y. Two or more *ply yarns, q.v.,* are twisted together to form a cord yarn. Also called *cord* and, in Great Britain, *cabled yarn*. A *ply yarn* is formed by twisting together several single yarns. Sometimes the term is applied to yarn where the plied twist is in the same direction as the twist of each component.

core y. Yarns made with a heavy center cord around which are wrapped finer yarns of different fibers, *e.g.,* synthetic-rubber core wrapped with rayon, cotton, or silk to improve absorption and feel. See *elastomeric* yarns, below.

corkscrew y. Novelty yarn, sometimes in two-color effects, made by winding heavy, slackly twisted yarn around thin, tightly twisted yarn in spiral fashion.

541

crepe y. Cotton, rayon, or silk yarn that is given a high twist during spinning; the yarn is stiff and wiry, contracts during finishing giving pebbled surface to fabrics.

crewel y. Two-ply, loosely twisted, fine worsted yarn used in embroidery.

crimp-set y. Man-made yarns that are heat-set into a sawtoothed or zig-zag shape, making them *elastic* for use in knitting or weaving *stretch fabrics, q.v.*

eider y. Soft knitting yarn made from loosely twisted wool of fine quality.

eis y. Fine two-ply worsted knitting yarn; also called *eis wool* and *ice wool.*

elastomeric y. Highly elastic *core yarns, q.v.,* made with center of rubber or synthetic rubber, e.g., Lycra *spandex, q.v.,* covered with cotton or rayon—producing a high degree of elasticity. Trademarks include Blue C., Spandelle, Orofil, Glospan, Spanselle, Lycra, Lastex, Surlane, and Ameliotex.

fiberglass y. See *glass yarn.*

fingering y. Combination of woolen and worsted yarn, usually two or more *ply,* used for hand-knitted garments. 2. Loosely twisted wool yarn used in Great Britain for *Berlin work, q.v.,* under *embroideries.*

flake y. Novelty yarn with tufts, similar to *slub yarn,* the tufts usually of a different color and loosely attached.

floss Embroidery yarn made of soft, lustrous, loosely twisted cotton or silk plies. Also called *embroidery floss.*

glass y. Yarn made from fine-spun filaments of glass; used principally for decorating fabrics. Trademark name is *Fiberglas.*

Lastex y. Trademark owned by U.S. Rubber Co. for synthetic-rubber *core yarn* wrapped with cotton, silk, wool, or man-made fibers; used for woven and knit fabrics in foundation garments, girdles, brassieres, swimsuits, and knit into the tops of socks. See *elastomeric,* above.

Lurex y. Trademark owned by Dow Chemical Co. for non-tarnishing metallic ribbon yarn in a variety of forms for different purposes, e.g., laminated yarn of aluminum foil sandwiched between two layers of polyester film.

Lycra y. Trademark owned by DuPont for filament *spandex* yarn, *q.v.,* in variety of types, both covered and bare, used for *foundations, girdles, brassieres,* and *swimsuits.*

metallic y. 1. Yarn formed by sandwiching aluminum foil between layers of acetate or polyester film or coating the film with metal particles. 2. Core yarn made by twisting thin metal foil around cotton, silk, linen, or rayon yarn.

monofilament y. Man-made yarn produced by extruding a mixture through a spineret with one hole into a single strand which can imitate straw, hair, horsehair, etc. For strength, diameter must be larger than *multi-filament yarns, q.v.*

multifilament y. Term used for rayon and continuous man-made yarns composed of many fine strands twisted together.

nub yarn Yarn made with lumps, knots, or flecks of fibers at intervals, sometimes of different colors giving mottled effect to the finished fabric. Also called *knop yarn*, *knickerbocker yarn*, and *nubby yarn*.

pigmented y. Rayon or other man-made yarns to which pigment (such as white titanium dioxide or a color) has been added to the spinning solution to produce a dull filament.

plated y. Yarn made of one fiber covered or wound with another fiber. Also see *core yarn*.

ply y. Textile-industry term referring by number to the individual yarns twisted together to form heavier yarn or *cord yarn, q.v.,* e.g., two-ply, three-ply.

ratine y. A curly knotty plied yarn made with one heavy and one or more fine single yarns twisted together under uneven tension; the heavy yarn is fed more freely, producing loops or nubs.

slub y. Yarns made with thick-and-thin texture, *e.g.,* as those used in *shantung* fabric, *q.v.* Also called *clouded yarn* or *flake yarn*.

solution-dyed y. A term used to describe a continuous filament yarn of man-made fiber of various types in which the coloring matter is introduced into the spinning solution before its extrusion through spinnerets and spinning of fibers into yarn. The coloring material is a pigment rather than a true dyestuff. See *pigmented yarn*, above.

stock-dyed y. Fibers, especially wool, dyed prior to spinning. After being dyed, the fiber is blended and made into yarn by the usual methods. See *gray flannel.*

stretch y. See *crimp-set* and *elastomeric*.

textured y. 1. Man-made continuous-filament yarns permanently heat-set in crimped manner or otherwise modified to give more elasticity, used to make *stretch fabrics, q.v.* 2. Man-made filament yarns processed to change their appearance; e.g., abraded.

torque y. Textured, curled synthetic stretch yarn, made by giving a *twist*—or torque—in S or Z direction, *q.q.v.*

tussah y. Coarse irregular natural-brown *silk yarn* spun from uncultivated silk-worm filaments used to make *pongee* and *shantung, q.q.v.,* under fabrics. Also spelled *tussore, tasar, tusser,* etc. *Der.* Hindu *tasar,* shuttle.

yarn number See *count of yarn.*

yarn-dyed Describing fabric that is woven or knitted from yarns already dyed rather than geige goods dyed after weaving; e.g., checked *gingham,* striped *chambray,* any *tartan, q.q.v.*

yashmak (yahsh-mahk) Turkish face *veil* worn outdoors by Moslem women, placed below eyes and hanging to chest. Also spelled *yasmak*.

yelek Type of long *coat* worn by Turkish women at home with the *salwar* (full trousers), *q.v.,* and over the *berundjuk* (a silk chemise); made with buttons to waist, long sleeves opened at wrist, and train in back that is slashed to waist; sometimes second *yelek* of more elaborate fabric, decorated with gold embroidery and pearls, is added for full dress.

yellow diamond See *diamonds.*

yemeni Head scarf painted with bright flowers and trimmed with fringe, worn by Jewish women in Turkey in latter part of 19th century.

yeoman hat Woman's fabric hat with puffed crown gathered into wide band, sometimes with upturned brim; worn with *walking dress* in early 19th century.

yeri Collar attached to the under-kimono, worn by Japanese men and women, shaped to accentuate V-neckline of kimono and pulled over top of outer kimono. See *shitagi.*

yoke Portion of garment across shoulders in front or back, usually a separate piece seamed to body, sometimes lined; in sweaters, yoke is knit in one with body, but may be of different stitch or color or patterned.

yoke blouse Woman's waist or blouse with square yoke in front and back outlined with a ruffle, fullness below yoke, elastic at waist and a ruffle below waist or a waistband; worn in 1890's. Also called a *yoke waist* or *shirtwaist.*

York-tan gloves Gloves of soft fawn-colored leather; worn mainly by women from 1780 to 1820's.

York wrapper Back-buttoned, high-necked woman's morning dress made of muslin trimmed with alternate diamond-shaped pieces of needle work in front; worn in early 19th century.

Youghal lace See *laces.*

young teens Size range between *girls* and *juniors, q.q.v.,* sizes 5/6 to 15/16; also called *young juniors.*

Yugoslavian embroidery See *embroideries.*

yumoji (u-mow-gee) Undergarment of soft cotton, like short *petticoat* in rectangular shape, draped around hips by Japanese women.

Z

zahones Spanish *chaps, q.v.,* worn for riding.

zarape, zerape Variants of *serape, q.v.*

zebra See *furs.*

zebra print See *stenciling.*

zendado Scarf, usually of black fabric, covering head and falling to waist in front where it is tied; fashionable in France and Venice in second half of 18th century.

Zepel Trademark of DuPont for durable, water- and stain-repellent fabric finish.

zephyr 1. Term used for lightweight clothing, *e.g.,* a shawl. 2. Belgian thin dress fabric, see *gingham* under *fabrics.* 3. Soft *woolen* or *worsted* yarn used mainly for crocheting and knitting.

zephyr flannel Light silk-wool flannel. See *fabrics.*

Zhivago Clothes inspired by those worn in the movie *Doctor Zhivago,* made in 1965, from the novel by Boris Pasternak; Russian styles of early 20th century adapted for coats and blouses in late 1960's. See *blouses, coats, collars, shirts.*

zibeline Fleecy wool. See *fabrics.*

zimarra 1. Italian robe or cloak. 2. See *simar.*

zigzag stitch See *Bargello* under *stitches.*

zip Short for *zipper, q.v.*

zip-in or **zip-out lining** Complete removable lining inserted into the coat by means of a *zipper, q.v.,* around the coat facing that starts at the hem, runs up side, across back neckline, and down the other side; making a dual-purpose coat. Also called a *shell.*

zip-off coat See *coats.*

zipper Name coined and patented by B. F. Goodrich Co. in 1923 for fastening device consisting of parallel rows of metal or nylon teeth on adjacent edges of an opening, interlocked by sliding tab; teeth may be covered by fabric tape and almost *invisible* or extra wide, called *industrial zipper,* and in various lengths to use on necklines, skirt plackets, jacket fronts, pockets, bags. (See *closings.*) Invented in early 1890's, sold by Talon Co. in 1917 for money belts and boots; used on men's trousers in 1930's and by designer Elsa Schiaparelli in Paris in 1933 for high fashions, and in use for all types of closures by 1960's. Generic name is *slide fastener,* but term *zipper* is in wide use.

zircon See *gems.*

zoot suit Man's extreme style of the 1940's, including high-waisted, wide-topped trousers, tightened at ankle; extra-long suit coat with wide shoulders and lapels; worn with wide-brimmed hat and extra-long key chain dangling from watch pocket, with keys placed in side pocket of pants.

zori See *sandals.*

Zouave (zoo-ahv) Term used to de-

scribe late 19th-century men's and women's costumes, derived from the short red embroidered vest worn by native Serbians, or the baggy trousers, bolero and shirt worn by members of a French infantry troop. 1. Man's *cloak* with quilted silk lining, velvet collar and cuffs; worn for riding, walking or the opera in last half of 19th century. 2. Man's peg-top *trousers*. 3. Woman's *bolero jacket* with three-quarter sleeves, fastened at neck, curved away to sides, decorated with military braid, worn with full skirt caught in at hem to give bloused effect; worn in latter half of 19th century. 4. Woman's collarless back-buttoned *shirt* with long full puffed sleeves, decorated down front with panel of sheer gathered fabric crossed by bands of lace, and trimmed with lace at cuffs and neck; worn under Zouave jacket in 1860's. 5. Woman's collarless *vest* coming down front, with long full sleeves finished with turned-back cuffs and embroidered down front and on cuffs to match Zouave jacket; worn in 1860's.

Z-twist Yarns twisted during manufacture so that the spirals slope in the direction of the center of a letter Z: from lower left to upper right. See S-*twist*.

zucchetto Ecclesiastical skullcap worn by Roman Catholic hierarchy: white for the Pope, red for a Cardinal, purple for a Bishop.

Zuckerman, Ben See *designers appendix, United States*.

zukin *Headscarf* consisting of square of challis worn by Japanese women wrapped around head when out of doors.

FASHION DESIGNERS
Introduction

Space does not allow the inclusion in this section of all the designers known and admired. Some who are listed were or are so successful that their names are literally household words. Others are less famed, but they have met these criteria: (1) Qualities of good taste and fine workmanship. (2) Originality of technique in construction, in use of color and fabrics. (3) A concept of fashion that accurately reflects the mood of his or her era. (4) A recognizable "look" identified with the designer's name. (5) One or more contributions of originality important enough to influence future designers and to be remembered in the history of fashion. (6) Success proven through five or more years of continuous evaluation.

ERMINA STIMSON GOBLE

About the Photographs

Supplementing the printed material about the world's great fashion designers are picture sections which require some explanation.

At the rear of each of the four major national groupings—England, France, Italy and the United States—we are running portraits of some of the outstanding designers, followed by photographs of representative styles by the designers included in this Appendix.

By no means is the photographic coverage definitive. In the style sections we have been selective in attempting to show the widest variety of fashion. Virtually all the styles shown were introduced in the 1970's or late 1960's.

In selecting portraits of the designers, we have attempted to include as many of the most famous as possible, providing suitable material was available.

In each of the designer and style sections, we have arranged photographs alphabetically.

The absence of any particular designer or style should not be considered as an editorial judgment in any way. Our editors worked with the best materials available.

E. B. Gold, Mgr.
FAIRCHILD BOOKS

ENGLAND

Amies, Hardy (1909–)

One of most important names in British couture for women in the 1940's and 1950's and top men's-wear designer in 1960's and 1970's. One of original members of the Incorporated Society of London Fashion Designers, 1942. Worked at Lachasse, q.v., 1934–41; for house of Worth during war years. Opened own house in Savile Row in 1948; specialized in tailored suits, coats, cocktail and evening dresses. Remembered for wardrobe made for Queen Elizabeth's Australian and New Zealand tour. Started men's designing in 1959; became leading consultant on ties, socks, scarves, shirts, handkerchiefs, etc. Considered forward-thinking in his breezy, contemporary clothes, pants-suits for women; wide yachting pants; casual classics. Big reputation in men's wear in U.S. helped by wide publicity of talk-show host David Frost's T.V. wardrobe in early '70's. Operates a women's couture and ready-to-wear business called Hardy Amies Ltd., acquired by Debenhams, a multiple retail chain in London, July, 1973.

Bates, John

Young designer, part of the "swinging London" scene in mid-'60s, designed for Jean Varon Ltd. in 1964. Remembered for white counterpane-lace dresses, roses appliquéd on white stockings and dresses, black and white Op Art prints, wardrobe for actress Diana Riggs in *The Avengers* on television.

Bellville, Belinda (1933–)

Young socialite designer of the '60's, specializing in wedding dresses for the aristocratic, diplomatic, theatrical, and social worlds. Started in 1955 in Knightsbridge; co-designer, husband, David Sassoon. Noted for romantic Victorian or Edwardian feeling. Especially popular with debutantes for party dresses from less expensive "Miss Bellville" collection in 1969.

Byrne, Kiki (1937–)

One of the originators of the Chelsea Look which made "swinging" London the leader in young fashion in the 1960's. Along with designer Mary Quant, she popularized off-beat, inexpensive dresses, pants tops, and accessories that put King's Road, Chelsea, on the map. Always ahead in her interpretation of the contemporary mood; first to exploit the mini, maxi, nostalgia for '30's and '40's. Designed children's clothes for New York department store Alexander's in '66; opened a boutique in New York discothèque "Salvation," in 1967.

Cavanagh, John

Irish; one of top British designers of the 1950's. Early training in Paris, first at Molyneux, then at Balmain, until 1951; opened own London house in 1952, Curzon St. Known for rounded-shoulder coats; "scarab" line in dresses; nipped-waist, full-skirt New Look; the sack dress a season before Paris promoted the chemise. In 1957, did wholesale line for Berg of Mayfair; 1965, hired Ronald Campbell as designer for boutique ready-to-wear.

Clark, Ossie (1942–)

Born Raymond Clark in Liverpool. Considered the *enfant terrible* of British fashion, starting at age 26 designing influential clothes for Quorum and for Radley in 1966. Always ahead with trends such as hot pants, maxi-coats, motorcycle jackets, see-through dresses, fringes, peplums, gypsy hems, etc. Began whole 1940's revival movement in 1968. Started Ossie Clark couture for Mendés, Paris. One of strongest creative forces in fashion, influencing *haute couture* in Paris and Italy by 1971. Married to textile designer Celia Birtwell.

Creed, Charles (1908–1966)

Fifth generation of the oldest name in British fashion. Ancestor opened men's tailoring shop in 1710; his descendant, Charles's grandfather, moved it to Paris in 1750, becoming a Francophile and establishing a reputation for finest tailored riding habits for women in Europe; clients included Rejané, Grand Duchess of Russia, Infanta of Spain, Empress Eugenie of France, England's Queen Victoria, notorious spy Mata Hari, and opera singer Mary Garden. Charles, born in Paris, studied in France and Switzerland, learned salesmanship in New York at Berg-

dorf Goodman. Had first showing in London in 1932; reopened after second World War; famous for elegant suits for town and evening as well as country. Married to Patricia Cunningham, fashion editor of British *Vogue;* published his autobiography, "Maid to Measure," in 1961. House ran from 1945 until his death in 1966.

Foale & Tuffin

Marian Foale and Sally Tuffin, team of young designers identified with mid-'60's "swinging London," making inexpensive, gay, off-beat clothes. Remembered for Rugby stripes, Pop Art prints, Oxford-bag trouser suits, bias-cut fluid dresses, mixed-up prints, quilting. In 1972, Sally Tuffin goes it alone, using circle cuts, clown look; maintains shop on Carnaby St. in London.

Hartnell, Norman (1902–)

Early experience designing for theatricals at Cambridge Unitersity; opened dress shop with sister in 1923, own house, 1930. Became largest couture house in London and famous as dressmaker to the British Court. One of original members of the Incorporated Society of London Fashion Designers, 1942. Known for Coronation gowns for Queen Elizabeth II in 1953, for which he received the Royal Victorian Order; lavishly embroidered ball gowns, fur-trimmed suits, city tweeds. Wrote and illustrated history of his career in *The Silver and the Gold* in 1955 and *Royal Courts of Fashion* in 1971. By 1970's was making collection in leather and expanding into furs and men's fashions.

Hulanicki, Barbara

Fashion artist turned designer; one of original group of young designers who created the Mod look in the early '60's, first selling dresses under $6 by mail order. Opened shop called Biba, in King's Road, London, in 1963 with partner-husband, Stephen Fitz-Simon; believes in the total look, coordinated color in clothes, cosmetics, hose. Trendsetter in the years of "Swinging London"; known for offbeat, muted shades of rose, mauve, brown, and orange, Art Déco prints, floppy hats, suede boots. Opened full-fledged department store with '20's-'30's flavor in Kensington High St. in 1969; special Biba boutique in Bergdorf Goodman's, N.Y., in 1971–73. In September 1973 opened new Biba department store in Kensington High St. London, old Derry and Toms 5-storey building, redecorated in Art Déco style and considered most theatrical and daring concept of department store planning in the world.

Lachasse

Made-up name for a house opened in London in 1929, specializing in city and country suits; a branch of Paulette couture. Frist designer, Digby Morton, 1929–1933; second designer, Hardy Amies, 1934–1941; third designer, Michael, 1941–1952; fourth designer Charles Owen in 1953, known as Owen of Lachasse.

Lucille (Lady Duff-Gordon; (–1937)

English; sister of novelist Elinor Glyn. First woman to enter couture; houses in Paris, London, New York, and Chicago. Contemporary of Poiret, Worth, and Doucet in the Edwardian—pre-World War I period. Famous for "boudoir lampshade" style of flowing pastel tea gowns, chiffon ballroom-dancing dresses laden with beads and lace, coat dresses and jacket costumes that faded from fashion after 1914. Employed Capt. Edward Molyneux in first job at age 17. Dressed dancers Irene Castle and Florence Walton and actresses; traveled with her celebrated mannequins, Hébé and Dolores, forerunners of type of glamorous models to be in every important couture house decades later. Died in 1937.

Michael

One of Britain's great designers of the 1950's–'60's, compared to Balenciaga for quality of tailoring. Designer at Lachasse, q.v., from 1941–1952. Opened own house on Carlos Place in 1953, specializing in spare, sophisticated suits, dresses with jackets, trouser suits; tied up with Canadian manufacturer in 1955. Closed couture operation in 1971, but continues in ready-to-wear and as fashion adviser to English department-store chain Marks & Spencer.

Morton, Digby (1906–)

First designer at Lachasse, q.v., 1929-33. Opened own couture house in 1933, specializing in tailored suits. One of the original members of the

Incorporated Society of London Fashion Designers in 1942. Known for design for W.V.S. (Women's Voluntary Service) uniform, Aran Island cable-knit sweaters and dresses, use of Donegal tweeds, pastel linen trench coats, ready-to-wear Lady Hathaway shirts. Closed couture house in 1957 and started ready-to-wear as "Couture Casuals by Digby Morton." Resigned 1969.

Muir, Jean

One of the new breed of anti-couture-establishment designers. Started as sketcher at Liberty's; designed six years at Jaeger's; designer for Jane and Jane, 1962–1966. Known for gentle, pretty clothes in soft printed chiffon, schoolgirl smock dresses, jersey tent or bloomer dresses, peasant dresses, shawls, wrapped judo coats. In 1967 opened Jean Muir Inc. in London and Jean Muir Shop in Henri Bendel in N.Y. In 1971, designed for Jaeger's New York shop.

Paterson, Ronald

Scotsman. Started in 1949; one of charter members of the Incorporated Society of London Fashion Designers. First made sweaters and designed fabrics. Highly successful in 1957 with his mohair coats and the curved sack dress in 1958. Closed couture business in 1967; but continued in ready-to-wear; expanded into men's wear, kept some private clients.

Porter, Thea (Dorothea Seal)

Offbeat London designer, typical of the late '60's and '70's, anti-couture in mood. Born in Damascus, lived in Beirut, Lebanon, and in Turkey 1950–1963, fascinated by Orientalia. Came to London in 1966 to open interior decorating shop in Soho, where her collection of embroidered caftans caught on. Became known for fantasy long clothes, Far Eastern, Japanese, Renaissance, Victorian Gothic, all timeless in unusual fabrics. In 1968, clothes sold at Vidal Sassoon's, London, and Henri Bendel, N.Y. By early '70's preferred the 1940's period, used drippy chiffon, mixing several prints in one costume. Opened New York boutique in 1971, closed in 1972. Appeals to wealthy private customers and actresses.

Quant, Mary (1934–)

Young designer credited with starting the whole Chelsea or Mod Look in the mid-'fifties, making London the most influential fashion center. At age 23, had two shops called Bazaar, selling her own idea of spirited, unconventional clothes; e.g., tight pants, shaggy sweaters, thick stockings, boyish knickerbockers. By 1967, started the miniskirt revolution, introduced denim, colored flannel, vinyl in "kooky" (her word) clothes, with 1920's flavor. Within ten years had made a cheaper "Ginger" line; joined huge U.S. department-store chain J. C. Penney Co.; received the O.B.E. on the Queen's Honor List; added furs, lingerie, and cosmetics; designed for New York dress house Puritan's Youthquake promotion in U.S. Always abreast of contemporary mood, likened to Chanel and Claire McCardell, she pioneered in body stockings, hot pants, night-time cosmetics, the layered principle of dressing, etc. Married to Alexander Plunkett-Greene, partner since the beginning. Son, Orlando, born 1971.

Rhodes, Zandra (1942–)

Young textile designer out of the Royal College of Art; producing her own designs by 1969. Considered an authentic young English eccentric, wearing fanciful face makeup, draperies with ragged ends flying, head swathed in scarves. Equally fanciful hand-screened prints on soft fabrics, Art Déco motifs, lipsticks, Teddy bears, zig-zags, big splashy patterns. By 1970, designing line of soft, butterfly dresses, slit-sided chiffons, edges cut by pinking shears, exclusive at Henri Bendel in N.Y. Also designed lingerie and wallpapers, and clothes for films in 1972. Her customers include Princess Anne (Mrs. Mark Philips), Mrs. David Bruce, Mrs. Alfred G. Vanderbilt, and Princess Lee Radziwill.

Stiebel, Victor (1907–)

One of leading London designers of the 1950's. South African born; came to London at age 17 and to Cambridge University; trained for three years starting in 1925. Opened house in 1932; interrupted by war, 1940. One of original members of the Incorporated Society of London Fashion Designers, started in 1942. In 1945, joined Jacqmar, called "Victor Stiebel of Jacqmar." Known as Princess Margaret's dressmaker; designed WREN's dress uniform; famous for "tulip" skirt, bouffant ball gowns, hour-glass dinner dresses, sculptured drapery.

Tinling, Teddy

Famous designer of women's tennis wear since 1927; Master of Ceremonies at tennis tournament at Wimbledon for twenty-two years until resignation in 1949 after scandal when he departed from classic plainness by putting lace on edge of woman champion Gussie Moran's panties. From then on has pioneered in custom designs for ten successive Wimbledon winners. Some innovations: A-line mini-dresses showing scalloped panties, Mao-collared tunics, jumpsuits, princess dresses with appliquéd embroidery, ruffled hems, hot pants, and pastel colors instead of traditional white. Also redesigned men's tennis shorts. Nicknamed "oldest living Mod."

FINLAND

Marimekko

Company founded in Helsinki, 1949, by Finnish textile designer, Armi Ratia. Name is combination of words: Mari (Mary—symbol of womanhood) and "mekko" (country woman's dress). Designer's theory is anti-fashion; simple, classic shapes in natural cottons, free of extraneous details. Characteristic: A-line, smock, or chemise shapes; floppy-brim hats or head scarves; clog shoes. Team of designers produce bold color prints in unusual two-toned combinations used for dress, also available for home decoration. Clothes first shown in conjunction with Scandinavian furniture at Design Research (D.R.), in Cambridge, Mass., where they became a status symbol at Radcliffe College from 1959 on. By early '70's, operated shop on E. 57th St. in N.Y., which is a laboratory of design for printed tablecloths, sheets, wrapping paper, plastic dishes, inflatable toys, etc.

FRANCE

Agnès (*ah*-nyess)

One of top Paris milliners of the '20's. Talented sculptress, friend of important artists of the time; prolific with avant garde ideas. Used fabrics designed by painters Léger, Mondrian, and Delaunay; abstract and zig-zag patterns in odd colors; one of first to do turbans inspired by French expedition to Africa ("La Croisiére Noir"). Used the new synthetic materials Cellophane and Vinylite in 1935.

Albouy

Important milliner of the 1940–50's. Inspired by current events or museum portraits, Louis XIV ballets, Persia and Far East, Napoleon; made wartime newsprint hats, clerical hats in Holy Year, 1950. Pleased private clients who appreciated the exotic and unconventional.

Alphonsine, Marie

Important milliner of the 1930's. Known for visor caps, side-tilted berets with cocardes, formal hats for coronation of Edward VIII in 1936.

Augustabernard (Augusta Bernard)

A Provençal who started as copyist, particularly of Chanel; opened own house in 1919. Great success in late 1920's and through 1930's, making custom clothes of unadorned simplicity for private clients and, in New York, custom departments of Henri Bendel and Bergdorf-Goodman. Specialties: slim, black, sleeveless crepe dresses with incrusted motifs matched to loose jackets; plain, pastel, bias crepe-satin evening gowns to set off jewels; shirring; cowl or scarf necklines; sunburst pleats for evening. Retired at peak of business in late 1930's.

Aujard, Christian (1942—)

Native of Brittany; early career in merchant seaman, then fisherman. Started in fashion about 1967 as a coat designer; expanded into soft dresses and sportswear; with wife, Michou, became one of most successful ready-to-wear firms, showing in both Paris and New York, young, inexpensive clothes, classic and sports-oriented.

Balenciaga, Cristobal (bal-lawn see *ah*-ga; (1895–1972)

Acknowledged one of three great fashion creators of the 20th century along with Vionnet and Chanel. Born in Guetaria, Spain, son of fishing-boat captain and a seamstress; after copying a Paris suit for rich marquesa at age 14, encouraged to leave home to study clothes design. Eventually supervised three of his own houses called "Eisa," in Madrid, San Sebastian, and Barcelona. Discouraged by Spanish civil war, he went to Paris. Opened own business on Ave. Georges V. in 1937 and was immediately successful. Continued until retirement in 1968, creating elegant clothes for cream of international society, royalty, and film stars. Considered a perfectionist in tailoring for the woman over forty; only couturier who could design, cut, sew, and fit a whole garment; revered as the "Master" by his staff and peers. Among his disciples were Givenchy, Courrêges, and Ungaro. With classic Spanish restraint, created many new silhouettes, always developed slowly from one season to the next, using somber browns and blacks, Goya and Velasquez colors in dramatic gowns. His innovations, particularly in the 1950's, still widely influential among designers. Partial list includes: revolutionary semi-fit jacket (1951); middy dress evolving into chemise (1955); cocoon coat; balloon skirt; short-front, long-back flamenco evening gown; bathrobe-wrap coat; pillbox hat, etc. A recluse; loathed publicity; refused commercial exploition except for his perfumes; collected antiques; refused to compromise when wave of "kooky" fashions started in 1960's. Came out of retirement to design wedding dress for Carmencita de Martinez Bordiu, married to Prince Alfonso de Borbon in 1972, two weeks before he, Balenciaga, died in Valencia at the age of 77.

Balmain, Pierre (bal-man, pee-air; 1914–)

Born in Aix-les-Bains; studied architecture at the Beaux Arts, designed at Molyneux 1934–1939. Wartime service. Assistant to Lucien Lelong, along with Christian Dior, 1940–1945. Opened own house 1945 in rue Francois I, which was immediate success. Known for, wearable, elegant clothes which change little from season to season; safe daytime classics for wealthy private clientele; extravagant evening gowns. Customers included Queen of Thailand, Empress of Japan, Barbara Hutton, Gertrude Stein, and Alice B. Toklas. One of most intelligent, astute businessmen among couturiers; designed men's wear, aimed at mass junior market in U.S.; blouses in Switzerland; sweaters in England; costumes for theater; movies, ballet; and famous perfume, "Jolie Madame." Owned villa on Elba, house in Marrakesh, apartment in Paris; loves luxury, travel; lectures on fashion and art.

Barthet, Jean (1920–)

One of the most influential, most copied milliners of the '50's and '60's. Came from the Pyrenees near Pau; dancing his avocation. First show in Paris in 1948. Youthful approach; inspired by current events. Designed Caribbean shapes, checked bandanna turbans; French Revolution bonnets; chef's hat in organdy; high crowned, wavy-brimmed town felts; chignon caps; check-wool visor caps. Customers included Princess Grace of Monoco, Sophia Loren, Brigitte Bardot, and Mme Hervé Alphand. In early 1970's, expanded into raincoats, shirt dresses, beach clothes, etc.

Beer

First couturier to have house on Place Vendome about 1905. Made fine lingerie as well as dresses; its label was a status symbol for many years.

Berge, Pierre

Business *alter ego* for Yves St. Laurent. In 1972, president Saint Laurent Inc., the American subsidiary, and president-director general of the French company. Partner with St. Laurent and Didier Grumbach in Saint Laurent-Rive Gauche ready-to-wear company.

Berthelot, Gaston (1929–)

Began as assistant to Christian Dior in 1950. Designed Miss Dior boutique clothes in Paris, 1960–1962. Replaced Guy Douvier at Dior-N.Y., February, 1963. Free-lanced from 1969–1971. Named artistic director for house of Chanel after Chanel's death in 1971. Continued the Chanel signature tweed suits, chiffon dresses, blouson jackets, pagoda-tiered skirts, and pants; same two-toned shoes and mixtures of jeweled necklaces. Left Chanel in 1973.

Bertin, Rose (ber-tan; 1744–1813)

Born Marie-Jeanne Laurent near Abbeville, France. Came to Paris at 16 to work in millinery shop, Pagalle. Sponsored by Princess de Conti; became confidante of Marie Antoinette and court milliner in 1772. Also made dresses and hats for many foreign courts and ambassadresses. Called "minister of Fashion," she was proud, arrogant, ambitious, and loyal to the Queen until her death. From her shop, "Au Grand Mogol," designed fantastic, humorous headdresses reflecting current events, on which fabulous sums were spent, one of the excesses leading to the French Revolution. First dressmaker to become celebrated and mentioned in contemporary memoirs and encyclopedias; her letters and account books preserved by couturier Jacques Doucet, *q.v.* Fled to England during Revolution; returned in 1800 and sold trinkets; died in poverty 1813.

Blanchot, Jane (blahn-show)

Veteran milliner of the '20's and '30's. A sculptress from the Auvergne, who catered to elegant, mature women. President in the '40's of the Chambre Syndicale de la Mode.

Bohan, Marc

Started career working successively with Molyneux, Piguet, and Madeleine de Rauch from 1945–53. Opened own business in 1953, but sold it in same year and worked with Jean Patou for short time. Free-lanced for Originala, N.Y., until August, '58. Joined house of Dior in '58, replacing Yves St. Laurent. Continues as chief designer with assistant, Philippe Guibourgé, designing the Miss Dior line. Noted for refined and romantic clothes, beautiful workmanship, suited to a wide range of types. His soft prints, details of ruffles, pleats, or embroidery, and flattering color sense make Dior clothes among most commercially successful of all couture.

Boussac, Marcel (boo-sak, mar-*sell*)

Called the Cotton King of France. Born in Chateauroux, son of cloth-factory owner whom he persuaded to add cheap, bright-color cotton prints to a drab line and inundated France, becoming millionaire at age 25. During first World War, organized government war production; produced airplane fabric and became even richer. After war, launched new fashion for surplus lightweight, tan airplane cloth for shirts, dresses, pajamas, etc. Bought more factories; owned successful racing stable. Backed Christian Dior in own house, 1946. By 1951 was estimated to be worth over $200,000,000.

Bruyère (Mme Marie-Louise)

Mme Bruyère worked for Jeanne Lanvin before opening own house in 1929. Became one of best sources for embroidered, peasant-style dresses, Chinese-inspired overblouses, practical trouser suits, and wool jumpsuits in earth colors. Also made hats and accessories. In the '50's, series of other designers kept the house on Place Vendôme going.

Cacherel, Jean (1932–)

Came to Paris from Nimes in 1957 as shirt manufacturer. By 1962, his body-tight flowered and striped cotton men's shirts had become the status symbol shirt for women. Since 1966, floral shirts, skirts, sweaters, socks, and soft crepe dresses are designed by sister-in-law, Corinne Grandval.

Callot Soeurs (kal-o sir)

One of great Paris dressmaking houses pre-World War I. Firm founded in 1895 by three sisters, daughters of antique dealer. Eldest and most talented, Mme Gerber, ran the business; was early influence on one of her modellistes, Madeleine

Vionnet, *q.v.* Firm reputedly financed by noted Spanish-American beauty, Mrs. Rita de Acosta Lydig, who was their best advertisement. Famous for delicate lace blouses; gold and silver lamé; Renaissance patterns; much chiffon, georgette, and organdy; rococo flower embroidery. Also had small establishment in New York. Closed November, 1953.

Cardin, Pierre (kar-danh, pee-air; 1922–)

Frenchman, born in Venice, grew up in St. Etienne. Studied architecture; designed costumes for Cocteau's movie *La Belle et la Bête;* Worked at Paquin, then at Schiaparelli and head of workroom at Dior in 1947. Considered one of most creative, intellectual avant-garde couturiers of the '50's and '60's. 1950, first showing in own house on Faubourg St. Honore, at age 25. House consisted of two shops, "Adam" and "Eve," for men and women; sold only ties, vests, and sweaters for men. Success began in 1957 with many innovations for women: coat with draped hemline and loose back panels; envelope, barrel, and bubble skirts; loose chemise; mini-dress; cartridge-pleated wool; scalloped edges; irregular hem; and first "nude" look in 1966. Called revolutionary for his metal body jewelry, unisex astronaut suits, helmets, bat-wing jumpsuits, and tunics over tights. Started men's-wear designing 1958 and now considered leader in field of couturiers designing for both sexes. First Paris couturier to sell his own ready-to-wear, designed by André Oliver, to department stores. In 1970, created new environment, "L'Espace Pierre Cardin" in old Theâtre des Ambassadeurs. Launched wig collection, fall 1972. Hopes to sell ready-to-wear in Russia.

Carven (Mme Carmen Mallet)

Daughter of Italian father and French mother; planned to study architecture and archaeology. Opened house in 1944 at Rond Point des Champs Elysée, backed by decorator husband. Specialized in dressing petite young women like herself in imaginative sports and beach clothes, emphasizing tiny waists and rounded hips. Got ideas from travels, e.g., samba dresses from Brazil, beach clothes in African cottons. Successful perfume, "Ma Griffe," packaged in her trademark colors, green and white stripes. Still designing in early '70's.

Castillo, Antonio Canovas del (kas-tee-yo)

Born in Spain. Studied architecture; aimed at diplomacy. Came to France during Spanish Civil War in 1936. Through friend, Missia Sert, wife of painter, José Maria Sert, entered couture by designing hats, dresses and jewelry. Worked for Chanel and then for Paquin during World War II. 1945–1950 with Elizabeth Arden in New York, where he was successful with private clientele; also designed for theater. 1950–1963, designer for Lanvin, Paris. Remembered for the Infanta silhouette; sack-chemise and big roomy coat with deep armholes in new, light, mohair fabric from Ascher. Continued theater designs, notably for Lynn Fontanne in the play *The Visit*. Also did ready-to-wear line. Left Lanvin to open own house in Paris, 1963. 1971, revived his couture collection in house called Canivet-Castillo.

Chanel, Gabrielle ("Coco"; 1883–1971)

Born in Auvergne region of France. Started with hat shop in 1913; opened own house on rue Cambon 1914; closed in 1940 for fifteen years; came back in 1954 to triumph again, hardly changing her original concept of simple wearability. One of three giants in 20th century fashion, along with Vionnet and Balenciaga. Called the *Grande Mademoiselle*. Dynamic non-conformist who interpreted the liberated woman's desires after World War I. Developed an empire consisting of couture house, textile and perfume laboratories, and costume-jewelry workshop, spanning years from early '20's to early '70's; success based on perfume Chanel No. 5, created in 1922. Early fame associated with casual clothes for working girl in plebeian fabrics, the *garçonne* or little-boy look, wool-jersey dresses with white collars and cuffs, pea jackets, bell-bottomed trousers, turtlenecks, bobbed hair, and sun tans. By the '60's, her trademarks were the Chanel suit—braid-trimmed, collarless jacket, patch-pockets, and knee-length skirt, in soft Scottish tweeds; multiple gold chain necklaces with fake jewels; chain-handled quilted handbags; beige and black sling-back pumps;

flat black hair bows and a gardenia. She loved to be copied; success was due as much to her personality as to skill and hard work. Personal life and love affairs were as colorful as her professional career; close friend of Duke of Westminster, Stravinsky, Picasso, Cocteau, Diaghilev, and Grand Duke Dimitri of Russia. Her life was basis of musical, *Coco,* starring Katharine Hepburn in 1969. Died in midst of preparing a collection, January, 1971. Business continues, designing directed first by Gaston Berthelot, then Ramon Esparza, and in 1974 carried on by veteran *directrices* of work-rooms, trained under Chanel.

Cheruit, Madame (share-oo-eet)

One of leading couture houses in early 20th century and one of first women leaders of *haute couture.* Took over house of Raudnitz (founded in 1873) in Place Vendôme. First to launch simple, almost severe models in contrast to fussy clothes of the time. Charming, vivacious, and her own best model; not a designer but a critical editor of her house's designs. Louise Boulanger, *q.v.,* designed for her and benefited from her exquisite taste; Paul Poiret, *q.v.,* sold her sketches at beginning of his career. Mme Cheruit retired in 1923.

Colombier, Janet

Milliner, Mme André Delannoy; opened 1942, Ave. Matignon. Trendsetter, 1940's. Known for small crescent shapes or calottes; flower-covered toques; open-back hats exposing curls; bandeaus held on by back straps; calots gripped to head by wires.

Courrèges, André (koor-ezh, awndray; 1923–)

Born in Basque country. Worked first for Jeanne Lafaurie, then with Balenciaga from 1952–1960. Own house opened 1961; collection shown on big healthy girls instead of emaciated models; impeccably tailored suits and roomy coats, classical, contemporary, balanced in architectural proportion similar to Balenciaga. Aimed to make functional clothes. Labeled "Couturier of the Space Age," the "Le Corbusier of Paris couture," "epitome of Tough Chic," anti-elegance. Remembered for all-white collections, above-knee dresses in crisp squared lines; suspender dresses in checked sequins or wide stripes; tunics over narrow pants with erotic seaming; flat, white baby boots; industrial zippers; slit-eyed tennis-ball sunglasses. Business sold to L'Oreal perfume company in 1965; retired for year, dressing only private clients. Returned in 1967 with more shockers: see-through dresses, cosmonaut suits, naked look in sheer fabrics and big oval cut-outs, appliquéd flowers on body and knee socks, knit cat suits. By 1972, designs less tough; used feminine ruffles, color pink, softer fabrics in evening gowns and loose pants. Operated boutiques, "Couture Futur" and "Hyperbole," and ready-to-wear in U.S. and other countries. Great showman, collections run like musical in fast movements.

Dressed eccentrically in white shirt, shorts, knee-socks, and baseball cap. Married to Coqueline, his model-assistant.

Crahay, Jules François

Belgian born. Started in 1951 at Jane Regny q.v., selling only. Chief designer at Nina Ricci q.v., 1954–1963. Went to Lanvin as head designer in 1963 where he remains. Known for young, uninhibited, civilized, soignee clothes. One of first to glamourize pants as evening wear in organdy or pleated silk; jeweled leather gauchos; Bermuda jumpsuits; updated leg-o'-mutton sleeves and fin de siécle evening gowns. In early '70's made ready-to-wear collection for Arkin's, N.Y.

de Rauche, Mme Madeleine (de-rok)

Renowned sportswoman of the 1920's; married to Count de Rauch, a Finn. Wanted proper sports clothes for herself and friends who played tennis, golf, skied and rode horses. In 1932, started business called "House of Friendship by Mme de Rauch," aided by two sports-minded sisters. Made beautiful wearable, functional clothes, adaptable to many types of women. Handled checks, plaids, and stripes precisely. House still open in early '70's.

Descat, Rose

One of the big names in French millinery in '20's and '30's; house active till early '50's. Made some of best felt cloches and brimmed hats with manipulated crowns in era when hats were as important as other clothes. Remembered for the Eu-génie and mannish fedora; silk turbans; baby sailors tilted forward with face veils; tiny pillboxes or Tyroleans feminized by feather quills and veiling. Died in 1954.

Dessés, Jean (des-say, zhon; 1904–1970)

Born in Alexandria, Egypt, of Greek ancestry. Studied law in Paris; aimed at diplomatic service but switched to fashion design in 1925, working for Jane, rue de la Paix, for 12 years. Opened own house in 1937 on Ave. Georges V. and in 1948 on Ave. Matignon in mansion of A. G. Eiffel, designer of the Eiffel tower. Designed directly on the dummy, draping fabric himself; inspired by ethnic garments seen on travels or in museums, especially from Greece or Egypt. Remembered for designing the stole in 1951; draped chiffon evening gowns in beautiful colors; treating fur like fabric; perfume, "Celui de." Admired American women; in 1950, designed lower-priced line for them, called "Jean Dessés Diffusion," the beginning of mass production in French couture. Gentle, refined man who loved luxury and Oriental objets d'art; customers included Princess Margaret, Duchess of Kent, and the Queen of Greece. Gave up couture in 1965 because of ill health. Returned to Athens and, in semi-retirement, had a boutique until his death in 1970.

Dior, Christian (dee-or, chris-ti-ann; 1905–1957)

Born in Granville, France (Normandy); son of rich industrialist.

Aimed at diplomatic career; operated art gallery 1930–1934; sketched hat designs for Agnès *q.v.*; designed for Piguet, *q.v.*, in 1938 and for Lucien Lelong, *q.v.*, in 1941. Backed by textile magnate Marcel Boussac, *q.v.*, opened own house on Ave. Montaigne, Feb. 1947; launched the revolutionary "New Look," an ultra-feminine silhouette: yards of material in almost ankle-length skirt, with tiny waist, snug bodice, rounded sloping shoulders, and padded hips. In next ten years, devised his own inner construction to shape a dress into the H, A, and Y lines, etc., each season a greater commercial success, his name standing for fashion to the masses. Sold 1½ times more clothes than all rest of couture together. In 1948–51, added perfumes, scarves, hosiery, furs, gloves and men's neckties and a young, less-expensive line, "Miss Dior"; became a vast international merchandising operation. Modest, retiring; liked gourmet food, canasta, late 19th-century art; believed in fortune-tellers. Died in 1957. House of Dior continued under designing leadership of his assistant, Yves St. Laurent, (1957–1960); since then with Marc Bohan, *q.q.v.*

Doeuillet, Georges (duh-ee-yeh)

Frenchman; started as silk merchant. Possessed combination of artistic, business, and social attributes; became business manager for Callot. Opened own house on Place Vendôme in 1900, year of great Exposition. First to make *robes-de-style,* later called cocktail dresses; specialized in all-over embroidered dresses in pastel crepes in Second Empire style. Still popular in 1920's. Inaugurated live mannequin parade at beginning of each season. In 1928 merged with Doucet, *q.v.*, to become Doeuillet-Doucet. Quality handmade goods still made up to late '50's.

Dorothée Bis

One of leading Paris trend-setting boutiques in '60's and '70's, run by designer-buyer, Jacqueline Jacobson and husband, Elie. Ten shops in Paris and boutique at Henri Bendel, N.Y., in 1972. Credited by some with starting hot-pants fad in 1969. Also remembered for long pants tucked into Tibetan boots; see-through knits; midi-coats over minis; skinny cardigans and scarves; knicker pants; sweetheart necklines; shrunken-crochet berets; dolman-sleeved Jacquard knits, etc. Trademark shop display: life-sized rag doll slumped in chair.

Doucet, Jacques (doo-seh, zhak)

One of the first couture houses in Paris in mid-19th century. Grandfather Doucet started in 1815 selling bonnets and fine laces; by 1844 had own building on rue de la Paix for gentlemen's haberdashery, laces, and a laundry for the frills of the dandies, aristocrats, and crowned heads. Grandson, Jacques, started his career as dress designer after the Franco-Prussian war (1870) in competition with Worth, *q.v.*; dressed demi-mondaines and actresses, notably the famous Réjane. Favored 18th-century styles and much lace. Apprenticed Madeleine Vionnet and

Paul Poiret. Flair for collecting 18th-century paintings and furniture; later one of first to collect paintings by Matisse and Picasso. In 1928, firm joined Doeuillet to become Doeuillet-Doucet.

Drécoll (dreh-caul)

One of most prestigious couture houses in Paris from 1900–1925. Actual designer was Austrian Mme de Wagner, who bought the name from Baron Christophe Drécoll, well-known Belgian dressmaker in Vienna. Designs were architectural, of elegant line, often black and white or two colors, reflecting the best of *La Belle Époque*. Drécoll sent a mannequin to the races in the first harem skirt in 1910. Son-in-law, M. Besançon de Wagner, took over business in 1925. Daughter, Maggy, formed her own couture house under name Maggy Rouff, *q.v.*

Esterel, Jacques (es-ter-el; 1918–1974)

Considered one of leading "*nouvelle vague*" (new wave) designers in late '50's and '60's. Major influence on teen-age design after creating Brigitte Bardot's red and white checked cotton wedding dress. Known for bouncy sexy dresses, snug bodices, full skirts, ruffles, sold in boutiques. In '70's, designed unisex clothes, furniture, and home accessories for boutique in Locust Valley, N.Y.

Fath, Jacques (fat, zhak; 1912–1954)

Enfant terrible of Paris couture in the 1940's. Great grandson of designer for Empress Eugénie, grand-son of a painter, son of Alsatian businessman; dabbled in theater and films. Opened his own house, 1937; kept open during war and for next 17 years was immensely successful, designing flattering, feminine, sexy clothes marked by showy elegance; had boutique for perfume, stockings, scarves, and millinary. Remembered for hour-glass shapes, swathed hips, plunging necklines, full-pleated skirts, wide cape collars and stockings with Chantilly-lace tops. Ran a close second to Dior in popularity in mid-'forties. Instinctive flair for publicity, sense of showmanship; loved pageantry and elaborate parties at his Corbeille chateau; married to actress, Genevieve Boucher de la Bruyere. Died of leukemia at age 42 in 1954. Business carried on by wife until 1957.

Feraud, Louis

One of the *nouvelle vague* (new wave) designers of the 1960's, antithesis of Balenciaga school. Native of Arles; had boutique in Cannes in late 1940's; opened in Paris 1958. Designed for young models and actresses—notably Brigitte Bardot. An athlete, designed active sportswear; promoted Rugby stripes, socks, helmets, knee-high boots. Married designer Mia Fonssagrives in 1967. Designed for 7th Ave.'s Andrew Arkin, N.Y., in 1970.

Giudicelli, Tan

Half Vietnamese, half Italian, trend-setting ready-to-wear designer of the '60's and early '70's. Trained at Dior, with Crahay at Ricci, and at Heim; made first success in St.-

Tropez at MicMac in 1968, after a period of free-lancing in Paris and for Youth Guild in N.Y. First to put women into maxi-coats in 1967. Known for sportive separates, ribbed jersey pants, polo shirts with epaulets. Opened boutique in Paris, 1970. Designed for Trell in Milan, 1972.

Givenchy, Hubert de (*zhee*-von-*she, u*-bare; 1927–)

Studied at École des Beaux Arts. At age 17, started designing at Fath, then at Piguet and Lelong; spent four years with Schiaparelli, designing separates, cardigan dresses, and blouses and became known for the "Bettina" blouse, a peasant shape in shirting material with wide open neck and full ruffled sleeves. Opened own house in 1952 at age 25, near Balenciaga whom he admired above all couturiers. Considered to have been influenced by Balenciaga's sober elegance and produced collections in same mood. Since death of Balenciaga, has taken on much of the Spaniard's reputation for super-refined couture. Shows ready-to-wear in his Nouvelle Boutique in many cities; does knitwear for Talbot (U.S.A.); launched perfumes in '60's and cosmetics for men, called "Givenchy Gentlemen," in 1972. Clientele includes many wealthy conservative women and his favorite movie star, Audrey Hepburn.

Goma, Michel (*go*-ma, mee-*shell;* 1931–)

Studied fine arts in Paris; worked for himself before becoming designer for Jeanne Lafaurie 1950–55. Bought out firm of Lafaurie (A.C.P.) 1958, renamed it Michel Goma and continued until 1963. Became designer for Jean Patou 1963–1973. Known for young, wearable clothes; sexy evening wear; and glamorous long slacks with halter tops.

Grés, Alix (gray, ah-*leex*)

One of the great original couturieres of the 20th century, on a par with Vionnet. Originally a sculptress, now dedicated to designing women's clothes. Served apprenticeship at Premet. Started in 1931–1932, making *toiles* under name of Alix Barton; in 1934, showed in house called Alix and, in 1942, used own name for present house of Grés. Closed by Germans in war; reopened in 1945. Noted for superb craftsmanship; moulded silhouette over uncorseted body; statuesque Greek-draped evening gowns in cobweb Alix jersey, named for her; bi-color pleated jersey gowns with criss-crossed string belts; cowled black jersey day dresses; asymmetric drapes, bias-cut caftans; loose top-coats with hoods and bat-wing sleeves; at-home and beach wear; perfume, "Cabochard." Shy, serious personality, approaching design as true artist; uninfluenced by others, difficult to copy. Has fanatical following of socialites and actresses in America and England as well as in France. In '70's, President of the Chambre Syndicale de la Couture Parisienne.

Griffe, Jacques (greef, zhak)

Born in Carcassone, son of dress-

563

maker. At age 16 worked with men's tailor in Carcassonne; then with couturier in Toulouse and finally with Madeleine Vionnet for seven years, where he learned to drape and cut on small wooden mannequin as she did, developing great sense of proportion and perfection of workmanship. Opened own house in 1939; interrupted by World War II, in which he was taken prisoner; reopened in 1942, making all types of clothes for smart private clients. Had boutique and ready-to-wear operation called "Jacque Griffe-Evolution." Considered the "spiritual son of Vionnet" who follows his career closely.

Guy, Maria

One of important milliners of the 1930's and '40's. Known for narrow, ripple-brimmed felts, worn slanted; gypsy bandanna, wrapped to side, one long hanging end; tricorns; folded-back brims, baring forehead in Bretons; Bengal Lancer turbans; collapsible-crown hats.

Hechter, Daniel (1938–)

One of leading ready-to-wear designers of 1960's–'70's. Designed for Pierre d'Alby 1958–62; opened own house 1962; aiming to dress the young girl in the street. Mass-produced separates, raincoats, sweaters, military maxi-coats for men, women, and children. Sold in 1000 stores all over world; many factories and seven boutiques in Paris. Made paper dresses for Scott Paper Co., U.S., in 1966; collection for Du Pont in 1970; opened own showroom on New York's 7th Ave. in

1972. Announced plan to quit business to write and produce movies, a longtime hobby.

Heim, Jacques (1899–1967)

Paris-born son of Isadore and Jeanne Heim who had founded a fur house in 1898. Jacques built house into a world-famous couture establishment, starting in 1923 and important for next 40 years. He reflected trends rather than creating them; was conservative editor of clothes. Well-known as favorite designer for Mme Charles de Gaulle and Queen Fabiola of Belgium; designer of the first bikini in 1945, which he named *Atome*. Also had success with youthful clothes in boutique, Heim Jeunes Filles. Worked with French underground during war in 1940's; president of the Chambre Syndicale de la Couture Parisienne 1958–1962. Died in 1967. Business continues under son Philippe Heim.

Hermès (air-mes)

Thierry Hermés, saddle- and harness-maker, opened shop in 1837 on Faubourg St. Honorè, adding sporting accessories, toilet articles, boots, scarves, and jewelry. Couture began in 1920 under Emile Hermés; mainly leather garments but also sweaters, shirts, capes, shoes, etc. Ready-to-wear called Hermés-Sport. Claims to have started boutique trend in 1918. Only store with whole floor as museum. Famous perfume: "Calêche." Present director-general, Jean-Louis Dumas, fifth generation descendent of founder. Opened a replica of shop at Bonwit Teller, New York, in 1973.

Jenny (Mme Jenny Sacerdote)

Educated to be professor of literature; switched to fashion; trained at Paquin. Opened own house 1911. Extremely successful with wearable, aristocratic clothes for private clients and theater personalities. Known for slim-skirted dresses with jabot collars, scarves, or shawls in tan and old rose. Popular with Americans in 1920's.

Kenzo (Kenzo Takada; 1945–)

Trend-setting star of French ready-to-wear in early 1970's. Came to Paris from Japan in 1965. Made twenty collections a year for a style bureau; designed for Madd boutique. Opened own boutique, Jap, in Passage Choiseul in 1970. By 1972 was hailed as trend-setter; noted for knit tank tops, wide-legged pants, sailor middies, smocks, blousons, fabrics like Oriental cottons and '30's crepes, anchor-motif sweaters, wide-top double sleeves, long lantern sleeves, '20's tennis looks with colored stripes on white. Designed patterns for Butterick Pattern Co. in U.S. Plans boutiques in U.S. Manager: Gilles Raysse.

Khanh, Emmanuelle (kahn, e-*man*-u-el; 1938–)

French, married to Nyuen Manh (Quasar) Khanh, Vietnamese engineer. Entered fashion world as mannequin for Givenchy. Began designing inexpensive ready-to-wear as rebellion against *haute couture;* sold in Paris and London boutiques. Attracted publicity in 1963; pioneer of the new wave of dress that swept the Paris streets as Mary Quant's

did in London. Typical: dog's-ear collars, droopy revers on long fitted jackets, loose cravat closings on coats and suits; dangling cuff-link fastenings; half-moon money-bag pockets; dresses with lanky '30's feeling. Labeled "antithesis of hard chic," "sloppy, casual," but reflecting a contemporary approach to individuality symptomatic of the '60's. Added men's fashions and designed for 7th Ave.'s Puritan Fashions in U.S., and, in early '70's, ski clothes, knits, and leather accessories.

Lagerfeld, Karl (1939–)

Came from Baden-Baden, Germany, in 1953. Based in Paris, designed ready-to-wear for Chloe; shoes for Jourdan, gloves for Guibert, etc. Known for love of Art Déco period, Op Art, '40's look, fabulous ultra-modern apartment. Believes in total look, elegant, sportive pants outfits, wrappy coats; long cardigans; Eskimo look, romantic big hats; halter evening dress. In 1972, still with Chloe, but also designing sweaters for Ballantyne in U.S. and clothes for Fendi in Florence.

Lanvin, Madame Jeanne (lahn-van, zhon; 1867–1946)

Born in Brittany, daughter of journalist, eldest of ten children, apprentice at 13; started as milliner in 1890; designed children's clothes for daughter and friends which led to Foubourg St. Honoré where she remained throughout a spectacularly successful period of nearly 50 years. Remembered for *robes de style* of 18th and 19th century flavor,

565

wedding gowns, fantasy evening gowns with metallic embroideries, tea gowns, dinner pajamas, dolman wraps and capes, Zouave bloomer skirt in 1936, and perfumes: "My Sin" and "Arpége." Her peak years were between two World Wars when she insisted on her brand of elegance, ignoring the simplicity of the 1920's Chanel school. Branch shops in French resorts added men's accessories, women's sport clothes, furs, children's wear, lingerie, and perfumes to a wide organization. Mme Lanvin represented France and the couture at numerous international expositions, such as the World's Fair in New York, 1939; received the Croix de la Légion d'Honneur. Died in 1946, age 79; but house continued under directorship of nephew, Jean Gaumont Lanvin; designing directed by daughter, Comtesse de Polignac, who hired Antonio del Castillo (1950–1962) and, since 1963, Jules Francois Crahay, q.q.v. who still designs for them. Today, house still run by members of the family and owned by Bernard Lanvin and wife, Maryll, serving such clients as the Rothschilds and Princess Grace of Monaco.

Larouche, Guy (1921–)

From cattle-farming family near La Rochelle. Dabbled in hair-styling and millinery; worked three years on New York's 7th Ave., eight years with Jean Dessés in Paris. First collection in fall of 1957, mostly coats and suits. At first followed Balenciaga line; later designed more in Fath mood, young and gay. Remembered for back cowl drapes; short puffed hems for evening; schoolgirl dresses; loose lines in soft coats. Creative but shrewd business man with following among actresses and socialities. Also designed for men and ready-to-wear for Maria Carine. By 1972 a big name in licenses: ready-to-wear and jersey knits (men and women), day and night lingerie, scarves, hats, bags, jewelry, shoes, belts, shirts, ties and perfume. In 1973, ready-to-wear collection designed by Guy Douvier.

Legroux, Germaine

House of Legroux Soeurs (Heloise & Germaine) began in Roubaix in 1913. Opened in Paris in 1917. Under Mme Germaine, became important milliner of '30's and '40's. Known for off-face sports hats, pork pies, padre hats, picture hats with wide brims trimmed with feathers or fur.

Lelong, Lucien (1889–1958)

One of great names in couture of the '20's and through the '40's; famed for elegant, feminine clothes of refined taste and lasting wearability. Couture house organized by his parents in 1886. Founded own business in 1919. Not a designer himself but an inspirer of a distinguished atelier of workers, including Christian Dior, Pierre Balmain, Hubert de Givenchy, and Jean Schlumberger. Launched Parfums Lucien Lelong in 1926; started "Editions" department of ready-to-wear, forerunner of boutiques, in 1934; President of the Chambre Syndicale de la Couture 1937–1947. Received Croix de Guerre in World War I; represented couture in World War II during German occupation, 1940–1945, frustrating plan to move couture to Berlin; responsible for revitalizing couture after war. Retired in 1947 because of ill health; died, May, 1958.

Lemmonier, Mme Jeanne

Popular milliner in the '20's and '30's, specializing in hats of fabric and felt worked in tucks, openwork rows, and fine gathers. Designed for such stage stars as Mistinguett.

Louiseboulanger

Combined her names, Louise Boulanger. Started at age 13 as workroom girl; period with Mme Cheruit. *q.v.* Established own house in 1923 on rue de Berri; flourished until early '30's. Never influenced by contemporary events or other designers; clothes were advanced in design, more super-chic than pretty. Known for beautiful colors in floral printed taffetas, bias-cut gowns, and evening gowns with billowing massed fullness.

Mad Carpentier (mad car-*pont*-e-ay)

Partnership of two women, Mad Maltezas, designer, and Suzy Carpentier, organizer and liaison with customers. Both having worked with Vionnet, carried on her tradition of excellence in own small establishment 1939; kept open during war, making best of poor materials and shortages; regained success after war.

Molyneux, Capt. Edward, (1894–1974)

Born in Ireland of Huguenot origin. Aristocrat, sportsman, officer in Duke of Wellington Regiment, art student. Started at age 17 as designer with Lucille (Lady Duff-Gordon), *q.v.*, working in London, Chicago, New York, until 1914. Captain in British Army during First World War, where he lost an eye. Opened own house in Paris in 1919, on rue Royale, next to Maxim's. Designed well-bred, elegant, fluid clothes for real ladies and stage stars — notably Gertrude Lawrence, Lynn Fontanne, Princess Marina, Duchess of Windsor, etc. Great success for next 30 years. Remembered for purity of line in printed silk suits with pleated skirts; timeless, softly tailored navy-blue suits, coats, capes; use of zippers to mould figure in 1937; handkerchief-point skirts; ostrich trim; bright Gauguin pink and *bois de rose* as accents with navy blue. Worked for national defense, established international canteen during World War II. Returned to Paris house in 1949, adding furs, lingerie, millinery, and perfumes. One of original members of the Incorporated Society of London Fashion Designers, 1942. Because of ill health, turned over house to Jacques Griffe in 1950; retired to Jamaica, W.I., to devote time to painting, his collection of Impressionist paintings, and travel. Persuaded to reopen in Paris, January, 1965, as Studio Molyneux, only for reproduction.

Oliver, André

Born in Toulouse; graduated from École des Beaux Arts in Paris. Joined Pierre Cardin in first men's-wear operation in 1955, selling shirts, ties and, ready-to-wear. By 1972, created clothes for both men and women in Paris boutique; responsible for Cardin U.S.A. women's collection; the official voice of Cardin in U.S.A. Collects antiques, paintings; vacations in the Camargue; sails in Mediterranean.

Orcel, Gilbert

From Burgundy; started as pianist, violinist; opened millinery house in 1938 at suggestion of wife. Specialty: finely draped hats, worked fabrics, tilted to side and curved to show forehead. Made hats for top couturiers and private clients.

O'Rossen

Half Irish, half French. Noted ladies' tailor in the 1920's. Famous for capes made for King Edward and Shah of Persia; tailored suits with velvet collars and riding habits for women.

Paquin (pak-ann)

House of Paquin founded in 1891 by Mme Paquin and banker husband on rue de la Paix. Name is synonymous with elegance in first decade of 20th century. First woman to achieve importance in *haute couture*. Specialties: fur-trimmed tailored suits, furs, and lingerie; noted for evening dresses in white, gold lamé, and pale green; blue serge suit trimmed with gold braid and buttons; fine workmanship and no two dresses alike. First to take mannequins to the opera or to the races, as many as ten in same costume. Customers included queens of Belgium, Portugal, and Spain; mistresses of the Prince of Wales

and the stars of *La Belle Epoque,* Liane de Pougy and La Belle Otero. President of the fashion section of the Paris Exposition, 1900; founded first foreign branch of a couture house, in London in 1912 and later in Madrid and in Buenos Aires. House closed in July, 1956.

Patou, Jean (pa-*too,* zhon; 1887–1936)

One of the great names in couture of 1920's, 1930's, who brought glamour and showmanship to fashion; more of a businessman than designer; specialized in lady-like country-club clothes, elegant and uncluttered. Showed first in 1914; interrupted by World War I in which he was Captain of Zouaves; reopened in 1919 in shop called "Parry" and after whole first collection was bought by an American, started new business as Jean Patou on rue St. Florentin, waging war against Chanel's low-waisted *garçonne* look. Remembered for sensation in 1929 when he lengthened skirts to the ankle, revived natural waistline; made long simple gown to go with important jewel; designed week-end wardrobes; imported six American mannequins to display his clothes better. Also one of first to have fabrics and colors produced especially for him; first to have gala champagne evening openings; cocktail bar in his shop; exquisite bottles for perfumes—"Amour-Amour" and "Joy." Personally dynamic, charming, fond of fancy-dress balls and devoted to American clientele. Died of stroke, age 49, in 1936. House remains open under Raymond Barbas with series of resident designers, including Marc Bohan in 1953 and Michel Goma 1963–1973.

Paulette (Mme Jacques de la Bruyere)

Opened house in 1939; during war created wool jersey turbans, ideal for bicycle era. Designed all hats for couturier Robert Piguet; worked with Christian Berard on theater costumes. Popular with private clients, many in South and North America. Known for small shapes, embroidered or ruched; flat berets; draped jerseys; peaked crowns; scarf hats; double hats. Salon at Saks Fifth Avenue specialty store in N.Y. in 1960. Made Mme Pompidou's hats for first U.S. visit of France's prime minister and his wife in 1970.

Pipart, Gérard (pee-par, zher-ar; 1933–)

One of youngest, brightest designers of the 1960's. At age 16, sold sketches to Balmain and Fath, and to Givenchy three years later; worked with Marc Bohan; in army two years. Early star of French ready-to-wear, working with Germaine et Jane, Chloe, and Jean Baillie Hemcey, gaining experience in youth-oriented fashion. In 1963, at age 30, joined Nina Ricci as chief designer, succeeding Jules François Crahay. Remembered for little-boy blazer suits; short-coats; swinging skirts; baby dresses; booted, hooded raincoats; wrapped blouses and skirts; beachwear and tunics. More sophisticated in the '70's: kimono coats, body dresses and sweaters, bareback halters, loose silk pants for evening, big clutch coats. House of Ricci shows ready-to-wear along with couture. Has boutique in Bonwit Teller, N.Y.

Piquet, Robert (pee-geh; 1901–1953)

Born in Yverdon, Switzerland, son of banker. Came to Paris at age 17 to study design with Redfern and Poiret from 1918–1928. Opened own house 1933. Known for refined simplicity of black and white dresses, afternoon clothes, tailored suits with vests, fur-trimmed coats, especially styled for petite women. Remembered as aristocratic, solitary man, super-sensitive, elegant, charming; loved painting, music; not physically strong so closed house in 1951. Great couturiers of the future worked for him: Givenchy at age 17 and Dior in 1937, who said Piguet taught him "the virtues of simplicity . . . how to suppress." Died in 1953.

Poiret, Paul (pwar-ay; 1880–1944)

Called King of Fashion from 1904–1924. Born in Paris, son of cloth merchant; began by dressing wooden doll; sold sketches to couturiers. First employed by Doucet in 1896, where he designed for actresses Réjane and Sarah Bernhardt; discovered passion for theatrical costuming. Short period at House of Worth. Opened own house 1904; became fashion tyrant over women, imposed his original ideas and strident colors; banned the corset; shackled legs with the harem and hobble skirts. Remembered for extreme Orientalism, turban with aigrette, minaret skirt, kimono-sleeved tunics, exotic foreign embroidery, barbaric jewels and eye make-up. Friend of ballet impresario

Diaghilev and important artists, Bakst, Raoul Dufy etc., who designed fabrics for him. First couturier to present perfume, called "Rosine." First to travel (1912) to foreign capitals with entourage of 12 live mannequins; designed new uniform for French soldier in 1914; founded crafts school called Martine. Spent fortunes on costume balls and decorations of his homes. After World War I refused to change his exotic image so faded from the fashion scene; his last display at the 1925 *Èxposition International des Arts Décoratifs et Industriels Modernes* in Paris. Died in Paris in 1944 after years of poverty and illness, leaving his mark on the taste of two decades.

Premet (*prem*-eh)

House of Premet started around 1911 with Mme Premet as designer; followed by Mme Lefranc; most successful under Mme Charlotte from 1918 on through the '20's. Her biggest commercial success in 1922 was simple black dress called "La Garçonne," which sold in the millions.

Rabanne, Paco (1934–)

Born in San Sebastian, Spain, son of Balenciaga's head dressmaker; studied architecture; moved into designing plastic accessories. Opened in Paris in 1966, age 32, causing a sensation with his metal-linked plastic-disc dresses, sun goggles and jewelry made of plastic in primary colors. Continued the linked-disc principle in fur-patched coats, leather-patch dresses, masses of buttons laced with wire, strips of aluminum. Also pioneered in fake-suede dresses in 1970; knit-and-fur coats; dresses of ribbons, feathers, or tassels linked for suppleness.

Reboux, Caroline (reh-boo; 1837–1927)

The most prestigious millinery house in Paris, both in *La Belle Époch* and later in the '20's and '30's. Founded by daughter of a journalist, who was discovered by same Princess Metternick who sponsored couturier Worth in 1865. Installed in rue de la Paix in 1870, creating tor leading actresses and society, but barring *cocottes*. After her death in 1927, house continued leadership under Mme Lucienne, making the head-fitting felt cloche the status symbol of fashion for many years. Noted for profile brims, dipping low on one side; forward-tilt tricorns; open-crown lamé turbans; flower bandeaus; shapes and colors inspired by paintings of Braque, Matisse, and Picasso, as late as 1950's.

Redfern, Charles Poynter

London house established in 1842 by Englishman John Redfern, dressmaker for Queen Victoria and the aristocracy, who sent his son, Charles Poynter Redfern, to Paris to represent firm in 1881. Opened house on rue de Rivoli, specializing in ladies' tailoring. Known for his sober, elegant dark-blue tailored suits. To satisfy his imagination, also designed elaborate theater costumes, notably for Mary Garden and Sarah Bernhardt.

Regny, Jane

Pioneer of couture sports clothes in the 1920's. Started in 1922 designing simple clothes for active or spectator sports, the kind of clothes suited to her own life and to that of socialite friends. Remembered for sweaters in geometric patterns, yachting suits with mess jackets and wide pleated pants, three-piece bathing ensembles, three- or four-color wool-jersey dresses with godet or pleated ease.

Ricci, Nina (ree-chee, neena; 1883–1970)

Born Marie Nielli in Turin, Italy; married to Louis Ricci, jeweler. Began by dressing dolls; at age 13 came to Paris to work as seamstress; by 1905 was designing own models on live mannequins. Opened her house, Nina Ricci, on rue des Capucines in 1932; specialized in dresses for mature, elegant women and trousseaus for young women, graceful with superb detailed workmanship, the antithesis of her contemporary Gabrielle Chanel. One of first to show lower-priced models in a boutique. Famous for her perfume, "L'Air du Temps," in a Lalique bottle. Since 1945, house has been managed by son, Robert Ricci, with various designers: Jules François Crahay (1954–1963) and, since then, Gérard Pipart. Died, 1970; age 87.

Rochas, Marcel (ro-shass, mar-*sell;* –1955)

Born in Paris. Opened couture house about 1930 on Ave. Matignon. Became popular after eight women appeared at same party wearing identical gowns of his design. Full of fantastic ideas: special bird- and flower-patterned fabric; combinations of as many as ten colors; lots of lace, ribbon, and tulle and a feminine, square-shouldered, hourglass silhouette several years ahead of the New Look. In 1948, invented new corset called *guépiere,* which cinched the natural waist. Had boutique for separates and accessories; designed for films; wrote *Twenty-five Years of Parisian Elegance 1925–1950.* Loved women, married three times, the last wife, Hélène Rochas. Packaged famous perfume, "Femme," in black lace. Died suddenly in 1955.

Roser, Maud (rose-eh mode)

Paris milliner, started 1926. Opened Maud et Nano in 1942. Known for: red-felt ear-hung beret, called "Danilo," shown with Dior's New Look in 1947; series of small hats called "Les Toits de Paris." Pioneered showing of hat collections before couture, claiming equal importance.

Rouff, Maggy (roof)

Daughter of Austrian, Besancon de Wagner, head of house of Drecoll. Planned to be surgeon but decided on couture in 1918, learning to cut and sew; considered herself an artist. Started own business in 1929 and for 25 years was among the leaders of Paris fashion, standing for refined, feminine elegance against Chanel's *garçonne* mode. Retired during World War II; house continued under M. Howald, with branch in London and ready-to-wear in Maggy Rouff-Extension. Died August, 1971.

Roy, Hippolyte (roy, ippo-leet; 1763–1829)

Napoleonic couturier in early 19th century, vain, garrulous, arrogant tailor, son of stagehand at Paris opera, encouraged by Rose Bertin q.v.. Switched to Republican side after French Revolution and designed red, white, and blue patriotic dress. Became dictator of fashion for Empress Josephine, Mme Tallien, Mme Récamier, Mme de Stael, and European royalty. Directed by Napoleon to design luxurious dress to encourage French industry. Created the modified classical lines to be known as Empire —e.g., slim high-waisted gowns in sheer fabrics, heavily embroidered borders, cashmere shawls, brocade and velvet court gowns. Peak of fame at Napoleon's coronation, staged by artist Jacques Louis David. Continued to work for Josephine's successor, his style unchanged through Directorate, Consulate, and Empire—although he never made two dresses alike.

Rykiel, Sonia

Important ready-to-wear designer of the late '60's and early '70's. Started making maternity clothes for herself; designed for husband's firm, Laura. Opened Sonia Rykiel Boutique in 1968, in Paris department store Galeries Lafayette. Known for tight, long sweaters; sheer gowns over body stockings, long, slit-sided day skirts, layered dresses and sweaters with thick, roll-back cuffs, high-rise wide pants. Her liberated, unconstructed clothes range from folkloric fantasy to basic classics. Plans to add perfume and household accessories to boutiques in U.S., Japan, and other countries.

St. Cyr, Claude (san-seer)

Milliner, opened in 1937. Excellent business woman who used designers to create her hats. Became one of top-rated houses in '40's and '50's; launched sports and tailored hats in "winter white." Asked to make hats for Queen Elizabeth II of England; had branch in couture house of Normal Hartnell in London.

Saint Laurent, Yves (sanh la-rahn, eve; 1939–)

Born in Oran, Algeria. Won prize for fashion sketch in design competition at Dior in 1953; worked there, 1953–1954. Inherited top designing post at Dior's death in 1957. Time out for army duty and illness, 1960–1962. Opened own house in 1962 at age 23. Since then has successfully interpreted the contemporary moods of fashion; considered the most influential modern designer for the sophisticated woman, 30 years old and under. Remembered for the trapeze line; pea jacket; blazers; chemises divided into Mondrian-blocks of bold color; sportive leather; city pants; military jackets; and the notorious nude look in see-through shirts and transparent dresses over nude body stockings in 1966. Also designed for theater and ballet especially for Zizi Jeanmaire. With partner, Pierre Berge, opened series of boutiques called Rive Gauche and created perfume "Y". By early '70's became almost anti-couture, believed in his lower-priced ready-to-wear and designed his couture mainly for private customers; now making soft, refined clothing with no theme, pleated shirtdresses, long-jacket suits, backless evening dresses, daytime pajamas.

Schiaparelli, Elsa (skap-a-*rell*-ee; 1890–1973)

Born in Rome, daughter of professor of Oriental Languages, niece of famous astronomer; has one daughter, Gogo, and grand-daughters, Marisa and Berynthia (Berry) Berenson (Mrs. Anthony Perkins). Became French citizen. One of most creative, unconventional couturieres of 1930's and '40's; an innovator whose clothes and accessories were startling conversation pieces, the epitome of hard chic. First designed dressmaker sweaters with designs knit in, e.g., white collar and bow-tie on black. By 1929, had own business, Pour le Sport, in rue de la Paix and first boutique at 4, Place Vendome in 1935. Spectacular success with avant-garde sweaters with tattoo or skeleton motifs; hot-pink color, "Shocking"; hour-glass-torso bottle of "Shocking" perfume; first evening dress with own jacket; guardsman's coat with square padded shoulders; trouser skirts for all occasions; use of zippers, jewelers' buttons, padlocks and dog-leash fastenings; doll hats, some shaped like lamb chops or pink-heeled shoes; printed newsprint and glass fabrics; flying and golf suits, etc. Traveled extensively in India, Portugal, North Africa, Peru, Tyrol, etc., using ideas from native costumes. Only couturiere to be in French Industries Fair in Russia.

Close friendship with artists Dalí, Cocteau, Van Dongen, Schlumberger, and Man Ray, all of whom contributed designs. Stopped designing in 1940 for duration of World War II. Reopened in 1945, returning to natural-shoulder line, stiff peplums, and timeless black dresses. Great flair for publicity; defied tradition, using aggressive colors and rough materials to shock. Her trademark of "ugly chic" was symptomatic of the snobbism of the prewar society. Published her autobiography, *Shocking Life* in 1954. Remained consultant for companies licensed to produce stockings, perfume, scarves etc. under her name after closing her business in February, 1954. In retirement lived in Mammamet, Tunisia and in Paris where she died in November, 1973.

Sherrer, Jean-Louis

Designer of soft, refined dresses; popular with wealthy private customers in the '60's. Began by designing for three years at Dior about 1959; three years with Louis Feraud; opened own house on Ave. Montaigne in 1962. Combines couture with ready-to-wear. Shows to private clients at Bergdorf-Goodman, N.Y. specialty shop.

Suzy

One of the most important milliners of the 1930's. Known for tiny forward-tilted "doll hats," miniature sailors, pillboxes; cone shapes with high quill, cocarde, or flower and veil; turbans; many fruit and flower trims. Came to Bergdorf-

Goodman specialty shop in New York after World War II, when hats were high fashion.

Svend

Popular milliner of the 1950's. Known for dinner half-hats in organza, ribbon, feathers, flowers; forward-draped fur berets. Associated with Jacques Heim in 1958.

Talbot, Suzanne

Established as couturiere in 1890's; became one of top Paris milliners in the 1920's and 1930's. Made small feminine shapes, caps, ribbon toques, worn to cover half of forehead. First to popularize the pompadour and off-the-face-hat.

Ungaro, Emmanuel (1933–)

Italian; in Paris called the "Young Terrorist." One of the ultra-modern designers. Interested in today and tomorrow, rather than the past. Worked with Balenciaga 1958–1963 and two seasons with Courrèges in 1964. His specialty, tailored coats and suits. Showed first collection in 1965, aimed at his own generation, similar to the "tough chic" of Courrèges. Remembered for short, straight, structured dresses in broad stripes or plaids; high-waisted coats; diagonal seaming; little-girl, A-line dresses; deeply cut-out armholes; shorts and blazers. Introduced above-knee socks; revived Mary Jane shoes; thigh-high boots; open lace nude dresses; low hipster pants; pinafores over tights and body jewelry. Ready-to-wear collection for specialty shop

Bonwit Teller, N.Y., widely copied in youth market. By early 1970's, showed softer lines and fabrics, more long pants and pastel leather coats; drawstring shirtdresses; elasticized shirring on jackets and coats.

Valois, Rose (Mme Fernand Cleuet)

Opened her own millinery business about 1927 after ten years training at Reboux. One of top six in 1920's and 1930's, catering to private clients for twenty-five years. Known for tailored felts, side-tilted berets, opulent dinner hats.

Venet, Philippe (ven-eh, feel-eep)

From Lyons, France. Started at age 14 learning tailoring. Worked two years (1951–1953) at Schiaparelli, where he met Givenchy; master tailor and cutter at Givenchy 1953–1962, where he cut clothes for Mrs. Loel Guinness among other famous elegants. First collection in own house, January, 1962. Known for immaculate, lean suits; rounded shoulders; round-back coats and curved seams; cardigan, caped, or back-wrapped coats in sportive mood; kimono and dolman sleeves. Wealthy customers included the Rothschilds; Jacqueline Onassis, Rose Kennedy, Doris Duke, etc. Also designed costumes for Rio de Janeiro Carnival in 1965; men's wear collection in 1970; and boutique in Bullock's Wilshire department store in California.

Vionnet, Madeleine (vee-o-neh; 1876–1975)

One of the three greatest creative fashion designers of the 20th century ranking with Chanel and Balenciaga in contributions of lasting influence. Called greatest technician of modern couture for her innovation of the bias cut and freeing of the body from corsetry and whalebone necklines. Born in Aubervilliers, France; began dressmaking at early age; trained in London and in Paris with Mme Gerber at Callot and later at Doucet. Opened own house 1912 at age 36. Closed during World War I; reopened 1918 and enormously successful for 20 years, finally closing before World War II in 1939. A Vionnet dress was noted for classical drapery, for wide-open necklines, easy over-the-head entrance, suppression of hooks and eyes, cowl or halter neck, handkerchief-point hem; faggoted seams; Art Déco embroideries; all difficult to copy. Personally draped and cut designs on small wooden mannequin; helpful to protegés Pierre Balmain, Jacques Griffe, Mad Maltezas and Suzy Carpentier, Marcelle Chaumont; made Chevalier of Légion d'honneur in 1929; hated the press and copyists. She died in March, 1975 in Paris.

Vuitton, Louis (*v*wee-ton, loo-ee)

Founder of firm producer of signature luggage with its yellow LV's and *fleuron* patterns on brown ground, first created for Empress Eugénie to transport her hoops and crinolines in mid-19th century. Today, family business is carried on by great, great grandson, Claude Vuitton, making everything from wallets to steamer trunks; still the number-one Status Symbol luggage and widely copied by other designers in the same coloring but different initials.

Worth, Charles Frederick (1826[5]–1895)

English, born in Bourne, Lincolnshire. Famous in 19th century as dressmaker for Empress Eugénie and the court of France's Second Empire. Considered to be founder of the industry of *haute couture*. Served apprenticeship in London drapery establishments. Came to Paris in 1845, age 20, to Maison Gagelin, dealers in fabrics, shawls, and mantles, soon showing unusual originality. In 1858, opened house on rue de la Paix, called Worth et Bobergh; closed during Franco-Prussian war, 1870–1871; opened as Maison Worth in 1874 with assistance of sons, Jean Phillipe and Gaston. For fifty years house was fashion leader without rivals, in the Second Empire and Edwardian eras, dressing ladies of the courts and society all over Europe and America in ceremonial opulence. Famous for the princess-cut dress, the collapsible steel framework for crinolines and later the elimination of crinolines (1867), the court mantle hung from the shoulders, gowns made of interchangeable parts, *i.e.,* various combinations of bodice, sleeve, and skirt with infinite variety of trimmings. Worth was the innovator in the presentation of gowns on live mannequins; first to sell models to be copied in America and England; was inspired by paintings of Van Dyck, Gainsborough, Velasquez, etc. Opened house in London and introduced Parfums Worth in 1900. Had great personal charm and tact; lived in the grand manner, surrounded by luxury. After death in 1895, house continued under sons and grandsons until sold in 1946. A London wholesale house now uses the name and Parfums Worth continues in Paris under great grandson, Roger Worth.

• **41** (left) Suit by Adele Simpson, American, 1949. See *suit, rolled collar, revers, ascot, brooch,* and *designers appendix, United States.* [Photograph by Coffin. Reprinted from Vogue Magazine. Copyright © 1949 by The Condé Nast Publications Inc.]

42

42 (above) Evening dress by Balenciaga, French, 1941. See *Chinese collar, train, bolero, ring,* and *designers appendix, France.* [Photograph by Rawlings. Reprinted from Vogue Magazine. Copyright © 1941, 1968 by The Condé Nast Publications Inc.]

43 (left) Sportswear, American, 1946. See *bangs, shirts, skirts, belts, ankle-strap shoes,* under *shoes, scarfs.* [Photograph by Kay Bell. Reprinted from Vogue Magazine. Copyright © 1946, 1973 by The Condé Nast Publications Inc.]

44

● **44** Sportswear, American, 1969. Over-the-knee boots by Cardin, see *designers appendix, France.* Also see *fall* under *hairpieces, turtleneck sweater, armlet, rib knit.* [Photograph by Penn. Reprinted from Vogue Magazine. Copyright © 1969 by The Condé Nast Publications Inc.]

45 (below) Short jumpsuit by André Courrêges, French, 1967. See *jumpsuit, organdy, appliqué, sequin,* and *designers appendix, France.* [Photograph by Penn. Reprinted from Vogue Magazine. Copyright © 1967 by The Condé Nast Publications Inc.]

45

46 (left) Evening dress by Mme Grés, French, 1963. See *one-shoulder dress, chiffon, jersey, topknot, hairpin,* and *designers appendix, France.* [Photograph by Penn. Reprinted from Vogue Magazine. Copyright © 1963 by The Condé Nast Publications Inc.]

47 (opposite, top left) Sweater by Irene Galitzine, Italian, 1973. See *pullover, metallic yarn,* and *designers appendix, Italy.* [Photograph by Pakchanian. Reprinted from Vogue Magazine. Copyright © 1973 by The Condé Nast Publications Inc.]

46

47

48

50

49

• **48** (top right) Coat from Dior, French, 1971. See *wrap coat, leather, fox* under *furs,* and *designers appendix, France.* [Photograph by David Bailey. Reprinted from Vogue Magazine. Copyright © 1971 by The Condé Nast Publications Inc.]

49 Dress by Oscar de la Renta, American, 1973. See *surplice neckline,* and *designers*

appendix, United States. [Photograph by Penn. Reprinted from Vogue Magazine. Copyright © 1973 by The Condé Nast Publications Inc.]

50 Bikini bathing suit and skirt by Emilio Pucci, Italian, 1965. See *swimsuits, wrap-around* under *skirts, designers appendix, Italy.* [Photograph by Henry Clarke. Reprinted from Vogue Magazine. Copyright © 1965 by The Condé Nast Publications Inc.]

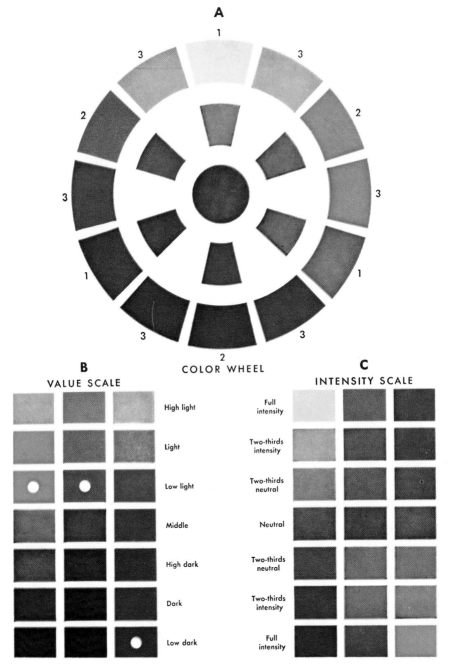

A

COLOR WHEEL

B

VALUE SCALE

			High light
			Light
			Low light
			Middle
			High dark
			Dark
			Low dark

C

INTENSITY SCALE

			Full intensity
			Two-thirds intensity
			Two-thirds neutral
			Neutral
			Two-thirds neutral
			Two-thirds intensity
			Full intensity

● A (top) The color wheel shows a sequence of hues in the following order, beginning with yellow at the top and proceeding clockwise: yellow, yellow-green, green, blue-green, blue, blue-violet, violet, red-violet, red, red-orange, orange, yellow-orange. The numeral 1 indicates primary hues; 2, secondary hues; and 3, tertiary hues. B (left) The value scale shows seven values each for three hues: green, orange, and violet. Those containing white disks are at normal value. C (right) The intensity scale shows two different degrees between full intensity and neutral for six hues. [Figs. A, B, and C adapted from *The Art of Enjoying Art* by A. Philip MacMahon as adapted from *Commercial Art* by C. E. Wallace; by permission of McGraw-Hill Book Company, Inc.]

IRELAND

Clodagh (Clodagh O'Kennedy)

One of top three Irish designers of the '60's and '70's, with boutique in Dublin and following in U.S. Known for heirloom clothes in vibrant Irish tweeds, linens, hand crochets; dramatic suits and coats; hand-painted velvet at-home gowns, maternity wear. Member of Montgomery Ward International Design Advisory Council in U.S.

Connolly, Sybil

Most prestigious Irish dress designer. In 1940, did custom dressmaking for Richard Alan in Dublin; discovered in early '50's by Carmel Snow of *Harper's Bazaar* magazine and showed in 1953 in U.S. where 80% of her clothes are sold. Known for evening gowns with horizontally mushroom-pleated handkerchief linen skirts and ruffled blouses, finely tucked linen shirts, Carrickmacross lace, iridescent Donegal tweeds, Aran Island white homespun, striped linen dish-toweling, Waterford quilting, crocheted-lace rosettes, fisherman's-knit caps, etc. In 1971,

made bedcovers for Parrish Woodworth in New York.

Davies, Donald

English shirtmaker, based in 18th century castle in Enniskerry, County Dublin. Started transforming shirts to dresses, in 1960; e.g., model called "Pygmalion" in featherweight Irish tweed in wide variety of delicate, off-beat colors; hand-blocked linens in plaids, checks, and solid colors. Opened shop on 57th St. in N.Y. in 1972, with basic shirtdresses, also long patchwork-tweed skirts, shirts, children's clothes, bed covers, etc.

Gilbert, Irene

One of the three great Irish dress designers. Apprenticed at age 17 to Dublin shop; studied in London in late '30's; opened small Dublin shop in 1950 selling mixture of fashions including ten of her own, later showed only her designs. Great success after first show in New York in 1954. Remembered for two and three-piece suits, coats and capes in Irish tweeds, linen; Carrickmacross lace; drawn thread-work on linen; mohair and crochet lace. Clients included top Irish society and British nobility.

ITALY

Antonelli, Maria

Pioneer of Italian high fashion, important for coats and suits from '30's through '60's; started as dressmaker in 1924. In 1933, operated Antonelli-Sport, assisted by daughter, Luciana; employed Guy Douvier and Andre Laug, future sucessful designers. Died in 1969; sport line continued by Luciana.

Brioni (Gaetano-Savini Brioni)

Internationally famous men's tailor, in Rome since 1959; noted for silk suits, black cashmere coats, pintucked batiste evening shirts, ancient Roman coins for buttons; designs complete outfits, including the umbrellas.

Capucci, Roberto

Called "boy wonder of Italian couture" in 1950's; worked anonymously for Emilio Schuberth, first showed independently in Rome in 1952 at age 21. Opened in Paris in 1962 and lost some prestige; reopened in Rome 1969. Known for masterly handling of drapery, imaginative cutting, no extra ornamentation, tapered-pants jump-suits, halter-neck hostess gowns, balloon drapes, huge bubble skirts, kimono and dolman sleeves, sculptured forms. Also designed children's wear, knits, furs, footwear and millinery. Sometimes compared to the American designer Charles James.

De Barentzen, Patrick (1933–)

rrom Denmark; French-trained. The "daring young man" of Italian couture of the '60's, comparable to Capucci in the '50's. First job at Jacques Fath in Paris, 1949–1953; opened own house in Rome in 1958. Considered spirited, young, with arrogant chic and a touch of whimsy. Remembered for enormous Infanta skirts, eye-high collars, deep cuffs, deep ruffled shawls, lace pantaloons peeping below hems, wide loose sleeves, round "turtle" capes, multilayers for beach, fake-animal-skin fabrics, hats designed by Gilles. Men's boutique added in 1969.

Fabiani, Alberto

Couture house started by parents in Rome in 1909, opened under his name about 1950. Considered one of top couturiers of the '50's, "the surgeon of suits and coats." Remembered for clean, conservative tailoring in all the popular themes, tapered oval chemise, draped waistless harem sheath, tent and poncho coats, rounded coats with wide cinched belts, tunic tops over pants-boots, and, in 1970, for furs. Married Simonetta Visconti in 1952, but kept fashion house separate except for brief trial of Simonetta-Fabiani combined house in Paris in early '60's.

Ferragamo, Salvatore

Italian shoemaker, emigrated to California in 1923, opening cobbler's shop in Hollywood. In 1936, opened business in Florence, Italy, and by 1960 had ten factories in Great Britain and Italy. Said to have originated the wedge heel, platform sole, and transparent Lucite heel. Died in 1960; business carried on by daughters, Fiamma and Giovanna.

Fontana, Sorelle (Fontana Sisters)

One of leading Italian couture houses in 1950's. Firm originated in Parma in 1907, then came to Rome, headed by mother, Amabile, assisted by daughters: Micol and Zoe as designers and Giovanna running boutique. Noted for evening gowns, delicate handwork, asymmetric lines, interesting necklines. Showed collection in U.S. in mid World War II. First in Italy to open doors to American students with awards, in 1957. Clients have included Margaret Truman Daniel and Ava Gardner in the movie *The Barefoot Contessa.*

Forquet, Federico

The "darling of Roman aristocracy" in the '60's. Worked five months at Balenciaga's in Paris; two seasons at Fabiani, five at Galitzine; started on own in 1961 on Via Condotti, Rome. Noted for coats and suits in blocks of bold color, horizontal seaming, bold stripes, imaginative sportswear, printed palazzo pants, long togas, short puffed pants, the stocking-shoe. Customers included Marella Agnelli and Jacqueline Onassis. Closed his high-fashion house in 1972 to concentrate on interior design.

Fortuny, Mariano (Mariano Fortuny y Madrazo; 1871–1949)

Famous for his long, slender mushroom-pleated silk teagowns, slipped over head, tied at waist by thin silk cord; the unique pleating technique was first shown in Paris in 1910 and never changed. Clothes considered a classic Status Symbol all through the '30's, now rare collector's items and worn by such fashion-conscious beauties as Gloria Vanderbilt Cooper. Fortuny printed fabrics, used in interior design, are manufactured in Venice.

Galitzine, Princess Irene

Russian, married to Signor Silvio Medici. Worked for Sorelle Fontana for three years; started own import business in Rome, 1948; first show of own designs, 1959. Remembered in the '60's for dinner or palazzo pajamas in silk, bead-fringed or with attached necklaces; at-home togas; evening suits; tunic-top dresses, lingerie; suits à la Balenciaga; bare-back or open-sided evening gowns; animal prints; decorative striped stockings. House declared bankrupt in 1968; continues in fashion, designing a cosmetic line, fur collection, table cloths, and sheets for various companies.

Gucci, Dr. Aldo (goo-chee; 1907–)

Family business in Florence since 1906, manufacturing and retailing luggage and leather accessories and, since 1969, collections of apparel for men and women. Most prestigious product, the walking-heeled loafer with metal harness-bit ornament across the vamp. The GG signature on bags and apparel as much of a Status Symbol as an LV (Vuitton) or Emilio (Pucci); sold in chain of Gucci shops in U.S. and Paris.

Lancetti, Pino

Young Roman designer, popular in the '60's, believing in stylization for day, madness for evening. First collection shown in 1961; previous training at De Luca (coats) and Carosa (day and evening.) Designed everything from shoes to hats and jewelry. Remembered for dinner-theater suits, military coats, tunics over pants. Still designing in early 1970's.

Marucelli, Germana (1906–)

Milan couturiere since 1935; considered avant-garde in '50's and '60's. Designed "corn-cob" line in '58, forerunner of the chemise; balloon chemise coats and chiffon evening dresses; rounded bias silk cape; unisex tunics and pants. Closed house in spring of 1973.

Micia

Knit firm run by Joseph Leombruno and Jack Bodi, American photographer and artist in Rome, started in 1962. Specialize in sophisticated knits: play clothes, ruffled sweaters, very cut-out swimsuits, bikinis. Customers have included Charlotte and Anne Ford, Sophia Loren.

Ognibene-Zendman

Firm composed of Peter Zendman, American and Sergio Ognibene, Italian (Zendman spent five years at Balenciaga); first show in Rome, January, 1965. Have specialized in youthful sports and casual wear; narrow-topped, flared coats in striped, dotted or plaid fabrics;

knit sweater-coats; long knit skirts; blazer suits and cardigan dinner jackets over pleated dresses.

Pucci, Emilio (Marchese Pucci di Barsento; poo-chee)

An aristocrat, living in Pucci Palace in Florence; sportsman, Olympic skier, Air Force pilot, member of Italian Parliament. Discovered as designer of own ski clothes by American photographer Toni Frissell, in 1947; designed ski wear for Lord & Taylor store in New York following year. Opened workshop in Florence in 1949, and by 1950 had couture house under name "Emilio," with boutiques in Capri, Rome, Elba, and Montecatini. Known for brilliant heraldic prints on sheer silk jersey, made into clinging chemises, at home robes, tights; signature scarves and dresses; resort shirts in designs from Sienese banners, Sicilian or African motifs; the "capsula," (jumpsuit tapered to cover feet with soft boots). The Pucci Look reigned as the Status Symbol throughout the '60's and was widely imitated in cheaper jerseys. In late '60's, designed uniforms for stewardesses of Braniff International airline; bath-towel ensembles; patterned pantyhose and rugs.

Schoen, Mila

One of important designers of the '60's and '70's, based in Milan but showing in Rome. Started in 1959 with the basic cut of Balenciaga and the adaptability of Dior. Known for use of reversible fabrics in suits and coats, long beaded evening dresses, bold horizontal stripes, sequin vests and shorts for evening, printed pantyhose. Customers have included Jacqueline Onassis, Princess Lee Radziwill, "Babe" Paley, and Jane Engelhard.

Schuberth, Emilio

Couturier of royal famlies, movie stars. Started designing in Rome in late '30's and extremely popular throughout '40's and '50's for his elaborate, inflated cocktail and evening dresses. Remembered for wedding dress for Maria Pia of Savoy, daughter of King Umberto II of Italy; dresses for Soraya, former Empress of Iran; personal tailor to film stars Gina Lollobrigida and Ava Gardner. Worked until his death in January, 1972.

Scott, Ken

American expatriate from Indiana. Fabric and dress designer who started in 1956 after traveling and painting in Guatemala. Designed fabrics for Falconetto specializing in massed flowers, vegetables; patterns reminiscent of the '30's or Art Nouveau. Remembered for clinging silk jerseys over body stockings, gypsy dresses, rajah tunics, bias skirts, Ban-lon prints in 1971, beachwear made of silk scarves. Operates boutique "Ken Scott" in Milan.

Simonetta (Countess Simonetta Visconti)

Born Donna Simonetta Colonna di Cesaro, married Alberto Fabiani in 1952, each having separate couture business. Began designing in mid-'40's and one of Rome's youngest couturieres with her house called Visconti, 1952. Remembered for ultra-feminine sports clothes and cocktail dresses; jumpsuit with long, tapered pants in '52; "collector's item" jackets over pants; bouffant ball gowns with strapless tops; full sweeping coats; oval cape-coats; harem-hem chemises. Moved to Paris in 1962, combining house with husband's briefly as Simonetta-Fabiani.

Tiziani (Evan Richards)

Ex-Texan cowboy, singer; opened house in Rome in 1963. Designed movie wardrobes for Gina Lollobrigida and Elizabeth Taylor movies. Known for all-over beaded dresses; lamé pants suits. Hired designers Gérard Penneraux and Guy Douvier in late '60's. Douvier left in 1973.

Valentino, Garavani (1932—)

Born near Milan; started at age 17 working for Guy Laroche and Jean Dessés in Paris, from 1950–1958. Opened own house, Valentino, in Rome, 1960. Called "Golden Boy" of Italian couture in '60's. Great success with wealthy international beauties including Jacqueline Onassis, Marella Agnelli, Gloria Guinness, Charlotte Ford, and Cristina Ford. Noted for refined simplicity, elegantly tailored coats and suits— usually marked with his signature V in seams as well as in gilt V's on belts, shoes, bags and V's woven in hosiery and silk pants; use of brown with off-white; patterned legs; chain prints; dark ruffled chiffons; blazers and wide-brimmed swagger hats; double sleeves and argyle sweaters. Also designs for men. Partner, Giancarlo Giametti; business bought by Kenton Corp. in 1969. In early '70's, designed bed linen, curtain and drapery fabrics, table and cookware, shown in boutique opened in Rome, 1972.

Veneziani, Jole

Ex-actress called the "designer's designer" important in the '40's and '50 s. Designed first dress collection to go with furs in 1947. Couture house and boutique in Milan, 1963. Since late '60's designs furs mainly.

JAPAN

Mori, Hanae

Leading fashion designer of Japan, working in Tokyo. Has exclusive shops in all principal Japanese cities; many chain outlets selling her designs. Creates collections sold exclusively at Bergdorf-Goodman in New York. Her special appeal is in unusually beautiful fabrics, mostly designed by herself, especially huge flowers, butterflies, and classic Japanese motifs on chiffon, sheer silk, or brocade. Styles are Western with Oriental details, usually for evening or at-home entertaining.

SPAIN

Berhanyer, Elio

Madrid couturier since 1960. A shepherd until age 17; studied architecture and painting; self-taught in fashion. Known for master tailoring; fond of seaming, spareness with single baroque touch; austere black dresses with typical lace ruffles and boleros. Designs beachwear for Condesa de Romanones and other private clients.

Mitzou

Micheline Stephen Isquierdo, Paris born. Opened in 1959 with salons in Madrid and Palma de Mallorca. With husband, Jose, specializes in suede and leather coats, dresses, boots, shoes. Counterpart, in youth and daring, of London's Mary Quant. 95% of customers are American. Dresses actresses Claudia Cardinale, Rita Hayworth.

Pertegaz, Manuel (pear-teh-gath)

Rated top Spanish couturier by mid-'60's. Opened in Madrid, 1940; now in Barcelona. Noted for pure cut, elegant details, starkness relieved by Goya-like color; like Balenciaga but younger, gayer. Also designs hats, scarves, shoes. Seldom leaves Spain.

Rodriguez, Pedro (roe-dree-geth)

Oldest couture house in Spain, ranked second to Balenciaga. Established in 1923 in Madrid, Barcelona, and San Sebastian. Typically Spanish in use of elaborate embroideries, dramatic silhouettes and fabrics. Catered to stage stars and such society as Marquesa de Villaverde, Duchess of Alba, and Condesa de Romanones.

UNITED STATES

Adolfo (1929–)

Adolfo Sardina, born in Cuba. Sent by aunt to study one year on staff of Balenciaga in Paris. Came to New York in 1948; designed millinery at Braagaard several years; joined milliner Emme, in 1953. Acknowledged as Adolfo of Emme in 1956. Started own millinery business in 1962, becoming favorite of young socialites. Known for the Panama planter's hat, banded in striped ribbon or jersey ('66); shaggy Cossack hat ('67); huge fur berets; packable jerseys; snoods; little-girl straw rollers; flower-braided pigtails. New career started in late '60's when he added imaginative separates, custom-created blouses, and long skirts for at-home entertaining; Pierrot ruffs at neck and wrists for Gloria Vanderbilt Cooper; soft caftans; Ultrasuede dresses and coats. Rivals Halston, another milliner-turned-couturier, in making the Status clothes of the 1970's.

Adrian, Gilbert (1903–1959)

Top Hollywood designer in '20's and '30's. Born Naugatuck, Conn.; career based in California. Designed for Metro-Goldwyn-Mayer Studios, 1923–1939, for stars Joan Crawford, Greta Garbo, Norma Shearer, Katharine Hepburn, Rosalind Russell, etc. Opened own business in Beverly Hills in 1942, for private clients. Noted for exaggeratedly wide shoulders on tailored suits; dolman sleeves; tapered waist; pin stripes or set-in patches of color; dramatic animal prints on sinuous black crêpe evening gowns; mixed gingham-check cottons; asymmetric lines; diagonal closings; huge ruffle-topped sleeves. Definitely opposed Dior's sloping shoulder of 1947. Influenced by wild animals, zoos, modern and Egyptian art. Retired to Brazil in 1952 with wife, movie star Janet Gaynor, devoting time to painting landscapes. Died in 1959.

Amey, Ronald (1932–)

Studied at Chouinard School, Los Angeles. In U.S. Air Force in World War II, where he met Joseph Burke; started couture house, Burke-Amey, in New York, 1959. Known for daring, unusual ideas in dresses, and ensembles in off-beat mixtures of rich fabrics and colors; anti-masculine suits; soft Racine jersey dresses; "chateau gowns" in unique fabrics; silk panel prints designed by him, executed by Bianchini. Favorite with wealthy women who appreciated something different from Paris copies. Formed Ronald Amey, Inc. in 1970.

Anthony, John (1938–)

Born New York, Gianantonio Iorio. Studied at N.Y. High School of Art & Design, Fashion Institute of Technology, and Academie de Alta Moda, Rome. Worked nine years at Devonbrook and with Adolph Zelinka. Started own business on New York's 7th Ave. in 1971, backed by Gunther Oppenheim and Sandy Smith of Modelia. Called a master tailor with impeccable taste and understated elegance. Designs for a young, sophisticated woman; likes natural fabrics, wool, crepe, chiffon and men's-wear fabrics; specially noted for cardigan sweaters with pants, mannish shirts and ties, pullovers with skirts, dramatic easy pants and gala dresses in soft satins with sequins and in sheer wool. Received Coty Award, *q.v.*, in 1972.

Beene, Geoffrey (1927–)

From Haynesville, Louisiana. One of New York's top-rated 7th Avenue designers of trend-setting women's clothes in the '60's and '70's; owner of business. Studied medicine five years; studied in Paris; worked for 7th Ave. firms for twelve years at Martini Designed Inc., Harmay, Teal-Traina, Abe Fetterman. Opened own house in 1963; received Coty Award in 1964. Known for casual, comfortable, feminine clothes in mood of Chanel, Cardin, and Norell —designers he admires; cotton suits, black bias dresses, baby chemises, gambler's stripes, djellabas, and gypsy looks. Made Lynda Bird Johnson Robb's wedding and bridesmaids' gowns in 1967; also dresses for Mrs. Richard Nixon. Started boutique, Beene Bag, in 1970; Beene Bazaar in 1969; men's wear and furs in 1970.

Blass, Bill (1922–)

Born in Fort Wayne, Indiana. In early '40's, came to New York to study at Parsons School of Design; sketched for sportswear firm David Crystal; enlisted in U.S. Army. After war, designed for Anna Miller & Co. In 1959 joined Maurice Rentner, Ltd. and in early '40's became sole owner of company, now called Bill Blass, Ltd. Rated as one of top quality designers and most versatile on New York's 7th Ave. Noted for women's classic sportswear in men's-wear fabrics, elegant mixture of patterns, knits, tweeds and shirtings, coordinated with sweaters, hats, shoes and hose for a total look; glamorous "drop dead" evening wear, laces, ruffles, feathers, completely feminine in contrast to mannish daytime look. Expanded into designs for furs, rainwear, watches, luggage, scarves, men's cosmetics, sheets and towels, and — most importantly — men's wear. Has reputation as leading American men's-wear designer, on a par with France's Pierre Cardin and England's Hardy Amies. Enjoys social life with his customers; a charming, cultured gentleman. Winner of Coty's Hall of Fame Award in 1970 and many other awards. Besides regular collections, designs active sportswear for women (Blassport), for men (Blasslook).

Brooks, Donald (1928–)

Born in New Haven, Conn. Studied Fine Arts at Syracuse University and Art History and Design at New York's Parsons School of Design where he has been critic-lecturer for some years. One of best-known names in American design. Noted for uncluttered day clothes in clear, unusual colors, carefully detailed; his own designed dramatic prints; romantic evening costumes; stage and screen costumes, notably for Diahann Carroll in the musical *No Strings;* Liza Minnelli in the movie *Flora the*

Red Menace; Julie Andrews in *Star* and *Darling Lili,* etc. New York 7th Ave. house, Donald Brooks, Inc., founded in 1965; boutique in 1969. Also designs furs, bathing suits, shoes, costume jewelry, wigs, and home furnishings. Recipient of many awards; customers include Mrs. Richard Nixon, Mrs. John Lindsay, Mrs. Aristotle Onassis, Mrs. Leonard Bernstein, and Mrs. Charles Robb.

Carnegie, Hattie (1886–1956)

Born in Vienna; worked in New York from 1909 to early 1950's. Designer of made-to-order and ready-to-wear for society and movie stars, about 20% copies or adaptations of Paris couture. Started in 1909 as Carnegie-Ladies Hatter; became Hattie Carnegie Inc. in 1918; and expanded into multi-million-dollar business with resort shops, wholesale business, factories, jewelry, and cosmetics. Tiny, feminine, shrewd, with great taste; influential through the '30's and '40's. Noted for "little Carnegie suit." nipped waist and rounded hips; embroidered, beaded evening suits; at-home pajamas; long wool dinner dresses and theater suits. Died in 1956. Name still significant in jewelry and cosmetics. Influential on many designers who worked for her; Norman Norell in '20's, Pauline Trigère in the '30's, and Claire McCardell in the '40's.

Cashin, Bonnie (1915–)

Californian, working in New York. Considered one of the most innovative of American designers, uninfluenced by Paris. Early career in '30's and '40's involved with designing for stage, and sixty motion pictures and collections for 7th Ave. sportswear houses, Adler & Adler and Philip Sills. Free lance after 1952. Specialized in comfortable country and travel clothes in wool jersey, knits, tweeds, canvas, and leather. Believed in functional layers of clothing, coordinated with her own designs of hoods, bags, boots, and belts. Influenced by travels to Japan, Portugal, India, Italy, etc. to collect ethnic fashions and fabrics of proven practicality. Among her specials, the toga cape, shell coat, sleeveless leather jerkin, the poncho, long fringed mohair plaid at-home skirt, kimono coat piped in leather, hooded jersey dress, double-pocket handbag, bag hat, and soft knee-high boots. Received Coty's Hall of Fame Award in 1972.

Cassini, Oleg (1913–)

Italian born; career in California designing for films in 1930's followed by years in own house on 7th Ave. in N.Y. Noted for sexy, fitted dresses and daring décolletages. Claims to have been first with the fitted sheath and knits in 1950. Best known as friend and official designer for Jacqueline Kennedy Onassis in her White House days, 1960-1963. Retired from couture in mid '60's, feeling unappreciated. Set up ready-to-wear business in Milan, Italy, in partnership with brother, Igor Cassini. Designs men's-wear collection, sold internationally.

Daché, Lilly

Leading milliner in U.S., from mid-

'30's to early '50's, expanding into custom dresses, cosmetics, and boutique accessories in '60's. Born in Beigles, France. Apprenticed at Reboux in Paris for four years. Came to New York in 1924; worked as milliner; sold hats at Macy's; opened small shop where she moulded hats on customers and established reputation. Opened own building on E. 56th St. in 1937, which became showrooms, work rooms, and home. By 1949, she was designing dresses to go with her hats, gloves, hosiery, lingerie, and lounge wear, wallets and jewelry; by 1954, added perfume and cosmetics. Remembered for draped turbans, brimmed hats molded to individual head, half-hats and war-workers' visor caps, colored snoods, romantic massed flower shapes, a wired strapless bra in '49, many fantasies for such movie stars as Marlene Dietrich and Rosalind Russell. Wrote two books on fashion and beauty, *Talking Through My Hats* and *Glamour Unlimited*. Boutique in Americana Hotel and cosmetics business continue into the '70's. Married to Jean Despres, vice president of Coty, Inc.

de la Renta, Oscar (1933–)

Born in Dominican Republic. Went to Spain to study painting. Discovered by Mrs. John Lodge, wife of American ambassador. Worked for Balenciaga's house "Eisa" in Madrid for twelve years, four years with Castillo at Lanvin, Paris; came to Elizabeth Arden, N.Y., in early '60's. Partner in Jane Derby in 1965, soon operating under his own name and becoming one of leading designers of luxury clothes and an important trend-setter. Noted ' for opulent fabrics in evening clothes like those of rich peasants or gypsies; long fur-edged Anna Karenina coats; see-through chiffons; jeweled shorts under mini-dresses; caftans in Klimt-inspired prints; bare-midriff dresses and sportive layers for day. Opened boutique in 1966 and "Something by Oscar de la Renta" in 1971. Married to Francoise de Langlade, former fashion editor of French Vogue, in 1967; leads international social life. Supports an orphanage in Dominican Republic in 1970's. Winner of a Coty award in 1967 and '68; elected to the Hall of Fame in 1973.

Di Sant' Angelo, Giorgio (1939–)

Born in Argentina; family home in France. Left at age 17 to go to Italy; won scholarship to study with Picasso; in U.S. created cartoons for Walt Disney; did industrial designs. Entered fashion field with his Lucite jewelry in 1964. Now, with partner, Michael Foley, operates widespread design service from offices on W. 56th St. in N.Y., making high quality women's ready-to-wear, called "Sant' Angelo 4U2"; accessories, hosiery, scarves, knitted and leather sportswear for various companies; fabrics for West German firm; boutiques in Japan. Noted for seasonal themes like the gypsy look, American Indian, Chinese; body stocking and body suit in brilliant bi- and tri-colors to match T-shirts and shorts; envelope clothes for today's lifestyles. Believes in diets, astrology, dramatic showing of collections in museum or theater background. Winner of the Coty Special Award in 1968 and a Coty Award in 1970.

Estevez, Luis (1930–)

Born in Havana, Cuba, of Spanish ancestry. Studied architecture. Worked in display department at Lord & Taylor, N.Y.; studied at Traphagen School; worked in Paris at Patou; joined Grenelle, Ltd. in N.Y. in 1955, becoming partner in Grenelle-Estevez. Won Coty Award in 1956. Known for restrained elegance in beautiful fabrics, reasonably priced for mass market; sexy, short cocktail and evening dresses with unusual cut-out necklines; much black and white; dramatic accessories. Designing based in Los Angeles. Leads very social life there and in Acapulco, Mexico. Designs special lines of furs, swimwear, dresses, and men's wear for various firms on West and East coasts.

Fogarty, Ann (Mrs. Tom Fogarty; 1919–)

Designer of junior-size dresses, outstanding since early 1950's. Remembered for "paper-doll" silhouette of 1951, a revival of crinoline petticoats under full-skirted, tiny-waisted shirtwaist dresses; the "camise," a chemise, gathered from a high yoke, 1958; lounging coveralls; and slim Empire dress with tiny puffed sleeves. In early 1970's, showed peasant look with ruffled shirts and long skirts with ruffled hems; hot pants under long quilted skirt.

Galanos, James (1925–)

Born in Philadelphia of Greek par-

ents. Studied fashion in New York; sold sketches; worked at Robert Piguet in Paris for three years, along with Marc Bohan; back to New York and finally to Los Angeles, where Jean Louis helped him start his own business in 1951. First show in New York in 1953 launched him on spectacular career; in five years received three Coty Awards and joined Hall of Fame. Considered greatest, most expensive, most independent designer in America, equal to great Paris couturiers. Known for luxurious day and evening ensembles in fabrics imported from Staron, Lesur and Bianchini; total look from hats, hairdos, shoes, makeup, hose designed by him; highest quality and timelessness at prices from $300 to $9000. Lives in California but shows only in New York; dresses many wealthy socialites and movie stars.

Gernreich, Rudi (roodee gernrick; 1922–)

Viennese, coming to work in California in 1938. Considered the most avant-garde, original designer in U.S. Specializes in dramatic sports clothes in striking color combinations and cut, bathing suits, underwear and hosiery—usually coordinated for total look. Remembered for maillot swimsuits with no bra and bare suits with deeply cut-out sides in the mid '50's; the topless swimsuit in 1964, along with see-through blouses; the No-Bra in skin color nylon net; knee-high leggings patterned to match tunic tops and tights in 1967; wrap-tied legs and dhoti dresses in 1968. After sabbatical year, 1969–1970, returned to designing, predicting future trend to bald heads, bare bosoms with pasties, and unisex caftans. Continues knitwear, hosiery, and scarves on free-lance basis.

Halston (Roy Halston Frowick; 1932–)

Born Des Moines, Iowa; studied at Chicago Art Institute; worked for Lilly Dache in N.Y.; and designed hats for Bergdorf Goodman, 1959-1968, where he made news with the pillbox hat for Jacqueline Kennedy at Pres. Kennedy's inaugural ceremony in 1961. Started own business on E. 68th St. in 1968 for private clients and entertainment world. His formula of casual throwaway chic, using superior fabrics for extremely simple classics made him most talked about designer in early '70's. Opened ready-to-wear firm, Halston Originals, in fall, 1972. Typical ideas: long cashmere dress with sweater tied over shoulders; long, slinky halter-neck jerseys; wraparound skirts and turtlenecks; evening caftans, lots of argyles, angora, and chiffon jersey; ivory jewelry. Customers include: Jacqueline Kennedy Onassis, Mrs. William Paley, Mrs. Vincent Astor, Baronne Guy de Rothschild, Liza Minelli, Lauren Bacall, and Catherine Deneuve. His business acquired by Norton Simon Inc., an American diversified company, in 1973, now called Halston Enterprises, Inc. Plans to be total designer, doing body-wear line, shoes, men's wear, and his own perfume.

James, Charles (1906–)

English born, from Chicago; had dressmaking salons in London and Paris in the '30's. Sponsored by Mary Lewis of Best and Co. in N.Y. in 1939. Operated own custom order business in '40's and '50's. Rated by his peers: "A genius . . . daring innovator in the shape of clothes . . . more of an architect or sculptor . . . independent, stormy, unpredictable, contentious." Acknowledged as an equal by top Paris couture in 1947. Remembered for new technique for dress patterns; new dress forms; elaborate, bouffant ball gowns in odd mixtures of colors and fabrics, notably for the exotic Millicent Rogers; bat-wing oval cape-coat; intricately cut dolman wraps and asymmetric shapes, many now in Brooklyn Museum or the Smithsonian Institution in Washington, D.C. Retired from couture design in 1958. After brief time of conducting seminars in costume design at Rhode Island School of Design and Pratt Institute in 1960 and a mass-produced line for E. J. Korvette in 1962, he now concentrates on painting and sculpture.

Mr. John (1906–)

Florence-born son of milliner; originally called John Pico John; later, John P. John. Partner in prestigious N.Y. firm of milliners, John-Frederics, Inc., from 1929–1948. Formed own firm, Mr. John, Inc. in 1948. Most successful in '40's and '50's in heyday of hats, putting on spectacular shows and developing his atmosphere in Napoleonic dress and décor. Remembered for forward-tilted doll hats, glorified Stetsons, scarf-attached hats, skull caps held by tight face veils, wig hats, huge flower or bushy fur toques. Added soft dresses, scarves, gloves, and finally coats and suits, in early '70's, to give total look.

Johnson, Betsey (1942–)

Graduate of Syracuse University; trained as dancer; started as Guest Editor for *Mademoiselle* magazine and illustrator. One of first American designers to head the Youthquake of anti-7th Ave. fashions in early '60's. At age 22, designed offbeat collections for all Paraphernalia shops; started, with partners, boutique, Betsey, Bunkie & Nini, in 1969. Known for basic, limp slipdress in clear vinyl with kit of paste-on stars, fishes, numbers, etc.; underwear dress; "noise" dress with loose grommets at hem; bell trousers; wrapped cowhide mini-skirt and thigh-high boots; loose smock over jeans; nightgown dress; quilted flannel coat; clunky shoes and thrift-shop accessories. Also designs shoes and clothes for I. Miller and for Alley Cat.

Kaplan, Jacques (1924–)

Chairman, designer, and chief personality at Georges Kaplan, fur house at 57th St. off 5th Ave New York. Third generation of family who founded fur business in Paris in 1889; moved to New York in 1942, becoming biggest volume fur business in country, owing to son Jacques's innovative ideas and flair for promotion. Known for pioneering in stenciled and colored furs; concept of "fun" furs in off-beat pelts, fur dresses, hoods, boots. Also designed classic furs. First to take stand against use of furs from endangered species. Company bought by Kenton Corp. in 1969, who wished to sell it in 1971; Jacques decided to close it and continue his interest in art.

Kleibacker, Charles

Born in Alabama; studied journalism at Notre Dame University; reporter and copywriter at Gimbel's department store in N.Y. under Bernice Fitz-Gibbon; three years on tour with singer Hildegarde; opened custom operation in New York briefly; three years with Antonio Castillo at Lanvin, Paris; one year in Rome; three years on N.Y.'s 7th Ave. with Nettie Rosenstein. Opened own business N.Y. in 1960, making custom designs for special clientele and stores. Known for handling of bias, exquisite workmanship in late-day dresses, simplicity and painstaking individuality of cut in black or neutral colors. Also acts as visiting designer-critic at Mt. Mary College in Milwaukee, Wisc.; lectures at St. Bernard College, Alabama; Virginia Commonwealth University, Richmond, Va.; Pratt Institute, N.Y. In 1971, started touring country to demonstrate use of DuPont's Qiana fabric to home-sewing seminars.

Klein, Anne (1923–1974)

New York-born designer, called the All American designer of classic sportswear for the woman 5' 4" and under. Designed for Jr. Sophisticates 1951–1964. Formed Anne Klein & Co. in 1968. Designed separates for Mallory Suedes, boots for Golo; belts for Calderon. Remembered in

1950's for nipped waist, full skirt; unbelted chemise; "little boy" look; use of white satin with gray flannel. In the '60's, classic blazers; shirt-dresses; long midis; leather gaucho pants; Western and American Indian accessories; Turkish rug coats; hot pants. In '70's more interested in non-gimmicky, inter-related wardrobe of classic jackets, twin sweaters, and pants for all occasions. Died 1974; firm continues.

Leser, Tina (1911–)

Born in Philadelphia, member of Wetherill family; traveled extensively in Far East and Europe as child; studied at School of Industrial Art and Academy of Fine Arts, Philadelphia, and at the Sorbonne, Paris. Lived in Hawaii 1936–1942, operating retail store, selling her own hand-blocked floral prints in play clothes. Came to New York in 1941 and showed her collection of Hawaiian-inspired fun clothes. Associated with Edwin H. Foreman, Inc. 1943–53; own business since then. Remembered for sarong play clothes; water-boy pants; painted and sequined cotton blouses; wrapped pareo skirt with bandeau top; costume jewelry in cork, coral, and shells, travel-inspired Mexican, Haitian, Japanese, Indian fabrics used in original trousers, easy cover-up tops, long at-home robes. Opened fabric factory in India 1965. Coty Award in 1944. President of Florida Gulf Coast Art Center, Clearwater, Fla., founded by her mother for good design in all fields. By 1970, concentrating on loungewear, caftans, and print beach ensembles.

Littell, Deanna (1930–)

Born Deanna Cohen, in New York: was graduated from Parsons School in 1960 with Norell Award. Worked at Evan-Picone and Mr. Mort; designed lingerie for Warner's. Exponent of the 1960's youth movement called Ye Ye in France, Mod in Britain. Had own collection of sports clothes at Henri Bendel's Studio in 1967. Known for jumpsuits and pants in fluorescent vinyl or knits; color-coordinated separates; long summer skirts and skaters's skirts; classics based on work clothes. Took year off from 7th Ave. to live in French village with husband and children, 1970–1. Backed by Marcel Boussac to make collections in France in 1971–2.

Louis, Jean (1907–)

Born Jean Louis Berthault in Paris Worked for Agnès, Drécoll; in New York for seven years at Hattie Carnegie, along with Claire McCardell and Norman Norell. Designer for Columbia Pictures in 1943 and stayed on in California to dress famous stars Ginger Rogers, Marilyn Monroe, Irene Dunne, Rita Hayworth, Marlene Dietrich, Loretta Young, etc. Nominated fourteen times for Academy Award. Known for pretty, flattering evening gowns; beaded chiffons and feather wraps for Dietrich's night club acts; wedding gown for Elizabeth Taylor's marriage to Eddie Fisher; furs, tunic suits, rainwear; costumes for 1972 movie of Lost Horizon. Went wholesale in 1961. Leads very social life with wife, former Maggy Fisher, on West Coast.

Mainbocher (man-bow-shay; Main Rousseau Bocher; 1891–)

Born in Chicago, Ill. Lived and worked in Paris 1917-1940. Aspired to be opera singer; editor of French *Vogue* for six years; had couture house on Ave. Georges V., 1930–1969. Opened N.Y. couture house 1940, one of few custom dressmaking establishments in U.S. Known for quiet good taste, simplicity, understatement at high prices. Clients included Mrs. Winston Guest, Mrs. Harrison Williams, Mrs. Wyatt Cooper, Duchess of Windsor, Katharine Cornell etc. Noted for Duchess of Windsor's wedding dress in 1936; WAVES' (Women in the Navy) uniform in 1942; Girl Scout uniform in 1948. Ideas widely copied: print-bordered and lined sweaters to match dresses; beaded evening sweaters; dirndl dresses with self-fabric incrustations, often in pastel check gingham; fur-lined coats; rain suits; tweed dinner suits with delicate blouses; embroidered-apron evening dresses; and always short white kid gloves, pearl chokers, plain pumps. Personally elegant, reclusive, exclusive, averse to publicity except on own terms; designer with most snob appeal for wealthy, conservatives. Closed business in June, 1971.

Maxwell, Vera (1904–)

One of small group of craftsmen-designers, truly original, independent of Paris, who flourished in '30's and '40's, with faithful followers up to present. Worked first with sportswear and coat houses, Adler & Adler and Max Milstein, before opening own business on 7th Ave. N.Y. Believed in classic approach to go-together separates in finest quality Scottish tweeds, wool jersey, raw silk, Indian embroideries, etc. Inspired by men's Harris-tweed jackets and gray flannel Oxford bags. Noteworthy innovations: weekend wardrobe, 1935; Einstein jacket, 1936; fencing suit, 1940; riding-habit suit; war-workers' clothes under L-85 rules; slit-side, braid-edged mandarin coat; wrap-tied blouse; three-piece vest suit; chesterfield coat with slacks; print dress matched to print-lined coat. In 1972, showed collection of week-enders and classics, knit coats over pants-dresses, sleeveless, slit-sided suede "paletot" coats. Likes ballet, opera, travel, admirer of Chanel; friend of and designer for Princess Grace of Monaco. Honored by retrospective show of designs at Smithsonian Institution in Washington, D.C. in 1970.

McCardell, Claire (1906–1958)

Studied at Parsons School in New York and in Paris. Worked at Hattie Carnegie and for nine years at Townley in N.Y. Considered top all-American designer of 1940's and 1950's, specializing in practical clothes for average working girl. Credited with originating the "American Look," *i.e.,* the separates concept inspired by travel needs, using sturdy cotton denims, ticking, gingham, and wool jersey. Gathered ideas from basic work clothes of farmers, railroad workers, soldiers and sportsmen, *e.g.,* hook-and-eye fasteners, Levi's top-stitching, rivets, side trouser pockets. Many firsts: the monastic dress with natural shoulders and tied waist; harem pajamas; the Popover, a surplice-wrapped housedress; kitchen dinner dress; bareback summer dress; long cotton Empire dress, tiny puffed sleeves; diaper-wrap one-piece swimsuit; shoulder bolero over halter dress; balloon bloomer playsuit; signature spaghetti belts; ballet slippers for street, etc. Received Coty's Hall of Fame Award. Died 1958 at age 52.

Norell, Norman (1900–1972)

Born Norman Levinson in Noblesville, Indiana, son of haberdashery store owner in Indianapolis. Came to N.Y. in 1919 to study at Parsons School of Design. Started with theatrical and movie designing for Paramount Pictures and Brooks Costume Co. In 1924 worked for Charles Armour, then for Hattie Carnegie from 1928 till 1940. Partnership in firm Traina-Norell followed in 1941. After death of Traina in 1960, formed own company, Norman Norell. Rated as top American designer on 7th Ave, "Dean of the fashion industry," "the American Balenciaga." Known for precision tailoring, dateless purity of line, conservative elegance in the finest imported fabrics. Remembered for trouser-suits for town and travel, widely flared day skirts, athome "smoking" robe, sweater tops with luxury skirts, straight wool jersey chemises, double-breasted coats over pussy-cat-bow blouses and straight skirts, slinky sequin sheaths, the sailor look. First designer elected to Hall of Fame by Coty Award judges in 1958. Founder and president of the Council of Fashion Designers of America. Modest, tough, independent; never followed fads; admired Balenciaga, Vionnet, and Chanel. Suffered stroke on eve of his retrospective show at the Metropolitan Museum of Art, Oct. 15, 1972; died ten days later.

Parnis, Mollie (1905–)

Born in New York City. One of the most successful women designers on 7th Ave. Started in 1939 as designer for Parnis-Livingston with husband, Leon Livingston. Has boutique and ready-to wear collections doing $6,000,000 a year business. Specializes in flattering, feminine dresses and ensembles for the well-to-do woman over 30, for the career girl and the wives of important businessmen. Clients include Mrs. Dwight Eisenhower, Mrs. Lyndon B. Johnson, Barbara Walters, Nancy Dickerson, Dinah Shore, etc. Leads busy social life; entertains politicians, actors, artists in beautiful apartment with collection of Impressionist paintings. Donated funds for creating small parks in underprivileged areas of New York City, 1972.

Pedlar, Sylvia (1901–1972)

Born in New York; studied at Cooper Union and Art Students League to be a fashion artist. Founded Iris Lingerie and designed there for forty years. Remembered for reviving the peignoir and matching long-sleeved gown, the Istanbul harem-hem gown, the toga nightdress, short chemise-slip, lace-trimmed silk gowns—sometimes doubling as evening dresses. Retired in 1970. Died in 1972.

Potter, Clare

One of the first group of all-American designers honored by Dorothy Shaver at Lord & Taylor in late '30's. Graduate of Pratt Institute; majored in portrait painting; entered fashion field designing embroidery. Own business on 7th Ave. under name Clarepotter in '40's and '50's, making classic sports clothes, at-home and dinner clothes. Noted for unusual color combinations, refinement of cut, and no extraneous trimmings. Worked under name Potter Designs Inc. in '60's; had wholesale firm, Timbertop Inc., in West Nyack, N.Y.

Pulitzer, Lilly (1932–)

Socialite daughter of Mrs. Ogden Phipps, living in Palm Beach, Fla., and married to Herbert Pulitzer when in 1960 she designed and sold a printed-cotton shift called a "Lilly," which proliferated into nation-wide fashion in '60's and '70's. Specially hand-screened floral prints now produced in Key West, Fla. Child's version, called "Minnie"; print slacks for men; "sneaky Pete" night shirts; new ruffled hems and short sleeves added to basic Lilly in '70's. Also home-furnishing fabrics, wastebaskets, laminated glassware, etc. Lilly shops in a dozen resorts. Now Mrs. Enrique Rousseau.

Sarmi, Ferdinando (Count, called "Nando")

Born in Ravenna, Italy. Studied law; trained in fashion design at Fabiani in Rome and with other firms. Chief designer at Elizabeth Arden, N.Y., 1951–59. Established Sarmi Inc. wholesale operation, 1959. Coty Award in 1960. Known for refined, romantic evening clothes in chiffon, lace and brocade, often fur-trimmed; elegant theater costumes; daytime wools; beaded sweater tops over chiffon skirts; subtle color combinations. After backruptcy in 1967, reorganized as Ferdinando Sarmi, Ltd., in 1971; business now closed.

Scaasi, Arnold (1931–)

Born Arnold Isaacs in Montreal, Canada; uses his name spelled backwards. One of last oldtime custom designers in U.S. Studied at school of Chambre Syndicale, Paris; spent thirteen years on 7th Ave., N.Y. 1950-63, eight of them in own custom business. Went wholesale in 1956, including furs, costume jewelry, men's ties, and sweaters. Custom salon on E. 56th St. since 1963; ready-to-wear for Maria Moutet in Paris, 1972. Coty Award in 1958. Known for spectacular evening wear in luxurious fabrics, often fur or feather-trimmed, appealing to glamorous actresses and socialite beauties; furs for Ritter Bros.; new habit for nuns in '67. Clients include Joan Crawford, Lauren Bacall, Lily Pons, Zsa Zsa Gabor, Sophia Loren.

Simpson, Adele (1903–)

Worked with husband, textile designer Wesley Simpson, before becoming designer for Mary Lee, 1942–1948. Took over company in her name in 1949 on 7th Ave. in N.Y. Dresses the typical American woman with conservative good taste, in upper income bracket. Known for pretty feminine clothes in delicate prints and colors, coordinated wardrobe, the opposite of avant-garde or "kooky." Remembered for the pink-and-white print dress with bow neck made for Mrs. Richard Nixon to wear to Republican Convention and the red wool coat and fur-lined hood for her trip to China in 1972. Loves travel; collects art, dolls, fabrics, and books related to fashion, which she hopes to leave to the Fashion Institute of Technology.

Stavropoulos, George

Born in Greece, studied dress design in Paris; had well-known custom salon in Athens 1949–1960. Married Greek-American; came to New York in 1961, opening house on 57th St., slowly building reputation for unusually beautiful, classically simple clothes. Known for draped, tiered, or pleated evening gowns, asymmetric folds, wrapped coats, kimono sleeves, floating panels, capes, bias jerseys. Mrs. Lyndon B. Johnson among distinguished clients.

Tassell, Gustave (1926–)

Philadelphian; studied at Pennsylvania Academy of Fine Arts; freelance designing in N.Y.; small couture business in Philadelphia; planned display at Hattie Carnegie; two years in Paris selling his sketches. Started own business in Los Angeles, California, in 1959. Won Coty Award in 1962. Known for refined, no-gimmick clothes with stark, clean lines à la Balenciaga; Spanish-shawl embroidered evening gowns. Chosen as design head at Norell, N.Y., after Norell's death in 1972.

Tiffeau, Jacques (1927–)

Born in Chenevelles, France. Trained with men's tailors there and in Paris; interrupted by war service. Came to New York 1952 and became outstanding Franco-American designer of spirited, youthful clothes in '50's and '60's. Studied at Art Students League and trained under friend Christian Dior while holding job with Monte Sano & Pruzan. In 1958, joined Beverly Pruzan Busch to form Tiffeau-Busch, Inc. making young, high-fashion clothes at lower prices. Known for modern, sportive, sexy clothes; uncluttered, uncollared, rounded suits and roomy coats; above-knee bouncy skirts; fanciful legs; mini-dresses with wide open areas of nudity; tweed pants-suits; hoods; swimwear for Catalina. Coty Award, 1960; Cotton Fashion Award, 1962, among others.

Trigère, Pauline (1912–)

Born in Paris. Came to New York in 1932, with husband, Lazar Radly, and two sons. Worked as assistant designer for Hattie Carnegie in late '30's. Started New York business 1942 with brother, Robert. Later helped by sons, Jean Pierre and Philippe. Owner-designer of firm on 7th Ave. Specializes in coats, capes, suits, dresses and accessories in unusual tweeds and prints, with intricate cut to flatter mature figures. Achieved Coty Fashion Hall of Fame. Gregarious and articulate; leads same social life as her customer; *au courant* in theater and art world; travels widely. Trademark is the turtle, which turns up in jewelry, scarf, and fabric designs and in her country home, "La Tortue."

Valentina (1904–)

Russian; came to U.S. with Revue Russe in 1922; opened own dressmaking establishment for private clients in 1928. Strikingly beautiful, with pale face, chignon of blond hair; modeled her own style of dramatic, fluid draperies, turbans, and veils. Known for simple, architectural, classic lines. Trademarks: all-black evening look, gown, cape, hood, hose; a Maltese-cross pendant. Credited with first short evening dress in early '40's; air-raid wrap coat with multiple pockets; one-bare-shoulder, one-long-sleeve black evening gown; bare-back halter gown with bolero; dolman sleeves; attached hoods. Strong-willed, shrewd business woman, dominating clients. Dressed Greta Garbo whom she resembled, Katharine Cornell, Zorina, Millicent Rogers, Katharine Hepburn in movie *Philadelphia Story*, Lynn Fontanne in play *The Visit* etc. Famous quotes: "Mink is for football, ermine is only for bathrobes"; "Fit the century, forget the year," Closed her salon in 1957; retired, Mrs. George Schlee.

Vera (1910–)

Artist-designer who has applied her bold floral and abstract designs to clothes, many household items. In 1945, started Printex firm with her art-director husband, George Neumann, and Werner Hamm, textile expert, to make place-mats, followed by scarves, sportswear, dinner-ware, sheets, towels, lingerie, sleepwear, by 1972. Influenced by wide travels; considers herself a painter; trademark is ladybug next to signature, "Vera." Honored in 1972 with show at Smithsonian Institution, Washington, D.C.; hailed as a "Renaissance woman."

Victor, Sally (1905–)

One of best-known U.S. milliners for thirty years from mid-thirties on. Born Sally Josephs in Scranton, Pa. Studied painting in Paris; worked in Macy's department store millinery department and at Bamberger's, 1923–30; designed for Serge, millinery house owned by Sergiu Victor, who became her husband. Established own firm on E. 53rd St. N.Y. in 1934 and became increasingly successful. Known for hats with themes taken from research in museums, fashion history, movies, and current events (e.g. Flemish and Renaissance portraits; American Indians; African, Caribbean, Czechoslovakian or Chinese headgear, etc.); clip-on half-hats; collapsible bonnets; chessmen-shaped pillboxes; innumerable new techniques of slashing, folding, and manipulating felt or fabric; unique names for each season's shapes. Coty award in 1956. "Sally V," inexpensive line, started in 1951. Lectured at F.I.T., Parsons School, and New York University. Customers included Mrs. Dwight Eisenhower, Mrs. Franklin Roosevelt, Queen Elizabeth, Judy Garland, etc.

Weinberg, Chester (1930–)

Started career on 7th Ave. with Harvey Berin; Herbert Sondheim; Patullo-Jo Copeland, etc. At Teal-Traina for ten years. Opened own house, Chester Weinberg, Ltd. in 1965. Boutique, Chester Now, in 1970. Known for sophisticated clothes for modern girl-on-the-go; beautiful fabrics; young ideas like ruffled hems, pantalettes, romantic peasant dress, jumpsuits. Aims at wealthy celebrity socialites.

Weitz, John (1923–)

Born in Berlin. Studied at St. Paul's and Oxford in England. Came to U.S. in 1940. Captain in U.S. Army; now married to actress, Susan Kohner. Sportsman: won the Sebring World Championship in sports-car racing; rides horses, sails, etc. One of most versatile pioneers in design of practical clothes for sports and specific life styles. Started with Lord & Taylor, making bulky sweaters and jeans after World War II. Known for women's sports clothes with men's-wear look; poplin car coats; hooded, zippered-up cotton jackets; pea jackets with white pants; town pants; strapless dress over bra and shorts, all new ideas in the '50's. In '60's, devised "ready-to-wear couture," chosen from sketches and swatches. Added Contour Clothes for men, inspired by Levi-Strauss jeans, cowboy jackets, fatigue coveralls, and jumpsuits. Since 1970, designs only for men, including accessories; compared to Cardin in Paris and Amies in London. In '50's, also designed uniforms for gas-station attendents.

Wragge, B. H. (1908–)

Owner-designer, Sydney Wragge, pioneered concept of sportswear separates; coordination or mix-matching pieces. Started by selling men's shirts; bought firm B. H. Wragge and kept name in 1931. Added skirts, suits, coats to man-tailored women's shirts. Became known for his all-American look; his great color combinations in natural fibers; sleeveless dresses and side-slit coats; jumpers; tapered pants with easy tops; tunics. A Wragge became a status symbol in the '40's and '50's in same way later names, Pucci, Gucci, or Halston meant quality. Received Coty Award in 1957. Closed 7th Ave. showroom in 1971. May franchise his name for men's and women's wear in future.

Zuckerman, Ben (1894–)

Born in Rumania; came to New York as child. Master tailor, rated highest through '50's and '60's. With partner-designer, Harry Shacter, created soberly elegant coats, suits, ensembles for day and evening in quality comparable to Balenciaga, whom he admired. Frankly adapted best of Paris for American tastes. At age 21, started with Zuckerman & Hoffman, remained eleven years; from 1924–49, firm called Zuckerman & Kraus; from 1950–1968, called Ben Zuckerman, Inc. Known for velvet coats and suits and jewel buttons, brocade blouses with tweeds, oval-back or princess coats with welt seaming, bell-hop jackets and round skirts, famous pink coat in 1959—starting vogue for bright colors in winter. Received Coty Awards for consistent, lady-like tailoring. Almost retired several times but urged to continue by fanatical clients; finally closed doors in 1968.

ENGLAND:
Designer Portraits

Ossie Clark

Jean Muir

Mary Quant

Zandra Rhodes

Thea Porter

ENGLAND:
Designer Styles

Ossie Clark

Ossie Clark

Ossie Clark

Jean Muir

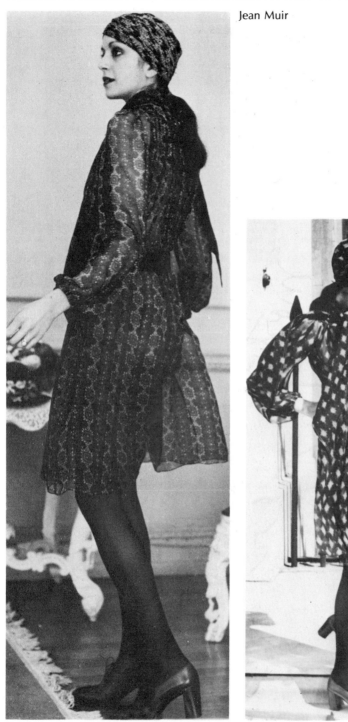

Jean Muir

Thea Porter

Thea Porter

Mary Quant

Mary Quant

Zandra Rhodes

Zandra Rhodes

FRANCE:
Designer Portraits

Cristobal Balenciaga

Pierre Balmain

Marc Bohan

Gabrielle Chanel

Pierre Cardin

André Courrèges

Christian Dior

Hubert de Givenchy

Jacques Heim

Alix Grés

621

Kenzo

Captain Edward Molyneux

Nina Ricci

Sonia Rykiel

Elsa Schiaparelli

Yves Saint Laurent

Emmanuel Ungaro

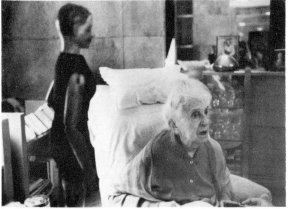

Madeleine Vionnet

FRANCE:
Designer Styles

Balmain

Cardin

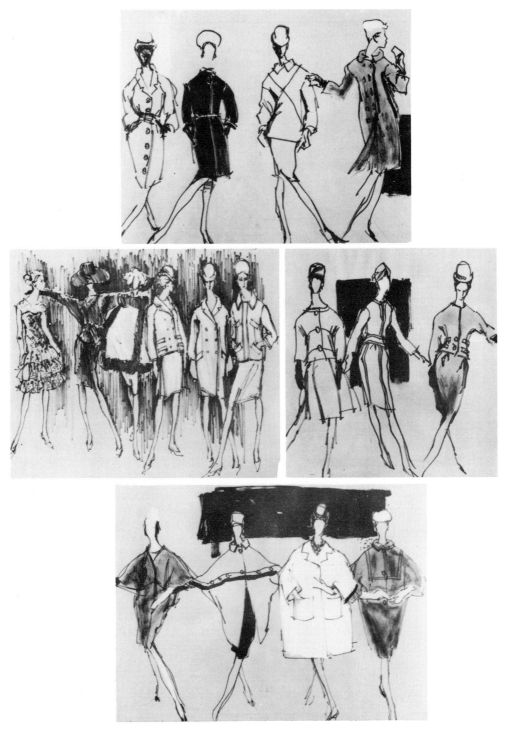

Balenciaga

Bohan

Bohan

Chanel

Chanel

Chanel

Courrêges

Courrêges

Dior

Givenchy

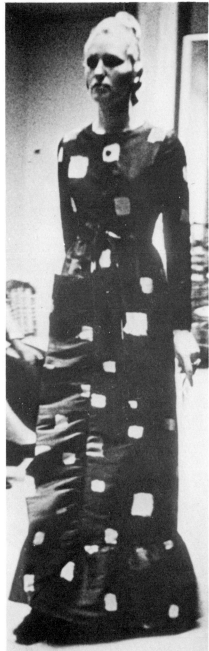

Givenchy

Madame Grés

Madame Grés

Kenzo

Kenzo

Ricci

Ricci

Rykiel

Rykiel

Saint Laurent

Saint Laurent

Ungaro

Ungaro

Madame Vionnet

ITALY:
Designer Portraits

Maria Antonelli

Dr. Aldo Gucci

Emilio Pucci

Simonetta

Garavani Valentino

ITALY:
Designer Styles

Maria Antonelli

Maria Antonelli

Gucci

Gucci

Pucci

Pucci

Valentino

Valentino

UNITED STATES:
Designer Portraits

John Anthony

Geoffrey Beene

Bill Blass

Donald Brooks

Bonnie Cashin

Oscar de la Renta

Giorgio Di Sant' Angelo

James Galanos

Rudi Gernreich

Betsey Johnson

Halston

Anne Klein

Vera Maxwell

Norman Norell

Adele Simpson

Jacques Tiffeau

Pauline Trigère

669

UNITED STATES:
Designer Styles

Adolfo

Adolfo

John Anthony

John Anthony

Geoffrey Beene

Geoffrey Beene

Bill Blass

Bill Blass

Donald Brooks

Donald Brooks

Bonnie Cashin

Bonnie Cashin

Luis Estevez

Oscar de la Renta

Oscar de la Renta

Giorgio Di Sant' Angelo

Giorgio Di Sant' Angelo

Galanos

Galanos

Rudi Gernreich

Rudi Gernreich

Halston

Halston

Betsey Johnson

Anne Klein

Anne Klein

Sarmi

Vera Maxwell

Vera Maxwell

Norell

Norell

Norell

Adele Simpson

Adele Simpson

Jacques Tiffeau

Jacques Tiffeau

Trigère

Trigère